The Revolution of 1905

Abraham Ascher

. . . .

THE
REVOLUTION
OF 1905

Russia in Disarray

Stanford University Press
Stanford, California

Stanford University Press
Stanford, California
© 1988 by the Board of Trustees of the
Leland Stanford Junior University
Printed in the United States of America

Published with the support of the
National Endowment for the Humanities,
an independent federal agency

CIP data appear at the end of the book

Original printing 1988
Last figure below indicates year of this printing:
03   02   01   00

To My Father
JAKOB ASCHER

Acknowledgments

In writing this book I received support and help from many institutions and individuals, and I should like to express my appreciation to them. Financial support from the National Endowment for the Humanities, the American Council of Learned Societies, the Hoover Institution on War, Revolution, and Peace, the Earhart Foundation, and the Research Foundation of the City University of New York made possible research trips to archives in the United States and Europe and enabled me to take time off from teaching. I was cordially received in various archives, all of which readily made available to me documents relevant to my subject: the Archives du Ministère des Affaires Etrangères in Paris, the Public Record Office in London, the Haus-Hof-und-Staatsarchiv in Vienna, the Politisches Archiv des Auswärtigen Amts in Bonn, the Hoover Institution, and the International Institute for Social History in Amsterdam. The National Archives in Washington, D.C., promptly sent me microfilms of diplomatic dispatches I requested. Librarians at Columbia University, the New York Public Library, and the library of the Graduate School of the City University of New York responded graciously to all my requests for books, pamphlets, and newspapers. The four summers I spent at the Slavonic Library of Helsinki University were especially profitable. I appreciate the courteous and efficient help of the staff and am particularly grateful to Ms. Päivi Paloposki, whose efforts in my behalf were beyond the call of duty.

I am grateful to all my friends who read the manuscript (or parts of it) and gave me the benefit of their thoughtful criticisms: Julian Franklin, Paula Franklin, John Keep, Guenter Lewy, Allen McConnell, Marc Raeff, and Richard Stites. Reginald E. Zelnik scrutinized the work with remarkable care and saved me from many mistakes and oversimplifications. J. G. Bell, Editor of Stanford University Press, not only encouraged me in this project from the very beginning of my work, but read the manuscript with his usual discernment; his spirited suggestions helped me to improve the book in many ways. Peter Kahn was in every way an ideal copy editor. He has a fine sense of style and an astute grasp of complicated historiographical issues; his close reading of the manuscript resulted in improvements in form and substance.

I especially want to thank my wife, Anna, who over the years supported me in more ways than I can express here. Her patience and encouragement lifted my spirits at moments when I felt overwhelmed by the complexity and scope of the project. Despite her own very busy schedule, she read the manuscript with extraordinary thoroughness and acuity. The final version owes much to her high standards of style and intellectual rigor. I suspect that our children, Deborah, Rachel, and Stephen, were exposed to more details about the Revolution of 1905 than could possibly have interested them, but they were always cheerful and indulgent toward my preoccupation with Russian history. Stephen even did a draft of the manuscript on the word processor before I had learned how to operate the computer, and I am pleased that the experience has had some influence on the direction of his own studies.

Although the book has benefited greatly from the help and advice of my family, friends, and editors, I myself am, of course, responsible for its shortcomings.

A.A.

Contents

Twelve pages of illustrations follow p. 144

. . . .

A Note to the Reader

In 1905 Russia was still using the Julian calendar, which was then thirteen days behind the Gregorian calendar used in the West. I have given all dates in the text according to the Russian calendar; I have also used the Russian date alone in the notes for issues of newspapers and other periodicals, which were often dated in both forms on their covers. Western dates do occasionally occur in dispatches from foreign diplomats stationed in Russia, but I always give the Russian equivalent in parentheses to avoid confusion.

The transliteration of Russian names inevitably poses a problem, and I have opted to use the forms most commonly known for the handful of people the reader is likely to be familiar with already: Tsar Nicholas, Count Witte, Kerensky, Trotsky. Otherwise I follow the Library of Congress transliteration system, modified to eliminate soft and hard signs. The list below is designed to define certain terms and offices mentioned in the text.

City Governor
: the chief authority in larger cities such as St. Petersburg, Moscow, Odessa, and Sevastopol; his powers were equivalent to those of a Governor.

Gendarmes
: members of a special police force under the direct authority of the Ministry of Internal Affairs.

Governor
: the chief authority in provinces; responsible to the Minister of Internal Affairs.

Governor-General
: the chief authority in a few important provinces (notably St. Petersburg and Moscow) and in the borderlands; his rank was equivalent to that of a minister, and he had direct access to the Tsar.

Guberniia   a province.

Kulak (literally, "fist")   a well-to-do peasant who owned a fairly large farm, who could afford to hire some laborers, and who often lent money to other peasants.

Chief Procurator of the Most Holy Synod   the chief administrator of the Russian Orthodox Church, with direct access to the Tsar.

State Council   an appointed body of dignitaries, established in 1810, that advised the Tsar on legislation.

Uezd   a county, including a city or town and several rural districts (volosti).

Volost   a district in rural regions.

European Russia in 1905

The Revolution of 1905

· ·

Introduction

ALTHOUGH the Revolution of 1905 was a turning point in modern Russian history, there is still no scholarly and comprehensive account of the event in any language. This remarkable lacuna in our historiography surely does not stem from a lack of interest in the subject or from a shortage of source material. Even as the upheaval was unfolding, Russian émigrés in the West published some official and confidential documents as well as numerous analyses of political trends. After the revolutionary tide receded in 1907, writers representing all shades of the political spectrum vigorously debated the historical significance of the turbulence that had shaken Russia. The *Complete Collected Works* of V. I. Lenin (the latest edition of which runs to 55 volumes) are filled with references to 1905, many dating back to the time of the revolution. Moreover, since the 1920's, Soviet scholars have explored 1905 more intensively than almost any other period in modern Russian history. The literature on the subject in Russian is already vast and continues to grow at a rapid pace.[1] The Revolution of 1917 still occupies first place in the Soviet historical consciousness, but the Revolution of 1905 does not lag far behind.

In 1920, Lenin referred to 1905 as the "dress rehearsal," by which he meant that without it the "victory of the October Revolution in 1917 would have been impossible."[2] But Lenin's description of 1905 was also meant to suggest the inevitability of 1917, since a dress rehearsal is always followed by the first performance. Soviet historians invariably quote Lenin's pithy comment on 1905, which, they believe, settles the question of why the revolution was a pivotal event in modern history. Although it is debatable whether the Revolution of 1905 was in fact the dress rehearsal for 1917, in one respect the link between the two is indisputable.

Bolshevism emerged as a distinct political movement during the first revolution. Strictly speaking, the movement originated in 1903, but only after the spread of unrest in 1904 did Lenin and his followers begin to formulate the strategies and tactics that became the essentials of Bolshevism, distinguishing it fully from other strands of Marxism.

Ultimately, the intense interest in the Revolution of 1905 in the Soviet Union must be seen as part of a general concern by the political leadership to enhance the legitimacy of Communism. If it can be demonstrated that Leninist policies were unimpeachable even in 1905, when the Bolsheviks suffered a major political and military defeat, the Communist Party's claims to preeminence in Soviet society and in the worldwide struggle for socialism are that much stronger. This concern with legitimacy explains the enormous outpouring of works on 1905 for mass circulation, generally written by well-established scholars.*

Over the past two decades or so, Western historians, too, have devoted a great deal of attention to Russia in the years from 1904 to 1907, which constitute the full span of the revolution. No single interpretation predominates, but a major theme that emerges from Western works runs counter to the Soviet view of 1905. The revolution is seen not as an event that made any one path of development inevitable, but rather as a critical juncture that opened up several paths. Under intense pressure from below for political and economic change, the autocracy appeared to suffer a loss of nerve. For an entire year, beginning in the fall of 1904, the government oscillated between leniency and repression, but neither policy succeeded in ending the unrest. On the contrary, the government's inconsistency was taken as a sign of weakness by the various groups within the opposition, which encouraged them to step up their agitation.

In October 1905, the pressure from mass movements became so acute that it drove the autocracy to the verge of collapse; it seemed as if Russia would be transformed into a constitutional state on the Western model. Even though that prospect did not materialize, some institutional changes introduced during the period of unrest survived the failure of the revolution. Most notably, Russia retained an elected legislature and political parties speaking for various social and economic interests. The partici-

---

* A recent publication nicely illustrates the determination of Soviet authorities to impress upon their citizens the historical importance of 1905 and the wisdom of Lenin even before 1917. It is a 300-page reference book written by noted historians for the general public; the first printing was issued in a run of 175,000 copies. After recounting the standard Leninist views on 1905, the authors discuss the "echo" of the revolution in five continents, including such countries as Cuba, Uruguay, and Algeria, where interest in Russia was altogether slight at the time. The book contains 99 footnotes, of which 95 are to Lenin's *Complete Collected Works*. See S. V. Tiutiukin et al., *Pervaia Rossiiskaia. Spravochnik o revoliutsiia 1905–1907 gg* (Moscow, 1985).

pants in the revolution failed to achieve their major goal, the dismantling of the autocratic regime, but the old order did not emerge unscathed from the three years of conflict. The autocratic system of rule, for centuries the bedrock of the Russian polity, was undermined.

Particularly striking features of the Revolution of 1905 were its scope and intensity. The challenge to the established order came from mass movements representing four different social groups: liberals among the middle class and gentry, industrial workers, peasants, and some of the national minorities. Serious disturbances broke out in various cities, agrarian regions, and outlying areas of the Empire, as well as in many cultural institutions and in the army and the navy. Virtually no social group or geographical region remained unaffected by unrest. The government was only able to survive these disorders because they did not occur simultaneously. But in some regions the onslaughts against the authorities forced Tsarist officials to flee, which left the responsibility for local government temporarily in the hands of insurgents.

The dynamism of the industrial workers was yet another striking and novel feature of the revolution. For a few weeks late in 1905, this group, a tiny segment of Russia's total population, spearheaded the political campaigns against the autocracy. It took the initiative in launching a general strike that gained the support of other groups and paralyzed the government. Moreover, in St. Petersburg and elsewhere, workers formed an institution (the soviet) that briefly assumed many of the prerogatives of government.

The currents of rebellion were so diverse that at times it seemed as though Russia were undergoing not one revolution but a whole series of parallel revolutions. However, since the numerous disturbances were part of a larger pattern of protest against the old regime, we can speak of a single revolution. The upheaval of 1905 was actually a new type of revolution, the first in which a Marxist movement made its mark on an agrarian society, and as such it foreshadowed in some important respects the convulsions that have taken place in developing countries in recent decades.

If the events of the first Russian Revolution are in themselves complicated, the ideological disputes among scholars and publicists over how to interpret them only add to the confusion. The original disputes were rooted in political conflicts between the two factions within Russian Marxism, the Bolsheviks and the Mensheviks, who until 1917 competed for supremacy among the industrial workers. Shortly after the revolutionary unrest ended, a group of Menshevik activist-scholars published an impressive study of the upheaval that was both a work of history and a political statement (*The Social Movement in Russia at the Beginning of the Twentieth Century*). Recoiling from the militancy to which many of them had subscribed in 1905, the Mensheviks now argued that under the economic and social conditions prevailing in Russia early in the twentieth century the country could not have moved beyond the limits of a bourgeois revolution, and that the attempt by workers to overthrow the autocracy by means of an armed uprising was a mistake. They further contended that although the industrial workers had greatly contributed to undermining the old regime, they had not been predominant within the opposition to Tsarism throughout the revolution.

To Lenin, and subsequently to Soviet historians, these notions were anathema, since they called into question the essentials of Bolshevism. With increasing fervor, Soviet historians have insisted that there was no alternative in 1905 to armed insurrection and that the industrial workers had indeed exercised "hegemony" over the entire opposition movement throughout the revolution. The doctrine of "the hegemony of the proletariat" has become so deeply embedded in Soviet historiography and Communist ideology that a brief discussion of it is in order. In fact, the doctrine is rather vague and over the years has frequently been redefined. Yet any hint by a scholar that it may not accurately describe the situation in Russia in the years 1904–7 raises a storm in Soviet academic circles, and the skeptics are quickly overwhelmed by an avalanche of rebuttal and denunciation.[3]

Russian Marxists first touched on the question of the proletariat's role in the 1880's and 1890's, while trying to delineate the political importance of industrial workers in a country such as Russia, where the middle class was not yet politically dominant and the proletariat was still weak, numerically and organizationally. The founders of Russian Marxism, G. V. Plekhanov and P. B. Axelrod, held that the industrial workers would be the most determined and consistent opponents of Tsarism and would take the initiative in the struggle against the old order, but without dominating the social classes that joined the struggle. Early in the twentieth century, Lenin defined the doctrine more narrowly, arguing that the Marxist party would be the decisive and dominant force within the opposition.*

Soviet historians have made the doctrine of proletarian hegemony the keystone of their interpretations of the Revolution of 1905. At the same time, since the 1930's they have claimed that the Bolshevik party was the only authentic voice of the industrial workers and that it exercised leadership over the entire opposition movement. It allegedly took the initiative in every campaign against Tsarism in 1905.[4] Because Soviet scholars

---

* For more on the doctrine of the hegemony of the proletariat, see Chapter 7 below.

rigidly adhere to this interpretive framework, their works contain a large number of fanciful assertions about 1905 and especially about the non-Bolshevik and nonproletarian segments of the population, which are assigned secondary and even insignificant roles in the revolution.

For the historian of 1905, the Soviet preoccupation with the subject both facilitates and complicates his work. It facilitates it because in their efforts to prove the correctness of the Leninist position, Soviet historians have published a vast number of primary sources that would otherwise not be readily available to Western scholars. For example, to commemorate the fiftieth anniversary of the revolution Soviet historians produced a collection of documents that runs to eighteen volumes and well over 13,000 pages—and this work constitutes only part of the total documentary output. Innumerable memoirs and monographs have also been published. Although much of the scholarship must be treated with caution, it includes some solid and sophisticated studies that enlarge our knowledge and understanding of 1905. I have made use of these works wherever appropriate.

On the other hand, the historian's task is made more difficult because he is forced to examine large quantities of polemical scholarship. It is time-consuming and tedious to disentangle fact from fiction and to discriminate between interpretations that are simply exaggerations and those that are made out of whole cloth. Detective work is part of the historian's calling, but anyone studying the Revolution of 1905 will have to devote more time than he would like to exploring bizarre claims and charges. A few examples will suffice: that "Comrade Stalin" led a strike of 30,000 workers in Baku in December 1904, "the most important event in the history of the revolutionary movement in Russia at the beginning of the twentieth century," and that he was the leader of the soviet in that city. In fact, Stalin spent at best a few days in Baku in 1904 and was not there at all at the time the soviet was formed in 1905. During the era of Stalin's rule, Soviet historians also argued without any convincing evidence that one reason for the failure of the Moscow uprising in December 1905 was that a day before the insurrection several important Bolsheviks fell into a police trap set with the help of their radical rivals, the Socialist Revolutionaries and Mensheviks.[5] Even the highly regarded works of scholarship published over the last decade and a half fail to do justice to revolutionaries such as Leon Trotsky who were important in 1905 but became rivals of Stalin in the 1920's. The very best studies avoid outright falsification by simply ignoring Trotsky altogether.

Although misleading and frustrating, Soviet writings on 1905 do sharply delineate many of the larger issues that must be addressed in a synthetic account of the revolution: What were the moving forces in the upheaval, the forces whose actions led to the tests of strength between the opposition and the autocracy? What was the role of organized political movements in the major events of 1905? Did the revolution provide a realistic opportunity for the establishment of a constitutional form of government? Was the overthrow of Tsarism by force feasible? Was the revolution bound to fail, and if so why? More generally, what light do the events of 1905 throw on the link between economic modernization and political change?

Of course, historians in the West have already examined these questions in numerous monographs, and I am pleased to acknowledge my indebtedness to them. We now have fine studies of Russian liberalism, the Socialist Revolutionaries, the Social Democrats, the workers' movement, the formation of political parties, the peasantry, the gentry, the development of the revolution in Moscow, and the role of the armed forces and of the most prominent statesmen, to mention only the more important topics.[6] Whatever the differences among the authors in approach, interpretation, and emphasis, they all stay clear of the highly tendentious or politicized interpretations of 1905. The overall picture is one of great complexity. No one social group dominated the opposition throughout the period. Many of the leading participants changed strategies and tactics in light of changing circumstances. There were ebbs and flows in the revolution, whose course was determined by various factors: a senseless war that Russia fought against Japan, the resolve of countless people to seek relief from their burdens, the government's clumsy attempts to halt the unrest, and, finally, the judgments of individuals about the strength of the movements they supported and the intentions and resilience of their opponents.

An approach to the study of 1905 that stresses complexity and ambiguity might seem to deprive the revolution of some of its excitement by not linking it directly to the more momentous Revolution of 1917. Such an approach, however, yields better—and ultimately more exciting—history: it is closer to what actually happened. The individuals who participated in the mass movements of 1905 did not believe that they were merely preparing the way for the real event at some future date. They were trying to bring about far-reaching changes then and there. Furthermore, an exploration of the first fifteen months of the revolution, the subject of the present volume, suggests that these endeavors were not necessarily doomed to fail. On several occasions the authorities considered daring reforms that would have satisfied enough of the opposition's demands to have brought the unrest to an end. The initial period of the revolution might aptly be designated as one of missed opportunities.

The problem was that the government always made its offers of reform too late. As the German Ambassador to St. Petersburg shrewdly noted in

January 1906, "the government is justifiably criticized for almost always failing to act at the right moment, for [not realizing] that the confidence it sought could be better achieved through timely checks of popular passions than through initial neglect and subsequent interventions, [for not realizing that] quick, even if incomplete reforms [are more effective] than constant groping, delays, [and] vain promises."[7] The government's stance proved to be costly. Concessions that would have been welcomed early in the spring of 1905 were rejected in the summer of that year by opposition leaders incensed at the pettiness, callousness, and obstinacy of the authorities. When the government at last (in October) did promise to introduce fundamental political changes, only a small portion of the opposition was willing to give up the struggle. The authorities, never enthusiastic about the reforms, soon began to renege on their promises. Poor judgment and bad timing played a large role in determining the course of the revolution.

Clearly, the men in positions of leadership in society and in the state were guided by their wish to defend their interests and the interests of social groups they claimed to represent. Yet by itself this does not adequately explain their behavior. Neither side in the revolutionary conflict was a monolith; in both camps important figures disagreed with each other over policies. Even more to the point, both statesmen and leaders of the opposition occasionally took positions out of keeping with their predilections. It was not uncommon for archconservatives to favor far-reaching concessions and for militants on the left to oppose bellicose tactics. A student of 1905 encounters many surprises, which is why the revolution is so complicated and fascinating a story.

I make no claim to have written a detailed history of every aspect of the Revolution of 1905 during its first fifteen months. That would require a volume at least twice the size of the present one. What I have attempted is a comprehensive account that makes sense of the critical episodes of the period.

Part I

. . . .

THE OLD REGIME
UNDER SIEGE

Chapter One

. . . .

The Fragmented Society

EARLY IN 1905 the distinguished historian and leader of Russian liberalism, P. N. Miliukov, wrote that "there exist two Russias, one quite different from the other, and what pleases one is quite sure to displease the other. . . ." One of the Russias was that of "Leo Tolstoy, the great writer; the other . . . that of Plehve, the late minister of the interior. The former is the Russia of our 'intellectuals' and of the people; the other is an anachronism, deeply rooted in the past, and defended in the present by an omnipresent bureaucracy. The one spells liberty; the other, despotism."[1] At about the same time, Maurice Bompard, the French Ambassador to St. Petersburg, warned that the deep divisions in the Russian Empire threatened to undermine the stability of the state. In August 1904 he reported to his government that "All classes of Russian society are, in effect, in a state of ferment" and that "a general explosion . . . a revolution" was quite possible. He could only hope that because the Russian people possessed a "robust temperament" the country would emerge from the social and political crisis "unharmed."[2]

These two assessments of the situation in Russia help to explain the magnitude and ferocity of the turmoil that engulfed the Empire during the three years from 1904 to 1907. By the fall of 1905 every social class was caught up in the turbulence and the country seemed indeed to be divided into two camps, one defending the old order and the other pressing for fundamental change. The notion of "two Russias," however, sheds light only on the causes of the upheaval. It does not help one to understand the convoluted course of events in that three-year period, which can in large measure be attributed to the absence of such a clear-cut division in Russian society.

In fact, the forces of change were themselves fragmented, which is why they failed to mount a unified onslaught on the despotic regime. And the forces of order, which revered the institutions of Russia and wished to preserve them, were similarly fragmented and failed to speak with one voice. The Tsar was the unquestioned leader of this camp, and he himself must bear much of the responsibility for the government's failings, but serious conflicts of interest among his supporters and differences over how to handle the growing discontent made it difficult for the authorities to pursue farsighted and consistent policies. Given the deep fissures in society, it seems best to speak not of two Russias but of one highly fragmented Russia. This notion makes more comprehensible the complexity of the Revolution of 1905 and the ambiguity of its outcome.

The conflicts over purely political issues, a central feature of the revolution, probably caused the most distinct divisions within Russia, though even on political questions neither the supporters nor the opponents of the prevailing order held monolithic views among themselves. Nevertheless, beginning approximately in the mid-nineteenth century, society, consisting of the educated, articulate strata of the population, became increasingly estranged from what its members perceived to be an anachronistic system of government. At a time when much of Western and Central Europe was moving toward the adoption of some form of constitutional government, the Russian Empire continued to be controlled by a hereditary monarchy that still claimed the right to rule autocratically. As the first article of the "Fundamental Laws" of 1832 stated, "The Emperor of all the Russias is a sovereign with autocratic and unlimited powers. To obey the commands not merely from fear but according to the dictates of one's conscience is ordained by God himself."[3]

The Tsar sought to impose his will on the vast Empire of some 129 million people through an imperial bureaucracy, which served at the sovereign's pleasure and whose reach extended to the lowest levels of local affairs. A revealing incident occurred in September 1905, during one of the more turbulent phases of the revolution. In an endeavor to calm student unrest, the rector of Moscow University, Prince S. N. Trubetskoi, asked the Minister of Education for permission to add 62 Jews to the previously established quota for admission (3 percent of the student body). Trubetskoi received the following reply: "The University's petition . . . will be submitted by me this week in my next report to His Imperial Majesty for an opinion."[4] Even on such a relatively trivial matter the minister did not feel free to take action on his own.

The power of the autocrat was matched by the weakness of public institutions, none of which can be said to have been substantially free from state control. Indeed, the principle of freedom of association was not recognized; very few laws had been enacted regulating public meetings or the establishment of private societies. All gatherings of groups of a dozen or more people were suspect and required police approval. No public lecture could be delivered without the formal permission of the police, which generally declined to issue permits. The organs of local self-government (zemstvos, city councils), established in the second half of the nineteenth century, were creations of the authorities in St. Petersburg, and during the era of counter-reform that began in the 1880's their functions and powers steadily eroded. The senior administrators of the Orthodox Church, a powerful institution in a country where the vast majority of the population was deeply religious, were servants of the state, appointed by the Tsar.

The government went to great lengths to prevent the emergence of an organized opposition to the autocratic regime. For one thing, it sought to shape public opinion by censoring books, periodicals, and newspapers. For another, it maintained an extensive system of police surveillance and arbitrarily meted out severe punishment (generally internal exile or imprisonment) to anyone considered "seditious," a term defined very broadly. The political police (the Okhrana and the more secretive "Special Section"), distinct and autonomous forces within the Department of Police, placed agents in educational, social, and political institutions as well as in factories, to keep an eye on actual and potential dissidents. In addition, governors and prefects throughout the Empire enlisted the help of janitors, who were required to report any unusual activities or gatherings in the buildings where they worked. When visitors sought entrance to an apartment building, they were required to show their identity cards or passports to the janitor, who was authorized to detain anyone suspected of illegal activities until the police arrived. Those who allowed a friend or relative to spend a night in their home without showing their guest's passport to the janitor risked a substantial fine.[5]

Despite Russia's deserved reputation as a repressive police state, the police were not notably efficient, primarily because the government was rather niggardly in its appropriations for the security forces.[6] As a result, corruption and other forms of dishonesty on the part of officials were perennial problems in Russia, though there is no way of measuring their extent. The stories of administrative malfeasance are legion; one example will indicate the kind of practices believed to have been widespread. The police chief of Ekaterinoslav, Rittmeister Krementskii, enjoyed a national reputation for efficiency because each year he succeeded in closing down three or four illegal presses. Krementskii's promotions came rapidly—until it was discovered that he himself had the presses set up so that he could make extravagant claims of vigilance to his superiors in St. Petersburg.[7]

Ultimately, of course, the reputation as well as the viability of an autocratic regime depend on the political sagacity and competence of the ruler. Whatever the judgments of historians about most Russian rulers of the nineteenth century, few would contend that the last autocrat of the Empire was endowed with the requisite qualifications to lead a large and powerful nation. Indeed, people acquainted with the future Tsar Nicholas II during the 1880's seriously doubted his ability to govern the country. On October 19, 1894, when it was clear that Alexander III was fatally ill, the Minister of the Navy, N. M. Chichaev, trenchantly assessed the 26-year-old heir to the throne: "The heir is a mere child, without experience, training, or even an inclination to study great problems of state. His interests are still those of a child, and it is impossible to predict what changes may be effected. At present, military service is the only subject that interests him. The helm of state is about to fall from the hands of an experienced mariner, and I fear that no hand like his is to grasp it for many years to come. What will be the course of the ship of state under these conditions the Lord only knows."[8] Also in 1894, Count V. A. Bobrinskii, who had served with Nicholas in a hussar regiment, was asked his opinion of the future ruler's intellect, education, and character. He would only say that the heir was a "very good colleague, notable for his affability, modesty, and honesty."[9]

Nicholas's private letters and diary confirm the accuracy of these assessments. A man of personal charm with strong religious convictions and deep affection for his wife and family, the Tsar showed no serious interest in politics. He took pains to record how he spent evenings with his family and to describe his various sporting activities, going so far as to note the number of birds he bagged on his hunts. He could be deeply moved by such events as the loss of his favorite dog, Iman. "I must confess," he wrote in his diary on October 20, 1902, "the whole day after it happened I never stopped crying—I still miss him dreadfully when I go for walks. He was such an intelligent, kind, and loyal dog!"[10] Yet the great events of his rule—the wars with Japan and the Central Powers, the demands of the liberals for a constitution, the industrial strikes, the violence of 1905, the breakdown of public order in that year—received scant attention from him. He venerated his father's memory and believed that it was his "sacred mission" to follow in Alexander III's footsteps. Like his father, he must be uncompromising in upholding the principle of autocracy, the only political idea for which he could muster any passion. On this issue he was very much influenced by K. P. Pobedonostsev, the reactionary Procurator of the Most Holy Synod after 1880, who contended that stability could be maintained in Russia only if society remained hierarchically organized and the masses unquestioningly obeyed the existing authorities.[11]

Although moderately intelligent, Nicholas lacked the personal drive and vision to take charge of the government, to familiarize himself with the workings of the administration, and to instill a sense of purpose and direction in the ministers and bureaucracy. He was also a narrow-minded, prejudiced man, incapable of tolerating people who did not fit his conception of the true Russian. He especially disliked Jews and attributed his refusal to abolish restrictions imposed on them to an "inner voice" that told him it would be wrong to do so.[12] Nor could he abide the intelligentsia. When Prince P. D. Sviatopolk-Mirsky, then Governor-General of Vilna, Grodno, and Kovno, accompanied the Tsar on a provincial tour, someone at a banquet mentioned the word "intelligentsia," provoking Nicholas to declare: "How repulsive I find that word." He added, wistfully, that the Academy of Sciences ought to expunge the word from the Russian dictionary. Nicholas firmly believed that all groups of the population except for the intelligentsia were completely devoted to him.[13]

At the time he ascended the throne, Nicholas was an unknown quantity to society at large, a fact that encouraged many enlightened people to hope that the new ruler would adopt policies more liberal than those of Alexander III. But Nicholas did not wait long before disabusing the optimists. On January 17, 1895, he told a delegation representing the nobility, the zemstvos, and the cities that they were entertaining "senseless dreams" of participating "in the affairs of internal administration." He intended to "maintain the principle of autocracy just as firmly and unflinchingly as did my unforgettable father."[14]

Actually, when the Tsar early in 1895 appointed I. L. Goremykin as head of the Ministry of Internal Affairs, the most important post in the government, society still had cause to be hopeful about the regime's political direction. Goremykin, a bureaucrat of many years' service, at that time was reputed to be an enlightened official who respected the rule of law. Apparently, the Tsar considered him acceptable for the high post because he had advocated revoking some of the judicial reforms introduced in the 1860's. But the likelihood of his being an effective minister was slight, for he lacked deep convictions and the energy to implement new initiatives of any kind. In 1899 Goremykin fell out of favor because he wished to establish zemstvos in the western provinces, where the law of 1864 on the formation of local organs of self-government did not apply. When he became embroiled in intense rivalries among other senior officials, he was dismissed. For the next five years Tsar Nicholas relied on two men who believed in the mailed fist as the principal tool of government.

Goremykin's successor, D. S. Sipiagin, was a 46-year-old country squire widely known as a bureaucrat whose intellectual endowments were slight even by the standards of the Russian civil service. His remedy for the growing political disaffection was to intensify repression.[15] Sipiagin was killed by a revolutionary in April 1902, whereupon the Tsar, disappointed with the mildness of the late minister's repressive measures, appointed V. K. Plehve to the post. In Plehve the sovereign had at last found a man who appeared to be ideally suited to carry out his wishes. Plehve was intelligent, devoted to the preservation of absolutism, and aware that Russia was undergoing a serious political crisis that required immediate attention. Although not reluctant to use force to crush the critics of the autocratic regime, he also favored more subtle approaches. For good reason, he has acquired the reputation of being the most reactionary and wiliest statesman of late Imperial Russia.

Born in 1846, Plehve joined the civil service in 1867 and by 1881 advanced to the post of Director of the Department of Police. In 1899 he became Minister for the Duchy of Finland, where he made his mark as a staunch proponent of the autocratic principle. He took the initiative in writing an imperial manifesto that, together with some other statutes of 1899, deprived Finland of the autonomy it had enjoyed ever since becoming part of the Russian Empire in 1809. These restrictive measures, totally unprovoked by the Finns, stimulated a protest movement in Finland that developed within six years into a major irritant to the Russian government.[16]

On assuming the post of Minister of Internal Affairs in 1902, Plehve became the preeminent figure in the Imperial government, even though he frequently feuded with the Minister of Finance, S. Iu. Witte, a powerful personality equally determined to shape the overall direction of the government. The jurisdiction of Plehve's ministry was immense. The ministry was composed not only of various branches of the police but also of separate departments responsible for the "peasant economy and rural life, mails and telegraph, medicine and statistics, non-Orthodox religions, the prison system, and censorship of the press." The governors of the provinces reported to the Minister of Internal Affairs, who also exercised substantial authority over the zemstvos and city councils. It is no exaggeration to say that hardly any aspect of domestic policy remained outside the jurisdiction of the department.[17]

Plehve's main concern was to pacify the country, which was rife with discontent. He was not averse to reform and actually devised several measures to conciliate the growing opposition; the most notable, the manifesto of February 26, 1903, was an ambiguous document that promised both decentralization of authority and continued control over national affairs by the Ministry of Internal Affairs.[18] But Plehve did not favor granting any class or social group in society a genuine voice in government. He considered both the masses and the educated groups inadequately trained for such a role, and he cherished autocratic rule as indispensable to the maintenance of order and stability. He was so obsessively committed to the latter notion that he could not tolerate the slightest expression of criticism of the authorities. In the words of V. I. Gurko, himself a conservative, Plehve "erred seriously in failing to differentiate between the revolutionary elements which strove to undermine the political and, to an even greater degree, the social structure of the state, and those public forces which, although in opposition to the government, were nevertheless opposed to the radical changes advocated by the socialists."[19]

The problem was that although Plehve talked about the need for reform, he really preferred repression, which achieved only superficial and temporary victories for the government over the forces of change. He ordered police searches and stepped up the policy of Russification throughout the Empire, but he directed his fire in particular against the zemstvos. He had their employees summarily arrested, he regularly overturned decisions of their assemblies, he frequently refused to confirm in office representatives elected by the zemstvo assemblies to serve on their boards, and he prohibited zemstvos from discussing such topics as universal education.

Nothing illustrates Plehve's intransigence more strikingly than his refusal in April 1904 to confirm D. N. Shipov as chairman of the zemstvo board of Moscow guberniia. Shipov, who had been active in zemstvo affairs since the 1890's and was regarded by all sectors of society as a responsible and thoroughly decent person, was devoted to the monarchy. He merely advocated an extension of the competence of local institutions of self-government and some form of national organization of the zemstvos. Plehve, however, believed that any such national body was bound in time to come into jurisdictional conflict with the central government, and he therefore would not permit its formation. If loyal monarchists such as Shipov could not even voice differing views on the issue without being punished, a serious clash between society and the radical opposition on one side, and the autocracy and the bureaucracy on the other, was unavoidable. Plehve's action against Shipov shocked "all of zemstvo Russia"; even the otherwise docile city council in Moscow formally expressed its sympathy for Shipov and asked that he be permitted to return to his work.[20] The government, it was widely believed, had mindlessly provoked society.

In truth, neither Plehve, the Tsar, nor most of the other leaders realized that the agitation for reform, far from being a passing phenomenon, was the outgrowth of a series of profound economic, social, and cultural changes, many of which the government itself had initiated. Russia's humiliating defeats on her own soil during the Crimean War (1853–56) had amply demonstrated that the country's economic and social backwardness had sapped its national strength. To a very large extent, those defeats prompted the government to undertake the Great Reforms of the 1860's and 1870's, which abolished serfdom, created the zemstvos, established the rudiments of the rule of law, and modernized the army. But by the 1880's and 1890's it was clear that by themselves the reforms, however far-reaching, could not maintain Russia as a European power such as she had been early in the nineteenth century. To remain a significant actor in the international arena, the country would have to be modernized economically. Unwilling to see their Empire slip into oblivion, the rulers of the late nineteenth and early twentieth centuries made the only possible decision, to embark on a program of rapid industrialization. Yet they did not understand the implications of their decision. They deluded themselves into believing that they could modernize the country economically without altering the traditional social and political order.

No one fostered the illusion more fervently than S. Iu. Witte, the brilliant architect of Russian industrialization who also played a central role in shaping government policies during the first fifteen months of the Revolution of 1905. Born in 1849 in Tiflis to a family that acquired hereditary nobility, Witte enjoyed the advantages of a cultivated upbringing and solid education.[21] At the age of sixteen he enrolled at Novorossiisk University in Odessa to study mathematics. He completed his studies with distinction and considered an academic career, but friends persuaded him that such an occupation was not worthy of a nobleman. In 1871 he entered the civil service, concentrating on railway administration. He advanced rapidly, turned to private business in 1877, and by 1889 had demonstrated such outstanding skills and imagination as an administrator that he returned to government service to head the Railway Department of the Ministry of Finance. Three years later, at the age of 43, he was appointed Minister of Finance, which marked the beginning of a fourteen-year period of extraordinary influence at the highest echelons of government.

Even Witte's sharpest critics acknowledged that he was a "rare Russian talent."[22] Highly intelligent and perceptive, he quickly grasped the essentials of any problem he tackled and devised ingenious, if not always effective, solutions. He was masterly in judging the abilities of subordinates and in inducing them to do his bidding. But he was also fiercely ambitious, arrogant, cunning, and given to backstage intrigues. If he encountered obstacles he could not overcome, he lapsed into depressions. He never accepted blame for the failure of any of his policies; it was always the fault of his opponents, whom he slandered mercilessly. Yet he could also be generous and loyal to the few people whom he counted as his friends. A firm believer in autocracy and the old order, he nevertheless was capable of defying the mores of high society. In the early 1890's he married a divorcée "of shady reputation" who was also believed to be Jewish. He could never bring his wife to Court and was excluded from many of the social functions in St. Petersburg, but by all accounts he remained devoted to her.

Shortly before his retirement from politics Witte's conception of economic modernization without political change would be tested to its limits, although by that time he had concluded that the traditional polity could no longer be maintained. Even later, in his memoirs, Witte claimed that primary responsibility for the political crisis must be laid at the feet of Tsar Nicholas, who lacked the wisdom to guide the ship of state through stormy waters. Witte's argument is not altogether without merit, but it suffers from two flaws. First, the very system of hereditary autocracy afforded no checks against the possibility of incompetent leadership. Second, as Witte occasionally acknowledged, by the early twentieth century the opposition to the autocracy had developed so large and devoted a following that at some point its campaigns for fundamental change would probably have produced a political crisis even if the ruler had not been incompetent.

Witte advocated industrialization not because he believed that modernization was desirable in itself or because he wished to raise the standard of living of the Russian masses. He wanted to transform the economy of Russia primarily to assure the political power and greatness of the state. It was this argument that appealed to Tsar Alexander III, who appointed him Minister of Finance in 1892, and to Nicholas II, who retained him in that office until 1903.[23] During those eleven years Witte's achievements were, by virtually every standard, remarkable.

Although some industries had been established by the 1880's, the real spurt occurred in the following decade, as a few statistics will indicate. In 1880, Russia had 22,865 kilometers of railway track. By 1890 almost 8,000 more kilometers had been laid, for a total of 30,596; but by 1904 trackage had virtually doubled, to 59,616 kilometers. Coal output in southern Russia jumped from 183 million poods in 1890 to 671 million poods in 1900 (1 pood equals 36.11 pounds). In the same region, the production of iron and steel rose from 8.6 million poods in 1890 to 75.8 million in 1900. Also between 1890 and 1900 the production of cotton thread almost doubled and that of cloth increased by about two-thirds. By 1914 the Russian Empire was the fifth industrial power in the world. But in some important respects economic progress was not as impressive as these figures suggest. Labor productivity and per-capita income rose much more slowly than in Western Europe. In 1910 per-capita income was only a third of the West European average, whereas in 1860 it had been slightly more than half.[24]

Reliable statistics on the size of the industrial proletariat at the turn of the century are hard to find. The government consistently used low figures to buttress its contention that the growth of an urban proletariat posed no threat to social and political stability. Many Marxists, most notably Lenin, vastly exaggerated the size of the proletariat by including various categories of workers that Marx himself never considered capable of developing the "proper degree of class consciousness." One Soviet historian has shown that Lenin, basing himself on the census of 1897, came up with a startlingly large number by categorizing the following groups as belonging to the proletariat, in addition to the 2,792,900 workers employed in large industrial establishments: 3.5 million agricultural laborers, 2 million forest workers, and 2 million people who worked in their homes. Altogether, according to this calculation, there lived in Russia over 10 million proletarians and "semi-proletarians" who, with their families, amounted to 64 million souls, 50.9 percent of the total population. On the basis of these statistics, Soviet historians have claimed that by 1917 the preconditions for socialism did indeed exist in Russia.[25] But M. I. Tugan-Baranovskii, a respected Marxist scholar, estimated in the late 1890's that the total number of industrial workers was about 3 million.[26] Even this figure is probably high, but if it is reasonably accurate it would still mean that the proletariat constituted no more than 2.4 percent of the country's total population. No student of Russian history can fail to wonder how such a small proportion of the population came to exert so significant an influence on the political evolution of the Empire.

To a large extent, the answer is to be found in the peculiarities of Russia's industrialization. The country was a latecomer to the process, and the state played an inordinately large role in stimulating industrial development. Determined to press forward quickly, Witte launched an array of interrelated programs, the main purpose of which was to amass capital investment. Among other things, he promoted foreign loans and investments, established confidence in Russia's financial system by adopting the gold standard, placed extremely high tariffs on foreign industrial commodities, and substantially raised the rates of taxation. A large share of the financial burden for these programs fell on low-income groups, especially the peasants, who had to pay high prices for manufactured goods and absorb the high indirect taxes on such items as tobacco, sugar, matches, and petroleum.[27]

The state not only adopted policies to encourage industrial development but also participated directly in the nation's economy to an extent unequaled in any Western country. For example, in 1899 the state bought almost two-thirds of all metallurgical production. By the early twentieth century it controlled some 70 percent of the railways. It also owned vast tracts of land, numerous mines and oil fields, and extensive forests. The national budgets from 1903 to 1913 indicate that the government received over 25 percent of its income from its various holdings. Thus, the economic well-being of private entrepreneurs depended in large measure on decisions of the authorities in St. Petersburg—a major reason for the political timidity of a substantial sector of the Russian middle class.[28]

On the other hand, the concentration of industry, a result of the adoption of the forms of production and factory organization of more advanced countries, facilitated the emergence of a militant labor movement early in the process of industrialization. At the beginning of the twentieth century Russia's manufacturing economy was more heavily concentrated than those of Germany and the United States, usually singled out as the pathfinders in this regard.[29] The existence of large factories was a boon to labor organizers and political activists, who could easily reach sizable numbers of workers resentful of the harsh conditions at the workplace.

The insensitive way senior government officials and industrialists handled the "labor question" also fueled working-class militancy. Until 1905 they frequently asserted that there was no labor problem at all, that relations between employers and their workers were patriarchal in character, comparable to the relations between landlords and peasants. Consequently, they argued, the Russian worker, who was in any event less well educated than his counterpart in Western Europe and still tied to the land, would not succumb to the enticements of outside agitators, the alleged fomenters of labor unrest. Many officials knew that these assertions were baseless;[30] but a frank acknowledgment by Imperial authorities that the patriarchal relationship was inapplicable to the urban setting would have constituted, in the words of one historian, "a denial of the validity of the social order on which the Tsarist regime was based."[31]

The disciplinary paternalism in industry, initially introduced by nobles who owned factories, grew harsher in the course of the nineteenth century, in part because the non-nobles who increasingly entered the entrepreneurial class lacked the tradition of *noblesse oblige*. The laws governing the contractual obligations of the worker were precise and stern, clearly designed to buttress the social and economic powers of the employer. Thus, amendments to the Penal Code in 1845 branded collective resistance to the employer as tantamount to an uprising against the state, punishable by fifteen to twenty years of hard labor. A strike for higher wages could result in prison sentences of three weeks to three months for instigators and seven days to three weeks for participants. In 1874 the Penal Code was further amended to make membership in an illegal organization that fomented strikes and unrest punishable by eight months' imprisonment in a fortress and exile to Siberia. During the next decade the government issued several decrees that increased these penalties.[32]

Conditions for factory workers were grim. After 1897 they normally worked eleven and a half hours a day five days a week and somewhat less on Saturdays. Their wages were exceedingly low, and since many of them (the exact numbers are in dispute) returned for part of the year to their villages to work in the fields, they were housed in large, unsanitary barracks during their service at the factory.[33] Many owners of industrial plants acted like "Tsars in their realm" and looked upon their workers "as servants and slaves."[34] The employers and their managers condescended to the laborers, addressing them in the familiar "thou," searching them for stolen goods at the end of the workday, and imposing fines on them for infractions of the intricate "Rules of internal order." Any act of insubordination was punishable by a fine.[35]

The wide cultural gulf between workers on the one hand and factory supervisors and government officials on the other only exacerbated relations between them. In 1897 about 50 percent of the proletariat was illiterate, and many who were classed as literate could barely read and write. That workers were not only economically exploited but also profoundly humiliated goes a long way toward explaining why they frequently gave vent to rage during the revolution.

In the meantime, it had become apparent that Russian workers would not permanently accept their status of inferiority and remain docile. Between 1862 and 1869 six strikes and 29 "disturbances" took place; from 1870 to 1885 the average number of annual strikes rose to twenty and the number of disturbances from three to 73. Some of the strikes, such as those in the St. Petersburg cotton mills in 1870, at Krenholm near Narva in 1872, and at Orekhovo-Zuevo in 1885, were so massive as to suggest a significant change in the proletariat's mood.[36] Increasingly, government officials acknowledged publicly that labor strife, far from simply being perpetrated by outside agitators, was in fact deeply rooted in working conditions. By 1884, the police in St. Petersburg and Moscow, who kept an eye on all potential sources of disorder, had issued several reports on the erosion of the paternalistic relationship between manufacturer and employee. The police contended that the masters paid their workers too little, showed no concern for their well-being, and had lost their respect. The social ideals of the Tsarist regime were manifestly not being implemented in the industrial sector of the economy.[37]

At the initiative of an enlightened Minister of Finance, N. Kh. Bunge, a child labor law was adopted in 1882 that prohibited the employment of children under twelve, limited the workday of children aged twelve to fifteen to eight hours, and placed restrictions on the use of children for night work. The law of 1882 also provided for factory inspectors to enforce the legislation. Beginning in 1884, inspectors regularly visited factories, examined conditions, listened to grievances of both workers and employers, and sought to achieve amicable settlements of labor disputes. Mostly professors and professionals with liberal sympathies, the inspectors gained some improvements for the workers, and their detailed reports on conditions are still a valuable source of information. There were too few inspectors, however; by 1897 only 267 had been appointed for the entire Empire. Some of the larger factories (especially among those owned by the government) and the smaller plants did not even come under their jurisdiction. Moreover, the Ministry of Finance, especially after Bunge's departure from office, directed the inspectors to concentrate on the maintenance of law and order in industrial enterprises and mines. At the same time, industrialists found ways to evade the laws protecting workers, either by misleading illiterate employees and gullible inspectors or by bribing unscrupulous inspectors. Not surprisingly, many workers looked upon the inspectors as government officials who could not be trusted to defend the proletariat's interests.[38]

In 1899 the government adopted new measures to prevent strikes. The third department of the Ministry of Internal Affairs established an elaborate network of police surveillance in industrial enterprises. Ostensibly the policemen were to study such matters as the "economic life of the factories" and workers' conditions, but in fact they devoted much of their time to ferreting out instigators of strikes and arresting them before the strikes were held. Discovering the leaders of a potential strike, however, was not easy. Indeed, labor unrest continued to rise rapidly, as the following ministry figures indicate: between 1886 and 1894 the annual average was 33; between 1895 and 1904, 176. During the massive strikes in 1896 and 1897 in the textile mills of St. Petersburg, workers revealed an unprecedented degree of sophistication, unity, and discipline. There could no longer be any doubt about the Russian workers' ability to act forcefully to advance their interests. The strike movement reached its highest level in the period before the Revolution of 1905 in 1903, when 138,877 workers engaged in 550 work stoppages.[39] The one policy that might have defused labor unrest, the legalization of independent unions and strikes, was never tried because the government feared that it would undermine the entire structure of autocratic rule.

In 1902 Witte actually proposed that strikes be legalized, on the assumption that they were a "purely economic phenomenon and not in the least threatening to the general order or peace." [40] But Sipiagin, the Minister of Internal Affairs, would not hear of it. He proposed instead that the police encourage conservative elements among the workers to form organizations to promote their economic interests. The difference between Sipiagin and Witte reflected an ongoing dispute between the Ministries of Internal Affairs and Finance that at times became acrimonious. Ever since rapid industrialization began in the early 1890's, the Ministry of Finance contended that economic efficiency demanded the government's noninterference in relations between labor and management. But the Ministry of Internal Affairs, concerned with the maintenance of order, wanted the government to press industrialists into pacifying labor through economic concessions. [41] Sipiagin and his successor, Plehve, gained the upper hand in the bureaucratic struggle. They even went so far as to arrange official sponsorship for some labor unions, but in the end their policies failed badly. In autocratic Russia any workers' organization, no matter how circumscribed by governmental regulations, would inevitably pose an intolerable challenge to the authorities. A case in point was the experiment in police unionization known as *Zubatovshchina*, or police socialism.

The scheme was the brainchild of S. V. Zubatov, one of the more colorful and imaginative police officers of pre-revolutionary Russia. Born in Moscow in 1863 or 1864, he early displayed a keen interest in intellectual pursuits and a strong sympathy for radical politics. But by 1884 his politics changed completely and he became an informant for the Okhrana. He formally joined the political police, probably in 1886, and rose rapidly through the ranks, attaining the post of head of the Moscow branch of the Okhrana within ten years. Zubatov was a fanatical believer in the cause he served as well as a highly intelligent and well-read official with a gift for turning a clever phrase. "You must look upon your colleague, the secret agent," he once told a group of subordinates, "as you would upon a woman with whom you are conducting a secret intrigue: one rash step and you have dishonored her in the eyes of the world." [42]

In 1898 Zubatov wrote a memorandum on the labor question for General D. F. Trepov, chief of police in Moscow, in which he urged the government to take the initiative in improving conditions for industrial workers and thus undermine the appeal of the socialists. Zubatov envisioned the development of the Tsarist regime into a "social monarchy," whose authority would be strengthened immensely by its assumption of the role of mediator in the struggle between capitalists and workers. Trepov found the arguments persuasive, and when the reactionary Grand Duke Sergei Aleksandrovich, Governor-General of Moscow and uncle of the Tsar, was also won over to Zubatov's scheme, the authorities in St. Petersburg gave their reluctant assent to the new approach.

Early in 1901 Zubatov began to organize educational activities for workers in Moscow. He enlisted liberal professors, unaware of his ultimate goals, to give lectures on a variety of subjects. In addition, Zubatov established three unions, which submitted demands to their employers; the latter, in turn, were pressured by police agents into making concessions to the workers. Soon "police unions" appeared in St. Petersburg, Vilna, Minsk, and Odessa. Deeply alarmed, employers and Witte urged the Ministry of Internal Affairs to call a halt to the scheme before the economy was irreparably harmed. Others feared that Zubatov's activities would politicize the workers.[43]

Nevertheless, the experiment was allowed to continue for another year and a half, in large measure because workers appeared to be rallying around the monarchy in response to Zubatov's enticements. On February 19, 1902, some 50,000 of them, organized by the police, marched to the monument of Alexander II to pay homage to the man who 41 years earlier had liberated the serfs. It was an orderly demonstration by workers confident that the monarch would once again turn his attention to his humble and deprived subjects and improve their lot. The Grand Duke Sergei Aleksandrovich and General Trepov were accompanied by P. I. Rachkovskii, a high police official from St. Petersburg, in reviewing this unprecedented display of working-class support for the "social monarchy." Rachkovskii, initially dubious about Zubatov's scheme, became a convert, and police socialism now gained other supporters in the upper reaches of the government. In July 1903, however, one of the police unions was believed to have been the moving force behind the general strike in Odessa, the first work stoppage of such dimensions in Russia. This unexpected turn of events alerted the authorities anew to the potential dangers of any legal workers' organization. They dismissed Zubatov and ended his experiment, which again left the government without an overall policy to defuse the protest movement of the working class. In 1904, Plehve, for lack of a better alternative, permitted a priest in St. Petersburg, Father Georgii Gapon, to revive "police socialism"—with results far more explosive than those in Odessa, as we shall see in Chapter 3.[44]

· · · · ·

Because the working class played a critical role in the events of 1905 and a party claiming to be its spokesman took power in 1917, scholars have taken great pains to recount the history of the Russian proletariat, its grievances and yearnings, its organizations, and the ideology of its various leaders. Yet early in the twentieth century the Empire was still a predominantly agrarian society and the people in the countryside constituted over 70 percent of the population. True, the vast majority of the peasantry was still devoted to the Tsar and considered him to be the only legitimate source of political authority. As they had for centuries, the peasants looked upon him as "God's vicar on earth," empowered to rule the land and committed to providing for his people's needs. They were convinced that the sovereign had their interests at heart; if only they could inform him about their grievances, he would overrule the landlords and officials and do his utmost to remedy them.[45] Most peasants also believed that in 1861 the Tsar had intended not only to emancipate them but to transfer all the land to them. The world of the peasants, it must be stressed, was highly circumscribed: they were mainly influenced by the Church, school, and the conscript army, institutions that placed a premium on loyalty to the autocracy.

Yet it would be a mistake to assume that the peasants did not nurture serious resentments. The agrarian disturbances in 1902 in Poltava and Kharkov provinces and the far more extensive outbursts of unrest in 1905 and 1906 testify to a profound malaise in the countryside. It is noteworthy, however, that the peasants focused their attacks not on the autocrat or his officials but on the landlords, whom they held primarily responsible for frustrating the Tsar's will.[46]

The principal cause of the peasants' discontent was their economic plight, which had deteriorated steadily since their emancipation.[47] In the first place, the rapid growth in population between 1887 and 1905 resulted in a decline in the average landholding of peasant households of over 20 percent, from 13.2 to 10.4 desiatinas (one desiatina equals 2.7 acres). Productivity remained abysmally low, in large measure because the system of communal landownership, which governed about four-fifths of the peasants' holdings, was not conducive either to long-range planning or to the application of modern methods of farming.[48] Many statistics could be cited to demonstrate the wretched conditions in the countryside, but none is more telling than the following: the death rate in Russia was almost double that in England.[49]

The government's fiscal policies, as already noted, also placed inordinate burdens on the peasantry. The expenses of the state treasury grew from 1861 to 1905 by 800 percent, from 414 million rubles to 3,205 million rubles, necessitating new taxes, many of which were levied on consumer goods. The peasant had to pay these taxes in addition to the redemption dues that had been imposed on him at the time of emancipation. Desperate to meet the tax bills, many poorer peasants were forced to sell their harvest in the fall, when plentiful supplies drove down prices. In the winter and spring, they would have to buy back some of the grain at exorbitant prices or take loans from landlords or kulaks (well-to-do peasants), which they would repay with labor if they lacked cash. For short-term loans, interest rates of 9.7 percent a month or 116.4 percent per year were not uncommon. If the peasant failed to make his payments, he might be subjected to whipping with a birch rod, or his property might be confiscated and sold. These measures did not have the desired effect. In the years from 1871 to 1875, the total peasant arrears in payments of various dues and taxes amounted to 29 million rubles. Twenty years later they totaled 119 million rubles.[50]

The peasants were also forced to endure the heavy hand of the bureaucracy. The emancipation of 1861 had freed them from serfdom, but they still could not move freely from one place to another and in numerous ways remained at the mercy of local landlords. Officials could imprison a peasant or exile him to Siberia without benefit of a trial. Only in 1903 did the government prohibit corporal punishment of convicted criminals. After the counterreforms of the late 1880's the land captains, appointed by provincial governors, assumed a vast amount of arbitrary power in the countryside. They could overrule decisions of all local institutions, appoint personnel to important governmental positions, and order the imprisonment of a peasant for five days or impose five-ruble fines on him without resorting to judicial proceedings.[51]

In view of these conditions in the countryside, the peasants' aloofness from revolutionary or other opposition movements may seem odd. But organized political action could hardly have been expected from a social class that was geographically dispersed, cut off from urban centers of intellectual life, and still largely (over 80 percent) illiterate. On the other hand, the rural masses did constitute yet another social group that could not be relied upon to side with the forces of order in times of crisis.[52]

Peasant unrest was not the only sign of social stress in the countryside. The *dvorianstvo* (nobility or gentry) was losing its grip economically and was declining as a social and political force. Still, the nobles were unquestionably the main prop of the autocracy, even though they constituted a small and highly diversified group. According to the census of 1897, 1.5 percent of the population were either hereditary or lifetime nobles, among whom one could find "rich . . . and poor ones, rustics and urbanites, reactionaries and liberals, capitalist operators of large estates, employers of hired or tenant labour (the majority of the landed gentry), rentiers, civil servants, officers, and professionals (one fifth or more) who, at best, kept a tenuous foothold or summer home in the countryside.

Half the nobility was non-Russian, and the 28.6 percent who were Poles and discriminated against by the state hardly contributed to the solidarity of the class."[53] Even the ethnically Russian nobles were so diversified in their interests that they did not form a common political front. Although the majority ardently supported the autocracy, quite a few became active in the liberal movement, to the dismay of the Tsar and officials at Court.

The decline of the nobility was probably unavoidable once the serfs were emancipated. Until that time, the nobility had performed important functions in the body politic, though it did not enjoy the kind of independence from the state that its counterpart in France (or other Western European countries) had achieved by the late eighteenth century. The Russian nobles exercised vast authority over the roughly 45 percent of the peasants who were their serfs, manned the judicial posts in their districts, supervised the collection of the soul tax, and oversaw the recruitment of men for military service. A few nobles, moreover, owned large estates that yielded a surplus for the export market. No matter how the other classes viewed these arrangements, they could not deny that the *dvorianstvo* discharged obligations useful to the state. After the reforms of the 1860's, however, the *dvorianstvo* lost much of its *raison d'être* and standing in society, though that was not the government's intention.

In fact, Alexander II's government went to great lengths to prevent the decline of the nobility. It designed the emancipation decree in such a way as to provide the nobles with a maximum amount of land. It also granted them tax privileges and assured them a dominant role in the local organs of government. Tsar Alexander III (1881–94) continued to be solicitous about the *dvorianstvo*, which he regarded as the preeminent class in society and the state.[54] In 1885 the government created the Gentry Land Bank, which offered loans at low interest rates to noble landowners. But neither this measure nor several others undertaken by the government in the late 1880's and the 1890's halted the decline of the *dvorianstvo*.

The most striking manifestation of the nobility's decline was its loss of land. Unable or unwilling to administer their estates on a capitalist basis, many nobles sold their land to townsmen or peasants. In the period from the Great Reforms until 1905, the nobility surrendered about one-third of its total landholdings. To appreciate the magnitude of the transformation in landownership, it should be kept in mind that in the 1860's the privileged classes owned one-half of all privately held arable land.

Economic trends played an important role in the nobility's decline. The severe agrarian crisis in the last decades of the nineteenth century, a worldwide phenomenon that caused a sharp drop in the prices of major crops, hindered the development of large-scale farming in Russia.[55]

Moreover, most nobles never mastered the rudiments of scientific farming and made only the feeblest efforts to obtain up-to-date machinery.[56]

In the last analysis, the nobles' inability to turn their estates into profitable ventures was rooted in their psychological disposition. Under serfdom, noble landlords had never been known for hard work, managerial skills, or frugality. Accustomed to receiving state handouts and dues as well as services from their serfs, they failed to develop the drive and initiative necessary for success in a market economy. The emancipation of the serfs made matters worse for the nobility. They became even more paralyzed, for now they had to fend for themselves under circumstances thoroughly alien to their experience.

Early in the reign of Tsar Nicholas II, senior officials became alarmed at the nobility's declining role in public institutions. So many nobles had fled the countryside that the supply of personnel qualified to hold positions of authority was seriously depleted. At times, not enough nobles could be found to fill all the seats to which they were entitled in the zemstvo assemblies. It has been estimated that in 50 provinces out of 78 the *dvorianstvo* was no longer capable of exerting a measurable influence on local affairs. The government was at a loss on how to reverse the trend.[57]

. . . . .

In the political arena, the government's policy of modernizing the economy without altering social and political institutions resulted in a unique phenomenon, the simultaneous appearance of organized liberalism and radicalism, both aspiring to mass support. But the autocracy refused to integrate either one of the new groups into the body politic in any meaningful way, which decisively affected the relationship between liberalism and radicalism virtually from the moment of their emergence as organized movements. Despite their shared hostility toward the autocratic regime, they were at odds with each other in vying for broad popular support on the basis of divergent visions of the country's future. Yet leaders of the two movements could not fail to realize that open warfare between them would inevitably play into the hands of the autocracy. Consequently, liberals and radicals faced tactical problems of enormous complexity.

Liberalism, in Russia and in the West, was such an amorphous movement that any attempt to define it necessarily runs the risk of oversimplification. At its core was the stress on individualism, the notion that the freedom of the individual must be protected against arbitrary encroachments by the state or social groups. There were important differences among Russian liberals, as we shall see, but all were critical of the bureaucracy and most favored limitations on the powers of the monarch. Liberals also tended (again with significant variations) to favor the rule of law, civil liberties, guarantees of private property, and the creation of a legislative body with a voice in shaping the laws of the Empire.[58] Finally, until the turn of the century, most of them believed that by means of peaceful agitation they would be able to persuade the Tsar and the bureaucracy to introduce reforms along these lines. When it became evident to liberals that they had misjudged the authorities' inflexibility, they faced the question whether to adopt more militant tactics and intensify their appeal for support to the lower classes. If they ignored the masses, they would risk being no more than an army of generals without soldiers, since the natural constituency for the liberal movement was not very large. On the other hand, if they sought the support of peasants and workers by championing some of their demands for economic and social reform, the liberals would risk alienating the moderates within their own ranks, who feared that such appeals would unleash the destructive impulses of the peasantry. Moreover, the latter tactic would provide ammunition for conservatives, who had insisted all along that the critics of the autocracy were without exception irresponsible agitators whose activities would, perforce, undermine the stability and integrity of the Empire.

The radicals, and in particular the Marxists, faced a dilemma no less difficult. Ever since the formation of the Russian Marxist organization in 1883 (the Group for the Emancipation of Labor, the forerunner of the Social Democratic Party), G. V. Plekhanov and his comrades had contended that the economic and political development of Russia would be similar, though not identical, to that of Western Europe. Russia would first undergo a bourgeois revolution, which would usher in the kind of polity that the liberals advocated; after an undetermined period of further industrial growth, a second, proletarian, revolution would occur. But whereas in Western Europe the proletariat had been a mere appendage to the bourgeoisie in the struggles against the old regime, in Russia workers would constitute an independent political force and would even take the initiative in the assault on Tsarism. As a consequence, the bourgeoisie in power would not be able to ignore the interests of the proletariat and the workers would not have to wait as long as their counterparts in the West before launching the socialist revolution. "Our capitalism," Plekhanov wrote in 1885, "will fade without having fully flowered."[59] Plekhanov's conception was appealing, but it proved not to be a satisfactory guide for the formulation of tactics by the workers' party that emerged late in the 1890's.

The problem was that liberalism and Social Democracy became political rivals even before the 1905 revolution. Ideological consistency as well as logic seemed to prescribe that the Social Democrats support the liberals. After all, the achievement of the goals of liberalism would vastly increase the scope of the working class's opportunities to operate openly in the political arena. This strategy ran the risk of losing the Social Democrats the backing of industrial workers, who might not understand why socialists should come to the political aid of their exploiters, the bourgeoisie. On the other hand, if Social Democrats pressed such demands as a democratic republic and extensive social legislation, not to speak of socialist measures, they would prolong the life of the autocracy by driving the bourgeoisie into its arms. Neither the Marxists nor the liberals could find an easy way out of their dilemma; the tergiversations of both movements throughout the turbulent period from 1904 to 1907 attest to that.

Although more deeply rooted in Russian history than is generally recognized, liberalism until the early twentieth century lacked an organization to promote its ideas and values. In a very general sense, the movement may be said to have originated during the reign of Catherine the Great (1762–1796), when intellectuals for the first time expressed independent opinions on public issues and began to be active in various charitable and educational enterprises. The intellectuals came to be known in Russian as the *obshchestvennoe dvizhenie*, a term whose meaning is not accurately conveyed by its literal translation as "social movement." The adherents of the obshchestvennoe dvizhenie, a small minority within the educated nobility, all deplored what they perceived to be the crudities and backwardness of life in Russia, though they differed over how to bring about change. Some called for the moral and spiritual improvement of man, whereas others contended that institutions had to be changed. Purely economic concerns were much less important to them than to their counterparts in Great Britain. The supporters of the obshchestvennoe dvizhenie were moved by rationalism, individualism, and patriotism, and they deeply resented their inability to give expression to those ideals.

In the 1860's the liberal idealists, now drawn not only from the gentry but also from the *raznochintsy* ("people of diverse rank"), were dubbed the intelligentsia, a word, as we have seen, that Tsar Nicholas II could not abide. Because of the stifling political and cultural atmosphere in Russia and the absence of independent interest groups that could mount an effective campaign for reform, a growing number of the intelligentsia turned to radicalism, which created a split within enlightened society. Although only a tiny social group driven essentially by moral passion, the intelligentsia played a critical role in undermining the legitimacy of the Tsarist regime.[60]

The zemstvos, established shortly after the emancipation of the serfs, afforded public-spirited men an arena in which to pursue the general good. To be sure, their scope was limited to such activities as charity, local education, health services, the building of roads and bridges, the maintenance of records, and the improvement of agricultural productivity, but the zemstvos were the only semipolitical institution at least partly free from bureaucratic control. And within their circumscribed sphere of competence, these local organs of self-government were remarkably effective, which accounts for the high hopes placed in them by the intelligentsia.

The law creating the zemstvos assured a predominant place in them to the gentry by stipulating that 42.1 percent of the deputies elected must come from its ranks; the peasants were allowed 38.5 percent, and the rest of the population (merchants, clergy) 19.3 percent. In 1890, as part of the counterreforms, the nobles' share was substantially increased and the bureaucracy's power to intervene in zemstvo affairs was enhanced. These measures of counterreform succeeded only in driving the *zemtsy* (activists in the zemstvo assemblies) to the left and in further energizing the so-called "third element," the technical experts employed by the zemstvos.* The latter—teachers, agronomists, engineers, statisticians, and doctors— were for the most part idealistic men and women who could find no other opportunities for public service. Their numbers increased steadily, reaching 65,000 to 70,000 by 1908. Committed activists and generally sympathetic to the left, these full-time employees of the zemstvos succeeded in persuading many elected zemstvo members to take up the cause of political reform. The employees also exerted influence along these lines in such professional organizations as the Pirogov Medical Society, the Moscow Law Society, and the Committees for the Advancement of Literacy in St. Petersburg and Moscow. Government officials came to look upon the third element as dangerous troublemakers and in some localities forced the dismissal of many experts. In 1902 Plehve went so far as to accuse the third element of instigating peasant riots and of favoring "the destruction of the entire existing order."[61]

By the mid-1890's the zemstvos began to turn their attention to national issues and to express opposition to the bureaucracy and, to a lesser extent, the autocracy. A sizable group of nobles, convinced that the government was ignoring their concerns, supported the call for a national congress of zemstvo representatives, the very idea of which was anathema to the authorities in St. Petersburg. Suspecting that sooner or later such a national body would challenge the prerogatives of the government, the Minister of Internal Affairs regularly prohibited gatherings of zemstvo

---

* The term "third element" was coined in 1899 by the vice-governor of Samara, V. Kondoidi, who dubbed government officials and elected members to the zemstvo boards the first and second elements, respectively.

activists. The zemtsy therefore organized "private meetings," often in conjunction with an official affair, such as the unveiling of a monument to Alexander II in Moscow in 1898.[62] To prevent these meetings, the government frequently banished zemtsy from certain cities, which further aroused their ire. For several years I. I. Petrunkevich, one of the more dynamic, radical, and outspoken zemtsy, was not allowed to live in Moscow. When asked for an explanation, I. N. Durnovo, the Minister of Internal Affairs from 1889 to 1895, replied: "There are no definite charges against him, but people gather around him."[63]

In the 1890's Russian liberalism began to attract the support of professional people—professors, lawyers, writers, doctors, and engineers—a group that soon exerted an influence on the national scene out of all proportion to its numbers. Even if "intelligentsia" is defined very broadly as the "white-collar class," it included only about 0.6 percent of the population, and many white-collar workers could not be counted upon to support the liberal movement.[64] Nor was the middle class a likely source of mass recruitment for the liberals, for the simple reason that a bourgeoisie in the Western sense—that is, a class capable of standing on its own feet economically—existed in Russia only in embryonic form. In fact, until 1905 the leaders of the Moscow merchantry either showed little interest in the ideals of liberalism or actually opposed them. They were much less interested in participating in the political process than in encouraging government policies that would foster economic development and protect them against foreign competitors.[65] It is therefore all the more remarkable that the relatively small group of liberal professionals could build an impressive political movement in less than a decade. Their main weapon was the pen, and they had access to "thick journals" of opinion and newspapers of rather high quality. Although government censorship was a hindrance, the regulations were loose enough to enable liberals to express their views in general terms, often couched in Aesopian language.

P. N. Miliukov, who is quoted at the beginning of this chapter and who was to become the most influential leader of liberalism from 1905 to 1917, is a prime example of a talented professional drawn to the movement. His interests and knowledge as well as his capacity for work were so prodigious that people thought he could on his own write a complete newspaper, beginning with the political coverage and ending with a section on chess.[66] The son of an architect, Miliukov (1859–1943) pursued two careers, one in history and one in politics. After he was graduated from Moscow University in 1882, he devoted himself to historical research and wrote an outstanding work on economic developments in the early eighteenth century. He taught history for a few years and continued his scholarly research, but he also became an activist in the liberal movement. Exiled several times by the government and jailed once, he nevertheless persevered in his political work. Most people who knew him considered him to be a cold person, but everyone, including even opponents in the revolutionary camp, admired him for his logical mind and tactical shrewdness.

P. B. Struve, a gifted political thinker who had abandoned Marxism, was another leading spokesman for liberalism. Also very erudite, he did not possess the requisite qualities for political leadership but was a brilliant publicist. In June 1902 he began to edit the journal *Osvobozhdenie* (*Liberation*) in Germany, where he was free of the Tsarist censorship; as a result, for the first time Russian liberalism was armed with a journal that could discuss with complete openness the aims of the movement.[67] Like other antigovernment publications printed abroad, *Osvobozhdenie* was smuggled into Russia. In the new journal, Struve urged liberals to represent the interests not merely of one class but rather of the entire nation. In keeping with his ideological position, the journal stood considerably to the left of the zemtsy. For about two years Struve not only ceased to advocate legal methods of struggle against the autocracy but also applauded vigorously the violent methods of the revolutionaries.[68]

In response to Struve's strategy, liberals in Russia in 1903 founded the *Soiuz osvobozhdeniia* (Union of Liberation), an underground organization (formally established in 1904) that included a sprinkling of moderate Social Democrats and Socialist Revolutionaries. The Union's program, adopted in October 1904, called for the liquidation of the autocracy, the establishment of a constitutional form of government, self-determination for the nationalities of the Empire, and economic and social reforms. Though the program did not spell out the latter reforms in detail, it did speak of "defending the interests of the working class."[69] Many zemstvo liberals strongly opposed the radicalization of liberalism and continued to favor retaining the monarchy and allowing it substantial powers.

The cause of liberalism's shift to the left in the years from 1901 to 1904 has been a source of controversy among historians. Some have suggested that it came about as a result of the rise to prominence after 1901 of the radical political intelligentsia, who prevailed over the more moderate zemstvo liberals. Gregory Freeze has argued, however, that the shift followed a "reappraisal by the liberals of the dynamics available for the liberation movement." That is, they no longer considered the zemstvos to be suitable vehicles for the realization of their goals. Increasingly, liberals came to believe that a "profound gulf separates the Russian government from Russian society" and that the opposition movements of all shades of opinion must therefore unite against the old order. In the words of *Osvobozhdenie*, "Russian revolutionaries and Russian liberals in essence move in the same direction and merely go to different terminal points."[70]

Given the government's intransigence over political reform, the Liberationists' strategy appeared to be logical, and there were occasions in 1904 and 1905, as we shall see, when the forces for change did in fact collaborate. All the opponents of the autocratic regime were then moving in the same direction in the sense that they all favored political change. But "terminal points" cannot be disregarded for long in politics, and it soon became evident that profound differences among the opposition groups precluded their prolonged cooperation. The liberal movement itself was sharply divided between the proponents of a constitutional order and the advocates of an autocracy that would respect the rule of law. The differences between the liberals and the revolutionary left could no more easily be bridged, for they involved not only "terminal points," as Struve and his followers believed, but also the means to be used to "move in the same direction." However much the liberal leaders turned to the left, the bulk of their supporters insisted that the main weapon against the government must be an aroused and unified public opinion demanding change. The revolutionaries' penchant for violent upheaval was bound to lead to a parting of the ways between them and the liberals, unfortunately (for the latter) even before the task of political liberation had been completed.

The liberals' drift to the left took place at a time of unprecedented unrest at institutions of higher learning, with which many Liberationists had close ties. Traditionally a breeding ground for antigovernment unrest, the universities had been politically quiescent since 1884, when the government imposed various controls on them, most notably by revoking their autonomy, which had only been granted in 1863. Rectors, deans, and professors were no longer to be elected by academic councils but appointed by the Minister of Education. In addition, the government deprived students of the right to organize their own associations and assigned inspectors to the universities to maintain order.[71] As long as society in general remained politically passive, these measures were not challenged.

In 1899 a tactless warning by the rector of St. Petersburg University against rowdyism at an annual festival, coupled with unwarranted police brutality toward students, triggered demonstrations and unrest that soon engulfed virtually all the institutions of higher learning in the country. For about three years student disturbances erupted frequently at the universities, which developed into prominent centers of hostility toward the government and attracted extensive public attention.[72] Students, after all, represented not only the educational but also the social elite of the country; the leading universities and institutes drew upon the children of nobles and officials for the majority of their places.[73] Not infrequently, their experiences at the troubled institutions of higher learning led young Russians to embrace radicalism in its Populist or Marxist form.

The doctrines of Russian Marxism (or Social Democracy) had been formulated in the 1880's and 1890's, but it was not until the publication of the paper *Iskra* (*The Spark*) in 1900 under the leadership of V. I. Lenin that an imposing network of illegal organizations appeared within Russia. Barely 30 years old, Lenin had already displayed impressive skills as a party activist and polemicist. He had turned to radicalism in 1887, the year his older brother was executed for his role in a plot to kill Tsar Alexander III. In 1888, Lenin (still known by his family name, Ulyanov) embraced Marxism, a creed that he never abandoned but that he effectively adapted to Russian conditions by fusing the doctrines of the Russian Jacobins, who championed a dictatorship by a revolutionary party, with those of Marx. A strategist and tactician of revolution rather than a profound theorist, he owed much of his success in creating his own movement (and later in making the first Marxist revolution) to his personal qualities: enormous drive, sincerity, self-assurance, modesty, and political sagacity. As one of his erstwhile comrades said of him: "Only Lenin represented that rare phenomenon, especially rare in Russia, of a man of iron will and indomitable energy who combines faith in the movement, in the cause, with no less faith in himself."[74]

These personal qualities enabled Lenin to become the guiding spirit of *Iskra*'s editorial board, whose members lived in Central and Western Europe, where the paper was also published. Brilliantly written, the paper not only dealt with ideological and tactical questions, but also reported on general political developments, paying special attention to events that seemed to demonstrate the growth of political consciousness among industrial workers. This was a matter of deep concern to the Marxists, for it touched on the question of how soon they could expect to win the workers' support.

At the time of its founding, in 1898, the Russian Social Democratic Workers Party (RSDWP) predicted that capitalist exploitation would inevitably transform the workers into a class-conscious proletariat committed to socialist revolution and that growing numbers of them would offer their support to the party. The Marxists' favorite refrain was that the "liberation of the working class can only be achieved by its own efforts." This tenet accorded with the deterministic strain in original Marxism: that material conditions would energize and politicize the proletariat. But politicization progressed more slowly than anticipated, too slowly in fact for some of the leaders of the party, who lacked the patience to await the gradual unfolding of that process. Statistics on the growth of the party are scarce, but it is generally accepted that in the early months of 1905 there were only 12,000 active Social Democrats in the entire Empire, and it is by no means certain that the majority were actually workers. The Marxist party, like every contemporary Russian political movement, was dominated by intellectuals, and its inner core consisted of professional revolutionaries, men and women dedicated full-time to radical politics.

The Marxists faced a problem that had plagued radicals in the 1870's and would be a perennial obstacle for them: the political inertia of the masses. If the *narod* (the people), revered by many Russian radicals, refused to be budged toward activism, how could the revolution ever be made? One could argue that a long period of preparation and mass education was needed before the people would be capable of shaping their own destiny; or that those with the proper degree of class consciousness should take matters into their own hands and organize the revolution in the name of the people, who would support it once they recognized that it was in their interests. Lenin turned to the issue of the masses' political inertia and analyzed it most comprehensively in 1902 in the pamphlet *What Is to Be Done?*

Although Lenin always insisted on his credentials as a genuine Marxist and repudiated deviations from orthodoxy such as Revisionism and Economism,* in *What Is to Be Done?* he himself deviated from traditional Marxism by placing primary emphasis on voluntarism as against determinism. His central point was that by itself the working class could never attain class consciousness. It was too subservient to bourgeois ideology and too preoccupied with immediate bread-and-butter issues. Lenin held that the "revolutionary socialist intelligentsia" must therefore imbue the workers with class consciousness, a contention that ran counter to Marx's deterministic view of the historical process. Significantly, Lenin did not confine his analysis to the working class in Russia, which was prevented by the oppressive police regime from engaging in the kinds of organizational activities necessary to develop the proper degree of political consciousness. He explicitly declared that

---

* Revisionism was founded by Eduard Bernstein, who called for the abandonment of several Marxist dogmas on the ground that historical developments had undermined their validity. For details, see Peter Gay, *The Dilemma of Democratic Socialism: Eduard Bernstein's Challenge to Marx* (New York, 1952). The Economists argued that the labor movement in Russia should concentrate on a struggle for economic improvements; in the course of that struggle workers would become politicized. See Ascher, *Pavel Axelrod*, pp. 126–29, 164–67, 177–79.

workers of *all* countries had been "capable of evolving only a 'trade union' consciousness."

Actually, this portion of Lenin's argument did not differ markedly from the positions of other European Marxists, most notably Karl Kautsky, the preeminent interpreter of the creed. The unique feature of *What Is to Be Done?* was the notion that, because workers could not develop class consciousness on their own, they should not be recruited en masse into the Social Democratic Party, which must be controlled by a small conspiratorial group of professional revolutionaries. Lenin's organizational scheme implied nothing less than the permanent tutelage of the proletariat by the radical intelligentsia. The ultimate justification for this voluntaristic approach to politics was summed up in his oft-quoted boast: "Give us an organization of revolutionists and we shall overturn Russia."[75] In short, Lenin maintained that human initiative, not general economic forces, would be the decisive factor in determining the political fate of the country.

When Lenin's closest collaborators saw the original draft of *What Is to Be Done?* they either did not grasp its political elitism or chose not to raise major objections for fear of offending their colleague. But at the Russian Social Democrats' Second Party Congress in 1903, convened to unite the various Marxist factions, Lenin's views on the organizational question provoked the most heated debates and, ultimately, a schism in Russian Marxism. Lenin introduced a motion that defined a party member as anyone who subscribed to the party's program, gave it material support, and took part in the work of one of its organizations. Iu. O. Martov, one of the editors of *Iskra*, simply wished to substitute for Lenin's wording of the third point ("personal participation in one of the party organizations") the phrase "regular personal support under the guidance of one of [the party's] organizations." Only as the debate unfolded did it become clear that whereas Lenin wanted a small party dominated by a hierarchy of professionals, Martov and his supporters wanted the party to be as broad as possible and to maintain the greatest possible degree of contact with the masses of workers. Although Lenin lost on this issue by a vote of 28 to 21, he succeeded, by a series of shrewd maneuvers, in winning majorities on other questions. He therefore called his faction Bolsheviks (Majoritarians) and the opposition Mensheviks (Minoritarians), appellations that both groups accepted.[76]

For the next two years the two factions seemed to devote more time to hurling invective at each other than to preparing their followers for the struggle against Tsarism. To the uninitiated, the differences between the factions were far from obvious, and many rightly suspected that personal animus played an important part in the ideological conflicts. Nevertheless, a careful reading of the Mensheviks' writings of the period reveals that they sensed in Lenin's organizational scheme a radical departure from the ideals of Social Democracy. As P. B. Axelrod, one of the spokesmen of Menshevism, pointed out, the party envisioned by Lenin would be a hierarchical and authoritarian organization; if it ever gained power, it would substitute one form of despotism for another. For Lenin's organizational plan amounted to "a very simple copy or caricature of the bureaucratic system of our Minister of Internal Affairs."[77]

These differences did not prevent Bolsheviks and Mensheviks from collaborating on several occasions during the turbulence of 1904 and 1905, especially at the lower levels of the two organizations, which suggests a blurring of distinctions between them. Yet in his writings of 1905 Lenin advanced ideas and tactics that in both tone and substance increasingly turned Bolshevism into a movement with a distinctive ideological thrust. More stridently and consistently than any other Marxist, he denounced the liberals for spinelessness, advocated an alliance between the proletariat and the peasantry (which he now considered to be potentially revolutionary), and urged his followers to prepare for an armed uprising against the government. Although Lenin was never explicit in suggesting a link between his views on party organization and the necessity of armed rebellion, he seems to have envisioned a logical connection between them. How could a small party of revolutionaries "overturn Russia" if not by means of armed struggle?

The Party of Socialist Revolutionaries (SRs), the third major revolutionary organization, was the heir of the Populists of the 1870's. Founded in 1901, it attracted a sizable following within five years (50,000 members and 350,000 sympathizers), in part because of its eclectic program and in part because it sought to enlist not only peasants, its primary constituency, but also workers. Although leading SRs had read Marx and were influenced by him, their political conceptions differed significantly from those of the Social Democrats, who had reason to fear the agrarian socialists as competitors in the scramble for mass support. The SRs repudiated Marxian notions of determinism, emphasizing instead individual activism and personal sacrifice. They had abandoned the belief of the former Populist organization *Narodnaia volia** that political terror could bring down the government, but they continued to tolerate the "Combat Organization," an independent organ of the party that carried out dozens of political murders.

The SRs believed that since the country was predominantly agrarian and most people had been exposed to the egalitarian practices of the

---

* Founded in 1879, *Narodnaia volia* was responsible for the assassination of Tsar Alexander II in 1881.

commune, Russia could attain socialism without passing through the stage of full-blown capitalism. The key social class in bringing about this transformation would be the toiling peasants, supported by their "natural allies" the urban workers, who also lived by their labor. In the SR vision of the future, land would be like air, free for anyone who needed it and would make proper use of it. The SRs favored the transfer of all the land to peasant communes or associations, which in turn would assign it on an egalitarian basis to everyone who wished to earn his living by farming. Industry would be similarly socialized. The SRs insisted that the final goal, socialism, must be achieved by means of persuasion. Believers in the natural goodness of man, they held that once the Tsarist edifice was dismantled, it would be possible to convince the people of the superiority of collectivism.

The short-range aims of the SRs hardly differed from the stated "immediate goals" of the SDs and had much in common with those of the left-leaning liberals. The SRs wished to replace the autocracy with a democratic republic in which local regions would be granted autonomy, and to introduce a wide range of social legislation. Although the Marxists rejected the SR land proposal as retrograde and utopian, in 1905 the radical movements cooperated quite extensively. In some respects the SRs were actually the most militant activists in 1905, since their experience with political terror and their idealization of individual heroism predisposed them toward mass violence. They betrayed few inhibitions about supporting an armed onslaught on the old order, and in 1905 they preceded the Marxists in arguing that a well-coordinated attack on the government by the peasantry and the proletariat could quickly bring about socialism.[78]

• • • • •

In sum, it can be said that three principal issues motivated the opposition to the old order in Russia at the turn of the century. The first was the constitutional question: How could the anachronistic political structure of the Empire be altered to introduce civil liberties and to assure a redistribution of power? The second was the labor question: How could the demands of the industrial proletariat for an improvement in its social and economic conditions be met? The third was the agrarian question: How could the land hunger of millions of peasants be satisfied? The liberals, workers, and peasants constituted fairly distinct social groups, each of which emphasized one of the three issues, but by the spring of 1905 their agitation overlapped and brought the country into a condition of social and political crisis. The government could restore political stability only if it addressed the aspirations of these protest movements, a state of

affairs the authorities found disagreeable not only because they were reluctant to make any concessions at all but also because they faced conflicting demands from various sectors of the opposition.

To complicate matters further, the national issue also provoked discontent, though national sentiments among most minorities were not yet
sufficiently aroused to pose a serious problem for the autocracy. But at
this time of political and social unrest, they served to exacerbate tensions.

The Russian Empire, the accretion of centuries of colonization, military conquest, and annexation by Muscovite rulers of weak principali-
ties, comprised over a hundred ethnic groups with a wide range of cul-
tures, languages, and religions. The Great Russians claimed to be the
dominant group and exerted paramount influence in politics, occupying
most of the important positions in the bureaucracy and military services.
By the late nineteenth century the authorities in St. Petersburg made plain
their determination to preserve the hegemony of the Great Russians and
even to increase their influence by reducing to a minimum the cultural
and political autonomy of the minorities. Tsars Alexander III and Nicholas II embarked on a policy of ruthless Russification partly for reasons
of security. Concentrated in the borderlands, the minorities were looked
upon as a potential danger in time of war. In addition, the Tsars feared
that the special rights and privileges, cultural as well as political, enjoyed
by some of the nationalities (notably the Finns and, to a much lesser
degree, the Poles) would serve as a model for other minorities, among
whom national consciousness was beginning to take root. If autonomy
were widely extended, the Empire would cease to be a "unitary state," to
use the parlance of the time, and the autocrat's power would be sharply
curtailed.[79]

The authorities in St. Petersburg were also motivated by sheer prejudice. They considered the minorities to be culturally inferior, and they
were especially antagonistic toward the Jews, who numbered about five
million. The government imposed economic, legal, and social restrictions
on the Jews that were more extensive and demeaning than the measures
taken against any other group. Forced, with few exceptions, to live in
one region of the Empire, the Pale of Settlement,* Jews also had to pay
special taxes, could not attain the rank of officer in the army, and were
almost completely excluded from employment in the bureaucracy. Moreover, their attendance at secondary schools and universities was con-
strained by rigid quotas. At bottom, the hostility toward the Jews derived
from the belief that they were marked by "innate vices" that made their

---

* The Pale of Settlement, established in a series of decrees issued from 1773 to 1791, was
the area in the western and southwestern provinces of the Empire in which Jews were
allowed to reside. Travel to other parts of the Empire required a special permit.

full assimilation into Russian society impossible.[80] The prominence of Jews in all the radical movements and, to a lesser extent, in the liberal movement was in large measure the fruit of the government's discriminatory policies.

The opponents of the autocracy did not adopt a uniform stand on the national question, which casts further doubt on the thesis that "two Russias" confronted each other in 1905. It is true that the entire opposition condemned the government's policies of Russification and oppression of minorities. The radicals, however, favored either full autonomy or self-determination for the minorities, whereas many liberals opposed the decentralization of political authority, a stand that antagonized some minority groups, especially the Polish nationalists. The liberals generally believed that a constitutional government in St. Petersburg that respected cultural differences would retain the loyalty of all the Empire's subjects regardless of their national identity. In light of the growing force of nationalism, the liberals may have been deluding themselves.

· · · · ·

Until 1904 the government managed to keep the opposition at bay. The agitation for political change, the industrial strikes, the agrarian unrest, and the increasing number of assassinations of prominent officials were ominous signs of profound malaise, but the autocratic regime could withstand such scattered, uncoordinated expressions of discontent. It was an unexpected event, a senseless adventure in the Far East, that opened the floodgates to the opposition and made possible a revolution. The ensuing struggle between the forces for change and the supporters of the status quo proved to be intense and at times savage. For at least fifteen months it also proved to be inconclusive, primarily because neither side offered a program that could command and retain the active support of large and diverse sectors of the population. The government insisted on preserving the autocratic regime, but beyond that it was indecisive, confused, and narrow-minded, yielding to pressure from below only belatedly and half-heartedly. The leaders of the opposition sought to put an end to the autocracy, but beyond that they were divided over ends and means. They cultivated neither unity of purpose nor agreement on tactics. In their confrontations, the two contending forces were disjointed and rudderless, incapable of the bold and imaginative action needed to score a quick and lasting political victory. Under the circumstances, the Revolution of 1905 dragged on for almost three years, and even then the autocracy, though victorious, did not succeed in turning the clock back to 1904.

Chapter Two

. . . .

War and Political Upheaval

THE RUSSO-JAPANESE WAR, which broke out on January 26, 1904, did not make a revolution inevitable in the Russian Empire, but it did create the preconditions for such an upheaval. The catastrophic defeats suffered by the Imperial army and navy seemed to justify every criticism that the political opposition had leveled at the autocratic regime: that it was irresponsible, incompetent, and reckless. Even at a time of national emergency, the government could not effectively mobilize the nation's resources.

N. I. Astrov, an activist in local government and in the liberal movement, accurately captured the mood of society when he wrote that "Impatience, feelings of resentment, indignation—these grew everywhere and became stronger. With each new defeat, with each new retreat to 'previously prepared positions' in 'accordance with prior plans,' indignation grew more intense and there took shape a mood of protest. There was no malicious joy. Oh no! There was a feeling of burning shame and undeserved injury." Increasingly, citizens raised a troublesome question: Who is responsible for this disgrace?[1] The realization that the government bore responsibility for the catastrophe could not but serve as a powerful impetus to all who had argued that the country's institutions needed to be overhauled. V. I. Gurko, a senior official who in 1906 rose to the position of Assistant Minister of Internal Affairs, contended in his memoirs that the disastrous course of the war actually "lent a noble, patriotic character" to the revolutionary movement.[2]

The war between Russia and Japan did not result from fundamental conflicts over national interests. This is not to say that the historical record sustains the claim endlessly repeated by scholars both in the West and the Soviet Union over the past few decades: that the Russian government's Far Eastern policies were inspired by the influential Minister of Internal Affairs, Plehve, who is supposed to have said that "In order to prevent revolution, we need a small victorious war."[3] The source for this pithy quotation is invariably Witte's memoirs, published posthumously in 1922. Witte in turn had derived his evidence for the charge against his implacable enemy from the unpublished diary of General A. N. Kuropatkin, the Minister of War, to whom Plehve allegedly made the comment. When Kuropatkin's diary appeared in print in 1922, however, Plehve did not emerge as a zealous advocate of war. The diary merely indicates that in December 1903 Plehve did not seem to object to Russia's going to war with Japan, on the assumption that a military conflict would divert the masses from political concerns. And there is evidence to suggest that Kuropatkin persuaded the Minister of Internal Affairs not only that a war in the Far East would fail to reduce domestic unrest in Russia but that defeats on the battlefield would intensify it.[4]

The basic cause of the war lies in the imprudent policies of expansionism in the Far East that were pursued by various senior officials and influential men at Court. In the mid-nineteenth century, when China's weakness became initially apparent, Russia was too preoccupied in the Balkans and Central Asia to pursue these policies in a systematic way, though it did make some minor penetrations into China. In the 1890's, however, Russian officials initiated a new phase in the Empire's forward policy in the Far East. Alarmed at Japan's emergence as a strong, aggressive power and eager to promote Russia's economic development, the government in St. Petersburg adopted various measures to extend its influence over two vast regions also coveted by Japan: Manchuria, which was part of China, and Korea, an autonomous kingdom under the suzerainty of Chinese Emperors. Plehve supported Russia's eastward drive and certainly made no effort to halt the actions of Russian adventurers that provoked the ire of the Japanese, but that is not the same as urging war so as to restore social harmony within Russia.

In 1891, the Russian government decided to construct the Trans-Siberian Railroad. Witte, who vigorously promoted the railway project during his tenure as Minister of Finance, was interested primarily in the economic exploitation of an area rich in resources and markets. At the same time, he favored a cautious foreign policy that would avoid needless provocation of other powers. Russian diplomats, however, adopted an aggressive stance toward Japan, a rapidly industrializing country with a strong interest in the economic development of the Asian mainland. On several occasions during the 1890's, Russia forced Japan to pull back from positions on the mainland. These humiliations produced a "paroxysm of public indignation," prompting the Japanese to embark on a program of massive rearmament.

Early in the twentieth century, the hostility between the two powers reached a climax. Japan had vastly expanded its economic and political influence over Korea, whereas Russia had extended its influence over neighboring Manchuria. When a Russian speculator, A. M. Bezobrazov, received a concession from the Korean government to cut timber on the Yalu and Tumen rivers, the Japanese government became alarmed. It proposed an arrangement whereby Russia would be granted predominance in Manchuria in return for Japan's predominance in Korea. In January 1904 the Japanese pressed for a speedy reply to their proposal. When none was forthcoming, they decided upon a course of action they had believed to be unavoidable for some time. On January 26, they launched a surprise attack on Russian ships at Port Arthur and Chemulpo.[5]

The incompetence of the Russian government during the last months of 1903 can hardly be believed. Tsar Nicholas, who did not want to go to war, had convinced himself that it would not break out because, in the words of Count Witte, "he did not wish it."[6] His Minister of Foreign Affairs, Count V. N. Lamsdorff, Witte (who after 1903 was Chairman of the Committee of Ministers), and Minister of War Kuropatkin all favored peaceful penetration of the Far East and urged strict avoidance of any action that could set off a military conflict. But the Tsar tolerated the witless machinations of adventurers and businessmen who pressed hard for Russia to extend its influence in the Far East. Irresponsible men such as Bezobrazov and Admiral A. M. Abaza became highly influential at Court and prevailed upon the Tsar not to yield to Japan's overtures for compromise. By 1903 Bezobrazov actually dictated Far Eastern policies, which foreclosed any possibility of a negotiated settlement of differences with Japan. It is not farfetched to suggest that in the months preceding the outbreak of hostilities Russia pursued two foreign policies: one conducted by the Ministry of Foreign Affairs, which was judicious, and one by the adventurers, which was reckless. The former was often kept in ignorance of the latter's activities.[7] Because of confusion and incompetence at the highest levels of government, Russia drifted into a situation that virtually invited Japan to attack.

Of course, it must be kept in mind that no knowledgeable people in St. Petersburg suspected that the Japanese could mount a sustained military campaign against their country. On every count—the size of its population, army, navy, annual budget, or gold reserves—the advantage seemed clearly to lie with Russia.[8] Under the circumstances, would the Japanese be so foolhardy as to provoke war? And if they did, was there any reason to be concerned?

The claims about Russia's superiority, of course, proved to be thoroughly misleading. For one thing, Russian forces were scattered over a vast area of the Far East, and reinforcements from the west had to be transported piecemeal, since the roadbed of the Trans-Siberian Railroad was not sturdy enough to bear heavy traffic. Even more serious, the railway still had a gap of over one hundred miles at Lake Baikal, where the line needed to be constructed around the lake in very mountainous terrain. In addition, much of the Russian navy was stationed in Europe and under the best of circumstances would not reach the theater of operations for several months. Clearly, Japan's active army of 180,000 men and reserve of some 670,000 were more than adequate to cope with the forces that Russia could field before the arrival of reinforcements.[9]

Japan enjoyed other advantages. Its troops and naval forces were better trained and its intelligence more effective than Russia's. In one blow on January 26, 1904, the Japanese managed to put out of action over half the Russian navy in the Yellow Sea, while suffering very minor losses: six of their men were killed and 45 wounded. Within a few weeks, the Japanese landed troops in Chemulpo and strengthened their forces in Korea, which proceeded to drive the Russian outposts back beyond the Yalu River. The Russian leaders had simply been outwitted. They had allowed the diplomatic negotiations to reach a critical point at a time that was, from a military standpoint, thoroughly unfavorable to them. The Japanese were in a position to pursue a military offensive that led them from one victory to another.

Though surprised by the attack and indignant at Japan's treachery, Tsar Nicholas and his closest counselors were at first not particularly apprehensive. They granted that Japan was better prepared than Russia, but they were convinced that in the end they would prevail because of the greater resources at their disposal. Since the fighting took place far from the Empire's centers of population, the Tsar and his advisers discounted the possibility of domestic unrest. A senior official recalled that "Everybody [at Court] regarded . . . [Japan's attack] as a mere episode; no one attached any importance to it. . . . Everyone was supremely confident that there would be a speedy termination of the 'adventure.'"[10]

The public buttressed the government's self-confidence by rallying to its support, often with passionate expressions of patriotism. The ultraconservative newspaper *Novoe vremia*, for example, alternated between crude denunciations of the Japanese and simpleminded assurances that Russia could not possibly lose: "The Japanese have attacked our fleet in a very treacherous way. But this should not disturb the Russian people. In our history there have been many examples [of such conduct]. The Asians always behave treacherously." But there were no grounds for concern, for Russia's resources were so much greater than Japan's.[11]

Moderate liberals were less boastful about Russia's putative strength but equally supportive of the government. The distinguished professor of philosophy at Moscow University, Prince S. N. Trubetskoi, who in June 1905 was to lead a delegation to the Tsar to plead for reform, contended that Russia was defending all of Europe against the "yellow danger, the new hordes of Mongols armed by modern . . . technology."[12] The liberal press referred to Russia's "historical destiny" to expand in the Far East and to the necessity of protecting the country against an aggressive and unscrupulous enemy.[13]

The Mayor of Moscow, V. M. Golitsyn, delivered an inspiring speech to the City Council urging the deputies to serve as an example for all cities of the Empire in supporting the army. The council responded by voting a subsidy of a million rubles for the military effort. Other city councils, numerous zemstvos, and various corporate bodies followed suit. At St. Petersburg University patriotic students replaced the revolutionaries as leaders of campus organizations and staged demonstrations in support of the war. Professors throughout the country openly criticized those students who aired unpatriotic views. The Council of Moscow University declared that the Russian government "in its foreign policy was steadfastly striving to realize moral ideals." The Council at Kiev University characterized the war as a Christian mission against "insolent Mongols." As women hurried to volunteer for the Red Cross, many doctors offered to serve in the Far East. "Everyone was occupied in the war effort, in work for the war," according to one observer. "Everyone was fully convinced of the complete necessity of a quick and decisive victory."[14]

The patriotic outburst bewildered the left-liberal movement and prompted some of its leaders to express confusing views on the war. P. B. Struve, a founder of the Union of Liberation, had in earlier years expressed strong reservations about Russia's adventurous policy in the Far East, but after Japan's attack he adopted a position that was "so ambivalent that his readers had great difficulty deciding where he stood." Although convinced that Russia would be defeated, he did not want liberals to appear unpatriotic. He therefore distinguished between the government, which he held responsible for provoking the conflict, and the army, which he believed would turn against the authorities once it had been humiliated in battle. In a celebrated "Letter to Students," he urged Russian youth to animate patriotic meetings by shouting "Long live the army!," "Long live Russia!," and "Down with Plehve!" Predictably, it was a strategy that gained him the opprobrium both of conservatives and of some colleagues in his own movement.[15] P. N. Miliukov, for example, questioned the practicality of Struve's position: "Down with Autocracy! is no less patriotic. Let us be patriots for ourselves, and for a future Russia."[16]

Among the revolutionary left, the war attracted surprisingly little attention. True, Plekhanov, Lenin, and Martov, to mention but a few prominent radicals, unequivocally denounced the adventurism of the Tsarist regime and gleefully predicted Russia's defeat, but their statements were very general. Thus they categorically opposed working-class support for the war effort and asserted that a proletarian revolution was needed to end the conflict and prevent future wars. "We are international socialists," Martov declared in March 1904, "and *therefore* any political alliance of the socialists in our country with any *class state* whatsoever, we regard as a betrayal of the revolution."[17] In April, Plekhanov wrote that the debacle at Port Arthur "promises to shatter to its foundations the regime of Nicholas II."[18] All in all, for much of 1904 the radical press barely discussed the possible impact of the war on Russian society or whether radicals should wage a special campaign against it. Lenin's writings for the year 1904 contain only three brief references to the war.[19]

Konni Zilliacus was the first activist on the left to perceive that the war created unique opportunities for revolutionary agitation. Born in Finland in 1855 and trained in the law, Zilliacus had led a colorful life. By the time he reached his early thirties he had made his fortune, enabling him to indulge his penchants for horse breeding and merrymaking. Then for some ten years he traveled widely, first in Costa Rica, where for a time he administered a railway construction camp, and then in the United States, where he became a successful journalist in Chicago. After spending some time in Japan and Egypt, he returned to Finland in 1898 to devote himself to journalism and to take up the cause of resistance to the Tsarist policy of Russification. When his newspaper was banned by the Russian authorities in 1900, Zilliacus moved to Stockholm to continue his writings in support of Finnish nationalism and his work as leader of the Finnish Party of Active Resistance. He closely followed political developments in Russia, and soon after the war with Japan broke out he concluded that conditions were now ripe for an assault against the autocracy.

In a letter of March 1, 1904, Zilliacus told F. V. Volkhovsky, a veteran of the radical movement of the 1860's then living in London, that the "Russian opposition of all shades" ought to launch an offensive against the old regime because "Russia and the Russian people" were passing through a profound crisis. Zilliacus had learned that "the greatest bewilderment as to what mode of action to adopt at present prevails among those surrounding the czar. The fact [is] that everyone has been deceiving him and therefore [he] does not trust anyone of his ministers but turns to his mother, whose influence is growing day by day." She herself, however, was confused; she no longer trusted Plehve and feared that the dynasty was in jeopardy. "A few more setbacks in Asia," Zilliacus predicted, "showing that the army has been no better prepared for war than the navy, will make her and many others amenable to reason—such as they conceive it!"

Zilliacus proposed that the various oppositional groups prepare a joint appeal to the Tsar for publication "after the first great disaster on land." Such an appeal would be of the "greatest effect, more especially if it were aided by demonstrations in various parts of the empire, showing that the people understands what there is at the bottom of the miserable situation." The appeal would promise to end the agitation for a revolution if the Tsar agreed to convoke a "congress of the people's representatives" and to grant "liberty of press, of speech, of electoral agitation and amnesty of all categories [of political prisoners]." Zilliacus acknowledged that such a constitutional order would probably be a "parody," but that did not disturb him. It would be "the beginning all the same, the first step that never could be recalled."

Even if the autocracy did not make concessions, a manifesto by all oppositional forces would serve many useful purposes. It would "throw consternation of the worst order into the enemy's camp and would raise the hopes of all those fighting the autocracy by making them feel that in a measure at least they stand shoulder to shoulder, and would . . . show the world at large that the opposition in Russia is not revolutionary in the common, sanguinary sense of the word, and still less anarchistic. . . ." Zilliacus thought it just possible that the Tsar might be reasonable, that he might come to understand that it would be in his interest to introduce reforms "before it is too late, before the revolution that is certain to come sweeps over the land and sweeps away all that may be good together with all that is bad."

Zilliacus's plan of action was not confined to the issuance of a manifesto. He also proposed that revolutionary literature be sent to Russian troops in Manchuria and that the opposition begin to acquire weapons. He indicated to Volkhovsky that he was already making progress in implementing these two schemes. One of his colleagues had suggested to the Japanese Consul General in New York that the Japanese government, which did not consider itself to be at war with "the Russian people but merely with its government, liberate all political prisoners in Siberia" who could be reached by the advancing army. Zilliacus conceded that the "scheme seems wild, yet it is nothing of the kind as the Japs undoubtedly are going to push along the [Amur] with a gunboat as soon as the ice goes, and consequently could pick up refugees anywhere along said river." Indeed, the scheme had been submitted to the Japanese government, which expressed interest and asked for the names and whereabouts of political prisoners in Eastern Siberia, especially the names of the more prominent prisoners. Zilliacus urged Volkhovsky to discuss the plan with colleagues and to begin collecting the necessary information.[20]

Zilliacus surely overstated the likelihood of impressing the Tsar with a manifesto issued by the opposition. Nor was it likely that all the various groups hostile to the autocracy, each with its own ideological position and constituency, could at that early stage in the war agree on forming a united front. Still, he understood before any other activist that the war would heighten unrest in Russia and that only when the opposition coalesced would the autocracy be forced to make far-reaching concessions. This is precisely what happened, though later than Zilliacus assumed and not in the manner he envisioned.

The Japanese government also sensed that the war would embolden the opposition in Russia and sought to encourage that process. It sent Colonel Akashi Motojiro, formerly military attaché in St. Petersburg, to Stockholm, where in 1904 and 1905 he established contact with Russians of diverse political persuasions: Prince P. A. Kropotkin, N. V. Chaikovsky, Miliukov, Maxim Gorky, Father Georgii Gapon, Zilliacus, and possibly Lenin. Colonel Akashi disbursed funds and helped arrange the transport of arms to revolutionaries. The Japanese are also said to have had a hand in organizing a conference of oppositional groups in Paris early in the fall of 1904. In Japan itself, the government allowed George Kennan, author of a famous report on the Russian penal system, to distribute revolutionary literature to the 4,000 Russian prisoners of war. Kennan, who obtained books and journals from Struve, was sure that Japan would win the war and that then "there is almost certain to be an upheaval of some kind. . . . I have strong hope that, as a result of the enlightenment that this literature will give [to the prisoners] . . . , three-fourths of them will go back to Russia at the end of the war confirmed revolutionists. At any rate, I shall have the satisfaction of knowing that some seed has been sown in fertile ground."[21]

The significance of the Japanese involvement in Russian internal affairs is difficult to assess. Edward Dillon, a well-informed observer of developments in Russia, claimed that the disorders there could be ascribed in "varying degrees" to Japanese largesse, but such assertions must be treated with the utmost caution. Disaffection was rife, and there is no reason to assume that disturbances would not have occurred even without outside help. All that can be said with confidence is that the Japanese eased the way for some opposition groups.[22]

Certainly, in 1904 the military defeats that the Japanese inflicted on the Russians proved to be the most potent stimulant to disaffection. The early retreats of Russian forces were rationalized as tactical moves to improve positions. But the war continued to go badly for Russia, and the rationalizations ceased to carry conviction. On April 13, the battleship *Petropavlovsk* struck a mine outside Port Arthur and sank, causing the loss of about six hundred men, including the much admired Admiral S. O. Makarov, who had only just arrived from Europe. Another battleship, the *Pobeda*, also hit a mine and was seriously damaged. On May 1, General Kuroki Tamemoto decisively defeated an army led by General M. G. Zasulich, a commander devoid of tactical skills.

Soon reports drifted back to European Russia that the army was performing poorly almost everywhere. Actually, the rank and file fought with determination, but they were utterly lacking in initiative. Much of the officer corps was incompetent, and technologically the Russian army was at a disadvantage because the government had failed to equip it adequately with modern weapons.[23]

By May 14, 1904, the Japanese had severed the Russian garrison at Port Arthur from all communication with the outside world, and it became more difficult than ever for local commanders to assess the enemy's strength. After a direct siege of 156 days, the commander at Port Arthur, A. M. Stoessel, surrendered on December 20, 1904. Over 28,000 Russians had been killed or wounded, and large quantities of equipment fell into the enemy's hands. Japan lost twice as many men, but it had scored a major victory.

In the meantime, the Russians had dispatched a large fleet under Admiral Z. P. Rozhdestvensky to the Far East with orders to engage the Japanese navy. When the fleet of eight battleships, twelve cruisers, and various auxiliary ships reached the Straits of Tsushima, it encountered the Japanese fleet commanded by Admiral Togo Heihachiro. In size the two fleets were about evenly matched, but Togo's intelligence included detailed information about the location and movements of the Russian ships, and his forces were well rested. The battle was joined early in the afternoon of May 14, 1905, and within 45 minutes it became clear that the Russian navy would endure a devastating defeat. All told, the Japanese destroyed 21 Russian ships and captured four battleships and two hospital ships. Six Russian ships escaped to neutral ports, where they were disarmed, and only four reached Vladivostok. With this triumph Japan gained undisputed mastery over the Pacific.[24]

On land, the Japanese had inflicted further humiliations on the Russians, most notably in the Battle of Mukden in March 1905. A key factor, as in previous battles, was the poor showing of the Tsarist officer corps. According to the Swedish military attaché, who had observed the battle from the Russian side, "the confusion and rout of the Russians was indescribable; many of the officers never stopped in their flight until they got to Tieling, and then immediately proceeded to get drunk. Eighteen are said to have been court-martialed. It is also reported that Kuropatkin lost two-thirds of his war maps and also [the] plans of the fortifications of Vladivostok."[25] By this time, the Japanese had come close to exhausting their human and financial resources, and Russia was in the throes of revolution. Early in August, President Theodore Roosevelt suggested to the belligerent governments that they enter negotiations to end hostilities. Both sides readily agreed.

The mood in Russian society had begun to sour long before the full dimensions of the military catastrophe became apparent. The change in attitude developed slowly. For several months early in 1904, the newspapers continued to exude optimism about Russia's chances, but that optimism grew increasingly guarded and defensive. By late April 1904, even the ultraconservative *Novoe vremia* conceded that the early defeats were demoralizing, though it still expected Russia to score a "complete victory."[26] The liberal *Vestnik Evropy* also became apprehensive, though it assured its readers that there was no reason for despair.[27] By the end of the year the left-liberal *Russkoe bogatstvo* spoke bluntly about Russia's military failures and placed the blame for them squarely on the authorities in St. Petersburg: "In the course of eleven months the greatest military power in the world not only could not handle a second-rate power, but was forced step by step to retreat in face of the enemy's successes, and could not rescue the courageous garrison at Port Arthur. This impotence of a powerful country . . . is, of course, a very significant event. The reasons for the impotence lie in the unpreparedness and improvidence, as well as in other defects, characteristic of a bureaucratic system."[28]

In the salons of society, questions were raised soon after news of the first defeats became known. Initially, people simply asked, "How could this have happened?" When one defeat followed another, questions grew more insistent and desperate, while the only answer from the authorities was a plea for "patience, patience, patience."[29] The moderate Prince Trubetskoi, who in January had strongly supported the war, argued in the spring of 1904 that "Russia could survive only if her government agreed to reforms."[30] Others were harsher, heaping ridicule on the government and the military leadership. Referring to the Tsar's effort to boost morale among the troops by sending them icons, General M. I. Dragomirov, a retired, highly respected soldier, quipped that "The Japanese are beating us with guns, but we will beat them with icons." He also claimed that the "heads" of the military services and government were to blame for Russia's plight. "As is known," he was fond of saying, "fish always begin to stink in their heads; is it any wonder that the army is incapable of fighting the Japanese!"[31]

It was not only the military humiliations that generated opposition to the war. The war also debilitated the economy, which was in the early stages of recovery after a prolonged slump. Usually wars tend to stimulate economic activity, and railway construction, arms factories, shipbuilding, and the metallurgical and mining industries did benefit in 1904 from the growth in government orders. But the decision by the Trans-

Siberian Railway to transport only military goods adversely affected some important sectors of the national economy. The production of silk goods, for example, declined by over 25 percent in 1904; that of woolen goods by about 15 percent; and that of cotton goods, chemicals, and some other industrial products by a smaller, but nevertheless significant, percentage.[32] Moreover, the call to arms of about 1,200,000 reservists, often the most productive workers, reduced output in the handicraft industries. In the province of Vladimir, officials in more than two-thirds of the county zemstvos reported a substantial decline in industrial production, which in turn hurt the economy in the countryside. In Moscow province, 75 percent of the zemstvo officials indicated that the war had led to a curtailment of seasonal work, an important source of income for many peasants. Peasants were therefore obliged to sell grain to pay their taxes, but their supplies were already inadequate. The town of Nizhnii-Novgorod reported a 20 percent drop in business from 1903 to 1904.[33]

The Polish Kingdom and the northwestern regions of the Empire, major centers of the textile industry, were especially hard hit, and the press accounts of the situation in these areas make for grim reading. The economic decline began in the spring of 1904; by early September, Warsaw was in the throes of a real crisis. "Stores are empty. Factories have curtailed production. Workers have been dismissed. Among artisans of Warsaw alone the severe consequences of the crisis are affecting up to 20,000 people."[34] By the fall, many industries in the Warsaw guberniia had dismissed between 25 and 30 percent of their workers, and wages had declined by anywhere from 33 to 50 percent. The total number of unemployed was so large that leaders of the Jewish community were forced to reduce assistance to needy families.[35] Such hardships were bound to reinforce doubts about the government's policies, and it is not surprising that the revolutionary turbulence assumed an especially intense form in the Polish Kingdom.

The drain on charitable resources became a serious problem in many parts of the Empire. The obligation to provide charity to indigent families of men called to the armed forces rested with the local organs of government. By the autumn of 1904, there were so many such families that zemstvos found the financial burden "completely unbearable." They appealed to the central government to take over the program, but it claimed to be in no position to do so. Consequently, the indigent families received much less help than they needed.[36]

· · · · ·

If there was a turning point in the evolution of the public mood in 1904, it was the assassination of Plehve, the Minister of Internal Affairs, in the summer of that year. The elimination of the most dynamic figure in the government both exposed the depth of despair over the state of affairs and opened up new possibilities for popular agitation against the war and the government.

Appointed to head the Ministry of Internal Affairs in April 1902, Plehve had come to symbolize the capriciousness and intransigence of the autocratic regime. He himself knew that he was widely despised, and feared that he might be a target of terrorists. His physician never wrote a prescription in his name, assigning the medicine instead to one of his servants.[37] Such caution minimized the chances of poisoning, but it could not prevent a terrorist from throwing a bomb at the minister's carriage, which is what happened soon after Plehve left his home early on July 15. After a tremendous explosion Plehve was found blown to pieces; his coachman and horse were also killed, and several pedestrians suffered severe injuries. Despite the ghastliness of the incident, very few people were shocked or particularly distressed.

The Tsar regretted the loss of a "friend and an irreplaceable Minister of Internal Affairs," and *Novoe vremia* lauded him as one of "The most steadfast and staunchest supporters of order . . . [against] the enemies of Russia." The assassination was such a vile crime, according to the paper, that it should receive a "moral rebuff from all reasonable [and] steadfast friends of order and legality."[38]

That this did not happen startled Count Aloys Lexa von Aehrenthal, the Austro-Hungarian Ambassador to St. Petersburg and a knowledgeable observer of conditions in Russia. "The most striking aspect of the present situation," Aehrenthal told his superiors in Vienna, "is the total indifference of society to an event that constituted a heavy blow to the principles of the government. One could hardly have expected sympathy for a minister who because of his authoritarian bent must have made many enemies. But . . . a certain degree of human compassion, or at least concern and anxiety with respect to the immediate future, would be natural. Not a trace of this is to be found. Up to now I have found only totally indifferent people or people so cynical that they say that no other outcome was to be expected."

Even conservatives and loyal servants of the Tsar expressed no regret over Plehve's murder. Aehrenthal was "genuinely surprised" that "barely 24 hours after the terroristic act, Count Lamsdorff, with startling candor, critically analyzed Plehve's activities in the tone of a man filled with a sense of moral relief at the disappearance of an inconvenient and uncongenial colleague." Witte, long at odds with Plehve, expressed similar sentiments, as did "most of Plehve's colleagues," even those who occupied high positions in the Ministry of Internal Affairs.

Aehrenthal also noticed a growing willingness on the part of people "publicly to expose the inadequacy of the present mode of government."

He continued, "it is significant that in the last resort this criticism is directed against the person of the Tsar, who is incapable of centralized and effective direction of the affairs of state." No one, not even the officials at Court, seemed to understand that the attack on Plehve, the man appointed by the sovereign as "guardian of law and order," signified an attack on the entire system of government. "It can be said that practically all strata of the educated population in Russia regard the government's struggle against the revolutionary opposition with total apathy, if not with *Schadenfreude* [malicious joy]."[39] Aehrenthal had put his finger on a critical fact: the fragility of the autocracy's popular support, a precondition for the eruption of a political storm.

It took Tsar Nicholas more than a month to decide on Plehve's successor. The monarch was expected to appoint a man committed to Plehve's harsh policies, but Nicholas could not ignore the growing restiveness in society. Some clashes between workers and police, the latter reinforced by Cossacks, had occurred in Warsaw in May and June, and on July 15 crowds in that city openly applauded the murder of Plehve.[40] Within the higher bureaucracy and in Court circles two factions offered conflicting advice to the Tsar: "The one affirmed that it was imperative to continue staunchly the course mapped out by the late minister [Plehve]; the other pointed out that it was impossible to continue much longer a policy which had aroused the indignation of all thinking Russia."[41] In the end, Nicholas decided on a conciliatory gesture. On August 26, he announced the appointment of Prince P. D. Sviatopolk-Mirsky as Minister of Internal Affairs.

Mirsky was a 47-year-old career bureaucrat who had occupied several important posts. In the late 1890's he had been Governor of Penza and Ekaterinoslav; from 1900 to 1902 he had served as Assistant Minister of Internal Affairs and commander of a special corps of gendarmes; in 1902 he became Governor-General of Vilna, Grodno, and Kovno. He was known to have expressed enlightened political views and was "universally held in high esteem for his intelligence, integrity, urbanity, and refinement." He was considered "a man of honor in the full sense of the term."[42]

At first, Mirsky declined this most important position in the government, pleading poor health. The real reason for his unwillingness to accept the new assignment was his disagreement with Plehve's policies, which he did not want to continue. Mirsky favored reconciliation between the government and society, and he believed that the authorities must distinguish between secret revolutionary groups and "those elements of the public which were not opposed to the existing order as a whole but only to the arbitrariness of the administration."[43] The Tsar insisted on Mirsky's appointment, which seemed to suggest that the sovereign would approve a new course in domestic policy. Under the circumstances, Mirsky could not refuse. He lost no time in announcing a change in direction in the conduct of affairs by the Ministry of Internal Affairs.

He made his most notable announcement to senior officials in his department: "Administrative experience has led me to the deep conviction that fruitful governmental work is based on sincere goodwill and sincere confidence between public and state institutions and the population in general." In an interview with foreign journalists, Mirsky was more specific about his contemplated reforms. For one thing, he favored decentralization of governmental functions: zemstvos should be granted more powers, and they should be established in provinces where they did not yet exist. He also spoke favorably of the press, suggesting that he would grant it greater latitude, and he promised a more tolerant policy toward national minorities. He conceded that he had not yet formulated a detailed program of reform. There were many issues—he himself singled out the agrarian question—that required attention, but he did not feel sufficiently informed to take a position on them.[44] He promised to do so in the future, but in the meantime he made important changes that reflected his commitment to act on the basis of the "principle of confidence." He relaxed the censorship, dismissed several of the more notorious hardliners from the Ministry of Internal Affairs, halted the harassment of the zemstvos, and restored full rights to many political prisoners and exiles. Several prominent liberals, among them Prince P. D. Dolgorukov, F. I. Rodichev, and I. I. Petrunkevich, could now resume their work in local government.

Mirsky's pronouncements and first measures received wide publicity in Russia and almost universal approval. The Mayor of Moscow warmly praised the new minister's vow to create a "government of confidence." "Moscow society," he declared, "views the coordination of government activities with those of the vital forces of society as the only path to the realization of national well-being and to the development and improvement of the internal system of Russia." The members of the City Council shouted their enthusiastic endorsement. Similar statements of support for what came to be known as the "political springtime" were made by many city councils and other public organizations.[45] *Russkie vedomosti* remarked that even though Mirsky had confined himself to generalities, his words nevertheless exhilarated society because the new minister was the first representative of the government in a long time to utter such conciliatory views.[46]

But discordant voices could also be heard. Liberals such as Struve and Miliukov suspected that Mirsky would eliminate only the most objectionable aspects of Plehve's regime and leave the autocratic structure of the government intact. As soon as the war was over and the unrest had subsided, the Tsar would return to Plehve's methods of rule.[47]

Conservatives were divided over the implications of Mirsky's policies. The editors of the right-wing *Moskovskie vedomosti* assured their readers that there was no reason to be alarmed by the pronouncements of the new Minister of Internal Affairs, for he had promised to be guided by the principles of the Manifesto of February 26, 1903, a document that referred ambiguously to future reform of the government. There will be no "unexpected innovations or dangerous experiments, such as the enemies of Russia have zealously prophesied. . . ." As for Mirsky's promise to seek the confidence of society, that, too, did not pose any danger, for it was not a new departure: the government of Russia had always "been favorably disposed toward our zemstvos and urban institutions."[48] On the other hand, the editors of the ultraconservative *Grazhdanin* expressed misgivings about Mirsky's policies. They praised the minister's demeanor and caution, but they feared that he might be acting precipitately, "under the pressure of terror." Such conduct, they warned, had prompted Count M. T. Loris-Melikov, the Minister of Internal Affairs who in 1881 sought to introduce some significant reforms, to "lead Russia to the edge of the abyss."[49] At bottom, the ultraconservatives suspected that Mirsky's fairly moderate reforms would only whet the appetite of society. There would be expectations of far more radical changes than Mirsky intended to implement, certainly more radical than the Tsar would tolerate. The ultraconservatives sensed that a government is at its weakest when it begins to yield to the demands of its critics.

The ultraconservatives were right. The time for niggardly concessions had passed. The military catastrophes had put the autocracy on the defensive, as the appointment of Mirsky made abundantly clear, and important elements of the public had concluded that in addition to being repressive and corrupt the government was thoroughly incompetent.

The new mood manifested itself in statements of unprecedented boldness in the aboveground press. An article of October 25, 1904, for example, ended with the following ominous words: "The government can save Russia from the horrors of revolutionary chaos only by acting with the greatest speed. Each day of delay will increase the torrents of blood and tears. In the sea of blood and tears the reforms will be swept away and on the stormy waves there will arise the spirit of destruction and revenge."[50] At about the same time, *Russkie vedomosti* carried an article that deplored the entire system of government and called on the authorities to introduce reforms that would allow representatives of the people to participate in legislative work.[51] Both these articles were symptomatic of the political offensive that liberals were determined to wage against the autocracy in the fall of 1904.

Historical analogies are always somewhat misleading, but the situation in Russia in the fall of 1904 may be compared roughly to that in France in the second half of 1788. Just as King Louis XVI's decision to convoke the Estates-General opened the dikes to a national movement against the old order, so Tsar Nicholas's inauguration of moderate reforms in mid-1904 unleashed a wave of oppositional activity against the autocracy. Indeed, it is no exaggeration to suggest that it was during the last four months of 1904, not in January 1905, that the Revolution of 1905 began.

. . . . .

Had the Tsarist government embarked on a consistent and imaginative program of reform in the fall of 1904, it probably could have conciliated society and restored political calm in the country. To be sure, the rhetoric of the opposition was turning strident, which inevitably frightened the authorities and their conservative allies; but the rhetoric was somewhat misleading. Some liberals no doubt believed that a revolution was necessary and desirable, whereas others thought that only the fear of one would prompt the autocrat to grant far-reaching concessions to the opposition. By and large, however, the liberals were not unalterably committed to a militant course of action. Nor did they agree on ultimate goals.

The discrepancy between the rhetoric of the left liberals and their political behavior had become evident in the spring of 1904, when a group of army officers approached the Council of the Union of Liberation with an offer to stage a coup d'état and establish the Council as a provisional government. The officers planned to act with the "same suddenness with which the Japanese had acted in disabling the fleet at Port Arthur": they would seize the military arsenals in St. Petersburg and quickly overthrow the old order. The liberal writer V. G. Korolenko attended a meeting with the officers but categorically opposed their plan, and everyone on the Council of the Union of Liberation sided with him.[52] At this time liberals also warned militant students that only by eschewing revolutionary tactics could they expect to attract society's support. Similarly, there is no evidence that liberals strove to organize workers or peasants or to agitate within the armed forces. Most liberals still pinned their hopes on appeals to the Tsar, who, they thought, might yet be persuaded to satisfy at least some of their demands.[53]

Overall, the range of opinion within the liberal camp continued to be broad. On the right stood D. N. Shipov, the highly respected leader of the so-called Slavophiles. Detesting the arbitrariness of the bureaucracy, he favored the introduction of a legal order in Russia but not the abolition of the monarchy or even its elimination as a significant institution. He would have been satisfied with the creation of a consultative legislative body composed of representatives chosen by the zemstvos and city councils, so long as the Tsar agreed to exercise his authority according to the law. On the other hand, the so-called zemstvo-constitutionalists were prepared to accept a legislative body elected either by reformed institutions of local government or by a highly restricted suffrage. As for the Union of Liberation, it advocated the introduction of universal suffrage (the "four-tail" suffrage)* to elect a constituent assembly responsible for determining the political future of Russia. To the left of these groups were some that supported radical democracy and republicanism. Of course, not all liberals fitted neatly into one of these ideological categories. The critical point is that in late 1904 the Tsar could have secured the support of many liberals—perhaps even some on the moderate left—without making the monarchy purely symbolic.

In the last analysis, the stumbling block was Nicholas's rigid conception of the autocracy—a realization that was impressed upon two leaders of the liberal movement, I. I. Petrunkevich and I. V. Gessen, when they visited Witte late in October. Although at the time Witte held the relatively unimportant position of Chairman of the Committee of Ministers, the two liberals hoped to persuade him to use his influence to prod the government into adopting reformist policies. Petrunkevich warned Witte that public pressure for the introduction of a constitutional order was intensifying so precipitately that in the end the autocrat would be compelled to yield to society's demands. Witte was not moved. "In making your judgment," he told his guests, "you do not take into account, first, that the sovereign considers the autocracy a dogma of faith, a trust that he must not give up, in part or as a whole. This is his faith and you are powerless to change it."

Witte also contended that society was much weaker than the liberals thought. It lacked the wherewithal to enter into a struggle against the autocracy, which "rests on three hundred years of history." Moreover, the Tsar could count on the support of the peasants; they "do not believe in the force of ideas and [they] know that humanity is moved not by ideas but by material interests. And the interests of the people are closely linked to the interests of the autocracy, which alone gave the people freedom and land in 1861 despite the wishes of the dvorianstvo. . . ."[54] Witte misjudged the mood of the peasants, as events in the countryside would soon show, but his assessment of the Tsar's character and intentions proved only too accurate.

Petrunkevich and Gessen, however, were right in predicting that the pressures for change would become too intense to be ignored by the government. The government was sharply divided over how to cope with the

---

*That is, a suffrage that was universal, equal, direct, and secret (though limited to males).

opposition, and therefore incapable of pursuing a consistent policy. Mirsky, who as Minister of Internal Affairs was the most prominent figure in the administration, led the moderate faction, which wanted to meet society halfway by making substantial concessions. The Tsar, however, tended to side with the hard-liners determined to resist change. As a result, for months the government acted in the worst possible way: it alternated between grudging reform and clumsy repression.

The reforms themselves did nothing to restore calm in society. On the one hand, they were so minor that they satisfied very few people. On the other, they were sufficiently innovative to suggest that the authorities were too weak to resist the growing pressure for change. At the same time, the government's crude police measures angered the opposition and inevitably cast doubt on the sincerity of Mirsky's announced program of "confidence in society." Confronted with these mixed signals, the opposition put the Minister of Internal Affairs to the test by going ahead with a massive campaign for political change that had been shelved when the war broke out. The government's response, it was hoped, would answer two critical questions: to what extent were the authorities prepared to tolerate public agitation for change; and would Mirsky proceed in a serious way with his program of liberalization? No clear answers to these questions emerged in the fall of 1904, which indicates the degree to which the government had lost its self-confidence. Of course, the autocracy and the police still wielded enormous power, but they could not exert the kind of authority to which they had been accustomed. The balance of political power in Russia between state and society was changing, slowly but perceptibly.

Before launching their campaign inside Russia, the opposition groups held a secret conference in Paris (September 30–October 9, 1904), organized by Zilliacus along lines first proposed by him in March. Not much is known about the proceedings of the "Conference of Oppositional and Revolutionary Organizations of the Russian State," but it unquestionably dramatized the opposition's sense of urgency: for the first time, many different parties (eight altogether) met and agreed—albeit after much discussion, controversy, and compromise—on a common program. The Russian Social Democrats were the only major opposition group that did not attend, although they had initially indicated that they would. Apparently, they pulled out at the last moment because they feared being outvoted and because they were distressed by reports that members of the Finnish and Polish opposition had been in touch with the Japanese government. The Russian Social Democrats maintained that the proletariat of Russia and Japan should not favor the victory of either power.[55]

Although the conference's statement, drafted by Miliukov, emphasized that no group was abandoning its own aims and tactics, the truth is that the goals on which they agreed were far-reaching by any criterion. The statement denounced the autocratic regime as "a fatal barrier to the progress and well-being" of all the Russian peoples, and urged the oppositional groups to coordinate their antigovernmental activities. "The present moment," the delegates concluded, "is especially favorable for harmonious action of all these parties against the autocratic government, which is discredited and [has been] made impotent by the terrible consequences of its adventurist war policy." The parties vowed to destroy the autocracy, restore the Finnish constitution, establish a democratic form of government on the basis of universal suffrage, and grant self-determination to national minorities within the Empire. In agreements never made public, the delegates seem also to have promised to support the campaign for constitutional reform that the Union of Liberation intended to inaugurate later in the autumn.[56] For at least a year, many liberals remained committed to an alliance with other opposition groups, which was to be a major reason for the effectiveness of the antigovernment agitation.

Of far greater importance was the zemstvo congress held from November 6 to 9 in St. Petersburg. The government always dreaded such national gatherings, which by their nature were likely to take up political issues that transcended the local matters on which they were supposed to concentrate. Since the congress organizers planned a debate on the country's political future, everyone expected the government to prohibit the meeting. The organizers were therefore delighted to discover that Mirsky, who had heard of the congress by chance, meant to give his approval and would ask the Tsar to do likewise. Within society, many came to believe that the government was eager to consult the public on political issues in order to evolve a consensus, as had been done in the late 1850's on the question of serfdom. The widespread belief that the Minister of Internal Affairs favored the meeting aroused enormous excitement and was a principal reason for the large attendance of zemstvo activists, who represented a wide range of views. The more conservative and nationalistic groups would otherwise not have participated.[57]

But on October 31, when Shipov, Petrunkevich, and Prince G. E. Lvov visited Mirsky to request official permission to hold the meeting, the liberals discovered to their dismay that the Minister of Internal Affairs did not approve of the kind of congress that was being planned. When he and the Tsar had given their blessing to the idea, it now emerged, they had in mind a gathering devoted solely to "technical zemstvo affairs."[58] Mirsky asked that the meeting be delayed until January 1, 1905, which the zemtsy refused, in part because several delegates were already en route to Petersburg. Mirsky then requested that the congress be moved to the provinces, where it would attract less attention, and again the zemtsy refused. After warning his guests about the Tsar's distrust of all public discussion of important state matters by people "incompetent" to do so, Mirsky gave in, promising that if zemstvo representatives met in the capital in private quarters "for a cup of tea, then I will order the police to wink [at the proceedings]." But he made clear that he had not formally sanctioned a public meeting, though he asked to be informed of the outcome. Mirsky then ordered officials to suppress all news about the congress.[59]

Petrunkevich was not perturbed by Mirsky's conduct, for he rightly suspected that the congress and its deliberations would be widely publicized anyway. As early as October 12, *Pravo* reported rumors of an impending congress on November 6 or 7. A week later *Russkie vedomosti* announced in a front-page article that representatives from all 34 provinces with zemstvos had been invited to a congress on November 6. "In all, about 75 people will be at the meeting."[60] The address of the first meeting, Fontanka 52 (the apartment of I. A. Korsakov, a wealthy landowner and industrialist who was active in the zemstvo movement), was kept secret to avoid demonstrations by students and workers, which might interfere with the deliberations and provoke a police crackdown. But the secret could not be kept for long. One participant recalled that his cab driver, when asked to go to Fontanka 52, expressed surprise, for he had already taken five people there. "Has someone there died?," he asked. Residents of St. Petersburg must also have been surprised by the sight of policemen near Korsakov's home. Posted on the street to keep nonparticipants away, the police officers went out of their way to be gracious and even directed the zemtsy to the right meeting place, which was changed every day so as not to place too great a burden on any one host.[61]

One hundred and three people attended the congress, though not all were present at each of the four sessions. Since the participants had not been elected by zemstvo assemblies, they were not empowered to act in the name of the zemstvos. Although they were zemstvo officials, they had decided on their own to take part in a national congress that would consider issues of vital concern to the country. This fact probably explains why the congress stood, politically, somewhat to the left of the zemstvo movement as a whole.

Quite aside from their own sense of mission, the delegates soon realized that they were engaged in a momentous enterprise. Liberal Russia learned about the meeting and expressed strong support, despite the officially imposed secrecy. Over 5,000 telegrams from all over the Empire arrived at the congress urging the delegates to press for fundamental changes in the "unbearable" state of affairs. Never before had telegrams with such daring messages been delivered to anyone in Russia. "In general," wrote a participant, "it seems that at this time there was a class of people in Petersburg who were convinced that freedom of speech already existed in Russia—the gentlemen telegraphists."[62]

The organizers of the congress had drafted a resolution, and deliberations on it proceeded in a businesslike manner. There was a remarkable absence of egotistical impulses, one delegate noted. Everyone agreed that whatever liberties were demanded for citizens should be extended to every Russian. "In no speech was there a particle of thirst for power or personal advantage." But a certain tension pervaded the meetings: "Each one of the participants felt that he must not say anything that was unnecessary, and at the same time must not leave out anything important, in view of the enormous responsibility that was ours." The tension produced great fatigue and made the delegates appear "boring and sluggish."[63]

The first nine points of the resolution evoked virtually no controversy. In addition to condemning the prevailing state system as "abnormal" and "arbitrary," the resolution proposed that officials be placed under the law and that the government grant civil liberties and abandon the "estate principle" in the election of deputies to the local organs of government, which assigned an inordinate proportion of deputies to the gentry, merchants, and clergy. Such organs should, moreover, be established in all regions of the Empire.[64] These points alone were far-reaching.

Most delegates, however, wished to go further, causing a rift at the congress. The sticking point was item 10 of the resolution, which called for the establishment of a "popular representative body" that was to participate "as a special, elective institution, in the exercise of legislative power, in the establishment of the national budget, and in the control over the legality of administrative acts." Out of deference to the moderates, the word "constitution" did not appear. Petrunkevich explicitly disavowed any intention of raising the question of a constituent assembly; he would be satisfied if the congress came out in favor of an arrangement that enabled the people and the government to share the power to make laws.[65]

Shipov was nevertheless distressed by the drift of the deliberations. He gave a fiery speech against point 10, in which he defended his Slavophile conception of the Russian polity. He stressed that the Russian people were basically different from Western Europeans. Russians were good-natured, patient, modest in their needs, religious, and full of love. Developing the Slavophile theme of the 1840's—"For the people, opinions; for the Tsar, authority"—he argued that Russia did not need formal arrangements, spelled out on paper, defining the relationship between the sovereign and the people. That relationship was based on moral principles and moral laws, the only kind that were eternal and truly effective. "The yearning for democracy [*narodovlastie*] is alien to the Russian people, [who] have a strong attachment to the idea of autocracy, which they want to regard as the expression of the people's conscience and which enjoys their confidence and love." According to Shipov, the principal cause of Russia's plight was the arbitrariness of the bureaucracy, which had separated the Tsar from the people.[66] Shipov's substitute for point 10 referred in very general terms to the necessity of providing for the "regular participation in legislative work of popular representatives in a special elected institution."[67] Such a body, it was understood by the delegates, would restrict itself to consultative functions.

The delegates found it extremely painful to oppose Shipov, a man who had made many sacrifices for the "social movement" and who was greatly admired for his knowledge, charm, and urbanity. In addition, Shipov, more than any other person, had taken the initiative in the past in planning zemstvo congresses. But Petrunkevich, V. D. Kuzmin-Karavaev, and Rodichev could not refrain from challenging his views. Love and moral principles alone, they contended, could not prevent arbitrary rule. Indeed, the despotism and slavery that Russia had endured for centuries were the direct result of the ethical-social approach to politics; "Among us only the principle of force, not love, prevails." The people, unwilling to tolerate this state of affairs, wanted to be masters of their fate. Only a state in which all subjects were protected by the law could be free of the arbitrariness that was so widely and properly resented in Russia.[68]

Although the precise number of delegates who supported Shipov's position is uncertain, only a minority did so. According to one account, probably the most reliable, the delegates rejected his formulation by a vote of 71 to 27.[69] In the end, the delegates, eager to avoid any rift, decided to include the language of both groups in point 10. Every participant at the congress signed the resolution containing all the points. The inclusion of Shipov's words on the functions of an elected institution did not affect the significance of the proceedings: for the first time, an overwhelming majority of zemtsy at a public meeting had demanded a constitution.

The congress chose a delegation of five people (Shipov; G. E. Lvov; Petrunkevich; Count P. A. Geiden, a Baltic German of moderately liberal views; and M. V. Rodzianko, a conservative liberal who was to play an important role in the Revolution of 1917) to submit the resolution to Mirsky, in accordance with the latter's request. But the minister feared that by granting a formal audience to the delegation he would be according the congress the status of an official body, which he was determined to avoid. He therefore met privately with Shipov, who reported to his colleagues that Mirsky had expressed sympathy for the resolution and promised to pass it on to the Tsar. The minister also asked for more information about the resolution and for suggestions on how it might be implemented. Prince S. N. Trubetskoi undertook to write a detailed memorandum on the congress's actions, which he read to the minister on November 28, 1904. Trubetskoi faithfully reflected the delegates' concerns about the fate of Russia and urged the sovereign to introduce major reforms. "At the present historical moment the political liberation of Russia, the organization of public forces on the principles of national representation—an organization without which we cannot rid ourselves of social chaos and disorder—is a state necessity. . . . Now, before it is too late, let the Supreme Sovereign take the initiative in this great and holy cause; he alone can accomplish this by peaceful means and thus consolidate his power for the future well-being of Russia on a deeper and firmer foundation."[70]

By all accounts, the congress made an enormous impression on society. Its unprecedented decisions were regarded as a bold declaration of principles by the opposition movement and dramatized the split that had taken place between the bureaucracy and the forces of change. The links between them had been cut. Officially, the meetings had been prohibited, yet they nevertheless were held. No one was arrested or exiled. The opposition, as one writer put it, grew bolder and decided that "not everything that was prohibited was in fact unfeasible."[71] It was an important lesson that the opposition would not soon forget.

Mirsky's interest in the liberals' proposals suggested that the government was prepared to continue its reformist policies. The liberals therefore believed that it was critical to keep up the pressure on the authorities. As Struve put it: "Despite the weakness of the Tsar and of Prince Sviatopolk [-Mirsky], owing to the decisiveness and courage of the zemtsy, the door to a peaceful constitutional transformation remains still unshut for the government. To take this road, firmly and decisively, will constitute an act of elementary political wisdom. Will such wisdom be available? History has given perhaps its final warning. Will it be heeded?"[72]

The liberals now took the offensive in local organs of self-government, seeking their support for resolutions favoring major political reform. It was not easy to persuade those bodies to pass motions critical of the government. Unlike the congress in Petersburg, they were official institutions with strict limitations on the issues they could discuss. Moreover, zemstvo assemblies were chaired by provincial marshals of the nobility, often men with conservative views. In any case, in many of the assemblies the constitutionalists did not enjoy the support of a majority of the deputies, which meant that resolutions had to be watered down to secure their passage. Also, the central government increasingly intervened at the local level to prevent the adoption of resolutions it considered unacceptable.[73] In view of these obstacles, it is all the more remarkable that the liberals secured as much support as they did on the local level.

Approximately one-third of the 34 provincial zemstvo assemblies adopted resolutions echoing the one passed at the November congress in St. Petersburg.[74] City councils also joined the campaign. On November 30, 1904, for example, N. N. Shchepkin, a member of the Moscow City Council, read a statement supporting the demands of the congress. None of the representatives objected to the publication of the statement, and, in the words of Astrov, "Thus the Moscow City Council joined the zemstvo movement."[75] Only strong pressure by the government prevented the St. Petersburg City Council from following suit. Soon other city councils showed interest in joining the protest movement and several representatives began to organize an All-Russian Congress of City Council Activists on the model of the zemstvo congress. In the months from October to January, several groups of industrial and financial leaders issued calls for political reform.[76] Finally, some 42 scholarly, cultural, and professional societies held meetings to press for changes in the political system.[77] All these manifestations of support for liberal goals were heartening to critics of the old order, but none could match in scope, drama, and effectiveness the banquet campaign that began on November 5, 1904, and ended on January 8, 1905.

The Union of Liberation had initially thought of launching a banquet campaign on February 19, 1904, to celebrate the anniversary of the emancipation of the serfs, but the wave of patriotism after the outbreak of the war made such a demonstration of opposition to the government inadvisable. Modeled on the famous banquets in Paris in 1847–48, the events were intended to unite "the bulk of the country's intelligentsia around the constitutional banner."[78] In light of the change in public mood that had taken place by the fall, the Union advised supporters throughout the country to organize banquets in honor of the fortieth anniversary of the judicial reforms. Again, the planners of the affairs had to negotiate with the government, which showed its usual reluctance to permit any meetings that would touch on political issues. In the end, the authorities relented, on the understanding that all the gatherings would be "private."

The rash of political meetings that ensued was unprecedented in Russian history. Never before had so many citizens, most of them from the educated classes, joined to give vent to their profound unhappiness with the state of affairs. Even some Social Democrats were sufficiently impressed to urge their followers in Russia to participate in the banquets. Lenin, who claimed not to be impressed, in effect acknowledged the significance of the campaign by publishing a long attack on it.

In all, 38 banquets were held in 26 cities. Zemstvo activists (physicians, lawyers, engineers, and "third element" people) were the most prominent participants, but some local bureaucrats, gentry, journalists, and teachers also took part. The "flower of literary and artistic Moscow" attended the banquet in that city, and many scientists showed up at its counterpart in St. Petersburg. At about a third of the affairs, Social Democratic activists, workers, and students attempted to drive the liberals to the left by staging street demonstrations and delivering speeches in the meeting halls.

The banquets adopted various kinds of resolutions, but to one degree or another all contributed to mobilizing support for the demands of liberal activists. Twenty banquets passed resolutions that echoed the views of the zemstvo congress held in November; eleven went beyond that and called for a constituent assembly. Most liberals sought to avoid demands that were bound to be immediately rejected by the government. They still hoped that reform would be granted from above without revolutionary violence from below. "Taking the constitutionalist campaign of late 1904 as a whole," the most recent and comprehensive study of the subject concluded, "the more moderate liberal tone prevailed."[79]

Although the banquets were "private" affairs, several major newspapers described most of them in detail. Thus, *Russkie vedomosti* reported on the banquet in St. Petersburg, held on November 20 and attended by more than 600 people. It named the speakers and noted especially the presence of the distinguished writers Maxim Gorky and Leonid Andreev. Most significantly, the paper carried a detailed account of the resolutions adopted by the diners. The judicial reforms of 1864, the St. Petersburg resolutions declared, had been thoroughly distorted. Indeed, under the "bureaucratic regime that has dominated the country," the most elementary conditions for a legal order could not be realized"; and no piecemeal changes in existing institutions could provide the necessary guarantees for the exercise of civil liberties and rights by the citizenry. The time had come to convoke a constituent assembly of freely elected representatives of the people and to grant a full and unconditional amnesty to all persons punished for political or religious offenses.[80]

Students at institutions of higher learning added their voice to the protest movement in the fall of 1904. As early as October 11, a group meeting at the Polytechnical Institute in St. Petersburg expressed its lack of confidence in the government and demanded "an end to the war and the convocation of a constituent assembly on the basis of universal suffrage." University students in the capital followed suit a week later and vowed to organize "a public demonstration in the very near future." Similar meetings were organized at the Women's Medical Institute, the Electrical-Technical Institute, the Mining Institute, and the Military-Medical Academy. In December, students in Moscow, Kharkov, Odessa, and Kiev flocked to demonstrations, often in support of the banquets that were being held in those cities. At one demonstration, on November 28 in St. Petersburg, the police charged the crowd and beat students cruelly, but on the whole the zemstvo campaign proceeded peacefully.[81]

Among Social Democrats the liberal offensive became an important factor in deepening the split between Mensheviks and Bolsheviks. The former had all along been more faithful than the Leninists to the orthodox Marxist position that in "backward" Russia the bourgeoisie constituted a potentially progressive force that deserved support in the struggle against the autocracy. Consequently, in November 1904, *Iskra*, which had come under Menshevik control a year earlier, responded favorably to the zemstvo congress, whose decisions, they said, "have acquired the significance of a political event of paramount importance. . . . The November resolutions can play an important role in the further development of the anti-Tsarist movement."[82] Having acknowledged that the liberals had taken a critical initiative, the Mensheviks contended that the proletariat must now play an important part in the next stage of the struggle against the government. They therefore distributed a "Letter to Party Organizations" outlining tactics for Social Democrats in the zemstvo campaign.

Basically an application of the theory of the leading role of the proletariat in the bourgeois revolution advanced by P. B. Axelrod, a leader of the Mensheviks, the "Letter" recommended a rather tortuous course of action. On the one hand, Social Democrats and workers should encourage the liberals in their campaign for a constitution and should even participate in it. This was desirable in order to strengthen the party's links with the masses and to heighten the latter's political consciousness. It was also desirable as a means of preventing the moderates in the liberal camp from wresting concessions only for themselves while ignoring the masses. But Social Democrats must not adopt an excessively militant approach, for that would only drive the liberals to the right. They should limit their demands to the election of a constituent assembly on the basis of universal, equal, direct, and secret suffrage. Although workers and Social Democrats should stage demonstrations wherever liberals were meeting and should seek to present their views to the bourgeois opposition, they must take every precaution to avoid street disorders, which would frighten the liberals. It would be wise, the "Letter" stated, for Social Democratic leaders to warn liberals ahead of time of an upcoming demonstration and to make clear that it would be a peaceful action.[83]

Lenin lost no time in attacking the Menshevik scheme, which, he contended, was shot through with a fatal contradiction. In advocating workers' demonstrations at the meeting places of liberals, the Mensheviks were in effect admitting that the liberals did not favor genuine democracy.

How then could the bourgeois opposition be gently prodded to press for democratic reforms? The truth is that, unlike the Mensheviks, Lenin no longer expected the bourgeoisie to play a progressive role under any circumstances. "Bourgeois democracy," he stated, "is by its nature not in a condition to satisfy these demands" [for total democracy], because it was unwilling to undermine in full the authority of the monarchy, standing army, and bureaucracy. It was "by nature condemned" to a course of "hesitation and halfway measures." Instead of wasting its strength on futile efforts to influence the bourgeoisie, the working-class party should focus on preparing for the "decisive battle" against the autocracy by means of an "all-national armed uprising." [84] The divergent tactics of the Bolsheviks and Mensheviks that emerged in late 1904—despite occasional periods of harmony—continued to be a source of friction between the two factions for most of the succeeding two decades.

As already noted, the tactics favored by the Mensheviks were applied at several banquets. In Odessa, for example, about 5,000 students and workers held a "democratic mass meeting," which was quickly dispersed by Cossacks and police freely using their rubber clubs. This was the first large street demonstration of the 1905 Revolution, though it cannot be said that "democratic interventions" of this kind greatly influenced the banquets to move to the left. Apparently, at only two or three meetings did the liberals adopt more democratic resolutions in response to pressure from Social Democrats. [85] Still, Lenin was sufficiently impressed to change his mind about the Menshevik tactic. Without explicitly retracting his previous position, he declared toward the end of December 1904 that demonstrations should be held at "zemstvo meetings and in connection with zemstvo meetings." After all, Lenin conceded, the government had been frightened by the "noisy meetings" into formally condemning zemstvos that had yielded to outside pressure in "discussing questions concerning the state, which are not within their competence." Lenin now even suggested that the need to organize demonstrations was self-evident. [86]

The various campaigns by Russian liberals in the fall and winter of 1904 had, in fact, created a new political climate in Russia. Some important new organizations appeared, and they also applied pressure on the government for reform. Professionals formed associations such as the Physicians' Union, the Academic Union, and the Engineers' Union, all of which were precursors of the Union of Unions, organized in May 1905. [87] It was all very bewildering. "The Russians," wrote Samuel Harper, a young American scholar then visiting Moscow, "cannot get used to the freedom (comparative of course) that they are enjoying these days. Men say many things they would have gone to Siberia for six months ago. The papers print the most rabid attacks against the bureaucracy, the war, and the government."[88] The critical question now was, How would the government handle the ferment that had gripped the people?

· · · · ·

Sometime in the fall, Tsar Nicholas concluded that further conciliatory gestures were necessary to pacify the country. He asked Witte, his most experienced and thoughtful official, to help compose a ukase granting reform. Much of the preparatory work had been completed by Mirsky, and it is not clear why Witte became involved in drafting the decree. Witte hinted in his memoirs, however, that Mirsky, though honorable and highly cultivated, was not suited for the post of Internal Affairs Minister. In Witte's view, Mirsky lacked experience in political affairs at the highest levels of government and was too gentle in character. The revolutionary process was already in full swing when he assumed office, and since the Tsar continued to heed the advice of "extreme reactionaries," Mirsky proved incapable of instituting the "new course in domestic policies." Witte suggested, though he did not say so explicitly, that his expertise was needed to enable the government to weather the storm. Indeed, he claimed that had the decree he drafted been "fully implemented," calm and stability would have been restored.[89]

But liberals (especially Petrunkevich) have charged that Witte himself was responsible for the failure of his decree to mollify the opposition. Much of the evidence for the charge may be found in Witte's own memoirs. On December 11, 1904, he and a group of senior officials met with the Tsar to discuss the concessions that should be made in the ukase. One of the proposals, the most significant by far, provided in very general terms for the participation of elected representatives in legislative work: some representatives from the provincial zemstvos and the larger city councils were to serve on the State Council (a body of dignitaries appointed by the Tsar to advise him on legislative proposals). Mirsky strongly advocated the reform. After some discussion, the sovereign agreed to a series of concessions, including the one on elected representatives. The officials at the meeting were profoundly moved, some of them bursting into tears. A major step had been taken to alter the political system of Russia, a step that even many of the Tsar's senior advisers now considered desirable.[90]

Shortly after this meeting and before publication of the ukase, however, Tsar Nicholas called Witte to his chambers for another discussion of the point concerning elected representatives. The Tsar, uneasy about making such a concession, wanted Witte's private and candid opinion on its advisability. In his memoirs, Witte frequently criticized Nicholas for being indecisive and vacillating, which suggests that he must have known at that meeting that only a straightforward statement in support of the concession would discourage the sovereign from changing his mind. Instead, Witte offered the following ambiguous advice: If the Tsar sincerely believed that he could not defy the course of world historical developments, then the point concerning elected representatives should remain in the ukase. But if the monarch considered it impermissible to allow elected officials to share power with the government, he should strike the point from the ukase, for the concession would amount to a first step toward granting society such a role in national affairs. Witte then indicated that he himself still favored the decree as adopted at the larger meeting.

Why did Witte respond so evasively to Nicholas's question? In part, no doubt, because he sincerely harbored reservations about the viability in Russia of a constitutional order. In a private conversation early in December with Sir Charles Hardinge, the British Ambassador, Witte made clear that though he was "in theory . . . willing to make certain concessions to the reform party to calm public agitation," he was "in reality their most bitter opponent" and "expressed himself quite openly as being opposed to any constitutional change, [and] as being of [the] opinion that a despotic autocracy was the only form of [government] suitable to this country."[91] It also seems likely that to ingratiate himself with Nicholas, Witte told him what he thought the monarch wanted to hear. By giving ambiguous advice, Witte was in a perfect position to dissociate himself from the ukase if it did not produce the desired effect. In any case, Nicholas seized on Witte's statement to justify changing his mind. He declared that "under no circumstances will I ever agree to a representative form of government, for I consider it harmful to the trust God gave me over the people, and therefore I will follow your advice and expunge this point."[92]

On hearing the news of the Tsar's decision, Mirsky lost heart. "Everything has failed," he said to some colleagues. "Let us build jails."[93] He offered to resign as Minister of Internal Affairs but was prevailed upon by the Tsar to remain. It would be difficult to prove that retention of Mirsky's point in the ukase would have satisfied society and ended the political storm. It was not that radical a measure. But its abandonment signified beyond any doubt that the government's attitude toward the demands of the opposition had not fundamentally changed. That perception demoralized the liberals who still hoped for reform from above and decisively influenced their conduct early in 1905, when the government faced its most serious crisis to date. The beleaguered autocracy could count on virtually no support from society. For that reason alone, Nicholas's decision on the ukase must be classed as among the most critical ones of his reign.

The decree, which was signed by the Tsar on December 12 and published two days later, announced that the government intended to propose legislation extending to the peasants rights equal to those enjoyed by other subjects. The ukase also promised that the Committee of Ministers under the chairmanship of Witte would prepare legislation with the following goals in mind: (1) to eliminate arbitrariness in the application of the law; (2) to extend the range of authority of zemstvos and city councils and to increase the number of persons eligible to be represented on these institutions; (3) to streamline the courts and guarantee them greater independence; (4) to establish a system of insurance for industrial workers; (5) to impose limitations on the application of exceptional laws; (6) to provide for greater toleration of religious dissenters; (7) to eliminate unnecessary legal restrictions on non-Russian peoples of the Empire; and (8) to ease restrictions on the press.[94] Witte was confident that the decree would be welcomed by society; he was quickly disabused by the liberal leader I. V. Gessen, who told him on December 20 that the measure was far too modest to satisfy the opposition.[95]

Not only did it fail to address the liberals' demand for some sort of popular participation in the political process, the decree also merely *promised* changes at some future date after further deliberations and, most ominously, was accompanied by a reassertion of the principle of autocracy. At the very moment that the government published the ukase, it issued a communiqué castigating liberal agitators for "unconsciously acting not for the good of the fatherland but for [the good] of its enemies." In addition, the communiqué rejected the liberals' "erroneous" resolutions and demands, and vowed to stop "by all legal means" every "violation of order and tranquillity." This attack on the liberals presaged a new campaign of repression. The authorities tightened the censorship over the press, dismissed several moderates from state service, imposed new limitations on local organs of government, and refused to allow several groups to organize political banquets.[96] To make matters worse, Mirsky issued a circular on December 31 that seemed to vitiate an important point in the Ukase of December 12: it stated that the ukase would not encroach upon the "peasant estate system."[97]

Liberals immediately vented their disappointment and frustration at the twists and turns of the government's policies. "The government," S. N. Trubetskoi declared, "is believed neither when it threatens nor when it promises."[98] In mid-December Struve warned that the decree would not pacify the country and, in fact, urged the opposition to "make ever tighter the ring of the blockade around the autocracy." Three weeks later he called on the liberal intelligentsia to organize the masses in urban centers and in the countryside for a more aggressive struggle against the regime.[99] The reaction of the liberal press to the ukase was "decidedly negative, and the only sincere expression of gratification has been the satisfaction evinced on all hands [*sic*] at the formal admission by the

Government of the error of its ways." Fearful about Russia's future, the editors of the liberal press exhorted "the Members of the Committee of Ministers to take a liberal and conscientious view of the duties imposed on them in the framing of the principles on which the subsequent legislation is to be based." [100]

Rebuffed by the opposition, the government also managed to confuse its own supporters with its vacillations. The senior police official in Kharkov, for example, was at a loss on how to respond to the agitation by liberals. "Where was the government? What were its intentions? We knew absolutely nothing about that. We, its local representatives, received no instructions at all and were condemned to observe general disintegration almost passively." [101] If the authorities in St. Petersburg could not formulate a consistent set of policies to deal with the unrest sparked by the liberal movement, which represented a relatively small sector of the population, how would they be able to handle unrest involving masses of people in most of the Empire's cities? The answer to this question would be forthcoming within a month of the issuance of the Ukase of December 12. But the government's conduct of affairs late in 1904 did not augur well.

Chapter Three

. . . .

Gapon and Bloody Sunday

"THE DOMESTIC situation is certainly bad," Witte privately conceded to the U.S. Ambassador in St. Petersburg, R. S. McCormick, during the first week of January 1905, but he assured him that "it did not forebode revolution or anything akin to it at the present time." Witte was still convinced that only the educated classes and urban workers had been seized by the mood of dissatisfaction. The "vast bulk" of the population, the peasants, "had not been touched with any deep longing for better things, of which their experience had taught them nothing," and they had not been "reached by the agitator," who promotes "a spirit bordering on revolt."[1] Usually an astute analyst of domestic affairs, Witte was far too sanguine on this occasion. Neither he nor most of the senior officials at Court and in the government realized that in articulating their own discontents, the liberals were speaking for many others as well.

There was no dearth of evidence of deepening agitation in Russian society. The liberal press had become bolder than ever in urging an end to the "futile war."[2] According to the German consulate in Riga, in such border regions as the Baltic provinces, virtually all sectors of the population, including "military circles," yearned for peace, even if the price was a loss to Russia's prestige.[3] Late in 1904 the security police learned that revolutionaries abroad had formed a committee of representatives of all antigovernment groups operating within the Empire so as to unleash simultaneous actions by underground organizations toward the end of January 1905. The revolutionaries, police agents reported, intended to stage strikes and disorders in many regions of the Empire as a prelude to an attempt at overthrowing the autocracy. Information about the planned actions was circulated among officials in a confidential *Weekly*

Intelligence Summary prepared by the Okhrana, which suggests that the authorities took the threats seriously.[4] To be sure, no one seems to have believed that the revolutionaries were strong enough to achieve their goals, but the official mood was clearly apprehensive, as the following incident demonstrates.

On January 6, 1905, the Imperial family and ranking military and diplomatic officials attended the annual religious ceremony honoring the Epiphany, during which the Metropolitan of St. Petersburg blessed the waters of the Neva River. At the conclusion of the service, a battery of artillery, some three to four hundred yards from the kiosk in which the dignitaries were standing, fired a salute. To everyone's amazement, the "walls of the Palace were bespattered with shots, one bullet passing through one of the windows of the room where the Corps Diplomatiques were assembled." The shots caused little damage, and only one policeman was wounded slightly. Still, rumors quickly circulated that someone had attempted to assassinate the Tsar. The *Manchester Guardian* announced that revolutionaries had "clearly intended" to kill the Emperor. Senior government officials insisted that the incident was nothing more than an accident, an assertion later confirmed by a commission of inquiry. But the British Ambassador, among others, was not convinced: "The serious aspect of the matter is that this is the first time on record that the troops have been implicated in an accident, or whatever else it may be called, by which the Emperor's life has been seriously endangered, if not deliberately attempted."[5] The nervous reaction of citizens in the capital to the incident may help to explain the intemperate behavior of officials a few days later when masses of people marched peacefully toward the Winter Palace.[6]

Inexplicably, a development more threatening to the regime than either the scheming of a few revolutionaries or the incident at the religious ceremony seems to have received scant attention from the authorities. That was the impact of the liberal campaign in the fall and winter of 1904 on a growing number of worker-activists. "I remember that outpouring of petitions," wrote the worker N. Simbirskii, "that was sent to Petersburg from all corners of Russia. . . . Petitions poured out in abundance, were printed in newspapers, workers read them and ardently discussed them at their meetings. . . . And then, at workers' meetings there emerged the idea: We must go to the people!" The activist A. S. Karelin recalled that "with the onset of Sviatopolk-Mirsky's spring I abandoned lectures and began to read only newspapers. At this time the zemstvo petitions began [to appear]. . . . [We] read them, discussed them, and discussed with [Father] Gapon whether the time had not come for us, workers, to come forward with our own petitions. He refused. . . . Beginning in the month of November there were heard vague rumblings: 'Suggest something we can do, from below.'" N. M. Varnashev, yet another activist among the workers, remembered that the newspaper articles, resolutions, and petitions provided him with material for his "agitation and propaganda." Finally, I. A. Pavlov wrote that as the workers read each evening about the liberal campaign in the newspapers *Nasha zhizn* and *Nashi dni*, their leaders began to think of joining the "general protests of Russian intellectuals." At a meeting on November 28, 35 workers' leaders in the capital considered formulating resolutions of "support for the intelligentsia, demanding freedom." Everyone at the meeting favored such action, but no one knew how to proceed.[7]

A few weeks earlier, Father Gapon himself, the preeminent leader of the St. Petersburg workers, had established contact with several members of the local branch of the Union of Liberation: V. Ia. Bogucharsky, V. V. Khizhniakov, E. D. Kuskova, and S. N. Prokopovich. The four Liberationists supplied Gapon and his colleagues with newspapers and information on the liberal campaign. The Liberationists also tried to persuade workers to agitate for both economic improvements for themselves and political concessions that the Union considered to be of paramount importance. The two newspapers that enjoyed a wide readership among industrial workers, *Nasha zhizn* and *Nashi dni*, had in fact been founded by the Union with the financial support of Savva Morozov, a millionaire manufacturer sympathetic to left-wing causes from liberalism to Bolshevism. In view of the various links between workers and liberals, it is not surprising that the demands of the former, put forth early in 1905, bore the imprint of the latter's influence.[8]

It is nonetheless a fact that by the time the liberal offensive was inaugurated, the workers of St. Petersburg had already developed on their own a remarkable organization destined to play a critical role in the events of 1905. The credit for the establishment of that organization belongs to Father Gapon, a man who was enigmatic as well as charismatic. About the only judgment on Gapon on which his associates, contemporary commentators, and historians can agree is that he was influential in triggering the second phase—the most turbulent and violent phase—of the revolution.

The U.S. Ambassador to St. Petersburg considered Gapon to be "a thorough-paced revolutionist" who "utterly deceived the workingmen into the belief that his sole aim was to aid them to better their condition." In actuality, he intended "to get possession of the Emperor and hold him as a hostage."[9] Count Aehrenthal, who contended that Gapon had "almost been elevated to the level of a historical figure" by the "Jewish press," denounced the priest as a depraved man. He had "a great predilection for material luxuries" and was believed to have violated a girl twelve years of age.[10] In historical works, especially those published in the Soviet Union but also in many that have appeared in the West, Gapon's ties to the police and the Tsarist government have been emphasized. The official Soviet view of him in the 1930's and 1940's was that he "undertook to assist the Tsarist Okhrana by providing a pretext for firing on the workers and drowning the working-class movement in blood."[11]

None of these characterizations does justice to the personality of Gapon, a man of extraordinary abilities and charm who appealed not only to workers but also to men in high government positions. For example, the Minister of Justice, N. V. Muraviev, was fascinated by the priest during a meeting on January 7, 1905. Muraviev confessed that Gapon had acknowledged that he supported revolutionary doctrines and that his "previous correct behavior had been a pose." Yet the minister could not bring himself to dislike the priest or to expose his deceptions. The Foreign Minister, Lamsdorff, expressed astonishment at Muraviev's reaction to Gapon and his failure to place the "dangerous charmer" behind bars.[12] Remarkably, each one of the divergent assessments of Gapon contains a grain of truth. He was an incredibly complicated man with a checkered career.

Georgii Apollonovich Gapon was born in 1870 in the small village of Beliki in Poltava province. His father, a man of modest means who had been educated by the village sexton, worked as a clerk for the volost administration. Both his mother, an illiterate, and his maternal grandmother were extremely pious. Young Georgii came under their influence and as a child revealed an intense interest in religion, spending an inordinate amount of time praying to the icons in his home. An intelligent child, he excelled in primary school and followed the advice of his priest that he continue his education at the Lower Ecclesiastical School in Poltava.

After graduation, Gapon entered the Poltava Seminary, but at some point he lost interest in the priesthood as a profession. He was distressed by the church's emphasis on ritual, its "religious formalism," and the hypocrisy and corruption of the clergy. Once he saw priests "celebrate the Eucharist in a state of intoxication," and he frequently encountered priests who were "positive leeches." His reading of some of Leo Tolstoy's works further led him to question his commitment to service in the church. In addition, exposure to people who lived in dismal poverty deeply stirred his sympathies. After recovering from two serious illnesses (a nervous disorder and typhus), Gapon decided that he preferred work among the "toiling and suffering classes" to the priesthood. He tried to transfer to a university to complete his studies, but a low grade for "behavior" at the seminary precluded his acceptance by any institution of higher learning.

Gapon went to work instead as a statistician for the Poltava zemstvo administration. In that position he came into further contact with the poor, which made him even more eager to serve them. In Poltava he married a local merchant's daughter, a pious woman who shared his concern for the downtrodden. She urged Gapon to enter the priesthood because as a man of God he would be better placed to pursue his interests. Gapon followed her advice, took orders, and served with great satisfaction and success as a "spiritual leader" in Poltava. He was very happy with his wife and two children, but after having been married for a few years he was struck by tragedy. His wife contracted a serious illness and died, a loss that deeply affected Gapon. He became something of a mystic, claiming to have visions. As an Orthodox priest he could not remarry, so in 1898 he entered the St. Petersburg Theological Seminary for further studies. In addition, he devoted himself to missionary work among poor workers and beggars. Before completing a year's studies in St. Petersburg, however, Gapon again suffered from a nervous disorder and approached total collapse. He went to the Crimea to recuperate, and there his future was decided: he met some intellectuals who reinforced his doubts about the "formalism and hypocrisy" of the church, and who convinced him to abandon religious work for his other interests.[13]

By all accounts, Gapon was an imposing man. Handsome, intelligent, and articulate, he impressed acquaintances with his deep dedication to humane principles and his loyalty to his associates. He was a fine speaker, and, when it served his interests, could be crafty and even duplicitous. He was also fired by a fierce ambition to make his mark in the world. When he returned to St. Petersburg after recovering from his nervous condition, he began to come into his own. While continuing his studies, he again worked among the downtrodden and attracted many people to his religious services and the various discussions he organized. His numerous schemes to help the poor attracted the attention of the Empress, who urged the Committee of Ministers to take an interest in his work and to invite him to one of its meetings. The priest now looked upon himself as a man destined for great achievements in improving the moral and material condition of the common people. He also had developed a strong faith in the Tsar's devotion to the well-being of the Russian people, especially those at the lowest rung of society.

At some point Gapon began to teach at the Orphanage of St. Olga, where he became embroiled in a scandal that gave rise to rumors that still cannot be fully disentangled. After being dismissed from his post in July 1902, he took with him a recent graduate, Aleksandra Uzdaleva, who became his common-law wife. Aleksandra's age is not known, but this incident seems to have been the basis for Aehrenthal's charge that

Gapon had violated a twelve-year-old girl.[14] Whatever the circumstances surrounding his liaison with Aleksandra, Gapon was not a lecher; certainly he was not given to the kind of sexual exploits for which Rasputin later gained notoriety. In any case, the incident did not affect his popularity among St. Petersburg workers. In fact, sometime in 1902 or early 1903—the exact date is uncertain—he seized on a new opportunity to enlarge his influence among them. He learned of the elaborate scheme by the chief of the Moscow Okhrana, S. V. Zubatov, to draw workers into organizations designed to mobilize mass support for the Tsar. It was the kind of endeavor that Gapon immediately found congenial.

For his part, Zubatov was eager to enlist the services of a man with Gapon's appeal to workers. A local Okhrana agent arranged a meeting between the two men, and although Gapon disapproved of Zubatov's stress on tight police control over workers' unions, they reached an understanding. Zubatov began to send the priest a monthly subsidy of 100 rubles (a substantial sum at the time), and in the summer of 1903 Gapon founded the "Assembly of the Russian Factory and Mill Workers of the City of St. Petersburg." He had secured Zubatov's agreement to minimize police involvement in the organization as well as to allow members to play a more active role in determining its work than had been the case in other police unions. The Assembly did not intervene in labor disputes, concentrating instead on organizing dances, concerts, and lectures, and on promoting various other projects for self-improvement. Gapon deliberately restricted the Assembly to activities that were politically innocuous because he planned eventually to expand the organization, both in the capital and in other cities, and wanted to avoid any action that might appear provocative or threatening to the authorities.[15]

Gapon succeeded in gaining the confidence both of workers who favored greater militancy than he did on the labor question and of high officials in St. Petersburg. He discussed the Assembly with General N. V. Kleigels, the city's governor, and A. A. Lopukhin, the Director of Police, assuring them that he was patriotic and law-abiding. Although the statutes of the Assembly, approved by the Ministry of Internal Affairs in February 1904, provided for popular election of various officers, the so-called Representative was clearly the central figure in the organization, and this office was occupied by Gapon himself. Nonetheless, his preeminence stemmed primarily from the fact that he was the most dynamic person in the Assembly, the man who made the key decisions, enjoyed the affection of the rank and file, and maintained the contacts with personages of high standing. When, early in 1904, I. A. Fullon, an amiable general of rather limited abilities, became Governor of St. Petersburg City, Gapon lost no time in visiting him and persuading him to look with favor on the Assembly. All these connections with high officials and with the police were known to the priest's associates, who nevertheless regarded him as sincerely devoted to promoting the workers' well-being.

Gapon was skillful—some might say cunning—in giving the impression to his lieutenants, several of them former Social Democrats interested in political issues as well as in economic improvements for the workers, that he really wished to go beyond the limited activities permitted by the statutes. For example, he set up a secret committee of workers' leaders who concerned themselves with political matters and even discussed illegal literature. Occasionally, political issues were brought up at general meetings of the Assembly. The police, having granted the Assembly virtual autonomy, seem not to have been aware of this "semi-secret political life" of the organization.[16] In his autobiography, Gapon claimed that as early as the summer of 1903 "there arose in my mind the question whether it might not be possible, by pretending adherence to Zubatoff's policy, to attain my own end of a genuine working-class organization." He thought of "influencing the Workmen's Association organized by Zubatoff in such a way as to completely paralyze the efforts of the Political Police to use it as a buttress of the Autocracy, and to direct it [the Assembly] into an altogether different channel. If I had had any faith in the genuineness of Zubatoff's intentions, it had by this time absolutely disappeared."[17] Gapon wrote these words after Bloody Sunday, when he had become thoroughly disillusioned with the Tsarist regime; there is reason to doubt whether his political views prior to 1905 were that unqualified. He himself conceded, also in his autobiography, that *at least* until late in the fall of 1904 (though almost certainly until January 9, 1905) he believed in the Tsar's benevolence and in his willingness to grant constitutional rights to the people.[18]

On the other hand, we know that as early as March 1904 he showed four leaders of the Assembly a document he had drafted containing demands that were subsequently incorporated in the famous petition submitted to the Tsar on January 9, 1905, and that he then knew to be anathema to the Tsar and most of his advisers. The March document called for, among other things, political rights for the Russian people, an eight-hour day, and the right of workers to form trade unions.[19] Gapon swore his associates to secrecy about the document, but in informing them of his ultimate intentions, if that is really what they were, he strengthened his hold on their loyalty. Moreover, these subordinates, pleased with the priest's ultimate goals, were determined to breathe new life into the organization. Those who had voiced reservations about Gapon's police connections now shed their suspicions. But for the historian, Gapon's true convictions and intentions still remain something of a mystery. Conceivably, he himself had not yet sorted out his beliefs and plans in his own mind and still held contradictory views on the autocracy, which would be consistent with his mercurial character. He cherished great ideals and great ambitions, but beyond that he lacked clarity of purpose.

His organizational skill was outstanding. By the spring of 1904 he had made sufficient progress in establishing the Assembly as a viable enterprise to conduct a ceremony marking its official opening. One hundred and fifty people attended the affair, which was held on April 11; by the end of the month the Assembly's membership had grown to 300. On May 30, he opened a branch in the Narva region of St. Petersburg in a large house where 2,000 people could be seated at any one time. The Governor of St. Petersburg City, General Fullon, attended the opening ceremonies, which naturally enhanced the priest's prestige. Within another five months, Gapon established a total of nine branches with a membership of about 5,000 people. The estimates of the Assembly's membership in January 1905 range from 6,000 to 20,000.[20]

Each branch of the Assembly engaged in a range of activities: lectures on the history of the labor and revolutionary movements; discussions of religious questions; concerts, singing lessons, and plays. No event could be scheduled without Gapon's personal approval. His authority was so great that some of his assistants actually referred to him as "dictator," an appellation he rather savored.[21] Intellectuals were wary of him, in part because he was not a cultivated man: he never mastered the pronunciation of foreign words and even had difficulty with the word "constitutionalists." They were also troubled by his lack of theoretical sophistication and ignorance of the history of radicalism. But none of these deficiencies reduced his appeal to workers. On the contrary, they liked the fact that he was, socially, of their class, did not talk down to them, treated them as comrades—in short, that he acted and spoke as they did. They also appreciated his openness in revealing his plans for a better future. And in the eyes of many workers, his priestly robe only added to his stature. To be sure, workers under the influence of revolutionary movements still distrusted him because of his police connections, but there is no question that he had "cast a spell" over large numbers of common laborers and that his adherents were "prepared to march with him through fire and water."[22]

In the last two months of 1904, when the liberal offensive was moving into high gear, Gapon intensified his efforts to turn the Assembly into a powerful organization. Contrary to the provisions of the statutes, he now admitted workers who were neither Orthodox nor ethnically Russian, and he considered organizing societies in Moscow and other industrial centers throughout the Empire. He sought to enlist women, arguing that

"If women are not drawn into the movement, if they do not help, they will hinder [our work]."[23] Increasingly, he gave evidence of planning to convert the Assembly into a genuine trade union, but he still took pains not to break his ties with the police. Most important, in November he invited several of his associates to his apartment for secret discussions on the desirability of drafting a petition, possibly containing political demands, that would be submitted to the Tsar on the occasion of a new military defeat or perhaps on February 19, to commemorate the emancipation of the serfs in 1861.[24]

A series of unexpected events at the Putilov plant, a large armaments and shipbuilding factory in the southwestern section of St. Petersburg, led Gapon to change the timing and to some extent the focus of the petition. In December 1904, four workers, all of them members of the Assembly, were dismissed. Many of the plant's employees belonged to the Assembly; S. I. Smirnov, the director, a rigid man not known for gentle treatment of workers, displayed growing hostility toward Gapon's organization, a hostility that reflected the attitude of the entire factory administration. Gapon himself at first thought that the issue would be settled amicably. He met with representatives of other branches of the Assembly; they decided to send delegations to General Fullon and to Smirnov with the request that the workers be reinstated and that the man directly responsible for the firings, an abrasive foreman named A. Tetiavkin, be dismissed. Smirnov refused to accede on the ground that the Assembly had no right to interfere in the affairs of the company.

The workers at the plant were now convinced that management was determined to emasculate their organization. It should be noted, however, that some evidence indicates that the four men did not have quite so strong a case as they claimed; as workers, they were neither industrious nor reliable.[25] In any case, it had become obvious that the Putilov administration was throwing down a gauntlet to the Assembly that could not be ignored. "If we abandoned . . . [the four men] to their fate," Gapon wrote in his memoirs, "the authority of the [Assembly] would be shaken, possibly fatally, and similar arbitrary action would be encouraged; while, on the other hand, if we succeeded in obtaining their reinstatement, our prestige in the eyes of the laboring population would be tremendously increased."[26]

On January 2, 1905, over 600 workers from various parts of the city attended a general meeting of the Assembly's Vasilii Island branch to receive reports on the latest developments at the Putilov plant and to map out future measures in support of their Putilov brethren. The gathering unanimously decided that workers at the plant should not begin work the next day until the four men had been reinstated and Tetiavkin dismissed. After management again refused to accede to these demands, the strike may be said to have officially begun. Gapon apparently did not attend the meeting at the Vasilii Island branch, but on January 3 he quickly expressed support for the work stoppage. On that day General Fullon informed Gapon that the company had reinstated three of the workers, but it was too late to prevent a confrontation. "It was no longer a simple question of the reinstatement of these men," Gapon later recalled. "There were other demands from each of the workshops, and I could only advise that the Putiloff administration should arrange a conference with the branch chairmen of [the Assembly] and delegates of the strikers."[27]

The strike spread with remarkable speed, which suggests that the dismissals were only the spark that ignited the flame. Delegations of workers from the Putilov plant marched from one factory to another to urge comrades to put down their tools. On January 4 the workers at the Franco-Russian works went out on strike; on January 5, those at the Nevskii Shipbuilding plant and the Shtiglits factory followed suit. By January 7 about two-thirds of St. Petersburg's factory force—some 100,000 people at 382 enterprises—had stopped working.[28]

The workers' initial demands focused on economic issues, but it did not take long for the strikers to voice political demands. This was bound to happen, since the leaders of the strike were seeking to maximize their support. On January 5 Gapon raised the question of preparing a petition for the Tsar, and a day later he suggested, for the first time, that a procession be organized to present the document to the sovereign in person. He had in mind a peaceful march and so informed the city governor. At that point no official tried to deter the priest from his scheme, which turned into the most momentous event of the Revolution.

For the next three days, Gapon and all the branches of the Assembly concentrated on securing support for the petition and for a march on Sunday, January 9. Gapon met endlessly with groups of workers, encouraging them not to abandon the plan. On one day alone he delivered 50 short speeches to workers. Generally, Gapon exuded unbounded confidence in the enterprise, arguing that the Tsar was a good man who would help the people once he understood their plight. But occasionally he acknowledged the possibility of failure. Nicholas might refuse to listen to his people, which would make it clear, Gapon said, that "we have no Tsar."[29] His listeners invariably showered him with expressions of support. The meetings were not only a powerful educational event for thousands of workers, who were almost always won over by Gapon to the Assembly's program, but also a profoundly emotional experience for them. At some branches, when a vote was taken on specific points in the petition, the workers signaled their approval by making a cross with their fingers so as to underline the sacredness of their demands.[30] As one contemporary put it, Gapon did not merely lead a strike movement or a political movement; he led "a crusade to the Tsar, that carried a banner inscribed with the word: 'Justice!'"[31]

Despite the religious fervor of Gapon's followers, it would be a mistake to view them simply as "politically backward workers" who blindly accepted the leadership of a charismatic priest. Certainly, many of the participants in Gapon's movement came from the unskilled and illiterate ranks of the Petersburg work force, but during the crisis over the firings at the Putilov plant workers flocked to the priest because they considered him a defender of "workers' rights on the job." They understood that their subservient position made them vulnerable to the arbitrary conduct of their employers, and they were persuaded that only if they took some dramatic action in their own behalf would they achieve better conditions. Their reliance on religious symbols and rhetoric was natural, given the enormous importance of Orthodoxy in the culture of the time. This is not to suggest that the participants in Gapon's movement were class-conscious workers in the sense that Marxists use the term. Neither committed revolutionaries nor superstitious dolts, they were men and women determined to vent their personal frustrations in the only way that made sense to them.[32]

Predictably, Social Democrats of both factions, who prided themselves on their class-consciousness, disapproved of the procession. On January 4, the Mensheviks distributed a leaflet warning the workers that the Assembly had been founded by "servants" of the government to divert them from pursuing their true interests. The Assembly's demands were dismissed as "insignificant," for they did not put sufficient stress on political issues. The Bolsheviks rejected Gapon's tactics even more stridently. It was futile, they said in a leaflet of January 8, to appeal to the Tsar, who would never agree voluntarily to the kinds of concessions demanded by the Assembly. "Freedom is bought with blood, freedom is won with weapons in a fierce battle. Don't beg from the Tsar, don't even demand [anything] from him; don't abase yourselves before our sworn enemy, but eject him from the throne and with him the entire gang around the autocracy—only in this way will it be possible to gain freedom."[33]

When Social Democrats tried to address workers along these lines at meetings of the Assembly branches, they were shouted down and occasionally hauled off the platform by irate workers. Social Democrats could speak freely only if they made clear their support for Gapon.[34] Most workers at this time were simply not interested in overthrowing the entire political system. They shared Gapon's proclaimed reverence for the Tsar, and consequently Social Democrats could do little more than contribute, in a general way, to stoking their emotions. The Social Democrats did not otherwise exert any influence on the events leading up to Bloody Sunday.[35]

Even while organizing the procession, Gapon made every effort to resolve the conflict between the employers and workers and, failing that, to assure a peaceful march. He tried twice to see Sviatopolk-Mirsky to urge the Internal Affairs Minister to prevail on the industrialists to make concessions to the striking workers, but without success. The Minister of Justice, whom Gapon did see on January 7, refused to intervene.[36] At the numerous meetings with his followers Gapon emphasized that everyone was to "go to the Tsar unarmed," and that the march was to be orderly.

Until January 7, the authorities appeared to be confused and failed to issue clear signals about their intentions. Rumors circulated that the army had been placed on alert, but there were also various hints that it was not being prepared for any kind of action. The police appeared to be well disposed toward Gapon's organization. They did nothing to obstruct the distribution of propaganda among the workers or to hinder the activities of the branches. A few policemen actually attended some meetings without interfering in any way. Under the circumstances, none of the workers had any reason to believe that they would be subjected to violent attack during the march. A few had even convinced themselves that the Tsar intended to invite 40 to 60 workers elected by the people to attend a "gala entertainment" at the Winter Palace.[37]

At the last moment, various prominent citizens became apprehensive and tried to forestall any untoward incidents. On Saturday evening, January 8, I. V. Gessen visited Witte and pleaded with him to persuade officials not to order the army to block the procession. Gessen sought to impress upon Witte that the workers were at such a high pitch of emotion that nothing could prevent them from marching. If the army tried to stop them, there would be a bloodbath. Witte received Gessen rather coolly, stressing his lack of influence at Court. He insisted that there was nothing he could do.

Gessen then went to a meeting of writers at the office of the newspaper *Syn otechestva* to discuss the situation. Here everyone feared a terrible tragedy; in a last-ditch effort to prevent bloodshed, the gathering decided to send a delegation to Witte to implore him once again to use his good offices to urge moderation on the government. I. F. Annenskii, K. K. Arsenev, Maxim Gorky, Professor N. I. Kareev, Professor V. I. Semevskii, V. A. Miakotin, A. V. Peshekhonov, Gessen, and a worker named D. F. Kuzin (who turned out to be a provocateur) appeared at Witte's house around midnight. Perhaps because this was so distinguished a group, Witte, after again pleading helplessness, agreed to telephone Mirsky and ask him to receive the delegation. The group proceeded to the Internal

Affairs Minister's house, only to be told that the Prince was in bed and that General K. N. Rydzevskii at the Department of Police would receive them. The general pointed out that all instructions to the police and army had been issued, that they could not be changed, and that if the delegation wished to avoid bloodshed, it should use its influence with the workers to have the procession called off.[38] Clearly, the government had been warned about the dangers in trying to halt the procession. A combination of callousness and mindlessness prevented it from taking appropriate measures to prevent a disaster. This unpardonable lapse would cost the old regime dearly.

Although none of the evidence suggests that the government wanted a violent confrontation, by January 7 it had reached two decisions that made a clash unavoidable: not to grant Gapon a meeting with the Tsar to present the petition, and not to permit marching workers to enter the center of the city. On January 7, General Fullon issued an appeal to the people to avoid any mass gathering, coupled with a warning that resolute, though legally prescribed, measures would be taken to handle disorders. He also declared that no procession would be tolerated. Troops were brought in from various regions to reinforce the local garrison, and by January 9 about 9,000 infantrymen and 3,000 cavalry were held in readiness in the capital.

On the evening of January 8, the government made a desperate attempt to deprive the procession of its leader: it issued an "absolutely secret" order for Gapon's arrest. The authorities deeply feared any mass demonstration designed to put pressure on them to grant political and economic concessions. They regarded this as an intolerable form of coercion in an autocratic regime; to yield to it would inevitably open the door to disorder on a massive scale. Hence, the government decided to place in police custody the man it now considered to be a dangerous ringleader of the lower classes. But Gapon either knew or suspected that the government intended to take action against him. He went into hiding, guarded by some 200 loyal workers.[39]

The evening before the procession, he sent a formal letter to the Minister of Internal Affairs requesting a meeting with the Tsar at the Winter Palace at 2 P.M. the next day to present the petition. Gapon assured the minister that there was no reason to fear the marchers and declared that the sovereign's acceptance of the petition "was necessary for His well-being, the well-being of the citizens of Petersburg, the well-being of our country: otherwise, these moral bonds that up to this time have existed between the Russian Tsar and the Russian people might be severed. . . . Tell the Tsar that I, the workers, and many thousands of subjects have reached the unalterable decision to come peacefully and with faith in Him to the Winter Palace."[40]

Gapon and his assistants put the final touches on the document on January 7 and then released it for distribution. Thus, the government had adequate time to absorb the message that Gapon was not planning a violent attack on the regime. The petition read as follows: [41]

A Most Humble and Loyal Address
of the Workers of St. Petersburg Intended for Presentation to HIS MAJESTY on Sunday at two o'clock on the Winter Palace Square

SIRE:

We, the workers *and inhabitants* of St. Petersburg, of *various estates*, our wives, our children, and our aged, helpless parents, come to Thee, O SIRE, to seek justice and protection. We are impoverished; we are oppressed, overburdened with excessive toil, contemptuously treated. We are not even recognized as human beings, but are treated like slaves who must suffer their bitter fate in silence and without complaint. And we have suffered, but even so we are being further (and further) pushed into the slough of poverty, arbitrariness, and ignorance. We are suffocating in despotism and lawlessness. O SIRE, we have no strength left, and our endurance is at an end. We have reached that frightful moment when death is better than the prolongation of our unbearable sufferings.

Hence we stopped work and told our employers that we will not resume work until our demands are fulfilled. We did not ask much; we sought only that without which there is no life for us but hard labor and eternal suffering. Our first request was that our employers agree to discuss our needs with us. But (even) this we were refused. We were prohibited even from speaking of our needs, since no such right is given us by law. The following requests were also deemed to be outside the law: the reduction of the workday to eight hours; our mutual participation in determining the rates for our work and in the settlement of grievances that might arise between us and the lower managerial staff; the raising of the minimum daily wage for unskilled workers, and for women as well, to one ruble; the abolition of overtime work; better medical attention for our sick without insults; and the arrangement of our workshops so that we might work there without encountering death from murderous drafts, rain, and snow.

According to our employers *and managers*, our demands turned out to be illegal, our every request a crime, and our desire to improve our conditions an insolence, insulting to *them* (our masters). O SIRE, *we are many thousands here* (there are more than 300,000 of us), but we are human beings in appearance only, for we, *with the rest of the Russian people*, do not possess a single human right, not even the right to speak, think, gather, discuss our needs, and take steps to improve our conditions. *We are enslaved, enslaved under the patronage and with the aid of Thy officials.* Anyone of us who dares to raise his voice in defense of the working class *and the people* is thrown into jail or exiled. Kindheartedness is punished as a crime. To feel sorry for a downtrodden, maltreated human being bereft of his rights is to commit a heinous crime! *The workers and the peasants are delivered into the hands of the bureaucratic administration, composed of embezzlers of public funds and robbers, who not only care nothing for the needs of the people, but flagrantly abuse them. The bureaucratic administration brought the country to the brink of ruin, involved her in a humiliating war, and is leading*

Russia closer and closer to disaster. We, the workers and people, have no voice whatsoever in the spending of huge sums collected from us in taxes. We do not even know how the money, collected from the impoverished people, is spent. The people are deprived of the opportunity to express their wishes and demands, to participate in the establishment of taxes and public spending. The workers are deprived of the opportunity to organize into unions in order to defend their interests.

O SIRE, is this in accordance with God's laws, by the grace of which Thou reignest? Is it possible to live under such laws? Would it not be preferable for all of us, the toiling people of Russia, to die? Let the capitalist-*exploiters of the working class* and officials, the embezzlers and plunderers of the Russian people, live and enjoy their lives.

These are the prospects that are before us, SIRE, and the reasons that brought us to the walls of Thy palace. Here we seek the final salvation. Do not turn Thy help away from Thy people. Lead them out from the mire of lawlessness, poverty, and ignorance. Allow them to determine their own future; deliver them from the intolerable oppression of the officialdom. Raze the wall that separates Thee from Thy people and rule the country with them. Thou reignest in order to bring happiness to Thy people, but this happiness is torn out of our hands by Thy officials, and there is nothing left for us but grief and humiliation.

Consider our demands attentively and without anger, for they are uttered not in malice but for good, ours as well as Thine, O SIRE. We speak not in insolence, but from the realization of the necessity to find a way out of a situation intolerable to us all. Russia is too vast, and her needs are too great and manifold to be dealt with exclusively by the bureaucrats. *Popular representation is essential*; it is essential that the people help themselves *and govern themselves*. Truly, only they know their *real* needs. Refuse not their help, accept it, and command representatives of the Russian land, of all her classes, of all her estates, *as well as representatives of the workers*, to gather without delay. Let these include a capitalist, worker, official, priest, physician, teacher—let everyone, whoever he may be, elect his representative. Let everyone be free and equal in his choice, and for this purpose let the elections to the constituent assembly be conducted under conditions of universal, secret, and equal suffrage.

This is our principal request, upon which everything else depends. This is the main and the only balm for our wounds, without which they will continue to fester and will *soon* bring us to death.

But a single measure cannot heal our wounds. Others are needed, and we have come to Thee, SIRE, openly and directly as to the father, to tell Thee, *in the name of the entire toiling class of Russia*, that the following are essential:

  I. Measures to eliminate the ignorance of and arbitrariness toward the Russian people.
     1. The immediate release and return of those who suffered for their political and religious convictions, for strikes and peasant disorders.*

  *In earlier versions Paragraph 1 was last and read: "Immediate release of those who suffered for convictions."

    2. An *immediate* proclamation of freedom and inviolability of the person, freedom of speech, press, association, and worship.

    3. Free universal and compulsory public education, financed by the State.

    4. Responsibility of the ministers before the people and guarantees that the government will act according to law.

    5. Equality of all before the law without any exceptions.

    6. *Separation of the church from the state.*

II. Measures to eliminate the poverty of the people.

    1. Abolition of indirect taxation and the introduction of a progressive income tax.

    2. Abolition of land redemption payments, cheap credit, and the gradual transfer of the land to the people.

    3. *Contracts for orders of the war and naval departments to be made in Russia and not abroad.*

    4. *Termination of the war in accordance with the will of the people.*

III. Measures to eliminate the oppression of labor by capital.

    1. *Abolition of the system of factory inspectors.*

    2. *Establishment in factories and plants of permanent elected worker committees, which are to participate with management in the consideration of worker grievances. Workers must not be discharged without the consent of these committees.*

    3. Freedom of cooperative associations and professional worker unions *to be allowed without delay.*

    4. An eight-hour workday and strict regulation of overtime work.

    5. *Freedom of the struggle for labor against capital to be allowed without delay.*

    6. *Immediate* establishment of normal wage rates.

    7. Participation of representatives of the (workers) *working classes* in the drafting of a bill for state insurance of workers is *indispensable, and is to be put into effect without delay.*

Here, O SIRE, are our principal needs which we have come to lay before Thee: *only with their fulfillment can our Motherland be emancipated from slavery and poverty, only then can the workers unite in order to defend their interests against the brazen exploitation of the capitalists and the plundering, stifling bureaucratic administration.*

Issue thy orders and swear to fulfill them, and Thou wilt make Russia happy and glorious, and Thy name will forever be engraved in our hearts and in the hearts of all our descendants. But if Thou withholdest Thy command and failest to respond to our supplications, we will die here on this square before Thy palace. There is no place for us to go, nor is there any reason for us to go any further. There are two paths before us: one to freedom and happiness, the other into the grave. . . . Let our lives be a sacrifice for suffering Russia. We do not regret this sacrifice, but offer it gladly.

No one reading the petition can fail to be struck by the difference between its content and its tone. In content it was in many ways quite radical. In calling for a constituent assembly elected on the basis of a democratic suffrage, civil liberties for all citizens, the right to establish trade unions, and an eight-hour working day, Gapon clearly aligned his movement with the political opposition that had become so vocal and militant in 1904. At the same time, it should be noted that the petition did not demand the abolition of the monarchy or the introduction of socialism. Nor did it contain threats of violence.

The petition took the form of a desperate plea to the Tsar, still referred to as "the father," to treat his subjects not as slaves but as human beings, and to institute the necessary reforms from above because such were the dictates of compassion. Significantly, the petition blamed the people's agonies not on the sovereign but on the bureaucracy, which was accused of robbing "the government and the people" and of having "devastated the country." Gapon included this statement because he and most of his followers genuinely subscribed to the age-old view of the Tsar as a benevolent patriarch who would right things if only the people could reach him and inform him of their anguish.

Without question, this tone of humility and supplication was sincere. The report of a commission of seven lawyers set up on January 16 to investigate the events surrounding Bloody Sunday emphasized that the participants in the march considered it "as nothing other than a religious procession; all the eyewitnesses also regarded it in this way." Even the police acknowledged as much.[42] Sir Charles Hardinge was "firmly convinced that had the police [force] been as efficient as that of London, three or four hundred policemen would have been amply sufficient to deal with the crowds without resort being had to . . . extreme measures."[43]

Early on the morning of the fateful day, people appeared in their Sunday best at designated places. Many women and children showed up, and all participated in the prayer meetings held before the procession began. Marchers carried icons and portraits of the Tsar, and sang "Save Thy People, O Lord" and other hymns. Many workers pointedly raised their hands and emptied their pockets to show that they were unarmed. As the lawyers' report put it, the people "went like children to weep out their grief on their father's breast."[44]

There is no consensus on the size of the procession. All eyewitnesses did agree, however, that it was large, probably ranging from 50,000 to 100,000 people. Certainly, Gapon attracted far more people that day than belonged to his organization, which lends support to the claim that the priest had come to be recognized by numerous workers in St. Petersburg as their true spokesman. But the procession probably also grew in size because people were moved to join it by a variety of considerations. A significant number—in all likelihood a substantial majority—believed that the Tsar would respond favorably to their pleas. However, workers with Social Democratic sympathies who did not share this optimism nevertheless considered it their duty to march with their "misguided" comrades so as to express solidarity with them. Some people joined the march because they looked upon it as a political demonstration. Even workers who expected the government to use force to repel the crowds felt that by marching they would drive home their point that the proletariat must rely on force to achieve its goals. Then there were the usual curiosity-seekers, those who wished to see the Tsar, to observe the ceremony of Gapon submitting the petition to the sovereign. "One old woman," we are told, "who wanted to give her son, a boy of seventeen, the opportunity to see the Tsar, gave him an icon and put him at the head of the crowd," never to see him again. Finally, quite a few workers took their families along to emphasize their peaceful intentions.[45]

The singing crowds marched toward the Winter Palace from different directions. Initially no one sought to stop them. The police not only refrained from interfering but in some cases walked in front of the crowds, as was customary in religious processions. In several neighborhoods no policemen at all could be seen. At the original meeting points, nowhere "was there any kind of warning, any kind of persuasion, or attempts by the authorities to interfere."[46] As the crowds approached their destination, soldiers in a few places told the marchers to turn back, but there was no one pattern to the behavior of the troops. The authorities seem not to have formulated a clear-cut plan of action.

The marchers did not heed the orders to disperse. When one large crowd that included Gapon, who was surrounded by a protective shield of workers, reached the Narva Gate, a bugle was blown as a signal to the soldiers to open fire. The workers, according to the lawyers' report, would have understood the meaning of the bugle call, but no one could hear anything over the din of the singing. Moreover, virtually no time elapsed between the signal and the shooting. Some 40 people were immediately killed or wounded. Gapon escaped injury, though two of his bodyguards and the chairman of the Assembly, I. V. Vaselev, died on the spot. Several other bodyguards threw Gapon over a fence, and the priest then hid in different private apartments, including that of Maxim Gorky. At the time of the violence Gapon is quoted as having exclaimed, "There is no God any longer! There is no Tsar!"[47]

Shooting also erupted at other places where marchers refused to retreat. Troops fired indiscriminately, hitting people who were trying to escape as well as innocent bystanders. There is no agreement on the total number of casualties on January 9, but the official figures, possibly on the low side, indicate the grimness of the carnage: 130 killed and 299 seriously wounded. The fury of the people in the streets was uncontrollable. Many were heard to shout: "Murderers! Bloodsuckers! Hangmen! You run away from the Japanese, but shoot at your own people."[48] Disorders continued for the rest of that day; people threw stones at officials in uniform and at windows; there were some incidents of looting. A few barricades were erected, but soldiers quickly dismantled them. Occasionally, in irrational outbursts of anger, workers attacked students, charging them with having caused the slaughter of their comrades.[49]

The day that immediately came to be known as Bloody Sunday could hardly have ended more disastrously. An occasion that the government could have exploited to its advantage became instead a rallying cry for the opposition. Had Tsar Nicholas received a deputation of workers and announced some concessions such as a reduction in the hours of work, he would have earned, in the words of the British Ambassador to St. Petersburg, "the admiration and undying loyalty of the workingmen. It is astonishing that the Emperor's Ministers should not have advised H[is] M[ajesty] in that sense nor have counselled him to receive the homage of his loyal subjects and have thus prevented the fusion of the socialistic and labouring classes."[50]

Although neither the Tsar nor his officials had planned a massacre, none of them had thought through the implications of preventing the procession from reaching its destination. Remarkably, the Tsar did not even bother to be at the Winter Palace on January 9; he stayed at his palace in Tsarskoe Selo, half an hour's drive from the capital. But even if he did not consider it advisable to meet Gapon himself, a minister or some other senior official could have been delegated to do so. Gapon and his supporters would have been deeply disappointed, but there would have been no carnage. The monarch and his advisers naively assumed that a mere show of force would cause the crowds to scatter. Nothing demonstrated more clearly how far out of touch the government had become with the mood of the workers who followed Gapon. "What could not fail to strike a disinterested onlooker," reported the British Ambassador, "was the absence of any direction, in fact of any Govt. at all. Events [were] allowed to drift without any cooperation between the Ministry of Finance which has control of the Govt. factories and the Ministry of Interior which is responsible for the public safety, the police acting without any knowledge or foresight, & the Military Auth[orities] without judgment or self-restraint."[51]

The massacre electrified public opinion throughout the Empire. In the words of the U.S. Consul in Odessa, "All classes condemn the authorities and more particularly the Emperor. The present ruler has lost absolutely the affection of the Russian people, and whatever the future may have in store for the dynasty, the present Czar will never again be safe in the midst of his people." Even the U.S. Ambassador to St. Petersburg, no friend of Gapon's, criticized the Tsar for not granting an audience to some of the workers and for not ordering an investigation of their grievances: "I have heard the assembled crowd accused of nothing worse than jeering at the troops, hustling the officers, and using language to them that will not bear repetition. . . . [The demonstrators] had not the look of revolutionists." The ambassador believed that "the Emperor will never be able to reestablish himself in his former unique position."[52]

The public outcry against the government began on the very evening of the procession; 459 intellectuals met at the Free Economic Society and signed a letter of protest expressing horror at the bloodshed and denouncing the government for incompetence and brutality. "It is impossible to continue to live this way," it declared. The letter also contained a special appeal to army officers: "If you are men of honor, do not raise your arms against unarmed people. . . . Turn your arms against the enemies of the people."[53]

That same evening at the Aleksandrinskii Theater a man urged the audience not to stay for the performance. Most followed his advice and the performance was canceled. A banquet for professors, scheduled for January 12, was also canceled; many who had bought tickets recommended that the money that had been collected be donated to the families of the victims. V. D. Nabokov, a member of the St. Petersburg City Council, formally proposed that 25,000 rubles be assigned for the same purpose. The intelligentsia began its own drive to collect money for the victims' families.[54] St. Petersburg remained tranquil in the days following the tragedy, but only because "the central part of the town was an armed camp both night and day, and all groupings of men were quickly dispersed." The same writer reported that "The strikers returned quickly to their homes, and whatever disturbances occurred after Sunday evening were due to hooligans and [the] worst elements in the town, who recognized the moment as favorable for breaking open the shops and looting in isolated quarters."[55]

Bloody Sunday shocked liberals in the zemstvos, which during the month of January 1905 experienced more political turbulence than ever before. Attempts by chairmen of zemstvo boards to silence criticism of the government were met by a rash of strikes by local assemblies and resignations on the part of elected officials and employees. Several zemstvos now adopted resolutions more radical than the resolution of the Zemstvo Congress of November 1904. It was not uncommon for zemstvos to set up funds for the victims of Bloody Sunday.[56]

The vast strike movement that ensued proved to be the most disruptive development and the one that the government found most difficult to handle. For the workers of St. Petersburg, the general strike in the days immediately preceding Bloody Sunday had been a crucial event. Strikes, it must be remembered, were illegal, and many workers faced a real psychological barrier in deciding whether to join one. Most had never defied the authorities in this way, and they needed to free themselves of the dread of the consequences before deciding to participate. Their fury over the dismissal of their four colleagues at the Putilov plant, coupled with their long-standing distress over the conditions of work, had led them to take the first and most difficult step. Having gone out on strike once, it was that much easier for them to do so again after the catastrophe of January 9.

On January 10, some 160,000 workers stayed away from their jobs, which meant that the capital continued in the throes of a general strike. Workers in other cities also reacted to Bloody Sunday with work stoppages, though the duration and intensity of the labor disorders varied. A few data and statistics will indicate the dimensions of the protests against the government. At the high point of the strike movement in 1903, 13,000 workers had laid down their tools in Moscow province. On January 10, 1905, 45,000 workers in the same province went on strike for eight days.[57] In the Baltic provinces, bitter strikes accompanied by clashes between soldiers and workers were quite common. In Riga alone 22 workers were killed and 60 wounded. In Lodz and Warsaw, more than 100,000 workers laid down their tools, crippling industrial production in both cities. Soldiers in Warsaw fired at peaceful crowds, killing at least 60 and wounding 79. In Vilna a majority of the industrial work force was on strike by January 11, and in Kovno the strike movement spread to "all factories and all artisanal establishments." In the latter city, too, trams and power plants were not functioning and shops were closed. Even in cities as distant from the capital as Tiflis, Baku, and Batum, workers in large numbers went on strike on hearing of the massacre. All told, some 414,000 people within the Empire participated in work stoppages during the month of January 1905. Bloody Sunday activated the working class to a degree unprecedented in Russian history.[58]

Serious disorders also erupted at institutions of higher learning, which for some time had been centers of oppositional agitation. Students at one school after another staged strikes, often after tumultuous meetings and with the support of many professors. At Moscow University, 3,000 students attended a rally where a portrait of the Tsar was publicly torn to pieces and a red flag triumphantly displayed. At the St. Petersburg Conservatory of Music, the administration's inept handling of a student strike provoked a storm of controversy, forcing the institution to close. In fact, by February virtually all institutions of higher learning in the Empire were closed, not to reopen until late August. To a lesser but nonetheless significant extent, students at secondary schools also stayed away from class and joined street demonstrations.

Officials tried to reopen the St. Petersburg Conservatory of Music on March 16, in the face of opposition from a majority of the council of professors, who had voted not to resume classes. N. A. Rimsky-Korsakov, the distinguished composer who for 35 years had been a professor at the Conservatory, made public a letter of protest he had written to the Director in which he argued that the atmosphere at the school was so tense—the building was surrounded by policemen—that no studies could be pursued. The letter prompted the composer's dismissal, which in turn evoked a torrent of protests from other professors and members of society. Teachers from 52 educational institutions joined in an expression of outrage that received wide publicity in the daily newspapers.[59] The incident further inflamed student passions, already at a high pitch.

Only a few voices could be heard in defense of the government's handling of the procession. The Moscow Assembly of the Nobility adopted a resolution exculpating the soldiers who had fired on the marchers and criticizing the latter for having participated in the affair. But even this conservative body could hardly be said to have shown enthusiasm for the government's conduct: it passed the resolution by a vote of 219 to 147.[60] Konstantin Pobedonostsev, the ultraconservative Procurator of the Most Holy Synod, persuaded his colleagues to circulate a pastoral letter charging foreigners with having fomented the unrest in Russia,[61] a claim that immediately became the official line of the government.

Throughout Moscow placards appeared blaming Anglo-Japanese agitators for the disorders of January 9. In Libava, a seaport in Kurland (Latvia), identical placards were posted over the signature of the governor of the province. The allegations were very specific: English and Japanese agitators had organized disturbances "for the purpose of delaying the departure of the Baltic and Black Sea squadrons. Enormous sums have been spent on furthering the agitation in Russia. . . . Any sympathy with the disturbances is crime and treachery. In Paris the Japanese are openly boasting of having originated the disturbances in Russia." Only after Sir Charles Hardinge sent an "urgent note" to Count Lamsdorff protesting the "obnoxious placards" did the Russian government take steps to have them removed from all public places. General I. D. Rudniev, Acting Prefect in Moscow, confessed to a British official that he had ordered that the posters be distributed "to gain time at a difficult moment." Hardinge's request that they be officially and publicly disavowed was at first ignored, apparently because Grand Duke Nikolai Nikolaevich strongly favored their use. Early in February the government yielded to the British protests and issued a disavowal, which was published in the foreign press.[62]

As a result of the massacre, Russia's image in the West, never exactly benign, plummeted to its lowest depth. The foreign press played up every detail, often exaggerating the horrors. The *Evening Sun* of New York, for example, claimed that 2,100 people had been killed and 3,900 wounded.[63] The newspapers in Berlin constantly referred to the "bloodbath in Petersburg" and the "Tsar's butchery." The Social Democratic *Vorwärts* published a detailed account of a speech delivered by August Bebel in the Reichstag in which he declared that the "Tsar, after having suffered so many defeats in the Far East, has finally won a victory over his own people." The *Berliner Tageblatt* spoke of "The cry of six thousand victims of this bloody Sunday, which reaches the Heavens and demands revenge."[64] The Italian press claimed that 5,000 people had been killed, about as many others wounded, and that "a revolution has burst out in Russia."[65] In Great Britain, one newspaper charged the Russian government with having killed 10,000 innocent citizens in one day and with having "excited emotions . . . which will not soon be appeased."[66]

The German government went out of its way to reaffirm its good relations with Russia, but senior officials entertained serious doubts about the durability of the autocratic regime. In a private conversation with the French Ambassador in Berlin, the Under Secretary for Foreign Affairs, Otto von Mühlberg, questioned whether Nicholas II had the necessary personal qualities to cope with the crisis and whether his advisers, especially the grand dukes, could be counted upon to recommend sensible domestic policies. When the ambassador expressed confidence in the Russian army's ability to restore order, Mühlberg indicated that "many German officers" did not share that optimistic assessment.[67]

Since Russia was heavily dependent on foreign loans, Count Lamsdorff, the Minister of Foreign Affairs, could not ignore the adverse reactions to Bloody Sunday in the West. He therefore asked the Ministry of Internal Affairs to prepare a detailed account of the disorders for circulation among Russian delegations abroad, which were to make use of it to enlighten foreigners. The final report of the ministry, purportedly a history of Gapon's movement, depicted the priest as a thoroughly unreasonable man who had fallen under the influence of "underground political agitators." It also claimed that the workers had been warned that a procession, which was really a "political demonstration," would not be tolerated and that Gapon had distributed icons to the marchers only to delude them into believing that no political demands would be made. The army had been "compelled" to fire on the procession because participants, guided by revolutionaries, had engaged in such provocative actions as the erection of barricades and the placing of red flags on them. Moreover, the first shots had been fired by civilians in houses near the barricades.

The report gave assurances that by January 11 St. Petersburg had returned to normal and that the army had been quickly withdrawn from
the city. "At this moment [January 24, 1905] the strike has finally ended
and all industrial enterprises have resumed work."[68] Though also fanciful, this account of recent events was at least more plausible than the
charge that foreign agents had instigated Bloody Sunday.

The government's most critical task was to halt the spread of disorder
within Russia. As usual, the government alternated between repression
and heavy-handed attempts at conciliation. On January 10, the Minister
of Internal Affairs sent instructions to officials in 194 cities recommending "decisive measures" to quell "strikes and disorders."[69] At about the
same time, the authorities closed down all branches of Gapon's organization and asked factory owners to supply them with lists of unreliable
workers, who were to be exiled. Not all employers complied with the
request, but the police nonetheless arrested so many people that for a
while the prisons and police stations were vastly overcrowded.[70] The police also arrested the writers who had visited Witte on January 8 (including Maxim Gorky) on the preposterous charge that they had declared
themselves to be a "provisional government." After vociferous protests
from abroad, the writers were quickly released.

On the other hand, the government sought to conciliate the workers,
but resorted to a clumsy gesture that completely misfired. At the suggestion of the newly appointed Governor-General of St. Petersburg, D. F.
Trepov, Tsar Nicholas on January 19 received a delegation of 34 workers, all of them chosen by factory managers and police officials because
the workers themselves refused to make the selection. Mindlessly, the
Tsar told his visitors that during the recent troubles the workers of St.
Petersburg had been misled by "traitors and enemies of our country."
Nonetheless, he went on, "I believe in the integrity of the workers and in
their unflagging devotion to me, and therefore I forgive them." He then
donated 50,000 rubles for the families of the victims of the bloodshed,
promised to see to it that the workers' lot was improved, and asked the
delegates to inform their colleagues of his sentiments. Trepov was pleased
with the meeting, having convinced himself that it would "leave a lasting
impression." But the Tsar's failure to acknowledge any wrongdoing enraged the entire opposition, and all the newspapers decided that it was
the better part of wisdom not to print any comment at all on the workers'
reception at Court.[71]

Still, some real concessions were made to workers shortly after Bloody
Sunday. Prodded by the government, but also moved by their own desire
to restore production, industrialists gave "grants" to workers who had
been out on strike, agreed to the election of workers' representatives to

negotiate with their employers, raised pay rates, and set limitations on fines imposed on delinquent workers.[72] Also, on January 19 the government established a commission, under the chairmanship of N. V. Shidlovsky, to examine the causes of the workers' discontent and to recommend measures to prevent future disturbances. Implicit in the formation of the commission was the government's acknowledgment that industrial unrest in Russia was not simply the work of foreign and domestic troublemakers. The creation of the commission was also significant because it allowed workers to elect representatives to participate in the inquiry, which facilitated the emergence of new labor organizations.

· · · · ·

The labor organization created by Gapon was a shambles and was not revived even after the release from prison in March and April 1905 of the second and third echelons of the Assembly's leadership. Gapon had escaped to the West, where he declared himself a convert to radical revolutionism and laid claim to leadership over the entire workers' movement. Indeed, on the very day of the massacre he had renounced his faith in reform from above; he castigated the "beast-Tsar and his jackal-ministers" and urged his followers to "tear up all portraits of the blood-sucking Tsar and say to him: be thou damned with all thine august reptilian progeny!"[73]

Gapon's brief sojourn in the West was stormy, for him as well as for his hosts and new comrades. To be sure, Plekhanov and several Menshevik leaders, delighted with Gapon's announcement that he was now a Social Democrat, received him warmly in Switzerland. But Gapon quickly tired of the Mensheviks' preoccupation with fine points of doctrine. Nor could he accept their view that objective laws, rather than individuals, determined the historical process. He regarded himself as a dynamic leader who had already shaped the course of events in Russia and would continue to do so. After a few days, he left the Marxists and joined forces with the Socialist Revolutionaries, who had all along claimed him as one of their own. Startled by the priest's sudden switch of loyalties, Plekhanov refused to return to Gapon the letter in which he had expressed support for Social Democracy. A scandal was prevented when the protagonists agreed on a compromise: Gapon would write a new letter calling for unity among all revolutionaries.[74]

Gapon's association with the Socialist Revolutionaries was of short duration, too, though he was sympathetic to their advocacy of the use of force against the old order. He actually learned to handle a pistol and to prepare dynamite. But he was too conscious of his fame as Russia's best-known revolutionary to accept a subordinate position in any organization. Within a few weeks he parted company with the Socialist Revolutionaries; he was now a lonely figure engaged in a futile effort to establish a unified revolutionary movement under his direction. His one lasting achievement abroad was the writing of his autobiography, *The Story of My Life*, which, despite some distortions, affords valuable insights into his personality as well as interesting information on the organization he had built in St. Petersburg.

The last phase of Gapon's erratic career began in the fall of 1905, when he returned to St. Petersburg incognito to reopen the Assembly. He called a meeting of workers, which was well attended, but all the revolutionary parties, much stronger now than in the early weeks of 1905, opposed his plan. The left did not consider him a true revolutionary and feared that if he succeeded in resurrecting his organization he would draw strength from other radical groups.

Gapon had in fact performed another volte-face: he had abandoned his extremist views and again established contact with the government. Count Witte was pleased with this turn of events because he thought that Gapon might eventually be useful to the government. Nonetheless, it seemed best to ship the priest out of the country, so Witte saw to it that Gapon was given 500 rubles on the promise that he would leave Russia immediately. In Western Europe Gapon now assumed the role of leader of a resurgent loyal workers' movement. He attracted maximum publicity in the press by appealing to workers to avoid violence and by assailing the extremism of the revolutionary parties. He even spoke favorably of Witte as the only man capable of saving Russia from the abyss. The revolutionary left, aghast at his sudden transformation, denounced him as a traitor.[75]

Gapon returned once again to Russia, late in December 1905, hoping to revitalize the Assembly. But the police had other plans. Wishing to make it impossible for him to lead another workers' movement hostile to the government, they demanded that he write a confession of his past misdeeds. Gapon agreed, though he produced a document that did not fully satisfy the police. He declared that he had tried to prevent Bloody Sunday and that his advocacy of revolution had been a mistake, but he still defended his overall behavior in 1904 and early 1905. The police then prevailed upon him to inform on the revolutionaries with whom he had established contact, only to discover that the priest knew very little about his erstwhile comrades.

In February 1906, Gapon conceived of a series of intricate maneuvers to secure permission from the police to reestablish his workers' organization. He approached Petr Rutenberg, the man who had marched next to him on Bloody Sunday and who was now a Socialist Revolutionary of some prominence, with a plan that can only be described as bizarre.

Rutenberg was to claim to have information about a conspiracy on the part of some of his comrades to murder the Minister of Internal Affairs. In return for informing on the plotters, Rutenberg would receive 100,000 rubles from the police, who would be able to boast of having foiled a dangerous conspiracy. But the conspirators would be forewarned so that they could escape apprehension. And Gapon, having done a good turn for the police, would be allowed to resume his organizational activities among the Petersburg workers. No one would be hurt and every participant in the scheme would benefit. To enhance the attractiveness of the plan, Gapon promised Rutenberg that he would adopt an extremely radical program once his Assembly was reconstituted. Gapon said that he was prepared to organize the assassination of several prominent officials in the government.

Rutenberg refused to commit himself to the incredible scheme until he had discussed it with his SR colleagues. Among others, he talked to E. F. Azef, then head of the party's "Combat Organization" and later exposed as a police agent, who insisted that Gapon must be killed. It is not clear why Azef decided on this drastic move. He may have been carrying out orders from police officials eager to get the priest out of the way; he may have wanted to accommodate the Socialist Revolutionaries, who considered Gapon a dangerous traitor; or he may even have wanted to get rid of Gapon because he feared that the priest knew he was working for the police. In any case, on March 28, 1906, after some further intrigues, Rutenberg and several other SRs lured Gapon to a cottage in a small town near the Finnish border and brutally murdered him.[76]

By the time of the murder, Gapon's reputation had been irreparably tarnished, especially among the intelligentsia and the radical parties. Nonetheless, his importance as a catalyst of the revolutionary process cannot be denied. This is not the role he had envisioned for himself in 1904. He organized the procession on January 9 to secure concessions from a ruler for whom he avowed the deepest affection, but the violence of that day unleashed a train of events that fundamentally changed not only the workers' movement in the capital but also the course of the entire revolution. For one thing, it greatly weakened the people's trust in the autocrat, a precondition for the spread and intensification of oppositional activity. For another, it made the working class a dynamic political force, whose agitation for change throughout most of 1905 the authorities could not contain. Already placed on the defensive by the liberals' campaign for reform, the government was incapable of putting a halt to the new protest movement. After January 1905 there actually existed a loose sort of alliance between the liberals and the working class, an ominous development for the autocracy. As an observer of the events that year correctly noted, in January "the Russian Revolution ceased to be the preserve of the conscious upper stratum and began to spread throughout the country, turning into a deeply rooted spontaneous movement."[77]

Bloody Sunday also marked the beginning of the second phase of the revolution. Until January 9, 1905, the struggle between the proponents of change and the authorities was conducted in the political arena. The opposition sought to mobilize public opinion by means of petitions, banquets, press discussions of reform measures, and occasional demonstrations. Although the government had at its disposal the usual tools of repression, in the second half of 1904 it resorted to them much less frequently than in earlier years. Its use of force on January 9, however, produced an entirely new situation: on the one hand, the authorities fell into disarray; on the other, lawlessness and mass violence on a scale unknown since the Time of Troubles early in the seventeenth century gripped the Russian Empire, although there was no dearth of political conflict. This violent phase of the revolution did not end until about a year after Bloody Sunday. Only then, early in 1906, did the third phase of the revolution begin, in which the predominant form of struggle between the adherents of the old order and the advocates of change was again political. Government violence and violence from below continued, but they were not as pervasive as in 1905.

Chapter Four

. . . .

The Government Flounders

BY TEMPERAMENT and ability, the men who occu-
pied the leading positions in the Empire were ill-equipped to cope with
the growing unrest sweeping across the country. The ruler, the linchpin
of the regime, showed no understanding at all of the turbulence that had
been set off by Bloody Sunday. In his diary he limited himself to brief and
superficial comments on the events of January 9: "It was a difficult day!
In Petersburg there were serious disorders owing to the wishes of workers
to go to the Winter Palace. The army had to open fire in different parts
of the city; many were killed and wounded. Good heavens, how terrible
and painful!" The other entries dealt with trivial family affairs: his
mother had joined him for dinner and stayed the night, and he had taken
a walk. On January 10, he noted that there were no serious incidents in
the city. For the rest, he merely referred to his appointment of Trepov as
Governor-General of St. Petersburg for the purpose of directing a "coordinated action in stopping the disorders" and noted that he had attended
a conference on "this subject" with senior officials. On January 11, he
ignored the events of Bloody Sunday altogether, confining himself to the
innocuous remarks that the city was quiet and that "it was a gray not
very cold day. Spent the evening all together. I read aloud."[1]

In his conversations with various officials and visitors, Nicholas insisted that since only a small area of the country had been affected by the
disorders, there was no reason to be overly concerned. He was sure that
the workers, left to their own devices, would be law-abiding citizens. On
January 15, he told Countess Alvensleben, wife of the German Ambassador, "that . . . English intrigues played a major role in instigating the
rebellion of the Petersburg laboring masses."[2]

Witte remained as unperturbed as he had been a few months earlier.
"The present ferment," he said in a confidential interview on February 12,

"is only a passing phenomenon: a form of influenza that suddenly causes a series of dormant illnesses to break out in a human body, but one that is not harmful if the organism is otherwise healthy. And Russia is a healthy organism that will not be destroyed by this influenza, nor by any other [such illnesses]. Russia is a strong, vigorous country that will for centuries to come remain as it is." The strikes in urban centers, Witte affirmed, were less dangerous to the existing order than many political commentators believed.[3] If Witte, justly regarded as the shrewdest statesman in the Empire, could be so shortsighted, what could be expected of the Tsar's closest advisers and senior officials, most of whom were either weak, incompetent, or simply unimaginative?

The leading minister, Mirsky, was thoroughly demoralized. Conservatives held him responsible for having "opened the doors to violent agitation" by advocating internal reform without taking adequate measures to keep the protest movement "within proper control." Others argued that although actuated by the "highest motives," he was "not a sufficiently strong man to grapple with the present political situation." These critics considered Mirsky to be an "amiable gentleman of no great force of character."[4] The attacks deeply wounded Mirsky. No longer confident that his policies would pacify the country, he asked to be relieved of his office. Mirsky's desire to leave government service became known and gave rise to the wildest speculation. Some liberal opponents of the regime persuaded themselves that the Tsar could not avoid making the most far-reaching concessions and that, in fact, he was contemplating a fundamental reorganization of the government. A few of them even discussed their role in a future government.[5] These liberals soon discovered that they had greatly underestimated the Tsar's determination to maintain the old order.

Convinced that Mirsky was to blame for the unrest, Nicholas accepted the minister's resignation on January 18 without any word of gratitude or reward. Never before had a Minister of Internal Affairs been let go so unceremoniously.[6] But Mirsky's replacement, A. G. Bulygin, was not the kind of person who was likely to undertake bold initiatives to restore calm in the country. Born in 1851 to a family of landowners in Riazan province and educated at the Imperial School of Law, Bulygin entered the civil service in 1871 and acquired over the next three decades the reputation of a solid, though not particularly creative, bureaucrat. In 1887 he was appointed Governor of Kaluga, and in 1900 Deputy Governor-General of Moscow, a post he left in 1904.

Bulygin was an easygoing, decent, honorable man endowed with common sense but lacking in "general knowledge and the capacity for statesmanship." He did not know, for example, that a sizable number of nobles had come to favor some form of popular government. He himself preferred the retention of the autocratic regime, not out of deep conviction, but rather because "he had never stopped to compare the merits of other forms of government." His main defect as a leader was that he disliked tense situations and always sought to avoid personal confrontations. Still, it was known that while in Moscow, even during the most repressive period under Plehve, he had never interfered with "the lawful aspirations of the local representatives in the Zemstvo or municipal assemblies."[7]

Most liberals were convinced that Bulygin was "a complete and absolute nonentity" and that with his appointment "a revolution [had] become inevitable, and soon."[8] In fact, it quickly became apparent that Bulygin's appointment did not portend a sharp break with Mirsky's conciliatory policies; no single personnel decision made by the Tsar in 1905 signaled a clear-cut political course. If he placed a moderate in one prominent position, he appointed a hard-liner to another, equally influential position. The Tsar looked to Bulygin as the moderate in the government and charged him with the formulation of new reform proposals.

Nicholas's advisers at Court saw to it that the Tsar wasted no time in placing a hard-liner in the government to counteract Bulygin. The Minister of the Court, Count V. B. Frederiks, who exerted a powerful influence over Nicholas, played a critical role in arranging the new appointment. Much of Frederiks's influence derived from the fact that he sifted all memoranda sent to the monarch and decided how the material should be presented to him. It is generally agreed that Frederiks was a man of limited intelligence, though he was probably not quite as dim as Witte claimed. "His colleagues," according to Witte, "taught him like a schoolboy before every report he gave to His Highness." Still, it is true that the Director of the Chancellery, A. A. Mosolov, a firm believer in the principle of autocracy and a rather clever man, could easily persuade Frederiks to do his bidding. Mosolov convinced Frederiks that Trepov (Mosolov's brother-in-law) was the man of the hour. The Minister of the Court, in turn, persuaded Nicholas that Trepov was the only person who could "restore discipline" in Russia.[9]

The 50-year-old Trepov impressed Nicholas as the ideal public servant. He was a "dashing general with terrifying eyes" who had served with the cavalry guards; he appeared to be a resolute and energetic man, and in private conversations with the monarch he had criticized the liberal views of Mirsky. Moreover, as chief of the Moscow police since 1896, he had demonstrated an ability to handle revolutionaries. Trepov clearly would serve as an effective counterweight to the ministers who argued for conciliatory policies toward the opposition.[10] On January 11, 1905, Nicholas announced his appointment as Governor-General of St. Petersburg, and on May 21 gave him the additional post of Assistant Minister of

Internal Affairs. In effect, Trepov now assumed charge of police affairs throughout the Empire.

By this time, Trepov had come to symbolize the arbitrariness and rigidity of the old order. Society looked upon him as a ruthless policeman, devoid of any understanding of the political situation in Russia. We owe the most colorful description of him, often repeated by his critics and historians alike, to Prince S. D. Urusov, who himself served as Assistant Minister of Internal Affairs in late 1905 and early 1906 before joining the liberal opposition. Urusov referred to Trepov as a "cavalry sergeant major by upbringing and a pogromshchik by conviction."[11] Witte, who frequently crossed swords with him, contended in his memoirs that Trepov had acquired so much power by late 1905 that he was really the "dictator" of Russia. Although this claim is clearly an exaggeration, in matters of internal security his position at Court and in the government was preeminent. By the same token, it is not accurate to depict Trepov simply as a bureaucrat whose only remedy for disorder was brute force. He was a more complicated and thoughtful man than his detractors recognized.

As police chief of Moscow, he had concluded that police measures alone would not suffice to stifle agitation against the autocracy. After a broad study of labor unrest, he became convinced that at least some of the blame for the growing industrial strife must be placed on employers, who would have to make concessions to satisfy the legitimate demands of workers for better conditions. Similarly, he argued that student unrest at institutions of higher learning would not end until the government's restrictions on them were loosened.[12] To be sure, in 1905–6 he often resorted to harsh measures to curb the opposition, but he was also prepared to make concessions as long as they did not undermine the existing system of rule. For example, at a secret meeting of senior officials in July 1905 on the formulation of reform measures, Trepov urged the Tsar to allow Jews to participate in the elections to the planned national assembly, arguing that only if the causes of their discontent were removed would the Jews cease to be active in the opposition. Nicholas followed Trepov's advice.[13]

Indeed, Colonel A. V. Gerasimov, the chief of the St. Petersburg Okhrana in 1905 and an unrepentant hard-liner on domestic unrest, criticized Trepov for inconsistency and leniency in handling the opposition. Gerasimov, who conferred with Trepov four or five times a week, contended that although the general was the single most powerful figure in the Tsar's entourage, he was not nearly so decisive as many people thought. His handsome and striking appearance, his confident glances and firm movements, conveyed the misleading impression of an independent and strong person with a clear vision of how to establish order in Russia. "Deep down highly indecisive and fickle," Gerasimov declared,

Trepov "easily fell under outside influences, and then he became the spokesman of the person who had just influenced him." His most distinctive virtue was his devotion to the sovereign. "He would have given up his life without any hesitation for the Tsar and the monarchy." But he failed to develop an effective plan to save the monarchy.

Whenever Gerasimov visited him in his office, Trepov was in the company of P. I. Rachkovskii, deputy director of the police. It was evident to Gerasimov that Rachkovskii, a man with close ties to several important political figures, advised the Assistant Minister of Internal Affairs on all matters and was especially influential in the formulation of policies on internal security. A talented police officer, Rachkovskii possessed a superficial, even primitive, grasp of politics. He believed it possible to solve all internal security problems with money. Everybody, including ardent revolutionaries, could be "bought" and thus rendered harmless. As a result, the directives that came out of Trepov's office "were characterized by uncertainty, confusion, and contradictions. In the atmosphere of 1905 in our country these directives practically led to the paralysis of governmental authority." [14]

If Gerasimov exaggerated Trepov's personal weakness, he was not far off the mark in his characterization of the government. By 1905 it was in disarray. Bulygin was the Minister of Internal Affairs, but he had been deprived of all authority in the most important sphere of his ministry, the maintenance of public order, which was Trepov's preserve. It was almost as though there were two Ministers of Internal Affairs; worse still, there was bad blood between them. [15] Much of the time Bulygin was not even consulted on major questions over which his department had jurisdiction. On several occasions he responded to questions about important new governmental decisions with the admission that "I myself have only read about it today in the newspapers." [16] He was shunted aside, forced to devote himself to economic issues and to devising a plan for a representative assembly. V. I. Gurko suggested that Bulygin was not distressed with the arrangement, "for thus he acquired more time to spend on his favorite occupation—whist." [17] Be that as it may, the fact remains that at a time of grave crisis, the man formally charged with defining policy on internal affairs did not enjoy the confidence of the Tsar.

The peculiar division of authority between Bulygin and Trepov was only the most striking sign of governmental disarray. In addition, several ministers and senior officials questioned the government's handling of unrest and advocated policies at variance with those of the Tsar. In a private conversation with the monarch on January 17, 1905, A. S. Ermolov, the Minister of Agriculture and State Properties, spoke with remarkable candor about the domestic situation. The bloodshed eight days earlier, he asserted, had succeeded only in preventing workers from reaching the Winter Palace, not in restoring order. On the contrary, Ermolov predicted, the protests would continue and grow more intense. There would follow a rash of assassinations of officials, the Tsar would no longer be safe, and disorders would break out in the countryside. Nor would the monarch be able to count on soldiers to continue obeying orders to shoot people who simply wanted their grievances to be heard. Nicholas responded in a conciliatory tone to these dire predictions: "I understand that the government would be in an impossible situation if it rested only on force." [18]

Ermolov then indicted the entire structure of government. "Permit me openly to tell your Highness that at present we have no government." Because no one minister held overall authority, each minister acted in isolation. High officials who had learned of the impending trouble shortly before January 9 were at a loss about what to do or whom to see to discuss ways of averting a catastrophe. It was therefore impossible to present the Tsar with sensible options from which he could have selected a reasonable approach to Gapon's procession. Ermolov urged the monarch both to reform the system of government and to satisfy the legitimate demands of the people. [19]

In a report on the domestic situation in Russia written two weeks after his meeting with the Tsar, Ermolov was even more pessimistic about conditions in the country and more specific in his recommendations. He contended that there existed "general disorganization in all spheres of our social life" and advised the ruler to enlist the support of the "healthy elements" of the people by establishing a legislative body of elected representatives. The radicals, he argued, could succeed in overthrowing the autocracy only if the "silent majority of your people" were prohibited from participating in national affairs and from expressing their views. Delay on Nicholas's part would invite the "destruction not only of the Tsarist throne, not only of autocracy, but of the entire Russian state." That was the "horror" that Ermolov wanted to avoid. [20]

The Minister of Finance, V. N. Kokovtsov, also urged Nicholas to adopt conciliatory policies. He suggested that the government enter into discussions with industrialists about ways to satisfy workers' demands without undermining the economic well-being of their enterprises. No other approach would persuade the workers to abandon "forceful actions" in seeking to improve their conditions. [21] In confidential memoranda, even high officials of the Okhrana rejected the notion that labor unrest—especially that of January 9—could be attributed to provocateurs. On February 7, 1905, L. A. Rataev, chief of the Okhrana office in Paris, reported that after talking at length with Gapon one of his agents became convinced that the priest had not intended to provoke bloodshed. Rataev also insisted that there was no conclusive evidence that Gapon's movement before January 9 had come under the influence of radical intelligentsia or activists of any revolutionary party.[22]

The disarray of the government, manifested in its inability to formulate a clearly defined response to the political storm unleashed by Bloody Sunday, was reflected more broadly in its failure to formulate a policy for dealing with unrest on a national scale. For all its concern with the threat to domestic tranquillity posed by radical agitators, the Ministry of Internal Affairs had not drawn up any directives on riot control for local officials. According to regulations issued in 1881, responsibility for police activities in local regions of the Empire rested with governors or governors-general, who were required to report to the ministry in St. Petersburg. However, officials in the capital never established clear lines of responsibility within the department or clear channels for reporting on local developments, with the result that provincial bureaucrats devised their own strategies to contain the disorders in their jurisdictions.[23] The differences in those strategies underline the degree to which bureaucratic centralization in late Imperial Russia was more myth than reality. The three following examples of how provincial governors coped with disturbances illustrate the point.

The Governor of Saratov province, P. A. Stolypin (who in 1906 became Prime Minister), adopted what may be called the hard-line approach to any sort of disorder. The city of Saratov was a center of internal exile to which the government sent "political criminals and unreliable elements of every kind,"[24] and Stolypin, who was in any case a strict law-and-order man, probably did not want to take any chances. On January 12, 1905, he announced that workers absent from their jobs for more than three consecutive days would be subject to dismissal under article 15 of the Industrial Regulations. Stolypin also prohibited workers from gathering in the streets or in public places. The slightest attempt by anyone to disturb public order would be met "by force."[25] Some two weeks later, workers in Saratov were contemplating a procession, and a deputation from the city council and provincial zemstvo asked Stolypin not to use force to disperse the marchers. One city council representative declared that the government would not be weakened by a workers' march, even if revolutionary songs were sung. Another suggested that city council representatives be allowed to serve as intermediaries in negotiating with the workers about the procession. "I answered," Stolypin reported to the Ministry of Internal Affairs, "that my response would be brief: 'I have taken an oath.' The city council members answered that they had also taken an oath. I reminded them that it was my duty to preserve order by all measures, that I would more willingly shed my own blood than that of a stranger, but that in the event of resistance by the crowd or any kind of violence on its part I would resort to the most extreme measures: that there is no revolution here and would not be, and that I would prevent not only a procession but even a simple gathering of people." Stolypin reported with no small measure of satisfaction that the organizers of the procession had understood his position: the marchers dispersed as soon as they saw troops lined up to halt their advance.[26]

The Governor of Poltava, N. P. Urusov, adopted a much more sophisticated and elaborate plan for coping with disorders. In a memorandum to zemstvo chiefs and local policemen, which was leaked to the press late in March 1905, he placed primary emphasis on preventive measures. He directed officials to observe the mood of the population more closely than before and to counteract antigovernment propaganda by touring areas of unrest and discussing the peasants' grievances with them. The officials should appeal to the peasants' patriotism, point out that the Tsar was introducing important reforms, and explain the consequences of disorders. As soon as officials learned of any serious discontent among the population, they themselves were to conduct an investigation and inform the governor if there was any likelihood of violence. The police and zemstvo chiefs should keep each other informed of any sources of trouble. The memorandum also noted: "It is desirable to maintain contact with the clergy, who have been given instructions by the hierarchy."[27]

In mid-April of 1905, the City Governor of St. Petersburg, V. A. Dediulin, sent a memorandum marked "strictly secret" to police officers that also focused on preventive measures. But Dediulin, concerned primarily with maintaining order in the streets, was not interested in influencing potential disturbers of the peace. He directed the police and civil servants to conduct constant patrols of the streets and issued detailed instructions on how the patrols should operate. For example, they should stand where they could see each other and quickly come to the aid of any unit that encountered massive disorders. The patrols must prevent the formation of crowds; but if crowds were to appear, they should "politely" ask them to disperse. Governor Dediulin stressed the need for courtesy; only after refusing polite requests should people be taken into custody. If large crowds nevertheless persisted in remaining in the streets, the patrols should call on troops to arrest the "instigators and leaders." Finally, Governor Dediulin directed police officers to rely on janitors, who were to report on suspicious people or activities in the buildings under their supervision.[28]

In the absence of detailed and reliable local studies, it is impossible to say whether one approach was more effective than any other in stemming disorder. In Saratov, where Stolypin imposed harsh measures, there was no prolonged strike in October, when general strikes broke out in many other cities, and no armed uprising in December. Yet Poltava was also spared an armed uprising. Moreover, strikes, political meetings, and occasional bloody clashes between demonstrators and soldiers occurred in both cities.[29] In St. Petersburg the preventive measures did not put a halt to strikes and demonstrations, but they may have helped to avert a recurrence of mass violence.

The government had at its disposal one weapon against disorder that, theoretically at least, made possible a degree of uniformity in its approach: it could proclaim emergency regulations in any region of the Empire. This power originated in a statute of August 14, 1881, which provided for two kinds of special measures, "Reinforced Security" (*Usilennaia Okhrana*) and "Extraordinary Security" (*Chrezvychainaia Okhrana*). The first could be imposed by the Minister of Internal Affairs or a governor-general acting with the minister's approval. The second could be imposed only with the approval of the Tsar. Designed to facilitate the eradication of sedition, the statute was vague about what conditions would justify placing a region in a state of emergency. In each case of unrest, the ultimate decision lay in the hands of the authorities in St. Petersburg. Initially enacted as a temporary measure, the statute remained on the books until 1917. In addition to these emergency powers, the government could declare an area under martial law, which meant military rule pure and simple.

The arbitrary power invested in local officials (governors-general, governors, and city governors) under the exceptional measures of 1881 was enormous. Under Reinforced Security, officials could keep citizens in prison for up to three months, impose fines, prohibit public gatherings, exile alleged offenders, transfer blocks of judicial cases from criminal to military courts, and dismiss local government and zemstvo employees. Under Extraordinary Security, a region was under the authority of a commander in chief, who was empowered to dismiss elected zemstvo deputies and even to dissolve zemstvos completely, to suspend periodicals, and to close universities and other centers of advanced study for up to one month. Implementation of the exceptional measures largely depended on the whims of local officials: in some provinces they acted with restraint, whereas in others they used their powers to the utmost. Frequently, officials operating under the emergency rules exiled "beggars, vagrants, and generally disorderly persons."[30]

The indiscriminate application of the statute of 1881—which one historian has called the "real constitution" of the Empire[31]—demonstrated more than anything else the absence of a legal order in Russia. But the

statute was of dubious effectiveness in maintaining order, as some government officials acknowledged. The people's resentment of the emergency regulations often intensified their defiance of authority, which, in
turn, provoked officials to apply even harsher measures.[32] In the Ukase of
December 12, 1904, the government promised to revise the statute of
1881, and to that end it appointed a commission in February 1905 under
the chairmanship of Count A. P. Ignatev. The commission's report sharply
criticized the conduct of the police and recommended that the force be
enlarged and more adequately trained. The commission also acknowledged that the use of emergency measures raised serious legal and practical questions, but beyond that it merely recommended that they be applied only in situations where "state security is really threatened."[33]

In the last analysis, the government refused to let the statute of 1881
lapse because it commanded no other effective weapon in the struggle
against unrest. Even in 1903, before political disturbances had become
critical, some thirty million people lived under one or another form of
emergency measure. During the revolutionary upheaval of 1905–6, the
government resorted to the regulations on a vast scale: by March 1906,
30 of the Empire's 78 provinces were entirely ruled by officials exercising
special powers; and in another 30 provinces sizable regions were ruled
by officials with such powers.

Generally regarded as the police state par excellence, Russia actually
lacked an adequate police force. In the rural regions of the Empire, where
some ninety million people lived, the Ministry of Internal Affairs could
dispose of only 1,582 constables and 6,874 sergeants.[34] True, the authorities depended on nonbureaucratic groups such as the gentry to assume some of the burdens of administering local regions, but such an
arrangement could not be very efficient, especially in times of crisis.

Even St. Petersburg, by 1905 the center of antigovernment agitation,
did not have a competent security force. When Gerasimov arrived in February 1905 to take charge of the Okhrana, he discovered that the police
did not take the most elementary precautions to protect their sources of
information. For example, civilian agents would casually walk into the
headquarters of the security police; no one realized that terrorists, who
were then known to be active in St. Petersburg, could easily spot the
agents, which eliminated their usefulness. At the same time, the police were
ill-informed about the activities and whereabouts of the terrorists, as the
following anecdote indicates. Trepov directed Gerasimov to liquidate a
new terrorist group that, the governor-general asserted, was planning
several assassinations. "Don't concern yourself about the cost," Trepov
said. "Seize these people, no matter what the cost. Do you understand?
No matter what the cost." But the Okhrana officials, to Gerasimov's dis-

may, knew nothing at all about the group. All they could do was to advise senior government employees to remain in their homes, virtually under "house arrest." [35]

Early in 1905, revolutionary terror once again struck down a person close to the centers of power. On February 4, a Socialist Revolutionary killed Grand Duke Sergei Aleksandrovich, a staunch reactionary, in the Kremlin in Moscow. The uncle and brother-in-law of the Tsar, Sergei had been the Governor-General of Moscow, and his assassination, the first of a member of the Imperial family since 1881, made a deep impression on society. The Tsar himself was apparently shaken by the incident, though it is a sign of his essential callousness that on the very evening of the assassination he went ahead with a planned dinner for Prince Friedrich Leopold of Prussia, despite the latter's suggestion that the event be canceled. By the time the festivities began, the Tsar seemed to have forgotten about his uncle's death. "Not a word was said about the murder of the Grand Duke. After dinner, the Tsar and . . . [another] brother-in-law amused themselves by trying to edge one another down from the long narrow sofa, before the eyes of the astonished German guest." [36]

Several of the Tsar's advisers, including the Minister of Internal Affairs, took a more serious view of the assassination and contended that substantial concessions must be made immediately to stem the unrest. Trepov disagreed with his colleagues, arguing that accommodation would be futile: "I am deeply convinced," he wrote on February 16, "that neither now nor in the immediate future will any sort of promise succeed in calming people: the so-called third element will not be satisfied with any concessions whatsoever." [37] Nicholas could not make up his mind, and when several ministers continued to press him for a decision, he turned to Bulygin: "One would think that you are afraid a revolution will break out." To this the Minister of Internal Affairs replied: "Your Majesty, the revolution has already begun." [38] This comment seems to have persuaded Nicholas to adopt a conciliatory course, but once again he followed a procedure that had become a pattern with him: he coupled the promise of reform with a savage attack on the instigators of unrest and a restatement of his commitment to the old order—all in one day.

On the morning of February 18, the monarch published an Imperial Manifesto denouncing the "ill-intentioned leaders" of disorders who, "blinded by arrogance," dared to "attack the foundations of the Russian Empire" and sought to "create a new government for the country based on principles alien to our fatherland." He asked all Russians to "stand firm around our Throne, true to the traditions of Our past . . . and support the autocracy for the good of all Our faithful subjects." In the evening Nicholas issued a ukase to the Senate that directed the Committee of Ministers to "examine and consider the ideas and suggestions presented to Us by private persons and institutions concerning improvements in the state organization and the betterment of the people's existence." Both pronouncements emanated from Tsarskoe Selo without the prior notification of any minister, which in itself was highly unusual. Then, to compound the confusion, the Tsar sent a rescript to Bulygin, also on the evening of February 18, informing him of his intention to permit individuals—the "worthiest people"—elected by the population of Russia to participate in the preliminary formulation and discussion of legislative proposals. The Minister of Internal Affairs was to head a commission to draw up plans for the implementation of this rather vague promise to establish some kind of legislative assembly.[39]

The ministers and society as well were "dumbfounded" to discover that within one day the Tsar had promised both to uphold the autocratic system and to draw the people into the process of governing the nation.[40] "Is it any wonder," asked Petrunkevich, "that the authority of a government that does not know in the morning what it will undertake in the evening declined in the eyes of the people to the point of complete rejection?"[41]

Although many liberals and all the radicals considered the Tsar's concessions far too limited, much of society chose to ignore the first proclamation and to take full advantage of the moderate reforms implied in the latter two. *Pravo*, a liberal publication, compared the rescript to Bulygin to a "door, behind which there are silhouetted the perspectives of future light." The editors rejoiced that the "bureaucratic regime [had] repudiated the monarch's will and that there can be no turning back. . . . The authorities want the support of the people, they want to govern with their agreement."[42] *Russkie vedomosti* hailed the rescript as "a highly significant historical act . . . [that] marks the beginning of a new era in our state." It had become increasingly evident that the "bureaucratic and police regime is not capable of pacifying society and of properly satisfying the demands of the people. For the well-being of the state and the people, the government must rely not only on the passive but on the active forces of the nation. . . ."[43] *Novoe vremia* showed no enthusiasm for the rescript, but acknowledged its importance and speculated on how it might best be implemented, which suggests that even this conservative paper considered the reform acceptable.[44]

For about four months—roughly from late February until July—organizations of various kinds, but most notably zemstvos, city councils, and cultural and professional societies, engaged in a "petition campaign" in response to the Tsar's request for ideas on how to improve the state. Hundreds of meetings were held throughout the Empire to discuss reform proposals and to adopt resolutions that were dispatched to the Minister of Internal Affairs. The newspapers carried accounts of the meetings and thus publicized the grievances and demands that were being voiced by growing numbers of people. Instead of curbing unrest, the monarch's ukase proved to be a catalyst that mobilized masses of people who had not previously dared to express opinions on political issues. Dominated by liberals and liberal demands, the petition campaign really amounted to a revival, in more intense form, of the liberal offensive of the fall and winter of 1904–5.

In Nizhnii-Novgorod, for example, 200 people attended a meeting late in March that passed a resolution stating that the Bulygin commission on the implementation of the rescript would be "useful" only if it recommended the democratic election of a constituent assembly and the granting of civil liberties to every citizen.[45] Early in April, the Tomsk Juridical Society devoted three days to discussing the rescript. The meeting hall overflowed with people, who endorsed a broad series of liberal reforms ranging from equality before the law to a system of popular government.[46] On May 24, the city council in Kazan unanimously approved sending a telegram to the Minister of Internal Affairs urging the speedy implementation of the promise to convoke an elected representative body.[47] On the same day, the city council in Kostroma called attention to recent developments in the war with Japan and unanimously resolved that a petition should be sent to St. Petersburg proposing the immediate convocation of a national representative assembly.[48] A special commission chosen by the provincial zemstvo assembly in Iaroslavl made a similar recommendation to the government, and took pains to stress that the elected legislature should be invested with real power, not with consultative functions.[49] The Saratov City Council pleaded politely with the Tsar not to delay: "Every moment of delay can entail fatal consequences."[50]

Realizing that it had opened a Pandora's box by encouraging the submission of petitions, the government tried on occasion to control the damage by rigidly enforcing the regulations on political meetings. Thus, when the Poltava zemstvo assembly voted to hold a public meeting to discuss political reform, the Ministry of Internal Affairs prohibited it on the ground that the zemstvo was empowered only to select a commission that could petition the Committee of Ministers; it did not have the right to organize a general discussion of the petition. To circumvent the ministry's order, the Poltava zemstvo assembly elected a commission composed of every member of the assembly, which then adopted a resolution with the usual liberal demands.[51]

There is no need to belabor the point. In the spring of 1905 the government was struck by an avalanche of petitions from groups of notables from virtually every corner of the Empire. As far as is known, no one organization planned the campaign. It was a spontaneous outpouring of popular sentiment, which at the time represented the only more or less coherent movement for change. All the petitions had in common one critical point: the call for major limitations on the power of the monarch.

Beyond that, a striking feature of the petitions is that they reflected a shift to the left since late 1904. Groups that a few months earlier had been quite conservative now joined in the demands for freedom and the rule of law. City councils, which had previously limited their deliberations to issues of local concern, now paid attention to general political matters. With increasing frequency, they advocated a national legislature that would not be confined merely to consultative functions. Many zemstvos went beyond their positions of 1904 and came out for a democratic suffrage or something akin to it. The city councils in the borderlands called not only for political reform but also for an end to national and religious discrimination and for some social and economic reforms. Finally, virtually all the groups among the intelligentsia proposed changes more radical than those advocated by liberals during the banquet campaign of 1904: they now stressed the introduction of a genuinely democratic suffrage. In addition, the resolutions of the opposition often contained demands for an immediate end to the war and for the convocation of a constituent assembly. Some of them also called for the lowering of the working day to eight hours, the introduction of a progressive income tax and workers' insurance, and the nationalization of the land.[52]

Parallel to this campaign for political reform from below, the national leadership of the zemstvo movement intensified its pressure on the government by calling for the convocation of a Second Zemstvo Congress to be held in Moscow on April 22. A day before the scheduled meeting, officials in Moscow, reverting to a hard line, announced that the congress would not be permitted. The delegates ignored the directive, and, surprisingly, no one made a serious effort to interfere with their deliberations. "The Administration," one participant recalled, "did not feel it had the power to wage open battle against public opinion."[53]

The meeting of some 125 delegates turned out to be a stormy affair. Shipov, satisfied with the promises contained in the Tsar's rescript to Bulygin of February 18, introduced a motion in support of a consultative legislative assembly. That was far too moderate for most delegates, 71 of whom voted for a series of resolutions that advocated a national legislative body representing the entire nation and consisting of two chambers, one to be chosen by universal, direct, equal, and secret suffrage, and one by the organs of local self-government. The democratically elected chamber was to serve as a constituent assembly. Thirty-seven delegates, the moderate constitutionalists, favored a system of indirect voting, and only seventeen supported Shipov's proposal. Shipov and his colleagues walked out of the Congress; a month later they met with a few moderate constitutionalists to adopt the Slavophile proposal for a consultative legislature.[54]

The zemstvo movement was now badly split, but in view of the calamitous defeat of the Russian navy in the Straits of Tsushima on May 14 and the spread of unrest, the leadership decided on a new effort to exert pressure on the Tsar to change his policies. It would seek an audience with the sovereign to present a petition embodying the view of a unified zemstvo movement that reform was urgently required. F. A. Golovin, the head of the organizing committee, persuaded the Slavophiles (including Shipov), as well as representatives of several city councils and some marshals of the nobility, to attend what came to be known as the "Coalition Congress" (May 24–25); they assented on the understanding that the meeting would seek not to confront the government but to reach agreement with it on steps to pacify the country.

After a considerable amount of wrangling over the contents of the petition, the size of the deputation, and the latter's composition, the Congress settled on a course of action and on the substance of the appeal to the Tsar. A delegation of fifteen men from all sectors of the zemstvo movement was elected. In the end Shipov refused to join, mainly because he considered the petition too militant, even though it had been modified to secure his support (which he had indeed given). He was not replaced, so the delegation remained at fourteen. The Congress asked Prince S. N. Trubetskoi to present the petition and to deliver an address to the Tsar. A moderate liberal who had initially supported the war, Trubetskoi was a man of rare charm; acquaintances almost invariably commented on his sincerity and decency. According to Petrunkevich, who stood far to his left politically, the opposition could not have selected a "more reliable, profound, and eloquent spokesman."[55] Trubetskoi was an excellent choice, acceptable to all zemtsy and to the Court.

Unfortunately, the delegates became embroiled in controversy with the Court before they ever reached the royal residence at Peterhof. In an unwarranted display of pettiness, Count Frederiks haggled over the size and composition of the deputation. The Count let it be known that the monarch was prepared to receive only three zemstvo leaders, an offer that all fourteen promptly rejected. Unwilling to assume the onus for the cancellation of the meeting, Frederiks suggested that half the delegation attend the audience with the Tsar; this proposal was also rejected. The Minister of the Court then raised the number to fourteen, but indicated that Petrunkevich, a firebrand who had in earlier years been exiled from the capital for his vigorous advocacy of a constitution, would not be welcome. The delegation again refused to proceed with the meeting, at which point Frederiks relented.[56]

This was not an auspicious beginning for an event that received wide publicity and was seen by a fair number of people within the opposition as a major—perhaps the last—attempt to achieve change in the structure of government by appealing to the Tsar. If at a time of national emergency the Tsar's advisers could devote hours to negotiating the makeup of a delegation that wished merely to submit a petition, could they be aware of the urgency of the situation? Could they be counted upon to advise the sovereign to steer a new course?

Trubetskoi made careful preparations for the audience. When he saw the Tsar early on the afternoon of June 6 he delivered a powerful speech eloquently and graciously. Trubetskoi expressed his gratitude for the audience and stressed that "Love of the motherland and the consciousness of our debt to You have led us here." The petitioners acknowledged "that this minute You are suffering more than all of us. We would like to be able to comfort You, and when we turn to Your Majesty in this unusual manner it is only, believe us, because we realize our debt and the general danger, which is great, Sire." Trubetskoi assured the Tsar that the Russian people continued to be patriotic, and that they retained confidence in his benevolence and in his intention of introducing reforms. Yet they could not fail to be distressed by the military defeats of Russia and the spread of internal disorder. They were also troubled by the realization that the Tsar's advisers and officials were perverting his announced policy to change course. "The only way out of our domestic crisis is the path You have chosen, Sire, in calling together elected representatives of the people."

Trubetskoi deliberately avoided specific recommendations on the nature of the future legislature: he wished only to "say that which unites all of us," that a legislature should be created and that it should represent all the people.

We would want all Your subjects, even if they profess a different faith and belong to a different race, to see in Russia their motherland and in You its Sovereign; to feel themselves the sons of Russia and to love Russia just as we love her. The national representation should serve the task of unification and of internal peace. It is impossible, therefore, to wish for a representative assembly based on the system of estates.* As the Russian Tsar is not the Tsar of the nobility, not the Tsar of the peasants or of the merchants, not the Tsar of classes, but the Tsar of

---

* The Russian word used here was *sosloviia* (plural for *soslovie*). The sosloviia were social groups—e.g., the nobility, the clergy, the merchantry, and the Cossacks—that possessed special rights and liberties and corporate organizations. For a recent study, see Freeze, "The *Soslovie* (Estate) Paradigm and Russian Social History."

all Rus, so also the elected people from the whole population, called to work with You on the affairs of state, should serve general and not estate interests. Representation based on estates will inevitably give rise to strife between estates even where none now exists.

One consequence of the establishment of a national legislature, Trubetskoi continued, would be to reduce the authority of the bureaucracy, which had usurped the Tsar's prerogative. Finally, the Prince urged Nicholas to permit free discussion of all issues affecting the well-being of the state. Not to do so would "undermine trust in the implementation of reforms . . . [and] stand in the way of their active implementation." He concluded: "Sire! The renewal of Russia should be based on trust."[57]

The Tsar seemed to be moved by the courteous, patriotic, and moderate address. He was clearly relieved not to have been exposed to a polemic. He even nodded a few times in apparent agreement with Trubetskoi's points, especially when he spoke of a legislature representing all estates. One of the delegates was so moved that he wept openly, and two others were on the verge of tears.

In his official response to Trubetskoi's address, Nicholas restated his intention of proceeding with major reforms. After expressing his confidence in the delegation's "love for the motherland," he uttered the following reassuring words: "Cast away your doubts. My will—the Tsar's will—to call together representatives from the people is unswerving. Attracting them to the work of the state will be done in an orderly fashion. I concern myself with this matter every day." He urged the delegates to inform the people of his intentions, and ended his short speech on a note calculated to inspire confidence in future collaboration between the government and the zemtsy: "I hope that you will help me in this work."[58]

The reaction of political activists to the meeting depended on their ideological orientation. Left-wing liberals criticized Trubetskoi for his lack of militancy and showed little faith in the monarch's promises. On June 20, Miliukov and Struve published a joint article ridiculing the entire affair: "'Cast away your—hopes!' No one will give you a constitution. It is necessary to know how to take it."[59] But more moderate oppositionists could not deny the significance of a formal meeting of the Tsar with known liberals, some of whom had previously been punished for their political activities. "The sixth of June will remain a memorable day in the history of Russia," declared *Vestnik Evropy*. "His Majesty the Emperor received and listened to people who were authorized—not formally but in fact—to speak on behalf of a significant segment of the Russian people."[60] Early in July even Struve acknowledged that the Tsar had in effect legalized a sizable portion of the opposition.[61] Indeed, many liberals skeptical of the ruler's motives came to realize that the meeting was bound to benefit their cause. If the Tsar kept his word, the encounter would mark a major step toward some sort of constitutional order. If he reneged, moderates would be driven to the left.

It took only two weeks for the Tsar and his advisers to confirm the worst suspicions of the skeptical liberals and to play right into their hands. On June 20 and 21, Nicholas made a point of greeting with singular warmth two groups of conservatives whom he considered to be a counterpoise to the zemstvo activists. The first group, nobles from Kerch, urged the monarch to create a consultative assembly composed only of noblemen and peasants. "I am fully conscious," Nicholas responded, "of the usefulness of a consultative institution in the future that will be composed of two basic landed classes, the dvorianstvo and the peasantry, which from time immemorial have shared joy and grief with their Tsar." A day later the Tsar received an even more conservative delegation, which went so far as to advocate the retention of autocracy.[62] Clearly, the Court was mobilizing public opinion against the constitutionalists, making a mockery of the Tsar's conciliatory words on June 6.

The meeting on June 6 marked the last occasion when leaders of a significant sector of the opposition sought reform by appealing to the Tsar. There is every reason to believe that if the delegates led by Trubetskoi had been met halfway by the government, they would have sought to calm the political storm. But the Tsar's intransigence and duplicity persuaded them that their goals could be realized only by aligning themselves with the more militant elements in the country, elements that were resorting increasingly to direct actions of various kinds to wrest concessions from the authorities. According to Petrunkevich, he and many of his associates now concluded that a revolution was necessary.[63] The nonsocialist opposition was seized by a new mood of political distemper, which lasted from late June until the fall of 1905.

. . . . .

In the meantime, the government's attempts to pacify the workers after Bloody Sunday also backfired. The most ambitious had been the creation of the Shidlovsky Commission, charged with examining workers' grievances in the capital and submitting proposals to improve working conditions. A unique feature of the commission was its composition. It was to include not only representatives from the government and industry but also delegates elected by workers themselves. On February 1, 1905, Senator Shidlovsky issued regulations on the elections, which were scheduled to be held in two stages. Factories of 100 to 500 employees were to select one elector; those with 500 to 1,000, two electors; and those with over

1,000 workers, one additional elector for each additional 500 employees. The electors were then to vote for 50 representatives to the commission in a rather complicated procedure. The elections, in which workers participated with varying degrees of enthusiasm, took place on February 6 and 13. Altogether, 145,295 ballots were cast "in the first basically free elections ever held in Russia by workers."[64] According to a Menshevik estimate of the time, 20 percent of the 417 electors belonged to Social Democratic organizations, 40 percent sympathized with the aims of the Social Democrats, and 30 to 35 percent were interested primarily in improved economic conditions. A clear majority, then, could be expected to speak for workers' interests in the broadest sense of the term.

The 417 electors were divided into eight groups, each one of which met separately to discuss various aspects of the commission's work. The eight groups then met as one body and agreed on a message to be sent to Shidlovsky. They asked for (1) freedom of expression for the workers' representatives on the commission, (2) assurances that the representatives would participate in all meetings of the commission, (3) representation for workers at enterprises employing fewer than 100 people, (4) uncensored publication of all the protocols, (5) reopening of the eleven branches of Gapon's Assembly, (6) release from prison of workers arrested since January 1, and (7) a promise of personal immunity for workers "freely discussing their needs." The electors declared that failure by the government to grant these demands would provoke a general strike.

Shidlovsky agreed to the first three demands but claimed that the others "are beyond the commission's competence and hence require no answer on my part." On February 20, the Tsar, unwilling to meet the workers' demands, followed Shidlovsky's advice that he disband the commission.[65] When between 50,000 and 60,000 workers protested by going out on strike, the government launched a new wave of arrests.

Although the Shidlovsky Commission must be pronounced a failure, its efforts did leave a deep imprint on the capital's industrial labor force. Workers in the larger factories retained the committees they had elected, and many of them looked upon the joint meetings of the city's electors as a "kind of first parliament" of the Petersburg proletariat. Thus, the elections for the Shidlovsky Commission laid the groundwork for the labor unions that were formed later in 1905 and for the Soviet that played so prominent a role in St. Petersburg during the last months of the year.[66]

Moreover, during the agitational campaign that accompanied the election of the Shidlovsky Commission, the Mensheviks and Bolsheviks further clarified their differences over tactics. The Mensheviks, eager to "create a platform for agitation" among the Russian proletariat, endorsed participation in the elections, though they differed among themselves on whether they should take part in the actual work of the commission. By contrast, the Bolsheviks—the activists in St. Petersburg as well as the leaders abroad—preferred to boycott the elections. Only pressure from below, from ordinary workers, induced them to take part in the voting. To the Leninists, the "notorious commission" was "no more than a commission of government hocus-pocus, . . . a vile, cheap Zubatov-Witte farce." It was a maneuver to divert the masses from political concerns. If only the Russian working class understood that the government planned "to dupe it behind a hypocritical, fawning mask," it would "drive its mighty fist in the face of the monarchist killers and swindlers and smash it to smithereens together with the mask."[67] In sum, the Mensheviks viewed the electoral campaign as a means of enlarging their political party and strengthening its ties to the workers. The Bolsheviks feared that participation in the elections would prompt workers to believe in the efficacy of the ballot and therefore deflect them from what ought to be the main goal of the Social Democrats—an armed uprising.

On the very day the Tsar disbanded the Shidlovsky Commission, he authorized the formation of another commission under the chairmanship of the Minister of Finance, V. N. Kokovtsov. It, too, was to study the labor question, but it was also to formulate legislative measures for the improvement of working conditions. An able bureaucrat with distinctly conservative views, Kokovtsov had concluded that labor reform was now essential. Among other things, he feared that further disorders would jeopardize Russia's chances of acquiring loans abroad, which the government desperately needed.

The new commission initially consisted solely of bureaucrats, though Kokovtsov was empowered to call on experts for information. Workers played no role in the commission's deliberations, but industrialists participated in large numbers in its plenary sessions, which began on May 16, more than four months after Bloody Sunday. Kokovtsov's proposals for reform were surprisingly progressive: they provided for legalization of certain workers' organizations, the creation of special funds for medical assistance for workers, shortening of the workday, and the establishment of a state insurance system for workers. Only Germany had a more generous program of labor legislation for the industrial sector.[68]

The industrialists at the plenary sessions of the commission, aghast at Kokovtsov's proposals, argued that the industrial unrest stemmed not from the workers' dissatisfaction with their economic plight but rather from their dissatisfaction with the political system. They also claimed that to yield on economic issues under the pressure of strikes would only raise workers' expectations and encourage them to make more far-reaching demands, which could not possibly be met without seriously harming the national economy. If the government wished to mollify the workers, it should grant political reforms.

The industrialists' assertions were only half true at best. On Bloody Sunday and during the strike wave afterward, workers had made clear their desperate plight and their yearning for better economic conditions. In any case, it soon became evident that the industrialists were looking for excuses to scuttle the Kokovtsov Commission. After news of Russia's naval defeat in the Straits of Tsushima reached the capital, they claimed that this was an inopportune time to continue the deliberations. "If the great misfortune that has befallen Russia does not pacify the workers and bring them to reason," declared F. A. Krestovnikov, the spokesman for the industrialists, "then the laws which we have devised and are laboring to bring to fruition will not pacify them in any case. Therefore we beg you [Kokovtsov] to defer the discussion of these questions until more peaceful times."[69] The representatives of industry then withdrew from the commission, whose bureaucratic members continued to meet from time to time during the revolutionary period without accomplishing anything of importance.

The dismal failures of the Shidlovsky and Kokovtsov commissions were only the most notable examples of government immobility. On January 17, 1905, the Deputy Minister of Finance, V. I. Timiriazev, formed a commission to implement the promise made in the Ukase of December 12, 1904, to establish a system of state insurance for people who, for one reason or another, had lost the capacity to work. Sixty-eight delegates from various industrial and insurance organizations served on the commission, but all they achieved was to list some general guidelines on an insurance system for invalids, victims of accidents, and older citizens, which were later used by the State Duma to formulate legislative projects.[70] Two "special conferences" on the peasant question in the spring of 1905 also failed to produce reforms that might have checked the growing unrest in the countryside.[71]

All in all, the government's response in the first months of 1905 to the spreading unrest was feeble. Beyond vague promises to establish a national legislature, it made so few genuine concessions to the opposition that they can be summarized in a few sentences. In February it began to ease restrictions on religious freedom. Administrative decrees that placed special burdens on the Old Believers were revoked, and on April 17 the Tsar issued a decree granting religious toleration. Over the course of several weeks, some 1,600 people who had been punished for religious dissent were either granted pardons or allowed to return from exile. But, determined to preserve the preeminence of Orthodoxy, the government appointed a "special commission" to seek ways of reconciling the principle of religious freedom with the maintenance of special privileges for the Orthodox Church.[72]

On April 15, the government bowed to reality by revoking two official circulars of 1897 on the punishment of strikers. One of them, issued by the Factory Inspectorate, had directed provincial governors to take all necessary measures to compel strikers to return to work. The second, drafted by the Ministry of Internal Affairs, had prescribed a series of punishments that governors should apply to stop strikes without recourse to judicial proceedings. They ranged from arresting intellectuals who were thought to have instigated the actions to exiling strikers to their native villages. Industrial strikes in 1905 were so immense that these measures could not possibly be invoked. Moreover, the government may finally have realized the foolishness of sending strikers to the countryside, where they could stir up unrest among the peasantry.[73] None of the measures succeeded in dampening labor unrest. Inevitably, hostility toward the autocratic regime continued to deepen and intensify.

Part II

. . . .

THE ASSAULT
ON AUTHORITY

Chapter Five

. . . .

Civil Disorder and
Labor Unrest

CAN THE EVENTS of 1904–7 be properly referred to as a revolution? Certainly an orthodox Marxist would be justified in disputing the designation, for political power was not transferred from one social class to another. Non-Marxists who define revolution as a fundamental change in the system of legality might also hesitate to use the term, since the Tsar emerged from the turmoil with only slightly less power.[1]

Yet it is understandable that the term should have been adopted by contemporaries and retained by political activists as well as historians. From mid-1904 until late in 1905, there occurred an assault on authority from below so massive, potent, and successful that to all appearances the old regime was disintegrating. Civil order broke down, and the government seemed capable of little more than biding its time until the defiant outbursts, generally unplanned and unorganized, had spent themselves. So effective a challenge to the state's monopoly of power, even though temporary, may justifiably be characterized as a revolution.[2]

The restlessness was not confined to workers, peasants, national minorities, and various political movements. Numerous other social groups and institutions, some traditionally known for their moderation and even conservatism, were seized by a rebellious mood that expressed itself in demands for economic, political, and cultural change. Significantly, the rebelliousness did not manifest itself only in petitions or requests for the redress of grievances. With increasing frequency, citizens took the law into their own hands; the power structure was so shaken by the onslaught that it lost the self-confidence and will—and sometimes also the power—to suppress the acts of defiance. Moreover, by the summer of 1905, the police in several cities could no longer cope with common criminality and therefore became tolerant of citizens resorting to mob law.

Among the most obvious signs that the government could be defied with impunity are the content and tone of the leading newspapers. Officially, censorship still prevailed in 1905 (in modified form), and the press was certainly mindful of it, but beginning in mid-1904 newspapers demonstrated real daring in criticizing the old order. After Bloody Sunday the press widely adopted a practice that came to be known as acting "iavochnym poriadkom"—"without prior permission." The government largely ignored the infractions of regulations, partly because it thought it wise in the tense circumstances to allow the opposition leeway to air grievances, and partly because it suspected that the opposition was simply too tenacious to be silenced completely. In effect, the government acknowledged *de facto* that freedom of the press had been vastly enhanced.

To be sure, readers of such newspapers as *Russkie vedomosti, Novoe vremia, Syn otechestva, Rus,* and *Slovo* could not piece together a comprehensive and fully satisfactory account of social and political developments in the Empire. The press could not entirely disregard the fact that the censorship was legally still in effect, nor could the revolutionary left publish freely. Indeed, many citizens refused to rely solely on Russian newspapers. In the summer of 1905, post offices in Moscow, Odessa, Kharkov, and many other Russian cities were "overloaded with orders for subscriptions to foreign newspapers, especially for [those published in] Berlin and Königsberg." German newspapers were popular because they provided detailed information about events in Russia.[3] Still, Russians who knew no foreign language could have learned a good deal about the turbulence in their country from their own press.

In 1905 the press reported extensively and vividly on the disorders in the cities and countryside, the clamor for basic reform, the political discussions among opponents of the autocracy, and the government's response to all these manifestations of popular discontent. On several occasions, highly confidential deliberations of senior bureaucrats or official committees were leaked to newspapers, which readily ran articles about them. *Syn otechestva,* a paper sympathetic to the Socialist Revolutionaries, even ridiculed the government for its clumsy efforts to prevent leaks. In mid-September the press printed the contents of a confidential conversation held at the Ministry of Education between the minister himself and several professors of the Historical-Philological Institute in St. Petersburg. The minister was so enraged that he ordered that the doors to his office be checked to see whether some defect in their construction allowed human voices to penetrate them. "No defect in the structure of the doors was discovered," *Syn otechestva* tells us. "Thus, the question of how the aforementioned conversation could have found its way into the columns of newspapers continues to be obscure. Indeed, is it worthwhile clearing it up?"[4]

The press devoted special sections to the disasters of 1905. On May 19, for example, the prominent liberal newspaper *Russkie vedomosti* carried no fewer than thirteen items that reflected the troubled state of the country. The first described the catastrophic defeat of the Russian navy in the Straits of Tsushima and ended by quoting approvingly Hannibal's plea after the battle of Zama: "Peace at all costs, even if the conditions are very severe!" To which the editors added: "Enough blood and tears." Of the remaining articles, eight reported on strikes in various regions, two on violent conflicts between religious groups, one on a clash between soldiers and demonstrators, and the last on a meeting of teachers of the Tiflis guberniia to discuss the "desperate conditions of schools at the present time."[5]

Russkie vedomosti was even bolder in its editorials. Although the paper welcomed every indication that the government intended to introduce reforms, it never ceased to denounce the incompetence and arbitrariness of the "disgraceful . . . bureaucratic system" and to assert that nothing short of a constitutional order with civil liberties guaranteed to all citizens would restore calm and stability. Each defeat in the war against Japan was cited as a new sign of the government's ineptitude; every promise by the government to grant concessions was hailed by the editors as merely a first step in the "renewal" of Russia.[6] In May *Russkie vedomosti* echoed the by now frequently heard cry of liberals: "We can no longer live like this."[7]

Not only in the ethnically Russian parts of the Empire were restrictions on the press loosened. In the Polish Kingdom, where the censorship had been particularly onerous, newspapers late in January 1905 no longer "hesitated to criticize actions of the government, to give advice to the Emperor, and to demand, at times in a strident tone, a national assembly and a constitution." The Polish papers often reprinted provocative articles from the Russian press. The censorship in Warsaw, like other branches of the Imperial administration, lacked the will to enforce the law.[8]

The authorities' weakness went beyond their failure to enforce regulations governing the press. They also failed to maintain order during the rash of attacks on innocent civilians by hooligans and right-wing extremist gangs known as Black Hundreds that broke out shortly after Bloody Sunday in many cities and towns. As *Russkie vedomosti* emphasized, the purpose was to intimidate anyone inclined to participate in antigovernment strikes or demonstrations. The editors of the paper made a point of reporting such attacks, though prudence apparently inhibited them from noting all of them.

In Moscow and Pskov, hooligans accused children, some of them only nine or ten years old, of "sedition" and then beat them in full view of the police, who did nothing at all. In Moscow merchants were subjected to so many wanton attacks that they provided for their own defense. In Kazan mobs beat up students and "other intelligentsia" while the police made no effort to protect them. Early in March, a drunken mob of peasants in Saratov, egged on by the local clergy's talk of "treason" and "internal enemies," made ready to stage a pogrom at a local school. The teacher had been warned of the impending attack and managed to evacuate the students; again the police did nothing. In Mogilev policemen themselves engaged in lawlessness. They arbitrarily arrested 50 people on charges of antigovernment activity. No evidence was uncovered to sustain the charges and all 50 were released, but only after having been physically abused.[9]

The Austrian Ambassador reported in mid-July that "innumerable rowdies have made the streets in the cities, even St. Petersburg, unsafe." He singled out Nizhnii-Novgorod as a city where the breakdown of order was particularly acute. Mobs regularly attacked well-dressed people and anyone who appeared to be educated. On a single day in July, between 70 and 80 people were injured. "The police were invisible; only in the evening of that day did the Governor issue a statement to calm the population."[10]

Pogroms against Jews were an especially virulent form of disorder. Though sporadic and scattered over a wide area of the Empire, they wreaked havoc on local communities. During the last four months of 1904, there were 33 anti-Jewish riots, many of them staged by soldiers in response to allegations in such anti-Semitic newspapers as *Novoe vremia* that Jews were helping the enemy of the fatherland. Then in the spring and summer of 1905 the Black Hundreds went on the offensive against Jews, believing them to be the main instigators of the opposition to Tsar Nicholas. Late in April, for example, they staged a pogrom in Zhitomir, a city whose population of 65,000 was about two-thirds Jewish. Supported by police and troops, the *pogromshchiki* went on a rampage for three days, though not without encountering stiff resistance from armed Jewish youths. One contemporary claimed that "in Zhitomir there was no pogrom but a war," in which, apparently, more Christians than Jews lost their lives. Twenty-nine Jews were killed and an enormous amount of property was destroyed.

In similar episodes, *pogromshchiki* killed 100 Jews in Kiev on July 10 and 60 in Bialystok on August 1. All told, from February through mid-October 1905, there were 57 anti-Jewish pogroms in the Empire. The available evidence suggests neither that the government in St. Petersburg inspired the massacres nor that it took adequate measures to prevent or stop them after they had begun. Very often the police and soldiers looked the other way for several days; occasionally they joined the marauders.[11]

"The question of the day," *Russkie vedomosti* stated in an editorial as early as February 20, "is the conduct of the police or, more accurately, the demoralization of the police." The reports of police attacks on innocent civilians were so widespread that there could be no doubt that the country faced a breakdown of public order. Only an immediate and drastic change in the police system could restore calm. Control over the police, the editors recommended, should be transferred from the central government to local organs of authority, which had a vital interest in maintaining "security and order" in the streets.[12]

Over the next few months, the demand that the police powers of the central government be curbed was taken up by one local organ of authority after another. A few city councils—in Riazan, Briansk, and Stavropol—even refused to allocate funds to reinforce the police or to pay for Cossacks.[13] Some councils asked provincial governors or the Ministry of Internal Affairs not to dispatch Cossacks to areas where disorders were taking place because they only made matters worse by provoking "irritation and resentment."[14] After an investigation of police and Cossack attacks on ordinary citizens on April 8, the city council in Rostov-on-Don unanimously voted to ask the town authorities to prepare a report on the organization of a city militia.[15] The councils of Saratov, Minsk, Nizhnii-Novgorod, and Zheleznovodsk also took up the question of organizing local militias.[16]

At least one city council, that of Blagoveshchensk, went beyond the mere discussion of the desirability of creating a local militia. On July 20, it decided to establish its own night patrols to protect the populace against thievery, which had become epidemic.[17] Sometimes, government officials allowed private citizens to organize their own paramilitary units; for example, in September the Acting Governor-General of Livland granted landlords permission to hire armed guards (one for each 500 desiatinas of land) to protect their estates.[18] Both these actions underline the police's inability to maintain order, a striking commentary on the state of affairs in Russia in the summer of 1905.

Nor could the police enforce regulations against political dissidents. For example, on August 21 several officers appeared at the apartment of

N. N. Bazhenov, a Muscovite of some prominence, with an order from the Governor-General of Moscow prohibiting him from holding a meeting of zemstvo and city notables in his home. The group, however, had already gathered and refused to disband, despite a threat by the police to use force. Informed of the impasse, the Governor-General announced that the meeting could take place, but only in the presence of the police. The condition was accepted and the discussions lasted about five hours.[19]

This incident was unique only in that it was reported in a major newspaper. I. I. Petrunkevich revealed that in 1905 illegal meetings in private homes in Moscow were quite common. The police always threatened to prefer charges, but they rarely did more than take notes. The local officials, Petrunkevich suggested, considered it prudent to give the appearance of not being lax, but they did not want to take any action against liberals, because there was the chance that their superiors might soon be replaced by others, "among them participants in [the illegal] conferences."[20]

This loss of nerve was not confined to political offenses. The police also became increasingly ineffective in coping with common criminality. Confidential reports of foreign diplomats in Russia expressed alarm at the mounting lawlessness. "Murder, pillage, massacre and riots," the U.S. Ambassador to St. Petersburg declared in a dispatch of July 7, "are rife in different parts of the country."[21] Three months later, the acting U.S. Consul in Batum reported that "the whole country is simply permeated with sedition and reeking with revolution, racial hatred and warfare, murder, incendiarism, brigandage, robbery and crime of every kind. . . . As far as can be seen we are on the high road to complete anarchy and social chaos." The consul went on to point out that "one of the worst signs is that the public under this long reign of anarchy and crime is growing callous and the news of the murder of an acquaintance or friend is, by the bulk of the population, received with indifference whilst cases of brigandage are looked upon as being quite in the ordinary course of events."[22]

In July of 1905, major newspapers carried a series of accounts on yet another form of civil disorder affecting Moscow and St. Petersburg, the spread of mob law. During the night of July 10–11, a group of Moscow workers tracked down as many as twenty thieves in a den in a district in the center of the city and proceeded to beat them. A thief armed with a knife ripped open the stomach of a printer from the Levenson plant. The police merely dispersed the people at the scene of the melee.[23] Four days later, a group of Moscow citizens assaulted thieves near the Riazan (now Kazan) railway station, and at Sukharev Square another group beat into unconsciousness a man who had impudently pestered a young girl at Strastnaia Square.[24]

The fear of criminals had become so acute that workers at the San-Galli factory in St. Petersburg and people living in the vicinity of the plant had formed a sort of militia of three hundred people who regularly patrolled several boulevards and streets looking for thieves. The members of the patrols regarded themselves as "voluntary guardians of order."[25] Between July 15 and 20, each night at 9 P.M. a group of 50–60 men moved from one street to another in search of "professional thieves, with the obvious aim of meting out mob justice." If they found no criminals, they returned to their homes "with decorum." But the "frightened public" took no chances and stayed clear of the streets being patrolled by the vigilantes.[26] On July 17, the volunteers encountered several suspected criminals and beat one woman and four men so mercilessly that all five had to be carried to a hospital.[27] Two weeks later a crowd on Tver Boulevard in Moscow attacked and seriously injured a robber who had grabbed a watch from a girl walking along the street.[28]

A striking feature of the accounts of mob action is the absence of any mention of police intervention. Of course, the Russian police had never been known for efficiency or scrupulousness, but in 1905 their performance seems to have reached a new low. More than likely they were demoralized by the rash of terrorist attacks on policemen, which could not be contained. "The assassination of police officials," according to a British diplomatic report of April 12, "continues on a large scale. Hardly a day passes without a victim being recorded, & in one day (March 30) no less than four murders of police officials were reported [in St. Petersburg] and fifteen political crimes between the 25th March & the 2nd April in various parts of the country. Other attacks on the police have occurred at Baku, Kutais, Lodz, Riga & Libau."[29]

Whatever the reason for the failure of the police to take effective action to curb the vigilantes, the seriousness of the situation is borne out by the fact that criminals increasingly saw to their own protection; they formed "fighting organizations" that struck back at the vigilantes. Sometimes they set up ambushes for small groups of workers, but quite often they operated in the open in large gangs. Thus, on July 19, "a crowd of armed hooligans on Naryshkin Boulevard [in Moscow] caught sight of workers leaving their factory and cried out 'There they are—beat them up!' and pounced on them and began a reprisal. The public was totally surprised by the attack and so confused that it offered no help to the workers. The hooligans were victorious. There are casualties among the workers."[30]

In Kishinev at this time the strife between hooligans and law-abiding citizens took an especially ugly turn. The main problems, again, were massive stealing and the failure of the police to put a halt to criminality.

People took the law into their own hands and began punishing suspects, killing a number of hooligans and injuring several others. The governor feared that Kishinev was being converted into "an arena of civil war" and noted that many residents were leaving the city. The governor held the police responsible for the violence because they had taken no action against the criminal elements, and he threatened to prefer charges against them if they did not immediately restore order in the streets.[31]

In Nowo-Minsk, a town near Warsaw, the police had literally ceased to function by the summer of 1905. Many thieves had moved there from the Polish capital, and stealing increased at such a rapid pace that the police simply gave up all attempts to curb it. Local workers therefore took it upon themselves to protect the property of the townspeople; the authorities not only raised no objection but by their conduct actually legitimized the new dispensation, as the following incident indicates.

A man whose horse had been stolen in Nowo-Minsk went to the police for help and was told that his only hope for redress was to turn to the workers who were the "guardians" of local property. The victim replied that he did not know any of the workers, whereupon one of the policemen made the necessary introduction. When the worker-guardians heard the story, they visited the local horse-thief and by means of threats compelled him to reveal that the stolen horse was being hidden in Kalyszyn, a nearby town. The workers gave the victim a letter to their comrades in Kalyszyn, the horse was found, and "finally . . . [it was] safely returned to the owner."[32]

The Polish railway system, too, was shot through with corruption, and rarely did the authorities seek to put a halt to it. For a relatively small bribe, anyone could ride the trains without buying a ticket. In August 1905, a zealous inspector sent by St. Petersburg to examine conditions on the Warsaw lines discovered that, in four trains picked at random, 778 passengers were enjoying a very inexpensive ride. "It is remarkable," according to the report on corruption, "that the culprits are never arrested and that the police are incapable of taking any preventive measures."[33]

By late spring in 1905, Warsaw may well have been the most lawless city in the Empire. According to the French Consul-General, the city was "absolutely terrorized by anonymous groups of veritable brigands who distribute proclamations ordering workers on pain of punishment to stop working, compel shop-owners to close their stores, force the comfortable classes to pay levies which, they say, will be handed out to the unemployed, and avail themselves of every opportunity to provoke violent disorders and terrorize the population." The police made no efforts to stop the malefactors. The consul-general himself witnessed incidents of street violence that could easily have been stopped by police officers who were at the scene but who refused to intervene. "Patrols that pass along the streets night and day do not appear to have any other instructions except to disperse crowds at the slightest provocation."[34]

Late in May, large-scale disorders of a particularly fierce kind broke out in the city. The initial cause of the upheaval was the abduction of a young Jewish woman and her forced employment in a house of prostitution. Her fiancé led a group of Jews in an attack on the brothel and then, under the pretext of a crusade against all such houses, scoured the city, invading apartments occupied by "women of easy virtue," pillaging, throwing furniture and pianos out of windows, and injuring many people. On the first day, Jews constituted the vast majority of the marauders, but then groups of poor people joined in the rampage and began to attack apartments occupied by well-to-do people. "These disorders lasted three days and three nights [May 24–26], accompanied by veritable scenes of savagery committed under the eyes of the police. . . ." Only during the night of May 26 did the Governor-General of Warsaw send troops to his capital from a nearby town to restore order. "It is impossible," the French Consul-General explained, "to form a precise conception in France of the mood of the population and of the incompetence, the negligence, and, I think I have the right to say, the knavery of the authorities."[35]

Attacks on brothels also occurred in other regions of the Polish Kingdom, most notably in Tomaszow and in Piotrkow province. The reasons for the spread of this particular kind of violence are not known. One historian has speculated that "workers sought to relieve some of their frustration by attacking one of the sources of workers' decadence."[36]

The prevalence of lawlessness in the Polish Kingdom may have resulted from a "tacit understanding" between Russian civil servants and the fomenters of civil disorder. Because of the Poles' strong nationalist antipathy to the Russians, the Tsar's officials came to think of themselves as administrators of a conquered land. One of their principal concerns was to protect themselves against physical attacks, and consequently they were prepared to tolerate violators of the law so long as the latter refrained from agitation for greater autonomy or independence. Moreover, civil disorder in the Kingdom made it less likely that the government in St. Petersburg would grant the Poles concessions that would reduce the privileges of Imperial officials serving in the territories. In short, Russian civil servants in Warsaw followed a dual policy: tolerance of civil disorder and suppression of political defiance of Imperial authority.[37]

The information available on the incidence of vigilantism and mob lawlessness suggests a serious deterioration in the maintenance of civil order in 1905. The government surely made every effort to avoid publicity about the loss of authority by the police, and it is clear that newspapers, technically still operating under censorship, exercised restraint on so sensitive a subject. "The newspapers," wrote the acting U.S. Consul in Batum, "teem with reports of crime of every class[;] and at the same time, we who live here know that not one tenth of the occurrences find their way into the press."[38] Of course, in many locales the police could still be relied upon to enforce the law and to deal swiftly with criminals as well as with political dissidents. But there can be little doubt that in the course of 1905 their effectiveness and standing in the eyes of society declined sharply. The very fact that major newspapers could with impunity report on the laxity and misconduct of local forces and call for their fundamental reorganization lends credence to such a conclusion.

. . . . .

Without question, labor unrest constituted the most dramatic, pervasive, and potent form of popular defiance of the government. As has already been mentioned, strikes and the formation of independent labor organizations were illegal, but after Bloody Sunday the authorities were either too weak or too demoralized to enforce the law. In the spring of 1905, some of the more liberal officials, among them Kokovtsov, came to terms with the realities of the new situation and proposed legalizing trade unions and the right to strike, only to be overruled by other, stronger elements at the highest levels of the government.[39] The government's intransigence on this issue further embittered workers, who increasingly supported various protest movements. By the end of February 1905, the strikes were adversely affecting the national economy. For example, many factories in St. Petersburg could not fill urgent orders for goods, and businessmen were turning to companies abroad to obtain industrial commodities previously produced in Russia.[40]

Several distinctive features of the labor unrest that swept across the Empire should be noted. In the first place, its magnitude was unprecedented. Industrial strikes had taken place in Russia before 1905, of course; many had been quite bitter, and some had ended in important concessions to workers. But none of the previous strike movements involved anywhere near as many workers as those in 1905. Nor did previous strikers touch as explicitly, directly, and frequently on political issues, though a few words of clarification are in order here. Factory inspectors who reported on strike movements tended to make a rigid distinction between workers' economic and political demands, a distinction often stressed also by historians. But in fact there was no clear line of demarcation between the two kinds of demands. To be sure, in many instances workers who went on strike emphasized economic grievances, but in autocratic Russia, where collective action against an employer was illegal, a work stoppage was inevitably a challenge to the authorities and therefore a threat to the political status quo. Moreover, early in 1905 many workers on strike called for the legalization of workers' committees, and this came very close to being an explicit political demand. In effect, the strikers were asking for the right of free association, which, if granted, would have amounted to a significant liberalization of the political order in Russia. The point is that although striking workers may have stressed economic issues, they were engaged in an activity with serious political implications. The authorities were never in doubt about this, and the reader should also keep it in mind whenever the workers' concern with economic issues is mentioned.

Nevertheless, it is useful to draw attention to a change in emphasis in the workers' articulation of demands during the first half of 1905. For several months early in that year, workers on strike concentrated on economic questions. Only rarely did they concern themselves with larger political issues, such as the abolition of the autocracy, alterations in the economic system, or even the ending of the war with Japan. When they began to do so with some frequency late in the spring and during the summer of that year, it was clear that the industrial workers had been radicalized.

During the early months of 1905, strikes also tended to erupt spontaneously and lacked firm leadership. By the end of the year, however, they often assumed the character of reasonably disciplined affairs; in some workers' organizations, political activists, generally Social Democrats but also Socialist Revolutionaries, attained positions of prominence. It is also significant that industrial and artisanal laborers were not the only ones to organize themselves. Professionals and white-collar workers also formed unions, a development of the utmost importance during the national crisis in October. Finally, it should be noted that until mid-November 1905 the strike movement commanded the support of many liberals, not because they approved of all the workers' economic demands but rather because they viewed the industrial disorders as an effective means of prodding the regime into granting political concessions.

The vast amount of statistical information on labor unrest in 1905 must be treated with caution. Not only was the collection of data incomplete; the strike movement was extremely complicated, and it is not easy to decide what criteria to apply in assessing its magnitude. Should a worker who laid down his tools three times in 1905 be counted as one or three strikers? Should workers who deliberately performed below capacity or who stopped working one or two hours before the end of their shift be regarded as strikers? Should an enterprise at which 25 percent of the labor force staged a job action be considered in effect closed down, especially in those instances where a large percentage of the strikers were skilled workers? These are only some of the problems encountered in any attempt to quantify the strike movement. Still, labor unrest was so critical a development in 1905 that a few statistics are worth mentioning.

Strikes occurred most frequently in the first and last quarters of the year. During the three months from January to March, over twenty times as many workers participated in work stoppages as in any *one year* between 1895 and 1905. There were also significantly more strikes during that three-month period in Russia than in any *one year* from 1895 to 1908 in Germany, the United States, or France.[41] According to official estimates, which include figures only on the 70 percent of Russian workers in factories under the supervision of the Factory Inspectorate, in January 414,000 workers were on strike and in February, 291,000.[42] In March and April the number declined to 72,000 and 80,000, respectively, but in May it rose to 220,000, in part because of the celebrations on May 1. In June and July the number of strikers decreased to 142,000 and 150,000, respectively. In the summer months of August and September, the strike movement reached its lowest point for the year: 78,000 and 36,000. In October it rose to its peak for the year, 481,000, and it remained high in November (323,000) and December (418,000). Altogether in 1905, 13,110 establishments were affected by work stoppages. Over 23.5 million working days were lost. The cost of labor unrest to employers has been estimated at 127 million rubles and to workers at over 17.5 million rubles.[43]

Triggered by the news of Bloody Sunday, strikes erupted in January and February 1905; they then developed spontaneously in various regions of the Empire. Provinces that in the years from 1895 to 1904 had been completely free of strikes, or had experienced very few, now witnessed labor unrest of major proportions. This was true of Novgorod, Smolensk, Tauride (Crimea), Samara, Saratov, Kaluga, and Tula.[44] Understandably, labor unrest was most extensive in St. Petersburg, where the work stoppages were marked by a considerable amount of confusion. At the Putilov plant, for example, on any one day some workers might not appear at all, some might appear but refuse to do any work, and some might work but stop before the final whistle was blown. Those who left early generally marched to other factories to persuade their employees to leave their jobs. In some factories whose workers showed up but refused to work the protesters would not declare a strike or submit any demands; they merely stayed on the premises and talked to colleagues. In yet other factories, workers performed "sluggishly," which caused a serious decline in productivity.[45] The amorphousness of the workers' protests is to be explained by the absence of trade unions or any other kind of proletarian organization that might have provided direction for those who wished to express their indignation at the massacre. What happened in the factories in January and February 1905 can only be described as an elemental outburst of anger. Workers were groping for an effective mode of protest.

As a matter of fact, in January 1905 workers in St. Petersburg as well as in other regions of the Empire drew up lists of demands only *after* going out on strike, further proof that the strikes themselves were spontaneous. Once formulated, the demands in the early period of the strike movement focused on the following issues: increased pay, the eight-hour day, improved medical care, and better cultural facilities such as libraries and schools. But workers also made what might be characterized as social demands: they insisted on polite treatment by foremen, who habitually demeaned workers by addressing them with the informal "thou," fining them for infractions of factory rules, and searching them to prevent theft of company goods. Finally, workers demanded the right to elect committees of their peers to represent them. According to S. P. Chizhov, the chief of the Factory Inspectorate in St. Petersburg, in the first three months of 1905 workers in the capital were more concerned with obtaining this right than improving their economic conditions. The workers feared that unless they formed strong organizations, employers would withdraw concessions as soon as the political storm subsided.[46]

According to the Menshevik scholar M. S. Balabanov, of all the workers who went on strike in the course of 1905, about 35 percent concentrated on "purely economic" issues.[47] Of these, approximately 84 percent engaged in offensive strikes; that is, they demanded better conditions and did not simply defend themselves against attempts by employers to lower wages or increase the hours of work. About 60 percent of the offensive economic strikes were conducted primarily to gain higher pay, 30 percent concerned reducing the workday, and about 9 percent had to do with working conditions in the factory.

Because this was a period of political instability, workers scored some notable successes: in 70 percent of the so-called economic strikes, they won partial or complete victories.[48] Workers attained a wide range of improvements, though some were not terribly significant. The working week of textile workers, for example, was reduced from 63 to 60 hours. But even this minor concession was often negated by the forcible imposition of overtime.[49] Nonetheless, the standard of living for a large number of industrial workers seems to have improved noticeably in many regions of the country. The precise increase in real income is difficult to estimate, in part because inflationary pressures reduced the value of higher hourly rates and in part because workers' annual income suffered from losses during work stoppages.[50]

A sign of the workers' growing sophistication in the spring and summer was the charges a number of them filed in St. Petersburg against employers for recovery of wages lost during a strike, two weeks' severance pay in case of dismissal, or extra pay when working hours were increased. Russian civil law permitted recourse to arbitration to settle disputes between workers and employers, but very few cases had been filed in the nineteenth century. Now, after Bloody Sunday, a thousand workers in the Nikolskaia textile mill joined in a suit against the owner; and there is evidence that similar actions were taken by workers in ten to fifteen other factories. In a majority of the cases, the board of arbitration decided in favor of the plaintiffs—clear evidence of a desire to placate workers.[51]

Although strikes that focused on economic issues lasted longer than those that stressed political demands, the latter had a greater impact on the economy because they were more extensive, involving workers in many different industries. But by the late spring, it was becoming more difficult than ever to disentangle the two; in mid-May, workers in St. Petersburg with economic grievances also expressed strong opposition to the war. A month later, workers at the Nevskii plant went on strike demanding, among other things, an end to the hostilities with Japan and to the mobilization of reservists; they also proclaimed solidarity with revolutionary sailors mixed up in a mutiny. Soon afterward, workers in the capital made clear their determination to commemorate the events of Bloody Sunday on July 9. Some employers decided to shut their factories for the day, and the police reported that approximately 35,000 workers from 43 other enterprises failed to show up. Many workers who did go to work nevertheless managed to attend memorials for their fallen comrades.[52]

The memory of Bloody Sunday kept workers in a state of agitation for some time. Incidents that would merely have been deplored before the march now provoked a strike. For example, the accidental death of a laborer at the Putilov plant (he was hit by a crane) kept the entire labor force away from work on April 1.[53] Workers were especially infuriated at foremen and supervisors who refused to treat them civilly. In one factory after another, workers demanded that the supervisors responsible for "insults to human dignity" be required to change their conduct or else be dismissed. Often, on the administration's refusal to discipline foremen, workers would subject the despised men to ridicule by carting them on wheelbarrows outside the gates of the factory and dumping them on the street. During the first three weeks of March there were twenty such

incidents in St. Petersburg. Administrators threatened workers with severe penalties for using force against foremen, but the latter often left
their positions "voluntarily" when they discovered that they were in danger of being subjected to the "carting humiliation."[54]

Within a few weeks after Bloody Sunday, it became clear that labor
unrest amounted to more than a temporary outburst and that it was a
movement that included virtually every occupational level of the work
force. Not only factory workers, but artisans, railway employees, and
employees in commercial establishments and banks staged work stoppages.[55] By early May, major newspapers carried special sections on the
labor situation; the reports that appeared in one daily on a randomly
chosen day (May 11) are instructive in this regard:

(1) *Rybinsk*: On May 10 the dockers on the piers began to strike.

(2) *Elizavetgrad*: On May 10 the workers in all the factories went on strike.

(3) *Lodz*: Eight factories, among them the Geintsel and Kunitser plants, have
been struck, involving altogether 5,320 workers. The latter factory is closed for
an indefinite period.

(4) *Minsk*: Following [the strike of] craftsmen on the Moscow-Brest Railway
Line, the [railway] station has been closed. . . . On the evening of May 9 the
workers on strike held a meeting in the . . . forest [nearby]. Five hundred people
participated. When the police and Cossacks appeared, the workers dispersed.

(5) *Rostov-on-Don*: A strike of waiters began in the Alexander Garden, where
a theater is located. At 9 o'clock in the evening, when an audience of more than
3,000 people had arrived, 75 waiters stopped working and insisted on the immediate implementation of their demands. Some volunteer waiters began to take
over. The owner incurred serious losses. On May 9 a group of waiters went to
other restaurants and persuaded waiters to stop working. The strike has spread.[56]

No one reading such accounts day after day could fail to be impressed by
the dimensions of the labor unrest. In August a journalist pointed out
that literally hundreds of locations in the Empire had experienced "bitter
strikes" and warned that it was naive to attribute them to "outside agitators." The wave of strikes constituted a "mass movement" of major
proportions.[57] To many citizens it must have seemed as though the social
fabric were disintegrating.

Moreover, there was every indication that the situation would deterio-
rate even further because workers were succeeding in creating a variety
of organizations capable of pressing labor's demands in a more disciplined way. The deputies elected by numerous factories in St. Petersburg
in response to directives of the Shidlovsky Commission continued to
function as local committees representing their constituencies. More significantly, in the spring of 1905 workers began to establish trade unions
in defiance of the law. There are some statistics on this development, but,

once again, they must be treated with caution. The evidence is meager, and quite a few unions remained in existence for only a very short period of time. With these caveats in mind, it can be said that by the end of September, sixteen unions seem to have been formed in St. Petersburg, 24 in Moscow, and a few others in scattered parts of the Empire. During the last three months of the year, 57 appeared in the capital and 67 in Moscow.[58] Industrialists were appalled by this development, but the movement toward unionization was too powerful, and the government too weak, for it to be stopped.

The intelligentsia also formed "unions," though strictly speaking that was a misnomer. Composed of individuals with similar professional interests, the unions of the intelligentsia directed most of their efforts not at obtaining improved economic conditions but at abolishing the autocracy. Lawyers in St. Petersburg took the lead. In defiance of police directives, they met on January 30, 1905, in the headquarters of the Imperial Free Economic Society and made preparations for a congress of lawyers on March 28–30. There the delegates hammered out a program for a national "Union of Lawyers." Some participants who belonged to the Social Democratic movement introduced a motion calling on the group to help the proletariat "prepare for an all-national uprising." That was too radical for the majority, which adopted instead a resolution advocating "material and moral support for revolutionary parties" and "help in arming the population." But many of the participants quickly realized that these two points also were dangerously provocative, and they therefore insisted on adopting a "compromise" resolution that simply expressed "solidarity" with the revolutionary parties. The Union vowed to wage a campaign of propaganda in favor of passive resistance to the autocratic regime. It would urge citizens to refuse to pay their taxes and to discharge other, unspecified, obligations. In addition, the Union announced its intention of forming an "All-Russian Union of Lawyers" dedicated to the political liberation of Russia and the introduction of a democratic constitution.[59]

One after another, professional groups organized themselves into unions during the next four months, and because of their social prominence their activities received a considerable amount of publicity in the press. At the Pirogov Congress in Moscow (March 21–24),[60] physicians formed a Union of Medical Personnel. They denounced the war and vowed to struggle "hand in hand" with the working class to establish democracy. The doctors also advocated the legalization of strikes, a system of progressive taxation, the allotment of public lands to the peasants, and the introduction of an eight-hour day, minimum wages, and comprehensive insurance for the elderly, invalids, and the unemployed.[61] Engineers met from April 22 to 24, adopting a similar program. Journalists and newspaper editors, who met somewhat earlier (March 3–4), disagreed sharply over aims. The editors were quite moderate, confining their demands to a legislative assembly with limited powers and freedom of the press and speech. But the writers advocated a constituent assembly democratically elected. In the end, the two factions agreed to set up an All-Russian Union of Writers that would campaign for the convocation of a constituent assembly and civil liberties.[62]

By late April, fourteen national professional unions had been established, several of them attracting a sizable membership. The Union of Lawyers enrolled 2,500 members; the Union of Medical Personnel, 2,000; the Union of Engineers and Technicians, 4,000; the Union of Pharmacists, 2,300; the Union of Academicians, 1,544; the Union of Office Workers and Accountants, about 6,000; the Union for Jewish Equality, 7,500; the Union for the Equality of Women, 6,000 to 8,000; and the Union of Railway Employees, 6,000 (a very rough estimate). The other five unions, for which statistics are lacking, were the Union of Agronomists and Statisticians and unions for writers, veterinarians, teachers, and zemstvo activists.[63]

On May 8–9, 60 delegates from the fourteen unions attended a congress in Moscow to found an umbrella organization, the Union of Unions. The new organization was structured as a federation of autonomous professional unions. Its central committee, composed of two representatives from each constituent union, was to confine itself to the dissemination of information, but that restriction was not observed for very long. To a marked degree, the central committee defined the policies of the Union of Unions.

Three decades after the events of 1905, P. N. Miliukov, chairman of the Union of Unions, explained that the main task of the new organization was to serve as the "connecting link" between liberals and revolutionaries. The overall strategy amounted to a fusion of "liberal tactics with the threat of revolution."[64] But, in actuality, Miliukov himself seems to have been converted to revolutionism in the summer of 1905. He was the author of a resolution adopted by the Union of Unions at its second congress in June that called for the most radical measures to topple the regime: "All means are now legitimate against the frightful menace that is posed by the very fact of the continuing existence of the present government: and all means should be employed."[65] At about the same time, a newspaper reported that the Union of Unions had decided to "refrain completely" from economic strikes and had set up a committee to undertake "the organization of a general political strike."[66] Two months later, the Union's central committee reaffirmed its support for a general strike and directed the autonomous units to make the necessary preparations. Miliukov's lunge to the left was an understandable response to the intransigence of the autocracy, but his strategy ran the risk of offending his more cautious colleagues.

Moderate liberals did indeed recoil at the thought of an alliance between their movement and the radical Union of Unions. "I am a convinced constitutionalist," Geiden announced, "but I will never sanction such aggressive, forceful activity."[67] Initially, Miliukov scorned Geiden's "parlor constitutionalism," but by the late summer Miliukov began to distance himself from the Union, though apparently not because he objected to its tactics in principle. He now feared that its radicalism and its outspoken hostility toward the moderate constitutionalists would prevent the formation of a broad liberal political party, which he considered essential and to which he now devoted his energies.[68]

The security police closely followed the activities of the Union of Unions, which appeared to be assuming leadership over the left liberal intelligentsia. The police had learned that even priests contemplated founding a constituent union and that some senior bureaucrats already belonged to one of the local units. Colonel Gerasimov of the St. Petersburg Okhrana, convinced that "under certain circumstances" the Union of Unions could be "more dangerous than the real revolutionaries," advised his superiors to order its liquidation. Rachkovskii, deputy director of the police, was fearful of provoking "too much of an uproar" and hence resisted taking such "energetic measures." In the end, he and Trepov agreed to approve the arrest of the executive committee, but only if Gerasimov could produce proof that the Union's leaders had engaged in "criminal activities." Gerasimov showed them resolutions of the Union that had a "revolutionary character" and received the promised authorization. He arrested some ten to twelve leaders of the movement (including Miliukov) early in August of 1905. The documents found in the Union's office were sufficiently incriminating to justify a trial, but liberal newspapers raised such a storm that Trepov ordered Gerasimov to release the prisoners. "Their transfer to the courts," Trepov said, "would excessively aggravate our relations with society." The police now felt hamstrung in trying to deal with other antigovernment organizations. "We were obliged to close our eyes in the face of many [developments]," Gerasimov recalled.[69]

· · · · ·

In 1905 one other mass organization worthy of discussion made its appearance: the soviet (council). Its importance in Russian and Soviet history is of course beyond dispute, but its impact on the turbulent events of 1905 has generated a considerable amount of controversy among

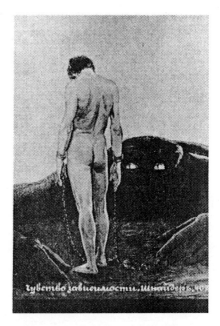

Contrasting views of the "monster" threatening Russia during the Revolution. *Left*: "Terror, horror and madness of our time." *Right*: The monster represents the autocracy, and the caption reads "Feeling of bondage." Postcards courtesy of the Helsinki University Library.

A postcard depicting "The solution of the agrarian question by Russian land-lords." Courtesy of the Helsinki University Library.

The Tsar and his agents of repression. *Clockwise from top left*: Tsar Nicholas II; V. K. Plehve, Minister of Internal Affairs, 1902–4; P. N. Durnovo, Minister of Internal Affairs, 1905; D. F. Trepov, Governor-General of St. Petersburg and Assistant Minister of Internal Affairs responsible for police affairs throughout the Empire, 1905.

Two leading ministers. *Left*: S. Iu. Witte, Chairman of the Committee of Ministers and Prime Minister, 1903–6. *Right*: Prince P. D. Sviatopolk-Mirsky, Minister of Internal Affairs, August 1904–January 1905.

Voices of reform. *Above, left*: A. I. Guchkov. *Above, right*: I. I. Petrunkevich. *Below, left*: Count P. A. Geiden. *Below, right*: P. N. Miliukov.

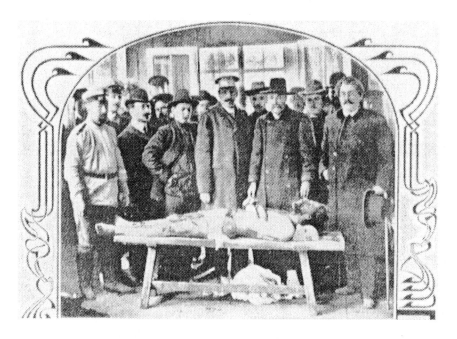

The death of Father Gapon. *Top*: The post mortem. *Below, left*: The dacha where the body was found. *Below, right*: An artist's rendering of the corpse. All from *Niva*, no. 20 (May 20, 1906), p. 318.

Above: The battleship *Potemkin*. *Below, left*: A. N. Matiushenko, a leader of the mutiny on the *Potemkin*. *Below, right*: G. N. Vakulenchuk, the spokesman for the sailors whose shooting set off the mutiny. All photos from S. I. Mitskevich, ed., *Albom*.

The birds represent the liberal
newspapers *Syn otechestva*
and *Nasha zhizn*, both of which
are muzzled but are trying to
get out the word "constitution."
Postcard courtesy of the Helsinki
University Library.

The aftermath of a pogrom in Rostov-on-Don. Houses and businesses belonging
to Jews have been sacked and in some cases completely gutted. The photos on this
page and the next were taken by a member of the German consulate staff and
have been preserved in the West German Foreign Ministry Archives in Bonn.

Mass demonstrations in October 1905. *Above*: The funeral procession in Moscow on October 20 of the revolutionary N. E. Bauman, who was murdered by a reactionary. Postcard courtesy of the Helsinki University Library. *Below*: A procession in St. Petersburg, in front of the University. From *Niva*, no. 45 (Nov. 12, 1905), p. 883.

Repression in the Baltic provinces. *Top*: A detachment arrives to search a peasant farmstead. *Bottom*: Soldiers watch as the farmstead burns. Both photos from S. I. Mitskevich, ed., *Albom*.

Russian justice. The front cover illustration of the December 24, 1905, issue of *Oskolki*, showing a woman labeled "Themis" (or Justice) harvesting the newspapers popping up like toadstools with the sword of "judicial discretion." The heavy weight in her scale reads "provisional regulations," those governing censorship.

Citizens man a barricade across a broad boulevard during the Moscow uprising of December 1905. From the collection of the Museiverket Historiska Bildarkivet, Helsinki.

Scenes of destruction in the Presnia district of Moscow, December 1905. From
S. I. Mitskevich, ed., *Albom*.

Two-faced Janus. The cover of the journal *Oskolki*'s issue of December 10, 1905. Even the figure on the bright side holding the proclamation that reads "Freedom" seems ominous in this view, and the dark side of repression and violence must have seemed as likely to triumph in the end as the year 1905 drew to a close.

scholars, who have not been able to agree even on how to define the word. The Soviet historian P. Gorin, for example, argued in 1930 that only those proletarian institutions that served both as strike committees and as political organizations devoted to a revolutionary conquest of power could be considered soviets. If this definition is accepted, then relatively few of them appeared in 1905. Indeed, V. I. Nevskii, also a Soviet historian, rejected Gorin's definition as "too narrow and too doctrinaire," arguing that soviets emerged gradually during the revolution and sought to achieve a variety of goals.

Nevskii's point is well taken. Most scholars agree that what distinguished the soviets from other proletarian organizations was that they represented not only people in one factory or trade but a wide range of workers in a variety of plants in one geographical region, generally in an entire city. Soviets were formed, as Oskar Anweiler put it, because "workers desired unity and leadership in their splintered struggle, and not because they wanted to seize political power." During the early phase of the council movement in 1905, there were no clear-cut distinctions between a strike committee and a soviet. The first organizations representing workers from a cluster of factories were "embryonic and tentative"; they developed into organs concentrating either on trade union matters or on revolutionary agitation. Many of them, however, evolved into organizations that fused the struggle for economic and political change. The emergence of soviets was a complex and confusing process, and no account that emphasizes only one of their functions does justice to them.[70]

An organization widely considered to have been the first soviet (even though it did not adopt that name) appeared in mid-May in Ivanovo-Voznesensk, a city of 80,000 inhabitants in the central Russian industrial region. Known as the "Russian Manchester," Ivanovo-Voznesensk was a center of the textile industry, one in which conditions of work were especially harsh—a fourteen-hour workday was common. A brief account of the origins and activities of the labor organization there, known as the Assembly of Delegates,[71] sheds light on the mood of workers in the late spring and summer of 1905. It also illuminates the approaches to labor unrest of local officials as well as the government in St. Petersburg. Although soviets did not assume national importance until the fall of 1905, the Assembly in Ivanovo-Voznesensk made a deep impression on public opinion. Never before had workers demonstrated such a high degree of solidarity and determination in waging a strike. The strike they launched lasted about 65 days, substantially longer than any previous one.

A few minor strikes had broken out in the city in 1904, but for the first few months after Bloody Sunday, Ivanovo-Voznesensk was relatively quiet. In an attempt to secure better conditions, workers at one factory went on strike on May 12; within a few days some 32,000 other workers joined the strike and every factory was closed. When the workers submitted a list of 24 demands to the district Factory Inspector, he suggested that deputies from individual plants be elected to conduct negotiations for them all. After some hesitation, the workers, who had already elected 50 of their number to a committee whose functions had not been clearly defined, agreed to hold elections in all the city's factories. But before proceeding, they asked the authorities to promise that they would not arrest the deputies; the Factory Inspector, with the approval of Governor I. M. Leontev of Vladimir, immediately yielded on this point. On May 15, the Ivanovo-Voznesensk Assembly of Delegates (composed of 151 deputies) was born, and it quickly elected a presidium to act as an executive. It is ironic that the first "soviet," an institution that came to be revered and romanticized by Russian revolutionaries, owed its origins, at least in some measure, to a suggestion by a Tsarist official.

Economic issues predominated in the strikers' list of demands. Indeed, when a worker at one factory meeting shouted "Down with the autocracy," his colleagues protested vehemently that they had not come to discuss political questions. If that were now to be the case, they warned, the unity of the striking workers would surely be destroyed.[72] For the most part, the strikers called for the kinds of concessions that were being sought by laborers throughout the Empire: an eight-hour day, an increased minimum wage, full pay during illness, limitations on the imposition of fines, better sanitary conditions in factories, and so on. But a few demands were novel: that pregnant workers be granted two weeks of paid leave before delivery and four weeks afterward, and that day nurseries be established in factories. Mothers of infants were to be given half an hour off every three hours to feed their children. In addition, workers asked for freedom of assembly and speech, two demands that were clearly political. Once the strike was in full swing, they also requested that May 1 and February 19 (the anniversary of the emancipation of the serfs) be declared official holidays.[73]

For the first three weeks of the strike there was no violence in Ivanovo-Voznesensk, in large measure because the Assembly quickly succeeded in establishing its authority over the city's labor force and because it took measures to avoid disturbances. On May 20, the Assembly voted unanimously to create a workers' militia, to which it assigned three tasks: to prevent the Black Hundreds and hooligans from provoking disturbances in the streets of the city; to forestall clashes between strikers and the few workers who chose to go to their jobs; and to keep workers in remote factories informed of the Assembly's decisions so that the strike would not be broken by local committees acting on their own. The Assembly warned the authorities that if the militia were hindered from carrying out its functions, a breakdown of public order might ensue.[74]

At the same time, the Assembly struck a note of moderation by responding favorably to a request from Governor Leontev. Unable to get some important decrees and instructions printed, Leontev asked the Assembly (with the chief of the Factory Inspectorate acting as intermediary) to allow printers to return temporarily to their jobs. The Assembly replied that it would not object so long as they volunteered for the work.[75] The local Social Democrats, who had set up the Ivanovo-Voznesensk Group of the Northern Committee of the RSDWP, agreed with the Assembly's overall goals and tactics. On May 22, the Northern Committee began to publish a daily *Bulletin* which urged that the *peaceful* strike be continued. The *Bulletin* stressed that only provocative actions by the authorities would lead to bloodshed. It did not urge workers to prepare for an armed uprising.[76]

For their part, Governor Leontev and his subordinates at first also took pains to avoid violence. Although Leontev expressed nervousness about the developing situation and asked for military reinforcements, on May 14 he allowed 10,000 workers to hold a meeting, which turned out to be peaceful and nonpolitical.[77] A few days later, however, the governor decided that such meetings posed a threat to public order. He now prohibited further mass meetings in the streets and town squares, which prompted the Assembly to move to the banks of the Talka River, where it continued to meet, unmolested, for several weeks. On May 23, two developments greatly agitated the strikers: the employers announced their refusal to make any concessions, and the authorities prohibited the creation of a workers' militia.[78]

The situation now deteriorated rapidly. On May 26, several plants were opened with strikebreakers. On June 2, the Assembly called a mass meeting for the following day, which the acting governor* forbade on the ground that workers were beginning to raise political issues at their gatherings. Some workers pointed out that the injunction against politics had not been fully observed during the previous two weeks, but the acting governor refused to rescind the order. On June 3, the mass meeting was held anyway, not in the city but in a nearby forest. Suddenly, Cossacks appeared and attacked the workers, beating them with whips and killing several. Many in the crowd—including the secretary of the meeting, who was also a workers' deputy in the Assembly—were arrested. Enraged, the workers went on a rampage; for eight days they threw stones at buildings and policemen, tore down telegraph poles and wires,

---

* From May 22 until June 8 the vice-governor, I. N. Sazonov, was acting governor.

and looted factories and liquor stores. A fire, apparently set by an arsonist, engulfed the Gandurin Factory. The acting governor received authorization to place the city under "Reinforced Security" and ordered Cossacks to conduct extensive searches. As one observer put it, they "snatched up anybody and everybody."[79]

On June 13, the employers finally made a concession: they granted a ten percent raise in wages (increased to fifteen percent two days later), which the workers rejected as inadequate. The strikers believed that the employers would have to be more forthcoming because they did not have enough goods to display at a city fair scheduled to open soon. Moreover, workers now pressed two other demands, which indicated that despite their original intentions they could not limit themselves to economic issues: the release of all prisoners and the right to hold public meetings.

Governor Leontev faced a dilemma. His principal concern all along had been to maintain order, but he feared that if he allowed meetings to be held, they would turn into antigovernment demonstrations. If he prohibited them, there would be more disorders. He decided on what he considered the lesser evil: to permit meetings, in the hope that the strikers would run out of steam. The workers were already in desperate economic straits, and hunger, he assumed, would force them to give up the struggle.[80] There were signs that workers were indeed becoming desperate. They had started to loot grocery stores, and small groups of them had attacked and plundered nearby estates.[81]

The Assistant Minister of Internal Affairs, Trepov, suspected that the situation in Ivanovo-Voznesensk had deteriorated so markedly because Governor Leontev had been altogether too lenient. On June 27, he directed the governor to apply "every repressive measure" permitted under Reinforced Security. "I place on you personal responsibility," Trepov wrote, "to clear up and arrest agitators among the laboring masses in Ivanovo-Voznesensk. I demand all your energy."[82] Trepov had reason to be suspicious of the governor, for Leontev, as he pointed out in a memorandum of July 5, placed much of the blame for the labor unrest in Ivanovo-Voznesensk on the manufacturers. He contended that working conditions were worse there than in other industrial regions of the country, and that employers had made huge profits and had treated their workers dreadfully, without any moral concern for their well-being. In the governor's view, that explained why workers had succumbed to the "intrigues" of agitators. His main concerns were to prevent bloodshed and the provision of further ammunition to the antigovernment press, which had gleefully publicized the violence in such cities as Lodz, Warsaw, and Odessa.[83] Leontev was one of the few senior officials who realized that the labor unrest sweeping the country had profound causes and that repression alone would not eliminate it.

But by mid-June, meaningful negotiations between the strikers and the industrialists in Ivanovo-Voznesensk were no longer possible. Not only had attitudes hardened on both sides, but after the disturbances many of the factory owners and their families had fled the city in fear. There were now too few people in positions of authority who could respond to the workers' demands. On June 24, those who remained announced that they would not make any additional concessions, would not pay strikers for the days of work they had missed, and would not even resume negotiations with the Assembly. Thirty-seven manufacturers sent a telegram to the Minister of Internal Affairs pleading with him to apply "energetic measures to put down the disorders."[84] The chief of the Factory Inspectorate of Vladimir province considered the manufacturers' attitude reprehensible because it suggested contempt for the workers. Meanwhile, the governor pleaded with factory owners to return to Ivanovo-Voznesensk to negotiate, but to no avail.

On June 24, angry workers went on another rampage, attacking 71 stores and causing damage estimated at 100,000 rubles. Ninety-one people were arrested, and many of them were whipped by Cossacks.[85] Three days later, a group of workers announced that "47 days on strike have exhausted our strength" and that they therefore intended to return to their jobs on July 1. At the same time, they vowed to resume the struggle as soon as they regained their strength.[86]

Most workers continued to hold out because the manufacturers now indicated that they would not make any concessions at all. But under pressure from the governor the employers relented and offered a moderate raise as well as maternity leaves of one month at reduced levels of pay. They also promised that workers were to be treated courteously and that all searches of women (for stolen goods) were to be conducted by women. Workers drifted back to the factories, and by July 18 the strike had ended. The Assembly, acknowledging failure, disbanded.[87]

The events in Ivanovo-Voznesensk inspired workers in neighboring Kostroma to take action against their employers. In July about 10,000 people went on strike and immediately elected an "Assembly of Deputies of the Strikers," which the Factory Inspector recognized as the bargaining agent for the city's entire labor force. The inspector's only conditions were that outsiders and people under the age of 25 be excluded from the Assembly. But the Assembly refused to change its composition and the employers refused to negotiate with it, preferring instead to deal with representatives from individual plants. After three weeks, the workers, economically exhausted, returned to their jobs, having gained no more than a one-hour reduction of the workday.[88]

Despite the failure of the Assembly in Ivanovo-Voznesensk to achieve most of its stated goals, the strike in that city was hailed by many workers as an historic event. Outside the Kingdom of Poland, it was the longest and most disciplined strike between January and October. Moreover, the Assembly in that city as well as in Kostroma marked a new development in workers' organizations. It was not the brainchild of any theorist; no one planned the formation of the Assembly and no one had defined its functions and goals. The Assembly made its appearance because workers as well as Tsarist officials were looking for a practical way of dealing with a serious crisis, a work stoppage of major proportions. Originally interested primarily in economic concessions for workers, the Assembly in Ivanovo-Voznesensk within short order asked for police powers, which was even more threatening to the authorities than the demands for freedom of speech and assembly. The evolution of this first "soviet" thus demonstrates anew the difficulty of attempting to draw a clear distinction between the workers' economic and political demands. In the Russia of 1905, protest movements could rarely avoid politics, even if they were disposed to do so.

· · · · ·

Labor unrest in 1905 constituted a critical aspect of the assault on authority because it relentlessly whittled away at the bureaucracy's ability to govern. But the claim advanced by Soviet scholars that the working class exercised hegemony over the revolutionary process throughout the year cannot be substantiated. During the first nine months of 1905, the workers were too disorganized, and their activities too disparate, for them to have assumed leadership in any meaningful sense. Nor did industrial workers as a group subscribe to any explicit or coherent political program. To be sure, they were in a rebellious mood, which led them to undertake vigorous protests against the authorities in various ways. But they devoted most of their energies to improving their economic conditions, even though their demands inevitably touched on political issues. The labor unrest still lacked a conscious political focus, and so long as that was the case the liberals were bound to be the dominant force in the political arena.

Remarkably, no group of political activists played a significant role in the emerging labor movement. In St. Petersburg and Moscow, "most Social Democrats, including Mensheviks, Bolsheviks, and non-faction Social Democrats, remained aloof from the incipient trade unions" during the early months of 1905.[89] The Bolsheviks' restraint, and to a considerable extent that of the Mensheviks, can be explained by their fear that unions would divert workers from revolutionary concerns. The impact of liberals, Socialist Revolutionaries, and syndicalists on the trade unions was also slight in this period, though members of the three groups did hold a few important positions in the workers' organizations.[90]

Eventually, all the political movements came to realize that labor unrest was in fact an "accelerator" of the revolutionary process. The turning point was the late spring of 1905, when Social Democratic activists began to show serious interest in labor unions. That interest increased steadily, and by the end of the year Social Democrats appear to have reached prominent positions in several unions.[91] By the same token, late in the spring the left liberals, convinced that appeals to the Tsar for political change were futile, persuaded some of their more moderate colleagues to adopt a new tactic, agitation among the masses. "Thanks to the government," Petrunkevich declared early in July, "a situation has been created that sanctions revolution. The revolution is a fact. We must divert it from bloody forms. We turn for this purpose to the people. We deserve their confidence. We must be bold enough to tell them everything. We must go with petitions not to the Tsar but to the people."[92] In sum, liberals were urged to exploit the burgeoning unrest and to steer it along lines they considered desirable.

The industrial strikes can thus be said to have helped produce a shift to the left on the part of the oppositional movement. Liberals now began to distribute agitational literature among the workers and peasants and to address their meetings. The success of the liberals in attracting working-class support for their political program is hard to assess, but there can be little doubt that it presaged the collaboration between liberals and workers a few weeks later during the revolution's most massive attack on the autocracy.

That attack, in the form of a general strike, could not have been mounted had the workers not gone through the eight-month experience of spontaneous assaults on authority. By engaging in strikes and by creating labor organizations, workers acquired a sense of their own power, of which they had been only remotely conscious before 1905. Even though they did not win many of the battles, they discovered that they were far from impotent. For this reason, the labor unrest from January to August 1905 must be considered one of the more critical developments of the revolution.

Chapter Six

. . . .

Minorities, Peasants, Soldiers, and Sailors

TWO FEATURES characterized the assault on authority in several borderlands of the Empire: it was notably violent from its inception, and it acquired an explicitly political thrust earlier than the mass protest movements in the ethnically Russian regions of the country. Deep national resentments intermingled with economic and social factors to produce particularly explosive conditions. Ever since the reign of Alexander III (1881–94), the government had sought to exploit Great Russian national sentiments to quash the growing social unrest. Ruthless policies of Russification and persecution of minorities, it was hoped, would prompt the masses of Great Russians to rally around the autocracy. Instead, as soon as the central government was perceived to be under siege, in the days following Bloody Sunday, disorders of special ferocity broke out.

Although many minority groups demanded that the measures of Russification be relaxed, three regions were particularly affected by revolutionary turbulence: the Caucasus, the Baltic Provinces (Estland, Livland, and Kurland), and the Polish Kingdom. It is worth paying special attention to them, for the inability of the government to enforce its will in these regions is further evidence of its weakness in 1905.

Even before the outbreak of the revolution, the structure of authority had collapsed in Guriia, a small, picturesque area in western Georgia bordering on the Black Sea and Turkey. It was a predominantly agricultural region where the vast majority of the population lived in unrelieved poverty. In the Kutais guberniia, which included Guriia, 89 percent of the peasant farms were no larger than 10.8 acres. "When I tie my cow to a tree in my yard," the peasants would say, "its tail is in my neighbor's land."[1] The main concern of the local population was to acquire more land, over 70 percent of which belonged to the state.

As early as the 1890's, Georgian intellectuals turned to Marxism and gained a considerable mass following, but they trimmed their sails to earn popular support. The Georgian Marxists advocated private ownership of land and avoided any criticism of religion, a powerful force among the peasants.[2] By 1903, "there was not one village that was not part of the general [Social Democratic] movement" in Guriia. In each village the Social Democrats established one or more circles of ten comrades, which then elected representatives to a regional committee. The regional committees, in turn, elected representatives to the "Guriian Social Democratic Committee." Such an extensive hierarchical structure of party organization, in place before the Second Party Congress in the summer of 1903, existed nowhere else in the Empire.[3]

Early in 1903, many peasants in Guriia, acting under the influence of Social Democrats (who later turned to Menshevism), stopped paying taxes, which provoked the authorities into adopting harsh countermeasures. Officials forced elders in a majority of the villages to make contributions to the treasury and arrested many of the recalcitrant taxpayers. The peasants retaliated by boycotting all government institutions. In some villages they tore up portraits of the Tsar and publicly burned them. Several government spies hired to inform on the instigators of the disorders were murdered. The clergy refused to perform burial rites for the victims, and no one showed up at the funerals. Within a few months, the local organs of government literally ceased to function. The police and civil servants remained at their posts, but they had nothing to do.

By this time, ultimate authority rested with the Guriian Social Democratic Committee, under whose auspices there emerged a unique form of self-government. Public meetings were regularly held at which all were free to express their opinions. These discussions served to guide the committee in its decisions on issues of local concern. Peasants elected their own judges, who were granted unusual powers to maintain order. They could forbid convicted criminals from attending the highly regarded public meetings, order the population to avoid contacts with them for a period of time, force them to work for the community, exile them from their place of residence or from all of Guriia, or simply require a public confession of guilt. For all intents and purposes, Guriia may be said to have seceded from the Empire by mid-1903.[4] In that year and throughout 1904 no attempt was made to crush the rebellion, probably because it was confined to a small, sparsely populated and remote region. It seemed unlikely that developments there would inspire similar popular movements elsewhere in the Empire.

Shortly after Bloody Sunday, however, the protest movement did spread to areas bordering Guriia and to other parts of Transcaucasia. "We want what [the peasants] in Guriia have," was a cry widely heard in January and February of 1905. On February 7, a local official in Georgia sent a telegram to the Minister of Internal Affairs warning that the protest movement "has assumed the character of an uprising, which expresses itself in open disobedience of the authorities [and] the killing of government officials, gentry, clergy, and other people whom the revolutionaries do not like. The population has freed itself from its oath of loyalty as citizens and has sworn allegiance to the revolutionary committee. All government employees are fleeing. All the measures taken until now, including the use of the army, have yielded no results. . . ."[5] A revolutionary peasant committee, the telegram continued, had seized power. The committee had abrogated all taxes as well as obligations to landlords and the clergy. It had confiscated state and private lands and distributed them, without compensating the owners, to the peasants. In addition, the committee had established a system of obligatory and free education for children and urged peasants in the villages to create organs of self-government. In short order, the insurgents had demanded the convocation of a democratically elected constituent assembly, the teaching of Georgian in every school, and the use of the Georgian language in the conduct of official business.

In the districts of Batum, Kinstrik, Ozaugueti, Echialauri, and Tiflis, and as far as the northwest area of Kakhetia, the peasants also proceeded to organize their own system of police and justice. In each village every group of ten families delegated one man "of good reputation" to serve as policeman and to dispense justice. Whenever a crime was committed, the plaintiffs would appear before the "deputy," who then formed a "sort of tribunal" with other deputies to investigate the case and pass sentence on the transgressors. In sum, in many parts of Transcaucasia "revolutionary peasants' self-governments" had replaced the Tsarist authorities.[6]

On February 18, 1905, the government in St. Petersburg placed all of Georgia under martial law and dispatched General A. M. Alikhanov-Avarskii with 10,000 troops and several pieces of artillery to quash the uprising. The general and his men spent four months in the region without launching an attack. Not only did the rebellious peasants enjoy enormous support, but Alikhanov-Avarskii feared that his troops would fraternize with them.[7] In July he withdrew his forces completely, only to return in October to assault the insurgents in earnest. But it was not until

January 1906, when the government was reasserting its authority throughout the Empire, that the insurrection in Georgia was fully crushed, and
then only after much blood had been shed.[8]

The Mensheviks abroad hailed the startling developments in Georgia.
"At a single word from their representatives," *Iskra* declared in March
1905, "[the Guriian peasants] are ready for fire and water. Marx, Engels,
Lassalle are worshipped like saints."[9] The Mensheviks looked upon the
events in Guriia as evidence that they had developed sound tactics in
calling on the working class to form "organs of revolutionary self-
government" even before the final collapse of the autocracy. But in their
understandable jubilation the Mensheviks ignored the uniqueness of the
situation in Transcaucasia. After all, it was the peasantry, not the working class, that was the most militant social force; and the government
was hardly likely to have been as indulgent toward "organs of revolutionary self-government" formed by workers in major cities as it was toward
such organs in a distant, isolated part of the Empire.

· · · · ·

The people of the Polish Kingdom,* incorporated into the Russian Empire in the aftermath of the Napoleonic Wars and subjected to Russification after the late 1860's, harbored profound grievances against the
Tsarist regime; but, for a variety of complex economic, political, and
cultural reasons, they failed to unite behind an anti-Russian program.
Economically, the Poles enjoyed several advantages as subjects of the Empire. Although the 11.3 million people in the Polish Kingdom constituted
only 7.9 percent of the Empire's population, their industrial output
amounted to about 25 percent of that of the entire country. For some
time, the metallurgical and textile industries in Poland had benefited
from the protective tariff imposed by the Tsarist government as well as
from the lucrative markets in Russian Asia. A growing number of Poles
also held high managerial positions in various sectors of the Russian
economy.

To be sure, the Tsarist government pursued policies that offset the attractiveness of these economic benefits. The Poles were not permitted to
form such organs of local self-government as zemstvos and city councils.
The autocracy tried in every way possible to hamper the development of
Polish culture. It prohibited the teaching of Polish or the Catholic religion
in the schools; it mandated the use of the Russian language in all public
institutions; and it refused to employ any person of Polish origin or even

* Also known as Congress Poland, from the fact that its boundaries were established at
the Congress of Vienna in 1815.

of the Catholic faith in government positions. On a per capita basis, less was spent on education in Poland than in Russia proper, and the Poles were required each year to contribute 150,000,000 rubles to the Imperial treasury.

The result was a steady cultural decline in Poland. According to a report of the Ministry of Internal Affairs, early in the twentieth century over 60 percent of Polish recruits to the army were illiterate. The comparable figure for recruits in 48 guberniias of European Russia was 37 percent. Most Poles, deeply patriotic, detested the Russians for seeking to crush their national and cultural heritage, but many also could not help being grateful for their economic advantages. Moreover, however repressive the Russians were, the Germans were even harsher in pursuing the "Germanization" of the Polish territory under their control. This complicated matters for Polish political leaders hostile to Tsarism: if they succeeded in weakening the Russian government, they might facilitate the expansion of Germany's influence in Poland.[10]

The outbreak of the Russo-Japanese War sharpened the political differences among the various political parties in Poland. The so-called Loyalists or conservatives, broadly representative of the gentry, supported Russia unconditionally because they feared that its defeat would give Germany and Austria-Hungary a free hand in the Balkans and in the Polish areas that each country controlled. Comfortable with the "paternalistic-autocratic form of government," and beneficiaries of Imperial economic policies, the Loyalists favored cultural autonomy for the Poles but did not want an independent Polish state.

The left, divided over the national issue, vigorously opposed the war, and the leader of the Polish Socialist Party (PPS), Josef Pilsudski, actually went to Japan to win support for his plan to stage an insurrection for Polish independence. The Social Democratic Party of the Kingdom of Poland and Lithuania (SDKPiL) advocated the overthrow of the autocracy and the introduction of socialism, but did not favor Poland's separation from the Empire. Finally, the National League, a middle-class party led by Roman Dmowski, sought conciliation between the Russians and the Poles, but only if the Kingdom were granted cultural and political autonomy within the Empire. Dmowski also traveled to Tokyo, but his aim was to dissuade the Japanese from supporting Pilsudski. Dmowski feared that an insurrection would be crushed by Russia, which then might be tempted to resurrect close relations with Berlin so as to restrain the movement for Polish autonomy.[11]

The attitude of the Polish masses toward the war and Russia was influenced more by economic developments than by the parties' ideological positions. As has already been noted, the war in the Far East had a devastating impact on the Polish economy. Many factories stopped operating, and people of means left the country in large numbers. By late 1904, some 100,000 workers had lost their jobs. In Warsaw alone, it was estimated, 50,000 people were receiving support from public charities. On November 13, 1904, the PPS organized a mass demonstration in Warsaw that was accompanied by a good deal of violence. Within four days of Bloody Sunday, major strikes broke out in Warsaw and Lodz.

Significantly, in Poland the strikers immediately emphasized political as well as economic demands. A police official reported on January 31, 1905, that workers in Lodz carried placards inscribed with the slogans "Down with the autocracy! Down with the war!" The Governor of Lodz persuaded employers to reduce the workday to ten hours and to raise wages by 5 to 15 percent, but, according to a police official, the workers made "absurd and unrealizable political demands" and called for an eight-hour day as well as raises of 166 percent. In a direct appeal for an end to the strike, employers opened the gates of their factories, but only between 15 and 20 percent of the workers showed up. The others remained in the streets, "electrified by the force they had created." These striking workers "often pressed impudently against military units, abused them, threw stones, and shot at them." Scuffles invariably ensued, causing numerous casualties.[12]

There was even more violence in Warsaw, where workers staged a general strike on January 14. Initially, peaceful demonstrations were held, but the presence of large numbers of troops in the city made clashes virtually inevitable. On January 16 alone, some 60,000 cartridges are said to have been fired at the demonstrators in Warsaw. Within a three-day period, according to official accounts, 64 civilians were killed and 69 wounded (of whom 29 eventually died). On January 17, the government placed Warsaw under a state of siege.[13] Three days later, the city was outwardly calm, but passions continued to run high. "No one now hesitates," wrote the French Consul-General in Warsaw early in March, "to express openly his Polish patriotism, [and] to rejoice at the humiliation imposed on the Russian flag by the Mikado's soldiers and at the government's embarrassments. The assassination of the Grand Duke Sergei was considered by many to be an act of justice."[14]

On April 18 (May Day—May 1 in the Julian calendar), the city was shut down by another general strike: economically, "it was as though the city were dead: there were no coaches, no horse-trams, no cabmen on the streets."[15] The police had prohibited demonstrations, but the crowds appeared in the streets anyway, carrying red flags. Once again, scuffles took place, shots were fired, and 31 people were killed.[16] On April 27, a group of Warsaw citizens appealed in person to Governor-General K. K. Maksimovich to appoint a special commission to investigate the conduct of the police and army during the May Day demonstration. Maksimovich pointed out that an investigation had already been completed and that it revealed that demonstrators had started the shooting. Under the circumstances, casualties were unavoidable, though he "sincerely regretted" it. He also reminded the delegation that the population had been warned that it might be dispersed by the army if it participated in demonstrations. His one conciliatory gesture was to agree to accept written accounts from eyewitnesses to the street clashes.[17]

By February 1905, the protest movement had spread to Polish educational institutions, where the major cause of discontent was Russification. Students at Warsaw University and the Polytechnical Institute, as well as pupils at high schools and even at some elementary schools, stopped attending class and joined street demonstrations.

Early in April and again in May, the government made some concessions to the Polish national movement. It permitted schools at all levels to teach the Scriptures in Polish and lifted several other restrictions on the use of Polish in the classroom. It also promised to establish chairs at the University of Warsaw in Polish language, literature, and history, all to be taught in Polish. On a limited scale, Polish as well as Russian would now be used in institutions of local self-government. Finally, zemstvos and city councils were to be introduced in Congress Poland.[18]

The concessions were too niggardly and came too late. The Polish working class, having entered the political fray, refused to give up. Nor was it the only social group that continued to be rebellious. Numerous professional groups met—as they did in the ethnically Russian part of the Empire—to pass resolutions in favor of a constituent assembly and autonomy for Poland or greater cultural freedom. In the meantime, disorder spread from the major cities to smaller cities and towns. From May to November 1905, it has been suggested, "the country was on the verge of civil war."[19]

For the Tsarist government, unrest in Poland proved to be very costly indeed. Even before the revolution, early in 1904, it maintained an army of 250,000 men in Poland, larger than the one then in the Far East; and by mid-1905, the government felt obliged to increase it by 50,000 men, this at a time when every soldier was needed at the front. It can also be argued that because such a large military force was tied down in Poland, the government found it more difficult to cope with unrest in other parts of the Empire, which compelled it eventually to grant concessions when it would have preferred not to.

. . . . .

The ferocity of popular unrest in the Baltic provinces in 1905 is explained by the fact that the national issue bred resentments of two kinds. On the one hand, the imperial authorities in St. Petersburg insisted on the use of the Russian language (instead of Latvian or Estonian) in most classes in the schools and encouraged the Orthodox Church to convert the local population, which to a large extent was Lutheran. Ever since 1885, for example, the permission of the Holy Synod in St. Petersburg had been required to build a new Lutheran church. At the same time, the governors of the Baltic provinces received generous supplies of funds from the Synod to be used for the construction of Orthodox churches. On the other hand, the local nobility, which owned a disproportionate share of the land, and the persons who occupied most of the managerial posts in the factories, were overwhelmingly of German extraction. Germans also held most of the important positions in the local organs of self-government, the police, the courts, and educational institutions. The Germans treated the Latvians and Estonians with contempt, a failing often reported by senior Russian officials to the ministries in St. Petersburg.[20]

Although the Baltic provinces were still largely agricultural, industrialization had taken root, and Riga and Revel (later Tallin) had become important centers of economic activity. In Estland, where the cultural level of the population was fairly high, a nationalist movement had been gaining strength for some time before 1905. Five periodicals were published in Estonian and a wide range of cultural societies had been established. The workers, apparently lacking organizations of their own, had fallen under the influence of the cultural societies. As soon as word reached them of the violence on Bloody Sunday, "all of the approximately 15,000 workers . . . [in Revel] participated in a strike." Their demands were principally economic, very similar to those put forth in St. Petersburg. There was relatively little violence, and after a few weeks of sporadic work stoppages the employers made some concessions, generally a reduction of the workday by one hour.[21]

In Riga, however, the strike that began on January 13 was marked by violence. This was owing in part to the greater militancy of the workers, but more importantly to the ruthlessness of Governor-General A. N. Meller-Zakomelskii, who later in the year became notorious for his brutality in conducting punitive expeditions against opponents of the regime. According to official reports, some 10,000 to 15,000 workers, in the streets of Riga to protest the bloodshed in St. Petersburg, surrounded a group of policemen and soldiers and demanded their weapons. In desperation, several soldiers fired into the crowd, killing 70 people and in-juring about 200. Meller-Zakomelskii was proud of the way he and his men had handled the tense situation. They had shown, he informed Tsar Nicholas, that if a small company of soldiers resorts to "energetic meth-ods," it can control hordes of unruly demonstrators. It was regrettable, he continued, that more local authorities were not willing to act as deci-sively to put an end to the disorders.[22]

Actually, Meller-Zakomelskii's methods were less effective than he be-lieved. Worker unrest continued in the Baltic provinces for much of the year and soon spread to the countryside, where the Germans were even more prominent than in the cities. Some 1,500 nobles, most of them German barons, owned about two and a half million desiatinas of land, whereas 1,300,000 Latvian peasants owned approximately two million de-siatinas. The average size of a landlord's estate was 2,000 desiatinas, but there were some huge latifundia of 46,000 and 66,000 desiatinas. Many of the poorer peasants owned between one-half and five desiatinas and could eke out a living only by becoming agricultural laborers.[23]

On several occasions, these agricultural workers joined forces with in-dustrial workers in staging general strikes, but they also engaged in other forms of protest. They refused to pay taxes and rents, boycotted Russian administrative offices, and organized attacks on the castles and estates of German barons. Because of a shortage of police and troops, the barons assembled their own military forces, and by the summer of 1905 the bloody clashes between them and the rebellious peasants had in effect turned into a civil war. In the fall the government imposed martial law, which only provoked more attacks on private estates. Toward the end of the year, Russian troops entered the Baltic region in force and crushed the peasants and the workers' movement.[24] Although the middle class did not participate in the violent actions, it did support the movement for local self-government and for the right to use the native language in schools, courts, and government offices.

With the breakdown of authority in the Empire, minority groups in several other regions gave vent to nationalist aspirations, though the agi-tation for cultural autonomy varied in intensity. In Lithuania, for ex-ample, a congress of 100 delegates in November 1905, controlled by the Lithuanian Democratic Party, voted for a democratic system of gov-ernment and for autonomy for Lithuania within the Russian Empire. In Belorussia and the Ukraine the nationalist movements were relatively docile, though people began to demand that the local languages be adopted in the schools and institutions of higher learning.[25] In Finland, the opposition to the Tsarist policy of Russification became so strong that in March 1905 the government made two concessions: it revoked the decree of 1901 that had abolished the autonomy of the Finnish army, and it accepted the principle of the irremovability of judges.

In view of these variations in the impact of the national issue on the opposition movements during the Revolution of 1905, the only safe generalization is that wherever nationalism was already a significant force, it tended to stimulate and intensify hostility toward the autocratic regime.

. . . . .

For the most part, Tsarist officials and radical historians have agreed that outside agitators played a critical role in provoking disorders in the countryside in 1905. But, of course, their reasoning has been quite different. Tsarist officials contended that the peasants were basically loyal to the Tsar and the old order; had it not been for troublemakers from the outside, motivated by political considerations, the villages would have remained calm. Thus, the relatively liberal Minister of Agriculture A. S. Ermolov reported to the Tsar on March 14, 1905, that "skillful agitators" in the Dmitriev district of Kursk guberniia had persuaded the peasants that a "golden charter" had been issued by the monarch depriving the landlords of their land and giving the peasants the right to take the landlords' stores of grain. The Tsar was said to have issued the charter because he wanted the peasants to punish the landlords for their refusal to provide supplies for the army in the Far East.[26]

Commentators on the left, eager to buttress their thesis that the working class took the leading role in the revolution, have argued that workers who returned to the villages stirred up peasant revolts. Thus, the Soviet historian S. M. Dubrovskii, also referring to the disorders in Dmitriev in mid-February 1905, contended that "an important role was played by the workers, who came to the countryside (especially during holidays), or who returned there, for the most part because of unemployment in the cities. . . . The workers . . . told the peasants what had happened in the cities and thus spread discontent in their native villages" (the last six words are quoted from Lenin).[27]

Neither of these interpretations is convincing. To be sure, outside agitators and peasants who had lived for a time in towns exerted some influence over the agrarian protest movement, particularly in helping peasants to define their demands. It is probably also true that news of the upheaval in the cities was a factor in the timing of the peasant movement. But outsiders were extremely unlikely to have had much success in provoking unrest among the peasants unless they were already deeply disaffected.[28] Unrest had frequently broken out in Russia's villages over the preceding three centuries; and no one can reasonably attribute those earlier outbursts to alien agitators, and certainly not to proletarian instigators.

There was no one pattern to the peasant movement of 1905, which refers to the more than 3,000 incidents that occurred throughout the Empire. Generalizations are therefore hazardous. It is possible to delineate the rhythm of peasant disorders in 1905, but even in this matter caution must be exercised. Dubrovskii has provided a welter of statistics on their incidence, but he has not distinguished major outbreaks of violence from minor disruptive acts by small groups of disgruntled peasants. Still, his data are useful in revealing the cyclical nature of the peasant movement. During the first few months of 1905 there were relatively few disorders in the countryside: 17 in January, 109 in February, 103 in March, 144 in April. In May, when the thaw had set in, the number grew substantially—to 299. It remained high for two more months: 492 in June and 248 in July. In August and September, when peasants were preoccupied with reaping the harvest and sowing the winter crop, the number of disorders declined to 155 and 71. In October it rose sharply (to 219), and in November and December reached the highest levels of the year—796 and 575, respectively.

In the Baltic provinces and the Caucasus, as has already been noted, peasant disorders were directed at governmental authority, but in European Russia most disorders—slightly over 75 percent of them—were directed at landlords' estates. For the rest, the European Russian peasants attacked the clergy (less than one-half of a percent of the disorders), kulaks (about 1.4 percent), and merchants, usurers, and liquor stores (roughly 8 percent). In slightly less than 15 percent of the incidents did governmental authorities bear the brunt of the peasants' rage.[29] It is noteworthy that the "rhythm" of the peasant movement was different from that of the labor movement. The months of greatest labor unrest, January, February, and October, were not the months of greatest peasant unrest, although the last two months of 1905 witnessed a considerable amount of disorder in both the industrial and the agrarian sectors of the economy. Had the two protest movements developed simultaneously throughout 1905, the autocracy would have found itself in an even more precarious condition than it did.

The first major disorders in the countryside were those in Dmitriev in mid-February 1905, and they spread quickly to the neighboring provinces of Chernigov and Orel. Although there is no evidence of an overall plan to the peasant actions, on the local level they were often well organized. Straw was burned as a signal to gather for an attack. In some localities "initiative groups" of peasants, after receiving the signal, moved from one village to another to incite people to action. Larger groups of peasants, numbering between 600 and 700, would then make for an estate, fire a few shots, break the locks on the granaries, load the grain on carts, and drive away. Frequently, peasants also divided the livestock and poultry among themselves and destroyed the offices where the records of their debts and obligations were stored. In about one-sixth of the incidents the peasants pillaged the estates; and in about the same proportion did they resort to arson. Rarely did they seize privately owned land or harm the landlords physically. Indeed, it was not uncommon for the peasants to tell landlords in advance exactly when they intended to appear; if the masters were still on the premises, they were permitted to witness the proceedings.

Apparently, peasants were reluctant to defy authority in a way that would imply a revolutionary challenge to the government. On the contrary, they assumed that the Tsar had authorized the actions against the landlords or that, at the very least, he was disposed to tolerate them. The peasants also assumed that after their actions, the owners, no longer considering their estates worthwhile, would abandon them; the peasants would then simply take over the land.[30] These notions may seem odd, but it was in keeping with the general outlook or mentality of the peasants. The legal concept of private property was alien to them; they believed that all the land belonged to the people who worked it.

One of the most persistent and widespread forms of peasant protest throughout the revolutionary period from 1905 to 1907 consisted of the illegal felling of trees and seizure of lumber. It has been estimated that 15 percent of all the unrest in the countryside involved this sort of action. It occurred wherever forests could be found and, significantly, was engaged in by quite a few well-to-do peasants. The woodlands mostly belonged either to the government or to landlords, who in recent years had begun to exploit the trees for industrial purposes. Once that happened, peasants were no longer permitted to roam the forests for firewood, as they had done in earlier years; and the well-to-do peasants could no longer sell the wood on the market.[31] The unrest in the countryside was also marked by strikes by agricultural workers, seizures of meadows and pastures by the peasants, and conflicts over rent between tenants and landlords.[32]

By the early summer of 1905, peasant disorders of one form or another had broken out in 62 districts, or 14 percent of European Russia. In some western provinces more than half the districts were affected.[33] It is not known precisely what proportion of the peasant population participated in the unrest: in most instances, between 10 and 30 percent joined in the actions, and sometimes as many as 50 percent did so.[34] Generally, peasants of all socioeconomic levels took part; the notion that the poorest peasants or agricultural laborers were invariably in the forefront of the agrarian movement is not borne out by the evidence.[35] In fact, these groups were sometimes the most restrained. A correspondent from Podolia gave the following report: "The leaders of the movement were the most prosperous peasants (none are rich); the most timid were the landless, because they cannot exist without their daily earnings, and they were soon compelled to bring the strike to an end, to avoid starvation."[36] It would seem that only two generalizations can safely be made about the social composition of the peasant movement: first, the "middling peasants" most frequently played an "active role" in the disturbances; second, the more successful peasants were more likely to engage in pillaging, whereas the "middling, poor, and landless peasants with the occasional exception of the most destitute" tended to participate in rent strikes and boycotts.[37]

A complex set of factors accounts for the outbreak of unrest in the countryside early in 1905 and its recurrence throughout the year. A basic reason, quite obviously, was the peasants' economic distress: the inadequacies of their landholdings; the lack of access to meadows, pastures, and forests; the high cost of leasing land; and the low wages of agricultural laborers. No doubt, peasants were deeply troubled by reports of the government's bungling of the war—all the more so since they suffered severe hardships from large-scale mobilization of their young men, many of whom were killed or maimed in the Far East. The news of Bloody Sunday and of the unrest in the cities also heightened the peasants' sense of despair. Then, in the summer of 1905, the harvests were poor, especially in the central black-earth regions, causing serious food shortages. Admittedly, these factors are so general that they do not amount to a very satisfactory explanation for the outbreak of unrest in 1905. But it is always difficult to account for the transformation of discontent into activism and violence. Moreover, since the movement was essentially a spontaneous one, unaffected in its initial stages by any revolutionary party or the intelligentsia, documentary evidence on motives is bound to be skimpy.[38]

Although violence was the most dramatic expression of peasant unrest, in the long run the petition campaign in the countryside, which developed in response to the Ukase of February 18, was probably more important, for it reflected the politicization of the peasantry. The bureaucracy did its utmost to prevent the ukase from being disseminated in the villages; where that failed, it tried to prevent the peasants from formulating petitions. But by the spring and early summer, the contents of the ukase had become fairly widely known in the countryside, in large measure because of the activities of the liberal movement and the liberal zemstvos. In the province of Kherson, for example, the zemstvo distributed 100,000 copies in April. Similar zemstvo initiatives took place in the provinces of Saratov and Orel, and it is reasonable to assume that zemstvos published the document in other parts of the Empire. Within a few months, some 100 peasant petitions were sent to St. Petersburg—and this despite initial coolness toward the campaign on the part of the Socialist Revolutionaries, who feared that the villagers would be diverted from the more militant struggle against the landlords and the authorities.[39]

Leaders of communes played a decisive role in organizing the petition campaign. In addition, peasants discussed their grievances at secret meetings in the forests attended by political activists unaffiliated with any commune. But the final drafts clearly represented the thinking and wishes of the peasants themselves, who voiced their concerns without hesitation and voted on the documents paragraph by paragraph. It is worth quoting at length the petition sent to the government by the villagers of Tashino, Kherson province, in mid-May 1905, because it typifies the messages emanating from the countryside:

Our needs are great, Your Majesty! For many centuries we peasants have endured all the adversities, all the blunders of the state: our ancestors spilled their blood for the expansion of Russia; for two and a half centuries we endured servitude and thereby made it possible for the privileged classes to live in clover; we alone carried the burden of harsh military service; for many centuries we have had to pay an unbearable amount in taxes and dues. For our unfailing centuries-old service to the state we received a wretched allotment of land with high redemption dues, [and] we were deprived of all rights; for centuries we stagnated in ignorance, and we remain in that condition today.

The petition then lists the following measures the peasants considered necessary to extricate them from their squalid circumstances: the convocation of a democratically elected constituent assembly; the granting of civil liberties; the transfer of all state and landlords' land to the peasants; the extension of local self-government; and the liberation from prison of all political dissenters. The petition ends with a plea to the Tsar: "Help us, Your Majesty! Maintain our faith in Your desire to aid us."[40]

In making these demands, the peasants not only expressed the age-old desire for land and freedom but also made common cause with the liberal movement, which was pursuing a vast campaign of agitation in the spring of 1905. To be sure, the petition of the villagers of Tashino, like those formulated in other parts of the Empire, was suffused with expressions of loyalty to the Tsar, but its most striking feature was its support for the liberal program. Never before had the peasantry articulated the same political demands as activists from other social groups. Moreover, in linking their expressions of loyalty to the Tsar with demands for extensive economic, social, and political changes, the peasants suggested that their continued allegiance was conditional: the Tsar would retain it only if he embarked on a program of far-reaching reform. Less than a year later, in 1906, the peasantry voted overwhelmingly for deputies to the

State Duma who openly opposed the autocratic regime, a clear indication of how profoundly the attitudes of the rural population had changed. "Indeed," one historian has concluded, "the picture that emerges from ... [the] petitions appears to be that of a peasant world that was revolutionary in spite of itself."[41]

The militancy of the peasants—in particular the violence—caught the government and landlords by surprise. Initially, in February and March, landlords in many of the affected regions panicked and fled to nearby towns, where they sought military help to crush the unrest. It took the authorities a while to react to the disturbances, but once they recovered from the shock, they applied force ruthlessly. Police and soldiers would swoop down on villages to search for stolen goods, and people found with such goods were flogged without mercy. In one village in Chernigov province, a group of peasants were forced to kneel in the snow for several hours, after which they were flogged. Half-dead, the peasants had to be carried away; some were so shaken by the ordeal that they tried to commit suicide.

In an attempt to intimidate the organizers of the disturbances, policemen and soldiers burned the homes of those peasants they believed to be at the head of the protest movement. "The impression was enormous," one officer wrote of this tactic, "but salutary."[42] In the southwestern provinces, Saratov province on the Volga, and Lublin province in eastern Poland, military courts were set up to hand down quick and severe sentences, not only on peasants who had engaged in illegal actions but on anyone who had submitted demands to landlords accompanied by threats of violence.[43]

On April 10, the government issued a ukase establishing temporary commissions in areas of unrest to identify the perpetrators and to determine the extent of the landlords' losses. Local officials and representatives of the gentry and the zemstvos were to serve on the commissions, but since the zemstvos refused to take part, not much was accomplished. Indeed, none of the police measures succeeded in pacifying the countryside, and during the summer landlords in some areas took matters into their own hands by forming armed detachments. In Saratov, for example, they organized the "Russian Union of Landowners," initially a secret society committed to "fighting the revolution." In September the Russian Union established branches in Moscow and St. Petersburg and began publicly to agitate for the vigorous suppression of the peasant movement.[44]

By this time, some sectors of the peasantry had entered the arena of national politics—an ominous development for the authorities, because it called into question the widely held notion that the countryside still abjured politics. Once again, as in the case of the soviets, a high Tsarist official unwittingly took an initiative that opened the way for the establishment of a mass organization hostile to the government. In the spring, the Governor of Moscow City urged some peasant communes to issue a statement in support of the war. A number of peasants responded to the governor's appeal by holding a congress in May in Moscow, but the gathering showed no interest in the governor's patriotic project. Instead, under the influence of reports about the formation of unions by the intelligentsia, the peasants' congress announced plans for the creation of an All-Russian Peasants' Union, which was to address economic conditions in the countryside and general political questions. The congress called for the election in each guberniia, uezd, and volost of representatives to a meeting that would set up the new organization.

On July 31 and August 1, the "Constitutional Assembly of the All-Russian Peasants' Union" met secretly near Moscow, first in a zemstvo hospital and then in a barn. Considering the peasantry's lack of organizational experience, attendance at the assembly was remarkable: over 100 delegates from 22 guberniias. Since so many provinces—especially those in the western regions of European Russia—sent no delegates, and since about 25 additional participants represented the Social Democratic and Socialist Revolutionary party organizations, it is difficult to say definitively whether the assembly was the authentic voice of the Russian countryside. But there can be little doubt that the resolutions reflected the political drift of a significant portion of the peasantry.

The assembly called for the abolition of private property in land, the confiscation without compensation of all lands owned by the Church, the Imperial Family, and the Tsar, the confiscation (partly with and partly without compensation) of privately held lands, and the convocation of a democratically elected constituent assembly. The assembly was ambivalent about the means to be used to attain these goals: it declared itself in favor of both conspiratorial methods and the orderly political processes of a constituent assembly. But it rejected a Bolshevik resolution that advocated a democratic republic, a reflection of the fact that sentiment for the monarchy in the countryside was still strong. Finally, the assembly elected a "Bureau of Assistance," which was to serve as the Union's executive committee. To emphasize the peasant character of the organization, the assembly voted not to permit members of any political party to serve on the Bureau.[45] That action, however, did not affect the real significance of the meeting, which was that the villagers had now turned to politics on a national scale.

· · · · ·

Ultimately, the fate of the autocracy during 1905 depended on the loyalty of the country's military forces. If they had refused in large numbers to obey orders, if they had gone over to the side of the striking workers, rebellious peasants, or minority groups in the borderlands, the autocratic regime would not have survived. It is true that General A. F. Rediger, the Minister of War, resented the use of the army to suppress civilian disturbances and frequently tried to resist requests for troops. Rediger argued, and other officers agreed, that the army's deflection to repressive services not only hindered military training but also lowered the army's prestige among the people.[46] Still, as a Soviet scholar ruefully conceded, "during the Revolution of 1905 Tsarism . . . succeeded in maintaining the army on its side—and this was one of the reasons for the defeat of the first Russian Revolution."[47]

An American historian, John Bushnell, recently challenged that interpretation. In a perceptive and interesting study, Bushnell argues that the army was not as "reliable [an] instrument of repression" as historians have assumed, because it was hobbled by a "social revolution within the armed forces."[48] Bushnell offers a spirited and thoughtful defense of his thesis, but, as he acknowledges, the most serious military mutinies took place late in 1905 (shortly after the general strike) and in the midsummer of 1906, and thus did not coincide with the greatest outbursts of urban revolutionary activity. More important, as Bushnell himself points out, the "revolution" in the military was largely a self-contained affair. Soldiers and sailors rebelled against the squalid conditions in the services, not against the Tsarist regime as such. Rarely did soldiers hand over arms to civilians: they did so in only 6 of the 211 disturbances during the last three months of 1905.[49] Although the government suffered some anxious moments, whenever it needed troops to quell unrest, it found enough to carry out the assigned task efficiently and ruthlessly.

In view of the wretched conditions of the rank and file in both the army and the navy, the relative quiescence of Russia's military forces during the first ten months of 1905 may appear, at first glance, to be somewhat puzzling. Privates earned 22.5 kopeks a month, and since they had to buy their own soap, spoons, boot brushes and polish, and blankets and bed linen, they were bound to be in dire financial straits. It has been estimated that 196.5 kopeks a month was the minimum needed to survive at a reasonable level. Over half the soldiers received some financial help from their families, but in most cases it did not cover all their expenses. It was not unusual for soldiers to sell part of their daily ration of bread (three pounds) to eke out an additional 30 kopeks a month. Nor was it unusual for them to be hired out by their officers for civilian work. The soldiers resented being treated as forced labor, and they resented even more the fact that part of their wages was retained by the officers for themselves. In addition, officers treated the ordinary soldiers with disdain and cruelty. They addressed them in the familiar "thou" and frequently beat them for minor infractions of the rules.

Even when not on duty, soldiers were treated as third-class citizens. They could not smoke in public places or ride in first- or second-class railway cars; and they could not enter clubs, bars, or restaurants. In many garrison towns, signs were posted prohibiting "soldiers and dogs" from walking along major streets or in public gardens. Soldiers were specifically forbidden to attend any meetings to discuss their grievances.[50]

There are several reasons why soldiers endured these conditions passively. The vast majority of them—about 90 percent—came from the countryside, where they had acquired a fatalistic attitude toward their position of social inferiority. About one-third of those drafted into service were completely illiterate, and many of the others could read little more than street signs. They served reluctantly, and their principal concerns were to make ends meet somehow for four years and to survive the ordeal. The severe and cruel discipline to which soldiers were subjected also militated against displays of defiance. In 1903, for example, only 1.5 percent of all ordinary soldiers were found guilty in military courts of having broken discipline. By the same token, the docility of the peasant soldier should not be overdrawn. Just as the peasants in the villages in periods of special stress were moved to rebel against their oppressors, so the soldiers in the Tsarist army could also rise up against their superiors. But throughout most of 1905 that did not happen on so large a scale as to endanger the Tsarist regime.[51]

Yet the high command and government did show some anxiety about the loyalty of the rank and file in the armed forces well before the rash of mutinies late that year. On July 22, for example, Lieutenant-General O. A. Bertel reported from Orel that he was concerned about the mood of the reserves recently called into service. The soldiers were calm, he noted, but lacked "special enthusiasm" for the war. He attributed this attitude in part to the resentment of the economic hardship inflicted on farming families by the loss of their young men to the army during the busiest agricultural season. In addition, the general was troubled by an "unfavorable element" among his troops, workers from Moscow who had links with revolutionary propagandists. These soldiers were suspected of concealing large stores of political proclamations. Some reservists had been arrested and one propagandist had been detained for inciting the men to disobey their officers. Three days later, General Bertel reported the presence of an "increasing number of unreliable people" among the lower ranks of his troops. He suspected them of belonging to a secret society that was waging propaganda about the "defects of the existing order and the pointlessness of the war." Also, soldiers had been observed attending meetings at a site near the camp. The general indicated that he intended to arrest the agitators.[52]

More serious signs of unrest appeared in the navy. Because the operation of modern warships required skilled personnel, the navy recruited a fairly large proportion (29 percent) of its men from the cities, the main centers of radical agitation. Fewer than a quarter of drafted sailors were illiterate, and peasants tended to receive at least a rudimentary education during their first months of service because otherwise they could not have performed their tasks. By mid-1904, disaffection had become apparent among the sailors of the Black Sea Fleet; they had not participated in the war and therefore had ample time for meetings and discussions of grievances. Late that year, some sailors in Sevastopol formed a revolutionary organization that acquired a degree of influence in the radical political movement in Southern Russia. After Bloody Sunday, these sailors talked of staging a mutiny throughout the fleet, which they hoped would ignite revolutionary action in that part of Russia and spread throughout the Empire. The Social Democrats in Southern Russia, however, were lukewarm toward the plan because they believed that the initiative for an armed struggle should come from civilians. In the end, nothing came of the plan.[53]

On June 14, 1905, an incident on the battleship *Potemkin*, patrolling in the Black Sea to test its guns, triggered a mutiny that resulted in carnage in Odessa more severe than that of Bloody Sunday. Commissioned only in 1903, the *Potemkin* was one of the most powerful ships in the Russian navy. But it was also one of the more volatile ships, since its crew of 800 men contained a fair sprinkling of active revolutionaries—perhaps as many as 50 belonged to one or another radical movement. Without any immediate plans to stage a mutiny, the sailors on the *Potemkin* were provoked to take dramatic action by the mindless conduct of several senior officers. Early on the 14th, the ship's cooks declared some meat that was being prepared for the evening meal to be rotten. However, the ship's doctor announced, after hastily inspecting the meat, that "those are not worms but flies' eggs; they'll wash off with vinegar. The meat is fit to eat."[54] The men thought otherwise, and in the evening a delegation of sailors complained to the captain and his executive officer (a Commander Giliarovskii), apparently "in crude words," that their *borshch* contained worms. In a fit of rage, Giliarovskii shot and killed the sailors' spokesman, G. M. Vakulenchuk, a 28-year-old seaman. At this—amid shouts of "Grab the rifles and cartridges," "Hurrah," and "Long live freedom"—several of Vakulenchuk's companions fell upon the commander, threw him overboard, and, as one of the assailants put it, "shot him, out of pity, since he was floundering in the water."[55]

Other members of the crew quickly joined the fray, killing four or five officers (among them the captain and the doctor) and locking the rest in a cabin. After hoisting the red flag, the mutineers summoned to their ship the commander of an accompanying torpedo boat; the hapless commander was immediately arrested and his ship seized by mutineers. Next, the men on the *Potemkin* elected a "people's committee" to take charge of their ship; the chairman, A. N. Matiushenko, was a dynamic person who quickly became the guiding spirit of the mutiny. Born into a working-class family in the Ukraine, the 26-year-old Matiushenko was a noncommissioned officer who had been a Social Democrat since 1903. At the time of the altercation over the rotten *borshch*, he had taken the initiative in shooting the commander. Matiushenko was determined to provoke mutinies in other ships, but he also wanted to attract mass support in Odessa, a major seaport within easy reach and then seething with discord. The *Potemkin* set a course for Odessa and arrived there during the night of June 14/15.

For about two weeks, strikes and demonstrations had been almost daily events in Odessa. There had also been several bloody clashes between workers and Cossacks. Unable to cope with the growing unrest, local authorities increasingly resorted to brute force, but this tactic backfired: the ranks of the strikers swelled, and the workers themselves turned more and more to violence. Their favorite ploy was to ambush individual policemen and beat them to death. On June 14, the city's public prosecutor, N. M. Levchenko, reported to his superior that over the preceding two days the striking workers had become transformed into an unruly mob. One group of strikers had destroyed the city's power station; another had fired at soldiers and policemen; and a third had stopped the movement of trains in the port. Moreover, the city was now in the throes of a general strike: most shops were closed and tram traffic had come to a standstill. A mass uprising appeared to be imminent.[56]

The strikers and demonstrators in Odessa were astonished by the appearance of the *Potemkin* in the harbor and deeply moved by the deposit at about 6 A.M. on June 15 of Vakulenchuk's body on a bier, surrounded by an honor guard, near a set of marble steps leading from the harbor up to the city proper. A message was pinned on the chest of the dead sailor: "This is the body of Vakulenchuk, killed by the commander for having told the truth. Retribution has been meted out to the commander." A harbor guard who approached the body was shot by the sailors. Within four hours, by 10 A.M., some 5,000 Odessans had gathered around the body, placed flowers near the bier, and offered food to the mutineers. When a group of Cossacks and policemen approached, a red flag was raised as a signal for sailors on the *Potemkin* to fire. The Cossacks and policemen immediately retreated, and a spokesman for the sailors warned the commandant of the harbor that any attempt to use violence to disperse the crowd would be met by the battleship's firing on the city. The sailors also invited representatives of local radical groups on board to discuss concerted action against the authorities.[57]

The size of the crowd in the area where the body rested grew steadily throughout the day (June 15); though clearly agitated, the people at first did little more than listen to revolutionary speeches and revolutionary songs. Late in the afternoon, however, at about 5 P.M., people turned violent, for reasons that are not clear. There is evidence to suggest that many in the crowd had consumed large quantities of vodka and that thieves and vagabonds played an important role in initiating the unrest. Be that as it may, once the tumult began, people looted warehouses at will, carrying away bolts of silk, champagne, tea, clothing, anything they could find. They also began to set fires, and soon the entire harborfront was ablaze. It was, one eyewitness declared, an "unforgettable spectacle, grandiose in its horror."[58]

The Assistant Minister of Internal Affairs, Trepov, had already taken steps to enable local authorities to deal firmly with the mutineers and the strikers in Odessa. Alarmed at the rumors that were circulating about the likely spread of mutiny to various ships, Trepov early on June 15 asked Tsar Nicholas to place the city under martial law. Nicholas promptly agreed to the request and informed Trepov that he had sent a telegram to the Governor-General of Odessa, I. S. Kakhanov, directing him to "take the most decisive measures to suppress the uprising."[59]

At about 9:30 P.M., after the fires had been blazing for over two hours, the army arrived in force and began to occupy strategic positions; shortly after midnight the troops began shooting indiscriminately into the crowd, which was hemmed in from all sides. Unable to escape, many people jumped into the sea, where they drowned, and many others perished in the flames. The shooting by the soldiers lasted several hours, and at first light the harbor was seen to be covered with bodies. (Apparently fearful about their own safety, the sailors on the *Potemkin* failed to respond to the government attack until the following evening, when they unleashed some 30 volleys from their guns—some of them blanks.) According to credible accounts, 2,000 people were killed and 3,000 seriously wounded. The damage to property was estimated at ten to fifteen million rubles.[60] "We have entered a period of anarchy," the French Consul in the city reported to his superiors. "Terror reigns in Odessa. . . . The people give vent to the most violent passions, and the worst excesses have been committed."[61]

Dazed by the massacre, and demoralized and intimidated by the sight of large numbers of soldiers (about 20,000 in all), the workers of Odessa became quiescent and many people tried to flee the city. By June 16 calm had returned to Odessa. The authorities permitted a solemn burial for Vakulenchuk on the 16th, but refused to grant the mutineers' demand for amnesty. Within four days, by June 20, factories had begun to operate again and most shops were open.

It had become clear even earlier that the men on the *Potemkin* had completely miscalculated not only the strength of the revolutionaries in Odessa but also the extent of practical support they would receive from sailors on other ships. Although Menshevik revolutionary groups were active on six capital ships of the Black Sea Fleet, no plans for a general uprising had been formulated. The six socialist organizations in Odessa were actually surprised by the appearance of the *Potemkin* and were at a loss about how to exploit the mutiny.[62] In a last act of desperation, on June 18 the *Potemkin* set out to sea, hoping that its renewed defiance of the authorities would spark mutinies on other ships. In fact, a mutiny of sorts had broken out on June 17 on the battleship *George the Conqueror,* and a few other ships experienced some disorders. But these proved to be halfhearted affairs; by June 19, loyal officers on the *George the Conqueror* and elsewhere had regained control.

Totally isolated, the *Potemkin* sailed toward the Rumanian port of Constanza in the hope of obtaining supplies and fresh water, which the crew badly needed. The Rumanian authorities turned down the mutineers' request, but offered them instead safe refuge in return for surrendering the ship. This was unacceptable to the mutineers, who decided on a bold move: they sailed into Feodosiia, a Black Sea port in the southeastern Crimea, and landed a small party of men to seize supplies, notably coal. But the men quickly came under fire from the local garrison and had to retreat without completing their mission. By June 25, the men on the *Potemkin* realized the hopelessness of their situation and, having returned to Constanza, agreed to the conditions of surrender previously offered by the Rumanian government. The Rumanians handed the *Potemkin* over to Russian naval officers. In serious disrepair because of neglect and vandalism during the 11-day exploit, the battleship had to be towed to the naval base at Sevastopol.

By itself, the mutiny on the *Potemkin* did not pose a threat to the regime, but it was nonetheless an embarrassment to the government and a source of concern about the depth of disaffection in the armed forces. Sailors on one of the most prized ships of the fleet had been influenced by revolutionary propaganda, and the government could not but wonder whether this was an isolated incident or a harbinger of things to come.

The entire affair, according to an analysis written by the British Ambassador at the time,

> made a very deep impression on public opinion & . . . brought home to many the very serious state of affairs prevailing in this country to which they have hitherto wilfully closed their eyes. Faith in the loyalty of the army & navy has hitherto been the corner-stone of the confidence felt that the prevalent disorders could not lead to really serious disorders. This confidence has now been rudely shaken & with that habit of rushing to extremes that is typical of the Russian character there are many who in their alarm think that the country is within a measurable distance of revolution.[63]

As a precautionary measure, the government placed some 5,000 men of the Black Sea Fleet on leave and for a time completely deactivated the fleet. The revolutionary left, however, took heart. For a few weeks, Bolsheviks, Mensheviks, and the Jewish Bund devoted an increasing amount of attention to agitation among soldiers and sailors.[64] To be sure, their influence never became a decisive factor in instigating mutinies. Nevertheless, the events surrounding the mutiny on the *Potemkin* contributed to a growing perception that the regime was losing its grip on the country.

Chapter Seven

. . . .

The Failure of Reform

DURING THE SUMMER OF 1905, civil order declined dramatically, but the conflict between the autocracy and the opposition passed through a phase characterized by contradictory developments. On the one hand, the campaign by liberals for political change continued to attract widespread support among various sectors of the population. On the other hand, industrial strikes subsided and relatively few units of the armed forces showed signs of active support for the opposition. Agrarian disturbances did increase early in the summer, but they abated considerably in August and September. In the midst of these divergent trends, the government took measures to shore up its position: it prepared a major reform project and conducted successful negotiations with Japan to end the war. An informed observer might well have concluded that the contending forces had reached a stalemate. But toward the end of the summer, the student movement unexpectedly came to life again, which injected new momentum into the revolution and set the stage for the opposition's most striking offensive against the old order.

After the fiasco of the audience with the Tsar on June 6, liberals not only intensified their campaign for reform but also defined with greater precision than ever before the kind of political order they envisioned for Russia. The liberals' renewed vigor was in large measure a response to signs that articulate spokesmen of society favored continued pressure on the autocracy. At the first national Congress of City Council Representatives on June 16, attended by 126 delegates from 87 towns, the constitutionalists were in the ascendancy. The congress endorsed the four-tail suffrage, which signified a marked shift to the left of this sector of public opinion. The delegates also advocated a two-chamber legislature, although they did not support the convocation of a constituent assembly.

Another sign of their leftward drift was that they condemned police brutality while refusing to criticize revolutionary terror. Finally, the delegates accepted an invitation from the organizing bureau of the zemstvo movement to attend a congress on July 6 in Moscow. It was to be the first time that representatives from the two systems of local self-government joined forces, and as such the meeting marked a new stage in the campaign for a constitutional order.[1]

Once again the authorities adopted heavy-handed methods to prevent a meeting of the opposition, and once again their ineptitude exposed them to ridicule. The government ordered the Governor-General of Moscow, A. A. Kozlov, to deny the organizing bureau's request for a permit to hold the congress, and it applied pressure on delegates from the capital and other cities not to attend. Nevertheless, about 200 people showed up. The Governor-General now faced two options, either one of which might have enhanced his stature: to disperse the delegates by force or to look the other way. But he chose a third course, which backfired. He sent the police to the meeting place, the home of Prince P. D. Dolgorukov, to ask the delegates to disperse. When they refused, a police officer decided to restrict himself to reporting on the affair. He requested a list of the participants, at which point someone shouted out: "Mark down all Russia." It was, as the Austrian Ambassador noted, a "thoroughly laughable intervention by the state authority." The government, many liberals suspected, was nervous, fearful that the congress would transform itself into a constituent assembly.[2]

The congress did not take so radical a step, but it did formally approve the new tactic that left liberals had proposed late in the spring—agitation from below instead of appeals to the autocrat for reform.[3] The delegates forced I. I. Petrunkevich and his sympathizers to tone down their original resolution, which had urged people "to act in a revolutionary manner," since that wording could be interpreted as an incitement to violence. But the final document, a direct appeal to the people, was still decidedly militant in tone and substance: after listing the usual demands of the constitutionalists, it called on the masses "to assemble quietly and openly" to discuss their "needs" and "wishes." It ended with the assurance that such a tactic would be successful without causing any bloodshed, for the government would be incapable of resisting the "collective voice" of the people.[4] Virtually all the delegates signed the appeal, fully conscious of the fact that they had taken "the first step along a new road." The congress marked "the beginning of political work . . . [by] political parties anxiously looking for contact with the masses."[5]

The Shipovites did not attend the congress. They continued to favor a special political path for Russia, that is, avoidance of a constitution on the Western European model. The split between the Shipovites and the rest of the liberal movement had become so pronounced that collaboration between them no longer seemed possible. A few weeks before the congress, Miliukov in effect invited a formal division of the movement when he addressed the following words to the zemstvo minority: "It is better that you go your solitary Byzantine way and leave us to our Western European straightforwardness."[6]

The July Congress of Zemstvo and City Council Representatives also published a draft of a "Fundamental Law of the Russian Empire" prepared by S. A. Muromtsev, N. N. Lvov, N. N. Shchepkin, and F. F. Kokoshkin. By anticipating the government, which was still working on proposals for political reform, the liberals intended to prepare public opinion for a critical stance toward any concessions on the part of the autocracy. But the action of the liberals served another purpose. In providing the most detailed statement to date of their goals in the form of a draft constitution, they made clear beyond any doubt that the differences between them and the radical opposition continued to be profound.

Actually, the draft "Fundamental Law" could not have surprised anyone who had followed the evolution of the liberal movement over the preceding few years. In its essentials it did not go beyond the demands voiced by liberals in the fall of 1904 and the spring of 1905; the eight months of extraordinary turmoil had not prompted Russian liberalism to abandon its ultimate goals. Only its tactics had changed. The draft provided for the rule of law, civil liberties, freedom of association, and the creation of a bicameral legislature, one branch of which was to be elected by "every citizen of the male sex." Although no proposal could become law without the approval of the legislature, which also was accorded "the right of controlling the finances of the state," it is noteworthy that the sovereign was to play more than a merely ceremonial role. He was granted the right to initiate legislation, though that prerogative could also be exercised by the legislature if the proposal was signed by 30 members of the lower house and fifteen of the upper. He also could refuse to approve legislation passed by the two chambers, in which case the proposal could not be reintroduced until the next session. Finally, the Tsar was to nominate the Prime Minister as well as the other members of the cabinet recommended by the Prime Minister.[7] Adoption of this constitution would certainly have entailed the end of the autocracy, though not of the monarchy.

About four weeks after the Congress of Zemstvo and City Council Representatives, the Bulygin committee at last issued its reform proposal.[8] The committee had begun its deliberations shortly after the issuance of the rescript of February 18, and in July the final draft of its proposal was discussed by a secret conference presided over by the Tsar himself and attended almost exclusively by grand dukes, ministers, and certain privy councillors and senators. Conservatives and moderates haggled over the specifics of the proposal. According to one report, the turning point came toward the end of the meeting when "[Count] Ignatieff made an unexpected & startling speech giving the result of his recent official visit to Odessa & Southern Russia & stating his opinion that unless wide reaching reforms were promptly introduced the dynasty would be in danger. . . . These words coming from an official well known for his reactionary views are said to have made a very deep impression on all those present." [9]

Even at this late date, however, the conference was divided on the question of granting a national assembly, the most sensitive issue. The Chief Procurator of the Most Holy Synod, Pobedonostsev, voted against the measure, as did Count V. B. Frederiks, the Minister of the Court, Count Lamsdorff, the Minister of Foreign Affairs, S. S. Manukhin, the Minister of Justice, and P. Kh. Schwanebach, the Minister of Agriculture. Three men, Kokovtsov, the Minister of Finance, V. G. Glazov, the Minister of Education, and General A. F. Rediger, the Minister of War, abstained. A majority of the conference participants did in fact vote for the measure, including Bulygin, most of the grand dukes, several other ministers, and General Trepov, "who appeared for the first time as a liberal." [10] Tsar Nicholas gave the impression of agreeing with the majority.

Yet it turned out that Nicholas was still not convinced that he must act with dispatch in instituting reform. He actually considered returning the project to Bulygin's committee for further study. When the Minister of Justice advised the Tsar that a quick decision was necessary, Nicholas replied that he saw no need to move hastily. The final decision would require more thorough deliberation and could easily be delayed for another year. [11] But on August 6 he was somehow prevailed upon to approve the project, which came to be known as the Bulygin Constitution. At the same time, the government announced that all further discussion of political issues, permitted on a limited basis in February, would now be prohibited.

Society was not surprised by the report on the Bulygin project. The press had printed accounts of the general drift of the Bulygin committee's discussions in May, and during the summer there were daily leaks on the deliberations of the secret conference. The eminent historian V. O. Kliuchevsky was a consultant at the conference, and every evening he sent his son to Miliukov with copies of the papers that had been distributed. After the conference ended on July 26, Miliukov also received a copy of the secret protocols. Miliukov, in turn, handed the materials over to *Pravo*, which published them abroad.[12] Thus the leaders of the liberal movement knew ahead of time that what had been billed as the most important reform measure to date would fall far short of their hopes.

Once again, the government had misread the mood of the opposition. A few months earlier, the Bulygin Constitution would almost certainly have been widely hailed as a bold and imaginative concession, but now society could muster no enthusiasm for so conservative a document. It provided for a State Duma whose functions were essentially consultative. The Duma could engage in "preliminary" discussions of legislative proposals that would be transmitted to the Tsar for final action only if they were also approved by the State Council (composed of dignitaries appointed by the Tsar himself). However, the Duma was not permitted to make any proposals to alter the structure of the state apparatus. On the other hand, bills introduced by the government and rejected by the Duma were not necessarily lost; the government could enact laws with the approval of the State Council alone.

The members of the State Duma were to be elected for five years, but the Tsar could dissolve the Duma at his pleasure and hold new elections. Moreover, the suffrage was to be based on high property qualifications and the elections were to be indirect, in two, three, or four stages. Much of non-European Russia was deprived of the vote altogether. Finally, not all the details of the new constitution had been worked out. Count D. M. Solskii was appointed to chair a commission to formulate regulations governing the elections.[13]

In the weeks following the Tsar's approval of the Bulygin Constitution on August 6, the newspapers subjected the provisions on the suffrage, which were hopelessly complex, to careful scrutiny and arrived at some astonishing conclusions. In St. Petersburg, for example, out of a population of approximately 1,400,000, only 7,130 would be able to vote for electors in the first stage of the election; in Moscow, 12,000 out of 1,100,000; in Tsaritsyn, 542 out of 85,000; in Kremenchug, 729 out of 75,000; in Kostroma, 600 out of 55,000; in Iaroslavl, 629 out of 95,000; in Riga, 3,900 out of 340,000; and in Kazan, about 1,000 out of 160,000.[14] Industrial workers were almost completely disenfranchised. In the final stage of the elections, 7,591 electors would select the 412 representatives to the State Duma.[15]

In addition, the electoral law was so cumbersome that absurd results were quite possible. Here is what might have taken place in Volhynia guberniia had the Bulygin project been implemented. The voters of the province were entitled to choose 195 electors who would meet in Zhitomir to select thirteen Duma representatives. First, 69 peasant electors would select one representative, and then all 195 would vote as a group for the remaining twelve seats. But it was very likely that the 69 peasants would vote for their own slate, the 86 landlords for theirs, and the 40 urban dwellers for theirs. Under the circumstances, no one would receive a majority on either the first or the second ballot. The regulations stated that on the third day of voting only a plurality was required for election. Consequently, "all the representatives, with the exception of the one peasant, . . . [would] be landlords." The townspeople in Volhynia guberniia would not have any representatives at all in the Duma.[16]

Writing some thirty years after the publication of the Bulygin project, Petrunkevich contended that "The sixth of August, the day on which this 'constitution' was published, was also the day of its demise. Nowhere did it meet with the slightest approval, and it was condemned in advance to a place in the archives of useless works of the Russian bureaucracy."[17] This was something of an exaggeration. The authorities, who attached great significance to the concessions, did evoke a favorable reaction from several sectors of the population, though some of the enthusiasm was clearly mobilized from above. At the direction of the Governor of Moscow City, the police suggested to all homeowners that they adorn their houses with flags, and on the evening of August 6, local officials illuminated the streets.

The next day, a public service of thanksgiving, attended by many dignitaries, was held at the Uspensky Cathedral. Similar services were conducted in all other churches and in other cities.[18] Prince P. N. Trubetskoi, the Marshal of the Moscow nobility and an adherent of Shipov's Slavophile liberalism, expressed strong approval of Bulygin's proposal: the sovereign, he declared, had demonstrated great wisdom, because the concessions signified confidence in the people and the country's social forces but did not break with Russia's historical traditions. The duty of all Russians, Trubetskoi continued, was to help restore calm in the country.[19]

Most of these reactions were to be expected. The critical question was, how would the center and left of the liberal movement respond? All of them expressed strong reservations about the project, though there were important differences among them. Struve dismissed the concession as a "cunning fabrication" that would lead not to domestic calm but to heightened conflict. Nonetheless, he did not seem to favor a boycott of the elections. "Russia has extorted a new instrument from Nicholas II," Struve wrote, "for the struggle against autocracy and should use it fully to achieve the final goal."[20] Other liberals emphasized the paltriness of the reform. *Russkie vedomosti* considered it to be "only a first step" in the restructuring of the country's political institutions, which did not satisfy the wishes of the progressive elements in Russian society.[21] The editors of *Vestnik Evropy* agreed with this overall assessment but nevertheless hoped that the reform would be a "first step toward the establishment of domestic peace after many years of hard struggle."[22]

In truth, the Bulygin Constitution placed the liberals in a difficult situation. On the one hand, it clearly did not meet their demands. The autocracy remained intact, and, as the liberal press emphasized, the police continued to prevent public meetings and the distribution of political literature, which made a mockery of the electoral process.[23] On the other hand, the election of a representative body would constitute a significant change for Russia. As Miliukov acknowledged, the parliament would provide a new arena for open political struggle, despite all its imperfections. He even went so far as to declare that "the bureaucratic system is no more." The reform of August 6, he continued, "was not simply a piece of paper. There can be no turning back from it. It is only possible to go forward, and only the public acknowledgment of all its consequences . . . can assure this act stability and durability."[24] Moreover, many liberals realized that a boycott of the election would not prevent it from being held but would virtually guarantee that reactionaries would control the Duma. The advocates of a boycott countered that the few moderates among the gentry who might win election to the Duma would be content to have achieved a measure of political influence and would cooperate with the government while ignoring the aspirations of other classes. Clearly, no tactic was without risk.

At the Second Congress of Zemstvo and City Council Representatives, held in Moscow from September 12 to 15, the supporters of participation in the elections for the Bulygin Duma gained the upper hand. But they made clear that their decision was tactical only, not an abandonment of their demand for a democratically elected parliament with real powers. On several other issues, however, the congress moved to the left. After a bitter debate, which anticipated a subsequent split within liberalism, the congress came out in favor of autonomy for Poland and for other borderlands after a "proper national representative body" was established. Also, for the first time organized liberalism formally supported specific economic and social reforms. The congress proposed the "alienation of state, appanage, and royal lands, and, in case of need, private lands with fair compensation to the landowner." In addition, it called for labor legislation reducing the length of the workday and granting the right to form unions and to strike. Finally, it recommended a revision in the system of taxation to bring about a fairer distribution of the tax burden.[25]

Over a three-month period Russian liberalism had undergone noticeable changes. In June, its leaders still hoped that personal appeals to the Tsar might persuade him to introduce major reforms; by July, they increasingly relied on mass actions from below to prod the authorities into concessions; in September, they sought to cement their ties with the people by championing economic demands put forward by industrial workers and peasants. Reacting to the intransigence of the Tsar and the politicization of the masses, liberalism had ceased to be simply a molder of the public mood. It had also become a follower of that mood.

· · · · ·

The government did not bank only on the creation of a duma to pacify the country in the summer of 1905. It also ended the war with Japan. Until late in March of that year, Tsar Nicholas had refused even to consider the possibility of peace, in large measure because he had "little conception of the real situation at the front." Several developments caused him to change his mind. The Russian government failed to secure a loan in Paris, whereas the Japanese had succeeded in floating loans in Berlin. Having lost confidence in Russia's military capabilities, the German Emperor actually intimated to the Tsar's officials "that the time had come to make peace."[26] And, finally, after the ignominious defeat of the Russian navy in the Straits of Tsushima on May 14, public support for the war virtually evaporated. St. Petersburg, according to one terse account, "for the first time since war commenced [was] really moved by fleet's defeat. Indignation and wrath are poured out freely upon bureaucracy, which alone is held responsible for all misfortunes of war. Press calls for Russian people themselves to say what should be done. Rather significant no universal cry for peace, but for immediate assembly of representation. Believe great mass of Russians realize war is futile."[27] A similar report emanated from Warsaw: "The events of the war interest the public here only insofar as they might have an impact on the political situation in the country, and this view, publicly proclaimed by the Poles, appears to be shared by a great many Russians who wish for peace and also want reform."[28]

Some time in late May or early June, Tsar Nicholas, finally convinced that victory was beyond reach, convoked a council of war to consider the question of "war or peace." Of the nine participants, seven opposed continuing the war.[29] At about the same time, President Theodore Roosevelt offered to act as an intermediary between Russia and Japan in arranging for peace; Nicholas consented on June 7 on the understanding that "it is to be kept absolutely secret" until the Japanese also agreed to enter the discussions. Nicholas was concerned throughout not to appear as the leader of a vanquished power begging for peace.[30] The Japanese, militarily and economically exhausted, quickly accepted President Roosevelt's proposal that peace negotiations be conducted in Portsmouth, New Hampshire.

Witte, Russia's negotiator in Portsmouth, had long favored an end to the war and was prepared to make extensive concessions to the Japanese, including the surrender of Sakhalin Island and the payment of a "disguised indemnity." But in a rare display of tenacity and independence, Nicholas formulated his own terms for peace, on which he did not waver. He now wanted peace, but under no circumstances would he agree to conditions that he considered a blot on Russia's honor. In a conversation with the U.S. Ambassador on August 23, he "remained absolutely firm in his decision not to pay to Japan any kind of war indemnity." Nicholas emphasized that "Russia [was] not in [the] position of France in 1870."

In the end, the Japanese, also eager to conclude the hostilities, backed down on most issues. Under the Treaty of Portsmouth signed on August 29, Japan obtained control over the Liaotung Peninsula, including Port Arthur and Dalny (Dairen), and one-half of Sakhalin, as well as preponderant influence in Korea. Russia did not have to pay an indemnity.[31]

Throughout the country, the outcome of the negotiations was greeted with satisfaction. "With a deep sense of relief," wrote one journal, "Russian society has received the happy news of the conclusion of peace on relatively moderate terms, without the payment of an indemnity and with the loss of only part of Sakhalin." [32] But even this achievement did no more than temporarily blunt some of the hostility toward the government. The protest movement had by now developed its own momentum and could not be stopped by minor reforms or triumphs that under different circumstances would have boosted the prestige and authority of the autocracy.

· · · · ·

The truth is that ever since Bloody Sunday it had become increasingly evident that the revolutionary upheaval was essentially an unpredictable and spontaneous affair. Neither the government nor the leaders of the opposition controlled the drift of events. Thus, although illegal groups of Mensheviks, Bolsheviks, and Socialist Revolutionaries operated in numerous cities, none of them planned or directed the strikes in the cities or the disorders in the countryside. There is no evidence, for example, that workers in large numbers responded favorably to a Bolshevik leaflet distributed in St. Petersburg in January 1905 containing the following political message: "Down with the Tsar! Down with Autocracy! Long live political freedom! Long live the Constituent Assembly elected by all the people on the basis of universal, direct, secret, and equal suffrage!" [33] The appeal of the Moscow Committee of the Russian Social Democratic Workers' Party (around January 20, 1905) to workers to focus on political issues also went unheeded,[34] as did Bolshevik calls in February and March for the proletariat to take up arms. Some time after Bloody Sunday, the Petersburg Committee of Bolsheviks created a "technical-combat group" to acquire and distribute arms, but not much was accomplished by this group or by the one other such unit founded in July. A Soviet historian who has carefully examined the attempt to arm the workers conceded as much when he wrote that he found it "difficult now to sum up the practical results of all the military work of the Petersburg Committee," though he did not doubt that it was significant in "workers' circles." [35]

Even four months after Bloody Sunday, on May 1—by which time radical activists had ample opportunity to acquaint themselves with the mood of the working class—the revolutionaries failed miserably in their attempts to organize mass meetings and street demonstrations. In the cities of European Russia, and especially in St. Petersburg, relatively few workers participated in the political activities. Only a few hundred people showed up at a demonstration in the capital that had been carefully planned by local Mensheviks.[36] The workers were simply not interested in the Social Democrats' political agitation.

Only in the Polish cities of Warsaw, Lodz, and Kalisz did workers heed the call of revolutionaries to join street demonstrations on May 1, some of which led to bloody clashes between workers and soldiers.[37] In large part this was probably the result of better party organization, but it may also reflect the fact that the national issue had contributed to the politicization of the masses in Poland.

Although the Social Democrats failed in their attempts to direct the mass protest movements, they (and other revolutionary groups) did gain a growing number of supporters. The available statistics on party membership are approximations and do not take into account the fact that most local cells had more sympathizers than members. Moreover, party structures were quite loose; most people had only a hazy notion of what a particular party stood for. It was not unusual for individuals to cross over from one radical group to another, since they were more interested in promoting the general cause of revolution than in any specific ideological tendency. Often, membership seems to have signified little more than occasional attendance at a political meeting. Contemporaries who discussed the size of the radicals' following apparently realized that they were dealing with a murky subject, for they used the vague term "organized workers." Still, the statistics that are available do provide a general picture of the revolutionaries' strength.

In St. Petersburg, between 1,200 and 1,300 workers belonged to the Menshevik organization and several hundred to the Bolshevik. In Riga, each faction had about 300 members. In Ivanovo-Voznesensk there were 600 Bolsheviks. The party in Iaroslavl was composed of 100 workers and 100 students. The "organized workers" numbered 200 each in Vilna, Vitebsk, and Minsk; in Dvinsk, 300; in Kiev, 500; In Kharkov, 300; and in Odessa and Ekaterinoslav, 1,000. In many other cities, too numerous to mention here, committees of "organized workers" were formed. Martov, a leader of the Mensheviks and not a disinterested observer, concluded that by the fall of 1905, "several tens of thousands of workers and several tens of thousands of students, soldiers, and peasants" belonged to illegal Social Democratic organizations.[38] David Lane, the author of a scholarly and comprehensive work on the size and social composition of Russian Social Democracy during the early years of its existence, suggests that there were 8,400 "organized Bolsheviks" and an equal number of Mensheviks in Russia in 1905.[39]

According to a reliable estimate, in the Kingdom of Poland the "labor-oriented parties" (SDKPiL, PPS, and the Jewish Bund) increased their membership from 5,000 to about 100,000 in the two years from 1904 to 1906.[40] The Bund had created a particularly impressive organization—the best in the Empire—and is said to have had a membership of roughly 30,000 in 1905 in Poland, Lithuania, and Russia.[41] As has already been noted, the Mensheviks in Georgia struck deep roots among the population and also established a strong organization. The only available estimate of party membership is for all of Transcaucasia: "several thousand workers and peasants" are said to have belonged to the Marxist movement.[42]

Party organizations devoted special attention to distributing newspapers and leaflets. Much of the material was printed in the West and shipped to Russia, sometimes in quantities ranging from 100,000 to 200,000 copies. A few statistics are instructive: during May 1905, the SD Committee in Moscow distributed 84,029 leaflets; the SD Committee in Odessa, 28,340; the Northern SD Committee, 39,500; and the Astrakhan SD Committee, 13,160. For the May 1 demonstrations, the Bund (which confined its activities to Western Russia, Poland, and Lithuania) distributed 130,000 broadsheets. The single largest number of leaflets was distributed in January by the Crimean SD Union: 232,000.[43]

The funds for the Social Democratic organizations came from a variety of sources. Members made regular contributions to local organizations: in Moscow during the first half of 1905, such contributions amounted to more than 4,200 rubles a month; in Petersburg during the last third of January 1905, slightly over 4,000 rubles were collected; and in Kiev, over 1,400 rubles were received each month during the first half of 1905. The central committee of the Bund collected 26,380 rubles over a ten-month period from October 1, 1904, to August 1, 1905.[44] In addition, Russian radicals received substantial contributions from sympathetic groups in Western Europe and the United States. "In Paris, Berlin, and other big German cities," a police memorandum indicated late in 1905, "there was hardly a day on which there was not a meeting at which the situation in

Russia was discussed; all end with collections for arms for the Russian people." In Paris, many members of the Chamber of Deputies and even some former ministers attended such meetings and hotly condemned the political regime in Russia. Also, the German Social Democratic Party is said to have given 160,000 marks to the Russian Marxists over the course of 1905. The International Socialist Bureau in Brussels sent over 80,000 francs. The Bund received contributions from organizations in England and the United States; in November and December 1905 alone, the sum was estimated at $20,000. A New Yorker known as "Richard" sent the Bund an additional 25,000 francs to buy weapons for the self-defense detachments that were being set up to protect Jewish communities against pogroms.[45]

The most difficult problem was to get weapons into the hands of revolutionaries. Several radicals had gone abroad to study how to produce bombs, and by the summer of 1905 they had set up small workshops in a few Russian cities, sometimes with the help of local scientists. But conditions and equipment were so primitive that not many bombs were actually made. Nor did the radicals fare much better in their endeavors to secure weapons from sympathetic army officers and from workers in arms factories. Only occasionally was it possible to smuggle out a few dozen rifles and revolvers.

Apparently, the revolutionaries found it easier to obtain weapons in Central and Western Europe. According to the Russian security police, various revolutionary groups (the Bolsheviks, the Mensheviks, the Bund, the Anarchists, and the Labor Zionists) were actively engaged in buying arms abroad and were using all the ingenuity at their command to smuggle them into the Empire. Russian students at foreign universities would hide revolvers, bullets, and even small bombs on their bodies when they went home on vacation. Such supplies were easily obtained at storehouses in Zurich, Bern, Liège, Hamburg, and probably other cities.[46] Manufacturers in almost all European countries readily sold weapons to anyone with the necessary cash—from a few pieces to entire crateloads. Since shipments of any size could only come in by sea, Russian police agents complained that all they could do was to bribe customs officials into naming the ships involved, which could then be tracked as they approached Russia. Such vessels generally unloaded in Finland or one of the Baltic ports, often dropping the arms at one of the "village piers" in Finland, of which there were literally hundreds. The Russian government despaired of trying to intercept the cargo. There were simply not enough policemen in the villages to patrol all the harbors.[47]

It is hard to estimate the quantities of arms that actually reached the revolutionaries, especially since the reports of the security police probably tended to exaggerate; but the evidence suggests that the amounts were not negligible. For example, in April 1905 the *Texas* arrived in Copenhagen from New York with eighteen boxes of weapons and bullets, which were then shipped to Russia. Somewhat later, the Berlin company of Paul Schwiedler sent 250 Brauning revolvers and several thousand bullets to the revolutionaries. A Danish firm by the name of Ashen at about the same time forwarded between 10,000 and 12,000 Bovling revolvers to Helsinki for transmission to Russia.[48] The revolutionaries used these arms to give some rudimentary training to their militia units (the *boevye druzhiny*), several of which participated in the Moscow uprising in December 1905.

However impressive all these activities may have been, it is still true that in the first nine months of 1905 the Social Democrats established close links with only a small proportion of the industrial proletariat. Many of the politically "mature" workers remained aloof from party organizations and often were even hostile toward them. To a large extent, the new recruits to the party who participated in its agitational work were members of the intelligentsia. The homes of the intelligentsia tended to be centrally located, which made gatherings easier to hide from the police; in working-class neighborhoods, which tended to be in outlying areas, the arrival and departure of numbers of people would have been immediately noticed. Consequently, the intelligentsia remained isolated from the mass of workers. Moreover, the professional revolutionaries devoted much of their time to conspiratorial work and too little to the immediate issues uppermost in the minds of the workers, which frequently led to conflicts between them. These conflicts became entangled in the controversies raging between Menshevik and Bolshevik activists. Splits were common, stunting the growth and consolidation of Social Democratic organizations at the local level.[49]

Although both factions were dominated by intellectuals, the Mensheviks appealed much more than their rivals to members of minority groups in the Empire. Georgians and Jews played an especially important role in the Menshevik movement. The prominence of Jews became evident from the earliest moments of the split in 1903. Out of 57 revolutionaries who attended the Second Congress of the RSDWP, 25 were Jews; fifteen of these were Mensheviks (there were only seventeen Menshevik delegates in all) and six belonged to the Bund, which after 1907 was generally allied with the Mensheviks.[50] It may well be that Menshevism owed its Western orientation—a dimension most notable a few years later and one that Bolshevism lacked—to the prominence in it of Jewish intellectuals, who traditionally maintained ties with the world beyond Russia and tended to be rooted in the more cosmopolitan centers.

Specifically, this meant that the Mensheviks took as their model for Russian Social Democracy Western socialist parties that were genuinely mass movements.

Until the fall of 1905, the leaders of the Social Democratic factions lived as émigrés in the West, where they formulated strategies and tactics in response to the turmoil at home. The events of 1905 were not unfolding as expected, which posed some knotty theoretical problems. In the 1880's, the Marxists had generally assumed that Russia would follow the European "model" of revolution, whose prime example was France in the late eighteenth century: the bourgeoisie would overthrow the old order and create a capitalist system, under which the proletariat would grow to maturity and eventually stage a second revolution for socialism. But by the 1890's, Russian Marxists realized that in some important respects developments in their country were taking a different turn. Among other things, an industrial working class was emerging *before* the bourgeois revolution. P. B. Axelrod therefore developed the notion, initially suggested by Plekhanov, that in light of the political and economic weakness of the bourgeoisie in Russia, the proletariat would play "a leading role" even in the first revolution.

The future Mensheviks and Bolsheviks interpreted this "doctrine of the hegemony of the proletariat" differently. The former contended that it was the proletariat's "historical mission" to "serve as the lever pushing all the enemies of absolutism into an organized attack against it." Axelrod, the Menshevik most concerned with the issue, argued that the proletariat should not direct or command other social classes opposed to the autocratic regime. On the contrary, the various classes must maintain independent political parties no matter how close the collaboration between them. In addition, he did not suggest that the Russian proletariat strive to seize power during the bourgeois revolution or in the period immediately following it. Lenin, however, gave the doctrine a much more constricted and sharper definition. He argued that Social Democrats must become the undisputed leaders of all the forces dedicated to overthrowing the autocracy, and he advocated that Marxists "utilize" for their own purposes the bourgeois opposition to the existing order.[51]

The course of events in 1905 played havoc with the theories evolved by both groups of Marxists. In the first place, at least during the initial six months of that year, the liberals were the leading force behind the political ferment. In the second place, the Marxists proved to be wrong in their assumption that the proletarians who did participate in the first revolution would be led by Social Democrats. The convolutions in the strategies and tactics of both Bolsheviks and Mensheviks must be seen as attempts by political leaders, saddled with a dogmatic view of the historical process, to cope with complexities they had not, and could not have, anticipated.

At the so-called Third Congress of the RSDWP in April 1905,* the Bolsheviks made preparation of the proletariat for an armed uprising one of the party's primary goals: the party must plan a direct, frontal attack on the autocracy.[52] Their emphasis on this point was not really new, but the Bolsheviks now conceived of the provisional government that would replace the autocracy in a way that did constitute a new departure from orthodox Marxism. The congress stated that it might be permissible for Social Democrats to participate in the provisional government, whose membership would presumably be mainly bourgeois. Finally, the congress urged Social Democrats to "support energetically all revolutionary measures of the peasantry to improve their lot, including the confiscation of state, gentry, church, monastery, and appanage lands."[53]

The resolutions of the congress anticipated the strategy Lenin developed at length in his *Two Tactics of Social-Democracy in the Democratic Revolution* (written in June and July), in which he advocated a provisional government that he called the "revolutionary-democratic dictatorship of the proletariat and the peasantry." Viewing the peasantry as a potentially revolutionary force, he contended that it, together with the proletariat, could form a government whose mission would be to introduce democratic reforms and arrange for the election of a constituent assembly. Although Lenin generally held that in view of Russia's primitive state of economic development the provisional government could not do more than establish democratic institutions, he casually mentioned the possibility of an immediate conversion to socialism. He was thoroughly unambiguous, however, about the primary duty of the party: with increasing urgency, he called on Social Democrats to devote all their energies to preparing an armed uprising.[54]

At their own conference in April and May in 1905, the Mensheviks phrased their resolutions so as to allow for most contingencies and satisfy a wide range of opinions on the revolution. The delegates indicated that they did not oppose an armed uprising but insisted that before military action could be contemplated, Social Democrats must engage in extensive agitational and organizational work. As the "party of the most extreme revolutionary opposition," Social Democracy must avoid participation in a provisional government. Nevertheless, the Mensheviks asserted that their approach "of course does not at all exclude the advisability of partial, episodic seizures of power and the formation of

---

*The Mensheviks refused to recognize this congress, which was convoked by Lenin and his supporters in the midst of some particularly intense intraparty feuding. The Mensheviks held their own conference at about the same time.

revolutionary communes in one or another city, in the exclusive interest of influencing the spread of the uprising and disorganizing the government."

Iu. O. Martov subsequently enlarged on this point, advocating the creation of a "network of institutions of revolutionary self-government." In effect, he was calling for an extension of the "municipal revolutions" that had already taken place in Georgia and Kurland early in 1905. Finally, the Mensheviks explicitly refrained from ruling out the possibility of a proletarian seizure of power in the near future: for this to happen, it was only necessary for the revolution to spread to the advanced countries of Europe, where conditions were already ripe for socialism.[55]

To the person untrained in the subtleties of Marxist doctrine, the tactical differences between the Bolsheviks and the Mensheviks may not seem all that momentous. Certainly, party members in Russia were often baffled by the passionate disputes between partisans of the two factions, especially since in their conduct they did not differ very much. Both factions tried to arm the proletariat and both formed "armed detachments"; both tried to extend their influence beyond the towns into the countryside. Indeed, cooperation between Mensheviks and Bolsheviks was not uncommon and became quite close during the last two months of the year. In short, in the excitement of the social and political stirrings of 1905, neither faction upheld the orthodox doctrine that the first revolution in Russia must be essentially a bourgeois affair. Ideology did not constrain activists who sensed that a proletarian revolution of sorts might be within reach.

Still, it is true that in their pronouncements the Leninists placed much greater emphasis than the Mensheviks on armed struggle and on an alliance with the peasantry rather than the bourgeoisie. Another major tactical difference between them can best be summed up as follows: the Leninists believed that the opposition should direct all its energies against the center of power, whereas the Mensheviks advocated partial seizures of power, to begin in those areas where Tsarist authority was most vulnerable to attack from below. This difference had less to do with theory than with divergent assessments of the strength of the autocracy and its ability to survive the disorders. The Revolution of 1905 eventually caused a new and profound ideological split between the two groups of Marxists, but only after the upheaval was over, when the theorists engaged in analyses of what had gone wrong and how their doctrine must be adjusted to take into account the lessons of defeat.

Although the two Marxist factions have received the greatest amount of attention from historians, the Socialist Revolutionaries (SRs) constituted the largest radical party during the years from 1905 to 1907. Committed to agrarian socialism, the SRs, also led by intellectuals, drew support from both the nonkulak peasantry and the industrial proletariat. They were instrumental in founding some working-class organizations, most notably the All-Russian Railway Union. The only known estimate of the party's strength is for November 1906, at which time there were about 50,000 "regular and organized" SRs, compared to a total of approximately 40,000 members of the two Marxist factions.[56]

In part, the Socialist Revolutionary Party enjoyed greater success than its rivals in attracting members because it was perceived, correctly, to be the most militant. For some time before 1905, the SRs had contended that only a unified uprising by the proletariat and peasants could overthrow the autocracy, and as soon as the party leaders learned of the events surrounding Bloody Sunday, they argued that this was the moment to launch an all-out attack on the old order. The party's paper, *Revoliutsionnaia Rossiia*, referred to the disorders in Russia as the "threshold of the Revolution" and urged workers not to confine themselves to mere economic demands. They should form armed militias, engage in individual and mass terror against officials, and at the earliest possible moment unleash an armed uprising. "Cast away your doubts and prejudices against militant means," the paper admonished its readers on February 10, 1905.[57]

In July 1905, *Revoliutsionnaia Rossiia* carried an article critical of radicals who still argued that the revolution would be a bourgeois affair. M. R. Gots, the probable author of the article, was a member of the SR Central Committee and co-editor with V. M. Chernov of the paper. That he did not speak merely for himself is suggested by the fact that even before the appearance of this particular article, the paper had argued that because the liberal bourgeoisie was weak in Russia, the revolution would have to be waged by workers and peasants led by the revolutionary intelligentsia. Moreover, in contrast to the Marxists, the SRs regarded peasants who owned small amounts of land not as petty bourgeois but as part of the working class, a premise that underlay their belief in the "socialist potential" of masses of people in the countryside. All things considered, it is not surprising that the July article advocated permanent revolution, anticipating by some four months the proposal of such a strategy by a small group of Marxist militants.

The forthcoming revolution will be achieved mainly by the efforts of the workers—proletarians and peasants. They should take from this revolution all that the social conditions permit them to take—the most important of these conditions is the extent of their own consciousness. They should not restrict the scale of this revolution in advance for the benefit of the bourgeoisie, but on the contrary they should turn it into a permanent one, oust the bourgeoisie step by step from the positions it has occupied, give the signal for a European revolution, and then draw new strength from there.[58]

The Socialist Revolutionaries were no more successful than the Social Democrats in influencing events during the first nine months of 1905. To be sure, SRs carried out numerous terrorist attacks on government officials of various ranks, but the overall strategy of the party failed. Neither the peasants nor the workers heeded its calls for a mass uprising with political goals. The SR activists in 1905 were yet another group of intellectuals out of touch with the popular mood, which was indeed militant but not revolutionary in an ideological sense.

Anarchism is another current within the radical camp that deserves to be mentioned. The doctrines of anarchism—that capitalism and the state should be immediately abolished and replaced by a decentralized society in which free individuals would voluntarily cooperate with each other—had been advocated for some time by M. A. Bakunin (1814–76) and P. A. Kropotkin (1842–1921), two Russian radicals who spent most of their adult lives as émigrés in the West. But it was only in 1903 that anarchism appeared as a lasting movement in Russia, and even then its following was very small. In Byalistok, for example, which was one of the more important anarchist centers, not more than 12 to 15 people joined the movement. But once the Revolution of 1905 began, some Social Democrats and SRs came under the spell of the anarchist creed. Within a few months the number of anarchists in Byalistok rose to 60 and small circles of anarchists appeared in other cities and small towns of the western provinces, as well as in some cities in the Caucasus and the Crimean Peninsula.

Although a few anarchist groups in Russia followed the more benign teachings of Kropotkin and devoted themselves to propaganda and agitation among the masses, in 1905 the advocates of terrorism held sway within the movement. Adhering to Bakunin's well-known dictum that "the urge to destroy is also a creative urge," and convinced that their acts of violence would stimulate the yearning for revenge by the masses against their exploiters, the terrorists carried out numerous armed robberies to enable them to secure weapons, which they used to assassinate officials. In the last months of 1905 hardly a day passed without some anarchist outrage being reported in the daily press. The terrorists scored their most spectacular successes in November and December 1905, when they exploded bombs in the Hotel Bristol in Warsaw and the Café Libman in Odessa. The violent exploits gained the anarchists a good deal of notoriety, but since they did not constitute a large, unified force they failed to exert a major influence on the course of the revolution. Still, the turn to fanaticism by activists on the fringes of the radical movement does indicate that the autocracy's intransigence was generating a mood of impatience and despair among some groups within the opposition.[59]

· · · · ·

"It seemed," N. I. Astrov recalled in his memoirs, "as though all of Russia had been seized by a fever and by convulsions."[60] A casual glance at newspapers for the late summer and fall of 1905 confirms Astrov's observation. No meeting of Russians, regardless of its ostensible purpose, could avoid some outburst of hostility toward the government. A case in point was a scholarly conference of psychiatrists in Kiev early in September. Academician V. M. Bekhterev delivered a paper on "Personality [and] the Conditions for Its Intellectual and Moral Development," in which he contended that social, political, and pedagogical circumstances in Russia were totally inhospitable to the healthy development of the human personality. He blamed the oppressive autocratic regime for the "inner demoralization" and weak personalities of many Russians. The 4,000 to 5,000 people in the audience "drowned the speech with long, endless applause. The young people carried Academician Bekhterev on their shoulders."[61]

Some of the "convulsions" were amusing; yet they, too, are symptomatic of the degree to which the population had been politicized by the many months of popular protest. In September a congress of apiarists in Moscow argued furiously over whether their deliberations should be restricted to "technical questions" or should also include resolutions of a "political character." In the end, the delegates decided to confine themselves to matters "dealing with beekeeping."[62] At about the same time, it was reported that "bribe-takers" in Warsaw had gone out on strike. Civil servants complained that in view of the inflation caused by the war, the bribes to which they had been accustomed were inadequate. Favors that used to cost three rubles were now refused for less than five. The crisis abated quickly, since "bribe-givers . . . made concessions."[63]

A protest movement genuinely deserving of sympathy developed among women, who launched a campaign for political equality. Some women had participated in the banquets organized by liberals late in 1904, and in February 1905 a group of activists established the All-Russian Union for the Equality of Women, whose goal was "freedom and equality before the law without regard to sex." The organization petitioned the Moscow City Council and the local zemstvo for the right to vote for deputies in those organs and then set up branches throughout the Empire. The

Union's first congress, held in May and attended by 70 delegates, adopted a political program that resembled that of the left liberals, though it contained one new demand—full political equality for all citizens. Many liberals, including P. N. Miliukov, were not overjoyed. They dismissed the demands of women as "inopportune," because they believed that the masses, especially the peasants, were not ready for so radical a measure as women's equality. The first two congresses of Zemstvo and City Council Representatives refused to support the women's demand, but a congress that met in the fall, subjected to intense lobbying, yielded on the issue. The Social Democrats and Socialist Revolutionaries had all along favored universal suffrage without discrimination by sex. But the efforts of women to achieve equality bore few concrete results during the revolution.[64]

· · · · ·

The assault on authority in Russia's educational institutions proved to be especially threatening to the autocratic regime. Because the educated classes generally considered university students to be the "barometer of the mood of society," the ferment in institutions of higher learning received the closest attention from the government, opposition groups, and the public at large. On some days, newspapers devoted close to one-fifth of their columns to such disorders. Most of the interest centered on secular institutions of higher learning—universities and specialized institutes—but they were not the only ones to be swept up by a spirit of rebelliousness. Secondary schools, seminaries, and theological academies joined the protest movement. Nor were the protesters' demands restricted to political issues. Quite often, students and their parents also demanded changes in the educational structure, the curriculum, and pedagogy. Though its primary impulse and thrust were political, the protest movement in education must also be seen as an attempt to effect important cultural changes.

Students reacted with indignation to Bloody Sunday. Many of them stayed away from the classroom, devoting their time to political meetings and demonstrations that not only protested the government's brutality against workers but also called for an end to the war and the granting of civil liberties. A few professors tried to continue teaching and urged students to resume their studies, but to no avail. On March 18, a committee of ministers, bowing to reality, in effect sanctioned the closing of all institutions of higher learning until the fall. The committee recommended that no punishments be meted out to striking students or faculty, but it warned that if the schools were not reopened for studies in the autumn, the government would dismiss the faculty, expel the students, and reorganize the educational institutions in accordance with "state needs."[65] Undistracted by studies or other obligations, the students proved to be an excellent source for a "new 'recruitment for the revolution.'"[66]

Although secondary schools also fell prey to strikes and other disorders immediately after Bloody Sunday, they were not closed down en masse. But that does not mean that they remained calm after the university students were sent home. Indeed, Patrick L. Alston did not exaggerate when he referred to the intense agitation for secondary-school reform as "The Revolutionary Assault on the Bureaucratic School, 1905–1906."[67] It was an assault, throughout the Empire, by pupils, parents, and teachers who sought a profound transformation of Russian education. Because of the pervasive unrest, the secondary schools in 1905 served as training grounds for future political activists.

The youngsters expressed their defiance in a variety of ways. In Kazan in April, for example, many high school students remained in class and refused to respond to the teachers' questions, while others engaged the headmaster in heated discussions about educational policies. At times, by prevailing upon others to participate in street demonstrations during class time, student activists prevented schools from functioning at all.[68] In Vilna, pupils at a Jewish religious school threw stones out the windows at policemen and Cossacks dispersing a crowd of demonstrators, which prompted the Governor-General to close down the school.[69]

In Skopin (Riazan province) pupils in grades 6 and 7 of the *realschule* submitted an audacious demand to the director that had nothing to do with politics or the curriculum but was nevertheless threatening to the administration. They asked that a certain Mr. Naumann, who taught mathematics, be dismissed because he knew less about the subject than the students themselves. "How can we understand trigonometry and pass an examination in it in a higher institution," they asked, "when our teacher teaches us nothing and knows nothing himself?" The director intended to take "repressive measures" against the pupils, but a trustee of the school, elected by the district zemstvo assembly, intervened and succeeded in settling the dispute amicably.[70] Unfortunately, the fate of poor Naumann remains unknown. The significant point here is that students had challenged the authorities and were not punished.

Most of the time, of course, the demands for educational reform had a more general thrust. Despite variations in the petitions submitted to officials in different regions of the Empire, some themes appeared in almost all of them. They may be summarized as follows: elimination of police surveillance; abolition of obligatory attendance at religious services; improvement in sanitary conditions; provision for parents to be allowed to select accommodations for their children; reduction of educational costs and fair distribution of stipends; permission for students to visit theaters, concert halls, libraries, and public reading rooms; access to all books authorized by the censorship; provision for parents to participate and vote in pedagogical councils; establishment of honor courts to settle disciplinary cases; and freedom for students to hold meetings at school and to organize mutual-aid funds.[71] In ethnically non-Russian regions of the Empire, citizens wanted schools to be mindful of local cultural traditions. For instance, a petition from Vilna and Kovno asked that teachers disrespectful of their pupils' religious and national feelings be dismissed; that students be permitted to speak Polish and Lithuanian at school; that native speakers of Polish and Lithuanian be taught in those languages; that Poles and Lithuanians be given appointments as teachers; and finally, that officials remove "from textbooks historical accounts that tendentiously distort the truth."[72]

The single most important demand, voiced by protesters throughout the Empire, touched on the governance of educational institutions. The protesters asked that parents be given the right to participate in the administration of the schools. In Kazan, to cite but one example, a committee of parents and pedagogues proposed that councils, consisting of representatives from the teaching staff and society, determine the curriculum, select the administrators and teachers, and set the salaries of all employees.[73]

It bears emphasizing that the demands for this radical transformation of Russia's educational system came from below. Pupils generally initiated the agitation at their schools, and parents, quickly drawn into the protest movement, played a major role in drafting the petitions. Teachers by and large supported the protest movement; indeed, on May 1, the Union of Secondary School Teachers of St. Petersburg issued a declaration that can only be described as a sweeping and moving indictment of Russian education at the high school level.[74] Local officials lacked authority to introduce major reforms on their own, but it was not unusual for them to pass the petitions for change on to senior bureaucrats. The police, however, often dealt brutally with student unrest and caused casualties and deaths.[75]

· · · · ·

Not until late in the summer did the government undertake any significant reform in the country's educational institutions. On August 27, it issued a decree restoring to the universities and advanced institutes the autonomy they had been deprived of in 1884. Councils of faculty members could now elect the rector and the faculty could elect the deans. The councils also assumed authority over educational matters and student affairs. For example, they could permit students to hold meetings on school grounds and, in the event of disorders, could close down the institutions. Courts of professors were established to rule on student infractions of disciplinary codes.[76]

General Trepov was the moving spirit behind the granting of autonomy. It seemed to him that among students "a form of insanity" prevailed, which required a "pathological form of treatment." By allowing them to hold meetings, Trepov expected that the "excited hotheads would exhaust themselves." He also thought that the autonomy measure would encourage students to concentrate on affairs at their own campuses, thus making it more difficult for them to maintain contact with other opposition groups. Trepov was confident that any attempt by students to radicalize workers would be met with ridicule. Count Aehrenthal, who discussed the autonomy measure with Trepov in some detail, expressed serious misgivings about the scheme. "It is to be hoped," he wrote to his superiors in Vienna, "that General Trepov is right in his assessment of the psychology of the Russian people, who, as is well known, quickly become enthusiastic about an idea but almost never persevere in any course of action." In Aehrenthal's view, if the government wanted to allow people to speak out on political issues, it could have permitted public meetings "under certain conditions," as was done in other countries. "Political meetings do not belong in universities, and if they are permitted, there necessarily exists the danger that clubs will be formed, which in the end the authorities will not be able to tolerate."[77]

Aehrenthal was remarkably prescient. Trepov's strategy misfired completely, as commentators on the right and left later recognized. In his memoirs, Count Witte contended that the "decree on university autonomy . . . was the first breach through which the revolution, having matured underground, emerged into the broad light of day."[78] N. Cherevanin (F. A. Lipkin), the Menshevik activist, attached even greater significance to the decree: "one can say with confidence that the great October strike was prepared within the walls of the higher educational institutions in the atmosphere of free speech and ardent exchanges of opinions. . . . Workers, railway employees, representatives of professional groups discussed their needs, decided whether or not to join the strike that had started, organized the forces of the strike, [and] discussed measures to be taken to bring about its spread."[79]

Ironically, it seemed unlikely that the decree on autonomy would have any bearing on the course of the revolution, for student activists at first showed little interest in the concession. Their slogan was "A normal life at school can [only] be guaranteed by a normal life in the country,"[80] that is, until the political system was fundamentally liberalized, the institutions of higher learning should not be reopened. But the Menshevik F. I. Dan had conceived of a tactic that came to appeal to a large number of students. In July Dan published an article in *Iskra* that developed an idea suggested by V. I. Zasulich, one of the founders of Russian Marxism and now a prominent Menshevik. Dan proposed that students abandon the strike at the start of the academic year in September, not to pursue their studies but rather to open the universities to the people for mass meetings.[81]

In September students representing 23 institutions of higher learning from all over the Empire met in Vyborg, Finland, and, after rejecting a proposal of Bolshevik and Socialist Revolutionary delegates to continue the strike and concentrate on a revolutionary struggle against the government, decided to implement the Menshevik plan. Evidently as a sop to the militants, the delegates also adopted a resolution that called on students to take "appropriate" steps so that at the right moment they would be prepared to join "a general political strike and an armed uprising."[82]

This was only the first step. It was now up to students at local institutions to vote on the question. If they decided to abandon the strike, they had then to decide whether or not to defy the decree on autonomy, which permitted meetings of students, but not of outsiders, within the confines of the schools. School administrators, to say nothing of the government, did not intend to lift the ban against outsiders.

Historians who have mentioned the autonomy decree have generally presumed that the students were so overwhelmingly radical that there was no serious disagreement among them about its implementation. Of the scholars who have deviated from the consensus, Samuel Kassow, the author of a detailed study of unrest at the universities, has been the most explicit: "It would be wrong," he wrote, "to assume that the majority of Russian students were prepared to take an active part in the revolution; despite the spate of political resolutions in September they were neither prepared to act as a political bloc nor were firmly committed to the Social Democratic Party."[83] Elsewhere, Kassow characterizes the students' political stance as "rhetorical commitment to the Revolution coupled with a strong desire to save the Universities for the sake of the students themselves."[84] These points are well taken.

An examination of the deliberations on the decree at the postsecondary level indicates not only that there were sharp divisions among the students but also that at several institutions the militants got their way only by manipulating mass meetings or disregarding their decisions. Although students who identified themselves as Social Democrats scored some impressive victories in various university elections (most notably in St. Petersburg),[85] and although there were few defenders of the status quo, moderate sentiment was far from extinct, despite the autocracy's callousness and intransigence over the preceding eight months. The British Consul in Moscow, who monitored developments at the educational institutions, claimed to have it on good authority that "about 6/7 of the students wished to continue work, but the obstruction was caused by the remaining 1/7 who were a united party."[86] Unfortunately, it is not known how the Consul's informant arrived at this statistical breakdown. More than likely, he made an impressionistic appraisal of the situation so as to emphasize the point that radicalism was not the predominant sentiment among students.

To be sure, students voted overwhelmingly in favor of ending the strikes, on the understanding that political agitation would be permitted in the schools. After a six-hour debate, a mass meeting at St. Petersburg University supported a resolution to this effect by a vote of 1,700 to 243 (the latter wanted to continue the strike), with 47 abstentions.[87] At a meeting attended by 300 people at the Electrotechnical Institute in St. Petersburg, only 51 opposed the reopening of the school.[88] At the Polytechnicum in Riga, an "overwhelming majority" of the 450 persons at the public meeting cast their ballots in favor of resuming classes.[89] In Dorpat the vote was 1,093 against 156.[90]

By themselves, however, these votes do not tell the whole story. To understand their full significance, two points must be kept in mind. First, the votes signified a defeat for the ultraradicals, who argued that the strikes should be continued because "there had been no decisive changes" in the political situation since January. The students who favored opening the universities contended that, on the contrary, a significant change had occurred that had to be taken into account. There had been, to use the language of the time, a change in the "mutual relations of social forces": former allies had become enemies, a reference to the growing rift between the bourgeoisie and the autocracy. Under the circumstances, students could not remain passive. They must support the working people, but a closed university is "tantamount to the political demise of the student body, whose strength lies only in its numbers."[91] Students ought to exploit the changing political conditions in Russia, not simply cling to revolutionary tactics that had seemed appropriate in the days after Bloody Sunday.

The second point is more interesting, certainly more important. The students voting to reopen the institutions of higher learning consisted of at least three groups with fairly distinct views on the role of the universities in public affairs: one group believed that the schools should be turned into centers of political action pure and simple; the second maintained that political meetings should be held at the schools only when they would not interfere with classes; and the third, dubbed "academics" and organized into "academic leagues," insisted that "the University is for scholarship" and should be open for academic pursuits only.[92] Initially, on the issue of reopening the institutions of higher learning, the three groups coalesced; but on the question of inviting outsiders into the schools for political meetings they split, and at times factional struggles became bitter. The accounts of the pertinent debates indicate that many students and professors favored the moderate positions.

At the Technical School in Moscow, students seem to have accepted the regulation against outsiders without much discussion.[93] But that was the exception. At Kiev University, a mass meeting of students on September 30 debated the issue at length and then voted 873 to 581 against admitting outsiders. The chairman, stunned by the outcome, ruled that those present were not representative of the entire student body and that a group of students in an adjacent room on other business should also be polled. The "academics" could not resist such a call for more democracy; but even though the new count was by a show of hands, the chairman could only muster a total of 797 votes, still not enough. At this point he ruled that it was unfair for 1,700 out of a total student body of 3,389 to decide so important an issue. He called for yet another vote; this time all students would have the opportunity to cast their ballots in secret. After some "quite stormy wrangling," this suggestion was adopted, but the result of the new vote, or even whether it was ever held, is not known.[94]

At the St. Petersburg Mining Institute, students were also split into bitterly hostile factions. The radicals wanted to end the strike, but only so they could transform the school into a forum for political activity. While one of them was giving a heated speech on September 22, someone in the audience shouted out that a column under the hall was cracking and that the floor was likely to cave in. Understandably nervous, a number of students left the meeting. An inspection of the column revealed that the warning had been "pure fiction." Although attendance had shrunk, the radicals submitted their resolution, which prompted several moderates to walk out in protest. Nevertheless, the motion did not pass. The sponsors of the resolution then refused to accept the decision as final on the ground that a large proportion of the students had failed to attend the meeting.[95]

Students at the Institute of Civil Engineering in St. Petersburg arrived at conflicting decisions on admitting outsiders to the lecture halls. This is probably explained by the fact that there were many meetings at that time and their composition varied. In any case, on September 16 a mass meeting voted overwhelmingly to permit anyone wishing to hear "the voice of truth" to attend lectures at the Institute.[96] But on September 29, the issue again came up for debate, and now the engineering students divided into two parties: the leftists who "openly appeared under the banner of Marxism," and their opponents, who had no clearly defined program but "instinctively" united against the radicals. The leftists contended that the assemblage had no right even to vote on the question of admitting outsiders and announced that they would not accept the legitimacy of a negative decision. When the students voted to allow outsiders to attend meetings, but with only a "consultative vote," the radicals became desperate, all the more because they could not count on any help from the chairman, who was a moderate. They therefore introduced a motion for adjournment, which was defeated, 172 to 171. The left then stalked out of the hall with an announcement that resolutions passed by the assembly were "not binding."[97]

At some institutions, students adopted resolutions designed to placate both moderates and radicals. On September 20 at the University of Dorpat, for example, 149 voted to reopen the school for academic pursuits only, 154 voted to use it exclusively for political agitation, while a majority of 454 supported reopening and permitting both kinds of activities. The latter approach was approved by another mass meeting on September 22.[98] Students at the Polytechnical Institute in St. Petersburg voted 711 to 22, with 5 abstentions, to accept outsiders, but they stipulated that the meetings should be held in the evening to avoid interference with academic lectures.[99] A public meeting at the Women's Medical Institute in St. Petersburg on September 26 rejected two radical resolutions and adopted one that both called for opening the school for political activities and specifically enjoined the students not to prevent their colleagues from studying.[100]

Even at the University of Moscow, a hotbed of radicalism, students at one of the first mass meetings, on September 8, failed to approve a resolution to open the institution exclusively for revolutionary agitation. By a vote of 1,202 to 517, they adopted, instead, a somewhat more moderate proposal: "to turn [the university] into a revolutionary center and our auditoriums into political schools," but yet still to permit it to be a "place . . . for those who at present want to spare time for academic studies and have the energy for that."[101] As a rule, classes scheduled during morning hours were to be allowed to proceed without interruption.

Administrators of the institutions of higher learning and councils of faculty members often pleaded with the students not to jeopardize the newly won autonomy by opening lecture halls to outsiders.[102] After all, students could hold political meetings with the approval of the rector, but if they persisted in inviting non-students, it would be impossible to guarantee anyone's safety. Occasionally, administrators temporarily closed institutions where violations occurred.

The militants, however, were in no mood to heed these warnings. Nor would they permit lectures by faculty members they considered politically undesirable. When Professor G. P. Georgievskii at St. Petersburg University began to lecture on September 20, he was met with shouts of "Boycott, boycott!" Georgievskii tried to explain that he did not oppose the "progressive movement," but the students continued to be disorderly, compelling him to leave the lecture hall.[103] Such disturbances occurred most frequently at Moscow University. On September 19 Professor A. A. Manuilov, the deputy rector, made a personal plea to students to refrain from interfering with the educational process. He reminded them that they could have held their meeting in the afternoon, when classes were not in session. "I consider your behavior an act of violence against the university and the student body, and protest against this violence. It is being said that some people are counting on our being compelled to turn to the police, which would provoke within the university a conflict between students and police. But we will not do this. I appeal to your sense of decency: I appeal to the students and to public opinion in the country." Manuilov's speech evoked "loud applause among some and sharp whistling among others." In the corridors people who had not been able to enter the hall applauded Manuilov.[104]

It is worth citing one other vote that indicates that moderates still commanded a substantial reserve of strength in institutions of higher learning in the fall of 1905. Early in October, students at Moscow University were polled on the weight to be assigned to decisions reached by general meetings of the student body. Although 1,384 held that such decisions should be considered binding on the university, even more, 1,507, maintained that they should be "consultative," that is, mere suggestions to the administration.[105] Still, it is not possible to make a definitive statement about the political allegiance of most university students shortly before the October strike. All that can be said with confidence is that the revolutionary left was not nearly as strong in the institutions of higher learning as its subsequent successes in the political arena would suggest.

The tactics of the left-wing students proved to be remarkably effective, far beyond anyone's dreams. Sensing that neither the university administrations nor the government any longer possessed the will or authority to enforce regulations, radicals simply went ahead with their plans to turn the schools into centers of political activity for students and non-students alike. Many of the demands that emanated from the innumerable meetings related directly to educational matters, and generally rectors and councils yielded without offering much resistance.

Rectors quickly responded to the call for the abolition of quotas on admitting Jews to postsecondary schools by urging the government to change its policy. Although the Minister of Education was not prepared to abandon the quota system entirely—he left the matter up to the State Duma scheduled to meet within a few months—he did secure the Tsar's permission to admit several dozen additional Jews to the universities in St. Petersburg and Moscow.[106] University councils also adopted measures to eliminate police surveillance, supported the abolition of discriminatory practices in the admission of women, and created curriculum committees consisting of both professors and students.[107] Not atypical was the case of the Polytechnical Institute in St. Petersburg, where the council established regular meetings between student and faculty representatives designed to familiarize them "with each other's wishes and opinions."[108]

At a few institutions, students, supported by some faculty members, demanded that "reactionary professors" be dismissed and that committees draw up "proscriptive lists of professors to be subject to boycott." At St. Petersburg University, for example, a commission of students examined the conduct of several faculty members and concluded that sufficient evidence existed that two professors and one privat-dozent had allowed political considerations to affect their academic judgments to warrant boycotting them. Several professors denounced the proscriptive lists, and one liberal academic accused the students of conducting "a trial by mob law, a moral lynching." After it emerged that one professor had been falsely accused by a privat-dozent of being an agent of the Okhrana, the students retreated. But they decided to continue the investigation and urged their colleagues to use their "own judgment" on whether to boycott the three teachers.[109]

The successes of students in attaining their goals within the academy paled in comparison with their achievements in the arena of national politics. Within a few weeks of the issuance of the decree on autonomy, it became clear that students in Moscow had not engaged in idle threats when they adopted the following slogan: "Let our open university become even more dangerous for the autocratic government than the university on strike has been."[110] At one school after another in the major cities of the Empire, people thronged to meetings that were blatantly political. In addition to university students, there appeared workers, soldiers, women, and secondary school pupils. To be assured admission into the university, many workers in Kiev, at least initially, donned rented double-breasted jackets, attire common among students.[111]

The gatherings were treated to lectures on such subjects as the political tasks of the working class and its relations with other classes, the State Duma, the tactics of progressive parties, the agrarian question, and the philosophical principles of scientific socialism. To attract the largest possible audience, a speaker on October 4 at the Polytechnical Institute in

Kiev delivered a political address in Yiddish, surely the first time that had occurred at a Russian institution of higher learning. The organizers of the meetings also attended to practical matters. They openly collected money for strike funds and for the acquisition of weapons. Some speakers urged their listeners to prepare for an armed uprising and for terrorist actions against the authorities. Invariably, the meetings would end with shouts of "Down with the autocracy." At the Veterinary Institute in Kazan, one speaker demanded that the portrait of the Tsar be removed from the hall. When this was refused, students had the portrait covered with a veil. In Kiev, students punched three holes into the portrait of Nicholas I.[112]

A few statistics will suffice to indicate the popularity of the meetings. Four thousand people attended meetings at the University of Kazan on September 20; 2,000 at the Polytechnical Institute in St. Petersburg on October 1; about 13,000 at St. Petersburg University on October 5; 4,000 at the University of Kiev on October 9; and 10,000 at the University of Odessa on October 9. At Moscow University on September 20, the crowd filled not only all the lecture halls but also the corridors, stairways, and, finally, the porter's lodge. The meetings would last for hours on end, but the crowds never seemed to tire. Nor did they heed the pleas of university officials to halt the illegal and occasionally dangerous gatherings. At St. Petersburg University, so many lecture halls were in use at night that many feared that the overloaded electrical system was threatened by fire, but this, too, dampened no one's enthusiasm.[113] It has been estimated that in the course of about three weeks in the capital alone, tens of thousands of workers attended one or more gatherings devoted to political indoctrination.[114]

The response of the government to the mass meetings of students and workers must have astonished Dan, who had first proposed the new tactic. Dan thought that the authorities would close the schools, "into which they had for so long and so unsuccessfully tried to drag the students by force." Moreover, he was sure that closure would constitute a moral and political victory for the opposition because the government would be held directly responsible. The reaction to such a lockout might well be so intense, Dan thought, as to prompt all "spheres of social and political life" to take the offensive against the government.[115]

Trepov, however, decided that the use of force was not called for in this situation. It is clear from several long memorandums that he sent to the Minister of Education that Trepov was well informed about the politicization of the institutions of higher learning.[116] But he continued to believe that in time his policy of permitting the popular movement to let off steam would succeed: people would tire of the endless discussions of revolutionary tactics. It is also conceivable that the government did not react forcefully to the student movement because it was "paralyzed by the fear of a general mutiny in the army, not yet demobilized after the war."[117] Whatever the reason, the authorities in St. Petersburg and in most other cities did little except station policemen and soldiers nearby when illegal meetings were in progress so that "the fire in the buildings . . . would not spread onto the streets." In a few places armed bands directed by plainclothesmen occasionally assaulted the participants, but generally the authorities looked the other way.[118]

The "meeting epidemic," as it has been called, could not but embolden the opposition. It was one of the more graphic signs of the collapse of authority. The administrations at the institutions of higher learning yielded to student activists on issue after issue, and the government was helpless in the face of the multitudes who were publicly defying the laws against political organization and agitation.

Even the Orthodox Church, presumed to be a solid pillar of the autocracy, had to contend with serious rebellions in its religious schools. In the spring, disorders had erupted at seminaries (training schools for the priesthood) in Kaluga, Zhitomir, and Kiev, and discontent had surfaced in many more places. The discipline at seminaries was brutal, the living conditions horrid, and the education archaic. Students especially despised the school inspectors, "who follow every step, every move of the seminarians, and try to penetrate their souls." In 1900 a student at the Kiev Seminary had tried to kill an inspector; when the man was subsequently removed from his post, he was replaced by someone just as tyrannical. In southwest Russia the seminaries were so discredited that "not a single professor at the Kiev Theological Academy, not one teacher at the seminary or theological school, enrolls his children at a theological school." Despite many warnings of unrest, the synod had failed to reform the schools.[119]

In the autumn of 1905, strikes broke out at 48 of the country's 58 seminaries, many of them severe enough to close the schools for prolonged periods.[120] The rebellious students were obviously influenced by the ferment in the country at large, but their demands focused on conditions at their own schools. They asked for better food, the abolition of the harsh disciplinary system, the transfer of the libraries to their control, and the introduction of a secondary school course of studies that would prepare them for admission to secular institutions of higher learning.[121] The last point underlines the unwillingness of many students at the seminaries to prepare for the priesthood. They attended church schools mainly because they had no other way to obtain an education.[122]

Early in October, student disorders at all four theological academies (in St. Petersburg, Moscow, Kazan, and Kiev) caused the suspension of classes. This turn of events astonished church officials, who looked upon the academies as elitist institutions immune to disaffection. Their students were carefully selected for both intellectual achievement and personal conduct. Moreover, their graduates faced good prospects for employment as teachers or in other moderately well-paying posts. "The more stormy spirits among the seminary students did not enter the academies, and a quieter spirit prevailed."[123] But in the fall of 1905, students at the academies joined the assault on authority, and their principal demand was that their institutions be granted the kind of autonomy that had been extended to secular schools. On October 9, students at the St. Petersburg Academy voted 157 to 26 against attending class until autonomy was achieved. The faculty supported them by a vote of 26 to one.[124] Within the church at large there was also sentiment favoring autonomy. A group of church employees in Moscow sent students and professors at the local academy a telegram wishing them success.[125]

Officials at the academies adopted sterner measures than their counterparts at secular schools to end the disorders. The administration of the Kiev Academy issued an ultimatum: if the students did not immediately certify in writing that they intended to return to class, they would be expelled. They were also told that their demands for reform would be considered by higher church authorities. The students, who seem to have been especially militant, paid no attention to the ultimatum.[126] Two weeks earlier, they had refused to participate in an annual commencement exercise that the academy's officials considered particularly important. In justifying their behavior the students revealed the extent to which even those who attended theological seminaries had become politicized. They declared "that this year the commencement exercises are extremely inappropriate in view of the difficult state of the country, the impending famine in many provinces, and the tense and difficult work in creating a new system of life in Russia and, in particular, in Russia's institutions of higher learning."[127] This statement suggests that had the academies been granted autonomy, attempts would have been made to turn them into centers of political agitation as well. But there was no such concession, and the academies remained closed until after the general strike in October.

· · · · ·

Two aspects of the assault on authority that occurred in Russia between Bloody Sunday and early October deserve to be emphasized. On the one hand, the indiscriminate shooting by government troops of unarmed people seeking to petition their sovereign for "justice and protection" had severed the psychological ties between the ruler and many of the ruled, ties that were intangible but indispensable for the maintenance of order. Masses of Russians no longer felt bound to obey the commands of a sovereign whose power had previously been accepted as hallowed by God and tradition. The attacks on authority that followed left few institutions untouched. In addition to the rampant disorder in the industrial and agrarian sectors of the economy, the autocracy was challenged and successfully defied by the media and students in religious as well as secular schools. For its part, the government proved incapable of using the police to contain the breakdown of civil order. A perspicacious observer might well have predicted that if several of the protesting groups ever joined forces—as in fact happened during the general strike in October—the government would be too weak to resist making far-reaching concessions. Its authority, moral and otherwise, seemed to have evaporated beyond immediate repair.

On the other hand, there was still a large group among those who opposed and defied the government whose political position can only be described as relatively moderate. The publishers of the major newspapers and many of their writers favored a constitutional form of government under which civil liberties would be guaranteed. A substantial portion of the liberal movement subscribed to a similar position. None of these groups favored socialism or insisted on the elimination of all the Tsar's prerogatives. Even among students at institutions of higher education—generally regarded as having been in the vanguard of the radical movement—there remained a large body of moderate opinion. This was, indeed, the single most surprising revelation to have emerged from press accounts about the decree on university autonomy.

The government, then, faced a delicate situation in the fall of 1905. To restore its authority, it needed to introduce fundamental change, but it had to devise a program of reform that would be acceptable to a broad range of opinion as well as to Tsar Nicholas and his closest advisers. Arguably, such a program could have appealed to large sectors of the opposition only if it provided for universal civil liberties and a broadly elected legislature vested with much more than consultative powers. The Tsar might have retained some voice in the legislative process and in the appointment of the government, which would have had to rely on support in the legislature to remain in office. In short, the autocracy and society would have had to share power. Since the educated sector, a critical element within the opposition, still contained a solid core that shied away from radical measures, such an arrangement probably had a reasonable chance of stemming the tide of social and political disintegration. But the autocrat and his coterie lacked the vision and boldness to undertake reforms that would fundamentally change the system of rule. They clung to the principle of autocracy and thus plunged the country into its deepest crisis, the general strike of October.

. . . .

Part III

REVOLUTION AND REACTION

Chapter Eight

. . . .

The General Strike

AT THE HEIGHT of the "meeting epidemic," a new wave of labor unrest erupted that within short order shook the autocratic regime to its foundations. Once again, events developed in an unplanned, unorganized, and unpredictable manner. Although a few opposition leaders had broached the idea of a general strike, no one sensed that the urban labor movement might be on the verge of its greatest show of strength and its most notable triumph. Indeed, the leaders of the revolutionary left were taken by surprise. Not until vast numbers of workers had laid down their tools did those leaders appreciate the significance of the strike movement and become active in it. In short, the general strike of October 1905 was a classic example of a momentous historical event that developed spontaneously.

On September 20, the printers in Moscow went on strike to press for higher wages and better working conditions. It was initially a peaceful affair, no different from most of the strikes that had taken place over the preceding nine months. But since the printing works were near the university, the strikers came into contact with students and soon began to take part in street meetings devoted to politics. Attempts by the police to clear the streets resulted in violence. Workers threw stones at policemen and stores, broke street lamps, overturned benches, and knocked down trees. On September 26, Cossacks fired into the milling crowds, killing ten people. By this time the strike had spread to 50 printing plants in the city and to several other industries; for thirteen days Moscow went without newspapers. Printers in St. Petersburg planned a three-day strike in solidarity with their comrades, to begin on October 3. Still, the total number of idle workers was relatively small, and by October 1, the Moscow Okhrana asserted that the situation was under control: "The mood among striking workers has noticeably subsided, and there is reason to believe that by Monday, October 3, a majority in the establishments on strike will resume work."[1] The Okhrana's assessment appeared to be correct; about one-half ended their walkout.

There were other indications, however, that the population of Moscow was still very restless. On October 3, several thousand people joined a funeral procession for Prince S. N. Trubetskoi, who had died unexpectedly at the age of 43 three days earlier during a business trip to St. Petersburg. The first elected rector of Moscow University, Trubetskoi had been a leading spokesman for moderate liberalism, and "all of Russia knew about his conversation with the Tsar" on June 6. Students, professors, and representatives from various professional groups looked upon the occasion of his funeral as an opportunity not only to honor a decent man but also to demonstrate their hostility toward the old order. Although Social Democrats chose not to participate in the procession, some marchers sang revolutionary songs and carried wreaths adorned with red ribbons. The streets were lined with sympathetic spectators. It was, in the words of one eyewitness, "the most grandiose political demonstration to date."[2]

After the religious ceremony at the cemetery hundreds of students, who had gathered at a separate location to listen to revolutionary speeches, made their way toward the university. En route, they were attacked by Cossacks; over twenty students were arrested. The educated public in Moscow was enraged by the violence, which was yet another sign of the authorities' refusal to tolerate free speech and the right of free assembly. The public's outcry was so intense that the police felt obliged to justify its conduct as self-defense against student provocations and to have the daily press print its version of the violent encounter.[3]

In the meantime, a strike movement of vast dimensions had begun, a movement instigated in large measure by the Central Bureau of the All-Russian Union of Railroad Employees and Workers. Formed in April 1905, largely at the initiative of the Socialist Revolutionary V. N. Pereverzev, the Railroad Union, with a potential constituency of 750,000 workers, had adopted a nonpartisan stance, focusing on broad political goals. It favored the convocation of a constituent assembly and the granting of political and civil rights to the people. To maintain unity among the railroad workers, who differed widely in economic status and political affiliation, the union deliberately subordinated economic demands to this very general program. The Central Bureau, however, which ran the organization, sympathized with the aims of the radical parties. At the union's second congress (July 22–24), the Central Bureau was authorized to agitate for a general strike of railway workers in support of the organization's aims and to call such a strike whenever conditions seemed propitious.[4]

Late in September the government unwittingly helped to further a greater measure of unity than had ever existed among the members of the Railway Union. To pacify workers who objected to certain rules governing the pension fund—notably the fact that dismissed railway employees lost their pension rights and merely retained their own contribution (6 percent of their salary) without interest—the authorities announced that a congress would be held on September 20 in St. Petersburg to consider changing the rules. Since most of the delegates to the congress were either professionals or managers of the pension fund, the government believed that it would be able to dominate the proceedings.

At the first session, however, the delegates rejected the chairman selected by the government and chose instead one of their own, a man named M. D. Orekhov. The congress also decided that only elected delegates, not managers, would vote on the issues before it. The delegates were "showered" with telegrams from railway workers throughout the country congratulating them on their coup.[5] The Central Bureau of the Railroad Union, which had been cool to the idea of a pension congress for fear that it would divert workers from political concerns, now viewed the gathering as a rallying point and as a possible catalyst for a massive strike movement. It decided to expand the local, uncoordinated strikes that were already a frequent occurrence by calling for a general strike of all the railways, to start on October 4.

For a variety of reasons, the work stoppage did not gain momentum until October 6, when engineers on the Moscow-Kazan line halted the trains on their branch. Having done that, they marched to nearby stations and persuaded others to join the strike. By October 10, service in Moscow had stopped completely, and since Moscow was the hub of the entire railroad system, the strike there had an enormous impact on transportation throughout the Empire.

False rumors that delegates to the pension congress had been arrested gave additional impetus to the work stoppage. In actuality, not only were the delegates free, but they viewed the Central Bureau's action with reserve and at first sought to mediate between the government and the strikers. The pension congress sent delegations to Witte, then Chairman of the Committee of Ministers, and to Prince M. I. Khilkov, the Minister of Transportation, to persuade them to come out in support of a constituent assembly and some economic concessions. Witte's polite response that the strike would have to end before discussions about reform could be undertaken drove the congress fully over to the side of the Central

Bureau. Once the congress opted for the strike, the railway workers in St. Petersburg gave their unanimous support to it.[6] The strategy of the Central Bureau had worked to perfection.

On October 9, General Trepov sensed the seriousness of the situation and urged the Minister of Transportation to take "the most drastic measures" to restore service on the railways. He suggested that workers who refused to return to their jobs be replaced with soldiers. Prince Khilkov, who had started his career as a railway worker and had spent two years in the United States laying track, thought that he would be able to end the work stoppage by personally appealing to the strikers. But his manner was less than ingratiating. He told a delegation from the Railway Union that he could not understand their grievances. During his years as a worker, he had put in sixteen hours a day and was glad to get the extra pay for overtime. He also claimed that workers abroad were paid less than their Russian counterparts, with the result that Russian goods were not competitive on the world market. A delegate pointed out that if he spent sixteen hours a day on the job, he would have no time to read or study, to which the minister replied that a sixteen-hour day still left one hour a day for reading. "In a year that comes to 365 hours." Finally, Khilkov declared that as a minister he spent many more hours on the job than the railwaymen; he arrived at his office at 7 in the morning, and "the strenuous work had spoiled his eyesight." Not surprisingly, Khilkov's callous remarks fell on deaf ears.[7] After hearing a report on the encounter with the Minister of Transportation, mass meetings on October 11 at the University of St. Petersburg, estimated at totaling over 30,000 people, unanimously adopted a resolution to join the "all-Russian railway strike."[8] By October 16 the strike had spread to every line in the country.

In the meantime, the strike had invaded other branches of the economy, despite the diffidence of revolutionary activists. For example, the Bolsheviks in Moscow, distrustful of any action not directed at a seizure of power, failed to come out in support of the general strike until October 10, and the Bolsheviks in St. Petersburg waited even longer, until the night of October 12–13.[9] But the movement had developed its own momentum. In St. Petersburg it attracted not only railway and industrial workers, but also telegraph operators, salesmen, and employees of private banks, government offices, and city utilities. Food stores were open from 11 A.M. to 2 P.M. daily, but pharmacies remained closed altogether. On October 15, the employees of the State Bank voted by a huge majority to stage a four-day political strike.[10]

On the same day, the director of the Imperial Theater asked the actors, "Does the nervous condition of the artists, provoked by current events, make it possible for them to continue working without doing violence to the performance?" Out of the 85 who responded, 55 said no, and the theater was closed. All private theaters and the Mariinskii Ballet followed suit.[11] In Moscow on October 13, employees at city hospitals and alms-houses quit working. The doctors at the Miasnitskii Hospital voted to support the liberation movement by donating 20 percent of their salaries to a general strike fund. They continued working only because they feared "the possibility of bloody events." Yet the doctors warned the government that if it sought to punish them for their stand, it would be responsible for bringing all work at the hospitals to a halt.[12] As for high school and university students, they stopped attending classes.

The crippling strike caused severe hardships in the cities and towns. Since no cattle were being shipped into St. Petersburg, the price of meat rose by 50 percent; other food items and water were also becoming scarce, and consequently the population of the capital faced the dangers of famine and disease. In Moscow the price of meat doubled, milk was completely unavailable, and the supplies of grain were rapidly being depleted. On October 9, Muscovites panicked because the water had become muddy. Rumors circulated that the strikers had contaminated the city's supply, which prompted the mayor to ask that guards be stationed at the waterworks. In the capital, where the public could not obtain medicine, the Governor-General ordered military pharmacies to fill civilians' prescriptions, but he warned that supplies were running low.[13] Large numbers of the deceased could not be buried for lack of transportation; as one newspaper reported, "The mortuaries at city hospitals are overflowing with bodies."[14]

On October 16, eight days after the beginning of the strike, Moscow was an eerie city: "Neither gas nor electric lights work," *Russkie vedomosti* reported; "the movement of trams, either horse-drawn or electrical ones, has not resumed. The telegraph system, telephones, and post offices do not work. A majority of the stores are closed, and the entrances and windows are boarded up with gates and shutters. The main business in stores is food items, conducted while the windows are blocked up by wooden shutters. The water lines have begun to work; in various parts of the city water is available [only] at certain times, from the morning until 1:30 P.M."[15] Fearing a catastrophe, the city council deputy A. I. Guchkov declared that "the present strike can only be explained as a psychosis that has seized our society."[16]

If Guchkov was right, then the disease was highly contagious. Virtually every urban center in the Empire was affected by it. In Kharkov, for example, railroad workers began to strike on October 10: "Crowds of people went into the streets demanding an end to all work in the mills and factories. Toward evening work stopped everywhere. Shops and bakeries closed. Some meetings were held. Crowds marched in the streets with flags. An isolated crowd marched with portraits of the Tsar. . . . Transportation has stopped. Prices of food products have risen."[17]

In the Belorussian town of Orsha "the demand of workers to close down was heeded by all the shops, artisanal and industrial establishments, and offices, and by the local branch of the commercial bank and the girls' high school."[18] In Batum "every shop was closed [by October 10]. At night the city has no electric light. Meat is bought by military officials under the guard of patrols. Citizens crowded around stores cannot obtain meat. The [city] council is not functioning. In private banks work has stopped. The mood is tense."[19] In Zhitomir the strike did not begin until October 16, when a "crowd walked along the streets demanding that stores be closed; workers left their jobs at all the shops, printing works, trams, electric stations, and water mains. Massive crowds gathered in the streets and squares shouting 'Down with the Autocracy!'" One group of marchers entered the city council building, sat down at the tables reserved for deputies, and drank in revolutionary speeches delivered in the presence of the hapless mayor and other officials.[20] It has been estimated that throughout the country more than two million workers and other employees joined in the general strike.[21] The Empire was paralyzed. Deprived of virtually all services, people believed that they were "experiencing the predicament of Robinson Crusoe."[22]

On the whole, the strike was peaceful, largely because the crowds had an outlet for their anger and frustration. They could attend innumerable meetings, most often at institutions of higher learning, where radicals excoriated the government and called for an end to the autocratic regime. "At one university [St. Petersburg]," wrote an eyewitness, "each day there gathered thousands of people, and the number who came grew and grew. The minds of the people were occupied, their attention was riveted [on the speeches]. To go to a meeting—that was the way to spend one's free time. And what kind of meetings there were! I remember that on one and the same evening there took place the following meetings at the university: public meetings of Social Democrats, railway employees, civil servants, dentists, teachers, [and] high school students; it was surmised that there was even a meeting of policemen. . . . There was apprehension about the irrepressible striving for gatherings and meetings. People feared the possibility of an accidental, instinctive outburst by the crowds, which could always lead to panic and catastrophe."[23]

The relatively small amount of violence during the general strike can also be explained by the authorities' hesitation to resort to force against the united opposition of so many different social groups. It was one thing to suppress groups of workers or peasants. But a protest movement that enjoyed the active support of white-collar employees, professionals, many government employees, and even a substantial sector of the business class had to be handled more gently. The extent of support lent by the middle class was remarkable. Some industrialists promised to pay their workers for days they missed during the strike—a promise that was kept.[24] Industrialists in Moscow organized breakfast meetings at the Metropol Hotel to collect money for the families of striking workers. On one such occasion they collected 14,000 rubles. At a different meeting, the middle-class participants contributed 603 rubles for Social Democratic workers; and at yet another, 2,500 rubles were donated for workers on strike. Some affluent sympathizers set up canteens in their homes for children of destitute families.[25]

So long as they emphasized political goals, the various social groups cooperated surprisingly well. To be sure, the railway employees' list of demands, published on October 9, included both economic and political items; and the Bolsheviks and Mensheviks promoted socialism as their goal in the many thousands of leaflets they distributed. Nevertheless, there was one overriding goal endorsed by all the protesting groups—the elimination of the autocratic regime.

And at least for the duration of the strike, all groups tended to place greater emphasis on their common demands than on economic and social issues over which they differed. As *Russkie vedomosti* put it on October 16: "There is only one way out of the situation: the immediate satisfaction of those demands that are the mainspring of the mass movement and that are displayed on its banner. It is necessary to secure full and complete amnesty, it is necessary to secure a guarantee of political freedom, it is necessary to secure the convocation of a legislative assembly elected on the basis of universal suffrage. At the present time, there are no other means of pacifying the country, and every minute of delay on these politically necessary steps threatens the country with an unprecedented disaster of anarchy and destruction."[26] Few who sympathized with the strike would have quarreled with these words, though some may have argued that they did not go far enough.

Although the general strike was by all accounts an extraordinary event, unprecedented for the high degree of discipline and self-sacrifice shown by masses of people, it had a darker side as well. For one thing, not every worker was prepared to engage in a prolonged strike. In Moscow and in other cities, it was not uncommon for workers to resort to physical intimidation of those who were reluctant to leave their jobs.[27] The organization that would within a few days assume prominence in St. Petersburg as the Soviet of Workers' Deputies encouraged such acts. On October 13, it issued the following declaration: "Comrades, those workers who do not wish to stop working, despite the resolutions of the Soviet of Deputies, should be removed from their jobs. Those who are not for us are against us, and against them the Soviet of Deputies has decided to apply more extreme methods—force."[28] The Soviet also sent deputies "to bosses with the demand that they immediately close their establishments on pain of destruction of their factories or workshops."[29] To prevent strikebreakers from running the railways, workers occasionally removed rails, broke semaphores, and overturned locomotives. On October 9, a crowd of strikers made its way into the Nikolaevskii Station in Moscow to let out the steam from all the engines.[30] Moreover, workers did not refrain entirely from vandalism. On October 10, a crowd attacked a post office in Moscow, drove out the employees and soldiers, and pilfered goods at will. Then it moved into the telegraph building where it caused further destruction.[31]

In some cities, armed clashes broke out between strikers and soldiers. In Odessa, for example, lives were lost during numerous disturbances. Officials claimed that, on October 14, demonstrators overturned trams and buses in the streets, erected eleven barricades, and opened fire on soldiers. Consequently, the army "was compelled" to shoot in order to disperse the crowd. When the fighting subsided, one Cossack and one gendarme had been injured and eight demonstrators lay dead.[32] In Ekaterinoslav, barricades appeared on October 11, and during three days of street clashes 28 people perished.[33] In battles between students and soldiers in Kharkov, fourteen civilians lost their lives.[34] Given the dimensions of the work stoppage and its political significance, the total number of casualties was relatively small. But the strike was by no means an entirely peaceful affair.

Many contemporaries were astonished at the discipline displayed by Russian workers, an element of the population widely regarded as ignorant, unruly, and politically timid. The bureaucrats, who had favored paternalism in the factories, looked upon the proletariat (and the peasants) as children who were incapable of independent, organized action in defense of their interests. It is therefore not surprising that shortly after the strike ended, defenders of the old order claimed that it had been German-inspired. As a dispatch from the U.S. Embassy put it, the strike was said to be "entirely organized by the German Socialists, they going so far even as to send representatives to insure the program being thoroughly carried out. This would account for the completeness of the organization which is entirely contrary to the Russian character. It is even said that the German Socialists were willing to take so much trouble on this occasion in order that it might serve as a rehearsal for what they intend to attempt some future day in the German Empire. The money on this occasion was furnished entirely by outside sources."[35]

Although never substantiated, the charge that Germans were responsible for the general strike is noteworthy on three counts: it is another example of the penchant of human beings to seek conspiratorial explanations for unexpected and undesirable occurrences; it demonstrates the unwillingness or inability of the defenders of the old order to come to terms with a new and threatening political force; and it anticipates a school of historians that attributes the outbreak and outcome of the Revolution of 1917 to foreign money also supplied by Germans, in this case the German government.

In truth, in October 1905 the industrial proletariat emerged as an organized—and for a time also as the most dynamic—force in the revolution. It was not the only class to go on the offensive against the government, but it clearly initiated the strike, kept it going, and provided most of the cannon fodder for the assault on the old order. The workers may not have been able to bring the government to its knees without the support of white-collar employees, professionals, and the middle class. But if the workers had not taken the lead, there would have been no general strike in the first place. In the nine months since Bloody Sunday, the proletariat had undergone a notable process of politicization, and the autocracy's reluctance to introduce fundamental reforms had induced a decisive shift to the left in society at large. It was the congruence of these two developments that furnished the essential backdrop to the general strike, the opposition's most impressive challenge to the autocracy during the revolution.

The establishment of the Soviet in St. Petersburg further testified to the growing political activism of the working class. On the evening of October 13, about 40 deputies, more or less formally elected by workers at the behest of Menshevik agitators, met at the Technological Institute to set up a "strike committee" to provide "unified direction" for the movement that was now engulfing the entire city. The newly formed committee called on all factories to elect deputies, one for every 500 workers. Within a few days, 562 deputies were chosen, the single largest group representing the metalworkers (351); 57 were textile workers, and the rest were distributed among other industries. Many of the deputies had previously served in positions of leadership, either on the short-lived Shidlovsky Commission or as *starosti* (factory elders).

The Soviet of Workers' Deputies (*Sovet rabochikh deputatov*) met in the building of the Free Economic Society. On October 17, the deputies elected an Executive Committee of 50, which made the major administrative decisions, though issues were publicly debated and voted upon by the entire Soviet. G. S. Khrustalev-Nosar, a left-liberal lawyer who later became a Menshevik, was selected to be chairman of the Soviet. In 1905, the Petersburg Soviet took pains to adopt a neutral stand on partisan politics, which was one of the reasons for its great popularity with the working class. Each socialist party (Menshevik, Bolshevik, and Socialist Revolutionary) was given seven seats on the Executive Committee. Leon Trotsky (L. D. Bronstein), who had aligned himself with the Mensheviks, was the only revolutionary Marxist of any prominence to play an important role in the Soviet. Twenty-six years old at the time, Trotsky had already made his mark as a brilliant polemicist, incisive dialectician, powerful orator, and dynamic personality. He served on the Executive Committee and, after Khrustalev-Nosar's arrest on November 26, became its dominant figure.

Because the Soviet in St. Petersburg attained great authority during the general strike and became even more prominent in 1917, Social Democratic activists and historians have argued at length not only about its origins but also about the way it was viewed by revolutionary Marxists. Bolsheviks have been extremely sensitive on the subject because in 1905 their party was ambivalent about the new organization. Initially, the Bolsheviks favored the Soviet; but as soon as it assumed political leadership of the St. Petersburg proletariat, they became hostile toward it. They were uncomfortable with any organization that strove to be nonpartisan, believing that such an organ could not genuinely speak for proletarian interests.

Only after Lenin arrived in St. Petersburg in November did the Bolsheviks desist from attacking the Soviet outright. Actually, Lenin himself also distrusted the Soviet because of its nonpartisan stance, though in a document that came to light only in 1940 he argued that the Soviet should represent various social classes and groups and that it might turn into the "nucleus of the provisional revolutionary government." However, this expression of strong support was uncharacteristic for Lenin. In 1905 he took part in only a few sessions of the Executive Committee and made no significant contribution to its work. Moreover, in Moscow, where the Bolsheviks were stronger than the Mensheviks, a Soviet was not introduced until November 21.[36]

On the other hand, the Mensheviks enthusiastically supported the Soviets, whose origins can in fact be traced to several ideas they had formulated in 1905. For some months before the general strike, the Mensheviks had advocated the creation of organs of "revolutionary self-government." In the summer of 1905 the Menshevik leader P. B. Axelrod had proposed the convocation of a "workers' congress," which was to be based on working-class elections in factories and local districts. On October 10, it was the Mensheviks who issued the call for the election of deputies to a Soviet. All these proposals and activities were part of the larger plan to create a broad proletarian political party. The function of the soviets would be to lead the working class into the Social Democratic movement and to help train cadres for the party. Once the Soviet in Petersburg came into existence, the Mensheviks rallied behind it; moreover, as a Soviet historian recently put it, "the leadership in the Soviet was assumed by the Mensheviks."[37]

The St. Petersburg Soviet became the headquarters of the general strike, exerting pressure on wavering workers, intimidating industrialists disinclined to close their factories, and keeping people informed of developments in the work stoppage. On October 17, it began to publish a newspaper, *Izvestiia Soveta Rabochikh Deputatov*, and over the next two months ten issues appeared in runs ranging from 35,000 to 60,000. The Soviet asked the editors of the left-leaning *Syn otechestva* to print *Izvestiia*, but they refused, no doubt fearful of the government's wrath. The first issue was therefore printed at night without the owner's knowledge. A few days later, several deputies appeared at the printing shop of *Syn otechestva* and announced to the workers: "Comrades! You're under arrest. Who wants to compose *Izvestiia* No. 2?" Everyone burst out laughing and confessed to wanting to print the paper. For one issue, the seventh, Soviet deputies even secretly used the press of the ultraconservative *Novoe vremia*.[38] *Izvestiia* was an informative paper eagerly read by workers hungry for news and political guidance. Its ideological thrust was clearly Social Democratic.

The Soviet sought to influence local government in a wide range of areas. On October 14, it called on the city council to assume responsibility for maintaining adequate food supplies for workers, to end financial subsidies for policemen and gendarmes, to secure removal of the army from the city, and to provide the Soviet with funds to form a workers' militia. The council, taken aback by the demands but unwilling to offend the Soviet, neither approved nor rejected them.[39]

The Soviet also took it upon itself to direct food stores to open their doors during the strike from 8 to 11 A.M. on weekdays and from 1 to 3 P.M. on Sundays and holidays. On October 19, it proclaimed freedom of the press and declared that only newspapers that did not submit their material to the censors would be printed by workers. On the other hand, in a less liberal spirit, the Soviet directed that "official publications" not be sold; the kiosks of vendors who disobeyed the directive were to be destroyed and the offending newspapers confiscated.[40] By the time the general strike ended, the Soviet in the capital had gone far toward arrogating to itself political powers normally exercised by a governmental authority. Over the succeeding ten weeks, the Soviet's powers increased substantially.

In all, workers in some 40 to 50 cities formed local soviets in the fall of 1905; in addition, soldiers and peasants established their own councils in several regions, bringing the total to about 80. The activities of these soviets varied considerably. Some acted primarily as strike committees, whereas several in the mining districts of the Urals and the Donets Basin concentrated on preparing for an armed struggle. The latter did not last very long, and consequently not much is known about them. In most of the soviets, Social Democrats predominated: in Odessa, Kiev, and Baku, and in the south of Russia generally, the Mensheviks had the upper hand; in Moscow, Kostroma, and Tver, and in the cities of the Donets Basin, the Bolsheviks were ascendant.[41]

Within a few days of the onset of the general strike, the authorities came under pressure to bring it to an end. On October 13, for example, a private group of industrialists in Moscow sent a delegation to Governor-General P. P. Durnovo urging him to resort to stern measures to stop the disorders and to resist demands for political reform. On the same day, a group of seventeen Moscow bankers recommended the imposition of martial law together with the granting of civil and political rights to the people. The bankers warned that repression alone would result in unnecessary shedding of blood.[42] Though appeals from private businessmen for strong action were not uncommon, public expressions of sympathy for the strike were more frequent. Wherever city councils met to discuss the crisis, most deputies supported the strike, though with varying degrees of enthusiasm. Although the city council in Moscow did not take a vote on the work stoppage, many deputies were known to favor the strikers' political aims.[43] The city council in St. Petersburg voted almost unanimously to ask the government to adopt "without delay measures to satisfy the pressing economic and political demands of the population."[44]

· · · · ·

The government itself vacillated for several days. "Nobody knows," the German Ambassador in St. Petersburg wrote on October 15, "who is to give orders. The ministers attack each other." The ambassador was also under the impression that "most ministers have in effect been dismissed, [but that] their successors have not been named or the [new] appointments have not been made public."[45] It has not been possible to substantiate this account, but it is true that until October 12, the government took no measures to bring the crisis to an end. On that day the Tsar ordered General Trepov, who had himself apparently concluded that concessions (such as autonomy for the universities) had been a mistake, to deal vigorously with the unrest. Trepov immediately sent a directive to police chiefs in all provinces with a sizable revolutionary movement to "act in the most drastic manner" to prevent any disorders, "not stopping at the direct application of force."[46] A day later Trepov ordered the Governor-General of Moscow to prevent any public meeting that had not been sanctioned. The police must disperse illegal meetings "with all means, including the overt use of force."[47] On October 14, Trepov issued a proclamation to the people of St. Petersburg that has since become notorious. Printed on the first page of the daily newspapers and posted on walls and fences in the capital, the proclamation began by promising that lives and property would be protected. The police and the army, it continued, had been ordered to put down all disturbances with the "most decisive measures." If crowds refused to disperse, policemen and soldiers were "not to use blanks and not to spare bullets." It was his duty, Trepov contended, to warn the people about the "painful consequences" that would result from participation in street disorders.[48]

Given the tense atmosphere in the streets, it is hard to imagine a government action less calculated to restore calm than Trepov's provocative proclamation. On the very day it was distributed, some 40,000 people defiantly streamed into the streets near the university. In addition, every auditorium in the buildings was filled to capacity with adherents from various labor unions. However, "at the time of the meetings," one eyewitness reported, "nowhere near the university could the army or police be seen; everyone was expecting them [in view of Trepov's proclamation]."[49]

Why the police and the army ignored Trepov is not clear. Conceivably, his subordinates realized that any action to disperse the crowd would have led to a bloodbath even more terrible than the one on January 9. They may also have doubted that success in scattering the crowds would guarantee an end to the strike. In fact, the public mood was so defiant that implementation of Trepov's order would probably have resulted in prolonged and bitter street fighting, which many officials wanted to avoid.

Once the dimensions of the strike movement became apparent, several senior advisers to the Tsar acknowledged that political reform was necessary to bring the crisis to an end. The main spokesman of this group was Witte, who had returned from the peace negotiations in September with a greatly enhanced reputation as a statesman and political leader. Witte still believed that a progressive autocracy with far-sighted leadership was the best form of government for the country, but he recognized that in view of the revolutionary assault on authority it was now impossible to reestablish the old order. He therefore hoped to salvage as much as possible of that order by means of moderate political concessions to the opposition.[50]

Most of the Tsar's advisers who favored the political option considered Witte to be the only person with the vision and political skill to lead the country during this turbulent period. Indeed, Count D. M. Solskii, one of Nicholas's most trusted counselors, urged Witte in mid-September not to go abroad for a rest since only he could save Russia from "collapse and ruin."[51] It seems that the Tsar himself ordered Witte "to remain among us [because] I will need you."[52] The trouble was that however much Nicholas recognized Witte's abilities, he could not abide the man, believing him to be overbearing and dangerously ambitious. At the same time, Witte nurtured a strong dislike for the monarch, whom he regarded as shallow, indecisive, and utterly devoid of political wisdom. Still, Witte was profoundly patriotic and eager to do all in his power to preserve some of the rudiments of the traditional order. And he was ambitious. The thought of being the savior of Russia, the man who would restore calm and stability, appealed to his vanity. It is inconceivable that he could have resisted Solskii's flattering plea to remain in Russia.

Soon after the outbreak of the general strike, Witte, at Solskii's suggestion, requested an audience with the Tsar to discuss the domestic crisis. When he arrived at the Palace on October 9, Witte had on his person a memorandum he had prepared on the sources of the unrest and the most effective way of dealing with them. In this document Witte unhesitatingly championed political reform. In his view, the "roots" of the crisis were to be found in the "disturbed equilibrium between the aspirations of the thinking elements and the external forms of their life. Russia has outgrown the existing regime and is striving for an order based on civic liberty. Consequently, the forms of Russia's political life must be raised to the level of the ideas that animate the moderate majority of the people." He recommended that civil liberties be granted immediately, even before the meeting of the State Duma. In addition to creating a "legal order," the government must permit the free election of a national Duma and must also "sincerely strive" to implement all the reforms promised in December 1904. Finally, Witte recommended "a firm tendency toward the elimination of extraordinary regulations" and the "avoidance of measures of repression directed against acts that do not threaten either Society or the State." Seditious actions must be suppressed only "in strict accordance with the law and in spiritual union with the moderate majority of the people."[53] The last few words are critical: Witte sought to detach the moderates from the opposition camp by introducing reforms that would establish a constitutional order without, however, reducing the monarchy to political impotence. This strategy was to become the core of Witte's policies over the next few months.

At the conclusion of his audience with the Tsar, Witte pointed out that the only alternative to the policy he proposed was the appointment of a dictator, who would have to subdue the opposition by force. He emphasized his preference for a political solution, but, as was his wont in the presence of the sovereign, Witte did not insist that his proposal was necessarily the best one.[54]

The depth of Witte's commitment to a political approach to the crisis emerges from a conversation he had with Count Aehrenthal on October 16. The Austro-Hungarian Ambassador argued against concessions to the opposition on the ground that "Civil liberties that are won by such brutal methods [strikes] could not be a blessing to the people." It seemed to Aehrenthal that only after the government had reasserted its authority should it contemplate reforms. Witte retorted that such an approach "was possible a year ago, not now." He considered it "absolutely" necessary to avoid a conflict between the 2,000-man garrison and the one million civilians in St. Petersburg. "Je ne veux pas être le bourreau du peuple russe [I do not wish to be the hangman of the Russian people]," Witte declared. Chaos could be avoided only if the "peaceful, calm population, which, to be sure, is resorting to unusual methods in demonstrating against the regime, is detached from the anarchistic elements. The detachment can only be achieved by means of a break with the existing [political] system, and repression can be applied only if disorders then continue." Although Witte considered it unlikely that the residents of St. Petersburg faced the danger of mass violence, he nevertheless advised Aehrenthal to leave the capital with his family "via Stockholm."[55]

Aehrenthal, who found these views anathema, shared the opinion of Russian ultraconservatives that Witte had become the champion of reform because he yearned to achieve "the highest power in Russia. . . . He had exploited the revolutionary upsurge in order to reach his goal." It was widely known, according to the Ambassador, that during the winter of 1904–5 there had already "existed a link between the revolutionaries and Witte. . . . If I speak of revolutionaries, then I have in mind the progressive zemstvo people and the followers of the Social Democratic Party, who are supported by the intelligentsia, or, more accurately, the intelligentsia proletariat. The army of strikes is being led by precisely these elements." And now, a year later, Aehrenthal reported, Witte had concluded a "pact" with the leaders of the Social Democrats by promising "to bring about a constitution, while numerous groups of revolutionaries promised not to disturb the peace." Accordingly, Witte, together with many spokesmen of society, was trying to "intimidate" Nicholas into granting a constitution.[56] Ultraconservatives searching for a sinister conspiracy to explain the plight of the country found these charges against Witte comforting. They continued to attack him in this vein after he became Prime Minister, which greatly reduced his ability to govern.

The notion that unscrupulous men had manipulated Tsar Nicholas and cynically converted him into an alarmist over the domestic situation in October is quite untenable. On the contrary, the evidence is overwhelming that the informed public, within Russia and abroad, genuinely believed that the fate of the autocracy hung in the balance. As early as October 11, the ultraconservative newspaper *Novoe vremia* declared that "We have gone the limit. . . . We need new measures and principles."[57] Count P. K. Benkendorf, the Palace Marshal, an intelligent man thoroughly devoted to the monarch, expressed distress over the fact that the Tsar's five children were with him at Peterhof. If Nicholas suddenly had to set sail from Peterhof in search of asylum, the five youngsters would be "a great impediment."[58]

Moreover, rumors circulated in St. Petersburg that Kaiser Wilhelm had invited Nicholas to Germany in the event of imminent danger to the Imperial family, although the reports on the political advice Wilhelm had given the Tsar were contradictory. Some claimed that he had urged the granting of a constitution, others that he had offered German troops to help suppress the revolutionary movement. A German army corps was said to be poised at the border, ready to march into Russia as soon as the Tsar requested its intervention. Several senior officials at Court thought that the Tsar should accept the Kaiser's offer of asylum, but Witte argued that Nicholas's departure would be a fatal blow to the existing order because it would remove the one person who could unite the forces opposed to the radicals.[59]

Many officials in St. Petersburg were apprehensive about the adequacy of the military forces at the government's disposal, since an armed uprising seemed to be a distinct possibility. The Austro-Hungarian Ambassador asked Count Lamsdorff in strictest confidence whether he would be able to provide protection for the embassy "in case of need."[60] At a meeting of several ministers on or about October 14, the Minister of War, General A. F. Rediger, and Trepov revealed that there were enough troops in the vicinity of the capital to quell an uprising but not enough to restore traffic between St. Petersburg and Peterhof, let alone in the rest of the country. The Minister of War also mentioned his concern about signs of disaffection among the reserves, who were distressed at not having been demobilized immediately after the conclusion of peace with Japan. He was even more concerned over the fact that soldiers in some units of the army had begun to grumble about being used for police work. Subsequently, Witte contended that it was only because the army could not be trusted to carry out orders that Nicholas in the end had decided against the use of "physical force" to crush the strike.[61]

· · · · ·

In the meantime, senior officials at Court discussed Witte's political program, which consisted of two main points: the issuance of a manifesto granting civil and political rights, and the establishment of a "unified ministry" headed by a Prime Minister who would have primary responsibility for running the government. Under the prevailing system, each minister reported directly to the Tsar, an arrangement that made it possible for ministers to pursue contradictory policies. Witte also suggested that the manifesto not be published over the Tsar's name. Instead, Nicholas was to approve, publicly, Witte's report promising reform. Witte pointed out that the monarch would thus be spared any blame if the new political system failed or if implementation of the reforms was delayed. But Witte's enemies at Court and the Tsar himself suspected that Witte really wanted to enhance his own prestige. There was even talk of his planning to become "president of the All-Russian Republic." [62]

On October 13, the Tsar indicated partial acceptance of Witte's program: he approved a decree creating a "unified cabinet" and asked Witte to coordinate the activities of the ministers. Witte, however, immediately informed the Tsar that this measure alone would not suffice to end the crisis. He again insisted that the autocrat faced only two realistic alternatives: to appoint a dictator, who would follow a policy of repression, or to allow extensive reform, which would have to include a manifesto promising political rights. Witte gave the monarch an outline of such a manifesto. On the evening of October 14, Witte received word from Prince A. A. Orlov that the Tsar wanted to see him again the next morning and that he should bring along a finished draft of a manifesto. Not feeling well that day, Witte asked his confidante, Prince A. D. Obolenskii, who had previously held the post of Assistant Minister of Internal Affairs and was now the Assistant Minister of Finance, to prepare the draft, which Witte himself took to the Tsar at 11 A.M. on October 15. One of the more important people to attend the meeting was the Grand Duke Nikolai Nikolaevich, the Tsar's cousin and the only person who possessed all the necessary qualifications for the post of dictator: he was a zealous defender of the autocracy, enjoyed the confidence of the sovereign, and was in the good graces of the Imperial family. The Grand Duke raised some questions but did not appear to be hostile to the manifesto.

The Tsar, however, continued to delay on a final decision. On the evening of October 16, Count Frederiks told Witte that the sovereign was still uneasy about making an irrevocable commitment to far-reaching concessions. Witte, dismayed, now suggested that someone else be appointed as Prime Minister and that he himself be made governor of a province. [63] Then, unexpectedly, on October 17 Witte was summoned to Peterhof to be informed that the Tsar had approved his draft of the manifesto. The decisive factor in the new turn of events was the dramatic refusal by Grand Duke Nikolai Nikolaevich to serve as dictator.

According to Witte, when Count Frederiks informed the Grand Duke that the Tsar wished him to take over as dictator, the following scene was played out. "The Grand Duke took a revolver from his pocket: 'You see this revolver,'" he said, "'I am now going to the Tsar and will implore him to sign the manifesto and Witte's program; either he signs or I will shoot myself in the forehead.'" "With these words," Frederiks continued, "he left me. After a while, the Grand Duke returned and transmitted to me an order to rewrite in final form the Manifesto and report, and then . . . bring them to the sovereign for his signature."[64]

What prompted the Grand Duke's emotional outburst is not clear. He was known as a reactionary, and his instinct would have been to apply repression against the opposition. Perhaps he was reluctant to undertake such a course with troops whose reliability was suspect. There is also some evidence that he was influenced by a labor leader, M. A. Ushakov, who had visited him on October 14 or 15 to plead for concessions and the appointment of Witte as Prime Minister. Ushakov had emphasized that the workers were still loyal to Russia but were determined to obtain a constitution.[65]

For Tsar Nicholas, the encounter with the Grand Duke Nikolai Niko-laevich was the last straw. Trepov had already informed him that for the army to reassert the autocracy's authority, a bloodbath would be re-quired, and even then Trepov was not altogether certain of success. He advised the ruler to accede to Witte's wishes. According to Mosolov, the Director of the Chancellery, Trepov claimed that previously he had not doubted his ability to restore order, but that the "discussions at the high-est circles about the necessity of reforms had stirred up the masses to such an extent that it was now necessary to give them something."[66] Without bothering to consult his Minister of Internal Affairs, Bulygin, Nicholas announced that he would sign the manifesto.

Clearly, Nicholas reached this decision not because he was now per-suaded of the wisdom of restructuring Russia's political system, but rather because he knew he had no choice. "My dear Mama," he wrote at the time, "you can't imagine what I went through before that mo-ment. . . . From all over Russia they cried for it, they begged for it, and around me many—very many—held the same views. . . . There was no other way out than to cross oneself and give what everyone was asking for."[67] Also, he appointed Witte Prime Minister not because he thought well of him and trusted his judgment, but because he had no choice. To a large extent, then, the new order would be shaped by a man who still did not believe in the desirability of reform. It was an inauspicious beginning for the "renewal" of Russia.

The Manifesto of October 17 was quite brief, basically an outline of reforms the government intended to introduce in the coming months. It read as follows:[68]

Unrest and Disturbances in the capitals and in many parts of Our Empire fill Our heart with great and heavy grief. The welfare of the Russian Sovereign is inseparable from the welfare of the people, and the people's sorrow is His sorrow. The unrest, which now has made its appearance, may give rise to profound disaffection among the people and become a menace to the integrity and unity of Our State.

The great vow of Tsarist service enjoins Us to strive with all the force of Our reason and authority for the quickest cessation of unrest so perilous to the State. Having ordered the proper authorities to take measures to suppress the direct manifestation of disorder, rioting, and violence, and to guard the safety of peaceful people to seek to fulfill in peace the duties incumbent upon them, We, in order to carry out more successfully the measures designed by Us for the pacification of the State, have recognized the necessity to coordinate the activities of the higher Government.

We impose upon the Government the obligation to carry out Our inflexible will:

(1) To grant the population the unshakable foundations of civic freedom based on the principles of real personal inviolability, freedom of conscience, speech, assembly, and union.

(2) Without halting the scheduled elections to the State Duma, to admit to participation in the Duma, as far as is possible in the short time remaining before its call, those classes of the population which at present are altogether deprived of the franchise, leaving the further development of the principle of universal suffrage to the new legislative order, and

(3) To establish it as an unbreakable rule that no law can become effective without the approval of the State Duma and that the elected representatives of the people should be guaranteed an opportunity for actual participation in the supervision of the legality of the actions of authorities appointed by Us.

We call upon all the faithful sons of Russia to remember their duty to their Fatherland, to aid in putting an end to the unprecedented disturbances, and together with Us to make every effort to restore peace and quiet in our native land.

Issued at Peterhof on the seventeenth day of October in the year of Our Lord, nineteen hundred and five, and the eleventh year of Our reign. The original text signed in His Imperial Majesty's own hand.

Nicholas

With relatively few exceptions, Russians from all walks of life greeted the October Manifesto with jubilation, or at the very least with profound relief. "Thank God," exclaimed General Trepov, "the Manifesto has been signed. Now a new life will begin." His assistant, Rachkovskii, agreed: "Thank God, thank God. Tomorrow the people of St. Petersburg will kiss each other on the streets as they do on Easter." Half in jest, Rachkovskii told Gerasimov, the chief of the security police, that "Your business will now do badly. You won't have any work." Gerasimov joined in the levity. No one, he said, would be more pleased than he if the security police could go out of business.[69] In fact, Gerasimov was thoroughly apprehensive about the new order. At a meeting of police chiefs in St. Petersburg to discuss how the manifesto should be publicized, someone suggested that it be printed in golden letters and read out to congregations at churches. Someone else suggested that heralds be used to announce the news. Gerasimov, however, was rather somber: "I fear that the revolution will begin tomorrow. We are talking about golden letters and imperial heralds, but I think that at the university they are already showing red flags."[70]

Shortly after the manifesto appeared in print, at close to midnight on October 17 in the Supplement to *Pravitelstvennyi vestnik* (*The Government Herald*), a student read the document aloud in the streets of the capital, evoking shouts of "Hurrah." Very quickly, other students acquired copies of the paper and hurried to street lamps to read the manifesto to milling crowds. "Everywhere joyous exclamations could be heard. The army and police were not in evidence."[71]

The next day in Theater Square in Moscow, some 50,000 people listened to speeches on the significance of the document. "The demonstrators branched off from here to all parts of the city. Many officers, ladies, workers, intelligentsia, civil servants, young students, merchants, salesmen, and railway employees wore red bands, scarves, ribbons. . . ." The entire city was draped in flags.[72] In the center of St. Petersburg, an unprecedented event "made a significant impression on all the people. A [very large] red flag with the inscription 'Freedom of Assembly' was raised and was greeted by a [great] procession of people who removed their hats. A large portion of the public [did the same] and joined in humming the melody of the Marseillaise. . . . From all the windows and balconies there were shouts of approval."[73] Such scenes of joy were evident throughout Russia. Few people had expected so far-reaching a victory so quickly.

City council representatives promptly supported the manifesto. On October 18, S. A. Muromtsev submitted a resolution to the Moscow City Council that lauded the Tsar's concessions; he also asked the deputies to stand for a minute in honor of those who had lost their lives in the cause of Russia's liberation. All but three deputies (A. I. Guchkov, K. A. Kaznacheev, and A. S. Shmakov) stood up. Muromtsev also introduced motions calling for full amnesty for political prisoners, an end to the state of emergency in all of Russia, free public education, and financial aid to the families of strikers. The motions passed by an overwhelming margin (62 to 24). Similar motions were passed in the city councils in Ekaterinoslav, Nikolaev, and Sevastopol.[74] The St. Petersburg City Council sent a telegram to the Tsar welcoming the granting of freedom to the people, "who firmly believe in the great future of our beloved, sacred land. Hurrah to the Tsar of a free nation."[75]

The change in mood in the capital profoundly moved the left-liberal Petrunkevich. He recalled that in June few people showed interest in the delegation that had visited the Tsar to plead for reform. But "now . . . the capital of the Empire buzzed like a huge garden full of bees on a hot summer day, and the entire atmosphere was saturated with revolutionary ferment. [There were] all sorts of gatherings, conferences, meetings in the morning and evening, halls full to overflowing, ardent speeches by orators, newspapers that had emerged without prior permission, printed leaflets, brochures, magazines filled with illustrations, and caricatures painted in bright colors. The censorship of the press did not function; the police were unusually obliging and polite, just like the English 'Bobby.' Never before had Russia experienced anything like it. . . . The twentieth century and European civilization had left their imprint on Russian life and subjected it to their influence. . . . Russia was like a powerful, icebound river whose ice was now breaking under the rays of the spring sun: the liberated masses poured out in all directions without encountering any obstacles whatsoever."[76]

The Tsar's promise to permit the election of a State Duma with legislative and not merely consultative functions was a decisive moment in the revolution. By conceding that he was no longer the sole repository of political power, Nicholas did what he had vowed never to do: he abandoned the principle of autocracy. Realizing this, the liberal press hailed the manifesto as a "great historical event," the "first step toward a Russian constitution," the beginnings of a "new order," the triumph of a "peaceful national revolution." "We can congratulate each other," wrote the editors of *Russkie vedomosti*, "on the realization of our cherished aspirations! Let us embrace as free people, as citizens of a free, constitutional Russia!" True, the manifesto did not mention a constitution, but now that political freedoms had been conceded to the people, the State Duma would formulate a Basic Law for the country.[77]

The editors of *Pravo* claimed that Russia "since October 17 has theoretically been a constitutional monarchy" and that "no contrivance or vacillations by the authorities" could stop the forward movement of the democratic idea. The old order had no choice but to retreat. Nonetheless, the editors warned that much needed to be done to safeguard the victory over the autocracy. Both martial law and the press censorship must be ended. The editors also warned that rifts between socialists and the democratic intelligentsia could weaken the new order. The two groups would commit "great sins" before history if they did not rise above their differences and maintain the unity of the "conscious forces of the social movement."[78]

Pravo's editors were not alone in fearing that intemperate behavior by political leaders might wreck the coalition that had broken the back of the autocracy. H. N. Brailsford, a prominent member of the British Labour Party, cautioned Felix Volkhovsky about the same danger. "To me," Brailsford wrote on November 1, "it seems that you have won your victory and even if some things are still incomplete . . . the bureaucracy is so utterly demoralized that you will obtain these also without bloodshed within three months when the Duma meets. It seems to me that the surrender this time is sincere, and though I distrust Witte as much as any of you do, I believe he is intelligent enough to see that the time has gone by for trying to trick the people. I've no doubt he would like to try, but I'm pretty sure he will not dare." Brailsford was worried about the "attitude of the Socialist parties," which did not seem to share his "inborn instinct of compromise" and would not give Witte a chance to demonstrate his sincerity. He acknowledged that he feared a repetition of the violence that accompanied the Paris Commune of 1871 and the subsequent reaction. "Is it really safe for the moment to go further than the Radicals [i.e., liberal democrats] will follow?"[79]

Indeed, few militants were disposed to give Witte time to implement the manifesto. Although the strike movement did wane quickly, there had been signs even before October 17 that it was losing support; within a few days of the Tsar's announcement of concessions, most workers returned to their jobs. Several political leaders, however, refused to take a conciliatory stand. Miliukov, who had been moderately pleased with the Bulygin Duma, is quoted as having remarked at a dinner on October 17 that "nothing is changed: the war continues." Even if he did not speak these words as he later claimed, he certainly left no doubt that he did not expect the manifesto to lead to a constitutional order.[80] The Union of Unions acknowledged that the manifesto constituted a significant concession, but it nevertheless rejected the document as inadequate.[81]

The St. Petersburg Soviet refused at first to call off the strike lest such a move be interpreted as a favorable response to the manifesto. On October 18, the Soviet actually urged that the strike be continued until "such a moment when conditions necessitate a change in tactics." One day later, on learning that workers in Moscow and other cities were returning to work en masse, the Soviet quickly began to retreat. On October 20, it voted to end the strike at midday the next day and advised workers at their factories to "discuss" the decision. By this time, all labor organizations in the capital had formally decided to resume work.[82] The strike ended as it had started: workers followed their own instincts, not the directives of labor activists or political agitators.

Social Democrats of both persuasions were merciless in denouncing the government's new policies. A leaflet "To the Russian People," put out by the Bolshevik Central Committee of the RSDWP on October 18, called upon the people to continue the strike until all near-term goals of the party were realized. The Tsar and his ministers, according to the SDs, were liars who could not be trusted to implement even the puny reforms promised in the manifesto. Among other things, strikers should insist on the immediate lifting of martial law, the formation of a people's militia, the convocation of a constituent assembly, and the introduction of an eight-hour day.[83] The Bolsheviks in St. Petersburg dismissed the manifesto with the argument that "Tsarist 'freedom' is the freedom to hang, to shoot; it is the freedom for new Tsarist guards, made up of hooligans and other Black Hundreds, to kill and rob peaceful citizens!" Only the complete destruction of the existing system of rule and "the transfer of state power to all the people can bring about real freedom in Russia."[84] In other cities of the Empire, local committees composed of Bolsheviks and Mensheviks issued equally strident denunciations of the manifesto.[85]

In the rural regions of the country, news of the manifesto reached people very slowly. According to one newspaper account, a month after the proclamation had been issued many villages still had not heard of it. Local priests tended to delay disseminating information about the manifesto as long as possible, and it was not unusual for them to ignore it altogether with the claim that they had not received it. When they did inform their flocks about the Tsar's concession, they often deliberately distorted its meaning. In one village, the priest told his parishioners that they were now "free" to be zealous in discharging their religious obligations.[86] Moreover, peasants themselves frequently misinterpreted the manifesto. For example, many asserted that it granted them the right to take trees for their own use from privately held lands. In numerous villages, peasants believed that they were no longer obliged to obey the land captain or town authorities. A police officer in Vladimir province warned his superiors that it would require a great deal of effort to explain the manifesto to the people.[87]

Among those who understood the significance of the concession and welcomed it, there were many who harbored serious doubts about the government's determination to implement it fully. They needed to be convinced that the authorities would allow the people to exercise their newly won civil rights, that they would remove bureaucrats known to be hostile to the reforms, restrain the police and army, create a genuine legal order, and move swiftly to hold fair elections to the State Duma.

Witte understood the magnitude of the tasks he faced. With a nice sense for public relations, he invited the editors of the mainstream St. Petersburg press to his office the day after he was appointed Prime Minister to convey his earnest desire for support for his policies. Witte frankly admitted that his policies could not succeed without the backing of the "vital social forces" of the country and that the press could help by fostering public confidence in the new government. Only after calm had been restored, Witte asserted, would it be possible to carry out the reforms that had been promised.

The editors, however, reversed the order of priorities. To a man, they contended that the country could not be pacified until the government offered practical proof that it intended to implement the manifesto. The government must immediately grant the four-tail suffrage and amnesty for political prisoners, and it must revoke the exceptional regulations wherever they were in force, remove the army from St. Petersburg, abolish capital punishment, and dismiss Trepov, the Governor-General of St. Petersburg. The editors also declared that the newly created Union for the Defense of Freedom of the Press would proclaim and protect that freedom. Witte promised to extend amnesty to political prisoners and to promulgate a law guaranteeing freedom of the press, but he did not commit himself on the other issues.[88]

The editors and Witte could not reach agreement because they took opposing views on the central question of the day: would further reforms produce social tranquillity or was tranquillity a necessary precondition for reform? In Witte's view, the uneducated masses were unprepared for sudden, dramatic changes in the political system. Witte's argument was not without merit, as events would soon show, but his record as a government official did not inspire confidence that he would ever carry out the announced reform program—and the other government officials, not to speak of the Tsar, inspired even less confidence. "We do not know," *Russkie vedomosti* declared sarcastically on October 20, "who will be appointed to the [new] cabinet, but we do know that it will be [made] of the same bone and flesh as the previous bureaucracy, which has governed with such success up to the present time."[89] In a real sense, the differences between Witte and the editors that emerged on October 18 were the same that divided Witte and society for the six months that he served as Prime Minister. He never could bridge them, and that, as much as anything else, explains the failure of his overall strategy—to turn the nonradical opposition, still a substantial force in Russia, into an ally of the government.

· · · · ·

The accelerated politicization of vast numbers of people, stimulated by the general strike and the manifesto, complicated the Prime Minister's task. In formulating policy, he was now obliged to take into account not only the wishes of the autocrat and his camarilla but also the conflicting pressures of three new political parties, each one representing powerful forces in Russian society. Liberal activists had taken the initial steps toward organizing a party during the summer so as to mobilize popular support in the elections announced by Bulygin on August 6. Their efforts came to fruition during the general strike, when the Constitutional Democratic Party (or Party of People's Freedom, generally known as Kadets) held its founding congress in Moscow (October 12–18). Somewhat later, Shipov and Guchkov took the lead in forming the Union of October 17, which spoke for conservative liberalism. Finally, the ultraconservatives founded the Union of the Russian People (URP) to activate the masses to defend the old order.

The Kadet party was essentially a movement of professionals and liberal landowners who subscribed to the political views of the zemstvo constitutionalists and the Union of Liberation. The professional class predominated in the party's leadership. Among the 26 men who composed the Central Committee of the party in 1905, eighteen were either professors or lawyers. Although the party intended to be "above class" and to represent the interests of the entire population, it never attracted many workers or peasants. Nor did it succeed in gaining a foothold in commercial and industrial circles, neither one of which contributed a single representative to the Central Committee in 1905.[90]

Despite their lack of a strong popular base, politically the Kadets achieved a remarkable degree of prominence, and eventually of influence. Their leaders were highly intelligent, articulate, determined, and skillful in the art of political maneuvering. Their main weapon was the press. Several Kadet leaders were first-rate journalists, and they had at their disposal several distinguished newspapers and journals. *Pravo, Birzhevye vedomosti, Narodnoe pravo,* and *Russkie vedomosti* were sympathetic to the party and readily opened their pages to Kadet writers. The informative and sophisticated newspaper *Rech,* founded in 1906, came to be regarded as the party's official organ, though that honor more properly belongs to *Vestnik partii narodnoi svobody.* No other political movement could broadcast its message as widely and effectively as the Kadets.

By January 1906, the Kadets had succeeded in creating an impressive organization. Approximately 100,000 people belonged to the party, which maintained local groups in 29 provinces and party sections in many districts and cities. Over a thousand activists ran the affairs of the movement at the local level.[91]

The Kadets suffered from one critical handicap: they were liberal democrats in the Western European mold in a country whose social and economic conditions were not hospitable to liberal ideals. Their program of 1905 was without question progressive and judicious, even though their tactics were often militant. The program called for a democratic system of government, the rule of law, a progressive system of taxation, an eight-hour day, and the distribution, "insofar as is necessary," of "land alienated from private landlords and paid for by the government at equitable, not market, prices." Whether the monarchy should be retained was left open.[92] With this broad program, combining political liberalism and social reform, the Kadet leaders hoped, on the one hand, to steer a course between revolution and reaction and, on the other, to preserve the unity of the opposition. But that proved to be too formidable a task in a society that was deeply fragmented.

The Kadet program could appeal neither to the Shipovites, who considered it to be far too radical, nor to the socialists, who considered it to be too moderate. Even those moderate socialists who had earlier been members of the Union of Liberation, as well as members of the Union of Unions, found the Kadet program insufficiently radical and refused to join the party. Moreover, the constant attempts of the Kadets not to alienate movements or social groups on their right or left prevented them from pursuing a steady political course. The founding congress, for example, applauded the general strike but passed a plank in favor of women's suffrage by only two votes (out of about 80); even then, support of the plank was not made binding on the minority. Miliukov, the most eminent figure in the movement, had opposed the plank for fear that its adoption would alienate the peasants. To the delegates' amusement, Mrs. Miliukov vehemently opposed her husband's petition. Her cause won only because I. V. Gessen and V. D. Nabokov had stepped outside to see what was happening in the streets (it was October 17), a lapse for which they were sharply rebuked by Miliukov.[93]

The party's reaction to the Manifesto of October 17 was another, more significant example of Kadet equivocation. When a newspaper reporter announced that the manifesto had been issued, loud applause and shouts of "Hurrah" broke out in the hall;[94] but after some reflection, the delegates adopted a rather reserved attitude toward the Tsar's concession. Although they did not denounce it categorically, they sharply criticized its vagueness on important political questions and its failure to eliminate all exceptional laws. They also gave vent to their lack of confidence in the men who were charged with implementing it. Disappointed at the government's failure to restructure society completely according to their political conceptions, the Kadets vowed to continue the struggle for a democratic suffrage and the election of an assembly to draft a constitution.[95]

The Kadets found it especially difficult to follow a consistent line toward the labor movement. In the fall of 1905, there was strong sympathy in the party's ranks for the workers, and in November some Kadets, most notably A. A. Chuprov, actually suggested that the Kadets and socialists form a single party.[96] But by this time most Kadets were recoiling from the growing militancy inspired by the socialists, especially the constant strikes, the attempts to introduce the eight-hour day by force, and the growing number of land seizures. "Yes, we are for the revolution," wrote Miliukov, "insofar as it serves the aims of political liberation; but we are against those who pronounce the revolution 'continuous,' because we consider that a continuous revolution serves only the aims of reaction."[97] To the socialists, it seemed as though the Kadets merely paid lip service to the cause of revolution.

Essentially, despite their advocacy of social reform, most Kadets were liberals committed to the establishment of a legal order and parliamentary government. Because of the autocracy's stubborn resistance to political change, many Kadets sympathized with the stirrings from below, which alone seemed capable of wresting concessions from the Tsar. Yet they did not approve of the ultimate goals of the socialists or their extremist tactics. Unwilling to align themselves permanently with the socialist left, they were forced to give up their ideal of a unified oppositional movement. Equally unwilling to cooperate with a government whose commitment to constitutionalism they did not trust, the Kadets soon lost the capacity to exercise decisive political influence.

. . . . .

To the right of the Kadets stood the Union of October 17 (also known as Octobrists), which may more properly be considered a political association than a political party. It never attained the status of a mass movement, relying for its support on commercial and industrial interests in the cities and the moderately conservative gentry in the provinces. Not until late in 1906 did A. I. Guchkov, a wealthy Muscovite industrialist, succeed in imposing an organizational structure on the Union that transformed it into a party.

Although the members of the Union of October 17 frequently clashed over issues, they all subscribed to several general political positions. Opposed to the arbitrariness of the autocracy and bureaucracy, they were generally content with the October Manifesto, which they confidently expected to lead to a political system according civil rights and equality before the law to all. They considered additional reforms desirable and believed that they could be achieved through the State Duma.

Unlike the Kadets, the Octobrists were strong believers in the monarchy, both as a symbol of national unity and as a center of political authority. "I am a monarchist," Guchkov said in his memoirs. "I remained one, and I will die a monarchist."[98] The Octobrists opposed calling a constituent assembly, which, they held, would signify a complete break with tradition. Much more than the Kadets, they tolerated and even sanctioned repressive measures against revolutionaries. They supported the right of workers to form unions and to strike over economic issues, but condemned attempts to make union membership or participation in strikes compulsory; and they repudiated political strikes. The Octobrists favored various measures to aid the peasants economically and were prepared, in "cases of state significance," to support the alienation of some private lands if these measures proved to be "insufficient."[99]

Nationalism was a key element in the Octobrist political outlook. An officer in a guards unit, Guchkov was a confirmed patriot who had fought bravely in the Russo-Japanese War. Any plan that even remotely suggested a federal system of government was anathema to him. He opposed political autonomy for Poland as well as all schemes to decentralize the legislative tasks of the government, though he did favor civil liberties and cultural autonomy for minorities. He was prepared to make an exception for Finland, which, he believed, should retain its autonomous status so long as it remained part of the Empire.[100]

Guchkov also favored lifting religious, educational, and certain other restrictions on the Jews, though he did not think that they should be allowed to own land, join the officer corps, or hold high posts in the government. He subscribed to what might be called "pragmatic anti-Semitism." "Personally," he told the Tsar, "I have little liking for the Jews and find that it would be very much better if we did not have them. But history has given them to us and we must establish some kind of normal relations with them. . . ." In any case, Guchkov contended, the restrictive laws had not solved the Jewish question, and their rescission might lead foreigners to take a more favorable view of Russia.[101]

Late in 1905 and in 1906, the Octobrists commanded too little mass support to play a major political role. Still, in two respects their impact on the course of the revolution was not altogether negligible: by creating their own party they weakened Russian liberalism; and by strongly backing the manifesto they accorded a measure of legitimacy to the new order.

. . . . .

For the first ten months of 1905, popular support for the autocracy manifested itself primarily in occasional visits of monarchists to the Tsar to declare loyalty to him or in outbursts of violence by Black Hundreds or other groups of angry mobs against opponents, or supposed opponents, of the old order. As early as February 1905, a few conservatives considered founding a mass political movement, but it was only in the fall that they took practical measures to that end. In order to compete with the left they adopted the organizational techniques of the opposition, much as that ran counter to their belief in autocratic rule.

Late in October or early in November of 1905, Dr. A. I. Dubrovin held a meeting in his St. Petersburg apartment with a group of right-wing activists to establish a new party, the Union of the Russian People (URP), which became by far the largest and most important of all the right-wing organizations among the approximately 200 that made their appearance during the revolutionary period. Not much is known about Dubrovin. Trained in medicine, he had served for some time as a military physician and reached the level of state councillor, which conferred a hereditary title of nobility in the Table of Ranks. After leaving military service, he opened a private practice in which, according to one source, most of his patients were Jews. He is supposed to have had liaisons with several Jewish women and to have fathered a few illegitimate children by them. These stories about his personal life, whose accuracy is in dispute, deserve mention only because anti-Semitism became a central feature of his political program.

The other people at the URP's initial meeting were for the most part (18 of 21) professionals, businessmen, landowners, and lesser officials. Only three came from the lower classes, two workers and a peasant. The upper reaches of Russian society were not represented at all and never became prominent in the URP leadership.[102]

Beyond that, not much can be said with certainty about the social composition of the URP, except that it apparently attracted the support of *Lumpenproletariat*, "backward provincials," disgruntled members of the middle class, and, at least briefly, some peasants and industrial workers. It is fair to say, however, that the leaders of the movement regarded themselves as spokesmen for a particular middle-class stratum whose position in society was especially precarious and threatened altogether by the revolutionaries. Although looked down upon by the upper classes, this stratum enjoyed a certain degree of social status under the existing order—a status that would be undermined by a successful challenge to the entire structure of privilege. The URP also sought to represent the interests of the peasants and workers by advocating that the government undertake a series of economic measures to improve the conditions of the masses. Above all, the URP's leaders were dedicated to mobilizing the people against the revolution, which they refused to regard as an authentic expression of popular disaffection. This disdain became an article of faith for them, which explains their flights of fantasy in accounting for the turbulence that engulfed Russia in 1905.

The single most important feature of the URP's ideology was anti-Semitism, derived mainly from two spurious documents that had been written in France and that until 1919 were hardly known outside Russian right-wing circles—the *Protocols of the Elders of Zion* and the *Rabbi's Speech*. According to these two works, the elders of international Jewry were engaged in an international conspiracy to take control of Europe and Russia by means of revolutions staged by Christians against their own leaders.

Because of pervasive economic crises, social chaos, and abuse of political power—all of which evils were allegedly perpetrated by the elders—the masses would in time be eager to turn power over to the Jews. Once in control, the elders would seize all the land for distribution among Jews, reshape the universities so that only subjects acceptable to Jews would be taught, and permit only the Jewish religion to be practiced. "Politics," according to the *Protocols*, "has nothing in common with morality. . . . Whoever wishes to rule must know how to resort to guile and hypocrisy. . . . *Thus , our watchword is Force and Hypocrisy.*" [103]

Basing itself on the *Protocols*, the URP contended that every catastrophe that had befallen Russia, and most notably the revolution, must be attributed to the machinations of the Jews. "Can it be," wrote one propagandist, "that we are still not convinced that the revolution [in Russia] was contrived and is being supported by the Jews? Can it be that it is not clear to us that the Jews wish to make of Russia a second France, where, having taken power into their hands, they have organized the persecution of Christians?" [104] Moreover, the Jews were responsible for Russia's defeat in the war against Japan and, "to the misfortune of our Homeland, the peace negotiations were entrusted to the traitor who was conducting the kike revolt in Russia." [105]

The URP branded not only such prominent liberals as F. I. Rodichev and Petrunkevich as "henchmen of the Jews," but even the Octobrist leader Guchkov; the Union also claimed that Jews managed "the stock exchange and the Constitutional-Democratic Party" and that socialists were tools of Jewish capitalists. [106] Some URP leaders advocated mass slaughter of the Jews to solve the Jewish problem. But in its official pronouncements the Union hewed to a less radical line: it urged that the authorities do everything in their power to encourage Jews to emigrate to Palestine. The Jews who remained in Russia should be regarded as foreigners "but without any of the rights and privileges extended to all other foreigners." [107]

Intensely nationalistic, the URP considered only Great Russians, Little Russians, and White Russians as "native Russians," defined in the official organ as people "whose father and mother, grandfathers, and forefathers were born in Russia, chose the Orthodox Christian religion as their own, and chose the Russian language." [108] All other national groups within the Empire were "aliens" who did not merit rights equal to those of the "natives" and must not be granted political or cultural autonomy.

The Union favored aggressive Russification of the minorities, by which it meant acceptance not only of the Great Russian culture and religion, but also of the principle of autocracy. "Can we call a man 'Russian,'" asked one of the URP's spokesmen, "who does not believe in the Church and sacraments; who does not recognize the Autocratic Tsar; and who wishes that in place of the Tsar, God's anointed Sovereign, there would be deputies as there are now in the zemstvos and the city councils? Would we not call such a man a Moslem?"[109] The URP welcomed the October Manifesto, but only because it believed that under the new order it would be possible to abolish the bureaucratic regime and reestablish a genuine autocracy. After the first elections to the State Duma, in which the liberals emerged as the dominant force, the URP heaped scorn on the legislature spawned by the manifesto.[110]

The URP sought to influence national politics in two ways. Like other right-wing movements, it engaged in a massive propaganda campaign, bombarding the Tsar with messages of loyalty. Its branches throughout the country, numbering about a hundred, also sent messages to the autocrat and his ministers recommending a wide range of measures to the government: that it dissolve the Duma, change the electoral law, and restrain the "revolutionary press." On occasion, the URP organized street demonstrations, but these did not attract very many sympathizers (except in Kiev and Odessa).[111] The URP's second tactic was more sinister: it organized "armed squads" that assassinated political leaders of the opposition. Among their victims were the Kadets M. Ia. Herzenstein and G. B. Iollos, shot in 1906 and 1907, respectively. The armed squads also made two attempts on the life of Count Witte, whom the rightists despised for his concessions to the liberals. Late in 1906 the leaders of the URP concluded that Witte was in fact the most effective agent of what they now called the "Judeo-Masonic conspiracy" to undermine Russia.[112]

The URP never succeeded in becoming a genuine mass movement. It won no seats in the first State Duma; and in the second, all the right-wing organizations together won a mere ten seats. The Union did better only after the extensive change in the electoral law in 1907 weighted the voting heavily in favor of propertied and conservative groups, when it won 51 seats. Because of its excesses, the URP may actually have inflamed popular opinion against the regime.

Still, the Tsar looked with favor on the Union. On December 23, 1905, he received 23 members of the URP, including Dubrovin, at his Court in Tsarskoe Selo and listened attentively to their expressions of loyalty. He accepted the gift of two URP badges, one for himself and one for his son, and indicated that he agreed with his visitors that the autocracy must be retained. "I am accountable for the exercise of my power [only] to God," the Tsar declared. One of the members of the delegation, a certain I. I. Baranov, then proudly announced that the URP did not accept Jews into their organization even if they had been converted to Orthodoxy. Baranov insisted that Jews were responsible for the "present troubles in Holy

Russia" and implored the Tsar not to grant them equal rights lest they "dominate us." Nicholas replied to this speech, which was not merely anti-Semitic but racist, with the words: "I will think about it."[113]

For the Tsar and his counselors the very existence of such organizations as the URP was heartening, because it allowed them to believe that far from being isolated, they actually enjoyed a groundswell of support among the people. Such reassurance could only have stiffened their resolve to hold the line against the forces of change.

. . . . .

The general strike and the October Manifesto fundamentally transformed the political contours of Russia. The working class, though numerically small, emerged as an organized group capable of exerting decisive influence on public affairs. Because it no longer focused on economic issues alone and because it had acquired a variety of organizational structures, the proletariat assumed a leading place within the opposition to the old order. Moreover, the formation of three new parties signaled the advent of Russia into the era of organized mass participation in the political process. At the same time, the opposition was now deeply divided, which was bound to make it more difficult to retain, not to say broaden, the concessions wrested from the Tsar in October. Yet the manifesto, despite its vagueness, represented a serious defeat for the autocracy; the Tsar had been forced to commit himself to granting some legislative power to a representative body elected by the people. That amounted to a break with the past. It was not as decisive a rupture as many within the opposition had hoped for, but it nonetheless altered significantly the relationship between state and society.

In the weeks immediately following the general strike, mass violence and various forms of disorder erupted, and for a time the authorities in St. Petersburg were even less in control of the ship of state than they had been in the days after Bloody Sunday. Russia also enjoyed a period of freedom that no one would have believed possible a few weeks earlier. The critical question now was whether the new government would be able to restore calm and stability without reneging on the commitments made in the manifesto.

Chapter Nine

. . . .

Concessions Endangered

THE OPPOSITION'S most stunning victory over the autocracy in 1905 led not to domestic tranquillity but to the dramatic disintegration of the social and political order. None of the enthusiasm for the October Manifesto translated itself into political support for the author of the document, Count Witte, appointed Prime Minister on October 17. At the head of a system of government that was an "absolute chaos," he immediately faced an array of intractable problems.[1]

First of all, more than a million soldiers were still in the Far East and clamoring to return to Russia for demobilization. Frequent strikes on the railways and administrative confusion had caused delays of up to six to eight weeks in bringing the men home. Frustrated and angry, many soldiers became unruly. "We saw only disorderly trainloads of reserves, drunk and destroying the railroad lines," recalled the Minister of War, Rediger.[2] On November 5, Witte told the Tsar that 162 "anarchists" had persuaded some railroad workers to go on strike, which held up the movement of 7,000 troops. Nicholas made the following notation on the Prime Minister's memorandum: "Will it really be possible for these 162 anarchists to corrupt the army? They should all be hanged."[3] Such brutality, Witte realized, would only set back the cause of pacification, his primary concern at the time.

Desperate to appease the army and to bring loyal troops back to European Russia, the government secretly sought "bids and proposals" to transport men by steamship from Manchuria to ports on the Black Sea. It actually concluded an agreement with the North German Lloyd Shipping Company; soldiers were to be sent from Manchuria at a cost of twelve pounds, ten shillings per man.[4] There is no evidence that the arrangement was carried out. More than likely, the Russian government could not afford it, for the national treasury was empty. As Witte recalled in his memoirs, "after October 17 I assumed direction of the government without money and without an army. My tasks were to obtain money and to bring back the army from the Far East."[5] It took him about two months to get the bulk of the reserves to European Russia and some six months to negotiate a loan with Western governments.

In the meantime, Witte faced what he considered to be a hopelessly divided society, one in which various social groups were jockeying for advantage. A sizable number of nobles favored limiting the powers of the autocracy, but they wanted to be the main beneficiaries of the new political arrangements. Among the merchant and industrial classes some people dreamed of a constitutional order in which they would predominate. Many in the professional classes sought a democratic constitutional monarchy. Several movements of the far left advocated socialism. Finally, the peasantry, constituting an overwhelming majority of the population, clamored for more land. Thus, though most of the people demanded change, there was no way of satisfying the demands of any one social group without giving offense to some or all of the others.[6]

Equally important, the new government encountered enormous resistance to the October Manifesto from established institutions. The intensity of that resistance was made clear by Prince A. D. Obolenskii, the newly appointed Chief Procurator of the Most Holy Synod of the Russian Church, in a confidential interview with the British Ambassador late in October. A man of moderate views on religion and politics, Obolenskii told Sir Charles Hardinge, in Hardinge's words, "that he had had the greatest difficulty to persuade the Synod to accept his proposals which were to the effect that a pastoral letter should be addressed to the faithful urging them in the name of Christianity to accept the new order of things in peace and quietness." He found it "absolutely impossible" to persuade the Synod to mention the Jews by name, though they were the main victims of the disorders that broke out on October 18. In the end, after much discussion and pleading, the Synod agreed to a pastoral letter with the rather tepid admonition that "he who thinks he renders true service to his Sovereign by sedition and violence incurs the guilt of a grievous sin." However, Obolenskii continued, the Synod had refused to issue a statement advising people to accept the manifesto until after the church dignitaries visited the Tsar *in corpore*, blessed His Majesty with an icon of the Savior, and heard Nicholas call on pastors to maintain "peace and tranquillity" among their flocks.

The problem, Obolenskii explained to Hardinge, was that Plehve and Pobedonostsev "had regarded the Church as a vast political machine and that all the parish priests who ought to be the centres of Christian influence were simply reactionary agitators who had no influence on their parishioners except for bad." Obolenskii was convinced that the opposition to his policies within the church "constituted a serious danger[,] and he doubted whether it was quite safe to have gone so far as he had insisted on going." To reverse the situation, Obolenskii believed, he would have to introduce major reforms and extensive changes in personnel. "And all this must be done within a week!" The Chief Procurator was not optimistic: "He spoke with undisguised fear of the growing organization of the forces of reaction as well as with disappointment at the impracticable nature of the demands of the reform party."[7]

The obstinacy within the church that frustrated Obolenskii was not unique. Devotees of the old order held the vast majority of posts in all branches of the bureaucracy. Prime Minister Witte found himself in the unenviable position of having to rely for the implementation of his reforms on officials who did not favor them.

Moreover, Witte knew that his position as head of the government was far from secure. Although widely regarded as the strong man in the capital, Witte had no circle of loyal supporters, and he had great difficulty finding competent men willing to serve in his cabinet. People at Court looked upon him as a necessary evil. Witte himself believed that Tsar Nicholas had appointed him Prime Minister only because "all the others that the monarch found acceptable had cold feet . . . and were completely confused in the chaos of very contradictory measures and events." He also claimed that the other candidates considered by Nicholas declined the post because they "feared bombs," but this charge can be dismissed as an expression of animus toward persons the Prime Minister suspected of having intrigued against him.[8]

The Tsar soon made known his lack of confidence in Witte. Two days after issuing the manifesto, Nicholas sharply criticized the Prime Minister for inaction. Russia, he declared, was "in the midst of a revolution with an administrative apparatus entirely disorganized, and in this lies the main danger. . . . But the ministry, instead of acting with quick decision, only assemble in council like a lot of frightened hens and cackle about providing united ministerial action."[9] Three weeks later, Nicholas complained that the ministers were "afraid of taking courageous action: I keep trying to force them—even Witte himself—to behave more energetically." Whereas others thought the Prime Minister to be "a very energetic and even despotic man who straightaway would try his utmost to re-establish order," the Tsar had already become "disappointed in him in a way."[10]

At about this time rumors began to circulate about Witte's imminent dismissal. On November 3 and 4, the general mood in Moscow was "exceedingly strained and nervous" because it was feared that Count Witte would resign and "would be replaced by a reactionary administration under Count Ignatieff. The local arms shops sold off virtually their whole stock of firearms and nearly everybody was in a very nervous state."[11] Late in November, newspapers in St. Petersburg reported that Witte was to be replaced by a military dictator, possibly the Grand Duke Nikolai Nikolaevich. It was even said that the Tsar intended to abdicate in favor of the Grand Duke.[12] On December 21, businessmen at the Stock Exchange spoke of Witte's dismissal "as though it were already a fact" that would be announced officially in the very near future.[13]

Actually, Witte never exercised the principal position in the cabinet that he had demanded and had been promised when he accepted the post of Prime Minister. Whenever Nicholas wanted some action taken that he suspected Witte would oppose, he dealt directly with other ministers. The Tsar also set up special Crown Councils, over which he himself or the bureaucrat Count Solskii presided, that formulated policies on internal matters. Consequently, Witte was forced to devote an inordinate amount of time to wrangling over his authority.[14]

Moreover, Trepov continued to serve as the Tsar's adviser. At the time the October Manifesto was issued, Trepov, still Governor-General of St. Petersburg and Assistant Minister of Internal Affairs, told Witte that he intended to resign. A few days later Witte was astonished to learn, from Trepov himself, that he had been appointed Commandant of the Court. The monarch's failure to consult with, or even inform, the Prime Minister about so important an appointment was a clear sign to Witte that he did not enjoy Nicholas's trust.[15]

Once ensconced near the summer palace at Tsarskoe Selo, Trepov continued to exert enormous influence on governmental policies. Witte went so far as to assert that "in the end, . . . Trepov was the head of the government without the burden of responsibility, and I was the responsible premier without much influence." Indeed, Trepov was "more or less the official dictator."[16] In voicing these charges, Witte surely exaggerated. Still, there is no doubt that Trepov, who controlled the flow of information to and from the Tsar, wielded undue power late in 1905, infinitely more than was consistent with a ministerial form of government. On January 26, 1906, Nicholas admitted as much in a letter to his mother: "Trepoff is absolutely indispensable to me: he is acting in a kind of secretarial capacity. He is experienced and clever and cautious in his advice. I give him Witte's bulky memoranda to read, and then he reports on them quickly and concisely. This is of course a secret to everybody but ourselves."[17]

In his memoirs, Witte raised the question whether he should not have been more diligent in trying to neutralize Trepov's influence. As the Tsar's protector, General Trepov saw the monarch frequently every day. Witte wondered whether he should have made a point of seeing Nicholas every day himself. But that was extremely difficult because the Tsar was staying in Tsarskoe Selo, some 15 miles from St. Petersburg where Witte lived. If the Prime Minister had traveled every day to Court, he would not have had enough time for his work; if he had moved to Tsarskoe Selo, he still could have seen Nicholas only at specified times.[18] The problem, in the last analysis, was that Nicholas still retained autocratic power and was unwilling to relinquish it. What Nicholas wanted, more than anything else, was to renege on the promises he had made in the October Manifesto. One can only reiterate one historian's astute observation that "the Prime Minister's most dangerous enemy was the Tsar."[19] To add to Witte's burdens, the extremists of the right viciously attacked him, hunting him down "like a wild beast."[20] The extraordinary pressures took their toll. "Thoroughly overworked," within six days of assuming office Prime Minister Witte looked "very exhausted."[21]

A relatively minor, but nonetheless significant, incident late in October revealed Witte's impotence to society. Petrunkevich asked the Prime Minister whether the noted liberal P. B. Struve, then in Paris, would be permitted to return to St. Petersburg. Witte could give no assurances on the matter until the Tsar reached a decision. Struve did arrive in Russia on October 25 and was not molested, but Petrunkevich recognized that if the chief minister could not act on his own on so trivial a request, the political system had not changed as much as people assumed.[22]

Nonetheless, immediately after the general strike, Witte made several moves in keeping with the spirit of the manifesto. On the evening of October 17, at a meeting at Trepov's house, he spoke vigorously in favor of an amnesty for political prisoners. The manifesto had not mentioned amnesty, but it was one of the major demands of the opposition, and the Prime Minister believed it should be granted quickly to attract support for the government. One of the participants at the meeting later recalled that Witte considered it critical "to show everyone who had been persecuted that old Russia was no more, that a new Russia was born, and—I remember his words—[he] 'called everyone to take part in her new life and to build a new and bright future.'"[23]

After overcoming some resistance from a few officials, Witte drafted a ukase incorporating his recommendations, which was issued on October 21. Various categories of political prisoners detained before October 17, 1905, among them strikers, were granted amnesty. The punishments of several other categories of prisoners were reduced; sentences to death or lifelong penal servitude were commuted into fifteen years of penal servitude.[24] The opposition was not satisfied, but the ukase unquestionably led to the release of many political prisoners. In the city of Warsaw alone, in the course of three days, 1,511 people who had been arrested on administrative orders were freed.[25] To Witte, the ukase constituted a vital part of the transition from a "police Empire to an Empire based on law."[26] To the left, it meant a substantial increase in manpower for political agitation.

On October 22, the government issued a manifesto abolishing all measures taken since 1899 in violation of Finland's legal system. The rights that the Finnish people had enjoyed during the period of autonomy were restored. On December 7, the Finnish diet was to meet to draft legislation for the election of a legislative assembly on the basis of a democratic suffrage. Moreover, late in November the government added 133 Russian towns to the list of places where Jews were permitted to reside.[27]

Liberals welcomed all these measures, but they refused to abandon their militant hostility toward the government, a stance Witte considered a terrible mistake. He told the British Ambassador in "a tone of deep conviction" that "the real danger which menaced Russia was not liberalism, as so many said, but the worst form of reaction, and the liberals were themselves playing into the hands of the reactionaries by their intemperate actions and still more intemperate words." The Ambassador agreed and predicted further that if the Prime Minister did not establish a stable government, "the alternative Govt. which will succeed will be of a very different character & will be based on principles of pure repression."[28]

Liberals remained suspicious of the new government in large measure because bureaucrats of the traditional mold continued to occupy virtually all the important posts. Although liberals applauded the departures of Trepov from the Ministry of Internal Affairs and Pobedonostsev from his position as Chief Procurator of the Most Holy Synod, they placed decisive importance on the composition of the new cabinet. Witte, on the other hand, was convinced that without the support of liberals, his chances of implementing his reform program would be gravely jeopardized. His government needed the aura of legitimacy that could only be conferred if prominent figures in society publicly demonstrated their confidence in him.

As soon as he assumed office, the Prime Minister began to court public men of a wide range of political views, from the moderate Shipov to the militant Petrunkevich. He sought their advice, offered them high positions in the government, and used threats, all to no avail. After nine days of discussions with liberals, Witte gave up. What each side said is fairly well known, but the motives for their more important decisions are still somewhat obscure. Since newspapers carried extensive accounts of the deliberations—a condition insisted upon by the liberals—Witte's failure was widely seen as a blow to his prestige.

On October 18, the Prime Minister sought the advice of the distinguished lawyer and prominent Kadet I. V. Gessen. Gessen suggested that to pacify the country an immediate "gesture" was called for, such as proclamation of freedom of the press. Highly agitated, pacing back and forth in his huge office, Witte could barely control himself: "You are really pushing me into something! As outstanding a scholar as [N. S.] Tagantsev was just here and he persuaded me that the formulation of a law on freedom of the press would require a lot of work and time." Gessen granted Tagantsev's point, but he nevertheless argued that the Prime Minister could take a first step by abolishing the system of preliminary censorship, which could be done "in five minutes."

Gessen's advice was astute. Indeed, Witte himself realized that he had to move assertively to establish his authority; that is why he held the press conference with newspaper editors on his second day in office. But he also believed that there were severe constraints on his freedom of action: reforms without adequate preparation might provoke excesses among the masses, who were unaccustomed to living in a free society, whereas bold reforms would arouse the wrath of the Tsar.

Witte's caution became most evident when Gessen stated that public men would serve in the cabinet only if it contained no one known to be deeply hostile to society. "You think it is so easy to do all this," the Prime Minister exclaimed. "It is extremely difficult for me to prevent terrible appointments." Gessen warned that his difficulty "does not at all interest public opinion."[29] Much to his discomfort over the succeeding few days, Witte did not take the warning to heart. He could not understand that by appointing even a few people distrusted by society to high positions, he would profoundly offend liberals and confirm all their suspicions about his lack of commitment to the new order. This failing led him to his greatest blunder as Prime Minister.

Shortly after talking with Gessen, Witte invited other leading moderate liberals (A. I. Guchkov; D. N. Shipov; Prince S. D. Urusov; and M. A. Stakhovich, marshal of the nobility in Orel province and for some years active in the zemstvo movement) to discuss their joining the government. The meeting proceeded amicably enough, everyone agreeing on the need to liberalize the electoral principles enunciated by Bulygin on August 6. But Witte struck a discordant note when he announced that he had selected P. N. Durnovo to head the Ministry of Internal Affairs. His four interlocutors immediately declined to serve with Durnovo, who, in the words of Guchkov, "was well known as a reactionary and had a very dubious moral reputation."[30]

The Prime Minister refused to withdraw the nomination, an act of stubbornness that remains a mystery. In insisting on Durnovo's appointment, Witte was not doing the bidding of the Tsar, who disliked Durnovo and did not want him in the cabinet. Witte had apparently convinced himself, as he told the four liberals, that Durnovo was uniquely qualified for the post and that he had recently shown himself to be an enlightened public servant. The Prime Minister also contended that there were no public figures with the necessary experience in police administration to run the ministry. He himself could not take the portfolio for the same reason.[31] The Durnovo affair became a cause célèbre, ending all chances for collaboration between the new government and the liberals.

It has been suggested that Witte could not yield on Durnovo because Durnovo had threatened that, if denied the appointment, he would make public certain documents that were extremely damaging to the Prime Minister. The evidence in support of this interpretation is rather meager. A more plausible explanation for Witte's behavior is that he wanted a strong man in that sensitive post to counterbalance the influence of the liberals he hoped to bring into the government.[32] Such a ploy would not have been beyond Witte, but it still leaves unanswered the question why he insisted on Durnovo after the latter so clearly became the chief stumbling block to a rapprochement with the liberals—which was the cornerstone of the Prime Minister's overall political strategy. He could have dropped Durnovo for another strong man unburdened by a shady past; one man actually proposed as Minister of Internal Affairs was P. A. Stolypin, who had dealt firmly with demonstrators in Saratov.[33] On the best available information, the mystery cannot be satisfactorily resolved.

Durnovo's credentials were indeed dubious. Born in 1844, he had joined the civil service in 1872 after serving for twelve years in the navy. He advanced rapidly and became Director of the Department of Police in St. Petersburg in 1884. A loyal supporter of Plehve, he appeared to be destined to rise even higher in the civil service. In 1893, however, Durnovo's career suffered a setback when his exploits as a womanizer led to a scandal. He had befriended a lady of easy virtue who was also the frequent companion of an ambassador representing either Brazil or Spain. Suspecting his paramour of betrayal, Durnovo ordered his agents to pilfer a batch of her love letters. The lady complained to the ambassador, who indignantly reported the theft to Emperor Alexander III. Aghast at this impropriety by one of his officials, Alexander issued an unambiguous order: "Get that swine out of here within twenty-four hours." Durnovo's career appeared to be finished, but soon after Alexander's death he managed to obtain new government appointments, first to the Governing Senate and then to the Ministry of Internal Affairs.[34]

Witte knew the details of Durnovo's past but persuaded himself that the man had reformed and was now a political moderate.[35] Actually, little is known about Durnovo's political views during the first ten months of

1905, for he took no public stand on the issues. But according to the chief of the St. Petersburg Okhrana, Colonel A. V. Gerasimov, Durnovo's politics were thoroughly primitive. Late in 1905, Gerasimov asked Durnovo which parties the government might be prepared to cooperate with in the Duma. "What kind of parties are you talking about?" answered Durnovo. "We will not permit any parties at all in the Duma. Every representative should vote only in accordance with his conscience. Why are parties necessary?"[36] Although Guchkov was not privy to this conversation, he knew enough about Durnovo to give Witte sound advice: "The capital you want to acquire by summoning us [to serve in your government] will be immediately dissipated if a responsible post in our cabinet is occupied by a resolute enemy of all of society."[37]

Nevertheless, Witte could not be swayed. He simply turned to other liberals, F. A. Golovin, F. F. Kokoshkin, and Prince G. E. Lvov, and urged them to support his government even if they could not join his administration. Again, he ran up against a stone wall. The three liberals advised the Prime Minister that if he wished to broaden the appeal of his government, he would have to convoke a constituent assembly, grant amnesty to political prisoners, and introduce without delay the reforms promised in the October Manifesto. Witte dismissed these "radical" reforms as unfeasible under the chaotic conditions then prevailing in Russia.[38]

In desperation, Witte approached two of the more militant liberals, Miliukov and Petrunkevich, asking them why leaders of society would not support him. Miliukov suggested that instead of troubling himself about the collaboration of society, Witte should choose as ministers serious civil servants who were not discredited. "Finally," Witte declared, "I hear the first sensible words. I have decided to do this."[39] Still, he appealed to Petrunkevich to use his good offices to persuade Guchkov to join the government. When Petrunkevich refused, the Prime Minister resorted to threats, warning that the government could easily crush the liberal movement. It had only to promise every peasant family 25 desiatinas of land, and all the landowners would be "swept away.... The government of course will not resort to this method, but you should not ignore it." Petrunkevich, however, did ignore this threat, which he understood to be Witte's "last resort in defending the monarchy against revolution."[40]

In the end, Witte's meetings with the liberals proved to be a fiasco. Inevitably, the rejections of his overtures embarrassed him. Even so conservative a liberal as Shipov made public his letter refusing the Prime Minister's offer to make him State Comptroller. Shipov claimed that it would be useless for him to be the only representative of the opposition to serve in an administration that clearly did not enjoy broad support.[41]

As for the Tsar, he was thoroughly dismayed at Witte's courting of "various extremists, especially as all these talks appear in the press the next day, and as often as not are distorted." He was amazed that "such a clever man [as Witte] should have deluded himself into believing that pacification of the country would be easy."[42]

By the same token, it is an open question whether the liberals acted wisely in turning down Witte's overtures. Though certainly not a democrat or a constitutionalist, Witte did believe in the weeks after the general strike that major reforms were necessary. Yet within the highest official circles he could count on few to support such a policy. The presence of committed liberals in the government might have strengthened his reformist proclivities and added weight to his argument that the country could be pacified only by political means. If after a few weeks it became evident that they were impotent or, worse, hostages to the reactionaries, the liberals could have resigned. It is not certain that such a course of action would have compromised them and irreparably harmed the cause of constitutionalism.

In part, no doubt, the liberals' rebuff of Witte was motivated by principle; but political considerations also played a role, perhaps a decisive one. "The gentlemen whom he [Witte] has consulted," Sir Charles Hardinge reported, "confess to him that their power would vanish as soon as they became ministers." To side with the Prime Minister, the liberals feared, might cost them the backing of the more militant elements in society.[43] If these fears were well grounded, which is quite possible, the liberals faced a dilemma. Lending support to Witte would threaten to erode their popular base, whereas withholding it might hinder the consolidation of the new order, so slowly and painfully won. This hard choice was compounded by the liberals' uncertainty about Witte's true intentions and their own lack of political experience, which prevented them from taking bold initiatives.

With Durnovo in his post (initially as Acting Minister of Internal Affairs), the cabinet consisted of fourteen people, eight of whom had not served as ministers before. All of them came from the bureaucracy, which did not enjoy the confidence of society. As one observer put it, "a provisional government has been formed without weight in the country, simply for the purpose of carrying out [the functions of] Government."[44] Moreover, the Tsar retained sole control over the appointment of four ministers (Court, War, Navy, and Foreign Affairs)—further evidence of Witte's inability to establish the kind of unified ministry he considered necessary for efficient administration. In the end, only one man from society, Prince S. D. Urusov, agreed to enter the government. He became Assistant Minister of Internal Affairs, but by himself he could not exert much influence on the government's policies. In any case, he soon resigned in disgust when he discovered that a high official in the Department of Police had helped incite pogroms.[45]

No sooner had Durnovo been appointed than he set about ingratiating himself with the Tsar, Grand Duke Nikolai Nikolaevich, the ultrareactionary Dr. Dubrovin, and Trepov. The Minister of Internal Affairs reported directly to Nicholas, took orders from him, and at every possible opportunity dropped strong hints that the Prime Minister was too liberal. Durnovo became so well established at Court that he succeeded in getting his daughter appointed a maid of honor without Witte's intervention on her behalf. Although Witte later scorned Durnovo as being "without principles" and acknowledged that his appointment had been "one of my most grievous mistakes," he asserted (not without justification) that Nicholas was the most to blame for Durnovo's abuse of power. If the Tsar was truly committed to creating a unified ministry, he should have impressed upon Durnovo that his duty was to report to Witte, not to the Court.[46]

· · · · ·

The attempts by Witte to recruit leading figures of the opposition into his administration took place against a background of unprecedented mass violence, one of the more puzzling outbursts of raw passion in 1905. For nine months, mass pressure for reform had seemed irresistible, and the government appeared to lack organized popular support. From time to time, defenders of the status quo had shown signs of life, but their efforts on behalf of the autocracy had been sporadic and ineffective. Yet, precisely at the moment when the autocracy was at its weakest, when it had been compelled to grant its first major concession, the defenders of the old order unleashed their most intense and ferocious attack on the advocates of change. This resort to brute force to silence the Tsar's critics threatened to undermine the new order before it could be consolidated.

The violence that erupted in the streets and countryside of the Empire was as sudden as it was widespread. "From the center, the north, the south, from all corners of Russia," *Syn otechestva* wrote, "there are telegraphic reports of attacks on demonstrators, of death and injuries; in many places exultant mobs attack Jewish streets and homes, plundering and demolishing whatever falls into their hands."[47] Although Jews were the principal focus of the pogroms in October, they were not the only ones to come under attack. The rampaging mobs also targeted the intelligentsia and students—anyone, in fact, who was presumed to have participated in the movement to extract the Manifesto of October 17 from the Tsar or who simply rejoiced in it.

The disorders began on October 18, the day after the concession was made, and within four days it seemed to one sober commentator that "complete governmental anarchy" prevailed in Russia. The shock to much of society was profound: "No one thought that the first day of a Russian constitution would end in tragedy."[48] After seven days the mobs largely ran out of steam, but sporadic incidents continued until late in November.

There was no one pattern to the disorders. For the most part, they appear to have started when organized gangs attacked demonstrators celebrating the opposition's victory over the autocracy. In the town of Volsk (Saratov guberniia), for example, on October 20 a crowd marched through the streets brandishing red flags and singing the Marseillaise. When the marchers reached the zemstvo house, they found it covered with national flags, which some of their number ripped down. At that point, a group of fifty to a hundred men armed with sticks rushed at the procession and beat the demonstrators mercilessly. The police joined in the attack and the crowd fled in a panic.[49]

In Zolotonoshka (Poltava guberniia), the day after the manifesto was granted, several hundred people celebrated by destroying the post office, which severed all telegraphic communications, and freeing inmates of the local prison. Jews had taken part in these activities, which served as a pretext for an anti-Jewish riot that began on October 19 and lasted "all day and night. . . ," with no effort made to stop it. On the second day of the disturbance a company of soldiers arrived, and within a few hours the violence stopped. But by that time, the destruction of homes and stores was extensive. "Five hundred families are starving," exclaimed Rabbi Fradkin; "for God's sake, help us immediately."[50]

In Vladikavkaz (Terek oblast) disorders broke out when two groups of demonstrators, one carrying red flags and the other portraits of the Tsar, ran into each other and began to argue excitedly. Shots were fired by some high school students leading the pro-manifesto cohorts and were met by a volley of gunfire from nearby soldiers. The Tsar's supporters then physically assaulted the marchers with the red flags, and, once again, a number of people were killed and wounded.[51] In Baku, the "patriots," as the Tsar's supporters styled themselves, attacked the Armenians, who were despised because they were not Orthodox Christians and because they were suspected of sympathizing with the opponents of the autocracy. The patriots, hoping to drive the Armenians from Baku, killed 60 of them and wounded more than a hundred. The city was turned into "a battlefield."[52]

Sometimes pogroms erupted after rumors circulated that Jews had perpetrated acts of wanton violence. On October 20, the Jews of Kiev were accused of having set fire to the Goloseevskaia Monastery and murdering all the monks. A senior military officer, General I. A. Karass, publicly denied that either the massacre or the fire had taken place, but a mob refused to believe him and went on a rampage. The rioters destroyed all the stores in the Jewish bazaar, killed twelve people, and injured 44.[53] In some localities, the pretext for a pogrom was the charge that Jews were planning to place one of their coreligionists on the throne.[54]

To counteract the demonstrations in support of the manifesto, the monarchists increasingly organized their own patriotic processions, which tended to degenerate into orgies of violence. Sometimes inspired by ecclesiastics, the patriotic crowds concluded their marches in a rage against "traitors," a term that as often as not referred to Jews. For several days attacks on Jews occurred with such frequency that newspapers carried special sections entitled "Jewish pogroms"; in fact, they told only part of the story. On October 23, *Rus* listed eleven serious incidents; on October 25, thirteen, which took place in eleven towns and cities. On October 27, *Syn otechestva* reported fifteen pogroms; on November 1, 26. Where none had as yet broken out, the Jews lived in dread of one. "The Jews of Moscow," the paper noted on October 24, "spent an extremely anxious night expecting a pogrom. Almost no one slept in his apartment; they all hid with Christian acquaintances."[55]

Odessa witnessed some of the worst mass violence. *Pogromshchiki* sacked innumerable Jewish stores and physically assaulted some 3,000 people; the police estimated that more than 500 were killed and over 300 injured. The population was in a state of panic, and many people left the city or sought refuge on ships in the harbor. In Rostov-on-Don, 34 Jews were killed and 159 injured. In Minsk, the bodies of 54 Jews were found after a day of rioting.[56] All told, according to the most reliable estimates, 690 anti-Jewish pogroms occurred, primarily in the southwestern provinces; 876 people were killed and between 7,000 and 8,000 injured. In a few cities the Jews lost property estimated at more than a million rubles. Altogether, the damage to property during the pogroms has been calculated at 62 million rubles.[57]

In the two largest cities of the Empire, no pogrom directed solely at Jews broke out, but there were so many attacks on people regarded as hostile to the Tsar that the populace succumbed to panic. In St. Petersburg on October 19, "Gangs of Black Hundreds, armed with flagpoles, hunted for intelligentsia and students in the streets until the next morning. Skirmishes between Black Hundreds and workers took place in various parts of the city."[58] For several days the citizens of the capital "lived in the expectation of some kind of catastrophe." Many residents left for Finland, and others sent their families to the suburbs. Some of the Russian Jews were evacuated, and some foreign Jews fled the country.[59] By the end of October, "All the stores that sell valuable items removed merchandise from the windows and placed it in storage for safekeeping. The banks in recent days have taken special pains to place boxes in fireproof storerooms. . . . Many shops are open, but they do no business, for there is no merchandise; it is hidden."[60] Officials in St. Petersburg tried to reassure the people that their fears were groundless, but they could not be calmed. Considering the extent of the irrational hatred that had infected the city late in October, it was not unnatural for law-abiding citizens to take fright.

October 22 in Moscow was a "day of terror and infamy." In various districts gangs of rowdies committed "brutal murders and tortured people, mainly students but also workers and other people who appeared suspicious to the crowds or aroused hostile feelings among them."[61] At least three people were killed and many were injured. Shopkeepers in the city trembled at the sight of patriotic processions, whose penchant for mischief seemed inexhaustible. On the afternoon of October 23, for example, a crowd "marching along Tver Street singing patriotic songs and screaming 'Hurrah' suddenly launched a completely unexpected attack on the furniture store 'Sovremennyi Rynok.' All the glass was knocked out and a major part of the store was destroyed. Then there occurred a clash between the crowd and the guards, two of whom were wounded."[62]

After the home of a well-to-do Muscovite was damaged by vandals, the upper class in the city gave credence to persistent rumors that Black Hundreds planned a general onslaught against private homes in affluent neighborhoods.[63] Students stopped wearing their special garb because of the rash of attacks on them in the streets.[64] The panic in Moscow persisted through mid-November, by which time many of the wealthy had fled the country. The foreign department of the Office of the City Governor reported that it was issuing between one hundred and two hundred passports a day.[65] Without question, the practitioners of indiscriminate violence had succeeded in disrupting the normal life of the two capitals.

An unexpected consequence of the unrest was a dramatic increase in the ranks of both revolutionaries and criminals. Frequently, supporters of the manifesto marched to local courthouses to demand the release of political prisoners, not all of whom had been covered by the amnesty of October 21. Eager to mollify the demonstrators, procurators quickly opened the prisons, unleashing large numbers of political activists. But the procurator in Moscow chose to interpret the decree on amnesty very broadly, as including common criminals. Consequently, "10,000 hooligans" began to "operate freely in the central sectors of the city," and crime rose sharply.[66] With his idiosyncratic interpretation of the decree, the procurator probably intended to discredit the entire concept of amnesty. He may also have believed that the criminals would make good recruits for the Black Hundreds who were assailing supporters of the manifesto.

The atmosphere was so tense that people readily credited rumors that the European powers had formally threatened the Russian government with armed intervention. If the disorders continued and the country slid into anarchy, it was reported, Central and Western European countries would act to protect their investments and to prevent the unrest from spilling over into neighboring states.[67]

In accounting for the disorders, critics of the autocracy claimed that the hooligans had been organized by reactionaries and abetted by officials at every level of government. Some critics also contended that the government in St. Petersburg had actually planned the violence so as to deal a crushing blow to all who had worked to wrest the manifesto from the Tsar.[68] These charges cannot be dismissed out of hand. The reports that the police looked the other way during pogroms and helped to organize patriotic processions are simply too numerous. In Moscow, for example, the police urged janitors—widely used to spy on their tenants—to mobilize "everyone who was 'for the Tsar.'" As for the janitors themselves, "participation in the demonstrations was obligatory."[69]

In various localities, investigations made shortly after the disorders confirmed that the police had indeed helped foment them. In Kostroma (Kostroma guberniia), the police were found to have played a "leading role" in the assaults on the intelligentsia and students on October 19. Several witnesses testified that the police had given money to the Black Hundreds and had thanked them for their work. Others testified that the governor himself, L. M. Kniazev, had also thanked the hooligans for their services. Finally, there was convincing evidence that the police had dragged people from their hiding places and handed them over to the hooligans for beatings.[70]

In Simferopol (Tauride guberniia), the city council conducted an especially thorough investigation of the disorders that had occurred in October. The commission of inquiry succeeded in interrogating 369 eyewitnesses, despite persistent efforts by the procurator and numerous police officials to terrorize them into silence. The commission reached two conclusions: first, that the pogroms had been designed to put a halt to political meetings and strikes; and second, that they had been planned with the participation of the "chief of the city police, the deputy chief, the colonel of the gendarmes, and the entire police staff, with the connivance or friendly neutrality of the governor." The commission recommended that a new procurator be appointed and that the entire police force of Simferopol be replaced immediately.[71] The deputy chief of police was actually tried and found guilty of misconduct; the chief of police, however, died before he could be brought to trial.[72]

A Bureau of Investigation of the Jewish Pogroms (apparently set up by the government) conducted a more general inquiry and concluded that "in almost every pogrom local authorities participated actively."[73] Historians of specific pogroms have reached the same conclusion.[74] Information found in the archives of the French Foreign Ministry also tends to implicate senior officials in the disorders.

In an astonishingly candid interview with the French Consul early in November 1905, the Governor-General of Odessa, A. V. Kaulbars, defended his conduct and that of officials under his command in great detail, and in the process revealed his sympathy for the pogroms. Without intending it, he also cast doubt on his claim that he had acted firmly to prevent violence. He was prepared to tolerate public meetings in support of the October Manifesto, Kaulbars declared, since freedom of speech and assembly had been conceded by the Tsar. But when he saw "the red flag and a lacerated portrait of the Emperor, I, an old soldier, veteran of fifteen campaigns, found it difficult not to unleash the Cossacks." He restrained himself only because he wanted "to avoid the shedding of blood on a day of joy."

The attitude of the Jews, however, became "singularly provocative," and Kaulbars expected that the "deeply offended" Russian people would "resort to reprisals." This is how he characterized his encounters with the Jews: "Many Jews came to me during the three fatal days. I proposed the following to them: you form a cortege displaying the Russian flag; I will place myself at its head, we will march through the city and I guarantee you that you will be respected and that there will even be a reaction in your favor. None of my visitors accepted. The Jews alone are guilty."

Although Kaulbars branded as "idiotic" the charge that the government had secretly incited the pogroms, he acknowledged that "*it is not impossible*" that policemen were "disguised as civilians in order to incite the people to take revenge and that they themselves fired more than one shot at houses occupied by Jews. I do not excuse them; but they obeyed the instincts of human nature." Kaulbars claimed that he himself had acted sternly at the first alert of impending disorder. True, on more than one occasion soldiers were "inactive" and "passive" when sent to the scenes of disorder, but that, too, was perfectly understandable. Initially, the troops "were given ovations, they were welcomed with hurrahs; officers were carried about triumphantly. Would such demonstrations not disarm them?" Kaulbars added that popular violence only began "in response to bullets and bombs that were thrown from houses." Thus, it was the Jews and revolutionaries who had provoked the pogroms.[75] Early in 1906 Kaulbars was quoted as having said about the governors in southwest Russia that "in our hearts we all sympathized with the pogroms." Because quite a few generals in the region shared this attitude, they refused to order their troops to put an end to the excesses.[76]

That a fair number of local officials tolerated and even abetted the pogroms is therefore beyond dispute. But the question of the culpability of the government in St. Petersburg is more complicated. On the one hand, Tsar Nicholas viewed the violence as a natural reaction of loyal citizens to the excesses of the left. On October 27, he wrote his mother that "the impertinence of the Socialists and revolutionaries had angered the people once more; and because nine-tenths of the troublemakers are Jews, the people's anger turns against them. That's how the pogroms happened. It is amazing how they took place *simultaneously* in all the towns of Russia and Siberia."[77] This expression of sympathetic understanding for the actions of the *pogromshchiki* merely confirms what every official knew, that their ruler despised Jews and opponents of the autocracy and was not likely to be distressed by physical attacks on them. But it does not prove that the Court planned or initiated the violence.

The most damaging evidence of complicity by the authorities in St. Petersburg came to light in February 1906. A. A. Lopukhin, Director of the Department of Police in the Ministry of Internal Affairs, informed Witte that in October and November 1905 a secret press in police headquarters in the capital had printed "thousands of proclamations" urging "all true Russians to rise and exterminate all foreigners, Jews, Armenians, etc. and all those who were advocates of reform and talked of restricting the autocratic power of the Sovereign." It also emerged that General Trepov had personally made corrections on the proofs of some of the proclamations. After an investigation confirmed the accuracy of Lopukhin's allegations, Witte ordered that the press and the remaining proclamations be destroyed.

Witte later claimed that he had not pressed charges against Captain M. S. Kommisarov, the officer directly responsible for the printing and distribution of the inflammatory material, because the Tsar had made it clear that he would not allow him to be punished. Nicholas held Kommisarov in high esteem for his work in military espionage during the war with Japan. But according to the British Embassy in St. Petersburg, Witte did request that all the officials involved in running the press be punished, only to be turned down by Durnovo, who actually gave them cash awards amounting to 70,000 rubles. The facts of the case were presented to Tsar Nicholas, who promised to "remove M. Durnovo immediately but expressed his objections to taking any definitive step until the Duma had met." Some of the details of this sordid affair appeared in the daily press in February 1906 and were not denied by the government.[78]

The secret machinations of the police officers were a perfect illustration of a point made by the Chief Procurator, Obolenskii: the bureaucracy contained within its ranks men bent on undermining the new order. The incident was one reason for Prince S. D. Urusov's resignation from his post as Assistant Minister of Internal Affairs early in 1906. As a Kadet deputy in the First Duma, Urusov delivered a powerful speech exposing the government's policies toward the pogroms.[79]

Witte himself, determined to maintain order and to enlist the support of liberals, publicly condemned the violence. On October 22, he branded the disorders as harmful to the state and vowed to take the "most decisive steps" to curb them. In response to a telegram from the Minsk City Council appealing for measures to end the violence, Witte promised an investigation.[80] In reply to a similar telegram from lawyers in Kazan and the city's rabbi, Witte directed officials to "take energetic measures to stop the destruction and violence."[81] Subsequently, two high officials who had brazenly shown their sympathy for the pogroms were punished. P. G. Kurlov, Governor of Minsk, and D. M. Neidhardt, the Prefect of Odessa, were dismissed and brought to trial (though both were cleared by the Senate in March 1906).[82] Finally, a report on the violence for official eyes only, prepared at Witte's request, gives no hint of collusion by the central government in the disorders.[83] In truth, the violence was not in Witte's interest since it discredited his government.

Moreover, some higher officials in local areas did not approve of the pogroms. In Astrakhan and Taganrog, for instance, they made it clear that they would not tolerate the violence, and the cities remained calm.[84] In Saratov the attacks on Jews were initially viewed with benevolent neutrality by the vice-governor, who was in charge during the absence of his superior, P. A. Stolypin. As soon as Stolypin returned, however, he ordered a halt to the violence, and "in the course of ten minutes the pogroms were stopped."[85] On October 28, the Governor announced that "every infringement of the rights of an individual or his property, regardless of his nationality or religion, will be suppressed with the most resolute measures, if necessary with the application of military force."[86] It seems highly unlikely that Stolypin would have issued such orders if they contravened the directives of the government in St. Petersburg. He surely would not have been promoted to head the government six months later (when he became Chairman of the Council of Ministers) had he done so. By the same token, Stolypin's actions and those of several other officials suggest that without the connivance of *local* administrators, the *pogromshchiki* could not have engaged in their criminal activities for very long.

One cannot agree, then, with the proposition that the pogroms began in response to a signal from St. Petersburg or that they would not have taken place at all without official inspiration or approval. The random character of the *pogromshchiki*'s acts of violence, the failure of local officials to follow one clearly defined policy, and the absence of evidence incriminating Witte's government argue against this interpretation. Most of the officials found wanting were charged not with instigating the disorders but rather with neglecting to take prompt action to end them.

The causes of the mass violence seem to lie elsewhere. In part, the violence can be traced to the rage of those who feared that the demonstrations applauding the manifesto signified the end of a social order in which they enjoyed a certain status that they wished to preserve. As one observer noted, ordinary people who had until October at least been able to take refuge in their superiority to Jews and other social outcasts "must undoubtedly have felt miserable [in seeing] the streets captured by new people, precisely those people who up to this time had stood outside the law, people against whom everything had been permissible. There are [such] malcontents even among the more solid elements of the population."[87] In short, to a substantial degree the violence from below late in October was a spontaneous response by various groups determined to crush the opposition and to preserve the old order.

Much of the reckless plundering and beatings of innocent civilians were the work of riffraff motivated largely by prejudice and a craving for loot. But peasants, shopkeepers, coachmen, janitors, and even some workers (though not any who belonged to trade unions) also lent a hand, for much the same reasons.[88] For these people, however, another factor played a role. They found unbearable the sight of multitudes of ordinary Russians, among them many Jews and rowdy students, celebrating their victory over the revered Tsar, often by defiling his portrait. For nine months the "upstarts" had defied authority more or less with impunity; now they had apparently succeeded in bringing down the entire political system, and with it the hierarchical structure on which Russian society had been based. If the autocracy could no longer restrain them, those who yearned to maintain the old order because they felt secure within it would have to take the law into their own hands. To some vigilantes, such conduct may not even have seemed to be a violation of legal norms, for the Tsar's capitulation signified to them that their revered leader—in their view the only legitimate source of authority—had been undermined by evil forces, and that they must therefore come to his rescue at all costs.

The prominence of Jews among the upstarts was especially galling to the *pogromshchiki*. For religious, social, and economic reasons, hatred of the Jews was deeply rooted among many sectors of the Russian population. Until 1905, the Jewish minority had been legally repressed, denied most of the few rights enjoyed by other citizens of the Empire. Now not only was there talk of granting rights of citizenship to Jews; they had even assumed positions of responsibility in the political movements that had dealt the Tsar so crushing a blow. Many people, including foreign observers, actually believed that "Jewish money had been a major main-spring" of the revolutionary movement. The government allegedly possessed incontrovertible evidence that Russian banks had disbursed huge amounts of money received from abroad in small sums to members of the Social Democratic and Socialist Revolutionary parties.[89]

The *pogromshchiki*'s resentment revealed itself with telling force in the humiliations they often inflicted on opponents of the Tsar seized during the unrest in October. They would force Jews and students to kneel in front of pictures of the Tsar or herd Jews into cathedrals to swear their allegiance to him.[90] These rituals—it is hard to think of a better word—were designed to impress upon the opponents of the old order that although the autocracy may have lost a battle, the symbols of authority were still generally venerated and the struggle over the future of Russia was far from over.

· · · · ·

During the October disorders, the left, too, emphasized rituals and symbolic gestures. Leftists turned funeral processions into events charged with emotion and made a point of adding the names of the fallen to the list of revolutionary martyrs. A notable example was the funeral in Revel (Tallin) on October 20 of 38 victims of a clash between demonstrators and soldiers. One description of the event, attended by 20,000 mourners, is worth quoting: "Multitudes of people sang in the chorale; the impression was overpowering; the lanterns and houses were draped with black cloth. There were almost one thousand wreaths and many natural fresh flowers. The streets were dotted with decorative branches. The windows along the route of the procession displayed lit candles. The funeral procession stretched over five versts [about three miles]. . . . City leaders and visitors took part in the procession. Stores and institutions were closed."[91] The elaborately staged affairs were meant not only to convey sympathy for victims of arbitrary violence but also to demonstrate popular hostility toward the old order. The Black Hundreds and Cossacks understood that very well, which explains why they frequently assaulted mourners peacefully returning from a funeral.

The most memorable funeral took place in Moscow on October 20 for N. E. Bauman. The 32-year-old Bauman had been a professional revolutionary since his early twenties and in 1896–97 had belonged to the St. Petersburg "Union of Struggle for the Emancipation of the Working Class." He was arrested and imprisoned in 1897; in 1899 he escaped and emigrated to Switzerland; and in 1900 he began to work for Lenin and became one of his closest collaborators. Bauman was *Iskra*'s first illegal agent inside Russia, establishing numerous links with local Social Democratic organizations. Early in 1902 Bauman was arrested again in Moscow, but within a few months he and ten other Iskraites escaped to the West. There, after surviving charges of personal misconduct,[92] he served as a delegate to the Second Congress of the Russian Social Democratic Party. He returned to Moscow in December 1903 to lead the city's Bolshevik party organization. In June 1904, the police found an illegal printing press in his apartment and imprisoned him in the Taganka jail. Released in October 1905, Bauman led a demonstration the day after the manifesto was issued, only to be shot and then beaten to death by a worker sympathetic to the Black Hundreds.

The stage was set for a spectacular procession. Bauman was the most prominent revolutionary to have been slain during the revolution, his brutal murder had shocked many Muscovites, and the Bolsheviks were resolved to exploit the popular hostility to the government. The liberal newspaper *Russkie vedomosti*, for instance, spoke glowingly of Bauman as a "fighter for freedom" and asserted that joining the cortege would be an expression of "protest against arbitrariness, violence, and oppression."[93] Far from weakening the opposition to the autocracy, the wanton violence by extremists on the right was only serving to solidify it.

The organizers of the funeral, the Moscow Committee of Bolsheviks, informed the Mayor that they did not want any police, Cossacks, or soldiers to be stationed along the route of the procession. Taken aback by the request, the Mayor turned for advice to the Governor-General, who agreed to remove his forces from the streets if the organizers submitted the route for his approval. The Bolsheviks, supported by the Mensheviks, signaled their sense of power by "categorically refusing" to comply with this condition.[94]

The estimates of the size of the procession vary widely. The government claimed that 30,000 Muscovites participated; one newspaper placed the numbers at 50,000 and another at 150,000.[95] Whichever figure is accepted, this "political funeral" was without doubt a major event. For the first time, the radical wing of Russian Social Democracy moved to center stage in the political life of Moscow. The Bolsheviks knew how to make the most of their opportunity.

The marchers began to gather early in the morning at the Technical School, where Bauman's body was reposing. Two Bolsheviks carrying a large red banner with the inscription "Citizens Preserve Order" led the procession. They were followed by well-armed militia bands, detachments of hospital workers, and representatives of various organizations, all holding flags and banners aloft. One group bore an enormous red velvet banner adorned with clusters of mourning bows. Emblazoned on this banner in gold letters were the words: "Social Democratic Workers'

Party. Moscow Committee." Middle-class liberals displayed a poster that hailed Bauman as a "Victim of Freedom without Guarantees." The coffin, draped in red, was at all times surrounded by bands of militiamen.

At several stops during the march, which lasted a total of eight hours, additional groups carrying banners of various kinds joined the mourners. Even some military officers and officials of the Gendarmerie participated. At the Conservatory an orchestra of students joined the procession, playing the mourning march "You Are a Victim of a Fateful Struggle." When the music stopped, the crowd vented its emotion by singing the "Marseillaise," "Red Banner," the "International," and "Eternal Memory." The cortege reached the cemetery at nine o'clock in the evening, and after the coffin was lowered, Bauman's widow pronounced the following oath: "I vow to seek revenge. I devote myself completely to this cause and you must vow to unite and to avenge this death." Thousands of marchers responded: "I vow! I vow!"[96]

P. A. Garvi, a Menshevik activist who witnessed the funeral, astutely observed that a sort of religious fervor had gripped the crowd: "It is difficult to communicate the feeling of rejoicing, pride, and triumph that filled our hearts. This was the day of our victory, the victory of the revolution. We did not think about Bauman in these happy hours, or thought of him without grief—it was as if this were not a corpse but a symbol of revolution, a sacred object carried forward in a procession surrounded by a chain of people who had resolved to die rather than forsake the sacred object."[97]

Some 35 years earlier, P. L. Lavrov, a theorist of Russian radicalism, had written that before a program of social and political change could be realized, "martyrs are needed, whose legend will far outgrow their true worth and actual service. Energy they never had will be attributed to them; the best ideas and best sentiments of the followers will be put into their mouths. For the multitude they will become unattainable, impossible ideals. But on the other hand their legend will inspire thousands with the energy needed for the fight."[98] For the Bolshevik persuasion, still in its infancy and lacking mass appeal, Bauman's murder and martyrization served precisely this critical function for the transformation of a political party into an influential movement. Even today, streets, schools, and a district in Moscow are named after Bauman.

Two episodes that grew out of the funeral further aroused popular sympathy for the Bolsheviks. At the conclusion of the procession, which had been entirely peaceful, about 4,000 mourners gathered at the university, where they unexpectedly came under attack, first from Black Hundreds and then from Cossacks. To ward off the assault, militiamen with the mourners fired their revolvers, and in the ensuing exchange of gunfire six marchers were killed and 30 injured, half of them seriously. The authorities promised to conduct a "strict investigation" of the incident, but it soon became apparent that they were not interested in bringing right-wing criminals to justice.[99]

On October 21, a prime suspect in Bauman's murder, a certain N. F. Mikhailin, was apprehended. Two days later, a mob of Black Hundreds besieged the courthouse demanding his release. The procurator immediately obliged, explaining lamely that the suspect deserved to be treated as a political criminal and consequently freed under the amnesty decree. The identification of a murder suspect as a political prisoner caused such an uproar that the procurator quickly retreated; he issued a statement that only the preliminary investigation of Mikhailin had been completed and that further testimony would be taken. In the end, Mikhailin was tried and sentenced to two years of hard labor, but the Tsar pardoned him. After the Bolshevik Revolution of 1917, Mikhailin was tried again; this time he was found guilty and shot.[100]

On the evening of October 21 the Moscow City Council met in urgent session to discuss the recent disturbances, which threatened to plunge the city into chaos. It had become evident that the authorities, the police, and the military were standing aside while revolutionaries and reactionaries were preparing to do battle. As the German Consulate in Moscow reported to Berlin, "Every day there are bloody clashes and no one can anticipate how this will end." There were rumors that monarchists, presuming that Bauman was of Jewish ancestry, planned to exhume his body from the Orthodox cemetery and publicly cremate it. Such a move, it was feared, would lead to new clashes and serve as a signal for a "general campaign of Jew-baiting."[101]

The city council now came under intense pressure to take action to restore order. A group of notables, appalled by the violence, decided on their own to set up a committee to investigate the "catastrophe of October 20," by which they meant the shooting of the mourners outside the university. In addition, a group of lawyers and other prominent citizens recommended the removal of all Cossacks from Moscow and the formation of a city militia. Arguing that the army was out of control, the group warned the city council that if measures were not taken quickly to protect Muscovites against arbitrary violence by private citizens and government troops, people would have no choice but to organize their own defense forces. Such measures, in fact, were already being taken. On October 25, however, the council voted overwhelmingly against establishing a militia. Only a tiny group of deputies was prepared to defy the central government on this issue and take the risk of placing arms in the hands of large numbers of people who might well be sympathetic to the revolutionary left. Nevertheless, the council did formally urge the Governor-General and Witte to remove the Cossacks from the center of the city. The Governor-General agreed to their removal, but he insisted on replacing them with dragoons, for whom the city was to provide proper quarters.[102]

In many other parts of the Empire, the breakdown of order in late October and early November also stimulated anew public interest in instituting militias of various kinds. In the Pale of Settlement, the Bund and two left-wing Zionist parties stepped up the organization of self-defense groups (*boevye otriady*; literally, "armed squads") charged with protecting Jewish communities from *pogromshchiki*. By 1905 such groups operated in almost one-third of the regions affected by anti-Semitic unrest, and early the next year the Bund alone maintained at least 550 men under arms. Their effectiveness in warding off the marauders is hard to gauge.

The Second Secretary of the British Embassy, who toured the Pale of Settlement in the summer of 1905, reported that "many Jews have recently procured arms to use in self-defence," but he doubted that they would be able to protect their fellows. "I was assured at Zhitomir," he wrote, "that when using their pistols they fired wildly into the air and seemed even more afraid of their own weapons than of the crowd which was attacking them."[103] Actually, in Zhitomir the self-defense units had acquitted themselves quite well. The problem there was that the police and troops helped the Black Hundreds. Wherever that happened, the self-defense groups could not possibly succeed in protecting Jewish communities and may even have provoked more bloodshed than might have occurred without their presence. That they were also poorly trained and inadequately armed, relying primarily on outdated revolvers, cannot be denied. Nevertheless, in some localities potential *pogromshchiki* were deterred by the knowledge that they would encounter armed resistance. In the last analysis, however, the growth of the self-defense groups was significant because it promoted a spirit of self-reliance among Jews.[104]

The movement for the creation of an effective police force was not confined to Jewish communities. On October 24, the St. Petersburg City Council adopted in principle a resolution to form a civil guard to maintain order in the capital, "since the existing police have ceased to be an organ guaranteeing the personal safety or property of the population."[105] In Zlatoust (Ufa guberniia) the city council set up a special commission to formulate plans for a militia. The council in Vinnitsa (Podolia guberniia) petitioned the government for permission to place the police under the command of municipal officials. In Kazan a huge crowd seized weapons at the police station, handed them over to the town council, and then demanded a militia.[106] These are just a few examples of the citizenry's growing loss of confidence in the government's exercise of police powers, which did not augur well for Witte's goal of achieving legitimacy for his government.

· · · · ·

The failure of Witte's government to stem the mob violence was only one symptom of its impotence. For a few weeks, it also could not cope with a new wave of disturbances in the countryside and a rash of mutinies in the army and navy.

The relative calm in the villages in the late summer and early fall came to an end with the large-scale disorders that broke out in Chernigov on October 23, when about 2,000 peasants plundered several landlords' estates. The unrest spread quickly, reaching its climax in November (when there were 796 major and minor incidents), by which time the turbulence in the cities had already receded. It has been estimated that during the last months of 1905, three times as many regions suffered major disturbances as in the spring and early summer; altogether, 478 districts in the 47 guberniias of European Russia were affected, as well as parts of Caucasia, the Baltic Provinces, and Poland.

The basic pattern was similar to that of the earlier period of unrest: peasants cut down timber, refused to pay taxes, and took grain from estates; and agricultural workers staged strikes. Now, however, the peasant movement assumed a more violent stance: in Tambov alone, 130 estates had buildings burned down. It was also more common for peasants to seize land for "temporary use"—that is, until the State Duma, expected to meet soon, approved the seizures. Although violence against individuals increased, it still was not widespread, in part because landlords made their escape before the arrival of the marauding peasants. The unrest subsided late in 1905, only to resume with renewed vigor in the period from May to August 1906. By the time the revolution ended in 1907, the Empire had endured the most intense wave of agrarian upheaval since the Pugachev peasant rebellion of 1773–75. Total losses in European Russia alone amounted to 29 million rubles.[107]

A major reason for the new wave of agrarian disturbances was the deterioration of economic conditions in the countryside. In two-thirds of the European provinces, the 1905 harvest was poorer than that of 1904.[108] But the impact on the peasants of the overall political situation should not be minimized. Although even this unrest can probably not be attributed primarily to agitators from the cities, the news that the Tsar had capitulated to the opposition and issued the October Manifesto did inflame the peasants, who placed their own interpretation on the document. According to one report, the peasants in Tambov, whose conduct was particularly ferocious, were convinced "that the Tsar had long ago ordered the landlords to give the land to the peasants, but they delayed, and now the Tsar gave a secret order to the peasants to take the land themselves." The landlords' abandonment of their estates before the disorders only confirmed the peasants in their view of the ruler's intentions.[109]

In many villages, it took some time for the peasants to receive detailed information about the manifesto, partly because of the poor system of communications and partly because the clergy deliberately held back the news. When rumors about the manifesto reached the peasants anyway, they assumed that they had been kept in the dark by the reactionary bureaucrats and landlords, who did not want them to know that the Tsar had granted "freedom" to the people. Freedom, as interpreted by the peasants, meant the right to attack landlords.[110]

Many peasants had simply lost faith in the government, which throughout 1905 had paid little attention to them. Nor was the October manifesto addressed to their concerns. To be sure, in a manifesto of November 3, the government reduced by one-half the redemption dues for almost all peasants as of January 1, 1906, and it promised their total elimination by January 1, 1907. The government also announced that the Peasants' Bank would soon provide more assistance to those with small holdings who wished to buy land. But these modest concessions did not meet the peasants' expectations.

In official documents of the time, one theme was frequently sounded: that unrest in so many localities could not be stopped because the authorities did not have adequate military force at their disposal. A sizable portion of the army continued to be bogged down in the Far East, and, as Trepov confided to the Tsar on November 17, "disquieting ferment" was noticeable among the lower ranks of various military units, making it hazardous to entrust even those troops that were available with duty against the troublesome villagers.[111] Two weeks earlier, the Governor of Tambov, V. F. Von der Launits, had sent an urgent plea to Witte that expressed the sentiments of many officials: "The agrarian movement is growing rapidly, numerous farmsteads have been destroyed, landlords are fleeing, the number of troops is insufficient. Persuasion has no influence on the masses. It is necessary to have an army in the province and to make a change from 'Reinforced Security' to martial law."[112]

Unable to supply the requested troops, Witte decided to send aides-de-camp of the Tsar to the provinces with the greatest ferment. He hoped that the presence of these personal emissaries of the highest authority would have a calming effect on the peasants and would also encourage local officials to resort to sterner measures to quell the unrest. General-Adjutant V. V. Sakharov was sent to Saratov, General-Adjutant A. P. Strukov to Tambov and Voronezh, and General-Adjutant F. V. Dubasov to Chernigov and Kursk.[113] It was a desperate gamble that did not pay off. The unrest subsided late in 1905 because the villagers seem simply to have run out of steam.

. . . . .

Many men in the army and navy also interpreted the October Manifesto according to their own lights. They chose to believe that the Tsar's concession gave them license to overturn rules and regulations that they found burdensome. Of course, the manifesto itself made no reference at all to civil liberties for soldiers and sailors, but that was immaterial. The Tsar had yielded to the opposition, authority in the civilian sector had collapsed, and to men in the military it seemed as though they, too, were no longer bound by the old restraints. They were convinced that they would not be punished for breaking the codes of military discipline. In short, the manifesto produced a profound change in the psychology of men who had been indoctrinated to accept discipline as the prime virtue.[114] With that psychological change in the soldiers, the dikes were opened for a veritable flood of mutinies.

The first occurred in Kronstadt, the city whose great naval base guarded the approaches to St. Petersburg at the head of the Gulf of Finland, on October 26–27, when 3,000 to 4,000 soldiers and sailors armed with rifles staged a riot. They plundered businesses throughout the city, destroying some 120 establishments and a few private houses; the damage to property has been estimated at a million rubles. The mutineers also attacked units that had not joined the riot. Revolutionaries, however, failed in their attempts to direct the rioters into disciplined political action. On October 26, the Commander of the Fleet and Ports of the Baltic Sea, K. P. Nikonov, reported to St. Petersburg that "the city is in a dangerous situation. . . . It is necessary to send as quickly as possible a large force to pacify the city." Even the sailors who were not participating in the riot, Nikonov reported a day later, were "passive" and could not be counted upon to restore order.[115]

The mutineers' demands, most of which dealt with conditions in the services, show that the men had been influenced by recent political developments. The first demand stated that "according to the manifesto that has been granted, sailors are Russian citizens. As such, they have the right to meet and to discuss their affairs. If it is inconvenient to have servicemen meet in [public] squares, then the riding arena should be assigned to them."[116] The mutineers' petition included the following justification for their demand for freedom of speech: "After all, military enlisted men are allowed to say only: 'Just so, sir,' 'No, sir,' 'Yes, sir.' They should have the right to say openly, to their commanders and everywhere, what they want."[117]

In addition, the mutineers requested a reduction in their term of service, a minimum salary of six rubles a month, and better food and clothing. They also asked to be allowed to buy alcoholic drinks without restrictions, "for they are not children," to attend meetings, and to spend their free time as they chose.

Although broader political demands (for universal suffrage, for example) appeared on the lists prepared by the mutineers in Kronstadt and in other localities, these were clearly of secondary importance. The soldiers and sailors evinced little interest in the political arrangements of the civilian sector. Indeed, they generally adopted political demands only to humor civilians, and the radical agitation often turned them into opponents of the revolution.[118]

On October 27, loyal troops from St. Petersburg and Pskov arrived in Kronstadt and quickly restored order. Although the rioters did not offer much resistance, there was nevertheless a good deal of bloodshed, much of it resulting from attacks by loyal troops on neutral barracks. Twenty-four people were killed, five of them civilians; 72 were wounded, including fourteen civilians.[119]

The bloody outcome of the riot did not act as a brake on other military units. On October 30 sailors and soldiers in Vladivostok, demanding the discharge of reservists, went on a rampage. By early the next morning, up to one-third of the city was in flames; drunken servicemen set fire to buildings and plundered stores at will. "Patrols on land behave violently," Rear Admiral N. R. Greve reported, "[and] in general there is complete anarchy." In the ensuing clashes between the mutineers and loyal troops, 24 insurgents lost their lives and 116 were wounded. Fourteen loyalist soldiers were killed and 28 were wounded before the disturbance ended.[120]

The most dramatic and clearly political mutiny took place in Sevastopol, a naval base in the Crimea. The guiding spirit was P. P. Schmidt, a charismatic 38-year-old lieutenant who attracted a sizable following among disaffected sailors and radical workers. The scion of a family with a tradition of service in the navy, Schmidt attended the Petersburg Naval School and served as a junior officer in the Baltic Fleet. As a student, he had come under the influence of the radical doctrines of N. K. Mikhailovsky and N. V. Shelgunov, which apparently prompted him to abandon the military for the merchant marine. Mobilized, however, when war broke out with Japan, he became commander of a torpedo boat stationed at Sevastopol at the time of the general strike in October, an event that drove Schmidt to political action. He was especially moved by the death of six civilians shot during an antigovernment demonstration on October 19. He attended the funeral, where he delivered a denunciation of the authorities. He then made several fiery speeches in the city council, which quickly turned him into a local hero and prompted the workers to elect him to that body "for life." Admiral G. P. Chukhnin, Commander of the Fleet in Sevastopol, ordered that Schmidt be arrested, but public pressure forced the authorities to release him.

On November 11, Chukhnin prohibited military personnel from attending public meetings, a directive ignored by many sailors. A company of soldiers sought to break up one such meeting with gunfire, which provoked a mutiny within the navy. By November 14, the cruisers *Svirepy* and *Ochakov* as well as several smaller boats had fallen under the control of mutineers, who called on Schmidt to assume command of the rebellion. Apparently, Schmidt hesitated at first because he doubted whether an isolated action against the government could avoid being crushed by local troops. In his view, only a coordinated effort by the masses throughout the Empire, directed by revolutionaries in St. Petersburg, could topple the regime. But an old revolutionary in Sevastopol, I. P. Voronitsyn, prevailed upon Schmidt to accept the challenge.

Once he had crossed the Rubicon, Schmidt acted boldly. He proclaimed himself commander of the fleet, raised the red flag on all ships under his control, sent a telegram to the Tsar demanding the immediate convocation of a constituent assembly, and formulated a grand plan to seize control of the entire fleet at Sevastopol and to secure the isthmus leading to the Crimea against outside military forces. Schmidt also ordered the arrest of officers opposed to his rebellion and threatened to hang them if the government tried to quell the rising.

Admiral Chukhnin immediately marshaled his forces for an attack. On November 15, he sent Schmidt an ultimatum demanding unconditional surrender. When the ultimatum was ignored, Chukhnin directed the loyal battleships and the artillery on shore to fire on the ships controlled by the mutineers. Within hours the *Ochakov* was ablaze, and by the morning of November 16 the mutiny had collapsed. Schmidt, disguised as a seaman, tried to escape but was captured, together with his sixteen-year-old son. Chukhnin's forces also arrested over 1,600 men and freed twenty officers held by the rebels. During the battle, one loyalist officer died; three mutineers lost their lives, and a large number were seriously wounded.

Early in 1906, Schmidt and three of his accomplices were court-martialed in a trial that lasted eleven days. Schmidt's eloquent defense, which included an elaborate attack on the Tsarist regime, attracted a great deal of sympathetic attention from the press but did not sway the tribunal, which sentenced all four defendants to death. On March 6,

1906, they were shot on the island of Berezan, some eight miles from the town of Ochakov in southern Russia. Many liberals were shocked, in part because Schmidt was the first officer to have been executed in decades and in part because it was widely believed that he had merely wished to defend the principles of the October Manifesto but had been carried away by the tensions of the moment into leading a mutiny.[121]

All told, 211 separate mutinies were recorded in the Russian army alone between late October and mid-December 1905, though very few were accompanied by serious violence. In fact, in only about 30 percent was there resort to arms. In most of them, the men simply refused to obey orders, left their barracks, held meetings to discuss current affairs, and talked back to their officers. Any one of a variety of incidents or orders could spark acts of insubordination: refusal by an officer to disburse money due, orders to arrest civilian troublemakers, or merely a command to go out on patrol.[122] The elite corps, the Cavalry and Cossacks, were virtually untouched by mutiny, but one-third of all infantry units experienced some form of disturbance, and the navy was so riddled with disorders that the government feared that it could no longer be relied upon to carry out its mission.

Moreover, late in November there were indications that even some officers (mainly in the Far East and Siberia) were openly supporting the opposition. In Chita, a large group of officers established a "Union of Officers and Military Specialists," which sympathized with the goals of the Soviet of Soldiers and Cossack Deputies of the RSDWP. Another group, including a major-general and two colonels, announced (also in the Far East) that it would remain loyal to the Tsar only if he implemented the October Manifesto. In Harbin, an assembly of officers opposed an order to shoot striking railway workers on the ground that the latter were "our brothers in the cause of freedom." A few junior officers, for the most part from the reserves, endorsed the revolutionaries.[123] Of course, the vast majority of officers remained loyal, but even the few incidents of radicalism involving officers were alarming to the High Command. The Minister of War, General Rediger, thought that the country was threatened with "total ruin."[124] After all, the upheaval in the military services occurred shortly after an enormous and unsettling outburst of popular violence. Witte could not afford a long delay in meeting the new challenge to his authority.

On December 6, the government instituted a series of military reforms. It increased pay and meat rations, provided servicemen for the first time with tea and sugar, and promised to abolish forced labor by soldiers in the civilian economy in January 1906. The government also reduced the term of service, from 4 to 3 years for infantrymen, 5 to 4 years for cavalrymen, and 7 to 5 years for sailors. Finally, the government removed a major source of discontent in the army by speeding up the demobilization of reservists, especially those in European Russia, most of whom resumed civilian life by mid-December 1905.[125]

The government's concessions helped to calm the soldiers and sailors. But a crucial factor in restoring military discipline seems to have been the decision by the government in mid-December to move forcefully against the civilians who had been defying its authority. Once the government embarked on that course, it became clear that the October Manifesto did not signify the dissolution of the old order after all. The psychology of the soldiers and sailors now changed as suddenly and drastically as it had in mid-October. With the restoration of authority in the civilian sector, the men in uniform again submitted to the orders of their superiors. Generally unsympathetic to political radicalism, they recoiled at the increasing violence of the revolutionaries, which on occasion was directed at the military itself. In thus desisting from their own "revolution," the soldiers and sailors removed a serious threat to governmental stability.[126]

Of course, the government was never totally bereft of loyal troops. Even among the infantry, the branch of the army most deeply affected by mutinies, two-thirds of the units did not engage in unrest. The thirteen regiments of the Guard Corps, elite soldiers who received special privileges, remained almost completely immune to disorder and played a major role in suppressing the revolutionary movement. Moreover, in late 1905 and early 1906, the government activated some 100,000 Cossacks, who were given generous grants of money and whose privileges were confirmed by special charters issued in the Tsar's name.[127] Relatively small, well-armed detachments of such loyal soldiers could be used with great effectiveness against poorly armed bands of workers or peasants. It was these loyal troops that the government began to unleash in mid-December, a move that proved to be instrumental in turning back the tide of revolution.

· · · · ·

"In no instance," Count Aehrenthal wrote his superiors in Vienna on December 3, "have any of Witte's actions achieved their aims."[128] Far from pacifying the population, the October Manifesto triggered disorders more violent and widespread than any that had occurred since the beginning of the revolution. Witte's attempts to detach the moderate liberals from the opposition movement ended in failure. The extremists on the right and the left had grown more determined and vocal, which only reduced the chances of a political settlement. All of these untoward developments occurred, yet it is an oversimplification to attribute each one of them to the Prime Minister's policies. He certainly blundered in pressing the candidacy of Durnovo as Minister of Internal Affairs. But when the October Manifesto was issued, no one could have foreseen the mass violence, the unrest in the countryside and the military services, and the growth of political militancy. To argue otherwise is to say that any major political reform in Russia in 1905 was doomed to fail, hence futile.

Witte's lack of success was not inevitable. Nor was the political situation altogether bleak in the days after the general strike. Witte did remain faithful to the essentials of the October Manifesto for about six weeks: it can reasonably be argued that during that time, the fate of the revolution was determined. Indeed, the Days of Liberty, as that brief period came to be known, were in many ways a remarkable political experiment—nothing like it would return to Russia until 1917, and then for only eight months. For the outcome to have been different, all political groups and social classes would have had to act with the greatest restraint and sense of responsibility. That was a great deal to expect in a country without a tradition of popular participation in the political process. How the experiment in political freedom came to grief is one of the more intricate and absorbing chapters of the revolution.

Chapter Ten

. . . .

The Days of Liberty

"WE HAVE ALL now arrived happily and without any difficulties in Petersburg," wrote F. I. Dan, a Menshevik leader, to Karl Kautsky, on October 27, 1905. "We live as though in a state of intoxication; the revolutionary air affects people like wine. As you can see from the enclosed announcement, we have already advertised our newspaper [*Nachalo*]. If Comrade Luxemburg translates the excerpts for you, then you will also note that the tone in which one can speak leaves nothing to be desired. There are in actuality almost no restraints on freedom of speech and assembly. The mood is splendid. To be sure, the Black Hundreds also operate quite openly." [1]

Prime Minister Witte quickly came to terms with the new atmosphere that pervaded the capital. The left liberal activist Petrunkevich later recalled that before he was to chair a private meeting of the Zemstvo Bureau, he received a polite telegram from Witte requesting that the group not engage in illegal activities and that it calmly discuss questions of interest to society and the government. "In other words, such meetings had in effect achieved independence [from the government], even though they were not legal. . . ." [2]

During the Days of Liberty, stretching from October 18 until early December, Russian society enjoyed so much freedom that some observers actually considered the new conditions dangerous because extremists would now be able to increase their support among the masses. To the German Ambassador in St. Petersburg, it almost seemed as though "the government wants to facilitate the work of revolutionaries." [3] That was certainly not the government's intention, but the left in fact did succeed in greatly strengthening its forces, which resulted in polarization of the political spectrum.

Revolutionary publications "increased like mushrooms." Newspapers and journals of all political movements—liberal, Marxist, Socialist Revolutionary, Anarchist—were sold freely on the streets of St. Petersburg and elsewhere. *Russkaia gazeta*, for example, a Social Democratic newspaper whose editorials were especially militant, appeared in runs of over 100,000 copies. The attacks on the authorities in these publications were often merciless. One of the more famous cartoons carried by a popular journal depicted the Tsar on a throne whose legs were being chewed up by mice. Some of the caricatures were beyond the comprehension of the Minister of Internal Affairs, Durnovo, who relied upon Gerasimov for enlightenment: "This is Count Witte and this here (represented as a pig or toad) is you, Your Excellency." Durnovo asked what could be done to "restore order." "If I were permitted to close down all revolutionary presses and to arrest 700 to 800 people," Gerasimov replied, "then I guarantee that I could bring calm to Petersburg." Durnovo, however, refused to authorize such sweeping action on the ground that the new constitutional order forbade it.[4]

Still, on occasion the police plied their old trade, though not with much success. On the night of November 2, 45 workers were arrested at the printing plant of *Novaia zhizn*, a Bolshevik paper that had published some articles the government considered to be unduly provocative and offensive. Within six days, however, the paper appeared again without any change in editorial policy.[5] A raid on the office of a satirical journal proved to be a boon to business. The police found only a few dozen of the tens of thousands of copies of the issue that was to be confiscated. The remainder, hidden by vendors, then "fetched, one, two, three, and sometimes five rubles instead of five kopecks."[6] During the Days of Liberty, police actions were nuisances, but they did not affect the flow of information.

On November 24, the government formally abolished preliminary censorship of periodicals. Some important, though vaguely defined, restrictions on freedom of the press remained, but no publication was to be suppressed without juridical proceedings. The government also announced that the State Duma would be charged with adopting comprehensive legislation on freedom of the press.[7]

Attendance at public meetings became even more common than it had been after the granting of autonomy to institutions of higher learning in late August. In Moscow alone, over 400 meetings were held between October 17 and December 8, not counting many that took place in factories and private homes. Of the legally sanctioned meetings, over half concentrated on trade union issues.[8] At the same time, the number of labor unions increased dramatically. There are some statistics on this development, but, as was pointed out earlier, they are rough estimates for which the evidence is sparse. In Moscow, 67 unions were apparently established, and in St. Petersburg, 58.[9] The author of a recent study of Odessa concluded that about 50 unions were formed in that city in November and December; however, this figure includes about twenty cases of workers holding a meeting to found a union without evidence that their plans bore fruit.[10] Trade unions also appeared in Saratov, Nizhnii-Novgorod, Baku, and other towns.[11]

Finally, proletarian political parties stepped up their organizational activities. Without abandoning clandestine operations entirely, the Bolsheviks adopted a new slogan: "Down with the Underground! We have long suffocated in it." Lenin boasted that between the spring and fall of 1905 the RSDWP became transformed from an "association of underground circles" into a party representing "a million proletarians." Although this claim can be dismissed as hyperbole, there is no doubt that the Bolsheviks' following increased substantially. The Mensheviks concentrated on creating political clubs at the local level, and their achievements were also impressive. On November 15, 120 people participated in the founding of a club at the Baltic Factory in St. Petersburg; on November 16, 300 attended the meeting of a unified club of Mensheviks and Bolsheviks; a third such event attracted 240 people. In provincial towns, Menshevik organizers were equally successful.[12]

During the Days of Liberty, the soviets vastly expanded their operations. They established regular contact with city councils and often secured access to public halls for their meetings; in some regions, local organs of government even honored the soviet's request that unemployed workers be given financial assistance. The Petersburg Soviet, the most prominent in the Empire, became especially influential. It made its presence felt in particular during strikes, when it sent directives to government agencies such as the Post Office and the railroads, and entered into negotiations with the St. Petersburg City Council—and once even with the Prime Minister himself. The Soviet also sent numerous inquiries to government offices, and the latter were often sufficiently impressed by the Soviet's authority to go to the trouble of answering.[13] It sponsored collections for unemployed workers and distributed 30 kopeks a day to adults and 10–15 to children. Moreover, it set up several inexpensive dining halls for the unemployed and their families.[14]

The boldest undertaking of the Soviet was the establishment of its own militia, whose members, identified by special armbands, "interfered in the affairs of the police, gave . . . [them] orders and made demands of them." It was not uncommon for "confused officers" to give in to the militiamen.[15] After partial amnesty was proclaimed on October 21, the

Soviet sent representatives to the police to make sure that the prisoners had in fact been released. On one occasion, a subordinate of Colonel Gerasimov, one First Lieutenant Model, "lost his head" and took the visitors on a tour of the entire building, including the colonel's office. Enraged, Gerasimov ordered that Model be transferred. On another occasion, one of the militiamen demanded that a policeman clean out a pit in a garbage-strewn yard because the odor was unbearable. The policeman meekly carried out the order.[16]

According to Trepov, by mid-November the militia numbered 6,000 men, who had at their disposal revolvers, hunting guns, knives, and heavy spades. About 300 workers belonged to a special militia of "self-defense," small groups of which patrolled the streets every night from 8 P.M. to 6 A.M. to protect merchants and residents. Trepov claimed that their real purpose was to protect revolutionaries from arrest. Allowance must be made for Trepov's penchant to exaggerate the danger to public order, but workers in growing numbers were definitely arming themselves.[17]

The Soviet posted armed militiamen outside its meeting place, the Free Economic Society, where the deputies gathered almost daily to discuss political developments and to adopt resolutions on current issues. The Soviet took it upon itself to demand that the government issue a general amnesty for all categories of political prisoners, send the army out of the city, end the state of siege everywhere in the Empire, and hold a democratic election for a constituent assembly. In mid-November, the Petersburg Soviet also took steps to achieve preeminence over the revolutionary movement nationwide. It sent delegates to other cities and regions of the country to establish contact with local soviets and various workers' organizations. It also received delegates from provincial towns and maintained close relations with the All-Russian Peasants' Union.[18]

Many workers in the capital looked upon the Soviet as their legitimate spokesman and saw it as a vehicle for the attainment of further social and political concessions from the government. Even some members of the middle classes turned to the Petersburg Soviet for help on specific issues.[19] Not surprisingly, the growing power of the Soviet aroused fear in non-working-class groups, and especially among conservatives. *Novoe vremia* complained that there were really two governments, one led by Count Witte and one by Khrustalev-Nosar (chairman of the Petersburg Soviet), and that no one knew who would arrest whom first.[20]

Flushed with success, the Petersburg Soviet succumbed to hubris. Instead of consolidating its achievements, it became increasingly militant, and even reckless. Many of its leaders reasoned that if the autocracy could be so easily brought to its knees, would it not be possible to gain more and more concessions for the working class and press ahead with a socialist revolution? They chose to ignore the fact that the general strike had succeeded only because it had been a unified effort by various social groups; and they failed to understand that they could count on middle-class sympathy only so long as the Soviet concentrated its fire against the autocracy.

In their defense, it must be said that the leaders of the Soviet were under pressure from their constituency, the workers, who quickly became impatient with the slow pace of economic and social reform. They had gone out on strike in October not merely to effect political change. They yearned for economic concessions and were not prepared to wait for them. The upshot was a wave of intense labor unrest, which proved to be an unmitigated disaster, for the workers as well as for the opposition movement as a whole.

On October 26 and 27, workers in several large enterprises in the capital decided on their own initiative to introduce the eight-hour day. The idea of shortening the workday by "revolutionary means" was not new. In May 1905 workers at various concerns had simply laid down their tools after nine hours on the job, and the government yielded on the issue for publicly owned plants. Now workers decided to use the same tactic to bring about an eight-hour day. They broached the subject on October 20 at factory meetings held at the initiative of the St. Petersburg Soviet to discuss ending the general strike; during the following few days an increasing number of workers supported the tactic. It was an ominous development, as V. S. Voitinskii, an activist in the capital, shrewdly pointed out: "The university meetings [in September and early October] marked the hegemony of the proletariat in the all-national movement. The factory meetings signified the beginning of the fatal isolation of the working class." [21]

When the Soviet took up the issue of the eight-hour day on October 29, a few deputies were bold enough to condemn what they considered to be a "syndicalist deviation." V. M. Chernov, leader of the Socialist Revolutionary Party, warned that approval of the workers' demand would be a major political blunder: "We are not yet done with absolutism, and you want to take on the bourgeoisie." Most deputies, however, either out of conviction or out of fear that the workers would proceed on their own, voted for the following resolution: "On October 31, the eight-hour day is to be introduced by revolutionary means in all factories." [22] Both wings of the Social Democratic movement supported the decision.

The government and many employers responded with a massive lock-out; the best estimate is that by early November over 100,000 workers were affected. It was an unprecedented collaboration by the employers, the result of their growing recognition that the defense of their interests required a unified stand. By a week after the general strike ended, on October 24, the "Petersburg Section of the Association for the Encouragement and Development of Russian Trade and Industry" had reorganized itself into the "Association of Manufacturers and Factory Owners," representing 150 companies that together employed more than 100,000 people, with the intention of adopting a common policy against further strikes. Among other things, the Association vowed not to pay workers for days lost during strikes and to cease giving those who were dismissed two weeks' severance pay. Late in October and again on November 1, representatives of 63 factories agreed to close down their plants if the workers tried to introduce the eight-hour day on their own.[23] The employers' tactic turned out to be highly effective, in large measure because the workers were exhausted and in desperate financial straits.

The campaign for the eight-hour day quickly became entangled with another conflict between the government and the Soviet. The government had decided to court-martial several hundred soldiers and sailors who had mutinied in Kronstadt and to impose martial law throughout Poland, which was then racked by disorders. On November 1, the Soviet voted in favor of a general political strike, to protest these actions. The strikers' slogans were "Down with Courts-Martial!," "Down with the Death Sentence!," and "Down with Martial Law in Poland and in All of Russia!"[24] By shifting the emphasis from economic to political issues, the Soviet sought to revive the solidarity and militancy of the strike movement by exploiting the government's repressive measures. As Trotsky declared some years later, the lives of "a few dozen sailors" were not the primary concern of the Soviet: "what does this matter in a revolution that has swallowed up tens of thousands of lives?" Nor was the imposition of martial law in Poland a critical factor. "The November strike was a call for solidarity, issued by the proletariat over the head of the government and the bourgeois opposition to the prisoners in the barracks."[25]

In an attempt to stave off a general strike, Prime Minister Witte on November 2 sent a telegram to all factories: "Brother workers! Remain at work, avoid disturbances, spare your wives and children. Do not listen to other advice. The Sovereign has directed us to pay special attention to the labor question. To this end, His Imperial Majesty has formed a Ministry of Trade and Industry that will establish just relations between workers and employers. Give us time, [and] everything possible will be done for you. Listen to the advice of a person who is well-disposed toward you and wishes you well." Witte's appeal did not sway many minds. On the contrary, workers were transported into "ecstasy" when they heard the Soviet's statement (drafted by Trotsky), which scornfully rejected the Prime Minister's appeal: "The proletariat is in no way related to Count Witte."[26]

In the end, however, relatively few workers outside the capital heeded the call for a general political strike. In St. Petersburg, some 100,000 people are said to have participated, but beyond that, only in Revel (Tallin) and Rybinsk did the strike attract substantial numbers. By November 4, even workers in St. Petersburg began drifting back to their jobs: that day, 4,500 returned at the Putilov plant; the next day, 5,000 followed suit.

Moreover, large sectors of the liberal intelligentsia refused from the very beginning to support the new strike, which they considered unwarranted. In their view, the opposition should now devote its energies to preparing for the elections to the State Duma. True, all but one of the constituent members of the Union of Unions supported the strike, but they did so reluctantly and halfheartedly. The Union of Teachers, for example, voted not to join "for pedagogical reasons," but then, to assuage its guilt, declared its "sympathy" and promised to donate three days' pay to the strike fund.[27] The liberal intelligentsia's attitude toward the strike, evident at a public meeting on November 5, astonished Voitinskii: "Three weeks earlier everybody glorified the workers, every arm was stretched out to the proletariat. And now it seemed as though an invisible wall had appeared between these people and the factory districts. Not a word was said about the strike."[28]

In short, the November general strike was in no way comparable to the October strike. In the capital, the banks, government institutions, commercial establishments, and public transportation remained essentially unaffected. Among the people, according to one reliable account, "neither revolutionary excitement nor revolutionary panic was noticeable." Even the Poles, who had stood at the forefront of every other antigovernment movement since 1904, failed to respond to the Soviet's summons.[29]

Clearly, the Soviet had misread the popular mood. As the liberal editors of *Pravo*, staunch supporters of the October strike, pointed out: "A general strike must, in essence, be regarded as an extreme revolutionary means. Only at moments of great revolutionary tension, when revolutionary fervor has seized broad circles of the public, should this means be quickly applied; only then can it have the necessary revolutionary effect." These conditions did not prevail early in November, for two reasons: there was no convincing evidence that the government planned to shoot the Kronstadt mutineers; and the imposition of martial law in Poland was not the kind of issue that could rouse public opinion in the rest of the Empire.[30] By November 4, a majority of the Executive Committee of the Soviet realized that the strike was a failure and voted, 9 to 6, to end it as of November 7.

Yet in the charged atmosphere of St. Petersburg, it was easier to begin a strike than to terminate one. The resolution of the Executive Committee touched off a storm in the Soviet itself; the highlight of the discussion was a plea by the deputy from the Aleksandrovskii factory: "When you [i.e. the Soviet] decided the question of the political strike three days ago, you realized what a responsibility the Soviet assumed in calling for it. But you realized that if you do not now protest, then you will lose all the positions you have won. . . . The political strike is an enormous weapon that one must not resort to lightly but that one must also not abandon lightly. If it appears that the masses are exhausted—and after such strikes this is no disgrace—then the Soviet of Workers' Deputies, of course, cannot disregard the wishes of the workers. But if there is any possibility of continuing the strike, it must be continued; the signal for a retreat must not be given before the enemy considers itself victorious."[31] Moved by this grandiloquent statement, the Soviet voted, 400 to 4, to continue the strike.

A day later, however, it reversed itself by an overwhelming margin and called for the strike to end as of 12 noon on November 7. The alleged reason for the sudden change was that the government had officially announced in the meantime that the Kronstadt mutineers would not be court-martialed. But that was simply a pretext for accepting the inevitable. The Soviet had suffered its first serious defeat, and in the process it had alienated the liberals, many of whom had previously been well disposed toward it.

The campaign for the eight-hour day also backfired. For one thing, it drew employers closer to the government, which supported resistance to the workers' demands by enforcing a lockout at its own plants and by making troops available to protect privately owned factories. Moreover, the excesses of the left prompted both moderate and militant liberals such as Miliukov to reconsider the advisability of basing their political strategy on an alliance with the revolutionaries.[32] A few years after the revolution, Martov, the Menshevik leader, conceded that the campaign had been misguided. He acknowledged that it might have been wiser to defeat "one enemy first, and then begin the struggle against another one." He also acknowledged that the Social Democrats had sanctioned the "battle" only because it had been unleashed from below.[33]

The Soviet's hasty retreat in the face of the successful lockout was embarrassing. At first, on November 6, the Soviet simply moderated its stand by calling for "practical means" to attain the eight-hour day. This vague formula seemed to mean that if workers wished to continue the struggle they could do so, but that the Soviet would not encourage them. Most employers, unimpressed, refused to open their plants. On November 12, the Soviet admitted complete defeat by calling for a temporary halt to the campaign. The Social Democrats offered two explanations for their retreat: workers should not prematurely provoke a counterrevolution; and they should wait for a new outburst of agrarian unrest so that the all-out battle against the employers could be coordinated with the peasants' attacks on the landlords.[34]

For the workers, the abandonment of the campaign for the eight-hour day proved to be a painful and humiliating experience. Although the workday was reduced in a few enterprises—in some to nine hours, in a few others to ten or ten and a half hours—most strikers, who had lost several days of pay, gained nothing. Some even had to accept more stringent conditions before being allowed to return to their jobs. At the Nevskii plant, for example, the workers were forced to pledge themselves to refrain from holding meetings on factory grounds and from calling wildcat strikes. They also had to agree to the same conditions of work and the same pay scale that had been in effect before the lockouts.[35]

In mid-November, white-collar employees of the postal service staged another major strike. These government employees had illegally formed the All-Russian Postal Union, and on November 15 they planned to convene a congress in Moscow. Shortly before the first session, the government dismissed three of the Union's leaders, an action that prompted the call for a nationwide strike. Then the police dissolved one of the first sessions of the congress and on November 20 arrested seven leaders of the Union.

Although the strike caused considerable inconvenience to the authorities and the public, it did not succeed in disrupting post and telegraph service. A fair number of postal employees, traditionally cautious, continued to work, and the government assigned firemen to fill in for the absentees. Moreover, the ultraconservative Union of the Russian People recruited volunteers to replace strikers. Consequently, the government could proceed with the dismissal of a large number of administrators and low-ranking employees who had joined the strike. Other unions and some businessmen expressed sympathy for the postal workers and even donated money to the strikers, but none offered to join their ranks. In an attempt to win broader support, the Postal Union affiliated itself with the St. Petersburg Soviet, which it had previously shunned. The strike still did not spread beyond the postal service, and by late November it fizzled out. The government agreed to reinstate the dismissed workers on condition that they sign a pledge not to join any unauthorized organization. Many administrators quickly accepted this condition; the rank-and-file employees also returned to their jobs, though at a slower pace.[36]

The defeat of the postal strike marked a turning point in the Days of Liberty. Until then, the government had mostly taken a defensive stance in the face of work stoppages and disorders. But it could not tolerate ruptured communications between St. Petersburg and the rest of the Empire, which explains why the Minister of Internal Affairs resorted to firm measures to break the strike. His success restored the government's self-confidence and demoralized the left, which had now suffered three major blows in three weeks. It soon became evident that this latest victory had emboldened the authorities to move to the offensive.

In a ukase of November 29, Tsar Nicholas decreed that in the event of a breakdown of telegraphic services or railway communications in any region of the country, the Governors-General, Governors, and City Governors were authorized to place such areas under "Reinforced Security" or "Extraordinary Security."[37] This was a striking departure from past practices, for such exceptional measures previously were to be taken only with the specific approval of the Minister of Internal Affairs.

On December 12, Nicholas issued another ukase in which he specified the punishments to be meted out to strikers at enterprises of "public or state importance" where a work stoppage could produce "ruinous consequences for the population." Agitators guilty of instigating strikes on the railways, at telephone companies, or in other establishments critical to the national well-being were to be imprisoned for periods ranging from eight to sixteen months. If the agitators were outsiders and no strike occurred, the term of imprisonment would be two to eight months. State employees who went on strike would be dismissed and imprisoned for periods ranging from three weeks to sixteen months. Government employees guilty of agitating for a strike that actually took place would be incarcerated for eight to sixteen months. Individuals belonging to an organization that agitated for strikes at railways or telephone companies would be jailed for sixteen months to four years and would be deprived of all rights and property.[38]

· · · · ·

The strike movement in November was only one aspect of the growing drift toward greater militancy by radical activists. Increasingly, the soviets and the publications of various socialist parties advocated an "armed struggle against the Tsarist regime" or another general political strike. By the fall of 1905, several Menshevik leaders and many lesser Menshevik activists threw caution to the winds and abandoned the Marxist dogma that a bourgeois revolution must precede a socialist seizure of power. In fact, at this time many Mensheviks in Russia were hardly distinguishable from Bolsheviks in their rhetoric and actions. In October and November 1905, the two factions set up Federal Councils (or Committees) in various towns, which generally consisted of an equal number of Bolsheviks and Mensheviks. In Moscow, for example, their collaboration became exceedingly close during the October strike. "Representatives of both ... [factions] found themselves in constant contact," wrote one Menshevik, "and from time to time organized joint meetings of the Committee and 'groups' [of party members or sympathizers]."[39] Some Mensheviks balked at the new arrangement, but since both factions favored revolutionary action against the government—the most pressing item on the radical left's political agenda—there seemed to be no reason to retain separate organizations.

Martov actually called for the formal reunification of the factions. He argued that the organizational issue, divisive in 1903, had ceased to be a source of conflict. True, the Bolsheviks considered it unfeasible for the workers' movement to maintain a democratic structure so long as it was forced to remain underground. But they had committed themselves to "democratism" once the party could operate openly, which was now the case. At the same time, many Mensheviks had come to believe in the necessity of a highly centralized party structure. "On the question of membership in the party," Martov declared, "many of us—adherents of the 'soft' formula at the Second Congress—willingly accept at present the 'hard' formula, since broad democratism in the organization will reduce to naught all fears of a conspiratorial degeneration of the party. . . . With [the party's] appearance in the arena of open struggle, [its] functions are first and foremost such as to require the greatest degree of uniformity, [and] the greatest degree of centralization. And the organizational apparatus must be adapted to the needs of this centralization of activities. We can therefore anticipate that the question of the powers of the party centers will not split the party into two sharply divided camps." Martov conceded that the Mensheviks and Bolsheviks still differed on such questions as the role of trade unions and soviets, "the tasks of an insurrection," and the composition of the provisional government after the overthrow of Tsarism. Nevertheless, he firmly believed that the differences could be ironed out.[40]

Martov published these views in *Nachalo*, the Menshevik paper that appeared legally in Russia and was in some respects even more radical than the Bolsheviks' *Novaia zhizn*. In the very first issue the editors of *Nachalo* made plain their conviction that the political order created by the October Manifesto would not be able to survive for long.[41] Trotsky, the leading figure on the editorial board, contended that though the bourgeoisie and liberal professionals had lent material support to the strikes in October, the actions of these classes were devoid of "any independent significance." Their participation "increased to a very small degree the political importance of the general strike of labor." The general strike, Trotsky maintained, "was a demonstration of proletarian hegemony in the bourgeois revolution. . . . The October days showed that in the revolution hegemony belonged to the cities; in the cities—to the proletariat." Because the general strike had unleashed an "orgy of reaction," the proletariat must now (in mid-November) organize the peasantry and establish contact with the army. Most important, the masses must arm themselves: "that is the simple and main conclusion the proletariat must draw from the October struggle and October victory. On this conclusion will depend the future of the revolution."[42]

Trotsky's analysis was remarkable as contemporary history and as political strategy. In denying the importance of the middle classes in the general strike, he ignored the fact that the protest movement had succeeded precisely because it had embraced all urban classes. Moreover, by urging the proletariat to arm itself for a new onslaught on the government, he was bound to alienate the radicals' allies among the liberals.

Trotsky's analysis also departed significantly from the doctrine of proletarian hegemony in the bourgeois revolution. Indeed, a few days before the appearance of Trotsky's article, Plekhanov, the author of the doctrine, gave an interview in Switzerland in which he took pains to disassociate himself from the maximalist claims that were being made by a growing number of Social Democrats in Russia. Plekhanov conceded having asserted in 1889 that the "Russian liberation movement will triumph as a proletarian movement or it will not triumph at all." But he hastened to add that "this did not mean then and does not mean now that the historical tasks of the present time will be decided by the proletariat alone. The bourgeoisie and the proletariat are interested in the renewal of the Russian [state] system. Therefore both society and the proletariat will play a decisive role in the events that are occurring. It would be a great mistake to diminish the value of one or the other factor."[43]

It soon became apparent that Trotsky had not only jettisoned the doctrine of proletarian hegemony as it had been developed by the founder of Russian Marxism; by advocating the theory of permanent revolution, he had also explicitly abandoned the traditional Marxist notion that backward Russia must undergo a more or less prolonged period of bourgeois domination before the socialist revolution could be effected. The Russian proletariat, Trotsky argued, had demonstrated greater energy and determination than its counterpart in Western Europe and would be the pathfinder in the struggle for socialism. "There is no stage," he wrote, "in the bourgeois revolution at which this force [the Russian proletariat] could become satiated, for it is driven forward by the iron logic of class interest. The law of self-preservation dictates to the proletariat a program of permanent revolution. The proletariat accomplishes the fundamental tasks of democracy and then, at a certain moment the logic of its struggle to consolidate its political power confronts it with problems that are purely socialist. Revolutionary permanency is established between our minimum and maximum programs."[44]

Trotsky's exposition of the theory of permanent revolution was not an isolated phenomenon in the Menshevik journal. An anonymous lead article stated that "it is entirely possible that in the event of a protracted civil war our revolution, which began as a democratic revolution, will end as a socialist revolution." The author did not think that such an outcome would violate Marxist doctrine, because Russian Social Democrats had never said how long the bourgeois stage would last. Even A. S. Martynov, the former "Economist," voiced such extremist views.[45]

The Marxist version of the doctrine of permanent revolution can be traced to several ideas first advanced by Parvus (A. L. Helfand), one of the more imaginative, eccentric, and controversial socialists of the early twentieth century. A Russian by birth, Parvus made his mark as a writer on politics in Germany. In 1895, at the age of 28, he predicted in *Die Neue Zeit* that Russia and Japan would wage war against each other and that the consequence would be a revolution against Tsarism. In addition to being a bold and clever writer, Parvus was fond of the good life. Convinced that he could achieve his aim of influencing the course of history by amassing a fortune—to be used for worthy causes—he began in 1912 to engage in a variety of economic speculations. He was so successful that people referred to him as the "socialist tycoon." After 1914, Parvus tried to forge an alliance between the German government and European, especially Russian, socialists. He liberally distributed funds acquired from the German Foreign Office to Russian radicals, on the assumption that their agitation, by weakening Tsarism, would hasten its military defeat, the prelude to the long-awaited revolution. By this time, his behavior corresponded to the Marxist caricature of a wealthy capitalist: he stayed at the most luxurious hotels, was almost always surrounded by "corpulent blond women," and had a penchant for big, expensive cigars and champagne. Most socialists now viewed him as a depraved man who had betrayed the cause.[46]

In 1905, however, Parvus still enjoyed high regard as a radical and exerted strong influence in left-wing circles. Trotsky, in particular, came under his intellectual sway, though the two soon drifted apart. During the Days of Liberty, Parvus wrote, also in *Nachalo*, that "we have arrived at a new stage in the development of the revolution. The struggle is now no longer for one or another legal rule in the state system, but for the immediate takeover of governmental power. Either by means of a constituent assembly or without it, the question of a revolutionary government is next on the agenda."[47]

In the same issue that carried this statement, *Nachalo* reprinted an article by Franz Mehring, the eminent German historian and theorist of Marxism, entitled "Permanent Revolution." In a footnote the editors explained that the article showed "that this outstanding historian and publicist of the German Social Democratic Party accepts a point of view on the Russian revolution that our sycophants and philistines try to depict as anarchism and Jacobinism."

Actually, Mehring did not agree with the arguments presented in *Nachalo*, even though he spoke glowingly of the achievements of the working class in Russia. He warned that the Russian proletariat could not count on "miracles"; they did not possess the power "to jump over stages of historical development and to create in one moment a socialist society out of the Tsarist autocracy." As if to emphasize the point, Mehring stated that the Russian workers could not impose "a dictatorship of the proletariat in the new conditions" prevailing in the country. At best, they could ease their struggle for emancipation and cut short the duration of that struggle. Furthermore, Mehring did not deprecate the contributions of the liberals to the political emancipation of Russia. Rather, he insisted that the freedoms the liberals had gained for themselves should be extended to the working class.[48]

Yet some radicals in Central Europe were as intoxicated by the turn of events as the proponents of permanent revolution. Their highly optimistic assessment of developments in the East seems to have been a factor in the radicalization of some German socialists.[49] On November 14, 1905, Rudolf Hilferding, a young Austrian socialist who in 1910 was to achieve renown as the author of *Das Finanzkapital*, wrote Kautsky that "the collapse of Tsarism is surely the beginning of our revolution, our victory, which is now attainable in the near future." The key development, Hilferding contended, was the upheaval in Poland, which would set off a chain reaction in Europe, just as Marx had predicted in 1849. If Poland succeeded in liberating itself from Russia, the revolutionary movement would spread to the Hapsburg lands and beyond. If Germany intervened to crush the Poles, war would break out in Europe, bringing with it "a catastrophe for the ruling classes and revolution in Germany." A free Poland would therefore be "the most effective ferment, the strongest stimulus for the permanent revolution." Confident that he was "thinking as a Marxist" in developing this scenario, Hilferding ended his letter on an exultant note: "This is a time in which one can justifiably be proud and happy to be a Social Democrat."[50]

Hilferding's favorable attitude toward Polish independence contrasted sharply with the views of Rosa Luxemburg, a founder of Polish Social Democracy in the 1890's and now a prominent figure in the German party. A radical Marxist, an original thinker, and a rather contentious person, Luxemburg disdained nationalism and considered Polish independence "a utopian mirage, a delusion of the workers to detract them from their class struggle."[51] But Luxemburg and other radicals in the German party such as Karl Liebknecht did believe that developments in Russia could be a factor in radicalizing the socialist movements in Central Europe. They were heartened by the "mass actions" of the Russian workers, which, they claimed, should serve as a model for the proletariat in Germany and perhaps elsewhere.

The German Social Democratic Party as a whole, however, was much less enthusiastic about the direction of events in Russia. It supported without reservation the opposition's attempts to dismantle the autocratic system of rule, but late in 1905 and early in 1906, leaders of the German party became very critical of the extremist tactics of the revolutionary left and its inclination to press for an immediate socialist revolution. German socialists also tended to reject the notion that the tactics of their Russian colleagues were relevant to the situation in Central Europe.[52]

Among the important Mensheviks in Russia, Martov was one of the few who held on to the previous assessment of the revolution as essentially a bourgeois affair. In the first issue of *Nachalo* he asserted that the proletariat lacked the strength "to push the revolution beyond the point it reached on the 17th of October."[53] But even Martov was a bit shaky in his convictions. In a private letter he declared that the influence and prestige of Social Democrats were so "incredibly high" that a "'seizure of power' at times begins to seem almost inevitable." He was not sure that Social Democrats should succumb to the temptation, but on the other hand he consoled himself with the thought that such a seizure of power would be no worse than "the Jacobin dictatorship" of 1792.[54]

Although some Bolsheviks shared Trotsky's optimism about the imminence of a socialist revolution, their leader, Lenin, who arrived in Russia on or about November 8, was more restrained. He hailed the October Manifesto as a "truly great victory for the revolution" and referred to October 17 as "one of the great days of the Russian Revolution." There could be no doubt that assent to a constitution was inevitable, and he advised the proletariat to take advantage of all the rights that had been won by forming workers' associations, organizing a militia, and demanding complete amnesty for political prisoners. At the same time, Lenin warned that the Tsar had by no means capitulated; he had only retreated. Lenin discerned a balance of power between the autocracy and the opposition. "Tsarism no longer has the power to suppress the revolution. The revolution still does not possess the power to crush Tsarism." The proletariat must now establish new alliances—for this he had in mind the peasantry—to prepare for new offensives against the government. Lenin still insisted that an armed insurrection and a provisional revolutionary government were necessary to eradicate the old order. In fact, he conjoined the two: "A provisional revolutionary government is the organ of the insurrection, having unified all the insurgents and politically directed the insurrection."[55]

Lenin left unanswered one crucial question: How long was the provisional government to remain in power? He was unequivocal in stating that the government was to represent both the proletariat and the peasantry and that it was to introduce democratic reforms as well as arrange for the election of a constituent assembly. But would its members give up power at that point and gradually prepare for the next revolution, the socialist revolution? The thrust of many statements by Lenin in 1905 seemed to be that this was the most likely option.

That strategy, however, raised other questions. If, as Lenin had been arguing for some time, the bourgeoisie was too weak and too uncertain in its commitment to democracy to make the first revolution, could it be trusted to preserve the gains achieved by the provisional government? Might it not be necessary for the leaders of the first revolution to retain power in the hope that Russia would move more rapidly than anticipated toward socialism? Occasionally, Lenin suggested that the provisional government would be obliged to follow precisely this path. Overall, then, Lenin's pronouncements on the role of the provisional government were so indefinite and equivocal that one could hardly have predicted his policy had the workers and peasants staged a successful uprising in 1905.[56] But the notion that the masses would shed their blood in a revolution against the autocracy and then voluntarily make way for other classes to take power is one of the less convincing tenets of Russian Marxism.

The writings of Marxist leaders were not merely theoretical effusions. On October 22, the Moscow Committee of Social Democrats adopted a resolution calling for the "immediate preparation for a new decisive battle." The party faithful were enjoined to intensify agitational work among the proletariat and to make full use of the freedoms won as a result of the October strike. The Committee also called for renewed efforts to arm the masses and urged workers to establish links with peasants and with dissident elements in the army. Finally, the Committee denounced the attempts of some socialists to rein in the revolutionary impulse in order to avert "anarchy."[57]

The Socialist Revolutionaries, the largest radical party, found the views of most militant Marxists congenial. As has been noted, the SRs had been the first to expound the theory of permanent revolution, and ever since the beginning of 1905 had favored an armed assault on the autocracy. Therefore, all the various sectors of the revolutionary left found it possible to cooperate in the campaign against the old order, despite lingering ideological differences among them.

· · · · ·

In the meantime, the challenges to the government's authority continued to mount. In St. Petersburg, even the police force faced a mutiny of sorts within its ranks. On November 20, a large number of janitors from three districts in the Kazanskaia section of the city held a meeting to protest their having to serve as police spies. They demanded that the government accept their status as employees of private owners of apartment buildings. If they had to serve the police, however, the janitors insisted on not being required to inform on citizens living in buildings outside their supervision. After passing a resolution that called for the abolition of all "administrative punishments," the janitors elected several deputies who were charged with organizing a Petersburg Union of Janitors.[58] How the government reacted to this rebellion of its police spies is not known, but it must have produced some anxious moments for officials in the Ministry of Internal Affairs.

In some outlying regions of the Empire, soviets were even more successful than the Petersburg Soviet in usurping the authority of local organs of government. This was especially true in Siberia, where revolutionaries whipped up sympathy for their cause among soldiers who were unhappy with the slow pace of demobilization and the shortages of supplies, both caused by the numerous strikes on the railroads.

In mid-November, the city of Chita in southeastern Siberia became a center of serious unrest. On November 16, some 4,000 workers and soldiers, under the influence of Social Democratic activists, attended public meetings that demanded a constituent assembly, a republic, and the immediate release of all reservists from service. A week later, revolutionaries organized a "Soviet of Soldiers' and Cossack Deputies of the RSDWP," and workers in the railway depot and workshops instituted the eight-hour day by "revolutionary means." On November 24, a large demonstration of workers and soldiers, attended by 600 fully armed Cossacks, forced the authorities to free many prisoners. By this time, local officials had ceased to govern, and Chita was in effect administered by Social Democrats, who formed committees of representatives of striking railway workers not only in the city but also in all major railway junctions in Manchuria. The committees organized the transport of troops to European Russia and the shipment of food supplies to the army in Siberia. On December 7, the Social Democratic Committee in Chita began publishing a newspaper, *Zabaikalskii rabochii*, which fully supported the cause of revolution. The Social Democrats remained in control of the city until January 12, 1906.[59]

In Novorossiisk, the local soviet seized control of the city administration on December 9 after troops had refused to fire on demonstrators. The soviet proclaimed a "Novorossiisk Republic," whereupon the governor and the chief of police fled. The city council as well as the mayor now submitted to the authority of the soviet, which immediately announced a series of radical measures. It promised to create new organs of self-government and a people's court, encourage the formation of trade unions and political clubs, deprive the propertied classes of political power, and prepare for an armed uprising against the government. The soviet remained in power for nineteen days. On December 26, a detachment of Cossacks, armed with artillery, subdued the revolutionaries.[60]

In Irkutsk, the revolutionaries exerted considerable influence over the city government but could not take power because the soldiers in the area were for some reason less militant. After a series of disturbances in the barracks on November 20, a military strike committee was elected; it demanded the immediate release of certain categories of reservists, a constituent assembly, universal suffrage, and amnesty for political prisoners. But by the end of November, the men began to waver in their support for the strike committee. Most notably, they refused to arrest the general who had rejected the committee's demands. A few days later, on December 2, the commander encountered no resistance in arresting several mutineers, an action that signaled the subsidence of the military unrest. Nevertheless, a soviet elected by the railway workers in Irkutsk took a hand in organizing the transport of troops to the West and assumed other local administrative functions. The government did not fully reassert its authority here until December 20.[61]

In Krasnoiarsk, a Soviet of Soldiers' and Workers' Deputies assumed control over the city administration late in November. The railroad workers enacted the eight-hour day, and on December 8 the soviet, dominated by Social Democrats, took over the provincial printing press. It published the *Krasnoiarskii rabochii*, a revolutionary paper widely distributed in the city. As in other regions, the soviet speeded up the transport of soldiers to the West. It also prepared for new elections to the city council, but on December 18, when news reached Krasnoiarsk that the government had crushed the rebellion in European Russia, support for the soviet began to wane. On December 24 loyal troops arrived, and within a few days the governor regained control of the city.[62]

In numerous districts in the Baltic Provinces governmental authority also collapsed, to be appropriated by elected officials. In Livland, agitators persuaded many people that with the promulgation of the October Manifesto the existing state system was defunct. At meetings held in almost all districts (volosti), speakers advised the populace not to recognize the legitimacy of any Tsarist official and to elect new officials; these in turn, when elected, urged everyone to stop paying taxes and interest to banks. In the Litensk district, a spontaneously organized assembly of the people ordered that all subjects in schools be taught in Latvian and that the curriculum of religion be replaced with moral philosophy. The elected officials also closed all inns and breweries (which were run by the state), permitted the people to sell liquor, and abolished the nobility's hunting and fishing privileges.

Violence often accompanied this transfer of power from the Tsarist government to the people: liquor stores were looted, several dragoons were ambushed and killed, and in a few areas near Riga and Wenden landlords' estates were burned down. In some localities, the people's assemblies issued warnings to the population that anyone who did not heed their directives would be subject to death sentences by revolutionary committees. On December 2, the Governor of Livland, N. A. Zvegintsev, informed Durnovo that "the complete elimination by revolutionaries of legitimate rural government, the open rejection of all governmental authority, the criminal actions by the masses against life and property, and a complete strike [by workers] have created a very threatening situation." The Minister of Internal Affairs replied, some two weeks later, that "it is necessary to act with military force against the insurgents and not to spare them. I beg you to accept this order as indispensable guidance." But, as one official after another pointed out, the authorities in the Baltic Provinces lacked adequate military forces to quash the disturbances.[63] Not until the spring of 1906 did the government achieve ascendancy over the revolutionary opposition, and then only because it resorted to the bloodiest repression.

· · · · ·

The deepening conflict between the government and the revolutionary left placed the liberals in a precarious position. A growing number of them became increasingly alarmed at the excesses of the extremists, yet they could not bring themselves to rally behind the government. At the Congress of Zemstvo and City Council Representatives from November 6 to 13 (which was to be the last meeting of this body), it was clear that the liberals faced several unpalatable options.

The underlying issues in the long deliberations can be summed up as follows: To what extent, if at all, did Witte's policies merit the support of liberals? Would such support encourage the implementation of the October Manifesto or would it give the authorities a free hand to turn back the clock? Would liberals promote their interests most effectively by strengthening their ties to the radicals? Or should they maintain an independent stance? By aligning themselves with the radicals, they might provoke more repression. By shunning the radicals, they would make it easier for the Tsar to reassert his authority. Finally, if they remained independent, they risked losing all influence. Several shadings of opinion emerged during the discussions, but overall the roughly 230 delegates may be said to have divided into three broad camps: a fairly radical left, a cautious and moderate right, and a center somewhere between the two.

The left, led by Petrunkevich, pressed for an alliance with the socialists of all persuasions. "People fear socialism," he declared. "I am not a socialist, but if I can be shown that the socialists can save Russia [from anarchy], I would be the first to stretch out my hand to them." He also indicated at a later session that he did not fear revolution, which "involves cultural tasks and leads to the replacement of a bad regime by a better one." Indeed, "for us to disavow the revolution would be tantamount to disavowing ourselves."

Petrunkevich's position was challenged by one of the leaders of the moderates, Count P. A. Geiden, who rejected collaboration with the socialists on the ground that many of their teachings were so extreme that no government could possibly implement them. To which Petrunkevich replied that the liberals and socialists differed only over means. "We want to act peacefully, [but] they—however only now and in Russia—favor violent methods. But, gentlemen, consider how much we have in common with regard to ultimate goals. Remember the words of a German politician: the ideals of the left and ours are progressive (though we and they pursue them in different ways); but between us and those who yesterday worshipped autocracy and today have become constitutionalists against their will [i.e., Witte], there exists an impassable abyss: their ideals are retrograde!"[64] This was an early version of the attitude "No enemies on the left," and it appealed to many delegates, who often responded to Petrunkevich with what the newspapers referred to as "stormy applause."

Nevertheless, in the balloting on specific resolutions, cooler heads prevailed. For example, Petrunkevich attracted little support for his suggestion that local government officials be replaced by representatives of the zemstvos and city councils, who would be sympathetic to a constitutional order. And the left's attempt to prevent the dispatch of a delegation to Witte on the ground that it would be a futile gesture was voted down, though by a fairly close margin, 88 to 57, with 3 abstentions.[65]

The cautious voices at the Congress, led by M. A. Stakhovich, N. I. and A. I. Guchkov, and Prince G. M. Volkonskii, marshaled even fewer votes for their positions. Their proposal for indirect (two-stage) elections was defeated by 174 to 32. On the issue of capital punishment, A. I. Guchkov proposed a "balanced" resolution to read as follows: "The Congress demands the abolition of capital punishment and unconditionally condemns violence and assassination as a means of political struggle." Guchkov intended, as he put it, "to enlighten the blind people in the extremist parties." This attempt to repudiate the revolutionary left was met with noisy disapproval and received only eight votes.[66] Guchkov's call on the liberals to end their opposition to the exceptional laws fared no better. "Not one country," he contended, "manages without martial law in times of exceptional stress." The issue aroused strong passions, not only because the arbitrary invocation of exceptional decrees throughout 1905 was widely resented, but also because the Polish Kingdom had just been placed under martial law.

That action by the government prompted the Congress to take up the question of autonomy for national minorities, to which it devoted more attention than any other. The moderates opposed the granting of autonomy in the borderlands because, as they put it, the "unity of Russia [guarantees] its might." Guchkov again took the lead in stating this view: "I know that the situation is as follows: in Poland there is an armed uprising. (*Shouts*: Lies! No! Give me the floor, give me the floor!) You know that the revolutionaries began the use of force. If you wish to speak of a prevention [of violence], then you must prevent both sides from using it. (*Shouts*: Enough! Keep Quiet! *Chairman*: We have freedom of speech!)" When the shouting died down, the Congress voted overwhelmingly that all legislation discriminating against religious minorities should be revoked, and defeated a motion supporting the denial of autonomy to Poland.[67] At this point, sixteen of the conservative participants, led by Guchkov, Geiden, and Stakhovich, walked out.

The delegates then reached a compromise on the ticklish question of the constituent assembly. The left favored holding an assembly as the only way to bring about a fundamental reordering of the Empire's political structure. The moderates feared that the very words "constituent assembly," or any other words suggesting a constitution, would conjure up the idea of a democratic republic, which, they claimed, was not consistent with the goals of the liberal opposition. Moreover, in the absence of strong governmental authority—an inevitable condition during preparations for a constituent assembly—"the revolutionary movement [would] lead Russia into anarchy." In the end, the resolution in favor of a constituent assembly was defeated by 137 votes to 80 and replaced by an ambiguous formula to the effect that the first State Duma would carry out "constituent functions" and create a constitution for the Russian Empire "with the approval of the sovereign."[68] This resolution passed by a vote of 204 to 23.

Overall, the Congress was a triumph for the centrist group, which commanded well over half and sometimes as many as three-fourths or four-fifths of the votes, depending on the issue. In the preamble to the final resolution, the Congress acclaimed the October Manifesto as a "priceless achievement of the Russian people"; at the same time, it declared that Witte's government could count on the "assistance and support" of the zemstvo and city council representatives, but "only insofar as it properly and consistently implements the constitutional principles of the manifesto." The delegates also issued a demand for the speediest possible election of a national representative body on the basis of the four-tail suffrage.

For the rest, the delegates appealed to the government to enact *immediately* the decisions of the Congress on emergency decrees, the death penalty, and Polish autonomy, and to eliminate discriminatory decrees against minorities, transfer police powers to local organs of government, prosecute officials who either provoked or tolerated pogroms, grant full amnesty to prisoners charged with political or religious offenses, and place all ministers with the exception of the Minister of the Imperial Court under the control of the Council of Ministers. Since the Congress no longer called for a constituent assembly pure and simple or for an eight-hour day, and did not mention the "compulsory alienation of land," the zemstvo and city council representatives had shifted perceptibly to the right since their last meeting in September. But it soon became clear that they still demanded much more than the government was prepared to yield.[69]

The troubled state of Russian liberalism is poignantly exemplified by a thoughtful article published in mid-November by the moderate Prince E. N. Trubetskoi (a professor of philosophy at Kiev University and brother of the late S. N. Trubetskoi, who on June 6 had pleaded with the Tsar to initiate reform). Trubetskoi sought to persuade his fellow liberals to steer a middle course between the extremes of the left and the right, and to warn the revolutionaries that they were courting disaster by pressing for an armed uprising. An uprising could succeed only if the country were "in a state of general ruin and the government were bankrupt." To be sure, the epidemic of strikes and the reluctance of foreign countries to extend loans to Russia were rapidly producing such a calamitous state of affairs. But no "provisional government" taking power under those circumstances would last. "The wave of anarchy that is advancing from all sides, and that at the present time threatens the legal government, would quickly sweep away any revolutionary government: the embittered masses would then turn against the real or presumed culprits; they would subject to destruction the *entire intelligentsia*; the masses would begin indiscriminately to slaughter all who wear German clothes [i.e., the well dressed]—conservatives, liberals, revolutionaries. Our unruly hordes will roam all over Russia, plundering and burning everything in their path."

Trubetskoi also warned that civil war was likely. Even radical parties would fall out with each other. In every city a provisional government would emerge that would refuse to recognize any other. The upshot would be an end to all parties and to Russian civilization. "The only question will be, who perishes first and who later on."

Trubetskoi believed that the catastrophe could be avoided only if an attempt were made, by peaceful means, to "renew, [and] improve, and thereby strengthen the existing weak, inconsistent, and, it goes without saying, bad government." Liberals, he pointed out, were caught between two stools—left-wing extremists on the one hand, and the government on the other—but he could see no alternative to the policy he recommended.

Trubetskoi predicted that he would be accused of favoring a "headlong embrace of the government," but he emphatically denied that that was his aim. Whenever the government violated the principles of the October Manifesto, it should be subjected to "firm, objective" criticism. But liberals must not turn every mistake of the government into a *casus belli*. And they must reject the notion "that *every* measure introduced by the government must be condemned simply because it emanated from the government." Trubetskoi ended by pleading with his fellow liberals not to be intimidated by the "shameless abuse" that the left heaped upon them. They must ignore the attacks from the left as well as those from the right. "Only he deserves respect who has the courage to be himself." He made an equally moving plea to the authorities: "Only a consistent, strict, and quick implementation of the principles proclaimed in the October Manifesto provides the possibility for society to unite [with the government] in common, creative work."[70]

Trubetskoi's analysis and recommendations might be dismissed as the ruminations of a patriot overly alarmed at the possibility that Russia might plunge into the abyss, or of a property owner too preoccupied with "law and order," or, more crudely, of a nobleman apprehensive about losing the privileges that he and his class enjoyed. None of these interpretations is convincing. Trubetskoi had long supported liberal causes and genuinely favored the liberalization of Russia's institutions; he had reluctantly reached the conclusion that his colleagues were following a course that endangered all the achievements of 1905. In truth, the history of violent revolutions in Russia and elsewhere suggests that his prognosis of the consequences of an armed uprising was not far off the mark.

The principal weakness of Trubetskoi's article was its premise: that the government could still be pressured into implementing the principles of the October Manifesto. Had Trubetskoi's advice been given and heeded a month earlier, when Witte had desperately sought liberal support and before disorder had become rampant in the country, it might have strengthened the Prime Minister's hand and enabled him to proceed more expeditiously with reform. But by mid-November Witte was politically too weak and too isolated. Moreover, even he was now beginning to embrace the application of repressive measures against the revolutionary left, though he was not yet ready to relinquish altogether his efforts to pacify the country by political means.

The Prime Minister's new attitude became evident after a meeting with Petrunkevich, S. A. Muromtsev, and F. F. Kokoshkin, who gave Witte a copy of the resolutions adopted by the Congress of Zemstvo and City Council Representatives. At the meeting, the three liberals also protested the recent arrest of members of the Bureau of the Peasant Union, which, they contended, violated the terms of the October Manifesto. Witte listened carefully and promised to respond to their concerns after studying the resolutions.

On November 29, the Prime Minister informed the liberals that although the cabinet remained committed to the manifesto, it would not enact the resolutions of the Congress. Witte declared that "the continuing troubles, the disturbances and revolutionary activities, directed against . . . authority in general" were undermining the state and could therefore "not be permitted by the government; in view of the responsibility [the government] had to the state, Russia, and history, it could not renounce the application of exceptional decrees and states of emergency in various localities."[71] *Russkie vedomosti* considered Witte's response as evidence that the government was determined to follow "its former policies."[72] Several actions by the government late in November, apparently undertaken by Durnovo without informing Witte, lent credence to that somber assessment.

·　·　·　·　·

At noon on November 26, infantrymen and Cossacks surrounded the headquarters of the Free Economic Society and arrested the president of the Soviet, G. S. Khrustalev-Nosar, together with several deputies. The decision to move against the Soviet seems to have been taken at a convergence of unnamed "influential people" at Tsarskoe Selo, who had concluded that the public, tired of "disorder and anarchy," would not oppose the action. The conferees also judged Witte's policies a failure and suggested that it might be necessary to place the capital under martial law.

Still, they did not believe that it would be advisable to unleash a full-scale counterrevolution. Indeed, they recommended that Witte be replaced by a former Minister of Internal Affairs, Sviatopolk-Mirsky, known as an outspoken advocate of political reform. The account of the conference unfortunately does not indicate why the participants believed that Sviatopolk-Mirsky—who in any case was not likely to accept the post after his disheartening experience earlier in the year—would succeed where Witte had failed.[73] It seems as though Nicholas's advisers were simply thrashing about for some way out of the deepening crisis.

The Soviet immediately elected a new presidium of three men, among them Trotsky, which wasted no time in launching a counterattack. On November 27, it passed a resolution calling on its followers to prepare for an armed uprising.[74] In addition, the presidium decided to strike at the government's soft underbelly, the precarious financial system. The country was on the verge of financial collapse, partly as a result of the enormous expense entailed by the war and partly because the rich, panicky over the continuing internal turmoil, were sending substantial amounts of capital abroad. During the second week in November, delegates at a meeting of the Peasants' Union had for the first time discussed possible measures that might be taken by the population at large to undermine the state's financial system. Parvus was familiar with the discussions and now became one of the moving spirits behind the drafting of a Financial Manifesto, which was published on December 2 in eight newspapers in St. Petersburg.

Signed by the Soviet, the Peasants' Union, the RSDWP, the Socialist Revolutionary Party, and the Polish Socialist Party, the manifesto sought to "cut the government off from the last source of its existence: financial revenue." It called on the people not to make any further redemption payments or other payments to the Treasury and to demand all wages in "gold, and in the case of sums less than five rubles, full-weight coin." The manifesto also urged the populace to withdraw all deposits from banks and to accept only gold. The leaders of the left did not ask that the payment of taxes be withheld because workers did not pay direct taxes. (Measures against indirect taxes were ruled out since these were charged on necessities for workers.) The assumption behind the drafting of the manifesto was that the government, deprived of an adequate supply of gold, would lose its credit rating and would then be unable to secure vitally needed loans.[75]

It was an original and imaginative ploy, but for a variety of reasons it is impossible to say whether the Financial Manifesto seriously affected the banking system. First, many people, concerned about the unrest, had begun withdrawing funds from their accounts even before the events of late November. Moreover, the police prevented the wide distribution of the manifesto by confiscating copies of the eight newspapers immediately after their appearance. The police also made clear their determination to punish anyone who advocated the tactics set forth in the manifesto. They arrested the chief editors of the eight newspapers, who remained in custody pending the payment of bail in the amount of 10,000 rubles. A day later, on December 3, the Soviet's Executive Committee and 200 deputies were also arrested, on Durnovo's orders.

According to Gurko, when news of this action reached the Council of Ministers, Witte turned ashen and "announced in great agitation: 'All is lost.'"[76] There is reason to believe that Gurko's account gives a misleading impression of Witte's mood at the time. In his memoirs, Witte argued that no state, no matter how liberal, could tolerate an attack on its financial system, which suggests that he favored the move against the Soviet.[77] Moreover, on December 1, the Tsar wrote to his mother that Witte had finally decided to take energetic measures against the revolutionaries. The Prime Minister now understood "that the well-disposed elements in the country are not pleased with him and are getting impatient with his inaction. He is now prepared to order the arrest of all the principal leaders of the outbreak. I have been trying for some time past to get him to do it—but he always hoped to be able to manage without drastic measures."[78]

Witte, a man given to contradictory moods and policies, probably was both shocked and relieved when he learned of the Soviet's arrest. Shocked, because he understood that the police action would trigger an all-out war between the government and the revolutionary left and that it marked an end to his policy of national renewal through reform. Relieved, because he could no longer resist the proddings of the Tsar and because he himself was increasingly alarmed over the spread of disorder, which, among other things, threatened to undermine his attempts to acquire a desperately needed loan for the government.

If Witte's reaction to the arrest of the Soviet confused Gurko, it was probably because Witte was not fully in control of his emotions. There is evidence to suggest that he had for some time been in a state of acute anxiety and that at times he acted irrationally. He turned against longtime collaborators and even against friends, of whom he had few to begin with.

The most notable example of Witte's irrational behavior was his cruel treatment of V. N. Kokovtsov, the Minister of Finance. Until Witte's departure for the United States, the two had been on the best of terms; and while Witte was abroad, Kokovtsov kept him informed about developments in Russia with a steady stream of telegrams. But after Witte returned, he treated Kokovtsov with contempt: he publicly criticized every opinion the Minister of Finance uttered. When Kokovtsov during one meeting raised some objections to a general amnesty for political prisoners, Witte shot back: "With such ideas as professed by the Honorable Minister of Finance one can govern only Zulus, and I shall suggest to His Majesty that he be selected for the post of Chairman of the Ministers' Council; but if this cross falls to my lot I shall beg the Emperor to free me from the cooperation of such statesmen."[79] A week later Kokovtsov resigned from the government.

It is true that the two men differed over several issues, such as the creation of a unified ministry and the issuance of the October Manifesto, but Kokovstov had remained loyal to Witte and could therefore not understand the latter's hostility toward him. It was only during a chance meeting with the Prime Minister, on December 14, that he came to realize that Witte was undergoing deep psychological stress. "I wish you knew in what a blind alley I find myself," Witte said. "There are moments when I am ready to commit suicide, and at such moments I recall my past and perceive how deeply I have wronged you."[80] He feared assassination, he could not sleep, and at an important meeting on December 5, he publicly confessed that the "whole revolution" had been a "nightmare for him."[81] His political failures since the October strike had completely broken him.

Although the revolutionary movement was severely weakened by the arrest of the Soviet's leadership, it was not completely crushed. The deputies of the Soviet who escaped arrest formed a second Soviet and elected a new Executive Committee, headed by Parvus, that called for a general political strike to begin on December 8. "Citizens," the committee declared in a ringing appeal, "freedom or slavery. A Russia ruled by the people or a Russia plundered by a gang of robbers, that is the question. . . . It is better to die in the struggle than to live in slavery."[82] The workers did not respond in very large numbers. Although the Union of Unions endorsed the strike, relatively few members of the intelligentsia did so. Neither the banks nor the zemstvo and municipal institutions stopped functioning. On December 19, the Executive Committee called off the strike.[83] In the meantime, the center of gravity of the revolution had shifted from St. Petersburg to Moscow, where the final drama of the first and most turbulent phase of the revolution reached its climax.

. . . . .

The Days of Liberty marked the culmination of a dual process that had begun in the fall of 1904: the decline of governmental authority and the concomitant increase in society's exercise of civil liberties. To be sure, there was still no constitution to guarantee those liberties. Nor was it certain that the autocrat and society would reach agreement on how to share power. Yet it appeared as though two principal institutions of the old regime, the bureaucracy and the police, were beginning to adopt new patterns of behavior, shaped largely by standards set by liberals. The Days of Liberty were thus a critical period in the revolution. Had the conditions prevailing from mid-October until early December been maintained, the cornerstone for a constitutional order would have been firmly set in place. However, with the arrest of the Soviet and the government's resumption of repression, the Days of Liberty—one of the more glorious chapters of the revolution—came to a close.

Yet even now the government did not completely abandon the October Manifesto. At the very moment that it sought to crush the opposition, Tsar Nicholas chaired a series of meetings at Peterhof on the new electoral law being designed to replace the Bulygin Project of August 6. Witte was expected to provide guidance to the conferees, but he was incapable of taking a clear-cut stand on the major issues. On various occasions he made statements that were either vague or contradictory. At times, he seemed almost to favor universal suffrage, but at others he clearly feared that the country was so unsettled that elections would provoke yet another outburst of mass violence. His dread of disturbances had paralyzed him. "Who can decide now," he asked pathetically at one session, "what kind of project will give us the better Duma?"[84] In the end, he supported the proposals of his cabinet, which were adopted by the conference and approved by the Tsar.

The electoral law of December 11, 1905, was far more liberal than the Bulygin Project, although it did not meet the demands of the opposition for the four-tail suffrage. The elections were still to be indirect, the suffrage was limited to males over the age of 24, and no student or person in active military service was allowed to vote. Moreover, the law was weighted heavily in favor of the gentry and the middle class. In European Russia, the peasants, who constituted over 70 percent of the population, were to choose 42 percent of the electors, who would in turn make the final selection of Duma deputies; urban dwellers were to choose 23 percent of the electors; workers, 3 percent. Or, to put it differently, in the countryside electors would represent 2,000 landlords or 30,000 peasants; in the cities, they would represent 7,000 middle-class people or 90,000 workers. Thus, the vote of one landowner "was equal to that of three and one-half city dwellers, of fifteen peasants, and of forty-five workers."[85]

With this elaborate electoral procedure, the government formally remained faithful to its promise in the October Manifesto to extend the suffrage to all classes. But it believed that the procedure would guarantee the election of a conservative Duma. Within four months it became evident that once again the government had thoroughly misread the mood of the nation. Even under the restrictive electoral law of December 11, the population elected a Duma overwhelmingly hostile to the old order.

As had happened with so many of the government's concessions, the electoral reform came too late. In the spring or summer of 1905 and perhaps even in the days immediately after the October strike, an election under the conditions specified on December 11 might have produced a legislature willing to cooperate with the government. But by April 1906, when the elections were finally held, the public mood had hardened. The government itself further contributed to that change in attitude by unleashing a new and savage campaign of repression late in 1905 and early in 1906.

Chapter Eleven

. . . .

Armed Uprising and
Counterrevolution

THE RADICAL LEFT's last hopes of overthrowing the autocracy were dashed in December 1905, when a violent confrontation erupted in Moscow between the government and the revolutionaries, which triggered the bloodiest domestic strife of the upheaval. At first glance, Moscow was an unlikely site for such a test of strength, for it had lagged behind St. Petersburg in revolutionary fervor. For example, the reaction to Bloody Sunday was not nearly as intense there as in the capital. About three and a half times as many people went on strike in St. Petersburg as in Moscow, whose population of 1.1 million was only 340,000 less than that of the capital. To be sure, the general strike of October began on the Moscow railway lines, but no soviet was formed in the city until November 21, some five weeks after the appearance of the St. Petersburg Soviet. This is not to suggest that Moscow in 1905 was not in turmoil. The universities and high schools, as we have seen, were centers of political unrest. Workers made a fair amount of progress in organizing unions, and both liberals and peasants held numerous illegal meetings to express their discontent with the existing economic and political order.

Nor was Moscow spared a breakdown in civil order. The incidence of violent crimes and the lack of effective police protection that had aroused public attention in the summer became even more serious by the end of the year. Henry Nevinson, an English journalist who was in Moscow during the Days of Liberty, noted that crimes of violence

tempered . . . our liberty. . . . For some weeks, the average of street murders was one a day. Barefooted, long-haired beggars, the very heroes of Gorky's tales, the ragged supermen of misery, sprang out from dark corners, and I always thanked them heartily for their mistake in regarding my money as more valuable than my life. People walked warily, kept one eye behind them, turning sharply round if they heard even the padding sound of galoshes in the snow. Often at night, as I went up and down the rampart of the Kremlin, and watched those ancient white temples with their brazen domes glittering under the moon, I noticed that the few passers-by skirted round me in a kind of arc, and if they came upon me suddenly they ran. My intentions were far from murderous, but all were living in that haggard element of fear.[1]

Another sign of pervasive tension in Moscow was the overreaction of people to any rumors of an impending catastrophe. To cite but one example, on November 17 a story circulating about the imminent collapse of the state savings bank immediately "produced panic. Everyone rushed to withdraw his deposits."[2]

Still, political radicalism did not emerge as a powerful force in Moscow until the late summer and early fall. Curiously, it then assumed a more violent form than in St. Petersburg; for a short period, developments in Moscow seemed to be propelling the revolutionary left into a dominant position within the opposition movement. That St. Petersburg had taken the lead throughout most of the revolution is not surprising. After all, it was the capital, the center of the nation's political life, the residence of the Tsar and the government. But that only makes more puzzling the emergence of Moscow as the focal point of the revolution in December. The differences in the economy, the composition of the working class, and the opposition movement in the two cities provide some clues to this curious phenomenon.

Heavy, large-scale industry was much more prevalent in St. Petersburg than in Moscow. As a result, steelworkers far outnumbered textile workers in the capital, whereas in Moscow the opposite was the case.[3] Relatively well paid, and more likely to be literate and settled urban dwellers, steelworkers especially inclined toward direct action against their employers. In 1905, they played a prominent role in initiating strikes and in persuading workers in other industries to join them.

Also, a significantly higher percentage of the plants in St. Petersburg than in Moscow employed at least 500 workers. Workers in such plants were more easily organized and tended to be more disciplined. By contrast, as one historian recently argued, the workers in the clothing, textile, and food industries, the dominant sectors of Moscow's industrial economy, were "unhappy and volatile, but culturally and politically unsophisticated."[4]

Much more so in Moscow than in St. Petersburg, the labor movement received its "organizational guidance" from the white-collar workers in the non-manufacturing sector of the economy. These workers were instrumental in organizing employees at the railroads and municipal institutions, without whose support the radical left in Moscow would have remained relatively insignificant. The differences in the development of the labor movement in the two cities were reflected in the leadership of the general strike. In Moscow, a "mixed committee of liberal professionals, white-collar employees, and representatives of industrial and crafts trades" directed the strike, whereas in the St. Petersburg Soviet, workers from metal and machine factories predominated.[5] The alliance in Moscow between "bourgeois" elements of the working population and the industrial workers held fast even during the armed uprising in December.

Two groups thus appear to have served as the cannon fodder of the insurrectionary movement: white-collar workers, who because of their greater exposure to radical ideas were more easily captivated by the slogans of extremists than skilled workers, and unsophisticated laborers, who felt that they had little to lose. Bolshevik commentators and Soviet historians, who regard the Moscow uprising as "the highest stage of the Revolution," bristle at the notion that "backward" workers might have been one of the main groups of participants in the armed assault on the government. In their view, the "advanced workers," politically the most sophisticated, risked their lives in an "inevitable" attack on the Tsarist regime. They make this claim even though it is now well established that the Bolsheviks' "main [political] support in Moscow lay among the less skilled and underprivileged workers."[6] On the other hand, Menshevik writers who after 1905 sought to explain the failure of the revolution held the backward workers responsible for the political violence in Moscow. Unfortunately, the controversy cannot be definitively settled because there is not enough information on the social background of the workers who actually took part in the street fighting.[7] However, one point is beyond dispute: in December 1905, Mensheviks as well as Bolsheviks in Moscow agreed on the advisability of launching an insurrection, and leaders of the two movements, supported by leaders of the Socialist Revolutionaries, collaborated in its direction.

According to P. A. Garvi, a Menshevik activist in Moscow, the strike committee there decided, after the issuance of the October Manifesto, to call a halt to the work stoppage so that the proletariat could "organize and arm itself for the future struggle." Indeed, if Garvi's memory can be trusted (and he was a remarkably reliable memoirist), the committee yielded to the inevitable in calling off the strike. A day or two before the Tsar's concession, Garvi tells us, "we knew very well that the general political strike was a spent bullet. . . . Everyone who lived through the events of that time can testify to the fact that had the Tsarist bureaucracy held out for another day or two, it would have been able to survive this phase of the revolution without making any concessions." The workers were incapable of sustaining the strike: "they were exhausted, poorly organized, and needed time to collect their strength for the final onslaught, and, above all, to organize themselves." As for the manifesto, the strike committee considered it merely "a partial victory," a "sop from the Tsar." The committee's task now was to formulate the principal political demands, "whose realization would inevitably remain the goal of the proletarian struggle."[8]

V. M. Zenzinov, a prominent Socialist Revolutionary, recalled that immediately after the general strike, his party also discussed at great length whether to prepare for an armed attack on the government. At meetings at the offices of the newspaper *Syn otechestva* in St. Petersburg, a majority of the SR leaders maintained that the suspension of terrorist activities was temporary and that "it was necessary to use the period of freedom for better preparation for the inevitable revolutionary offensives in the future."[9] But the policy of individual terror was now to be abandoned in favor of mass violence. Early in November, Zenzinov himself was sent to Moscow to help organize the workers. "To Arms! To Arms!—that was the slogan of all revolutionaries in November 1905. Everyone understood that a decisive clash could not be avoided." The radicals stepped up their efforts to secure weapons, especially the German Mauser pistol, which was highly regarded because it could fire nine bullets automatically. At various locations near Moscow and Petersburg and in Finland, workshops had been established for the production of bombs, and by the fall of 1905 they were all functioning at top speed.[10]

In mid-November of 1905, the German Consul in Moscow, a close observer of the political scene, warned of the likelihood of "serious disturbances with an anticapitalist thrust" in the near future. Because of the absence of street demonstrations and any unusual movement of troops during the preceding few weeks, Moscow appeared to be tranquil. On the other hand, "a simple glance at the newspapers here suggests that beneath the apparent calm of the city there is concealed a feverish movement that is gradually affecting ever more strata of the population. . . . Every week, new publications appear that openly preach violent revolution, and every day one can read about the emergence of new groups of employees or workers, who for the most part immediately join socialist organizations." Moreover, workers were staging an increasing number of strikes over "purely political" issues. Frequently, strikers made threats or used force against their employers as well as against workers who crossed the picket line. The authorities' failure to halt the violence, according to the German Consul, only encouraged lawlessness.

The revolutionaries scored a startling success during the night of November 9–10, when they managed to cut various telephone lines guarded by the police and thus prevented administrators of several factories plagued by disorders from appealing for help. But even when the telephones did function properly, the authorities could not be relied upon to maintain order because the police and army failed to cooperate. All things considered, the German Consul cannot be faulted for having been "more pessimistic than before" about future developments in Moscow.[11]

Many ordinary Russians also sensed that some sort of cataclysm was imminent. On a brief visit to Berlin early in December, the U.S. Ambassador to St. Petersburg discovered that "Russians with their families are moving to Germany in great numbers: 2,500 refugees in Königsberg alone; Berlin also crowded." The German Emperor claimed to have information that the Russian government had mobilized "450,000 Cossacks, who can be absolutely depended upon," and he believed that the Tsar would try "to reconquer the country."[12]

In light of all these developments and the theoretical pronouncements of the revolutionary left (described in the last chapter), the question often raised by contemporaries and historians of who provoked the violent clash, the government or the revolutionaries, seems irrelevant. Of course, in unleashing its offensive against the left, the government aroused intense resentment within the radical movement. But it is difficult to avoid the conclusion that the revolutionary left was waiting for just such a provocation. Indeed, its behavior suggests that it had deliberately invited the provocation. Considering the moods of the authorities and the radicals late in 1905, a violent confrontation between them seems to have been unavoidable. As Zenzinov put it many years later, "the revolution and the government were like two persons who had already taken aim at each other with pistols. The only question was, who would be the first to pull the trigger."[13]

The Moscow Committee, the main organization of Bolsheviks in the city, was the driving force behind the uprising. About fifteen people nominally belonged to the committee, but the principal decisions were made by three intellectuals, M. N. Liadov, M. I. Vasilev-Iuzhin, and V. L. Shantser (Marat). The Moscow soviet and the district (raion) soviets, as well as the Federal Council (composed of an equal number of Bolsheviks and Mensheviks), did not play a significant role, though the leaders of the uprising considered it important that all these organizations issue statements of support. Actually, the city soviet had met only four times before the violent clash and had not evolved into a very influential institution—certainly not nearly as important a one as its counterpart in St. Petersburg.[14]

The immediate background to the revolutionary leadership's decision to engage the government in armed conflict is still somewhat hazy. The left was certainly perturbed by the police crackdown. Not only had the

St. Petersburg Soviet been wiped out, but in addition, on November 28 the police rounded up the leaders of the Union of Ticket Collectors of the Moscow–Brest-Litovsk Railway, and two days later they invaded the Museum for Assistance to Labor, an important meeting place for workers, and confiscated publications and money.[15] Enraged activists on the left wanted to retaliate, but they were inadequately prepared, both politically and organizationally, for an armed action.

Most significantly, there was no assurance that if the proletariat of Moscow took the initiative, either workers elsewhere or the peasants would follow suit. On December 4, a messenger from the St. Petersburg Soviet appeared before the Moscow one to report on the workers' mood in the capital. Remarkably, there are three divergent accounts, all by Bolsheviks, of how the messenger assessed the chances of a strike by the Petersburg workers.[16] People seemed to hear whatever they wanted.

At local gatherings in Moscow where tactics were discussed, a few activists voiced serious reservations about launching an attack. For example, a Socialist Revolutionary of the district soviet in Presnia-Khamovniki, a certain Comrade Martyn, argued against an uprising because he did not think that the peasants would join the revolution en masse. Without the peasants, Martyn predicted, the workers and revolutionary intelligentsia would not prevail against the regime, which, though badly shaken, still had at its disposal impressive military force.[17] In his memoirs, V. M. Chernov recalled that neither in St. Petersburg nor in Moscow were the revolutionary leaders really ready to take the initiative: "The Moscow Soviet decided to declare a strike and transform it into armed insurrection principally because such a decision had been taken in St. Petersburg; and in St. Petersburg the decision had been made because events in Moscow were 'leading up to an insurrection.'"[18]

The military preparations were equally unimpressive. Although revolutionaries had been collecting weapons for about a year, their supplies hardly sufficed for a prolonged battle with the army. Ever since late October, the left had been organizing detachments of militiamen, primarily at the factory level but also among intellectuals; yet early in December, according to the most reliable accounts, not more than 1,000 militiamen were armed and only a few had been exposed to more than the most rudimentary military training. Their weapons, mainly revolvers and a small supply of bombs, could hardly make them the match of a modern army. Moreover, their leaders had not developed any tactics appropriate for street fighting. Not until December 11, four days after the fighting began, did the Combat Organization of the Moscow Committee issue directives on the conduct of military operations.[19] In his warning against military action, Comrade Martyn had referred to the militia's weakness and poor equipment, and he was not alone in pointing out these deficiencies.

Most of the revolutionary leaders in Moscow, however, would not listen because they were intoxicated with their own rhetoric. For months they had talked endlessly about the need for a violent revolution, and by now they believed that the masses were as bewitched as they by the thought that only by force would they be able to smash the autocracy. Garvi's response to Comrade Martyn nicely illustrates the mood of many who favored military action. Garvi granted that there was good reason to be chary of engaging the government in armed conflict, but added: "we have no choice." Although he felt that it would have been better if the revolutionaries, and not the government, had chosen the time to strike, the government's attack on the Petersburg Soviet had forced their hand. If the left did not resist now, the regime would crush all the soviets and workers' organizations. Admittedly, the peasants were quiescent, "but the thunder of the present struggle will perhaps awaken them."

In any case, the decision to fight had already been made by their leaders, and now all revolutionaries were obliged to support them. Neither Garvi nor anyone else at the meeting (except Martyn) showed "any hesitation or doubt" in this regard. On the contrary, Garvi later claimed to have "experienced a kind of enthusiasm that I did not have even during the days of the October general strike. I felt that now we had staked everything, that during this fight the fate of the revolution would be decided." Garvi realized that he and his colleagues faced a real possibility of death, but he was prepared to "make this sacrifice convinced that it was necessary for the final triumph of our cause."[20]

Reports of a mutiny in Moscow greatly encouraged the revolutionaries. On December 2, between 200 and 300 soldiers of the Rostov Grenadier Regiment held an unauthorized meeting and elected a committee to lead what amounted to a mutiny. They prepared a list of 37 demands, most of which dealt with conditions in the army. They asked that they be addressed in the polite form; that no one be punished for the mutiny; that reserves drafted in 1901 and 1902 be released immediately; that no more than four hours a day be devoted to drill; that their mail not be censored; and that medical services and food be improved. Some of the demands were clearly political: for example, that soldiers be granted all the freedoms that the October Manifesto had promised the civilian population, and that soldiers not be used to pacify workers and peasants involved in disorders. One demand that must have especially disturbed the officers called for the election of platoon commanders and sergeant majors.

At one point, some of the mutineers were met by officers with drawn swords, but there was no bloodshed. The government, however, took no

chances and had a few suspect officers summarily arrested.[21] General
N. N. Malakhov, the commander of the Moscow military district, reacted with alarm: "In view of the extremely small size of the Moscow
garrison," he wrote the Minister of War, A. F. Rediger, on December 2,
"and the probable organizational [strength] of revolutionary propaganda
in the army, I consider necessary the immediate dispatch to Moscow of
two regiments of infantry guards and one brigade of artillery." A few
hours later, Malakhov reported that on December 3 other units were
expected to join the mutiny.[22] During the preceding five days, soldiers in
at least three regiments (aside from the Rostov Grenadiers) had in fact
already held illegal meetings and submitted demands to their officers.

The leaders of the revolutionary parties were jubilant, for they knew
that in the last analysis the outcome of their insurrection would depend
on the conduct of the army. As soon as they received word of the mutiny,
therefore, civilian agitators made extensive contacts with the rebellious
soldiers. On December 3, representatives of several units formed a soviet,
which further encouraged the radicals. "From the speeches of the soldier-
deputies," declared the Bolshevik paper *Vpered* on December 4, "it was
clear that there is a mood of elation in all the regiments, that all sympathize with the revolutionary movement, that they might join an uprising
of the people, and, at any rate, that they will not shoot at their brothers. . . . The liberation movement is flowing in large torrents within the
army despite the desperate efforts of the commander to arrest [and] to
slow down its powerful progress."[23] This proved to be a complete mis-
reading of the soldiers' mood.

On the very day the soviet was formed, the Rostov Regiment became
apprehensive about the presence of so many civilians in the barracks. The
soldiers also had second thoughts about the mutiny because they had
learned that Tsar Nicholas would make concessions to the soldiers (the
reforms of December 6) and that some reservists would soon be demobilized. Within hours of its establishment, the soldiers' committee promised that civilians would henceforth be barred from the barracks. When,
early on December 4, a few leaders of the mutiny tried to breathe new
life into the rebellion, soldiers shouted back: "We promised not to fire at
the people, why are you demanding that we go openly against the
Tsar?"[24] Loyal soldiers now arrested 57 leaders of the revolt, which
quickly fizzled out.

Clutching at straws, the revolutionaries refused to accept the possibility that the soldiers' insubordination could be traced primarily to a desire
for better conditions for themselves. The radicals had convinced themselves that the soldiers concurred in their hostility to the government and
that as soon as civilians took to the streets, large segments of the army
would join the battle on their side. At various meetings of revolutionar-

ies, a few speakers again tried to sound a note of caution: the mood of the soldiers, they warned, was not all that volatile. The party leaders paid no attention.

A difference over tactics now emerged between Bolsheviks and Mensheviks, a difference that subsequently was blown up into a quarrel of major proportions. Ever since the 1905 revolution, Bolshevik polemicists and historians have claimed that the Mensheviks were halfhearted in their support of the uprising. The Mensheviks, in turn, have alleged that they opposed their rivals' adventurism. According to Garvi, the Mensheviks waged a "stubborn struggle against the Moscow Bolsheviks in the Federal Council and in the Soviet." Garvi supports his claim with the following evidence: "The Bolsheviks insisted on a simultaneous appeal for a general political strike and for an armed uprising. We [Mensheviks] insisted on an appeal for a general political strike, but categorically objected to a simultaneous appeal for an armed uprising. As a result of intense discussions, agreement was reached on a compromise formula: the Soviet would appeal for a general strike in order to 'strive in every way possible to transform it into an armed uprising.'"[25] Only a gifted semanticist would have detected a significant difference between the Bolshevik position and the compromise. In truth, the leadership of the radical left in Moscow was not seriously divided over the question of an uprising.

On the evening of December 5, some 400 Bolsheviks attended a six-hour meeting at the Fiedler Academy, a Protestant church school whose director, I. I. Fiedler, was a prominent liberal, for what turned out to be the decisive discussion about whether to initiate an armed assault on the government. A. N. Vasilev, the Bolsheviks' military expert, gave an optimistic appraisal of the situation. He reported that the revolutionaries could dispose of roughly 1,000 armed men and declared that not more than 4,000 of the 14,000 troops presumed to be in the city would follow orders to crush a workers' uprising.[26] All the factory representatives announced that the workers would heed a call to strike. Several party leaders, however, were still not persuaded that an insurrection would succeed and warned against precipitate action.

In the midst of the deliberations, it was learned that at another meeting taking place at the same time, representatives of 29 railroads had agreed to support a strike, though with some reluctance. Bolshevik speakers at that gathering had pressured the representatives by threatening to take the case for an uprising directly to the workers. On hearing about the action of the railroad workers, the Bolsheviks at the Fiedler Academy renounced all thought of caution and voted to proceed with the strike, which was to be transformed into an insurrection.

The Mensheviks and Socialist Revolutionaries held similar meetings, and despite the misgivings of some, both parties formally opted for the rising.[27] On December 6, the Moscow soviet, attended by about 120 deputies, issued the official appeal to all workers to begin a "general political strike" at 12 noon the following day. "With our joint efforts we will finally overthrow the criminal Tsarist government, convoke a constituent assembly on the basis of universal, equal, direct, and secret suffrage, and proclaim a democratic republic, which alone can safeguard our freedom and the inviolability of our persons."[28]

The mood at all the mass meetings during the final hours before the military action was highly emotional. On December 7, for example, one of the more eloquent orators ended his address to a throng of railway workers by urging: "Let us start not a strike but the great Russian Revolution." The crowd responded with thunderous applause. "Everywhere [in the city] the same resolutions [were passed]—to join the general political strike."[29] According to Zenzinov, all the activists were "at heart . . . certain that our defeat was inevitable. . . . But we were all young, we were seized with revolutionary enthusiasm." The activists readily accepted the notion that it was "better to perish in a struggle than to be bound hand and foot without engaging in a struggle. The *honor of the revolution* was at stake."[30] Those radicals who harbored reservations about the drift of events nonetheless supported their comrades out of a sense of solidarity. For several days it actually seemed as though the most ardent advocates of an armed uprising had accurately gauged the government's fragility in Moscow. Local authorities failed to move forcefully against the insurrections and thus gave the impression of being helpless.

Admiral F. V. Dubasov was now Governor-General of Moscow, the third person to occupy that post since the assassination of the Grand Duke Sergei Aleksandrovich in February 1905. The announcement on November 24 of Dubasov's appointment had been greeted with some surprise, because the admiral lacked experience in civilian administration and was in poor health. The choice of Dubasov, a reactionary who favored firm measures to suppress the radicals, signaled a further shift to the right by the government. But there is also reason to believe that he was chosen because the authorities in St. Petersburg could not find a more suitable candidate willing to undertake this arduous assignment. Hurriedly recruited, Dubasov arrived in Moscow on December 4 without detailed instructions on how to deal with the growing unrest there.[31]

Dubasov had under his command about 6,000 soldiers, 2,000 policemen, and a division of gendarmes,[32] a force large enough to quell an insurrection quickly in open battle. Apparently out of fear that his men might not be reliable, Dubasov withdrew them from the streets, which provided the rebels with an opportunity to roam large parts of the city at will. Had they been better organized and had their leaders planned their moves ahead of time, the radicals most probably could have seized the centers of government authority. Still, Dubasov did place Moscow under a state of "Extraordinary Security," and he arrested two important Bolshevik leaders, Vasilev and Shantser (as well as the heads of the Menshevik printers' union), which was a severe blow to the insurrection. Otherwise, the Governor-General confined himself to repeated pleas for reinforcements from St. Petersburg.

Witte telephoned Trepov to urge him to persuade the Tsar to send the troops. "I consider it absolutely essential," he told the Commandant of the Court, "to send a special army to Moscow. . . . If Moscow falls into the hands of the revolutionaries, it would be such a blow to the government of His Majesty that it could have incalculably harmful consequences."[33] Durnovo agreed with Witte. Indeed, according to Gerasimov, the news of the uprising transformed the Acting Minister of Internal Affairs. "Durnovo suddenly became a different person. He no longer vacillated; he gave the impression of a strongly determined man."[34] But others at Court, in particular Grand Duke Nikolai Nikolaevich, feared that moving troops out of St. Petersburg would make the capital vulnerable to an insurrection. Only after Witte insisted that no such danger existed did the Tsar order the Grand Duke to reinforce the garrison; but the new forces did not arrive until December 15.[35]

In the meantime, the economy of Moscow ground to a virtual standstill. By the second day of the strike over 80,000 workers had left their jobs,[36] which made this the largest work stoppage by far in the city's history. Shopkeepers also closed their doors, either voluntarily or under pressure. On December 7, parties of deputies from the Moscow soviet traversed the city, street by street, asking proprietors "very politely" to lock up their stores. "Another party would come around an hour afterwards to see if the shops were closed; if they were still open, they said, they would not be responsible for the windows or the goods."[37] Occasionally, militiamen fired shots at shopkeepers to force them to close. By the evening of December 7, many stores were boarded up, public transportation had stopped, and there was no electricity.

A majority of public institutions, including the city government and the provincial and district zemstvo boards, were also closed. "The mood is especially anxious," *Pravo* noted, "bordering on panic, to a degree not observed in previous strikes. . . . All over the city agitated people are running about, fussing, buying food, kerosene, candles." On December 8, private banks, theaters, schools, and most shops were closed. "Life in the city seemed to be extinct." People began to run out of food, especially dairy products. All railway lines except one were idle. But the exception was significant: it was the Nikolaevskii line, which linked the two capitals. Additional troops could be sent to Moscow.[38]

A mass meeting in the garden of the Aquarium during the night of December 8 threatened to turn into a bloodbath. Dragoons, soldiers, and Cossacks surrounded the crowd of more than 6,000 and insisted on conducting a search for weapons. Defiantly, the participants handed most of their weapons over to revolutionary militiamen, who slipped through a fence to a nearby house and then vanished into streets where no policemen were stationed. Most of those in the garden refused to leave; a few taunted the soldiers to "slaughter everyone at once." But the troops, who were only interested in seizing weapons, held their fire. At nine o'clock in the morning, the crowd left peaceably. A police search of the garden turned up about two dozen small arms.[39]

So far, only scattered violence had broken out in the city. The first major clash occurred on the evening of December 9 at the Fiedler Academy, where some 500 people and 100 armed militiamen were attending a meeting of the railway union. At 10 P.M. troops surrounded the building and ordered those present to surrender and give up their weapons. The officer in charge promised that if the militiamen obeyed within two hours, they would be freed after being disarmed, but no one believed him.

At the expiration of the grace period, the infantrymen opened fire and advanced to storm the academy; a bomb thrown from the building killed a lieutenant and seriously wounded a captain, which prompted the soldiers to withdraw. Shortly after midnight, however, the troops resumed the attack. For the first time, they made use of light artillery; the shells caused a considerable amount of damage and quite a few casualties. At this point, Fiedler advised the unionists to yield, but to no avail. Finally, the militiamen offered to surrender, but now the soldiers showed no interest in ending the confrontation peacefully. When the militiamen quietly walked out of the building at 3 A.M., they were attacked by troops with drawn swords. As usual in these instances, there are different estimates of the number of casualties, but it is certain that at least five revolutionaries lost their lives and that sixteen were wounded. One hundred and twenty were arrested. The soldiers seized a small quantity of bombs, rifles, and revolvers left behind by their adversaries.[40]

The use of artillery, highly unusual in a domestic disturbance, aroused profound anger even among people unsympathetic to the insurgents. It was assumed that Dubasov resorted to that form of warfare because he did not trust the soldiers under his command in hand-to-hand combat. Whatever the reason, the shelling of the Fiedler Academy marked the beginning of the bloody phase of the insurrection. Barricades appeared in the streets for the first time, and on the evening of December 10, a group of Socialist Revolutionaries, responding to the violence at the Fiedler Academy, threw two bombs at the headquarters of the Moscow Security Police, which damaged the building slightly. At a meeting the same evening, the Governor-General decided to apply the "most severe measures to put down the uprising." He also approved a proposal to permit the ultra-right-wing Union of the Russian People to form a militia, subject to the authority of local officials.[41]

The next day, December 11, four days after the start of the antigovernment action, the Combat Organization of the Moscow Committee of the RSDWP issued instructions to its militia on how to wage an armed struggle in the streets. In effect, they amounted to a manual on guerrilla warfare. The militiamen were advised to form detachments of three or four, on the assumption that if the city were saturated with small, mobile units that could not be pinned down, the "police and army will be impotent." Under no circumstances should militiamen occupy fortified places, which could be destroyed by artillery fire without much difficulty. The revolutionaries must also avoid large meetings, where they would be particularly vulnerable to arrest. Militiamen should fire at officers and Cossacks from behind closed doors and then quickly disappear. But they should refrain from attacking low-ranking soldiers and policemen, who were potential recruits for the people's cause. Policemen known for their cruelty, however, were to be shot on the spot. Finally, the militiamen were to see that janitors did not lock any doors, so that insurgents were assured easy access and escape routes. "Then, each courtyard will serve as our hideout and [as a potential] ambush [for the enemy]." Janitors who refused orders to keep all doors open were to be beaten; those who still refused were to be killed.[42]

In many parts of the city, Muscovites now came to the aid of the militia by erecting barricades, which greatly hampered the flow of traffic. The barricades consisted of whatever was found at hand: telegraph poles, poles from streetcars, placards, stones, garden fences, doors ripped from private homes, lampposts, and old pieces of wood. To one eyewitness, it seemed as though the barricades "literally grew up from the ground."[43] Soldiers and firemen would dismantle them, only to see them restored in short order.

To bolster morale, the insurgents circulated two rumors: that the soldiers sympathized with the strikers and would soon join them, and "that a large party of revolutionists from the Baltic provinces was on the way to Moscow, all well armed with guns and cannon."[44]

The partisan tactics of the insurgents baffled and confused the authorities. Soldiers were being disarmed and officers manhandled by people not easily recognizable as insurgents. As a result, troops became trigger-happy. "It was dangerous being on the streets," one foreign resident reported, "as one never knew when firing would commence all round, the troops firing at anybody they saw."[45] By December 12, senior government officials expressed great alarm: Durnovo confessed to Witte that Moscow did not have enough policemen to make the necessary searches and arrests and that the barricades prevented the movement of troops, who thus could not take control of the city. Durnovo also took seriously the insurgents' threat to cripple the government by assassinating everyone in a position of authority.[46]

Meanwhile, Admiral Dubasov sent the Minister of Internal Affairs a disheartening telegram: "The situation has become very serious: a ring of barricades is enveloping the city ever more tightly; the army is clearly inadequate for action against [the insurgents]. It is absolute necessary to send at least temporarily a brigade of infantry from Petersburg."[47] On December 11 and 12, police officers in the various districts of Moscow sounded the same alarm in reports to their superiors: disorders in the streets were increasing rapidly, and more troops were needed to handle them.[48] Actually, it was not simply a matter of too few soldiers; those available for duty were tired and unenthusiastic about again risking their lives so shortly after the conclusion of peace with Japan. Moscow appeared to be within the rebels' grasp.

Surprisingly, the insurgents lacked drive, so much so that some contemporaries believed that the revolutionary leaders had been forced to launch their assault prematurely. According to information received by the British Consul, the "dress rehearsal" was supposed to have "come off" in January and the "real business" in March. The dates had been moved up in response to demands by impatient workers, who threatened to "wash their hands of the whole revolution" if some action were not taken immediately. How else could one explain the failure of Moscow's revolutionaries both to have acted "in concert with Petersburg" and to have formulated a detailed military campaign ahead of time? Most significantly, how could one explain their failure to have directed their forces against "really vital spots" in the center of the city, such as the Imperial or other banks, the Governor-General's house, or the town hall?[49] The series of unconnected brushes between rebels and the army, many of them on the outskirts of town, vexed the authorities in Moscow but could not lead to their overthrow.

In the political arena, the revolutionary left was more adroit and more successful. The soviets—both the all-city soviet and the local ones in the districts—exercised a remarkable degree of authority over the civilian population. When shopkeepers wanted to open their stores, they sought permission from the all-city soviet. On December 8, that soviet's Executive Committee directed local committees to recommend which shops should be allowed to do business. The Executive Committee ruled that permits to that effect would be issued only if the owners accepted two conditions: not to raise prices, and to allow strikers to buy merchandise on credit. The Executive Committee also took the precautionary measure of permitting employees at the sewage system to report for work.[50] It even attended to affairs that in themselves would appear to have been trivial but evidently carried symbolic significance; for example, bakers were prohibited from producing "white bread, since the proletariat needs only black bread." On December 10 no white bread could be found in Moscow.[51]

In the Presnia district, the center of the textile industry and of an especially militant sector of the working class, the local soviet assumed full powers of government. Here, too, the insurrection lasted longer than anywhere else. The District Combat Committee, which commanded all the militiamen in the area (estimated at between 200 and 600), had perforce to act on its own because contact with other districts was cut off after December 11. In any case, because of the arrest of two of the three leaders and poor overall planning and organization, there was very little centralized direction of the rising.

Garvi, a member of the Presnia Combat Committee, claimed that the militia was so weak that two battalions of 200 to 300 Cossacks could have taken the district by storm. But initially, Dubasov did not order such an assault. On the contrary, the policemen in the district were so intimidated that they donned civilian clothes (on orders from their superiors) to avoid being recognized. Meeting little resistance, the insurgents simply took control. Their greatest triumph came on December 12, when they seized a police station and captured a cache of revolvers and various documents. Their prestige soared.[52]

The militiamen patrolled the streets of Presnia, disarmed persons recognized as police officers, and conducted searches of apartments occupied by Tsarist officials. They arrested several such officials and placed them in makeshift prisons in workers' apartments. The militiamen's most notable captives were a police officer, Sakharov, and the chief of the Criminal Investigation Department, A. I. Voiloshnikov. Sakharov was known as an implacable enemy of the workers, an officer given to ruthlessly suppressing revolutionary groups.

A fierce quarrel broke out within the Combat Committee over the fate of the two prize prisoners. Z. Ia. Sedoi (Litvin), one of the most fanatical zealots among Moscow's Bolsheviks, insisted that both men should be executed immediately. But I. F. Dubrovinskii, a high-ranking SD activist, urged restraint, on the ground that during the Paris Commune shootings by revolutionaries had given the authorities a pretext for dealing harshly with the Communards. Dubrovinskii could not fairly be accused of being soft toward Tsarist officials, for he contended that if the insurrection were defeated, the two prisoners could still be liquidated at the last minute "if that were to be considered necessary." In the end, the Combat Committee decided to set up a "kind of military court" to pass judgment on the prisoners. Then, after "mature reflection," the entire committee was to reach a final decision.

During the night, however, Sedoi took it upon himself to have the captives shot because he feared that his recommendation would not be adopted by the committee. A "stormy scene" ensued in which Garvi and Dubrovinskii denounced Sedoi for this "outrage" and he berated them for excessive timidity. For his part, Sedoi indicated that he had not even given a thought to "formalities," by which he meant legal procedures. Garvi and Dubrovinskii threatened to bring the matter before the soviet and the party, but there is no information on what action, if any, was taken.

Many years later, Garvi viewed Sedoi's conduct as a precursor of judicial procedures in the Soviet Union: "In embryonic form there arose institutions in Presnia during the uprising that, on a different scale and in a different form, developed in the February and then in the October revolution of 1917. The embryos of Soviet power were the militia, the Red Army, revolutionary tribunals, and the Cheka. Sedoi's arbitrary reprisal against Sakharov and Voiloshnikov, without a trial, anticipated the future system of the Bolsheviks' Extraordinary Commission and its executions without trial."[53]

The revolutionary tribunal, or people's court, established in Presnia was more humane than Sedoi, though its procedures were idiosyncratic. Presnia was not merely a working-class district; it was also a center of the underworld. Hence the revolutionaries considered it necessary to create some organ that could take quick, punitive action against criminals. Indeed, most of the miscreants brought before the revolutionary tribunal had not committed offenses of a deeply political nature; they included a prostitute who had plied her trade with a Cossack, a citizen who had tripped on the barricades and in a fit of temper cursed the revolution, and some mischievous children and hooligans. The prisoners were brought into a courtroom filled with people who acted as an impromptu jury. One of the revolutionary leaders would question the suspects, and after handing down his judgment he would turn to the people and say:

"Do you agree with the decision, comrades?" "We agree!" the "people" would answer. The sentences were generally light: those found guilty were reprimanded or kept in custody for a short time.[54]

In the meantime, the government began to use artillery fire against the Presnia insurgents with deadly effect. As soon as rebels fired one shot from a building, artillerymen trained their guns on the building and blasted it. And in keeping with orders issued by Governor-General Dubasov on December 12, troops fired their rifles on any group of more than three that gathered in the streets. "In the battle," wrote *Pravo*, "hundreds have fallen and there are perhaps thousands of victims; in all streets, bodies are scattered about, the cemeteries and hospitals are overcrowded, and the end of the battle is still not in sight. The rapidly depleted ranks of revolutionaries, literally shot like birds, are constantly replenished by more and more new forces. The combat unit has been transformed into a kind of many-headed hydra: in place of every head that is chopped off, two new ones grow. . . . Barricades increase as though by the wave of a wand."[55] The writer was indulging in hyperbole, but there can be no doubt that the army inflicted very heavy casualties on the rebels. By December 14, many insurrectionists had also been arrested.

Nevertheless, the leaders of the uprising exuded confidence in their ability to prevail. On December 15, the British Consul in Moscow reported that he had met various persons who were in touch with the revolutionaries, all of whom declared that the leaders "are very well content with affairs here, that they have lost but a few of their own men here, and that they can carry on the struggle here for a good month more, by which time they hope to have worn the troops out." The revolutionaries asserted that their "plan of campaign" had been drawn up by ex-officers of the army in Manchuria and that they had at their disposal about 40,000 trained men. They also claimed to have captured three field guns and two Maxim machine guns. The British Consul acknowledged that he could not vouch for the accuracy of these claims.[56]

Actually, on the very day the consul wrote his report the tide turned decisively against the insurgents. The long-awaited help from St. Petersburg arrived in the form of the Semenovskii Regiment, commanded by Colonel G. A. Min, a soldier made to order for Tsar Nicholas. Min had no scruples about shelling buildings harboring revolutionaries. By the time he arrived, Presnia was the primary center of resistance; the unrest in much of the rest of Moscow had subsided.

Min's force of 1,500 trained soldiers was large enough to storm and overpower the militiamen with a minimal loss of lives. But Governor-General Dubasov was determined to teach the revolutionaries a lesson.

He ordered Min to "exterminate the gangs of insurgents and seize the leaders of the insurrection." If he met with resistance, Min was to "act ruthlessly."[57]

Late in the day on December 15, the troops, supported by sixteen artillery pieces, surrounded a large area of the Presnia district that included the Prokhorov cotton mill and the Schmidt furniture factory, two major centers of the insurrection. (The owners of the two enterprises, N. I. Prokhorov and N. P. Schmidt, sympathized with the radicals and supplied them with shelter and food.) On the morning of December 16, Min sent Schmidt an ultimatum: the militiamen must surrender in fifteen minutes or his factory would be destroyed. Schmidt agreed to comply on condition that he be set free. Min rejected these terms, gave Schmidt a bit more time to reconsider surrendering, and then ordered his men to fire.

The barrage of artillery fire continued for over two days, causing an enormous amount of damage and many casualties.[58] "It seemed," Garvi recalled, "as though Presnia were surrounded by a ring of fire."[59] The militiamen offered little resistance, firing a few shots here and there. To engage in a full-scale battle would have been futile, as the insurgents quickly realized. The leaders of the uprising and captains of the militia, as well as the militiamen themselves, had in fact been ordered by the local soviet in Presnia to disperse into the central parts of the city. Most managed to escape.

Even before the bombardment of Presnia, a meeting on December 15 of 90 members of the Moscow soviet (out of a total of 170) had considered calling for an end to the rising. According to Garvi, the Mensheviks urged the adoption of a resolution to this effect, though there is some question about how vigorously they pressed their case. The Mensheviks had good reason to be pessimistic about the insurrectionists' prospects. V. N. Krokhmal, a member of the party's Central Committee, had brought a somber report from the capital: the workers in St. Petersburg were far too exhausted to join the uprising. Indeed, they had not even succeeded in preventing the dispatch of fresh troops to Moscow.[60] The Bolsheviks at the meeting, however, convinced that uprisings were about to erupt in other parts of the Empire, insisted on continuing the struggle.

The Bolsheviks based their optimism in part on a report by a delegate from the Union of Postal and Telegraph Employees, who claimed to have overheard a conversation between Dubasov and senior officials in St. Petersburg that revealed the government's precarious situation. According to this delegate, Dubasov's request for more troops had been met with the following response: "We cannot provide more troops; there are few reliable troops available, and they are needed to protect the Tsar and the government." There was therefore no cause for alarm. Moreover, the delegate contended that the workers in St. Petersburg were bound to rise up "with renewed vigor. . . . All of Russia is now watching Moscow: if we throw down the banner of insurrection and lay down our arms, we will be giving a signal for retreat to all of Russia and then the revolution will be crushed."[61] No self-respecting revolutionary could resist an appeal based on so optimistic, though wildly unrealistic, an appraisal of the situation. The 90 delegates failed to decide to end the rising.

However, it was so obvious that the rebels had been crushed that within one day the Moscow Bolsheviks felt obliged to reverse themselves. On December 16, they conceded defeat and called on their followers to stop fighting in three days. On December 18, the Executive Committee of the Moscow soviet adopted a resolution to the same effect. The Committee assured the people of Moscow that the week of bloody combat had not been in vain, that it had brought closer the demise of the autocracy: "Our duty was to show that the working class guards its own political interests, that it can stand up for itself with weapons in its hands, if necessary. We have fulfilled our duty." Now the task would be to "prepare more actively for an all-Russian political strike and a national armed uprising."[62]

The December uprising was a costly affair. According to the Medical Union, 1,059 Muscovites, most of them civilians not involved in the fighting, were killed. Of these, 137 were women and 86 children. Twenty-five policemen and nine soldiers lost their lives.[63]

But this was only the beginning of the carnage in Moscow, for the authorities unleashed a brutal crackdown. There were numerous reliable reports of executions, without any judicial proceedings, of workers and students on the mere suspicion of their having taken part in the rising. Hundreds of others were arrested, and many of them were cruelly beaten by their captors. According to Henry Nevinson, the police had been ordered "to arrest all suspected boys and girls in the Moscow schools and bring them to the police stations. There they were handed over to soldiers, who stripped them, and if they were under fifteen, beat them with their hands. Between fifteen and eighteen, the girls and boys alike were stripped and beaten with rods, though the girls received only five strokes and the boys twelve."[64] Even people who had opposed the excesses of the revolutionaries were appalled. The Tsar and his advisers, they believed, "brought the country to this state of affairs and now, having been beaten by the Japanese, . . . make short work of us."[65]

Much of the responsibility for the failure of the Moscow uprising must be attributed to the organizers' military and political ineptitude. For months revolutionary leaders had stressed the inevitability of a military action against the old order and the need to prepare for it. Yet, at the moment when they chose to wage the final battle, they could muster only a small militia that was inadequately armed and poorly trained. They had also failed to pay sufficient attention to tactics. The guerrilla tactics they formulated in the course of the conflict were essentially those that the militiamen were already applying in the streets. For a day or two, the revolutionaries baffled their opponents and even inflicted some casualties on them. But as it turned out, a relatively small force of disciplined and ruthless soldiers could easily crush the militia. Revolvers and partisan tactics were no match for artillery.

Perhaps even more significant, each one of the revolutionaries' political calculations proved to be utterly wrong. From the beginning of the insurrection, it was clear that the Muscovites could succeed only if workers elsewhere also took up arms. The events in St. Petersburg in November, however, had demonstrated that the workers were becoming increasingly isolated politically and that their revolutionary zeal was waning. They suffered one defeat after another during the strikes, and the arrest of the Soviet deprived them of leadership. Exhausted, demoralized, leaderless, the workers in the capital could not realistically have been expected to make the ultimate effort, a military attack on the government.

To be sure, in some two dozen cities of Great Russia, the Ukraine, the Kingdom of Poland, Transcaucasia, and Siberia, workers staged disturbances, prompting a foreign resident to comment that "the country appears to be suffering, as it were, from some malady of the blood, which is cured in one place only to break out in another."[66] But none of these disorders was serious enough to force the government to divert a large number of troops from Moscow or any other major trouble spot.

In Aleksandrov on December 8, for example, a manufacturer named S. N. Baranov led workers from three factories in an attempt to seize control of the city. The insurgents succeeded in disarming the local police, but they failed to persuade a battalion of sappers to join the rebellion. Baranov professed to be a moderate who simply wanted to implement the October Manifesto. He repudiated violence and declared that his followers were hostile not to the Tsar but only to the bureaucracy. I. M. Leontev, the Governor of Vladimir province, was not convinced. He placed Aleksandrov under martial law and asked Durnovo for additional troops. Some violence broke out in the city and at a factory in nearby Strunino, but after the arrival of 30 Cossacks from Ivanovo-Voznesensk, the local commander began "active operations" against the insurgents. By December 15, after the arrest of numerous workers, the disorders ended.[67]

In Rostov-on-Don, the local soviet called a strike for December 8, which within five days turned into an insurrection. About 1,000 protesters, mainly railroad workers, occupied the railway station in the suburb of Temernik. On December 16, troops surrounded the station and ordered the workers to surrender. When the insurgents refused, the commander resorted to the same tactics that were being used in Moscow: he trained artillery fire on the station, killing 28 and wounding 107. All the insurgents could do with their light arms was to wound one officer and six men of lower rank. The soldiers cleared the station of strikers, many of whom were taken into custody. By December 20, Rostov was pacified.[68]

In the Polish Kingdom late in December three socialist parties called for a strike, and one of them urged its followers to attempt a seizure of power. The response was pitiful. In Warsaw, only a tiny minority of the workers left their jobs, and in Lodz, where a larger proportion did so, the strikers did not stage an armed uprising. The entire movement fizzled out within a few days without ever having posed a serious threat to the authorities.[69]

In Transcaucasia, the Social Democrats, enjoying broader popular support than anywhere else in the Empire, made a determined effort to coordinate their activities with those of their colleagues in Russia. On December 10, the Social Democrats of Tiflis proclaimed a general strike and stepped up their agitation within the armed forces. The tactics were only partially effective. A fair number of workers went out on strike, crippling the systems of transportation and communication. Food supplies dwindled, and toward the end of December officials lived in dread of a famine. For 25 days the French consulate in Tiflis could not communicate with any other city in the Empire or with French officials abroad.

But the army, far from supporting the revolutionaries, went on a rampage against actual and presumed opponents of the regime after two bombs thrown into a bazaar in the center of town on December 22 wounded several Cossacks. First, the local commander ordered his artillery to shell the building from which the bombs had allegedly been hurled. Then, once the building was demolished, rank-and-file soldiers defied orders from their officers and began to pillage shops and steal merchandise from railway trains idled by the strike. The soldiers' riot lasted two days. Life in Tiflis began to return to normal toward the end of the month after General Alikhanov-Avarskii, newly appointed Governor-General, imposed a state of siege.[70]

Ironically, the spread of disorders after the outbreak of the Moscow insurrection was impeded by an action that workers themselves had taken. Because many of the postal and telegraph employees were on strike early in December, communication between cities was extremely difficult. On December 7, a telegram that reached Rostov-on-Don announcing that the soviets in Moscow and St. Petersburg had called for a general political strike caused great excitement. But how could the local revolutionaries be sure that the news was accurate, that it was not a trick by the government to provoke precipitate action? The infeasibility of speedy consultation among leaders in various localities prevented the radicals from developing a common strategy. By the same token, the inability of revolutionaries in Moscow to obtain a reliable and steady flow of information from provincial towns helps to explain their unrealistic appraisals of their own situation.[71]

Wishful thinking had thus led to poor political judgments. That revolutionary leaders in Moscow would have been gratified by the news, early in December, that members of the Rostov Regiment had mutinied was understandable, but the assumption that large numbers of other troops were on the verge of joining the revolutionary movement was unwarranted. Members of the armed forces—even those who had participated in mutinies—had shown little evidence of sympathizing with radical political and economic goals. What reason was there to believe that those in Moscow would behave differently?

· · · · ·

The impact of the Moscow uprising on the course of the revolution can hardly be exaggerated. As a result of it, the liberal movement, which until October had played a decisive role in undermining the autocracy, became politically more cautious and increasingly distanced itself from the radical left. A case in point is the Moscow City Council, which met several times during the fighting. On December 13, S. A. Levitskii, one of the more liberal members of that body, introduced a motion that placed responsibility for the "consequences of the uprising" on the government and urged the immediate convocation of a constituent assembly elected by universal suffrage. The motion was defeated, 42 to 16. Instead, the council adopted a much more moderate resolution introduced by A. I. Guchkov. It acknowledged that the violence had resulted from lack of confidence in the government and the slow pace of reform, but it affirmed that the uprising would "not delay the implementation of those reforms that alone can lead the country along the path of peaceful development"—a muted expression of support for Witte's overall program.[72] The Mayor rejected a suggestion that the council censure the military and the police for indiscriminately killing civilians on the grounds that such an action "would only pour oil on the fire. It would appear to the workers as a new call to violence."[73] On most issues, the liberals, who until the uprising enjoyed a majority in the Moscow City Council, could count on no more than 20 to 25 votes out of a total of 100.[74]

In Kiev, the city council decided to punish all students at institutions of higher learning because a large proportion of them had taken part in disturbances in December. It voted overwhelmingly not to grant any stipends to students, and it rejected a proposal to give a small subsidy to the Society for Promoting Literacy, contending that instead of educating the people it "sowed the seeds of revolutionary sedition." Councils in other cities took similar actions against stipends for students.[75]

The liberals and moderates varied in their reactions to the uprising, though most expressed some degree of criticism. The Octobrists and other moderate liberals (such as the Party for a Legal Order) condemned the revolutionaries and called on the people to oppose them.[76] The Octobrist N. I. Guchkov (brother of A. I. Guchkov) went so far as to offer a toast of gratitude to Governor-General Dubasov for having crushed the rebellion.[77] Some Kadets now abandoned the tactic of solidarity with the radical leftists on the ground that the latter had demonstrated that they were interested not in national liberation but in a democratic republic and in social as well as political revolution. These Kadets denounced both revolution and reaction. Struve, for example, declared that the authorities and the revolutionaries constituted two strike committees battling each other to the detriment of the national interest. The committee of the radicals, he warned, would lead the country into "complete economic disorganization," whereas the committee of "Witte-Durnovo-Dubasov," "feeding" the madness of the extreme left, had declared a "strike" against the October Manifesto with the intention of abolishing the freedoms granted by the Tsar.[78]

The Kadet Central Committee found itself in a quandary. It disapproved of the insurrection, but did not wish to issue any condemnation that might be interpreted as either support for the government or a threat to the alliance between the liberals and the radicals. Consequently, the Kadets criticized both the rebels and the government; but they placed most of the blame for the outbreak of violence on the authorities.

Miliukov, the leader of the party, at first did not know how to react to the uprising; but on December 8 he appealed to the revolutionaries to end the insurrection. As time passed, however, and the dimensions of the government's offensive against the insurgents became apparent, he appealed for an end to the massacre. "Moscow is being bombed by cannon," he wrote. "Bombarded with a fury, with a persistence, with an accuracy with which the Japanese positions were never favored." Yet he warned the left that it was playing into the hands of Witte by driving the moderates into his camp. "Witte," he wrote in January 1906, "found unexpected support in the Russian revolutionary movement which, by its childish goals of 'armed uprising' and 'a democratic republic,' made that frightening impact on the average citizen on which Count Witte relied."[79] Years later, Miliukov concluded that "the Moscow uprising, flippantly undertaken and lost before it started, created between us [liberals and revolutionaries] an impassable gulf."[80]

The liberal press, most notably *Russkie vedomosti*, held the government responsible for the Moscow uprising. In a lead editorial on December 19, the paper contended that the cause of the violence could be traced to a single source: the "government, its policies, its blind obstinacy and failure to understand the needs of the time and the urgent needs of the people." Specifically, the government was to blame for not having convened a national representative assembly, for not having guaranteed the freedoms granted in the October Manifesto, and for having violated those freedoms repeatedly. The editors urged the authorities not to pursue a repressive policy now that the uprising had been crushed but to proceed with basic reform.[81]

Given the rhetoric of the radicals during the Days of Liberty and their preparations for armed action, the editors of *Russkie vedomosti* can fairly be charged with having presented a one-sided assessment of the causes of the uprising. Still, their advice to the government was humane and politically sound, but no one heeded it. Tsar Nicholas had decided that the time was propitious for an assault on the militant opposition, especially since the liberals, more divided than ever, were in no position to offer serious resistance. Indeed, many moderates increasingly came to believe that the restoration of order must be the first item on the government's agenda. For their part, the workers were so thoroughly demoralized that they could not begin to stop the government's offensive. A major consequence of the Moscow uprising, therefore, was the weakening of the opposition movement. Only ten weeks after the government had tottered on the verge of collapse, it felt free to shed virtually all inhibitions in a drive to reassert its authority.

$$\cdot \quad \cdot \quad \cdot \quad \cdot \quad \cdot$$

As has already been noted, Prime Minister Witte had concluded late in November and early in December that order would have to be restored before he could proceed with reform.[82] After the outbreak of the Moscow uprising, he became preoccupied with finding a way to quell unrest. On December 15, he informed Nicholas that the Council of Ministers had decided that a new approach was needed. In the past, the government had considered it undesirable for the army to take energetic measures against disturbers of the peace; force was to be used sparingly, primarily to intimidate crowds. But the situation had changed; the danger to the state was much greater than ever. Consequently, if the army was called upon to pacify an unruly crowd, it must deal "decisively and mercilessly" with "all who resist with weapons in their hands."[83]

On December 21, Witte recommended that Nicholas dismiss certain aged and incompetent generals and assign a new role to the army: "The army has been deployed in accordance with strategic considerations and not in accordance with the needs of domestic politics. Now the army must be called upon [to serve an active role] . . . in the struggle against sedition and for support of the foundations of the state." Witte suggested that it might be advisable to resort to a "radical solution": place a military man at the head of the government and entrust him with the coordination of all its operations.[84]

When Witte learned of the uprising in Rostov-on-Don, he promptly sent a telegram to the ataman in Novocherkassk ordering him "not to stand on ceremony" in crushing the disturbance.[85] Finally, on December 25, the Prime Minister told General V. U. Sollogub in Riga that "in view of the small number of soldiers and the weakness of the police on the one hand, and the bloodthirsty behavior of local revolutionaries on the other, there is no way to suppress the revolution except by ruthless means."[86]

Even Tsar Nicholas was startled by Witte's new determination to move forcefully against the left. "As for Witte," the Tsar wrote his mother on January 12, 1906, "since the happenings in Moscow he has radically changed his views; now he wants to hang and shoot everybody. I have never seen such a chameleon of a man. That, naturally, is the reason why no one believes in him any more. He is absolutely discredited with everybody, except perhaps the Jews abroad."[87] With Witte's blessing, the army now unleashed a savage attack on suspected disturbers of the peace. For about three months late in 1905 and early in 1906, several regions of the Empire were subjected to a ghastly bloodbath.

The crackdown began with some relatively mild police actions in St. Petersburg. In the weeks following the issuance of the October Manifesto, Gerasimov had mobilized a special police force of 250 men for an eventual roundup of revolutionary activists, a step that he believed the government would have to take sooner or later. He preferred to move sooner rather than later, but Witte, Durnovo, and Rachkovskii restrained him. In the meantime, he kept tabs on the revolutionaries through an extensive network of some 120 to 150 agents placed in working-class districts. Gerasimov recruited many of his agents in the prisons of St. Petersburg. Some turned police agent to avoid long terms of incarceration, some were lured by money, some bore personal grudges against individual radicals, and a few were genuinely disillusioned with the revolutionary movement. The agents had little difficulty in tracking down agitators, who did not bother to conceal their identity during the Days of Liberty. Each agent reported to "secret apartments" located in various districts. Any one apartment was known to only three to five agents; the more important agents reported directly to Gerasimov.

When the Moscow uprising began and the police chief in St. Petersburg received the order to move against the left, Gerasimov quickly implemented his plans. In one day his special squad conducted 350 searches and arrests, closed down three "laboratories" for the production of dynamite and several printing presses, and confiscated 400 bombs. The next day his men carried out 400 searches and arrested dozens of political activists, among them A. F. Kerensky, who twelve years later, as the SR Minister of Justice in the Provisional Government, signed the order for Gerasimov's arrest. Gerasimov claimed that his swift crackdown prevented the kind of armed uprising in the capital that had broken out in Moscow. This was a bit of puffery, but there is no doubt that he dealt the radical left a severe blow.[88]

In the week from December 15 to 22, the police in St. Petersburg also closed down 32 printing presses of nonrevolutionary publications. Durnovo justified this action by claiming that the editors had failed to comply with the regulations on censorship: pamphlets had not been submitted for preliminary screening, and periodicals had not been submitted for official authorization. With these measures, Durnovo violated the spirit if not the letter of the directive on freedom of the press that the Prime Minister had issued only a month earlier. When the publishers appealed to Witte for help, he replied that he did not find Durnovo's moves unwarranted. It seemed to him "that there is no other way to fight against unruly presses except to close them down." Nevertheless, he promised to see that the presses were allowed to operate again, though he did not indicate when that might be.[89] On December 23, the Governor-General of Moscow closed down *Russkie vedomosti* for a week on the ground that the paper had supported the uprising and had collected substantial sums for the insurgents. The editors pointed out that most of the 55,000 rubles the police confiscated from the paper's accountant had been donated for charitable and educational purposes. The 1,771 rubles that were to go to the strike committee had been received before the December uprising.[90]

The government also launched a campaign against the "Third Element." In a circular memorandum of December 16 to all Governors, City Governors, and the Warsaw chief of police, Durnovo charged that a significant number of "politically unreliable" people had in recent years been employed by various urban and zemstvo institutions. Many of them had at one time or another been convicted of "state crimes," and others belonged to revolutionary organizations. These employees were agitating among the peasants and workers, inciting them to violence. He singled out statisticians, teachers, and doctors' assistants as the worst offenders and urged officials to take the "most drastic measures in accordance with the law" against them. What Durnovo had in mind was their dismissal, an action that he claimed would be legal if taken to preserve "state order and tranquillity."[91] On this basis, hundreds of such employees were discharged. In some places, most notably Chernigov, a large percentage of them were also arrested.[92]

The government's most devastating and brutal weapon against the revolutionaries was the punitive expedition, an organized attack by small groups of specially selected troops in regions either controlled by radicals or in a state of unrest. The idea behind the punitive expedition was not only to root out disorder but to intimidate the population by publicly, quickly, and ruthlessly punishing participants in disturbances or people suspected of having participated in them. It was, in short, a form of state terror directed at the state's own citizens.

How the expeditions originated and who bore responsibility for them is not quite clear. In his memoirs, Witte claimed that some expeditions were dispatched without his knowledge; this may be true of the first, relatively small raids in the south-central provinces early in November to quash peasant disturbances. Witte also suggested that the Tsar, more than anyone else, encouraged the soldiers in the field to treat radicals brutally, without regard for due process. Thus, when Nicholas read a report about summary executions in the Baltic provinces by a certain Captain O. Richter, he noted on the document: "What a fine fellow!" On the other hand, the Prime Minister himself defended the punitive expeditions in December along the Trans-Siberian Railway, which he is known to have initiated, by arguing that even though they involved "sacrifices," traffic had been restored and the army's evacuation from the Far East had been hastened.

Witte further acknowledged that he favored the use of force "without any sentimentality," but only if a revolt had actually broken out. Once order was restored, Witte said, his policy was not to sanction acts of revenge or the arbitrary use of force. Local authorities were then to govern in accordance with the law. He conceded that they did not always do so. To his dismay, he was blamed for the unnecessary repression, which was one reason he asked to be relieved from office late in 1905.[93]

In truth, Witte had few scruples about the punitive expeditions, as he himself revealed in a rather poignant story about his own family. While one of the first expeditions was in progress in Siberia, Witte's son-in-law and step-daughter (with their one-year-old child) were in Brussels on a government mission. After Lieutenant General P. K. Rennenkampf sentenced several revolutionaries in Chita to death, Witte's wife received a message from émigrés in Western Europe warning that if the Chita radicals were executed, her daughter and grandchild would be assassinated. Mme. Witte tearfully pleaded with the Prime Minister to stop the executions. He refused to intercede, and the revolutionaries were killed. We are not told whether the émigrés made any attempt to carry out their threat.[94]

It seems that the initial decision to resort to punitive expeditions was taken in great secrecy by senior officials at Court in consultation with several army generals. Even the Minister of Internal Affairs apparently played no significant role in the deliberations. Moreover, military commanders were given full control over the expeditions. Nevertheless, there is no evidence that Witte or any other members of the Council of Ministers argued against them after they had begun. Only in January and February 1906, when most of the country had already been pacified, did Witte try to put a halt to the worst excesses.[95]

At least ten punitive expeditionary forces were sent out, ranging widely in size and firepower. Major General A. A. Orlov's force in the Baltic provinces appears to have been the largest, consisting of three infantry regiments, fourteen cavalry squadrons, four heavy guns, and twenty machine guns. Colonel A. K. Riman, whose task was to wrest control of the Moscow-Riazan railroad from the rebels, commanded the smallest force, a single infantry detachment. The expeditionary forces' orders were formulated in general terms, but there could be no doubt that whatever steps were taken to pacify a region would be approved in St. Petersburg. Each commanding officer was told to apply "measures he considers necessary to restore order"; the commander understood that these words granted him carte blanche and that he would not have to answer for any excesses committed by his men.[96]

In mid-December 1905, a major expeditionary force began to operate in Siberia, which was in effect cut off from European Russia (the telegraph system did not work, and the railways were controlled by strike committees that decided which trains could move westward). On December 13, Tsar Nicholas sent a ciphered telegram to General M. N. Danilov in Nagasaki, Japan, for transmission to General N. P. Linevich in Siberia (this was the only way the ruler could communicate on sensitive matters with his generals in the Far East), ordering General Rennenkampf to begin forcing workers on the Siberian and Trans-Baikal railway lines to obey local authorities. Rennenkampf was to start out in Harbin and move his troops westward on the railway line, making sure, wherever necessary, "to break the spirit of resistance and rebellion." Outside agitators attempting to persuade railway employees and telegraphists not to work should be dealt with "quickly and with merciless severity, with every kind of measure."[97]

Meanwhile, on December 21, Lieutenant General A. N. Meller-Zakomelskii left Moscow for Siberia with a detachment of about 100 infantrymen, six cavalrymen, and two machine guns. Each of the two generals was to restore order along his route until they met. On January 31, 1906, General Meller-Zakomelskii sent word to the Tsar that in four days he would reach Cheliabinsk and that he had accomplished his mission: "The revolutionary elements on [the railway] lines have been eliminated, arrested, dismissed; a portion of them have fled. The line is protected by reliable troops of the 4th Siberian Corps."[98]

Meller-Zakomelskii, who by all accounts was a sadist, achieved his success by shooting or hanging dozens of people, flogging hundreds, and arresting thousands. One example will suffice to indicate how he operated. When his train reached a railway depot in the Yenisei region in mid-January and encountered a crowd of protesting workers, he ordered his men to disembark and begin firing. Seventeen people were killed, 22 wounded, and about 80 arrested. Thereupon, the entire force reboarded the train and headed for Irkutsk. Meller-Zakomelskii counted on the news of his atrocities to travel fast and to intimidate troublemakers in a wide region, which is precisely what happened.[99]

General Rennenkampf was equally successful on his westward trek, though he behaved with somewhat more restraint, at least at first. According to one source, he even criticized Meller-Zakomelskii for the zeal and haste with which he opened fire as soon as he reached a trouble spot. Rennenkampf prided himself on not acting as a bloodthirsty monster, though he can hardly be accused of leniency.

When he reached the border of Trans-Baikalia and Manchuria on January 7 with some 1,500 well-armed troops, Rennenkampf appealed to the railway workers to submit voluntarily to "legal authority." Anyone who refused would be dismissed from his job. Then he posted a public notice: if anyone attempted to assassinate his men, gendarmes, or railway guards, all those in custody (how many there were is not clear) would be shot. In addition, Rennenkampf ordered that the teacher A. I. Popov (Konovalov), who was a Social Democratic agitator, be tried by a field court-martial, which sentenced him to death.

After the execution, which was clearly designed to cow the local population, "Rennenkampf traveled along the railway line, conducted a general's inspection, and carried out mass arrests." Subsequently, four other suspects were brought before a field court-martial and sentenced to death. No one could be found to hang them, so they were shot in full view of the local population.[100] Thanks to the efforts of Rennenkampf and Meller-Zakomelskii, all of Siberia was pacified and fully restored to the government's control by late January 1906.

Punitive expeditions wreaked the greatest amount of havoc in the Baltic provinces, large portions of which had been taken over by rebels. On November 28, a special conference at Court under the chairmanship of Grand Duke Nikolai Nikolaevich decided on a crackdown in the region and appointed a strong advocate of repression, Lieutenant General V. U. Sollogub, as Acting Governor-General. Within a few weeks Sollogub assigned seven trusted officers to conduct punitive expeditions in specific areas. Altogether, the officers had at their disposal about 19,000 men by the end of March 1906.[101]

In keeping with their orders, the troops in the Baltic provinces unleashed an unspeakable reign of terror. Late in December, Major General V. M. Bezobrazov and Lieutenant General P. N. Voronov instructed their officers to "act in an extremely energetic and decisive manner, [and to] shoot the main agitators; [do not] be fastidious in the choice of means to attain the pacification of the country." Bezobrazov assured his subordinate that they would not be held responsible for any "major errors."[102]

In their sweep through the Baltic region, troops summarily executed numerous citizens and mercilessly flogged peasants and workers, men, women, children, and even the elderly. In the Kharius district, Bezobrazov organized a public spectacle of beatings and executions, which he then held up as a "model exercise in dispensing justice." General Orlov boasted to the Tsar that his troops had burned 70 buildings, killed 22 rebels in armed encounters, and shot 78 others, while suffering only one casualty.[103] "The state of the country," according to one contemporary report, "is pitiable as the landlords have suffered from the action of the peasants and the peasants have in turn been harried by the troops."[104]

It has been estimated that 1,170 people were killed in the Baltic region between December 1905 and late May 1906. Property damage amounted to 2,000,000 rubles.[105] The Tsar, believing that "terror must be met by terror," did not flinch; on the contrary, he praised General Orlov for "acting splendidly."[106] But the Governor-General, Sollogub, began to have misgivings about the behavior of the soldiers. He contended that the punitive expeditions were in some instances acting illegally and ordered his officers to punish only those known to be guilty of rebellion, not whole groups of people. The excesses, in his view, stirred up public hostility against the government and made it more difficult to reestablish order. In the spring of 1906, Sollogub was replaced by General Meller-Zakomelskii, a man made of sterner stuff.[107]

Punitive expeditions also operated in the Ukraine and the Caucasus, though not on the same scale as in Siberia and the Baltic provinces. But the brutality was comparable. On December 17, 1905, the Governor-General of Kharkov, V. V. Sennitskii, sent the following instructions to a commander of one of the punitive detachments: "In the event that peasants in a region support insurgents and do not disperse on first demand, you are to announce that the entire village will be burned; if they disperse, they will not be harmed."[108]

Perhaps the most explicit instructions on the application of terror were issued by the Minister of Internal Affairs himself on January 6, 1906. Durnovo had learned that unrest had broken out in the small town of Kagarluka in Kiev province. He feared that the local police would not be able to protect nearby landed estates, and therefore issued the following directive to the Governor-General of Kiev, V. A. Sukhomlinov: "I earnestly request, in this and in all similar cases, that you order the use of armed force without the slightest leniency and that insurgents be annihilated and their homes burned in the event of resistance. It is necessary once and for all to stop, with the most severe measures, the spreading willfulness that threatens to destroy the entire state. Under the present circumstances, the restoration of the authority of the government is possible only by these means." Arrests, Durnovo asserted, were useless, for it was impossible to bring hundreds of people to justice in small, remote regions of the Empire. "The army must be inspired with such orders [as Durnovo had issued]."[109]

In the Caucasus, General Alikhanov-Avarskii's military operations created, in the words of one report, "a state of things hardly credible in a civilized country. Whole districts seem to have been given over to military executions by the Cossacks who appear to have behaved with inconceivable brutality. The surviving inhabitants have fled to the mountains where they endure great privations from hunger and cold. At one place 15 political prisoners were killed by letting steam into the cells where they were confined and this statement, though often repeated, has not been denied. The result of these operations has been to restore the tranquillity which is not likely to be disturbed for some time to come." General Alikhanov-Avarskii, a Tatar by origin, is said to have boasted that "the Georgians will have cause to remember me for four generations."[110]

Two other aspects of the government's policy of repression should be noted. First, the authorities vastly increased the number of regions placed under exceptional laws. From mid-October 1905 until March 1, 1906, the government imposed martial law on two entire guberniias and 48 districts or cities, "Reinforced Security" on one guberniia and eighteen districts or towns, and "Extraordinary Security" on five guberniias and 32 districts or towns. All told, by the spring of 1906 about 69 percent of the provinces and regions of the Russian Empire were either completely or partially subjected to one of the various emergency codes.[111] This development stood in stark contrast to Witte's public declaration of October 17 that he would seek to eliminate the exceptional laws.

Second, on December 6, 1905, the Tsar signed a ukase that granted governors and commanders in any region not under exceptional laws the right to issue permits to wealthy landowners to form militias with their own funds. These militias were to operate only on specified estates unless the owners permitted their transfer to other estates. How many landlords actually availed themselves of this opportunity to provide for their own defense is not known; but a larger number of semi-independent armed forces sprang up in the countryside early in 1906 and played a significant role in the campaign against agrarian unrest.[112]

The government's repressive policies proved to be highly effective. Within about four months, the revolutionary movement was in retreat everywhere, incapable of holding the line against the authorities. This was in a sense a puzzling development, for the autocracy used relatively few troops against the rebels. As has already been noted, the combined strength of the largest of the punitive expeditions—that in the Baltic provinces—added up to less than 20,000 men. Some of the units operating elsewhere consisted of fewer than 200 soldiers. The point is that by indiscriminately applying brute force, small contingents of troops succeeded in intimidating multitudes of people, many of whom had grown weary of the fifteen-month-old struggle with the autocracy. Needless to say, the fickleness of formerly disgruntled soldiers played into the hands of the government. As soon as the authorities demonstrated their determination to crush the civilian revolution, mutineers turned into their loyal tools.[113]

The government's victory exacted a heavy toll in human lives and property. No precise figures are available, but the number of deaths surely ran to thousands and the damage to property amounted to millions of rubles. The jails overflowed with political prisoners: estimates range from 20,000 to 100,000.[114] Whatever the exact count, the repression clearly cast a pall over the lives of huge numbers of people.

Public opinion was shocked by the brutal punitive expeditions. The chances for a reconciliation between society and the government, slight in the fall of 1905, virtually evaporated in the winter and spring of 1906. A large sector of the liberal movement, never convinced that the government had been sincere in granting the October Manifesto, now claimed that the autocratic regime had indeed not undergone any fundamental change.

This sentiment was most vividly expressed by the historian E. D. Grimm in a lead article in the liberal journal *Pravo*. Grimm contended that the government had reverted to the practices of Russia's most brutal rulers. In support of his indictment, he argued that the "'constitutional' regime established by Count Witte's Manifesto" was even more repressive than that of "Plehve's regime . . . [for] even Plehve did not hit upon the idea of shooting [people] without a trial according to prepared lists of the security police, [or] of administrative exile for parents whose children had been involved in disorders at their schools, et cetera."[115]

Clearly, Witte's political program and his personal career had suffered a severe blow. Undermined by the Tsar and his Court camarilla, thwarted in his attempts to gain the support of liberals, buffeted by mass unrest, Witte failed to establish the rule of law, the sine qua non for the survival of his experiment. He remained in office until April 1906, but no one looked to him any longer as the man to steer Russia along a path of reform and pacification. That task was taken up by another statesman, as was the attempt to institutionalize the political changes that had been introduced since October. For despite the government's repression, the revolution was not fully beaten back and the Tsar's concessions could not be entirely nullified. In his last weeks in office, Witte played a role in the deliberations on the Fundamental State Laws, which defined the powers of the Tsar and the upcoming Duma and the rights of the people, but he was not the guiding spirit. His main achievement was to secure a long-sought foreign loan; other than that, it seemed to many people, Witte was simply marking time. The Tsar, who had never trusted or liked him, was now listening to very different voices.

Conclusion

THE POLITICAL SITUATION in Russia early in 1906 was bewildering. After fifteen months of revolutionary turbulence a climax had been reached in the conflicts between the state and society, but it was not clear whether this portended a lasting settlement or merely a lull. No consensus had emerged among either the articulate defenders or the opponents of the government on the meaning of the frightful events that had brought the Empire to the brink of collapse. Nor did either group formulate a political strategy that commanded the assent of broad sectors of public opinion. With the exception of an occasional note of optimism emanating from senior officials, the dominant mood was one of foreboding; the revolution, it was widely believed, had not yet run its course.

Count Witte, temporarily out of the doldrums, indicated in a private conversation on January 7 that he was "in good spirits and full of confidence as to the future." He regretted having had to use force against the radical left, but he affirmed that the revolution was now crushed and that order would be completely restored within a few weeks. Heartened by the "thorough loyalty of the troops," Witte anticipated no new rebellions and looked forward to the opening of the State Duma in April, which would consolidate the political arrangements outlined in the October Manifesto. He also expected Western nations soon to abandon their insistence on the reestablishment of order everywhere in the Empire before granting Russia a loan. After all, if the Russian economy collapsed, "the shock would resound throughout the whole financial world." To Western financiers he would say: "Give me the money and I will restore tranquillity." [1]

Less than three weeks after Witte made these remarks, Count A. K. Benkendorf, the Russian Ambassador to London, voiced radically different views. During a brief stay in St. Petersburg, Benkendorf confided to his British counterpart that conditions in Russia were "worse than he had expected." In his conversations with senior officials in the government and activists in various political parties, Benkendorf could not "discover any proof that there existed anywhere the elements of a permanent reorganization of society." Although he did not believe that the elections to the Duma would be canceled, he detected a "general feeling of uncertainty" about the political role of the legislature. He himself feared that since the October Manifesto was a general document, the government would easily find ways of nullifying "the most important points in it." Most distressing of all, Benkendorf had met no one who trusted Witte to carry out his promises of reform.[2] The German Ambassador to St. Petersburg was even more pessimistic. Convinced that the revolution had not been "definitively crushed," he compared Russia to a volcano that shortly might erupt much more violently than it had in 1905.[3]

The ultra-right, which, as we have seen, maintained close ties with the Tsar and the Court camarilla, denounced the revolution and the October settlement as an unmitigated and intolerable disaster: the educational system was a shambles, undermined morally and intellectually by the radicals; mindless reforms had corrupted the religious foundations of the country; and the political reforms could only result in the continuation and intensification of domestic strife. "One of two things will happen," the right-wing *Moskovskie vedomosti* declared: "either the Duma will deprive the Tsar of His Autocratic Powers or the Tsar will deprive the rebellious Duma of its powers. In either case, unrest and civil war are inevitable."[4] As the Russian Monarchist Party made clear, the ultra-right did not acknowledge that the authority of the Tsar had been in any way diluted: "As for the Manifesto of October 17, the Sovereign, as always, bore the title of 'Autocrat,' [and] did not [say] any words renouncing autocracy or proclaiming any kind of constitution." Ultimately, the extreme right believed that Russia could solve its problems solely by turning to the religious realm: "Without God's help we can do nothing. We humbly beseech Him to save Russia. We place all our hopes in Him!"[5]

Political activists in the opposition movement also disagreed among themselves over the outcome of the revolution thus far. The Octobrists, who represented the industrial and commercial classes and the moderate gentry, were divided into two broad factions. One group insisted that anarchy was now the main threat to the country; it therefore placed primary emphasis on the restoration of law and order and refused to criticize the government's repressive policies. The other faction, eager to see the October settlement consolidated, warned that the government was jeopardizing its own proclaimed program by its failure both to hold elections at an early date and to end the arbitrary punishment of suspected rebels and agitators. D. N. Shipov, a founder of the Union of October 17 whose views were very moderate, feared that the party had been penetrated by "frightened" elements who, "if not hostile, were not very sympathetic to the liberation movement." Their only concern, he said, was to protect "their wealth and narrow class interests."[6]

The Kadet Party oscillated in its assessments of the political situation in Russia and hence could not settle on a consistent strategy. Early in January, when the revolutionary tide was receding, the party stopped excoriating the October Manifesto and in effect conceded that the reforms of the previous fall constituted a fundamental change in the political system. Three months later, when the autocracy had shown a new resolve to assert its authority and the masses had given evidence of continuing hostility toward the government, the Kadets once again turned militant. Persuaded that a new revolutionary impetus might be in the offing after all, they adopted a more radical stance than before. They now declared that they would rely on the activism of the masses to bring about further political changes as well as extensive agrarian reforms.[7]

The radical left parties were the most steadfast in predicting renewed revolutionary momentum and in rejecting any accommodation with the new government. But even among them, differences emerged that affected their strategies. The Bolsheviks and Socialist Revolutionaries firmly expected new stirrings from below in the spring of 1906; hence they urged their followers not to take part in the elections to the Duma, whose only purpose, they claimed, was to confuse the masses and divert them from the revolutionary path.[8] The Menshevik leaders also foresaw a new and massive outbreak of unrest in the near future, but several argued that workers should still vote because the Duma could be useful in accelerating the revolutionary process. By the summer of 1906, however, both the Social Democratic factions and the Socialist Revolutionaries would come out in favor of participation in future elections.[9] Apparently they had concluded that the masses wanted to take part in the voting and that the State Duma could indeed be exploited for antigovernment agitation.

That the state of affairs in Russia was unsettled is revealed by the fact that the proponents of each of the positions described here could marshal an impressive array of evidence in support of their case. Prime Minister Witte had brought the October general strike to an end, but he had not resolved any of the basic issues that had provoked the political crisis in the first place. The government and the opposition remained at loggerheads; new confrontations were inevitable.

Although Witte indulged in some wishful thinking in his survey of conditions in the Empire, he was right about the general drift of events: unrest had subsided and the revolutionaries were lying low. The radicals in Moscow, who had made the boldest attempt to overthrow the autocracy, had been effectively muzzled. Accordingly, by early February the government eased the extraordinary measures imposed on the city in December: restrictions on traffic were lifted and theaters and restaurants were again permitted to remain open at night. Patrols of armed policemen and Cossacks still roamed the streets to ward off potential troublemakers, but the population appeared to be calm. Many workers who had left Moscow for the countryside were returning, and only two factories in the city and surrounding regions still remained idle. The government had closed down the radical press; *Russkie vedomosti* was now the sole legally published newspaper in Moscow that was openly sympathetic to the opposition.[10] Similar trends were at work elsewhere in the Empire, prompting foreign residents in St. Petersburg to conclude that the government was making "gradual progress" throughout the country in "restoring external order" and that the people were becoming resigned to the status quo.[11]

But this account of Russia's return to tranquillity tells only part of the story. From one city after another, reports reached the capital of assassinations of officials, politically inspired robberies, and incidents of arson. The number of assassinations had actually declined from 31 in October 1905 to 4 in November and 21 in December, but it rose to 34 in January and remained fairly high in February and March (19 each month). Moreover, revolutionaries continued to operate illegal presses and bomb factories, despite the best efforts of local authorities to stamp them out. In various outlying regions of the Empire, there were still pockets of unrest, and the calm in the countryside appeared to be merely a symptom of the peasants' winter lethargy.[12] Some of the violence from below was a response to the government's repressive policies,[13] but much of it was perpetrated by revolutionaries (mainly SRs) who had all along favored terror as a political weapon.

Finally, Witte's continuing inability to assert firm leadership over the government inevitably raised questions about its durability. The Tsar had reneged on his promise to create a unified ministry, which left Witte with little more than the title of Prime Minister. Four ministers were not obliged to report to him at all, and the reactionary Minister of Internal Affairs, Durnovo, was known to settle many of the most important questions with Nicholas himself, without even bothering to inform the Prime Minister. Witte also clashed with the Ministers of Commerce and of Industry and Agriculture, which led to the resignation of two of the more competent and enlightened members of the government.[14] The press speculated endlessly about the date of Witte's removal from office, and it was widely believed that the Prime Minister held on as long as he did only because "no one else [had] the courage to assume the task of controlling the nation" and no one else commanded the prestige to float a loan in Western Europe, without which the government would soon be bankrupt.[15]

That Russia was still in the midst of a political crisis early in 1906 is not surprising, considering the nature of the cataclysm it had endured. The revolution, by every standard, was unique. Unprecedented in scale and ferocity, the upheaval had achieved only a partial victory for the opposition. Not only were there no fundamental changes in the economic and social structure of society, but even in the political realm the changes were so general as to leave open the question of their ultimate significance. To be sure, in October Tsarism had been on the verge of collapse and had survived only by yielding important ground to the opposition. But three months later the bureaucracy remained essentially intact and the army, though riddled with unrest, for the most part retained its loyalty to the Tsar. The old regime still disposed of adequate means for a reassertion of autocratic authority.

Nevertheless, even after the balance of power had shifted in favor of the government in the wake of the Moscow uprising, the Tsar did not dare rescind all the concessions of 1905. Much as he wanted to, Nicholas did not cancel the elections to the State Duma, outlaw political parties, suppress all the trade unions or the workers' cultural organizations, or reimpose the pre-1904 censorship. He was inhibited by the working of a critical, if intangible, change in the people in the past fifteen months; they had become accustomed, as one foreign observer put it, "to think and to talk freely."[16] These six words neatly summarized one of the most fundamental consequences of the revolution: the political mobilization of masses of people in all walks of life. Once having been galvanized to political action, the people would not easily revert to their previous status of apathetic subjects. Or, as the eminent sociologist Max Weber noted at the time in his otherwise pessimistic assessment of the situation in Russia, "after all that had happened [in the relations] between the Tsar and his subjects," the autocrat would find it very difficult to rule as he had before the revolution. Too many people had successfully defied his authority.[17] Nicholas had no choice but to tolerate some form of mass participation in the political process.

The second fundamental consequence of the revolution, inseparable from the first, was the Tsar's acknowledgment in the October Manifesto that he was no longer an autocratic ruler in the sense that his word, and his word alone, was law. However much he and his advisers might later try to circumvent this interpretation of the manifesto, it was clear beyond doubt that in committing himself to the "unbreakable rule that no law can become effective without the approval of the [elected] State Duma," Nicholas had renounced his prerogative to rule as an absolute monarch. This action marked a decisive departure from a system of rule that had prevailed in Russia for centuries, and as such constituted a signal achievement for the opposition.

Yet it remains something of a puzzle how, after a period of immense political and social turbulence that threatened the Empire with total collapse, the outcome could be so unclear and ambiguous. One of the more intriguing aspects of the revolution in 1904 and 1905 is that on several occasions the autocracy could have obtained a clearer and more lasting settlement of the conflict, a settlement it would have found preferable to the one it accepted to end the general strike. Late in 1904, moderate sentiment was still strong enough among zemstvo activists and the middle classes for these groups to have been mollified by the concessions offered in the Bulygin constitution (of August 1905). A more forthcoming and sincere response to the personal appeal of the zemstvo activists on June 6, 1905, would most probably have had the same effect—as would the promulgation of the electoral law of December 11, had it occurred two months earlier. Tsar Nicholas never seized the opportune moment to conciliate the opposition. Unswerving in the conviction that he must defend the principle of unlimited autocracy at all costs and that the overwhelming majority of the people did not want the principle violated, he made concessions grudgingly, only when he had no choice, and even then he failed to act boldly and sincerely.

Intransigence and narrow-mindedness account for the behavior of the Tsar and his most powerful advisers at Court. They could not bear to yield one iota of their prerogatives and they could not grasp the significance of the changes Russia had undergone over the previous few decades, changes that made it impossible to maintain the status quo. This unyielding mentality of rigid conservatism explains their failure not only to take timely measures to halt the revolutionary upsurge but also to distinguish between moderate critics of the old order and radicals determined to overturn it altogether. In addition, it explains their callous reaction to Gapon's peaceful procession and their willingness to resort to brute force to crush their opponents.

In view of the autocracy's inability to bring about a viable settlement of the national crisis, why was the opposition unable to score a decisive and lasting victory over the old regime? Although initially, in 1904, the opposition constituted a numerically small force, it gained steadily in adherents as the government committed one blunder after another. In response to the growing activism of workers and peasants, the opposition moved continually to the left, and by the fall of 1905 it was strong enough to bring the government to its knees. Yet it could not consolidate the rather liberal order—the Days of Liberty—that emerged after the general strike.

No one familiar with the major events of 1904 and 1905 can be surprised at the opposition's failure thoroughly to dismantle the autocratic system of rule. As has been shown in this study, the groups that propelled the revolution—the liberals, the workers, the peasants, and the national minorities—never coordinated their campaigns against the government. That a simultaneous offensive by all segments of the opposition could have toppled the old regime is suggested by the fact that when only two groups (workers and liberals) cooperated in October, they brought a decisive victory within reach. Then the natural divisions within the opposition, fed by both the growing militancy of the workers and the radical left and the liberals' fear of anarchy, greatly weakened the movement. Finally, when the revolutionary left decided to act on its own and sparked an armed uprising, the authorities could again count on their ultimate weapon, the army, which faithfully did their bidding.

These factors, however, do not explain the collapse of the experiment in freedom, which lasted for six weeks during the fall of 1905. The question is worth pondering, not only because the Days of Liberty marked the high point of the revolution, when Russia appeared to be well on the road toward an open society, but also because their preservation was in the interest both of the most prominent statesman, Witte, and of important social groups. The Prime Minister's whole program of pacification through reform depended on the success of the experiment in freedom. For the liberals, the new dispensation marked the realization of one of their most cherished dreams, a political order in which all the people exercised civil liberties. Such an order did not enjoy the same esteem among the revolutionary left, but the radicals could not dismiss the advantages of an open society. Their principal constituency, the industrial workers, had become a powerful factor in the political arena. Never before had radicals in Russia (or anywhere else, for that matter) enjoyed so many opportunities to articulate their views, organize mass movements, and exert influence over public affairs. Yet all the individuals and groups who stood to benefit from the preservation of the experiment in freedom contributed to its demise.

Educated society's deep distrust of the authorities was a major factor in deterring liberals from serving in Witte's government and thus helping him to carry out his program. But the Prime Minister himself did not help his cause by insisting on the appointment of the reactionary Durnovo to the all-important post of Minister of Internal Affairs. The radical left, responding in part to the impatience of the masses, adopted militant tactics bound to frighten the government as well as many liberals otherwise inclined to sympathize with the revolutionaries. As if these developments were not enough to endanger the new political arrangements, the country unexpectedly experienced an outbreak of mass violence against Jews and opponents of the Tsar, which further undermined the public's confidence in the Prime Minister's ability and even determination to establish a legal order in Russia.

At bottom, what all the failed negotiations between Witte and the liberals and the extremism of the radicals and of unruly sectors of the populace comes down to is that in the Russia of 1905 citizens of all classes lacked political experience, itself a legacy of the long-standing exclusion of the people from the political process. By experience in this context I do not mean simply service in the government. Witte had that in abundance, but he was still not politically experienced in the larger sense of the term. Though very intelligent, thoughtful, and shrewd, he was handicapped by the fact that all his life he had operated in a political system which was highly centralized and inhospitable to the idea that power should be shared. A serious challenge of authority seemed inconceivable to Witte. In this connection, it is noteworthy that he himself was obsequious and irresolute in the presence of the Tsar. During meetings with the sovereign he often behaved "like a junior officer—bowing excessively, his hands at the seams of his trousers, and displaying little of his bold and independent mind." [18] By the same token, Witte was not accustomed to exchanging ideas with men who occupied positions less exalted than his and who differed with him, or, more important, to reaching compromises with political opponents. What was true of Witte applied with even greater force to the liberals and radicals, whose involvement in practical affairs was much more limited.

The charged atmosphere made it impossible for the Days of Liberty to survive without a corps of senior officials and an educated public prepared to enter into compromises and to exercise self-restraint. The county teetered on the edge of anarchy, and passions ran high in every sector of the population. Supporters of the old regime for the first time sensed that all might be lost; opponents glimpsed the possibility of total victory. Both were thoroughly mistaken, for the essential meaning of the Days of Liberty was that the government had acknowledged a significant, but by no means total, victory by the opposition. The consolidation of that new, precarious balance between state and society required political experience—or wisdom—of the highest degree. When virtually everyone in a position of leadership failed to show wisdom, the Days of Liberty came to an end. This was the political tragedy for Russia in 1905.

Even so, the revolution had changed the political landscape of the Empire. Although the government still controlled the levers of power and had regained much of its self-confidence and authority, the opposition remained vibrant enough to continue the struggle, for it had forced Tsar Nicholas to yield on the principle of autocracy. The revolution now entered its third phase, comparable to the initial stage in 1904 because politics came to be the most characteristic, though not the only, mode of struggle.

Of course, the similarities between the first and third phases should not be overdrawn. In 1904, relatively small groups of the population (mostly from the middle class and the gentry) engaged in illegal campaigns for political reform. By contrast, the upheaval of 1905 had resulted in a vastly expanded political arena. The suffrage enacted in December was restricted, unequal, and indirect, but it nevertheless allowed hundreds of thousands of citizens to register their political preferences at the polls. Although operating under constraints, political parties could broadcast their message and organize their followers. Because of the activism of the workers and peasants, political parties increasingly emphasized economic and social reform. If the political process had not been democratized, it had been made accessible to hitherto powerless segments of the population.

The critical question early in 1906 was the durability of the new relationship between the state and society that had been created by the October settlement. It was an untidy settlement, suggesting a form of power-sharing between the Tsar and the people without defining the role of each and without depriving the authorities of the capacity to reassert their lost position. Good will and political sagacity of a high order would be required to breathe life into the new arrangements and make them work. Judging from the history of the revolution in 1904 and 1905, the prospects for success were not reassuring.

. . . .

Reference Matter

Notes

The following abbreviations are used in the Notes. Complete authors' names, titles, and publication data are given in the Bibliography, pp. 383–97.

AMAE Archives du Ministère des Affaires Etrangères. Russie: Direction Politique, nouvelle série, Paris.

BDFA British Documents on Foreign Affairs. Public Record Office, London.

Dokumenty i materialy *Revoliutsiia 1905–7 gg. v Rossii: dokumenty i materialy.* Eds. A. Pankratova et al. 8 vols. in 17 parts. Moscow, 1955–65.

HHSA Haus-Hof-und-Staatsarchiv. Russland, Berichte. Vienna.

Hoover Inst. Hoover Institution on War, Revolution, and Peace. Stanford University, Stanford, Calif. FV Coll.: Felix Volkhovsky Collection; OA: Okhrana Archive.

Obshchestvennoe dvizhenie *Obshchestvennoe dvizhenie v nachale XX-go veka.* Eds. L. Martov, P. Maslov, and A. Potresov. 4 vols. St. Petersburg, 1909–14.

PAAA Politisches Archiv des Auswärtigen Amts. Abteilung A, Russland. Bonn.

USDMR U.S. Dispatches from U.S. Ministers to Russia, 1808–1906. National Archives, Washington, D.C.

Introduction

1. A scholarly bibliography on the upheaval published in 1930 ran to 715 pages. See Kommunisticheskaia Akademiia, *Pervaia russkaia revoliutsiia: Uka-*

zatel literatury. On Soviet scholarship on 1905, see also Sablinsky, "The All-Russian Railroad Union," p. 114.

2. V. I. Lenin, *"Left-Wing" Communism—An Infantile Disorder*, in Tucker, ed., *The Lenin Anthology*, pp. 555–56.

3. See Ascher, "Soviet Historians and the Revolution of 1905."

4. See, for example, Derenkovskii et al., "Osnovnye itogi i izucheniia istorii pervoi russkoi revoliutsii," p. 47, and A. L. Narochnitskii, "Istoriografiia revoliutsii 1905–1907 gg. Osnovnye itogi i zadachii izucheniia," in Naumov et al., eds., *Aktualnye problemy sovetskoi istoriografii*, p. 17.

5. See Ascher, "Soviet Historians and the Revolution of 1905," pp. 484–85, 488. See also Isaac Deutscher, *Stalin: A Political Biography* (London, 1949), p. 66.

6. I have in mind the works of the following scholars: Victoria Bonnell, John Brock, John Bushnell, Laura Engelstein, Shmuel Galai, Sidney Harcave, Manfred Hildermeier, J. L. H. Keep, Roberta Manning, Howard Mehlinger and John Thompson, Maureen Perrie, Richard Pipes, Walter Sablinsky, Jonathan Sanders, Robert Slusser, Nathan Smith, and Theodore Von Laue.

7. German Ambassador in St. Petersburg to Berlin, Jan. 15, 1906, PAAA.

Chapter 1

1. Miliukov, *Russia and Its Crisis*, pp. 14–15.

2. Bompard to Delcassé, Aug. 30, 1904, AMAE, I.

3. *Svod zakonov Rossiiskoi Imperii*, eds. A. F. Volkov and Iu. D. Filipov (St. Petersburg, 1904), I, p. 2.

4. *Russkie vedomosti*, Sept. 21, 1905, p. 3.

5. Miliukov, *Russia and Its Crisis*, p. 148.

6. Weissman, *Reform in Tsarist Russia*, p. 11.

7. Gerassimoff, *Der Kampf gegen die erste russische Revolution*, p. 35.

8. Gurko, *Figures and Features of the Past*, p. 14.

9. Petrunkevich, "Iz zapisok obshchestvennogo deiatelia," p. 287.

10. Bing, ed., *The Secret Letters of the Last Tsar*, p. 160.

11. Byrnes, *Pobedonostsev*, p. 24; Adams, "Pobedonostsev and the Rule of Firmness," pp. 132–39.

12. Rogger, "The Beilis Case," p. 623.

13. Vitte, *Vospominaniia*, I, p. 269.

14. Quoted in Struve, "My Contacts with Rodichev," p. 350.

15. Rogger, *Russia*, p. 32.

16. Judge, *Plehve*, pp. 29–31.

17. *Ibid.*, pp. 2–3.

18. *Ibid.*, pp. 78–79.

19. Gurko, *Figures and Features*, p. 120.

20. Astrov, *Vospominaniia*, pp. 274–75.

21. The details on Witte's biography in this and the next paragraph are taken from Von Laue, *Sergei Witte*, pp. 39–70. See also Dillon, "Two Russian Statesmen," pp. 411–17.

22. Miliukov, *Vospominaniia*, pp. 316–17, gives a vivid portrayal of Witte's personal qualities. The quoted phrase is on p. 316.

23. Von Laue, *Sergei Witte*, pp. 1–3.

24. Rogger, *Russia*, p. 107.

25. Dubrovskii, *Krestianskoe dvizhenie*, p. 34.

26. Tugan-Baranovskii, *Russkaia fabrika*, p. 303.

27. Arcadius Kahan has argued that the government's fiscal policies were actually an "obstacle" to "more vigorous industrial development of Russia." See his "Government Policies and the Industrialization of Russia," pp. 460–77.

28. Blackwell, *The Industrialization of Russia*, p. 47; Seton-Watson, *The Decline*, p. 118; Miller, *Economic Development*, pp. 125–30 and *passim*.

29. Rimlinger, "Management," p. 227.

30. More realistic discussions of the "labor question" had been conducted as early as the 1850's and 1860's. See Zelnik, *Labor and Society*, pp. 69–159.

31. Rimlinger, "Autocracy," p. 91.

32. *Ibid.*, p. 70; Rimlinger, "Management," p. 232.

33. We have some statistics on the number of seasonal workers. From 1886 to 1893, about 30 percent of all workers still spent some time in the villages, but there were marked variations between industrial regions. For example, only about 11 percent of the laborers in St. Petersburg retained ties with the countryside, whereas 76 percent in the Voronezh district did so. Skilled workers were more likely than unskilled workers to remain permanently in industrial regions. See Rimlinger, "Management," p. 228. For an interesting study of the cultural and political significance of the ties between workers and their villages, see Johnson, *Peasant and Proletarian*. See also Reginald E. Zelnik, "The Peasant and the Factory," in Vucinich, ed., *The Peasant in Nineteenth-Century Russia*, pp. 158–90. Good accounts of working-class conditions and official policies toward workers can be found in Glickman, *Russian Factory Women*, pp. 5–21; Owen, *Capitalism and Politics*, pp. 120–36; Von Laue, "Tsarist Labor Policy," pp. 135–45; and Laverychev, *Tsarizm*.

34. Owen, *Capitalism and Politics*, p. 131.

35. Some very moving accounts by workers themselves of conditions in factories are now available in English: Zelnik, trans. and ed., *A Radical Worker*; and Bonnell, ed., *The Russian Worker*. Both books contain informative and perceptive introductions.

36. Rimlinger, "Autocracy," pp. 72–73.

37. *Ibid.*, p. 78.

38. Laverychev, *Tsarizm*, pp. 60–62; Rimlinger, "Management," pp. 239–41. On the background to the factory legislation, see Giffen, "In Quest of an Effective Program of Factory Legislation in Russia."

39. Laverychev, *Tsarizm*, pp. 133–35; Rimlinger, "Autocracy," pp. 81–89. On the strike movement, see also Varzar, *Statistika*, p. 5. The statistics on the strike movement refer only to the establishments under the supervision of the Factory Inspectorate.

40. Quoted in Gordon, *Workers*, p. 29.

41. Judge, *Plehve*, pp. 124–25.

42. Quoted in Wolfe, *Three Who Made a Revolution*, p. 272.

43. Gerassimoff, *Der Kampf*, p. 32.

44. The most detailed discussion of Zubatov's scheme is in Schneiderman, *Sergei Zubatov and Revolutionary Marxism*.

45. Pipes, *Russia Under the Old Regime*, p. 161.

46. Robinson, *Rural Russia*, p. 174.

47. There has recently been a controversy over whether the lot of the peasants actually worsened. See Simms, "The Crisis in Russian Agriculture"; Hamburg,

"The Crisis in Russian Agriculture"; Simms, "On Missing the Point"; John T. Sanders, "'Once More into the Breach, Dear Friends'"; Simms, "Reply."

48. Dubrovskii, *Krestianskoe dvizhenie*, p. 26; Miliukov, *Russia and Its Crisis*, p. 333.

49. Rogger, *Russia*, p. 88.

50. Dubrovskii, *Krestianskoe dvizhenie*, pp. 22–23.

51. For a recent analysis of the background to the introduction of the land captains, see Pearson, "The Origins of Alexander III's Land Captains."

52. Robinson, *Rural Russia*, pp. 138–39.

53. Rogger, *Russia*, p. 89.

54. *Ibid.*, pp. 90–91.

55. Hamburg, "The Russian Nobility."

56. On the difficulties of introducing modern methods of farming, see Queen, "The McCormick Harvesting Machine Company in Russia," pp. 172–73.

57. Rogger, *Russia*, pp. 88–94; Von Laue, *Sergei Witte*, pp. 172–73.

58. The problems encountered in any attempt to define Russian (or Western) liberalism rigidly are perceptively analyzed in Raeff, "Some Reflections on Russian Liberalism," pp. 218–30.

59. Quoted in Frankel, ed., *Vladimir Akimov*, p. 10. For a discussion of Plekhanov's Marxism, see *ibid.*, pp. 7–17, and Baron, *Plekhanov*, pp. 89–116.

60. On the intelligentsia, see Malia, "What Is the Intelligentsia?" The most comprehensive works on Russian liberalism are Leontowitsch, *Geschichte des Liberalismus in Russland*, and George Fischer, *Russian Liberalism*. See also Pipes, *Struve: Liberal on the Left*, pp. 284–88, for a brief analysis of liberalism in the last decades of the nineteenth century.

61. Judge, *Plehve*, p. 59; Seton-Watson, *The Decline*, pp. 471–72. The best overall study of the role of the zemstvos is Emmons and Vucinich, eds., *The Zemstvo in Russia*.

62. Zimmerman, "Between Revolution and Reaction," p. 15.

63. Gessen, *V dvukh vekakh*, p. 182.

64. Emmons, *Formation*, pp. 3–4.

65. On the politics of the entrepreneurial class, see Owen, *Capitalism and Politics*, and Rieber, *Merchants and Entrepreneurs*.

66. Pipes, *Struve: Liberal on the Left*, p. 310.

67. The funds came from a certain D. E. Zhukovsky and from contributions by the constitutional zemtsy. See *ibid.*, pp. 311–12.

68. *Ibid.*, p. 326.

69. *Ibid.*, p. 319.

70. "Demarkatsionnaia liniia," *Osvobozhdenie*, no. 19 (Mar. 19, 1903), p. 329, quoted in Freeze, "A National Liberation Movement," p. 86.

71. Kassow, "The Russian University in Crisis," pp. 40–43.

72. For details, see *ibid.*, pp. 130–208.

73. Emmons, "Russia's Banquet Campaign," p. 81.

74. The quotation, by A. N. Potresov, is taken from Tucker, ed., *The Lenin Anthology*, p. xlvi. For a good analysis of Lenin's political ideas and his personality, see Tucker's introduction to the *Anthology*.

75. Lenin, *What Is to Be Done?*, pp. 33, 119.

76. For details, see Wolfe, *Three Who Made a Revolution*, pp. 230–48.

77. Quoted in Ascher, *Pavel Axelrod*, p. 211.

78. Radkey, *Agrarian Foes*, pp. 3–46; Hildermeier, *Die Sozialrevolutionäre Partei Russlands*, pp. 58–108; Rogger, *Russia*, pp. 151–54.

79. For good overviews of the national problem in Russia, see Pipes, *The Formation of the Soviet Union*, pp. 1–49, and Rogger, *Russia*, pp. 182–206.

80. Rogger, *Russia*, pp. 199–206.

Chapter 2

1. Astrov, *Vospominaniia*, p. 281.

2. Gurko, *Figures and Features of the Past*, p. 253.

3. See, for example, Dukes, *A History of Russia*, p. 179; Malozemoff, *Russian Far Eastern Policy, 1881–1904*, p. 227; *Istoriia KPSS*, II, p. 11; Piaskovskii, *Revoliutsiia 1905–1907 gg. v Rossii*, p. 28.

4. Vitte, *Vospominaniia*, I, p. 239; "Dnevnik A. N. Kuropatkina," p. 94. For an analysis of the reliability of Witte's memoirs, see Ananich and Ganelin, "Opyt kritiki memuarov S. Iu. Vitte." On Plehve's doubts about the wisdom of going to war against Japan, see also L. Aehrenthal to His Excellency Count Goluchowski, July 24/Aug. 6, 1904, HHSA, and Judge, *Plehve*, pp. 173–74.

5. The preceding two paragraphs are based on White, *The Diplomacy of the Russo-Japanese War*, pp. 78–81; Von Laue, *Sergei Witte*, pp. 147–57, 239–48; *Obshchestvennoe dvizhenie*, II, part 1, pp. 10–12.

6. Esthus, "Nicholas II and the Russo-Japanese War," p. 397.

7. *Obshchestvennoe dvizhenie*, II, part 1, pp. 15–16; Galai, "The Impact of War on Russian Liberals in 1904–5," pp. 87–88.

8. *Obshchestvennoe dvizhenie*, II, part 1, p. 19.

9. Maurice, "The Russo-Japanese War," pp. 577–79.

10. Kokovtsov, *Out of My Past*, pp. 9, 14.

11. *Novoe vremia*, Jan. 28, 1904, p. 3, and Jan. 25, 1904, p. 3.

12. Bohachevsky-Chomiak, *Sergei Trubetskoi*, p. 120.

13. *Russkie vedomosti*, Jan. 26, 1904, p. 1; *Vestnik Evropy*, 39 (Mar. 1904), p. 345.

14. Astrov, *Vospominaniia*, p. 280; Galai, "Impact," p. 88; *Novoe vremia*, Jan. 28, 1904, p. 3, and Mar. 31, 1904, p. 1; Voitinskii, *Gody pobed i porazhenii*, I, p. 10; *Obshchestvennoe dvizhenie*, II, part 1, p. 36.

15. Pipes, *Struve: Liberal on the Left*, pp. 338–44.

16. Riha, *A Russian European: Paul Miliukov*, pp. 57–58.

17. Quoted in Getzler, *Martov*, p. 97.

18. Plekhanov, quoted in Baron, "Plekhanov and the Revolution of 1905," p. 136. On Plekhanov and 1905, see also Baron, *Plekhanov: The Father of Russian Marxism*, pp. 261–73.

19. Wolfe, *Three Who Made a Revolution*, p. 278; Keep, *The Rise of Social Democracy*, pp. 183–84.

20. Konni Zilliacus to Felix Volkhovsky, Mar. 1 and Mar. 31, 1904, Hoover Inst., FV Coll., Box 5.

21. George Kennan to Felix Volkhovsky, Dec. 14, 1904, *ibid.*, Box 9.

22. Dillon, *The Eclipse of Russia*, pp. 291–93, 184; White, *Diplomacy*, pp. 14–42; Futrell, "Colonel Akashi and Japanese Contacts with Russian Revolutionaries in 1904–5."

23. Hart, "The Russo-Japanese War."

24. See Maurice, "The Russo-Japanese War," for an analysis of the military campaigns.

25. The information on the Swedish attaché's report is in a dispatch of the

U.S. Embassy in St. Petersburg to Secretary of State John Hay, Apr. 12/25, 1905, USDMR.

26. *Novoe vremia*, Apr. 24, 1904, p. 3.

27. *Vestnik Evropy*, 39 (July 1904), p. 362; *ibid.* (Aug. 1904), p. 782; *ibid.* (Nov. 1904), p. 374.

28. *Russkoe bogatstvo*, no. 12 (Dec. 1904), pp. 182–83.

29. Astrov, *Vospominaniia*, pp. 280–81.

30. Bohachevsky-Chomiak, *Sergei Trubetskoi*, p. 130.

31. Petrunkevich, "Iz zapisok obshchestvennogo deiatelia," pp. 343, 345.

32. *Obshchestvennoe dvizhenie*, IV, part 1, p. 37.

33. *Ibid.*, pp. 39–41, 43.

34. *Russkie vedomosti*, May 8, 1904, p. 2.

35. *Ibid.*, Oct. 5, 1904, p. 2.

36. *Russkoe bogatstvo*, no. 9 (Sept. 1904), part II, pp. 157–58.

37. Gessen, *V dvukh vekakh: zhiznennyi otchet*, p. 175.

38. *Novoe vremia*, July 16, 1904, p. 1; Judge, *Plehve*, pp. 238–39.

39. Ascher, trans. and ed., "The Coming Storm: The Austro-Hungarian Embassy on Russia's Internal Crisis, 1902–1906," pp. 154–55.

40. Galai, "Impact," p. 92.

41. Gurko, *Figures and Features*, p. 292.

42. Bompard to Delcassé, Sept. 28, 1904, AMAE.

43. Gurko, *Figures and Features*, p. 194.

44. *Russkie vedomosti*, Sept. 18, 1904, p. 1, and Sept. 29, 1904, pp. 2–3.

45. *Ibid.*, Sept. 22, 1904, p. 3, and Sept. 28, p. 2.

46. *Ibid.*, Sept. 24, 1904, p. 1.

47. Pipes, *Struve: Liberal on the Left*, pp. 361–62.

48. *Moskovskie vedomosti*, Sept. 18, p. 1.

49. *Grazhdanin*, Sept. 12, 1904, pp. 18–20.

50. *Pravo*, no. 41 (Oct. 25, 1904), column 3400.

51. *Russkie vedomosti*, Oct. 26, 1904, p. 1.

52. Gessen, *V dvukh vekakh*, pp. 176–77.

53. Smith, "The Constitutional-Democratic Movement," pp. 216–17.

54. Petrunkevich, "Iz zapisok," p. 354.

55. Treadgold, *Lenin and His Rivals*, p. 81. The following eight organizations attended the Paris meeting: Union of Liberation, Polish National League, Finnish Party of Active Resistance, Latvian Social Democrats, Socialist Revolutionaries, Georgian Socialist-Revolutionary-Federalists, Polish Socialists, and the Armenian Revolutionary Federation. The Soviet historian K. F. Shatsillo minimized the importance of the meeting in Paris. See Shatsillo, "Iz istorii osvoboditelnogo dvizheniia v Rossii."

56. The statement is reprinted in Smith, "The Constitutional-Democratic Movement," pp. 220–21; see also Pipes, *Struve: Liberal on the Left*, pp. 365–66, and Miliukov, *Russia and Its Crisis*, pp. 381–84.

57. Pipes, *Struve: Liberal on the Left*, pp. 367–68.

58. Fischer, *Russian Liberalism*, p. 178.

59. Rainey, "The Union of 17 October," p. 40; Budberg, "Sezd zemskikh deiatelei 6–9 noiabria 1904 goda v Peterburge," p. 72; Petrunkevich, "Iz zapisok," p. 357.

60. *Russkie vedomosti*, Oct. 12, 1904, p. 2, and Oct. 19, p. 1.

61. Budberg, "Sezd zemskikh," p. 75; Petrunkevich, "Iz zapisok," p. 358.

62. Budberg, "Sezd zemskikh," p. 81.

63. *Ibid.*, p. 79.

64. The resolution is reprinted in *Chastnoe soveshchanie zemskikh*, pp. 141–43, and may be found in translation in Smith, "The Constitutional-Democratic Movement," pp. 240–43.

65. *Chastnoe soveshchanie*, p. 81.

66. *Ibid.*, pp. 58–61.

67. *Ibid.*, p. 14.

68. *Ibid.*, pp. 61–63, 65–66; Petrunkevich, "Iz zapisok," p. 359; Budberg, "Sezd zemskikh," pp. 82–84.

69. *Ibid.*, p. 84.

70. Shipov, *Vospominaniia i dumy o perezhitom*, p. 583.

71. *Obshchestvennoe dvizhenie*, II, part 1, p. 38; Petrunkevich, "Iz zapisok," p. 360.

72. Quoted in Pipes, *Struve: Liberal on the Left*, p. 370.

73. See Smith, "The Constitutional-Democratic Movement," p. 263, for a discussion of the difficulties faced by zemstvo assemblies.

74. *Ibid.*

75. Astrov, *Vospominaniia*, p. 288.

76. Smith, "The Constitutional-Democratic Movement," pp. 270–73.

77. Emmons, "Russia's Banquet Campaign," p. 69.

78. D. I. Shakhovskoi, quoted in *ibid.*, p. 52.

79. *Ibid.*, p. 76. I have relied heavily on Emmons's thorough study of the banquet campaign.

80. *Russkie vedomosti*, Nov. 24, 1904, p. 3.

81. *Obshchestvennoe dvizhenie*, II, part 2, pp. 161–63.

82. *Iskra*, no. 79 (Nov. 20, 1904), p. 1.

83. The "Letter to Party Organizations" is reproduced in Lenin, *Sochineniia*, VII, pp. 410–16.

84. Lenin, "Zemskaia kampaniia i plan *Iskry*," *Sochineniia*, VII, pp. 5–20.

85. Emmons, "Russia's Banquet Campaign," p. 63.

86. On Lenin's change of mind, see Schwarz, *The Russian Revolution of 1905*, p. 49.

87. Emmons, "Russia's Banquet Campaign," p. 81; S. D. K. [Kirpichnikov], *Soiuz soiuzov*, pp. 20–21.

88. S. N. Harper to his father, Dec. 10, 1904, quoted in Smith, "The Constitutional-Democratic Movement," p. 260.

89. Vitte, *Vospominaniia*, I, pp. 263–64, 276.

90. *Ibid.*, pp. 271–72.

91. Sir Charles Hardinge to Lord Landsdowne, Jan. 3, 1905, FO 181/851, BDFA.

92. Vitte, *Vospominaniia*, I, pp. 273–74.

93. Gurko, *Figures and Features*, p. 303.

94. On the eight points, see the succinct summary in Smith, "The Constitutional-Democratic Movement," p. 257; see also the discussion in Weissman, *Reform in Tsarist Russia*, pp. 96–99.

95. Gessen, *V dvukh vekakh*, p. 187.

96. Smith, "The Constitutional-Democratic Movement," pp. 274, 277; Galai, *The Liberation Movement in Russia, 1900–1905*, p. 238.

97. *Obshchestvennoe dvizhenie*, II, part 2, p. 3.

98. Quoted in Smith, "The Constitutional-Democratic Movement," p. 274.

99. *Ibid.*, p. 275.

100. Quotations are from an analysis by the British Embassy in St. Petersburg of press reaction to the Ukase of Dec. 12, dated Jan. 4, 1905. FO 181/451, BDFA.

101. Gerassimoff, *Der Kampf*, p. 28.

Chapter 3

1. Askew, "An American View of Bloody Sunday," p. 41.

2. *Russkie vedomosti*, Jan. 1, 1905, p. 2. The article also stated: "The time has come to acknowledge that we possess too little strength and too few means to pursue an aggressive policy on the shores of the Pacific Ocean." Once hostilities ceased, the country would be able to devote its energies to the "creative work" of internal reform.

3. German Consulate in Riga to Berlin, Feb. 13, 1905, PAAA.

4. Hoover Inst., OA, Box 153, Folder XIII, C(2). It is possible that the report was based on misinformation about decisions taken by the secret conference in Paris in the fall of 1904.

5. British Embassy in St. Petersburg to Lord Landsdowne, Jan. 19, 1905, FO 181/851, BDFA.

6. See Sablinsky, "The Road to Bloody Sunday," pp. 485–86. I generally cite the more comprehensive dissertation, as here (and subsequently as "The Road"). Occasional references to the book of the same title are distinguished by italics (*The Road*).

7. The information and quotations in this paragraph are from Shuster, *Peterburgskie rabochie v 1905–1907 gg.*, p. 68.

8. Galai, *The Liberation Movement in Russia, 1900–1905*, pp. 236–37; Pipes, *Struve: Liberal on the Left*, pp. 371–73; Gurevich, "Narodnoe dvizhenie v Peterburge," esp. pp. 202–3; Gapon, *The Story of My Life*, p. 134.

9. Askew, "An American View," p. 41.

10. L. Aehrenthal to His Excellency Count Goluchowski, Mar. 1/Feb. 16, 1906, HHSA.

11. *History of the Communist Party of the Soviet Union*, p. 57.

12. L. Aehrenthal to His Excellency Count Goluchowski, Feb. 11/Jan. 29, 1905, HHSA; for different accounts of the meeting, see Sablinsky, *The Road*, pp. 203–4, and Gapon, *Story*, pp. 165–67.

13. Gapon, *Story*, pp. 7–58; I have also relied on the account in Sablinsky, "The Road," pp. 84–103.

14. For details on the incident, see Sablinsky, "The Road," pp. 120–25.

15. Surh, "Petersburg's First Mass Labor Organization," part 1, pp. 244–45.

16. *Ibid.*, p. 253.

17. Gapon, *Story*, pp. 94, 99.

18. *Ibid.*, pp. 134–35.

19. Sablinsky, "The Road," pp. 250–53.

20. *Ibid.*, pp. 259–96.

21. *Ibid.*, p. 302.

22. *Obshchestvennoe dvizhenie*, II, part 1, p. 44; Gurevich, "Narodnoe dvizhenie," p. 202.

23. Gurevich, "Narodnoe dvizhenie," p. 204; Gapon, *Story*, p. 126.

24. Sablinsky, "The Road," pp. 339–51, 363–64.

25. *Ibid.*, p. 379; *Dokumenty i materialy*, I, pp. 3–4.

26. Gapon, *Story*, p. 143.

27. *Ibid.*, pp. 155–56.

28. *Obshchestvennoe dvizhenie*, II, part 1, p. 189; the Ministry of Finance estimated that 87,926 workers were on strike on January 7. See *Dokumenty i materialy*, I, pp. 24–27.

29. Gurevich, "Narodnoe dvizhenie," p. 208.

30. *Ibid.*; Gapon, *Story*, p. 171.

31. *Obshchestvennoe dvizhenie*, II, part 1, p. 44. The Russian word is *pravda*, which generally means "truth" but can also mean "justice."

32. Surh, "Petersburg's First Mass Labor Organization," part 2, p. 438. See pp. 436–41 for an interesting discussion of the question of the political consciousness of Gapon's supporters. Surh's conclusion is different from mine. He writes: "Precisely because Gapon spoke a traditional language and acknowledged time-honored folk and religious practices, large numbers of workers were able to overcome their habitual caution and join the bold and radical activities of the Assembly in January 1905. The very acknowledgment of 'backwardness' therefore granted the possibility of revolutionary action" (p. 441).

33. Valk et al., eds., *1905 god v Peterburge*, I, pp. 10–12, 15–17.

34. Sablinsky, "The Road," pp. 455–56, 459; Shuster, *Peterburgskie rabochie*, p. 76.

35. See Nevskii, "Peterburgskaia sotsial-demokraticheskaia organisatsiia v ianvare 1905 goda," which argues that the organizational weakness of the Social Democrats accounts for their failure to influence the workers in the capital.

36. Sablinsky, "The Road," pp. 499–500.

37. Gurevich, "Narodnoe dvizhenie," pp. 211–12.

38. Gessen, *V dvukh vekakh*, pp. 191–92.

39. The most detailed and best account of the last few days before the procession may be found in Sablinsky, "The Road," pp. 485–583.

40. The text of the letter is in *Obshchestvennoe dvizhenie*, II, part 1, pp. 45–46.

41. The text of the petition is from Sablinsky, "The Road," pp. 503–9 (with minor changes). I have left out Sablinsky's explanatory notes. It should be noted that there were two versions of the petition; the italicized words were added to the final text. According to Sablinsky (*The Road*, p. 349), the "words in parentheses were either deleted or replaced."

42. *Dokumenty i materialy*, I, p. 108.

43. Sir Charles Hardinge to Lord Landsdowne, Jan. 27, 1905, FO 181/851, BDFA.

44. *Dokumenty i materialy*, I, pp. 107, 114.

45. *Ibid.*, p. 108; Shuster, *Peterburgskie rabochie*, pp. 87–89.

46. *Dokumenty i materialy*, I, p. 107.

47. *Ibid.*, p. 108; Sablinsky, "The Road," pp. 609–14.

48. Gurevich, "Narodnoe dvizhenie," p. 224.

49. Sablinsky, "The Road," p. 637.

50. Sir Charles Hardinge to Lord Landsdowne, Jan. 27, 1905, FO 181/851, BDFA.

51. *Ibid.* Hardinge was mistaken in ascribing control over government-owned factories to the Ministry of Finance; various agencies such as the Navy and the Transportation Administration ran them.

52. Askew, "An American View," pp. 41–42, 43.

53. *Dokumenty i materialy*, I, pp. 63–65.

54. *Russkie vedomosti*, Jan. 15, 1905, p. 3.

55. Sir Charles Hardinge to Lord Landsdowne, Jan. 27, 1905, FO 181/851, BDFA.

56. Manning, *The Crisis of the Old Order in Russia*, pp. 82–83.

57. Engelstein, *Moscow, 1905*, p. 64.

58. *Dokumenty i materialy*, I, p. 164; *Obshchestvennoe dvizhenie*, II, part 1, pp. 51–52; *Russkie vedomosti*, Jan. 15, 1905, p. 2. On the strike movement in Russian Poland, see Lewis, "The Labor Movement in Russian Poland," pp. 98–140.

59. On the Rimskii-Korsakov affair, see *Russkie vedomosti*, Mar. 17, 1905, p. 3, Mar. 24, p. 4, Mar. 31, p. 4, Apr. 10, p. 3, Apr. 16, p. 3.

60. Bohachevsky-Chomiak, *Sergei N. Trubetskoi*, p. 140.

61. Sablinsky, "The Road," p. 660.

62. Sir Charles Hardinge to Lord Landsdowne, Jan. 26 and Feb. 5, 1905, FO 181/844 and 851, BDFA.

63. *The Evening Sun*, Jan. 23, 1905, p. 1.

64. There is a summary of the accounts in the German press in Bihourd to Delcassé, Jan. 25, 1905 (from Berlin), AMAE, I.

65. French Embassy in Rome to Delcassé, Jan. 26, 1905, AMAE, I.

66. French Embassy in London to Delcassé, Jan. 27, 1905, AMAE, I.

67. French Embassy in Berlin to Delcassé, Jan. 25, 1905, AMAE, I.

68. Report of Feb. 3/16, 1905, Russian Imperial Legation in Weimar, Hoover Inst., OA, Box 2, Folder 22.

69. *Dokumenty i materialy*, I, pp. 133–34.

70. Gurevich, "Narodnoe dvizhenie," p. 228.

71. Sablinsky, "The Road," pp. 698–701; *Obshchestvennoe dvizhenie*, IV, part 1, p. 286; Kokovtsov, *Out of My Past*, p. 40.

72. Shuster, *Peterburgskie rabochie*, p. 101.

73. Sablinsky, "The Road," pp. 675, 680.

74. *Ibid.*, pp. 723–26.

75. *Ibid.*, pp. 727–56.

76. For details on Gapon's dealings with the police and Rutenberg, see Sablinsky, "The Road," pp. 757–73. See also Nikolajewsky, *Azeff the Spy*, pp. 137–48.

77. Gurevich, "Narodnoe dvizhenie," p. 200.

Chapter 4

1. *Dnevnik Imperatora Nikolaia II*, p. 194.

2. Kokovtsov, *Out of My Past*, pp. 49–50. L. Aehrenthal to His Excellency Count Goluchowski, Jan. 15/28, 1905, HHSA.

3. See the report on the interview dated Feb. 12, 1905, in PAAA.

4. Sir Charles Hardinge to Lord Landsdowne, Jan. 3 and Feb. 5, 1905, FO 181/851, BDFA.

5. L. Aehrenthal to His Excellency Count Goluchowski, Jan. 15/28, 1905, HHSA.

6. Verner, "Nicholas II and the Role of the Autocrat," p. 259.

7. Sir Charles Hardinge to Lord Landsdowne, Feb. 14, 1905, FO 181/851, BDFA; Gurko, *Figures and Features of the Past*, pp. 355–56.

8. Petrunkevich, "Iz zapisok obshchestvennogo deiatelia," p. 364.
9. Vitte, *Vospominaniia*, I, p. 286.
10. *Ibid.*, pp. 284–86.
11. Petrunkevich, "Iz zapisok," p. 385.
12. Schneiderman, *Sergei Zubatov and Revolutionary Marxism*, pp. 61–62, 86.
13. *Petergofskoe soveshchanie . . . Sekretnye protokoly,* p. 163.
14. Gerassimoff, *Der Kampf,* pp. 45–47.
15. Vitte, *Vospominaniia*, I, p. 285.
16. *Ibid.*, pp. 286–87.
17. Gurko, *Figures and Features,* p. 360.
18. "Zapiski A. S. Ermolova," *Krasnyi arkhiv,* 8 (1925), pp. 51–52.
19. *Ibid.*, pp. 53–57.
20. *Ibid.*, pp. 58–67.
21. *Dokumenty i materialy,* I, p. 165.
22. Hoover Inst., OA, Index XI, C(5), Folder 1.
23. Naimark, *Terrorists and Social Democrats,* p. 18.
24. Zelnik, trans. and ed., *A Radical Worker,* p. 178.
25. *Dokumenty i materialy,* I, pp. 377–78.
26. *Ibid.*, pp. 390–91.
27. *Syn otechestva,* Mar. 23, 1905, p. 4.
28. *Dokumenty i materialy,* II, pp. 262–64.
29. Derenkovskii et al., "1905 god v Saratove."
30. Harper, "Exceptional Measures in Russia," pp. 92–105; Pipes, *Russia Under the Old Regime,* pp. 305–7.
31. Pipes, *Russia Under the Old Regime,* p. 305.
32. Weissman, *Reform in Tsarist Russia,* pp. 205–6.
33. Quoted in *Obshchestvennoe dvizhenie,* IV, part 1, p. 306.
34. Weissman, *Reform,* p. 11.
35. Gerassimoff, *Der Kampf,* pp. 15–17.
36. Von Bülow, *Memoirs,* II, p. 178.
37. Quoted in Chermenskii, *Burzhuaziia i tsarizm v pervoi russkoi revoliutsii,* p. 60.
38. Quoted in *ibid.,* p. 58.
39. The manifesto and the ukase were published in *Pravitelstvennyi vestnik,* no. 39, Feb. 18, 1905, and the Imperial Rescript appeared in the same paper in no. 40, Feb. 19, 1905; see also Gurko, *Figures and Features,* pp. 369–70.
40. Gurko, *Figures and Features,* pp. 371–72.
41. Petrunkevich, "Iz zapisok," p. 366.
42. *Pravo,* Feb. 20, 1905, column 475.
43. *Russkie vedomosti,* Feb. 20, 1905, p. 1.
44. *Novoe vremia,* Feb. 21, 1905, p. 1.
45. *Syn otechestva,* Mar. 23, 1905, p. 4.
46. *Russkie vedomosti,* Apr. 7, 1905, p. 1.
47. *Syn otechestva,* May 26, 1905, p. 5.
48. *Ibid.*
49. *Russkie vedomosti,* May 31, 1905, p. 3.
50. *Ibid.*, June 1, 1905, p. 2.
51. *Ibid.;* see also the issue of June 3, 1905, p. 2.
52. See the analysis in Smith, "The Constitutional-Democratic Movement," pp. 299–302.

53. Petrunkevich, "Iz zapisok," p. 374.
54. Shipov, *Vospominaniia*, pp. 310–12; Rainey, "The Union of 17 October," pp. 71–73.
55. Petrunkevich, "Iz zapisok," p. 382.
56. *Ibid.*, pp. 375–76.
57. Trubetskoi's address was published in *Pravitelstvennyi vestnik*, June 8, 1905, p. 1. For an English translation (which I have used with some emendations), see Bohachevsky-Chomiak, *Sergei N. Trubetskoi*, pp. 150–54.
58. Bohachevsky-Chomiak, *Sergei N. Trubetskoi*, pp. 154–55.
59. *Listok "Soiuza Osvobozhdeniia,"* no. 4 (June 20, 1905), quoted in Smith, "The Constitutional-Democratic Movement," p. 373.
60. *Vestnik Evropy*, 40, no. 7 (July 1905), p. 332.
61. Smith, "The Constitutional-Democratic Movement," p. 372; [Struve], "Nezhnaia uvertiura k groznomu konfliktu," pp. 369–70.
62. Sef, *Burzhuaziia v 1905 godu*, pp. 41–44; Petrunkevich, "Iz zapisok," p. 384.
63. Petrunkevich, "Iz zapisok," p. 384.
64. Schwarz, *The Russian Revolution of 1905*, p. 94. For more details on the Shidlovsky Commission see *ibid.*, pp. 75–128. See also the treatment of the commission in Bonnell, *Roots of Rebellion*, pp. 110–16.
65. Schwarz, *The Russian Revolution of 1905*, pp. 118–19.
66. Bonnell, *Roots of Rebellion*, p. 115; Anweiler, *Die Rätebewegung in Russland, 1905–1921*, p. 45.
67. Quoted in Schwarz, *The Russian Revolution of 1905*, p. 107.
68. *Obshchestvennoe dvizhenie*, IV, part 1, p. 189; the most thorough discussion of the Kokovtsov Commission may be found in Snow, "The Kokovtsov Commission."
69. Quoted in Snow, "The Kokovtsov Commission," p. 792. On the controversy between industrialists over the source of labor unrest, see Menashe, "Industrialists in Politics: Russia in 1905"; and Roosa, "Russian Industrialists, Politics, and Labor Reform in 1905."
70. *Obshchestvennoe dvizhenie*, IV, part 1, pp. 289–90.
71. *Ibid.*, pp. 292–96.
72. *Ibid.*, pp. 301–3.
73. *Ibid.*, p. 290.

Chapter 5

1. Keep, *The Rise of Social Democracy in Russia*, p. 150.
2. See the definition of "revolution" in Amann, "Revolution: A Redefinition," pp. 38–39.
3. *Russkie vedomosti*, June 28, 1905, p. 1.
4. *Syn otechestva*, Sept. 18, 1905, p. 3.
5. *Russkie vedomosti*, May 19, 1905, pp. 1, 2, 3.
6. *Ibid.*, Feb. 20, p. 1; similar views were expressed by *Nasha zhizn*, Aug. 9, 1905, p. 1, and *Syn otechestva*, Apr. 15, 1905, p. 1.
7. *Russkie vedomosti*, May 21, 1905, p. 1.
8. French Consul in Warsaw to Delcassé, Mar. 16, 1905, AMAE.
9. *Russkie vedomosti*, Feb. 26, 1905, p. 2; Mar. 1, p. 2; Mar. 5, p. 2; Mar. 31, p. 3.

10. L. Aehrenthal to Count Goluchowski, July 16/29, 1905, HHSA.

11. "From Kishineff to Bialystok. A Table of Pogroms From 1903 to 1906," *The American Jewish Yearbook* (Philadelphia, 1906), pp. 38–48; Frankel, *Prophesy and Politics*, p. 147 and *passim*. In addition to describing the pogroms, Frankel provides an excellent analysis of their impact on the politics of the Jewish communities in Russia and abroad.

12. *Russkie vedomosti*, Feb. 20, 1905, p. 2.

13. *Obshchestvennoe dvizhenie*, I, part 2, p. 115.

14. *Russkie vedomosti*, June 1, 1905, p. 2; June 9, p. 3.

15. *Ibid.*, June 10, p. 2.

16. *Nasha zhizn*, Aug. 3, 1905, p. 3; *Obshchestvennoe dvizhenie*, II, part 2, p. 115.

17. *Nasha zhizn*, July 21, 1905, p. 3.

18. *Ibid.*, Sept. 6, 1905, p. 3.

19. *Russkie vedomosti*, Aug. 22, 1905, p. 2.

20. Petrunkevich, "Iz zapisok obshchestvennogo deiatelia," p. 367.

21. U.S. Embassy in St. Petersburg to Department of State, July 7, 1905, USDMR.

22. Report of Acting Consul W. H. Stuart in Batum, Oct. 13, 1905, USDMR.

23. *Nasha zhizn*, July 17, 1905, p. 2.

24. *Ibid.*, July 16, 1905, p. 3; *Syn otechestva*, July 16, 1905, p. 4.

25. *Nasha zhizn*, July 16, p. 3.

26. *Syn otechestva*, July 17, 1905, p. 4.

27. *Ibid.*, July 19, 1905, p. 5; *Nasha zhizn*, July 19, 1905, p. 3.

28. *Nasha zhizn*, Aug. 2, 1905, p. 3.

29. Sir Charles Hardinge to Lord Landsdowne, Apr. 12, 1905, FO 181/857/4, BDFA.

30. *Syn otechestva*, July 20, 1905, p. 3.

31. *Ibid.*, July 23, 1905, p. 3; *Nasha zhizn*, July 20, 1905, p. 2.

32. *Syn otechestva*, Aug. 25, 1905, p. 3.

33. French Consul-General in Warsaw to Ministry of Foreign Affairs, Aug. 26, 1905, AMAE, IX.

34. French Consul-General in Warsaw to Delcassé, May 5, 1905, AMAE, IX.

35. *Ibid.*, May 29, 1905; Lewis, "The Labor Movement in Russian Poland in the Revolution of 1905–1907," p. 146.

36. Lewis, "The Labor Movement," p. 146.

37. This interpretation of the widespread lawlessness in Poland was suggested by the French Consul-General in Warsaw in a report of May 5, 1905, AMAE, IX.

38. Report of Acting Consul W. H. Stuart from Batum, Oct. 13, 1905, USDMR.

39. Bonnell, *Roots of Rebellion*, pp. 119–21.

40. *Russkie vedomosti*, Feb. 24, 1905, p. 3.

41. Piaskovskii, *Revoliutsiia 1905–1907 gg. v Rossii*, p. 41; Amalrik, "K voprosu o chislennosti"; *Dokumenty i materialy*, I, p. 466.

42. Grinewitsch [M. G. Kogan], *Die Gewerkschaften in Russland*, pp. 231–35.

43. Varzar, *Statistika stachek rabochikh*, pp. 44, 61; *Obshchestvennoe dvizhenie*, IV, part 1, pp. 49–50; Mavor, *An Economic History of Russia*, II, pp. 476–77.

44. *Obshchestvennoe dvizhenie*, IV, part 1, p. 59.

45. Shuster, *Peterburgskie rabochie v 1905–1907 gg.*, p. 97.
46. *Dokumenty i materialy*, I, p. 221; on the workers' demands, see *ibid.*, pp. 320–21.
47. Balabanov, *Ot 1905 k 1917*, p. 1. Balabanov uses the words "purely economic" to describe some strikes, but immediately points out that political demands "invariably accompanied" the economic demands.
48. *Ibid.*, pp. 2–3.
49. *Ibid.*, pp. 18–19; *Obshchestvennoe dvizhenie*, II, part 1, p. 201.
50. Balabanov, *Ot 1905 k 1917*, p. 23.
51. Shuster, *Peterburgskie rabochie*, p. 125; See also Bonnell, *Roots of Rebellion*, chaps. 3 & 4.
52. Shuster, *Peterburgskie rabochie*, pp. 131–34.
53. *Dokumenty i materialy*, II, p. 254.
54. Shuster, *Peterburgskie rabochie*, p. 120; *Russkie vedomosti*, Aug. 2, 1905, p. 3.
55. *Ibid.*, Mar. 17, 1905, p. 2. On the strikes of railway workers, see Reichman, "Russian Railwaymen and the Revolution of 1905."
56. *Russkie vedomosti*, May 11, 1905, pp. 2–3.
57. *Ibid.*, Aug. 2, 1905, p. 3.
58. Bonnell, *Roots of Rebellion*, p. 123. See the cautionary note at *ibid.*, p. 468, on the available evidence on the founding of unions in 1905.
59. *Obshchestvennoe dvizhenie*, II, part 2, pp. 171–72; [Kirpichnikov], *Soiuz soiuzov*, pp. 25–26. The most detailed study is Sanders, "The Union of Unions."
60. For details on the Pirogov Congress, see Frieden, *Russian Physicians in an Era of Reform and Revolution*, pp. 197–305.
61. *Obshchestvennoe dvizhenie*, II, part 2, pp. 172–73.
62. *Ibid.*, pp. 173–77.
63. *Ibid.*, pp. 178–79, 182–83. The figures on the membership in the various unions is given in [Kirpichnikov], *Soiuz soiuzov*, pp. 20–28, and Sanders, "The Union of Unions," p. 373.
64. Miliukov, *Vospominaniia*, I, pp. 284, 316. See the discussion in Pipes, *Struve: Liberal on the Right*, p. 6.
65. Quoted in [Kirpichnikov], *Soiuz soiuzov*, p. 10.
66. *Syn otechestva*, June 10, 1905, p. 4.
67. Quoted in Rainey, "The Union of 17 October," p. 91.
68. *Ibid.*, p. 92; Smith, "The Constitutional-Democratic Movement," pp. 429–31.
69. Gerassimoff, *Der Kampf*, pp. 48–51.
70. Anweiler, *Die Rätebewegung in Russland*, pp. 48–49.
71. Only after the appearance of N. Podvoiskii's book *Pervyi sovet rabochikh deputatov (Ivanovo-Voznesenskii-1905 g.)* (Moscow, 1925) did Soviet historians refer to the organization in Ivanovo-Voznesensk as a soviet. Western historians such as Oskar Anweiler and Sidney Harcave have also used that designation, which, given the range of activities of the Assembly in Ivanovo-Voznesensk, is not unreasonable. On this issue, see Schwarz, *The Russian Revolution of 1905*, pp. 335–38. On developments in Ivanovo-Voznesensk in the summer of 1905, see the informative article by Gard, "The Party and the Proletariat."
72. *Dokumenty i materialy*, II, part 1, p. 409.
73. *Ibid.*, pp. 406–7, 409, 415, 426–27; Anweiler, *Die Rätebewegung*, pp. 50–51.

74. *Dokumenty i materialy*, II, part 1, p. 421.
75. *Ibid.*, p. 411.
76. *Ibid.*, pp. 422–23.
77. *Ibid.*, pp. 407, 409–10, 422, 433.
78. *Ibid.*, p. 425.
79. *Ibid.*, pp. 439–40, 448–49.
80. *Ibid.*, pp. 450–53.
81. *Ibid.*, p. 886.
82. *Ibid.*, pp. 459, 886.
83. *Ibid.*, pp. 463–65.
84. *Ibid.*, pp. 454–55, 458.
85. *Ibid.*, pp. 460–63.
86. *Ibid.*, p. 460.
87. *Ibid.*, p. 475.
88. Anweiler, *Die Rätebewegung*, p. 52.
89. Bonnell, *Roots of Rebellion*, pp. 153, 156–57.
90. For details, see *ibid.*, pp. 164–68.
91. *Ibid.*, pp. 160–64.
92. *Osvobozhdenie*, no. 76 (Sept. 2, 1905), pp. 453–54; Smith, "The Constitutional-Democratic Movement," p. 422.

Chapter 6

1. Uratadze, *Vospominaniia gruzinskogo sotsial-demokrata*, p. 107.
2. *Ibid.*, p. 53.
3. *Ibid.*, pp. 79–80.
4. *Ibid.*, pp. 81–83, 88, 99.
5. *Revoliutsiia 1905–1907 gg. v Gruzii*, p. 98.
6. Piaskovskii, *Revoliutsiia 1905–1907 gg. v Rossii*, p. 49; *Obshchestvennoe dvizhenie*, IV, part 2, p. 224; French Consul in Tiflis to Delcassé, Mar. 29, 1905, AMAE, VII.
7. Uratadze, *Vospominaniia*, pp. 104–10; Piaskovskii, *Revoliutsiia 1905–1907 gg.*, p. 50.
8. Piaskovskii, *Revoliutsiia 1905–1907 gg.*, p. 122.
9. "K vosstaniiu v Gurii," *Iskra*, no. 91 (Mar. 6, 1905), quoted in Leopold Haimson's Preface to Uratadze, *Vospominaniia*, p. vi.
10. Dziewanowski, "The Polish Revolutionary Movement," pp. 377–79, 381; *Obshchestvennoe dvizhenie*, IV, part 2, p. 153.
11. Dziewanowski, "The Polish Revolutionary Movement," pp. 377–82.
12. *Dokumenty i materialy*, I, pp. 554–59.
13. *Obshchestvennoe dvizhenie*, II, part 1, p. 52.
14. French Consul-General in Warsaw to Delcassé, Mar. 3, 1905, AMAE, IX.
15. *Russkie vedomosti*, Apr. 22, 1905, p. 3.
16. *Ibid.*, Apr. 23, 1905, pp. 2–3; Lewis, "The Labor Movement in Russian Poland," pp. 98–140.
17. *Russkie vedomosti*, Apr. 29, 1905, p. 3.
18. *Obshchestvennoe dvizhenie*, IV, part 2, p. 167.
19. Dziewanowski, "The Polish Revolutionary Movement," p. 387.
20. *Dokumenty i materialy*, I, p. 498, and II, part 1, pp. 337–38. For a comprehensive discussion of the national question in the Baltic provinces and in Fin-

land, see Thaden, ed., *Russification*. Raun, "The Revolution of 1905," presents a thoughtful overview of the upheaval in the Baltic provinces and provides some interesting statistics on the ethnic composition of the region's population. Raun points out that "The outlying areas and borderlands helped prolong the government's woes, but the primary motivating force at each stage came from the central Russian core." *Ibid.*, pp. 458–59.

21. *Dokumenty i materialy*, I, pp. 498–501.

22. *Ibid.*, pp. 496, 505–6.

23. *Obshchestvennoe dvizhenie*, IV, part 2, pp. 190–91.

24. *Ibid.*, p. 196.

25. *Ibid.*, pp. 187–88, 206–7; on the relatively slow development of Ukrainian nationalism, see Elwood, *Russian Social Democracy in the Underground*, pp. 22–23. See also Pipes, *The Formation of the Soviet Union*, pp. 9–12.

26. *Dokumenty i materialy*, I, pp. 747–48.

27. Dubrovskii, *Krestianskoe dvizhenie v revoliutsii 1905–1907 gg.*, p. 46.

28. See Perrie, "The Russian Peasant Movement of 1905–1907." Perrie concludes that "The peasant movement of 1905–7 was partly related to, partly independent of, the parallel movement in the towns" (p. 155).

29. Dubrovskii, *Krestianskoe dvizhenie*, pp. 42, 65.

30. *Obshchestvennoe dvizhenie*, II, part 2, p. 214. Robinson, *Rural Russia Under the Old Regime*, p. 156; Dubrovskii, *Krestianskoe dvizhenie*, pp. 46–48.

31. Dubrovskii, *Krestianskoe dvizhenie*, pp. 75–77.

32. For statistics on these disorders, see Perrie, "The Russian Peasant Movement," pp. 128–29.

33. *Obshchestvennoe dvizhenie*, II, part 2, p. 61.

34. Dubrovskii, *Krestianskoe dvizhenie*, p. 84.

35. Perrie, "The Russian Peasant Movement," p. 138.

36. Quoted in *ibid.*

37. *Ibid.*, pp. 141, 142.

38. *Obshchestvennoe dvizhenie*, II, part 2, pp. 228–29.

39. See the excellent study by François-Xavier Coquin, "Un aspect méconnu de la révolution de 1905: les 'motions paysannes.'"

40. *Dokumenty i materialy*, II, part 2, pp. 278–79.

41. Coquin, "Un aspect méconnu," p. 196. See this article for more details on how peasant attitudes changed in 1905–6.

42. Dubrovskii, *Krestianskoe dvizhenie*, p. 49.

43. *Obshchestvennoe dvizhenie*, II, part 2, p. 234.

44. *Ibid.*, p. 233.

45. *Ibid.*, pp. 236–37; Robinson, *Rural Russia*, pp. 160–63; Dubrovskii, *Krestianskoe dvizhenie*, p. 99; Kiriukhina, "Vserossiiskii krestianskii soiuz v 1905 g.," pp. 95–141.

46. For details, see Fuller, *Civil-Military Conflict in Imperial Russia*, pp. 129–68, 259–63.

47. Muratov, *Revoliutsionnoe dvizhenie v russkoi armii v 1905–1907 gg.*, p. 332.

48. Bushnell, "Mutineers and Revolutionaries," pp. 2–3. See also the more up-to-date figures in Bushnell, *Mutiny amid Repression*, pp. 76, 232–47.

49. Bushnell, "Mutineers and Revolutionaries," p. 88.

50. *Ibid.*, pp. 16–22; Muratov, *Revoliutsionnoe dvizhenie*, pp. 9–10. For a good treatment of the Tsarist officer corps, see Bushnell, "The Tsarist Officer

Corps, 1881–1914." For an excellent overall discussion of the army in late Imperial Russia, see Wildman, *The End of the Russian Imperial Army*, pp. 3–40.

51. Bushnell, "Mutineers and Revolutionaries," pp. 15, 24.

52. *Dokumenty i materialy*, II, 1, pp. 710–11.

53. Bushnell, *Mutineers*, pp. 167–72.

54. Quoted in Bennett, "Potemkin Mutiny," p. 60.

55. *Dokumenty i materialy*, II, part 2, p. 265.

56. *Ibid.*, p. 257. For a thorough account of the events in Odessa, see Weinberg, "Worker Organizations and Politics in the Revolution of 1905 in Odessa," pp. 223–37. Weinberg provides a full bibliography of works on the mutiny and gives a very good narrative and analysis of the revolution in Odessa.

57. *Dokumenty i materialy*, II, part 2, pp. 265, 464.

58. French Consul in Odessa to Rouvier, June 29, 1905, AMAE, I; *Dokumenty i materialy*, II, part 2, pp. 265–66.

59. *Dokumenty i materialy*, II, part 2, pp. 257–58.

60. *Ibid.*, p. 268; French Consul in Odessa to Rouvier, June 30, 1905, AMAE, I.

61. French Consul in Odessa to Rouvier, June 29, 1905, AMAE, I.

62. Keep, *The Rise of Social Democracy in Russia*, pp. 161, 174–75.

63. Sir Charles Hardinge to Lord Landsdowne, July 4, 1905, FO 181/831, BDFA.

64. Bushnell, "Mutineers and Revolutionaries," pp. 177–78.

Chapter 7

1. King, "The Liberal Movement in Russia, 1904–1905," p. 129; Rainey, "The Union of 17 October," pp. 81–83.

2. L. Aehrenthal to Count Goluchowski, July 16/29, 1905, HHSA; Smith, "The Constitutional-Democratic Movement," p. 384.

3. See p. 151 above.

4. Pogorelko, ed., *Doklad kharkovskogo gorodskogo golovy*, p. 195; see also Smith, "The Constitutional-Democratic Movement," pp. 420–24. The protocols of the July Congress were initially published in *Osvobozhdenie*, no. 76 (Sept. 2, 1905), pp. 447–60.

5. Astrov, *Vospominaniia*, pp. 311–12.

6. Miliukov, "Novyi variant slavianofilskoi politicheskoi doktriny," p. 132.

7. For an English summary of the draft constitution, see King, "The Liberal Movement," pp. 130–33.

8. For a comprehensive discussion of the Bulygin committee, see Doctorow, "The Introduction of Parliamentary Institutions in Russia," pp. 40–161.

9. Sir Charles Hardinge to Lord Landsdowne, Aug. 9, 1905, FO 181/22A, BDFA.

10. U.S. Ambassador Meyer in St. Petersburg to Department of State, Aug. 6, 1905, USDMR.

11. L. Aehrenthal to Count Goluchowski, July 16/29, 1905, HHSA.

12. Riha, *A Russian European*, pp. 84–85. For details, see *Petergofskoe soveshchanie . . . Sekretnye protokoly*, and Snow, "The Peterhof Conference."

13. *Polnoe sobranie zakonov Rossiiskoi Imperii* (1905), no. 26661; King, "The Liberal Movement," pp. 133–35; see the analysis in Emmons, *The Forma-*

tion of Political Parties, pp. 10–13. For an English translation of most of Bulygin's project, see Raeff, ed., *Plans for Political Reform*, pp. 142–52.

14. *Syn otechestva*, Aug. 19, 1905, p. 1; *Rus*, Oct. 2, 1905, p. 1, Oct. 8, p. 3, Oct. 11, p. 1, Oct. 13, p. 1; *Russkie vedomosti*, Aug. 30, 1905, p. 1. The figures for the population of these cities are my estimates, based on census statistics for 1897 and 1910 given in Fedor, *Patterns of Urban Growth*, pp. 183–214.

15. *Russkie vedomosti*, Aug. 18, 1905, p. 2.

16. *Syn otechestva*, Aug. 17, 1905, p. 1.

17. Petrunkevich, "Iz zapisok obshchestvennogo deiatelia," pp. 388–89.

18. *Russkie vedomosti*, Aug. 7, 1905, p. 3, Aug. 8, p. 2.

19. *Syn otechestva*, Aug. 23, 1905, p. 4.

20. [Struve], "Iz ruk tsaria," p. 441.

21. *Russkie vedomosti*, Aug. 7, 1905, p. 1.

22. *Vestnik Evropy*, 40 (Sept. 1905), p. 365.

23. *Russkie vedomosti*, Sept. 2, 1905, p. 2.

24. *Pravo*, 31 (Aug. 6, 1905), column 2517; Riha, *A Russian European*, p. 85.

25. Rainey, "The Union of 17 October," pp. 94–98.

26. U.S. Embassy in St. Petersburg to Department of State, Mar. 24, 1905, USDMR.

27. *Ibid.*, June 2, 1905 (cable).

28. French Consul-General in Warsaw to Minister of Foreign Affairs, June 1, 1905, AMAE, IX.

29. Based on Tsar Nicholas's reminiscences in conversation with Aehrenthal in January 1906. See L. Aehrenthal to Count Goluchowski, Jan. 14/27, 1906. This dispatch was found in PAAA.

30. U.S. Embassy in St. Petersburg to Department of State, June 7, 1905, USDMR.

31. *Ibid.*, Aug. 24, 1905; Maurice, "The Russo-Japanese War," pp. 600–601; Esthus, "Nicholas II and the Russo-Japanese War."

32. *Vestnik Evropy*, 40 (Sept. 1905), p. 365.

33. Valk et al., eds., *1905 god v Peterburge*, I, p. 50.

34. *Dokumenty i materialy*, I, pp. 279–81.

35. Shuster, *Peterburgskie rabochie*, p. 137. The Bolshevik leaflets calling workers to arm themselves are reprinted in Valk et al., eds., *1905 god*, I, p. 83, and in *Dokumenty i materialy*, I, pp. 309–11, 317–18.

36. *Obshchestvennoe dvizhenie*, II, part 1, p. 64.

37. *Ibid.*, p. 65.

38. *Ibid.*, III, pp. 572–75.

39. Lane, *The Roots of Russian Communism*, p. 12. This work contains a great deal of interesting statistical information on various aspects of the Marxist movement in Russia in 1905. Lane also discusses the difficulty of defining a party member at this time (pp. 11–12).

40. Lewis, "The Labor Movement in Russian Poland," p. 450.

41. Tobias, *The Jewish Bund in Russia*, p. 239. For estimates of the Social Democratic Party's membership in the Ukraine, see Elwood, *Russian Social Democracy*, p. 38.

42. *Obshchestvennoe dvizhenie*, III, p. 574.

43. *Ibid.*, II, part 1, pp. 567–68. For a content analysis of party propaganda in St. Petersburg in 1905, see Lane, *The Roots of Russian Communism*, pp. 80–81.

44. *Obshchestvennoe dvizhenie*, II, part 1, pp. 568–69. For additional figures on party finances, see Lane, *The Roots of Russian Communism*, pp. 78, 105–9, 184, 201–2, and *passim*.

45. Hoover Inst., OA, Box 213, Folder XXIV, h-4. For details on the contributions of the German Social Democratic Party to Russian revolutionaries, see the excellent article by Dietrich Geyer, "Die russische Parteispaltung im Urteil der deutschen Sozialdemokratie 1903–1905," p. 432.

46. Hoover Inst., OA, Box 213, Folder XXIV, h-4.

47. *Ibid.*, Box 209, Folder XXI, i.

48. *Ibid.*, Box 213, Folder XXIV, h-1 and h-4. For more details on the acquisition of arms by the radicals, see A. Fischer, *Russische Sozialdemokratie und bewaffneter Aufstand im Jahre 1905*, pp. 117–25, and Futrell, *Northern Underground*, pp. 59–61, 66–84. Futrell gives an account of the ill-fated *John Grafton*, a ship that carried 15,500 rifles, 2,500 cartridges, 2,500 revolvers, and three tons of explosives for revolutionaries in Russia. The shipment was organized by Konni Zilliacus with financial and other help from Colonel Motojiro Akashi. After a series of mishaps the boat ran aground off the coast of Finland early in September 1905, with most of the cargo still aboard. It was by far the most ambitious attempt to smuggle weapons into Russia during the Revolution of 1905.

49. *Obshchestvennoe dvizhenie*, III, p. 570.

50. These statistics are taken from Getzler, "The Mensheviks," p. 20. For an analysis of the evidence available on the social composition of the two factions, see Lane, *The Roots of Russian Communism*, pp. 11–51.

51. Ascher, *Pavel Axelrod*, pp. 134–36; Pipes, "The Origins of Bolshevism," pp. 45–52.

52. See Schapiro, *The Communist Party of the Soviet Union*, pp. 61–62.

53. *Tretii sezd RSDRP*, p. 454; Kingston-Mann, "Lenin and the Challenge of Peasant Militance"; Schapiro, *Communist Party*, pp. 60–62.

54. For an analysis of Lenin in 1905, see Meyer, *Leninism*, pp. 120–44.

55. *Pervaia obshcherusskaia konferentsiia*; Getzler, *Martov*, pp. 106–7.

56. Perrie, "The Social Composition and Structure of the Socialist-Revolutionary Party Before 1917," pp. 223–350.

57. Hildermeier, *Die Sozialrevolutionäre Partei Russlands*, pp. 142–45 and *passim*.

58. Quoted in Perrie, "The Socialist Revolutionaries on Permanent Revolution," p. 411.

59. The preceding two paragraphs are based on the excellent discussion in Avrich, *The Russian Anarchists*, pp. 3–71. For full accounts of Russian syndicalism, a political tendency closely related to anarchism, and of the "anti-intellectualism" of the anarchists, see *ibid.*, pp. 72–119.

60. Astrov, *Vospominaniia*, p. 289.

61. *Syn otechestva*, Sept. 13, 1905, p. 3.

62. *Ibid.*

63. *Ibid.*

64. For more details on the women's movement in 1905, see the excellent account in Stites, *The Women's Liberation Movement in Russia*, pp. 198–210.

65. *Russkie vedomosti*, Mar. 23, 1905, p. 3. For details on the developments in higher education, see Kassow, "The Russian University in Crisis," pp. 274–349.

66. Garvi, *Vospominaniia sotsialdemokrata*, p. 530.

67. Alston, *Education and the State in Tsarist Russia*, pp. 172–95.

68. *Russkie vedomosti*, Apr. 9, 1905, p. 2.

69. *Ibid.*, Sept. 21, 1905, p. 2.

70. *Syn otechestva*, Mar. 23, 1905, p. 5.

71. *Russkie vedomosti*, Mar. 1, 1905, p. 2; see Alston, *Education and the State*, pp. 175–88, for a more detailed discussion of the demands.

72. *Russkie vedomosti*, May 23, 1905, p. 2.

73. A. Anin, "Nekotorye vyvody iz shkolnykh volnenii," *Syn otechestva*, Mar. 27, 1905, p. 1; *Russkie vedomosti*, Apr. 9, 1905, p. 2.

74. Alston, *Education and the State*, p. 181; see *ibid.*, pp. 260–66, for a translation of the teachers' declaration.

75. *Ibid.*, pp. 175–80.

76. For more details on the autonomy decree and the professors' reaction to it, see Kassow, "The Russian University," pp. 350–62.

77. L. Aehrenthal to Count Goluchowski, Oct. 8/21, 1905, HHSA. The analysis of Trepov's motives is based on Aehrenthal's report, which in turn seems to have been prepared after discussions with Trepov himself.

78. Vitte, *Vospominaniia*, I, p. 449. Translation taken from Keep, *The Rise of Social Democracy in Russia*, p. 217.

79. *Obshchestvennoe dvizhenie*, II, part 2, p. 187.

80. *Syn otechestva*, Sept. 16, 1905, p. 2.

81. Dan, "K nachalu akademicheskogo goda," p. 1.

82. Harcave, *First Blood*, p. 167; Bovykin and Latysheva, "Moskovskii universitet v revoliutsii 1905–1907 godov," p. 52.

83. Kassow, "The Russian University," p. 371. Other historians who have suggested that there was a large number of nonradical students are Keep, *The Rise of Social Democracy*, p. 217, and Morrison, "Political Characteristics of the Student Movement," esp. p. 72.

84. Kassow, "The Russian University," pp. 403–4.

85. *Ibid.*, pp. 402–3. The results of student elections given in these pages refer only to St. Petersburg.

86. British Consulate in Moscow to Sir Charles Hardinge, Oct. 11, 1905, FO 181, 859/9, BDFA.

87. *Russkie vedomosti*, Sept. 14, 1905, p. 3.

88. *Syn otechestva*, Sept. 16, 1905, p. 2.

89. *Ibid.*, Sept. 17, p. 4.

90. *Russkie vedomosti*, Sept. 22, 1905, p. 2.

91. *Nasha zhizn*, Sept. 14, 1905, p. 3.

92. *Syn otechestva*, Sept. 20, 1905, p. 3.

93. *Nasha zhizn*, Oct. 6, 1905, p. 3.

94. *Ibid.*, Oct. 7, p. 3; see also the report on this meeting in *Rus*, Oct. 2, 1905, p. 1.

95. *Syn otechestva*, Sept. 24, 1905, p. 2.

96. *Ibid.*, Sept. 17, p. 2.

97. *Ibid.*, Oct. 1, p. 3; *Rus*, Oct. 1, 1905, p. 4.

98. *Syn otechestva*, Sept. 24, 1905, p. 2.

99. *Ibid.*, Sept. 14, p. 2.

100. *Pravo*, no. 39 (Oct. 1, 1905), column 3268.

101. *Dokumenty i materialy*, III, part 1, p. 38.

102. *Russkie vedomosti,* Sept. 10, 1905, pp. 2–3; *Rus,* Oct. 2, p. 1.
103. *Syn otechestva,* Sept. 21, 1905, p. 2.
104. *Russkie vedomosti,* Sept. 20, 1905, p. 2.
105. *Syn otechestva,* Oct. 13, p. 4.
106. *Ibid.,* Sept. 29, p. 3; *Russkie vedomosti,* Sept. 30, 1905, p. 2.
107. *Russkie vedomosti,* Sept. 30, 1905, p. 2; *Rus,* Oct. 1, 1905, p. 1; *Syn otechestva,* Sept. 18, 1905, p. 3.
108. *Syn otechestva,* Sept. 23, 1905, p. 2.
109. *Ibid.,* Sept. 28, p. 2, and Oct. 9, p. 3; Woytinsky [Voitinskii], *Stormy Passage,* pp. 28–29; Voitinskii, *Gody pobed i porazhenii,* I, pp. 77–84. For more details on the boycott issue, see Kassow, "The Russian University," pp. 391–92.
110. *Dokumenty i materialy,* III, part 1, p. 23. See also Kassow, "The Russian University," pp. 382–87.
111. *Dokumenty i materialy,* III, part 1, pp. 151–52.
112. *Ibid.,* pp. 124–26, 152–55.
113. *Ibid.,* pp. 100–102; *Syn otechestva,* Oct. 7, 1905, pp. 3, 7; Oct. 8, p. 4; Oct. 9, pp. 3–4; *Russkie vedomosti,* Sept. 22, 1905, p. 3.
114. Voitinskii, *Gody pobed,* pp. 91–92.
115. Dan, "K nachalu," p. 1.
116. *Dokumenty i materialy,* III, part 1, pp. 25–27.
117. Woytinsky, *Stormy Passage,* p. 27.
118. *Ibid.;* Vitte, *Vospominaniia,* I, p. 446; *Nasha zhizn,* Oct. 8, 1905, p. 4.
119. M. Volynskii, "Volneniia v seminariiakh," *Syn otechestva,* May 14, 1905, p. 2; see also the discussion in Curtiss, *Church and State in Russia,* pp. 188–91, 206–8.
120. Curtiss, *Church and State,* p. 207; see also Cunningham, *A Vanquished Hope: The Movement for Church Renewal in Russia, 1905–1906,* pp. 296–97.
121. *Syn otechestva,* Sept. 22, 1905, p. 4; *Rus,* Oct. 14, 1905, p. 1.
122. Curtiss, *Church and State,* p. 189.
123. *Ibid.,* p. 191.
124. *Syn otechestva,* Oct. 10, 1905, p. 1.
125. *Ibid.,* Oct. 30, 1905, p. 4.
126. *Rus,* Oct. 13, 1905, p. 1.
127. *Syn otechestva,* Oct. 2, 1905, p. 4.

Chapter 8

1. *Dokumenty i materialy,* III, part 1, p. 98; *Obshchestvennoe dvizhenie,* II, part 1, pp. 75–79; Engelstein, *Moscow, 1905,* pp. 87–92.
2. Garvi, *Vospominaniia Sotsialdemokrata,* p. 535.
3. For details, see Engelstein, *Moscow, 1905,* pp. 95–96.
4. Sablinsky, "The All-Russian Railroad Union," pp. 115, 117, 123.
5. *Obshchestvennoe dvizhenie,* II, part 1, pp. 77–78; see also Reichman, "Russian Railwaymen and the Revolution of 1905," p. 361.
6. Sablinsky, "The All-Russian Railroad Union," pp. 125–31.
7. *Rus,* Oct. 11, 1905, p. 1.
8. Voitinskii, *Gody pobed i porazhenii,* I, pp. 93–94.
9. Schwarz, *The Russian Revolution of 1905,* pp. 138–40.
10. *Dokumenty i materialy,* III, part 1, pp. 363–64.

11. *Ibid.*, pp. 364, 674.
12. *Russkie vedomosti*, Oct. 14, 1905, p. 3, and Oct. 17, p. 2.
13. *Ibid.*, Oct. 14, 1905, p. 1, Oct. 16, p. 1, and Oct. 17, p. 1; Engelstein, *Moscow, 1905*, p. 123.
14. *Rus*, Oct. 14, 1905, p. 2.
15. *Russkie vedomosti*, Oct. 17, 1905, p. 2.
16. *Ibid.*, Oct. 15, 1905, p. 3.
17. *Ibid.*, Oct. 14, p. 2.
18. *Ibid.*, Oct. 15, p. 2.
19. *Ibid.*, Oct. 10, p. 2.
20. *Dokumenty i materialy*, III, part 2, pp. 96–97.
21. Chermenskii, *Burzhuaziia i tsarizm v pervoi russkoi revoliutsii*, p. 129.
22. *Vestnik Evropy*, 40 (Nov. 1905), pp. 445–46.
23. *Ibid.*, p. 446.
24. *Obshchestvennoe dvizhenie*, II, part 1, p. 113.
25. *Russkie vedomosti*, Oct. 17, 1905, p. 2, and Oct. 20, p. 3.
26. *Ibid.*, Oct. 16, 1905, p. 1.
27. Engelstein, *Moscow, 1905*, p. 112.
28. *Dokumenty i materialy*, III, part 1, p. 367.
29. *Ibid.*, pp. 369–72.
30. *Rus*, Oct. 11, 1905, p. 1; Voitinskii, *Gody pobed*, p. 134.
31. *Nasha zhizn*, Oct. 12, 1905, p. 2; *Syn otechestva*, Oct. 12, 1905, p. 3.
32. *Dokumenty i materialy*, III, part 2, pp. 177–78.
33. *Ibid.*, pp. 103–9; Weekly Intelligence Summary, Nov. 3, 1905, Hoover Inst., OA, Index no. XIII, C(2), Folder 6C.
34. *Obshchestvennoe dvizhenie*, II, part 1, p. 82.
35. U.S. Embassy in St. Petersburg to Secretary of State, Dec. 18, 1905, USDMR.
36. Shuster, *Peterburgskie rabochie v 1905–1907 gg.*, pp. 150–52. The document is reproduced only in the 4th edition of Lenin, *Sochineniia* (Moscow, 1947), X, pp. 3–11. Keep, *The Rise of Social Democracy in Russia*, pp. 230–34.
37. Shuster, *Peterburgskie rabochie*, p. 152; on the Menshevik proposal for a workers' congress, see Ascher, *Pavel Axelrod*, pp. 233–39.
38. Shuster, *Peterburgskie rabochie*, pp. 177–78.
39. *Obshchestvennoe dvizhenie*, II, part 1, pp. 89–90; *Dokumenty i materialy*, III, part 1, pp. 368–69.
40. *Ibid.*, pp. 369–70; Shuster, *Peterburgskie rabochie*, pp. 158–59.
41. Anweiler, *Die Rätebewegung in Russland, 1905–1921*, pp. 58–63.
42. *Russkie vedomosti*, Oct. 14, 1905, p. 3; Owen, *Capitalism and Politics in Russia*, p. 190.
43. Engelstein, *Moscow, 1905*, p. 134.
44. *Russkie vedomosti*, Oct. 14, 1905, p. 2.
45. German Embassy in St. Petersburg to Berlin, Oct. 28, 1905, PAAA.
46. *Dokumenty i materialy*, III, part 1, p. 429.
47. *Ibid.*, p. 432.
48. *Syn otechestva*, Oct. 14, 1905, p. 1.
49. *Russkie vedomosti*, Oct. 15, 1905, p. 2.
50. Von Laue, "Count Witte and the Russian Revolution of 1905," p. 31.
51. Vitte, *Vospominaniia*, II, p. 25.
52. French Embassy in St. Petersburg to Rouvier, Oct. 21, 1905, AMAE, II.

53. "Zapiska Vitte ot 9 oktiabria," pp. 51–57.

54. Mehlinger and Thompson, *Count Witte and the Tsarist Government in the 1905 Revolution*, p. 36.

55. L. Aehrenthal to Count Goluchowski, Oct. 13/26 and Oct. 17/30, 1905, HHSA.

56. L. Aehrenthal to Count Goluchowski, Oct. 17/30, 1905, HHSA. For the source of Aehrenthal's charges against Witte and more details on the conspiracy against the Prime Minister, see Heilbronner, "An Anti-Witte Diplomatic Conspiracy."

57. *Novoe vremia*, Oct. 11, 1905, p. 3.

58. Vitte, *Vospominaniia*, II, p. 29.

59. Gerassimoff, *Der Kampf gegen die erste Russische Revolution*, p. 57.

60. German Embassy in St. Petersburg to Berlin, Oct. 27, 1905, PAAA.

61. Vitte, *Vospominaniia*, II, pp. 9–10, 26–27.

62. *Ibid.*, p. 27.

63. *Ibid.*, pp. 11–12.

64. *Ibid.*, p. 32.

65. *Ibid.*, pp. 33–34; Mehlinger and Thompson, *Count Witte*, p. 44.

66. Mosolov, *Pri Dvore Imperatora*, p. 135.

67. Bing, ed., *The Secret Letters of the Last Tsar*, p. 185; *Dnevnik Imperatora Nikolaia II*, p. 222.

68. I have used the translation of the manifesto in Mehlinger and Thompson, *Count Witte*, pp. 331–32.

69. Gerassimoff, *Der Kampf*, p. 58.

70. *Ibid.*, p. 59.

71. *Russkie vedomosti*, Oct. 18, 1905, p. 2.

72. *Rus*, Oct. 22, 1905, p. 2.

73. German Embassy in St. Petersburg to Berlin, Oct. 31, 1905, PAAA.

74. *Obshchestvennoe dvizhenie*, II, part 1, pp. 105–6.

75. *Russkie vedomosti*, Oct. 19, 1905, p. 1; Owen, *Capitalism and Politics*, p. 192.

76. Petrunkevich, "Iz zapisok obshchestvennogo deiatelia," p. 410.

77. *Russkie vedomosti*, Oct. 18, 1905, p. 1.

78. *Pravo*, no. 41 (Oct. 25, 1905), columns 3397–3400.

79. H. N. Brailsford to Felix Volkhovsky, Nov. 1, 1905, Hoover Inst., FV Coll., Box 9.

80. Zimmerman, "Between Revolution and Reaction," p. 132; Miliukov, *Vospominaniia*, I, p. 329.

81. *Obshchestvennoe dvizhenie*, II, part 1, p. 106.

82. Shuster, *Peterburgskie rabochie*, p. 155; *Dokumenty i materialy*, III, part 1, p. 383; Voitinskii, *Gody pobed i porazhenii*, I, pp. 172, 176–77.

83. *Dokumenty i materialy*, III, part 1, pp. 196–97.

84. Valk et al., eds., *1905 god v Peterburge*, I, p. 329.

85. See, for example, the leaflet published by the Unified Committee of the RSDWP in Perm reprinted in *Dokumenty i materialy*, III, part 2, p. 14. See also Keep, *The Rise of Social Democracy in Russia*, pp. 226–27.

86. *Syn otechestva*, Nov. 13, 1905, p. 5.

87. *Materialy i dokumenty*, III, part 2, pp. 379, 398.

88. *Syn otechestva*, Oct. 22, 1905, p. 4.

89. *Russkie vedomosti*, Oct. 20, 1905, p. 1.

90. Rosenberg, *Liberals in the Russian Revolution*, p. 20; Zimmerman, "Between Revolution and Reaction," pp. 55–56; for the most comprehensive discussion of the early history of political parties in Russia, see Emmons, *The Formation of Political Parties and the First National Elections in Russia*.

91. Zimmerman, "Between Revolution and Reaction," p. 53.

92. An English translation of the Kadet program may be found in Harcave, *First Blood*, pp. 292–300.

93. Gessen, *V dvukh vekakh*, p. 205.

94. *Russkie vedomosti*, Oct. 18, 1905, p. 3.

95. *Sezd 12–18 oktiabria 1905 g.*, pp. 20–22.

96. Zimmerman, "Between Revolution and Reaction," p. 146.

97. Quoted in Riha, *A Russian European*, p. 101.

98. Quoted in Menashe, "Alexander Guchkov and the Origins of the Octobrist Party," p. 77.

99. *Ibid.*, p. 219; Emmons, *The Formation*, p. 110.

100. Rainey, "The Union of 17 October," pp. 118–24; Pinchuk, *The Octobrists in the Third Duma*, pp. 8–23.

101. My discussion of Guchkov's attitude toward the Jews is based on Menashe, "Alexander Guchkov," p. 170.

102. Brock, "The Theory and Practice of the Union of the Russian People, 1905–1907," pp. 8–20.

103. For a succinct summary of the *Protocols* and the *Rabbi's Speech*, see *ibid.*, pp. 66–87; for an excellent study of the *Protocols*, see Cohn, *Warrant for Genocide*. On the history of the Russian right, see three perceptive studies by Hans Rogger: "The Formation of the Russian Right, 1900–1906"; "Was There a Russian Fascism? The Union of the Russian People"; and "Russia," in Hans Rogger and Eugen Weber, eds., *The European Right: A Historical Profile* (Berkeley, Calif., 1965), pp. 443–500.

104. "Kto vinovat," *Russkoe znamia*, no. 79 (Mar. 28, 1906), p. 1, trans. from Brock, "Theory and Practice," p. 100.

105. V. M. Purishkevich, ed., *Kniga russkoi skorbi*, II (St. Petersburg, 1908), p. 190, quoted in Brock, "Theory and Practice," p. 107.

106. *Ibid.*, pp. 108–9.

107. Quoted in *ibid.*, p. 121.

108. "Besedy po dushe," *Russkoe znamia*, no. 260 (Oct. 20, 1906), p. 3, trans. from Brock, "Theory and Practice," pp. 29–30.

109. "Russkie Soiuzi," *Russkoe znamia*, no. 38 (Feb. 14, 1906), p. 2.

110. Brock, "Theory and Practice," pp. 131–43.

111. *Obshchestvennoe dvizhenie*, III, pp. 412–17.

112. Brock, "Theory and Practice," pp. 162–68, 203, 201–50.

113. *Moskovskie vedomosti*, Jan. 15, 1906, p. 2.

Chapter 9

1. Sir Charles Hardinge to Lord Landsdowne, Nov. 9, 1905, FO 181/841, BDFA.

2. Quoted in Bushnell, "Mutineers and Revolutionaries," p. 113.

3. Semennikov, ed., *Revoliutsiia 1905 goda i samoderzhavie*, p. 23.

4. Cable from U.S. Embassy in St. Petersburg to Department of State, Jan. 7, 1906, USDMR; *Russkie vedomosti*, Oct. 22, 1905, p. 2.

5. Vitte, *Vospominaniia*, II, p. 76.

6. *Ibid.*, pp. 106–7.

7. Sir Charles Hardinge to Lord Landsdowne, Nov. 20, 1905 [o.s. Nov. 7], FO 181/841, BDFA.

8. Vitte, *Vospominaniia*, p. 45; German Embassy in St. Petersburg to Berlin, Nov. 6, 1905, PAAA.

9. Bing, ed., *The Secret Letters of the Last Tsar*, pp. 183–86.

10. *Ibid.*, p. 192.

11. British Consulate in Moscow to British Embassy in St. Petersburg, Nov. 20, 1905, FO 181/827, BDFA.

12. *Russkie vedomosti*, Nov. 28, 1905, p. 2; German Embassy in St. Petersburg to Berlin, Nov. 17, 1905, PAAA; U.S. Embassy in St. Petersburg to Department of State, Nov. 20, 1905, USDMR.

13. *Russkie vedomosti*, Dec. 21, 1905, p. 3.

14. Vitte, *Vospominaniia*, II, p. 90; Von Laue, "Count Witte and the 1905 Revolution," pp. 32–33.

15. Vitte, *Vospominaniia*, II, p. 62.

16. *Ibid.*, pp. 64–65, 71.

17. Bing, ed., *Secret Letters*, p. 211.

18. Vitte, *Vospominaniia*, II, pp. 70–71.

19. Keep, *The Rise of Social Democracy in Russia*, p. 224.

20. Vitte, *Vospominaniia*, II, p. 58.

21. German Embassy in St. Petersburg to Berlin, Nov. 6, 1905, PAAA.

22. Petrunkevich, "Iz zapisok obshchestvennogo deiatelia," pp. 436–37.

23. Kokovtsov, *Out of My Past*, pp. 69–70.

24. *Polnoe sobranie zakonov Rossiiskoi Imperii*, XXV, part 1, pp. 766–67.

25. *Rus*, Oct. 28, 1905, p. 1.

26. Vitte, *Vospominaniia*, II, p. 99.

27. *Obshchestvennoe dvizhenie*, IV, part 1, pp. 352–53, 362. The manifesto on Finland may be found in *Polnoe sobranie zakonov*, pp. 772–73.

28. Sir Charles Hardinge to Lord Landsdowne, Nov. 9, 1905, FO 181/841, BDFA.

29. Gessen, *V dvukh vekakh*, pp. 207–8.

30. Guchkov, "Iz vospominanii A. I. Guchkova," p. 1.

31. Vitte, *Vospominaniia*, II, pp. 82–87.

32. Mehlinger and Thompson, *Count Witte and the Tsarist Government in the 1905 Revolution*, pp. 79–80.

33. Startsev, *Russkaia burzhuaziia i samoderzhavie v 1905–1917 gg.*, p. 15. In his memoirs Shipov indicated that Stolypin's name came up during the discussions with Witte, but he was not seriously considered because he was not well known. See Shipov, *Vospominaniia i dumy o perezhitom*, p. 343.

34. Santoni, "P. N. Durnovo as Minister of Internal Affairs in the Witte Cabinet," pp. 32–40.

35. Vitte, *Vospominaniia*, II, pp. 58–60.

36. Gerassimoff, *Der Kampf gegen die erste Russische Revolution*, p. 80.

37. Guchkov, "Iz vospominanii A. I. Guchkova," p. 1.

38. *Russkie vedomosti*, Oct. 23, 1905, p. 2.

39. Miliukov, *Vospominaniia (1859–1917)*, I, pp. 325–28.

40. Petrunkevich, "Iz zapisok," pp. 429–33.

41. *Russkie vedomosti*, Oct. 29, 1905, p. 1; for more details on Shipov's discussions with Witte, see Shipov, *Vospominaniia*, pp. 334–49.

42. Bing, ed., *Secret Letters*, p. 188.
43. Sir Charles Hardinge to Lord Landsdowne, Nov. 9, 1905, FO 181/841, BDFA.
44. *Ibid.*
45. See below, pp. 259–60.
46. Vitte, *Vospominaniia*, II, pp. 61, 87–89; see also Gerassimoff, *Der Kampf*, pp. 78–79.
47. *Syn otechestva*, Oct. 23, 1905, p. 1.
48. *Russkie vedomosti*, Oct. 22, 1905, p. 1, and Oct. 30, p. 3; see also the report of the German Embassy in St. Petersburg to Berlin, Nov. 16, 1905, PAAA.
49. *Rus*, Oct. 23, 1905, pp. 1, 2.
50. *Ibid.*
51. *Ibid.*, Oct. 22, 1905, p. 4.
52. *Ibid.*, Oct. 28, 1905, p. 1.
53. *Russkie vedomosti*, Oct. 22, 1905, p. 2.
54. *Obshchestvennoe dvizhenie*, II, part 1, p. 101.
55. *Syn otechestva*, Oct. 24, 1905, p. 2.
56. *Ibid.*, Oct. 22, 1905, p. 2, and Oct. 27, p. 3; *Rus*, Oct. 22, 1905, p. 2; German Consulate in Odessa to Berlin, Nov. 11, 1905, PAAA. See also Weinberg, "Worker Organizations and Politics in the Revolution of 1905 in Odessa," pp. 276–306, for an excellent treatment of the background, development, and aftermath of the pogrom. The figures on casualties in Odessa are from Weinberg.
57. Löwe, *Antisemitismus und reaktionäre Utopie*, p. 87. The most comprehensive account of the anti-Jewish pogroms in October may be found in Linden, ed., *Die Judenpogromme in Russland*.
58. *Russkie vedomosti*, Oct. 20, 1905, p. 2.
59. German Embassy in St. Petersburg to Berlin, Nov. 11, 1905, PAAA.
60. *Russkie vedomosti*, Oct. 29, 1905, p. 2.
61. *Ibid.*, Oct. 24, 1905, pp. 2–3.
62. *Ibid.*, p. 3.
63. *Syn otechestva*, Oct. 25, 1905, p. 3.
64. *Rus*, Oct. 23, 1905, p. 1.
65. *Ibid.*, Nov. 17, 1905, p. 1.
66. *Syn otechestva*, Oct. 27, 1905, p. 3.
67. *Russkie vedomosti*, Nov. 3, 1905, p. 3.
68. This view is also held by some historians. Louis Greenberg, for example, wrote without supporting evidence that "the emperor and his camarilla had decided to crush the revolutionary spirit by diverting it toward bloody attacks upon the Jews." Greenberg, *The Jews of Russia*, II, p. 76.
69. *Russkie vedomosti*, Oct. 22, 1905, p. 3.
70. *Syn otechestva*, Nov. 13, 1905, p. 5.
71. *Ibid.*, Nov. 17, 1905, p. 4.
72. Löwe, *Antisemitismus*, p. 92.
73. *Syn otechestva*, Nov. 25, 1905, p. 4.
74. See Weinberg, "Worker Organizations and Politics," pp. 288–90, and Linden, ed., *Die Judenpogromme*.
75. French Consul in Odessa to Paris, Nov. 7, 1905, AMAE, II.
76. For details, see Löwe, *Antisemitismus*, p. 94.
77. Bing, ed., *Secret Letters*, pp. 187–88.
78. British Embassy in St. Petersburg to London, Feb. 28, 1906, FO 181/869, BDFA; Mehlinger and Thompson, *Count Witte*, pp. 64, 359; Vitte, *Vospominaniia*, II, pp. 67–70.

79. The speech is reprinted in Baring, *A Year in Russia*, pp. 233–39. The speech was delivered on June 8, 1906.

80. *Rus*, Oct. 23, 1905, p. 1.

81. *Russkie vedomosti*, Oct. 2, 1905, p. 2.

82. Löwe, *Antisemitismus*, pp. 96, 243.

83. *Ibid.*, p. 96.

84. *Obshchestvennoe dvizhenie*, II, part 1, p. 104.

85. *Russkie vedomosti*, Oct. 22, 1905, p. 1.

86. *Rus*, Oct. 30, 1905, p. 2.

87. *Syn otechestva*, Oct. 23, 1905, p. 1. On the government's role in the pogroms, see also Rogger, "The Jewish Policy of Late Tsarism: A Reappraisal," pp. 46–47.

88. Löwe, *Antisemitismus*, p. 90; *Rus*, Oct. 22, 1905, p. 3.

89. German Consulate in Moscow to Berlin, Nov. 8, 1905, PAAA.

90. Harcave, *First Blood*, p. 205.

91. *Rus*, Oct. 22, 1905, p. 2.

92. Getzler, *Martov*, pp. 66–67.

93. *Russkie vedomosti*, Oct. 21, 1905, p. 1.

94. Garvi, *Vospominaniia sotsialdemokrata*, p. 585.

95. *Russkie vedomosti*, Oct. 21, 1905, p. 1; *Pravo*, nos. 48–49 (Dec. 4, 1905), column 132; *Dokumenty i materialy*, III, part 1, p. 469.

96. *Syn otechestva*, Oct. 22, 1905, pp. 5–6.

97. Garvi, *Vospominaniia sotsialdemokrata*, p. 587.

98. Lavrov, *Historical Letters*, p. 172.

99. *Russkie vedomosti*, Oct. 21, 1905, p. 1; *Syn otechestva*, Oct. 22, 1905, p. 6.

100. *Syn otechestva*, Oct. 23, 1905, p. 3, Oct. 24, p. 2, Oct. 25, p. 3, Oct. 26, p. 3; *Dokumenty i materialy*, III, part 1, p. 682.

101. German Consulate in Moscow to Berlin, Nov. 7, 1905, PAAA.

102. *Russkie vedomosti*, Oct. 22, 1905, pp. 2–3, Oct. 26, p. 4; *Rus*, Oct. 23, 1905, p. 1; Engelstein, *Moscow, 1905*, p. 145.

103. Report of the Second Secretary of the British Embassy in St. Petersburg, dated July 18, 1905, FO 181/831, BDFA.

104. On the Jewish self-defense groups, see Lambroza, "Jewish Self-Defense During the Russian Pogroms of 1903–1906"; Tobias, *The Jewish Bund in Russia*, pp. 222–31, 313–16, and *passim*; and Frankel, *Prophesy and Politics: Socialism, Nationalism, and the Russian Jews, 1862–1917*.

105. *Russkie vedomosti*, Oct. 26, 1905, p. 3.

106. *Rus*, Oct. 22, 1905, p. 2; *Syn otechestva*, Nov. 9, 1905, p. 4, and Nov. 10, p. 4.

107. Robinson, *Rural Russia Under the Old Regime*, pp. 174–76; Dubrovskii, *Krestianskoe dvizhenie v revoliutsii 1905–1907 gg.*, p. 53.

108. Robinson, *Rural Russia*, p. 174.

109. *Russkie vedomosti*, Nov. 25, 1905, p. 3.

110. *Obshchestvennoe dvizhenie*, II, part 2, p. 240.

111. *Dokumenty i materialy*, III, part 2, p. 369; see also the Tsar's complaint about the shortage of troops in Bing, ed., *Secret Letters*, pp. 192–93.

112. *Dokumenty i materialy*, IV, part 2, p. 387.

113. Vitte, *Vospominaniia*, II, p. 115.

114. For an incisive analysis of this development, see Bushnell, "Mutineers and Revolutionaries," pp. 69–71.

115. *Dokumenty i materialy,* IV, part 1, p. 195.
116. *Ibid.,* p. 199.
117. *Ibid.,* p. 200, quoted in Bushnell, "Mutineers and Revolutionaries," p. 63.
118. Bushnell, "Mutineers and Revolutionaries," pp. 62–63, 67, 87–89. The demands are listed in *Dokumenty i materialy,* IV, part 1, pp. 199–200.
119. *Dokumenty i materialy,* IV, part 1, p. 227.
120. *Ibid.,* pp. 228, 847.
121. My account of the mutiny and the reaction to Schmidt's execution is based on contemporary reports in *Russkie vedomosti,* Nov. 14, 1905, p. 2, Nov. 18, p. 2, Mar. 7, 1906, p. 1; and in *Pravo,* nos. 45–46 (Nov. 20, 1905), columns 3761–62, and no. 47 (Nov. 17, 1905), columns 3842–43. Chukhnin's secret report of November 22 on the events in Sevastopol may be found in *Dokumenty i materialy,* IV, part 1, pp. 284–301. For Soviet accounts, see Gelis, *Noiabrskie dni v Sevastopole v 1905 godu,* and Genkin, *Leitenant Shmidt i vosstanie na "Ochakov."* For one of the many "historical tales" on Schmidt published since 1917, see M. Charnyi, *Leitenant Shmidt: istoricheskaia povest* (Moscow, 1960).
122. Bushnell, "Mutineers and Revolutionaries," p. 76.
123. The information in this paragraph is taken from Wildman, *The End of the Russian Imperial Army,* pp. 58–60.
124. [Rediger], "Zapiski A. F. Redigera o 1905 g.," p. 91.
125. Bushnell, "Mutineers and Revolutionaries," pp. 116–17.
126. On this point see *ibid.,* pp. 145–52.
127. *Ibid.,* pp. 126–27.
128. L. Aehrenthal to Count Goluchowski, Dec. 3/16, 1905, HHSA.

Chapter 10

1. Dan to Kautsky, Oct. 27, 1905, Kautsky Archive, International Institute for Social History, Amsterdam.
2. Petrunkevich, "Iz zapisok obshchestvennogo deiatelia," p. 368.
3. German Embassy in St. Petersburg to Berlin, Dec. 2, 1905, PAAA.
4. Gerassimoff, *Der Kampf gegen die erste Russische Revolution,* pp. 65–66.
5. *Russkie vedomosti,* Nov. 5, 1905, p. 2.
6. Gerassimoff, *Der Kampf,* p. 67.
7. Ruud, *Fighting Words: Imperial Censorship and the Russian Press, 1804–1906,* p. 222; Healy, *The Russian Autocracy in Crisis, 1905–1907,* p. 57.
8. Engelstein, *Moscow, 1905,* p. 150.
9. Bonnell, *Roots of Rebellion,* p. 123.
10. Weinberg, "Worker Organizations and Politics in the Revolution of 1905 in Odessa," p. 311.
11. *Obshchestvennoe dvizhenie,* III, pp. 583, 584–85.
12. *Ibid.,* pp. 584–85; *Istoriia KPSS,* II, p. 116.
13. Anweiler, *Die Rätebewegung in Russland,* pp. 71–72.
14. *Obshchestvennoe dvizhenie,* II, part 1, pp. 238–39.
15. Gerassimoff, *Der Kampf,* p. 68.
16. *Ibid.,* pp. 62–63, 68.
17. *Dokumenty i materialy,* IV, part 1, p. 49.
18. Anweiler, *Die Rätebewegung,* p. 72.
19. *Ibid.*

20. Vitte, *Vospominaniia*, II, p. 78.

21. Voitinskii, *Gody pobed i porazhenii*, I, p. 181; Zelikson-Bobrovskaia, ed., *Pervaia russkaia revoliutsiia v Peterburge 1905 g.*, I, p. 112.

22. Zelikson-Bobrovskaia, ed., *Pervaia russkaia revoliutsiia*, pp. 114–16; Anweiler, *Die Rätebewegung*, pp. 69–70.

23. Shuster, *Peterburgskie rabochie v 1905–1907 gg.*, pp. 163, 193–94.

24. *Russkie vedomosti*, Nov. 3, 1905, p. 2.

25. Trotsky quoted in Keep, *The Rise of Social Democracy in Russia*, p. 238.

26. Voitinskii, *Gody pobed*, pp. 244–45; Shuster, *Peterburgskie rabochie*, p. 164.

27. *Obshchestvennoe dvizhenie*, II, part 1, p. 112.

28. Voitinskii, *Gody pobed*, p. 254.

29. *Russkie vedomosti*, Nov. 3, 1905, p. 2; *Pravo*, no. 44 (Nov. 13, 1905), columns 3582–83.

30. *Pravo*, no. 44 (Nov. 13, 1905), column 3582.

31. *Izvestiia Soveta rabochikh deputatov*, Nov. 7, 1905, quoted in Shuster, *Peterburgskie rabochie*, p. 165.

32. Miliukov, *Vospominaniia (1859–1917)*, I, pp. 335, 344.

33. *Obshchestvennoe dvizhenie*, III, p. 599.

34. *Ibid.*, II, part 1, pp. 237–38.

35. Shuster, *Peterburgskie rabochie*, pp. 192–93.

36. *Obshchestvennoe dvizhenie*, II, part 1, p. 114; Engelstein, *Moscow, 1905*, pp. 174–79.

37. *Dokumenty i materialy*, IX, part 1, p. 145.

38. *Ibid.*, pp. 147–50.

39. Garvi, *Vospominaniia sotsialdemokrata*, p. 582.

40. Martov, "Zadachi obedineniia," p. 2.

41. "Nashi zadachi," *Nachalo*, no. 1 (Nov. 13, 1905), p. 1.

42. Trotskii, "Stachka v oktiabre," p. 5.

43. "Beseda s G. V. Plekhanovym," *Rus*, Oct. 23, 1905, p. 3. For a full discussion of Plekhanov's views of the revolution, see Baron, *Plekhanov*, pp. 254–78, and Baron, "Plekhanov and the Revolution of 1905."

44. "Sotsialdemokratiia i revoliutsiia," *Nachalo*, no. 10 (Nov. 25, 1905), p. 1. Translation taken from Keep, *The Rise of Social Democracy in Russia*, p. 274.

45. "Krestianskii vopros i revoliutsiia," *Nachalo*, no. 7 (Nov. 20, 1905), p. 1.

46. Scharlau and Zeman, *Freibeuter der Revolution*.

47. Parvus, "Khod revoliutsii," p. 2.

48. Mehring, "Die Revolution in Permanenz," p. 171. See also the discussion in Keep, *The Rise of Social Democracy in Russia*, pp. 274–75.

49. Schorske, *German Social Democracy, 1905–1917*, pp. 36–38, 73–74.

50. Rudolf Hilferding to Karl Kautsky, Nov. 14, 1905, Kautsky Archive, International Institute for Social History, Amsterdam.

51. Quoted in Nettl, *Rosa Luxemburg*, I, p. 76.

52. For details on the German party, see my "German Socialists and the Russian Revolution of 1905," forthcoming in Ezra Mendelsohn and Marshall S. Shatz, eds., *Imperial Russia 1700–1917: State, Society, Opposition*.

53. Martov, "Noiabrskaia zabastovka," p. 1, quoted in Getzler, *Martov*, p. 111.

54. Martov to Axelrod, end of Oct. 1905, *Pisma P. B. Akselroda i Iu. O. Martova, 1901–1916*, p. 146.

55. Lenin, *Sochineniia*, VIII, pp. 352–57, 405–8.

56. On Lenin's tergiversations, see Wolfe, *Three Who Made a Revolution*, pp. 294–96.

57. *Obshchestvennoe dvizhenie*, III, p. 582.

58. *Rus*, Nov. 23, 1905, p. 4.

59. *Obshchestvennoe dvizhenie*, II, part 1, pp. 167–71. For details on the soldiers' revolts in the Far East and Siberia, see the excellent account in Wildman, *The End of the Russian Imperial Army*, pp. 52–57.

60. Anweiler, *Die Rätebewegung*, p. 76; Sokolskii, "Novorossiiskii sovet rabochikh deputatov v 1905 godu," pp. 76–86; *Obshchestvennoe dvizhenie*, II, part 1, pp. 149–51.

61. *Obshchestvennoe dvizhenie*, II, part 1, pp. 171–72.

62. *Ibid.*, pp. 173–74.

63. *Dokumenty i materialy*, IV, part 4, pp. 364–67, 375–76, 416–17, 426–27, 431, 464.

64. *Pravo*, no. 44 (Nov. 13, 1905), columns 3615–16, 3621, 3628; *Pravo*, no. 45–46 (Nov. 20, 1905), column 3723. See also Emmons, *The Formation of Political Parties*, p. 414.

65. *Pravo*, no. 45–46 (Nov. 20, 1905), column 3726.

66. *Ibid.*, column 3705.

67. *Pravo*, no. 44 (Nov. 13, 1905), column 3624.

68. *Ibid.*, column 3611; *Pravo*, no. 45–46 (Nov. 20, 1905), columns 3700, 3703.

69. The introductory section may be found in *Pravo*, no. 45–46 (Nov. 20, 1905), columns 3702–3, 3706–7; see also Rainey, "The Union of 17 October," pp. 110–17; *Obshchestvennoe dvizhenie*, II, part 2, p. 18.

70. E. N. Trubetskoi, "Dve diktatury," *Russkie vedomosti*, Nov. 16, 1905, p. 2.

71. *Russkie vedomosti*, Dec. 2, 1905, p. 1.

72. *Ibid.*, Dec. 3, 1905, p. 2.

73. *Ibid.*, Nov. 30, 1905, p. 2.

74. *Obshchestvennoe dvizhenie*, II, part 1, p. 132.

75. Garvy, "The Financial Manifesto of the St. Petersburg Soviet, 1905." The article contains a translation of the manifesto.

76. Gurko, *Figures and Features of the Past*, pp. 443–44.

77. Vitte, *Vospominaniia*, II, p. 51.

78. Bing, ed., *Secret Letters*, p. 195.

79. Kokovtsov, *Out of My Past*, p. 70.

80. *Ibid.*, p. 89.

81. Von Laue, "Count Witte and the 1905 Revolution," p. 38.

82. Valk et al., eds., *1905 god v Peterburge*, I, p. 371.

83. *Obshchestvennoe dvizhenie*, II, part 2, p. 201; Anweiler, *Die Rätebewegung*, p. 74.

84. Healy, *The Russian Autocracy in Crisis*, pp. 97–98.

85. Mehlinger and Thompson, *Count Witte and the Tsarist Government in the 1905 Revolution*, p. 123.

Chapter 11

1. Nevinson, *The Dawn in Russia*, pp. 118–19.

2. *Syn otechestva*, Nov. 18, 1905, p. 4.

3. Engelstein, *Moscow, 1905*, p. 27.

4. *Ibid.*, p. 4.

5. *Ibid.*, p. 6.

6. Lane, *The Roots of Russian Communism*, p. 132.

7. *Ibid.*, pp. 127–28.

8. Garvi, *Vospominaniia sotsialdemokrata*, pp. 572–74.

9. Zenzinov, *Perezhitoe*, p. 206.

10. *Ibid.*, pp. 222–23.

11. German Consulate in Moscow to Berlin, Nov. 27, 1905, PAAA.

12. U.S. Embassy in St. Petersburg to Secretary of State, Dec. 8, 1905, USDMR. The Emperor was mistaken about the number of Cossacks that could have been mobilized. The correct figure is much closer to 300,000.

13. Zenzinov, *Perezhitoe*, p. 226.

14. Keep, *The Rise of Social Democracy in Russia*, pp. 243–46.

15. Engelstein, *Moscow, 1905*, p. 179.

16. *Ibid.*, p. 188. The three Bolsheviks were M. N. Liadov, M. I. Vasilev-Iuzhin, and S. I. Chernomordik.

17. Garvi, *Vospominaniia sotsialdemokrata*, pp. 611–12.

18. Chernov, *Pered burei: vospominaniia*, p. 259, quoted in Engelstein, *Moscow, 1905*, p. 188.

19. *Dokumenty i materialy*, IV, part 1, p. 665.

20. Garvi, *Vospominaniia sotsialdemokrata*, pp. 611–13.

21. *Dokumenty i materialy*, IV, part 1, pp. 612, 623–24.

22. *Ibid.*, pp. 613–14.

23. *Vpered*, Dec. 4, 1905, quoted in *Dokumenty i materialy*, IV, part 1, p. 615.

24. Quoted in Bushnell, "Mutineers and Revolutionaries: Military Revolution in Russia, 1905–1907," pp. 214–15.

25. Garvi, *Vospominaniia sotsialdemokrata*, pp. 609–10.

26. On Vasilev's report see Engelstein, *Moscow, 1905*, p. 190.

27. *Ibid.*, pp. 190–91; Keep, *The Rise of Social Democracy*, pp. 248–50.

28. *Dokumenty i materialy*, IV, part 1, p. 650.

29. *Pravo*, no. 50 (Dec. 18, 1905), column 4011.

30. Zenzinov, *Perezhitoe*, p. 225.

31. German Embassy in St. Petersburg to Berlin, Dec. 6, 1905, PAAA.

32. Keep, *The Rise of Social Democracy*, p. 251.

33. Vitte, *Vospominaniia*, II, pp. 139–40.

34. Gerassimoff, *Der Kampf gegen die erste Russische Revolution*, p. 75.

35. Vitte, *Vospominaniia*, II, p. 140.

36. Engelstein, *Moscow, 1905*, p. 195.

37. British Consulate in Moscow to British Embassy in St. Petersburg, Dec. 25, 1905, FO 181/827, BDFA.

38. *Pravo*, no. 50 (Dec. 18, 1905), columns 4011, 4018–20; Report from U.S. Consulate in Moscow, Jan. 5, 1906, USDMR.

39. *Pravo*, no. 50 (Dec. 18, 1905), columns 4019–20.

40. *Ibid.*, columns 4023–24; Engelstein, *Moscow, 1905*, p. 204; British Consulate in Moscow to British Embassy in St. Petersburg, Dec. 25, 1905, FO 181/827, BDFA. The author of the report, H. Montgomery Grove, was an eyewitness to the events at the academy.

41. *Pravo*, no. 50 (Dec. 18, 1905), column 4024.

42. *Dokumenty i materialy*, IV, part 1, pp. 665–66. See also Engelstein, *Moscow, 1905*, p. 209, on the Combat Organization's instructions.

43. Zenzinov, *Perezhitoe*, p. 247.

44. U.S. Consulate in Moscow to U.S. Embassy in St. Petersburg, Jan. 5, 1906, USDMR.

45. British Consulate in Moscow to British Embassy in St. Petersburg, Dec. 25, 1905, FO 181/827, BDFA.

46. *Dokumenty i materialy*, IV, part 1, pp. 677–78.

47. *Ibid.*, pp. 676–77.

48. *Ibid.*, pp. 669–70.

49. British Consulate in Moscow to British Embassy in St. Petersburg, Dec. 25, 1905, FO 181/827, BDFA.

50. *Dokumenty i materialy*, IV, part 1, p. 656. For a comprehensive account of the soviet in Moscow, see Slusser, "The Moscow Soviet of Workers' Deputies of 1905."

51. *Pravo*, no. 50 (Dec. 18, 1905), column 4026.

52. Garvi, *Vospominaniia sotsialdemokrata*, pp. 635, 640–41.

53. *Ibid.*, pp. 639–45.

54. *Ibid.*, p. 646.

55. *Pravo*, no. 50 (Dec. 18, 1905), column 4037.

56. British Consulate in Moscow to British Embassy in St. Petersburg, Dec. 28, 1905, FO 181/827, BDFA.

57. *Dokumenty i materialy*, IV, part 1, p. 730.

58. *Ibid.*, pp. 729–35.

59. Garvi, *Vospominaniia sotsialdemokrata*, p. 669.

60. *Ibid.*, p. 644.

61. *Ibid.*, pp. 655–56.

62. *Dokumenty i materialy*, IV, part 1, pp. 713–15.

63. *Obshchestvennoe dvizhenie*, II, part 1, p. 148; *Russkie vedomosti*, Dec. 21, 1905, p. 3.

64. Nevinson, *The Dawn in Russia*, pp. 194–95; for reports on summary executions, see *Russkie vedomosti*, Dec. 21, 1905, p. 2.

65. Astrov, *Vospominaniia*, pp. 332–33.

66. Report on the General Situation from St. Petersburg, dated Dec. 28, 1905, FO 181/828, BDFA.

67. *Dokumenty i materialy*, IV, part 2, pp. 21–37.

68. *Ibid.*, pp. 460–72.

69. Lewis, "The Labor Movement in Russian Poland," pp. 271–82.

70. French Consulate in Tiflis to Paris, Feb. 5, 1906, AMAE, VII. For a brief, polemical account of events in Tiflis toward the end of 1905, see Makharadze and Khachapuridze, *Ocherki po istorii rabochego i krestianskogo dvizhenie v Gruzii*, pp. 189–99; see also *Dokumenty i materialy*, IV, part 3, pp. 855–60, 872–73. On the outbreaks of violence in Siberia, see Chapter 10 above, pp. 291–92.

71. *Obshchestvennoe dvizhenie*, II, part 1, p. 244.

72. *Ibid.*, p. 146, and part 2, p. 123; *Russkie vedomosti*, Dec. 20, 1905, p. 4.

73. Quoted in Owen, *Capitalism and Politics in Russia*, p. 202. On the general rightward drift of the Moscow business community after the uprising, see *ibid.*, pp. 200–205.

74. Astrov, *Vospominaniia*, p. 334.

75. *Novoe vremia*, Dec. 23, 1906, p. 6.

76. *Ibid.*, Dec. 16, 1905, p. 1.

77. *Obshchestvennoe dvizhenie*, II, part 2, p. 123.

78. *Poliarnaia zvezda*, no. 1 (Dec. 15, 1905), pp. 3–4; *ibid.* (Dec. 30, 1905), pp. 223–28, both cited in Smith, "The Constitutional-Democratic Movement in Russia, 1902–1906," p. 500.

79. Riha, *A Russian European*, p. 102.

80. Miliukov, *Vospominaniia (1859–1917)*, I, p. 350.

81. *Russkie vedomosti*, Dec. 19, 1905, p. 2.

82. See Chapter 10 above, pp. 298, 300; see also Mehlinger and Thompson, *Count Witte and the Tsarist Government*, p. 125.

83. *Dokumenty i materialy*, IV, part 1, pp. 156–57.

84. Semennikov, ed., *Revoliutsiia 1905 goda i samoderzhavie*, pp. 31–32.

85. *Ibid.*, p. 34.

86. *Ibid.*, p. 36.

87. Bing, ed., *The Secret Letters of the Last Tsar*, p. 211.

88. Gerassimoff, *Der Kampf*, pp. 74–75, 77, 86–87.

89. *Russkie vedomosti*, Dec. 22, 1905, p. 3.

90. *Ibid.*, Jan. 1, 1906, p. 3.

91. *Dokumenty i materialy*, IV, part 1, pp. 157–58.

92. Semennikov, ed., *Revoliutsiia 1905 goda i samoderzhavie*, pp. 197, 204; Chermenskii, *Burzhuaziia i tsarizm v pervoi russkoi revoliutsii*, p. 182.

93. Vitte, *Vospominaniia*, II, pp. 125–28.

94. *Ibid.*, pp. 122–23.

95. Mehlinger and Thompson, *Count Witte*, pp. 88, 106–7, 164–65; Santoni, "P. N. Durnovo as Minister of Internal Affairs," pp. 237–38.

96. "K istorii karatelnykh ekspeditsii v Sibiri," *Krasnyi arkhiv*, I (1922), p. 232.

97. *Ibid.*, p. 330.

98. *Ibid.*, p. 343.

99. *Dokumenty i materialy*, V, part 1, pp. 818–19, 915.

100. "Iz vospominanii I. K. Okuntsova," *Byloe*, no. 7 (1908), pp. 80–85.

101. Kariakhiarm et al., *Revoliutsiia 1905–1907 godov v Pribaltike*, pp. 73–74.

102. *Dokumenty i materialy*, IV, part 5, p. 591.

103. Kariakhiarm et al., *Revoliutsiia 1905–1907 godov v Pribaltike*, p. 74.

104. "Report on Internal Affairs" (from St. Petersburg), Feb. 14, 1906, FO 181/866, BDFA.

105. *Obshchestvennoe dvizhenie*, II, part 1, p. 175.

106. Bing, ed., *Secret Letters*, pp. 205–6.

107. Mehlinger and Thompson, *Count Witte*, p. 109.

108. *Dokumenty i materialy*, IV, part 3, p. 413.

109. *Ibid.*, V, part 2, pp. 76–77.

110. British Embassy in St. Petersburg to London, Feb. 28 and Mar. 26, 1906, FO 181/869, BDFA.

111. *Pravo*, no. 10 (Mar. 6, 1906), columns 909–16.

112. Santoni, "P. N. Durnovo," p. 249.

113. Bushnell, "Mutineers and Revolutionaries," p. 146.

114. Nevinson, *The Dawn in Russia*, p. 138; for details on government repression in the period from October 1905 to April 1906, see Obninskii, *Polgoda russkoi revoliutsii*. This work reproduces telegrams received by the newspaper *Russkoe slovo* from all over Russia on disturbances and measures taken by the authorities to quell them.

115. *Pravo*, no. 4 (Jan. 29, 1906), column 283.

Conclusion

1. British Embassy in St. Petersburg to Sir Edward Grey, Jan. 7, 1906, FO 181/866, BDFA.

2. British Embassy in St. Petersburg to Sir Edward Grey, Jan. 26, 1906, *ibid.*

3. German Embassy in St. Petersburg to Prince Bülow, Feb. 19, 1906, PAAA.

4. *Moskovskie vedomosti,* Jan. 1, 1906, p. 2.

5. *Ibid.*; the statement on the powers of the autocrat is in the issue of Jan. 10, 1906, p. 1.

6. Shipov, *Vospominaniia i dumy o perezhitom,* p. 421; Menashe, "Alexander Guchkov and the Origins of the Octobrist Party," pp. 184–91.

7. Pipes, *Struve: Liberal on the Right,* pp. 35–36.

8. Keep, "Russian Social Democracy," pp. 183–84; Hildermeier, *Die Sozialrevolutionäre Partei Russlands,* p. 176.

9. Hildermeier, *Die Sozialrevolutionäre Partei Russlands,* p. 178; Keep, "Russian Social Democracy," p. 198.

10. German Consulate in Moscow to Prince Bülow, Feb. 19, 1906, PAAA.

11. British Embassy in St. Petersburg to London, Feb. 14, 1906, FO 181/866, BDFA.

12. *Pravo,* no. 2 (Jan. 15, 1906), columns 143–45; Obninskii, *Polgoda russkoi revoliutsii,* p. 152; German Embassy in St. Petersburg to Prince Bülow, Feb. 19, 1906, PAAA.

13. German Embassy in St. Petersburg to Prince Bülow, Feb. 19, 1906, PAAA; *Pravo,* no. 2 (Jan. 15, 1906), columns 150–51.

14. Mehlinger and Thompson, *Count Witte and the Tsarist Government in the 1905 Revolution,* pp. 127–28; Santoni, "P. N. Durnovo as Minister of Internal Affairs in the Witte Cabinet," pp. 443–57; British Embassy in St. Petersburg to Sir Edward Grey, Jan. 7, 1906, FO 181/866, BDFA.

15. British Embassy in St. Petersburg to London, Feb. 14, 1906, FO 186/869, BDFA. On the rumors about Witte's imminent resignation, see *Russkie vedomosti,* Mar. 13, 1906, p. 1; Mar. 16, pp. 2–3; Mar. 17, p. 2; Mar. 19, p. 3.

16. British Embassy in St. Petersburg to London, Feb. 28, 1906, FO 181/866, BDFA.

17. Weber, "Zur Lage der bürgerlichen Demokratie in Russland," p. 353.

18. See Rogger, *Russia in the Age of Modernisation and Revolution, 1881–1917,* p. 29.

Bibliography

The Bibliography is in three sections, each arranged alphabetically. I begin by listing the newspapers and journals cited so frequently in the Notes, with some indication of the political orientation of each. The main body of the Bibliography follows, divided into one section titled "Memoirs and Published Documents" and another titled "Other Sources."

Newspapers and Journals

Die Neue Zeit. Stuttgart. Official theoretical journal of the German Social Democratic Party.

Grazhdanin. St. Petersburg. Conservative political and literary journal.

Iskra. Munich-London-Geneva-Vienna. Organ of the Russian Social Democratic Party.

Izvestiia soveta rabochikh deputatov. St. Petersburg. Newspaper of the St. Petersburg Soviet.

Moskovskie vedomosti. Moscow. Conservative newspaper.

Nachalo (1905). St. Petersburg. Menshevik paper.

Nasha zhizn. St. Petersburg. Left-liberal; sympathetic to the Socialist Revolutionaries.

Novoe vremia. St. Petersburg. Pro-government newspaper.

Osvobozhdenie. Stuttgart-Paris. Bi-weekly journal of the Union of Liberation.

Poliarnaia zvezda. St. Petersburg. Liberal theoretical journal.

Pravitelstvennyi vestnik. St. Petersburg. Official government newspaper.

Pravo. St. Petersburg. Weekly juridical journal. Liberal, close to the Kadets.

Rus. St. Petersburg. Liberal daily newspaper.

Russkie vedomosti. Moscow. Liberal newspaper; after 1905, close to the moderate Kadets.

Russkoe bogatstvo. St. Petersburg. Liberal Populist, anti-Marxist.

Russkoe znamia. St. Petersburg. Official organ of the right-wing Union of the Russian People.

Syn otechestva. St. Petersburg. Initially a liberal paper; came under the influence of the Socialist Revolutionaries.

Vestnik Evropy. Moscow. Moderate-liberal historical and political journal.

Memoirs and Published Documents

Ascher, Abraham, tr. and ed. "The Coming Storm: The Austro-Hungarian Embassy on Russia's Internal Crisis, 1902–1906," *Survey: A Journal of Soviet and East European Studies*, 1964, no. 53, pp. 148–64.
Askew, William C. "An American View of Bloody Sunday," *Russian Review*, 1952, no. 2, pp. 35–43.
Astrov, N. I. *Vospominaniia*. Paris, 1941.
Baring, Maurice. *A Year in Russia*. London, 1917 (original ed., 1907).
Bing, Edward J., ed. *The Secret Letters of the Last Tsar*. New York, 1938.
Bompard, M. *Mon Ambassade en Russie, 1903–1908*. Paris, 1937.
Bonnell, Victoria E., ed. and intr. *The Russian Worker: Life and Labor Under the Tsarist Regime*. Berkeley, 1983.
Budberg, R. Iu. "Sezd zemskikh deiatelei 6–9 noiabria 1904 goda v Peterburge (Po lichnym vospominaniiam)," *Byloe*, 1907, no. 3/15 (Mar.), pp. 70–88.
Chastnoe soveshchanie zemskikh deiatelei proiskhodivshee 6, 7, 8 i 9 noiabria 1904 goda v S. Peterburge. Moscow, 1905.
Chernov, V. M. *Pered burei. Vospominaniia*. New York, 1953.
Dillon, Edward J. *The Eclipse in Russia*. New York, 1918.
Dnevnik Imperatora Nikolaia II. Berlin, 1923.
"Dnevnik Kn. Ekateriny Alekseevny Sviatopolk-Mirskoi za 1904–1905 gg.," *Istoricheskie zapiski*, 1965, vol. 77, pp. 240–88.
"Dnevnik A. N. Kuropatkina," *Krasnyi arkhiv*, 1922, no. 2, pp. 6–112.
Drezen, A. K., ed. *Tsarizm v borbe s revoliutsiei 1905–1907 gg.: Sbornik dokumentov*. Moscow, 1936.
Gapon, G. A. *The Story of My Life*. London, 1905.
Garvi, P. A. *Vospominaniia sotsialdemokrata: stati o zhizni i deiatelnosti P. A. Garvi*. New York, 1946.
Gerassimoff, Alexander. *Der Kampf gegen die erste Russische Revolution. Erinnerungen* (tr. Ernst Thälmann). Frauenfeld and Leipzig, 1934.
Gessen, I. V. *V dvukh vekakh: zhiznennyi otchet*. Berlin, 1937.
Guchkov, A. I. "Iz vospominanii A. I. Guchkova," *Poslednie novosti*, Aug. 9, 1936, p. 1.
Gurko, V. I. *Figures and Features of the Past; Government and Opinion in the Reign of Nicholas II* (tr. Laura Matveev). Stanford, Calif., 1939.
"Iz vospominanii I. K. Okuntsova," *Byloe*, 1908, no. 7, pp. 80–86.
[Zelnik, Reginald E., tr. and ed.]. *A Radical Worker in Tsarist Russia: The Autobiography of Semen Ivanovich Kanatchikov*. Stanford, Calif., 1986.
"Karatelnaia ekspeditsiia polk. Rimana," *Krasnyi arkhiv*, 1925, no. 4–5 (11–12), pp. 398–420.
Kokovtsov, V. N. *Out of My Past: The Memoirs of Count Kokovtsov*. Stanford, Calif., 1935.
Lopukhin, A. A. *Otryvki iz vospominanii (po povodu "Vospominanii" gr. S. Iu. Vitte)*. Moscow and Petrograd, 1923.
"Manifest 17 oktiabria," *Krasnyi arkhiv*, 1925, no. 4–5 (11–12), pp. 39–106.
Miliukov, P. N. *Vospominaniia (1859–1917)*. New York, 1955.
Mosolov, A. A. *Pri dvore Imperatora*. Riga, 1938.
Nevinson, Henry W. *The Dawn in Russia: Or Scenes in the Russian Revolution*. New York, 1906.
Pervaia obshcherusskaia konferentsiia partiinykh rabotnikov. Otdelnoe prilozhenie k No. 100 'Iskry'. Geneva, 1905.

Petergofskoe soveshchanie o proekte o gosudarstvennoi dumy pod lichnym Ego Imperatorskogo Velichestva predsedatelstvom: Sekretnye protokoly. Berlin, n.d.

Petrunkevich, I. I. "Iz zapisok obshchestvennogo deiatelia," *Arkhiv russkoi revoliutsii* (Berlin, 1934).

Pisma P. B. Akselroda i Iu. O. Martova, 1901–1906. Ed. F. Dan, B. I. Nicolaevsky, and L. Tsederbaum. Berlin, 1924.

Pogorelko, A. K., ed. *Doklad kharkovskogo gorodskogo golovy o rezultatakh soveshchanii zemskikh i gorodskikh deiatelei po voprosam, kasaiushchimsia usovershenstvovaniia gosudarstvennogo blagoustroistva i uluchsheniia narodnogo blagosostoianiia.* Kharkov, 1905.

Polnoe Sobranie Zakonov Rossiiskoi Imperii. Third Collection, St. Petersburg, 1908.

Raeff, Marc, ed. and intr. *Plans for Political Reform in Imperial Russia: 1730–1905.* Englewood Cliffs, N.J., 1966.

[Rediger, A. F.]. "Zapiski A. F. Redigera o 1905 g.," *Krasnyi arkhiv,* 1931, no. 2 (45), pp. 86–111.

Revoliutsiia 1905–1907 gg. v Gruzii. Sbornik dokumentov. Tiflis, 1956.

Revoliutsiia 1905–1907 gg. v Latvii. Dokumenty i materialy. Riga, 1956.

Revoliutsiia 1905–1907 gg. v Rossii. Dokumenty i materialy. Eds. A. N. Pankratova et al. Vols. I–IV. Moscow, 1955–1961.

Revoliutsiia 1905–1907 godov v g. Samare i Samarskoi gubernii: Dokumenty i materialy. Kuibyshev, 1955.

Semennikov, V. P., ed. *Revoliutsiia 1905 goda i samoderzhavie.* Moscow, 1928.

Sezd 12–18 oktiabria 1905 g. St. Petersburg, 1905. A publication prepared by the Kadet party.

Shipov, D. N. *Vospominaniia i dumy o perezhitom.* Moscow, 1918.

Struve, Peter. "My Contacts with Rodichev," *Slavonic Review,* 1934, no. 35, pp. 347–67.

Svod zakonov Rossiiskoi Imperii. Eds. A. F. Volkov and Iu. D. Filipov. St. Petersburg, 1904.

Tretii sezd RSDRP, Aprel-Mai 1905 goda: Protokoly. Moscow, 1959.

Uratadze, Gregory. *Vospominaniia gruzinskogo sotsial-demokrata.* Stanford, Calif., 1968.

Valk, S. N. et al. *1905 god v Peterburge.* 2 vols. Leningrad-Moscow, 1925.

Vasilev-Iuzhin, M. I. *V ogne pervoi revoliutsii.* (Reprint in abbreviated form.) Moscow, 1955.

Vitte, S. Iu. *Vospominaniia.* 3 vols. 2d ed. Leningrad, 1924.

[———]. "Zapiska Vitte ot 9 oktiabria," *Krasnyi arkhiv,* 1925, no. 11–12, pp. 51–57.

Voitinskii, V. S. *Gody pobed i porazhenii.* 2 vols. Berlin-Petersburg-Moscow, 1923.

Von Bülow. *Memoirs of Prince Von Bülow.* Tr. Geoffrey Dunlap. Vol. II, Boston, 1931.

Woytinsky [Voitinskii], W. S. *Stormy Passage: A Personal History Through Two Russian Revolutions to Democracy and Freedom, 1905–1960.* New York, 1961.

——— *Wehe der Besiegten. Erinnerungen aus der russischen revolutionären Bewegung 1906/1910.* Berlin, 1933.

"Zapiski A. S. Ermolova," *Krasnyi arkhiv,* 1925, no. 8, pp. 49–69.

Zenzinov, V. *Perezhitoe*. New York, 1953.
Zhordania, Noah. *Moia zhizn* (tr. Ina Zhordania). Stanford, Calif., 1968.

Other Sources

Adams, Arthur C. "Pobedonostsev and the Rule of Firmness," *Slavonic and East European Review*, 32 (1953), pp. 132–39.
Alston, Patrick L. *Education and the State in Tsarist Russia*. Stanford, Calif., 1969.
Aluf, I. A., et al., eds. *Problemy gegemonii proletariata v demokraticheskoi revoliutsii (1905–Fevr. 1917 gg.)*. Moscow, 1975.
Amalrik, A. S. "K voprosu o chislennosti i geograficheskorn razmeshchenii stachechnikov v evropeiskoi Rossii v 1905 godu," *Istoricheskie zapiski*, 1955, no. 52, pp. 142–85.
Amann, Peter. "Revolution: A Redefinition," *Political Science Quarterly*, 77 (Mar. 1962), pp. 36–53.
Ananich, B. V., and R. Sh. Ganelin. "Opyt kritiki memuarov S. Iu. Vitte," in S. N. Valk et al., eds., *Voprosy istoriografii i istochnikovedeniia istorii SSSR. Sbornik statei* (Moscow and Leningrad, 1963), pp. 298–374.
Anweiler, Oskar. *Die Rätebewegung in Russland, 1905–1921*. Leiden, 1958.
———. "Die russische Revolution von 1905," *Jahrbücher für Geschichte Osteuropas*, n.s. 1955, no. 1, pp. 161–93.
Ascher, Abraham. *Pavel Axelrod and the Development of Menshevism*. Cambridge, Mass., 1972.
———. "Soviet Historians and the Revolution of 1905," in Coquin and Gervais-Francelle, eds., *1905*, pp. 476–96.
Avrich, Paul. *The Russian Anarchists*. Princeton, N.J., 1967.
Balabanov, M. *Ot 1905 k 1917: Massovoe rabochee dvizhenie*. Moscow, 1927.
Baron, Samuel H. "Plekhanov and the Revolution of 1905," in John S. Curtiss, ed., *Essays in Russian and Soviet History* (New York, 1963), pp. 133–48.
———. *Plekhanov: The Father of Russian Marxism*. Stanford, Calif., 1963.
Becker, Seymour. *Nobility and Privilege in Late Imperial Russia*. DeKalb, Ill., 1985.
Bennett, Geoffrey. "The *Potemkin* Mutiny," *United States Naval Institute Proceedings*, 1959, no. 9, pp. 58–66.
Blackwell, William L. *The Industrialization of Russia: An Historical Perspective*. New York, 1970.
Bloomfield, Edith. "Soviet Historiography of 1905 as Reflected in Party Histories of the 1920's." Ph. D. diss., University of Washington, 1966.
Bohachevsky-Chomiak, Martha. *Sergei N. Trubetskoi: An Intellectual Among the Intelligentsia in Prerevolutionary Russia*. Belmont, Mass., 1976.
Bonnell, Victoria E. *Roots of Rebellion: Workers' Politics and Organizations in St. Petersburg and Moscow, 1900–1914*. Berkeley, Calif., 1983.
Bovykin, V. I., and O. I. Latysheva. "Moskovskii universitet v revoliutsii 1905–1907 godov," *Voprosy istorii*, 1955, no. 4, pp. 49–58.
Bovykin, V. I., et al., eds. *Rabochii klass v pervoi rossiiskoi revoliutsii 1905–1907 gg.* Moscow, 1981.
Brock, John Joseph, Jr. "The Theory and Practice of the Union of the Russian People, 1905–1907: A Case Study of 'Black Hundred' Politics." Ph. D. diss., University of Michigan, 1972.

Bushnell, John S. "Mutineers and Revolutionaries: Military Revolution in Russia, 1905–1907." Ph. D. diss., Indiana University, 1977.

———. *Mutiny amid Repression: Russian Soldiers in the Revolution of 1905–1906.* Bloomington, Ind., 1985.

———. "The Tsarist Officer Corps, 1881–1914: Customs, Duties, Inefficiency." *American Historical Review*, 1981, no. 4, pp. 753–80.

Byrnes, Robert F. *Pobedonostsev: His Life and Thought.* Bloomington, Ind., 1968.

Chermenskii, E. D. *Burzhuaziia i tsarizm v pervoi russkoi revoliutsii.* 2d ed. Moscow, 1970.

———. "Zemsko-liberalnoe dvizhenie nakanune revoliutsii 1905–1907 gg.," *Istoriia SSSR*, 1965, no. 5, pp. 41–60.

Chernomordik, S. I. "Dekabrskoe vooruzhennoe vosstanie 1905 goda i Moskovskii Sovet rabochikh deputatov," *Voprosy istorii*, 1946, no. 1, pp. 3–36.

Cohn, Norman. *Warrant for Genocide: The Myth of the Jewish World-Conspiracy and the Protocols of the Elders of Zion.* New York, 1969.

Coquin, François-Xavier. "Un aspect méconnu de la révolution de 1905: les 'motions paysannes,'" in Coquin and Gervais-Francelle, eds., *1905*, pp. 181–200.

Coquin, François-Xavier, and Céline Gervais-Francelle, eds. *1905: La Première Révolution Russe.* Paris, 1986.

Cunningham, James W. *A Vanquished Hope: The Movement for Church Renewal in Russia, 1905–1906.* New York, 1981.

Curtiss, John S. *Church and State in Russia: The Last Years of the Empire, 1900–1917.* New York, 1940.

Dan, F. "K nachalu akademicheskogo goda," *Iskra*, no. 107 (July 29, 1905), p. 1.

Demochkin, N. N. "Revoliutsionnoe tvorchestvo krestianskikh mass v revoliutsii 1905–1907 godov," *Istoriia SSSR*, 1980, no. 1, pp. 45–61.

Derenkovskii, G. M., and S. V. Tiutiukin. "K voprosu ob ispolzovanii opyta pervoi russkoi revoliutsii v period podgotovki Oktiabria," *Istoriia SSSR*, 1977, no. 5, pp. 105–19.

Derenkovskii, G. M., et al. "1905 god v Saratove," *Istoricheskie zapiski*, 1955, no. 54, pp. 74–104.

———. "Osnovnye itogi izucheniia istorii pervoi russkoi revoliutsii za poslednie dvatsat let," *Istoriia SSSR*, 1975, no. 5, pp. 42–60.

Dillon, Edward J. *The Eclipse of Russia.* New York, 1918.

———. "Two Russian Statesmen," *The Quarterly Review*, vol. 236, 1921, pp. 402–17.

Doctorow, Gilbert S. "The Introduction of Parliamentary Institutions in Russia During the Revolution of 1905–1907." Ph.D. diss., Columbia University, 1975.

Drezen, A. *Armiia i flot v revoliutsii 1905 g.* Moscow, 1931.

Drozdov, I. G. *Agrarnye volneniia i karatelnye ekspeditsii v Chernigovskoi gubernii v gody pervoi revoliutsii. 1905–1906 gg.* Moscow, 1925.

Dubrovskii, S. M. *Krestianskoe dvizhenie v revoliutsii 1905–1907 gg.* Moscow, 1956.

Dukes, Paul. *A History of Russia.* New York, 1974.

Dziewanowski, M. K. "The Polish Revolutionary Movement and Russia, 1904–1907," in Hugh McLean et al., eds., *Russian Thought and Politics* (The Hague, 1957), pp. 375–94.

Elwood, Ralph Carter. *Russian Social Democracy in the Underground: A Study of the RSDRP in the Ukraine, 1907–1914.* Assen, 1974.

Emmons, Terence. "Russia's Banquet Campaign," *California Slavic Studies*, 10 (1977), pp. 45–86.

———. *The Formation of Political Parties and the First National Elections in Russia*. Cambridge, Mass., 1983.

———. "The Statutes of the Union of Liberation," *Russian Review*, 1974, no. 1, pp. 80–85.

———, and Wayne S. Vucinich, eds. *The Zemstvo in Russia: An Experiment in Local Self-Government*. Cambridge, Eng., 1982.

Engelstein, Laura. *Moscow, 1905: Working-Class Organization and Political Conflict*. Stanford, Calif., 1982.

Erman, L. K. "Borba Bolshevikov za demokraticheskuiu intelligentsiiu v 1905 godu," *Voprosy istorii*, 1955, no. 2, pp. 17–31.

———. *Intelligentsiia v pervoi russkoi revoliutsii*. Moscow, 1966.

———. "Uchastie demokraticheskoi intelligentsii vo vserossiiskoi oktiabrskoi politicheskoi stachke," *Istoricheskie zapiski*, 1954, no. 49, pp. 352–90.

Esthus, Raymond A. "Nicholas II and the Russo-Japanese War," *Russian Review*, 1981, no. 4, pp. 396–411.

Fainsod, Merle. "Soviet Russian Historians, or: the Lessons of Burdzhalov," *Encounter*, 1962, no. 3, pp. 82–89.

Fedor, Thomas S. *Patterns of Urban Growth in the Russian Empire During the Nineteenth Century*. Chicago, 1975.

Fischer, Alexander. *Russische Sozialdemokratie und bewaffneter Aufstand im Jahre 1905*. Wiesbaden, 1967.

Fischer, George. *Russian Liberalism: From Gentry to Intelligentsia*. Cambridge, Mass., 1958.

Frankel, Jonathan. *Prophesy and Politics: Socialism, Nationalism, & the Russian Jews, 1862–1917*. Cambridge, Eng., 1981.

———, ed. *Vladimir Akimov on the Dilemmas of Russian Marxism, 1895–1903*. Cambridge, Eng., 1969.

Freeze, Gregory L. "A National Liberation Movement and the Shift in Russian Liberalism, 1901–1903," *Slavic Review*, 1969, no. 1, pp. 81–91.

———. "The *Soslovie* (Estate) Paradigm and Russian Social History," *American Historical Review*, 1986, no. 1, pp. 11–36.

Frieden, Nancy M. *Russian Physicians in an Era of Reform and Revolution, 1856–1905*. Princeton, N.J., 1981.

Fuller, William C. *Civil-Military Conflict in Imperial Russia, 1881–1914*. Princeton, N.J., 1985.

Futrell, Michael. "Colonel Akashi and Japanese Contacts with Russian Revolutionaries in 1904–5," *Far Eastern Affairs*, 1967, no. 4, pp. 7–22.

———. *Northern Underground: Episodes of Russian Revolutionary Transport and Communications Through Scandinavia and Finland, 1863–1917*. London, 1963.

Galai, Shmuel. "The Impact of War on the Russian Liberals in 1904–5," *Government and Opposition*, 1965, no. 1, pp. 85–109.

———. *The Liberation Movement in Russia, 1900–1905*. Cambridge, Mass., 1973.

———. "The Role of the Union of Unions in the Revolution of 1905," *Jahrbücher für Geschichte Osteuropas*, 1976, no. 4, pp. 512–15.

Gard, William G. "The Party and the Proletariat in Ivanovo-Voznesensk, 1905," *Russian History*, 2 (1975), pp. 101–23.

Garvy, George. "The Financial Manifesto of the St. Petersburg Soviet, 1905," *International Review of Social History*, 1975, no. 1, pp. 16–32.

Gelis, I. *Noiabrskie dni v Sevastopole v 1905 godu. Istoriia vosstaniia v Chernomorskom flote, rabocham Sevastopole i chastiakh garnizona 11–15 noiabria 1905 g.* Kharkov, 1924.

Genkin, I. I. *Leitenant Shmidt i vosstanie na "Ochakov." K dvadtsatiletiiu 1905–1925.* Moscow-Leningrad, 1925.

Getzler, Israel. *Martov: A Political Biography of a Russian Social Democrat.* Cambridge, Eng., 1967.

———. "The Mensheviks," *Problems of Communism*, 1967, no. 6, pp. 15–29.

Geyer, Dietrich. "Die russische Parteispaltung im Urteil der deutschen Sozialdemokratie 1903–1905," *International Review of Social History*, 1958, nos. 2 & 3, pp. 195–219, 418–44.

———. *Lenin in der Russischen Sozialdemokratie. Die Arbeiterbewegung im Zarenreich als Organisationsproblem der revolutionären Intelligenz 1890–1903.* Cologne, 1962.

Giffen, Frederick C. "In Quest of an Effective Program of Factory Legislation in Russia: The Years of Preparation, 1859–1880," *The Historian*, 1967, no. 2, pp. 175–85.

Girault, René. "La révolution russe de 1905 d'après quelques temoignages français," *Revue Historique*, July–Sept. 1963, pp. 97–120.

Glickman, Rose L. *Russian Factory Women: Workplace and Society, 1880–1914.* Berkeley, Calif., 1984.

Gordon, Manya. *Workers Before and After Lenin.* New York, 1941.

Gorin, Pavel. *Ocherki po istorii Sovetov rabochikh deputatov v 1905.* Moscow, 1925.

Greenberg, Louis. *The Jews of Russia.* 2 vols. New Haven, Conn., 1951.

Grinewitsch, W. [M. G. Kogan]. *Die Gewerkschaften in Russland.* Berlin, 1927.

Gurevich, L. Ia. "Narodnoe dvizhenie v Peterburge 9-go ianvaria 1905 g.," *Byloe*, 1906, no. 1, pp. 200–229.

Hamburg, G. M. "The Crisis in Russian Agriculture: A Comment," *Slavic Review*, 1978, no. 3, pp. 481–86.

———. *Politics of the Russian Nobility, 1881–1905.* New Brunswick, N.J., 1984.

———. "The Russian Nobility on the Eve of the 1905 Revolution," *Russian Review*, 1979, no. 3, pp. 323–38.

Harcave, Sidney. *First Blood. The Russian Revolution of 1905.* New York, 1964.

Harper, Samuel N. "Exceptional Measures in Russia," *Russian Review*, 1912, no. 4, pp. 92–105.

Hart, Sterling. "The Russo-Japanese War, 1904–05," *Strategy and Tactics*, 1976, no. 59, pp. 28–43.

Healy, Ann E. *The Russian Autocracy in Crisis, 1905–1907.* Hamden, Conn., 1976.

Heilbronner, Hans. "An Anti-Witte Diplomatic Conspiracy, 1905–1906: The Schwanebach Memorandum," *Jahrbücher für Geschichte Osteuropas*, 1966, no. 3, pp. 347–61.

Hildermeier, Manfred. *Die Sozialrevolutionäre Partei Russlands: Agrarsozialismus und Modernisierung im Zarenreich (1900–1914).* Cologne, 1978.

History of the Communist Party of the Soviet Union (Bolshevik). Ed. Commission of the Central Committee of the C.P.S.U.(B). New York, 1939.

Hoetzsch, Otto. *Russland. Eine Einführung auf Grund seiner Geschichte von 1904–1912.* Berlin, 1913.

Hough, Richard. *The Potemkin Mutiny.* Englewood Cliffs, N.J., 1960.

Iakovlev, N. N. "Moskovskie bolsheviki vo glave dekabrskogo vooruzhennogo vosstaniia 1905 goda," *Voprosy istorii*, 1955, no. 12, pp. 3–18.

———. *Vooruzhennye vosstaniia v dekabre 1905 goda.* Moscow, 1957.

Istoriia KPSS. Ts. N. Pospelov et al., eds., *Istoriia Kommunisticheskoi partii Sovetskogo Soiuza.* Vol. II: *Partiia Bolshevikov v borbe za sverzhenie tsarizma 1904–Fevral 1917 goda.* Moscow, 1966.

Ivanov, L. M., et al., eds. *Rossiiskii proletariat: Oblik, borba, gegemoniia.* Moscow, 1970.

Johnson, Robert E. *Peasant and Proletarian: The Working Class of Moscow in the Late Nineteenth Century.* New Brunswick, N.J., 1979.

Judge, Edward H. *Plehve: Repression and Reform in Imperial Russia, 1902–1904.* Syracuse, N.Y., 1983.

Kabanov, P. I., et al. *Proletariat vo glave osvoboditelnogo dvizheniia v Rossii (1895–1917 gg.).* Moscow, 1971.

Kahan, Arcadius. "Government Policies and the Industrialization of Russia," *Journal of Economic History*, 1967, no. 4, pp. 460–77.

Kariakhiarm, T., et al. *Revoliutsiia 1905–1907 godov v Pribaltike.* Tallin, 1981.

Kassow, Samuel D. "The Russian University in Crisis, 1899–1911." Ph. D. diss., Princeton University, 1976.

Keenan, Edward L. "Remarques sur l'histoire du mouvement révolutionnaire à Bakou (1904–1905)," *Cahiers du Monde Russe et Soviétique*, 1962, no. 2, pp. 225–60.

Keep, J. L. H. "Russian Social Democracy in the First State Duma," *Slavonic and East European Review*, 34 (1955), pp. 180–99.

———. *The Rise of Social Democracy in Russia.* Oxford, 1963.

King, Vladimir. "The Liberal Movement in Russia, 1904–1905," *Slavonic and East European Review*, 14 (1935), pp. 124–37.

Kingston-Mann, Esther. "Lenin and the Challenge of Peasant Militance: From Bloody Sunday, 1905, to the Dissolution of the First Duma," *Russian Review*, 1979, no. 4, pp. 434–55.

Kirillov, V. S. *Bolsheviki vo glave massovykh politisheskikh stachek v period podema revoliutsii 1905–1907 gg.* Moscow, 1961.

Kiriukhina, E. I. "Vserossiiskii Krestianskii soiuz v 1905 g.," *Istoricheskie zapiski*, 50 (1955), pp. 95–141.

[Kirpichnikov, S. D.]. *Soiuz soiuzov.* St. Petersburg, 1906. Signed S. D. K.

"K istorii karatelnykh ekspeditsii v Sibiri," *Krasnyi arkhiv*, 1 (1922), pp. 329–43.

Kommunisticheskaia Akademiia. *Pervaia russkaia revoliutsiia: Ukazatel literatury.* Moscow, 1930.

Kostomarov, G. D. *Moskovskii sovet rabochikh deputatov v 1905 godu.* Moscow, 1948.

Krivoguz, I., and P. Mnukhina. *Mezhdunarodnoe znachenie revoliutsii 1905–1907 godov.* Moscow, 1955.

Kuznetsova, L. S. "Stachechnaia borba rabochikh Peterburga v ianvare 1905 goda," *Voprosy istorii*, 1955, no. 1, pp. 11–25.

Lambroza, Shlomo. "Jewish Self-Defense During the Russian Pogroms of 1903–1906," *The Jewish Journal of Sociology*, 1981, no. 2, pp. 123–34.

Lane, David. *The Roots of Russian Communism. A Social and Historical Study of Russian Social Democracy, 1898–1907.* Assen, 1969.

Laverychev, V. Ia. *Tsarizm i rabochii vopros v Rossii, 1861–1917 gg.* Moscow, 1972.

Lavrov, Peter. *Historical Letters.* Tr. and ed. James Scanlon. Berkeley, Calif., 1967.

Lenin, V. I. *Sochineniia.* 3d ed. Moscow, 1926–37.

Lenin, V. I. *What Is to Be Done?* New York, 1929.

Leontowitsch, Victor. *Geschichte des Liberalismus in Russland.* Frankfurt, 1957.

Levin, Alfred. "Russian Bureaucratic Opinion in the Wake of the 1905 Revolution," *Jahrbücher für Geschichte Osteuropas,* 1963, no. 4, pp. 1–12.

Levin, Sh. M. "V. I. Lenin v Peterburge v 1905 g.," *Voprosy istorii,* 1955, no. 6, pp. 3–12.

Lewis, Richard D. "The Labor Movement in Russian Poland in the Revolution of 1905–1907." Ph. D. diss., University of California, Berkeley, 1971.

Linden, A., ed. *Die Judenpogromme in Russland.* Cologne and Leipzig, 1910.

Long, James W. "Russian Manipulation of the French Press, 1904–1906," *Slavic Review,* 1972, no. 2, pp. 343–54.

———. "The Economics of the Franco-Russian Alliance, 1904–1906." Ph. D. diss., University of Wisconsin, Madison, 1968.

Löwe, Heinz-Dietrich. *Antisemitismus und reaktionäre Utopie: Russischer Konservatismus im Kampf gegen die Wandel von Staat und Gesellschaft.* Hamburg, 1978.

Makharadze, F. E., and G. V. Khachapuridze. *Ocherki po istorii rabochego i krestianskogo dvizheniia v Gruzii.* Moscow, 1932.

Malia, Martin. "What Is the Intelligentsia?," in Richard Pipes, ed., *The Russian Intelligentsia* (New York, 1961), pp. 1–18.

Malozemoff, Andrew. *Russian Far Eastern Policy, 1881–1904: With Special Emphasis on the Causes of the Russo-Japanese War.* Berkeley, Calif., 1958.

Manning, Roberta T. *The Crisis of the Old Order in Russia: Gentry and Government.* Princeton, N.J., 1982.

Martov, L. "Noiabrskaia zabastovka," *Nachalo,* no. 1 (Nov. 13, 1905), p. 1.

———. "Zadachi obedineniia," *Nachalo,* no. 8 (Nov. 23, 1905), p. 2.

Martov, L., P. Maslov, and A. Potresov, eds. *Obshchestvennoe dvizhenie v Rossii v nachale XX-go veka.* 4 vols. St. Petersburg, 1909–11.

Martynov, A. S. "Krestianskii vopros i revoliutsiia," *Nachalo,* no. 7 (Nov. 20, 1905), p. 1.

Materialy k istorii russkoi kontr-revoliutsii. St. Petersburg, 1908.

Maurice, F. B. "The Russo-Japanese War," in A. W. Ward et al., eds., *The Cambridge Modern History* (New York, 1910), vol. XII, pp. 576–601.

Mavor, James. *An Economic History of Russia.* 2 vols. New York, 1914.

Mehlinger, Howard D., and John M. Thompson. *Count Witte and the Tsarist Government in the 1905 Revolution.* Bloomington, Ind., 1972.

Mehring, Franz. "Die Revolution in Permanenz," *Die Neue Zeit,* 24, no. 1 (1905–6), pp. 169–72. This is a German version of an article titled "Nepreryvnaia revoliutsiia," *Nachalo,* no. 10 (Nov. 25, 1905).

Menashe, Louis. "Alexander Guchkov and the Origins of the Octobrist Party: The Russian Bourgeoisie in Politics, 1905." Ph. D. diss., New York University, 1966.

———. "Industrialists in Politics: Russia in 1905," *Government and Opposition,* 1968, no. 3, pp. 352–68.

Meyer, Alfred G. *Leninism.* Cambridge, Mass., 1957.

Miliukov, P. N. "Novyi variant slavianofilskoi politicheskoi doktriny," *Russkoe bogatstvo,* 1905, no. 4, pp. 127–32.

———. *Russia and Its Crisis.* Reprinted with a new Foreword by Donald W. Treadgold. New York, 1962.
Miller, Margaret S. *The Economic Development of Russia, 1905–1914, with Special Reference to Trade, Industry and Finance.* 2d ed. London, 1967. Orig. ed. 1926.
Morrison, John D. "Political Characteristics of the Student Movement in the Russian Revolution of 1905," in Coquin and Gervais-Francelle, eds., *1905*, pp. 63–75.
Muratov, Kh. I. *Revoliutsionnoe dvizhenie v russkoi armii v 1905–1907 gg.* Moscow, 1955.
Naimark, Norman M. *Terrorists and Social Democrats. The Russian Revolutionary Movement Under Alexander III.* Cambridge, Mass., 1983.
Naumov, V. P., et al., eds. *Aktualnye problemy sovetskoi istoriografii pervoi russkoi revoliutsii: sbornik statei.* Moscow, 1978.
Nechkina, M. V., et al., eds. *Istoriia i istoriki.* Moscow, 1965.
Nettl, J. P. *Rosa Luxemburg.* 2 vols. London, 1966.
Nevskii, V. I. "Peterburgskaia sotsial-demokraticheskaia organizatsiia v ianvare 1905 goda," *Krasnaia letopis*, 1925, no. 1 (12), pp. 145–56.
———. *Rabochee dvizhenie v ianvarskie dni 1905 goda.* Moscow, 1930.
Nikolajewsky, Boris. *Azeff the Spy.* Tr. George Reavey. New York, 1934.
Obninskii, V. *Polgoda russkoi revoliutsii: Sbornik materialov k istorii russkoi revoliutsii. Oktiabr 1905 g.–aprel 1906 g.* Moscow, 1906.
"Ob odnom nepravilnom tolkovanii roli proletariata v revoliutsii 1905–1907 godov," *Kommunist*, 1955, no. 2, pp. 124–27.
Owen, Thomas C. *Capitalism and Politics in Russia: A Social History of the Moscow Merchants, 1855–1905.* Cambridge, Eng., 1981.
Pankratova, A. M., ed. *Pervaia burzhuazno-demokraticheskaia revoliutsiia v Rossii 1905–1907 gg., kratkii ukazatel literatury.* Moscow, 1954.
———. *Pervaia russkaia revoliutsiia 1905–1907 gg.* 2d ed. Moscow, 1951.
Pares, Bernard. *Russia and Reform.* London, 1907.
Parvus. "Khod revoliutsii," *Nachalo*, no. 10 (Nov. 25, 1905), p. 1.
Pearson, Thomas S. "The Origins of Alexander III's Land Captains: A Reinterpretation," *Slavic Review*, 1981, no. 3, pp. 384–403.
Perrie, Maureen. *The Agrarian Policy of the Russian Socialist-Revolutionary Party from Its Origins Through the Revolution of 1905–1907.* New York, 1976.
———. "The Russian Peasant Movement of 1905–1907: Its Social Composition and Revolutionary Significance," *Past and Present*, 1972, no. 57, pp. 123–55.
———. "The Social Composition and Structure of the Socialist-Revolutionary Party Before 1917," *Soviet Studies*, 1972, no. 2, pp. 223–50.
———. "The Socialist Revolutionaries on Permanent Revolution," *Soviet Studies*, 1973, no. 3, pp. 411–13.
Perris, G. H. *Russia in Revolution.* 2d rev. ed. London, 1905.
Petrova, L. F. "Peterburgskii sovet rabochikh deputatov v 1905 godu," *Voprosy istorii*, 1955, no. 11, pp. 25–40.
Piaskovskii, A. V. *Revoliutsiia 1905–1907 gg. v Rossii.* Moscow, 1966.
Pinchuk, Ben-Cion. *The Octobrists in the Third Duma, 1907–1912.* Seattle, Wash., 1974.
Pipes, Richard. "Max Weber and Russia," *World Politics*, 1955, no. 2, pp. 371–401.
———. *Russia Under the Old Regime.* New York, 1974.

——. *Struve: Liberal on the Left, 1870–1905.* Cambridge, Mass., 1970.

——. *Struve: Liberal on the Right, 1905–1944.* Cambridge, Mass., 1980.

——. *The Formation of the Soviet Union. Communism and Nationalism, 1917–1923.* Rev. ed. Cambridge, Mass., 1964.

——. "The Origins of Bolshevism: The Intellectual Evolution of Young Lenin," in Pipes, ed., *Revolutionary Russia*, pp. 26–52.

——, ed. *Revolutionary Russia.* Cambridge, Mass., 1968.

Pokrovskii, M. N., ed. *1905: Istoriia revoliutsionnogo dvizheniia v otdelnykh ocherkakh.* 3 vols. Moscow, 1925–27.

——. *Brief History of Russia.* Tr. D. S. Mirsky. Vol. 2. London, 1933.

Queen, G. S. "The McCormick Harvesting Machine Company in Russia," *Russian Review,* 1964, no. 2, pp. 164–81.

Radkey, Oliver H. *The Agrarian Foes of Bolshevism: Promise and Default of the Russian Socialist Revolutionaries. February to October 1917.* New York, 1958.

Raeff, Marc. "Some Reflections on Russian Liberalism," *Russian Review,* 1959, no. 3, pp. 218–36.

Rainey, Thomas B., Jr. "The Union of 17 October: An Experiment in Moderate Constitutionalism (1905–1906)." Ph. D. diss., University of Illinois, 1966.

Raun, Toivo U. "The Revolution of 1905 in the Baltic Provinces and Finland," *Slavic Review,* 1984, no. 3, pp. 453–67.

Reichman, Henry F. "Russian Railwaymen and the Revolution of 1905." Ph. D. diss., University of California, Berkeley, 1977.

Rieber, Alfred J. *Merchants and Entrepreneurs in Imperial Russia.* Chapel Hill, N.C., 1982.

Riha, Thomas. *A Russian European: Paul Miliukov in Russian Politics.* Notre Dame, Ind., 1969.

Rimlinger, Gaston V. "Autocracy and the Factory Order in Early Russian Industrialization," *Journal of Economic History,* 1960, no. 1, pp. 67–92.

——. "The Management of Labor Protest in Tsarist Russia: 1870–1905," *International Review of Social History,* 5 (1960), part 2, pp. 226–48.

Robinson, Geroid T. *Rural Russia Under the Old Regime: A History of the Landlord-Peasant World and a Prologue to the Peasant Revolution of 1917.* 2d ed. New York, 1949.

Rogger, Hans. *Russia in the Age of Modernisation and Revolution, 1881–1917.* London, 1983.

——. "Russian Ministers and the Jewish Question, 1881–1917," *California Slavic Studies,* 1975, pp. 15–76.

——. "The Beilis Case: Anti-Semitism and Politics in the Reign of Nicholas II," *Slavic Review,* 1966, no. 4, pp. 615–29.

——. "The Formation of the Russian Right, 1900–1906," *California Slavic Studies,* 1964, pp. 66–94.

——. "The Jewish Policy of Late Tsarism: A Reappraisal," *The Wiener Bulletin,* 1971, nos. 11–12, pp. 42–51.

——. "Was There a Russian Fascism? The Union of the Russian People," *Journal of Modern History,* 1964, no. 4, pp. 398–415.

Roosa, Ruth A. "Russian Industrialists, Politics, and Labor Reform in 1905," *Russian History,* 1975, no. 2, pp. 124–48.

Rosenberg, William G. *Liberals in the Russian Revolution: The Constitutional-Democratic Party, 1917–1921.* Princeton, N.J., 1974.

Ruud, Charles A. *Fighting Words: Imperial Censorship and the Russian Press, 1804–1906.* Toronto, 1982.

Sablinsky, Walter. "The All-Russian Railroad Union and the Beginning of the General Strike in October 1905," in Alexander Rabinowitch et al., eds., *Revolution and Politics in Russia: Essays in Memory of B. I. Nicolaevsky* (Bloomington, Ind., 1972), pp. 113–33.

———. "The Road to Bloody Sunday: Father Gapon, His Labor Organization, and the Massacre of Bloody Sunday." Ph. D. diss., University of California, Berkeley, 1968.

———. *The Road to Bloody Sunday: Father Gapon and the St. Petersburg Massacre of 1905.* Princeton, N.J., 1976. A revised and shortened version of the dissertation above.

Samoilov, F. *Pervyi sovet rabochikh deputatov.* Leningrad, 1931.

Sanders, John T. "'Once More into the Breach, Dear Friends': A Close Look at the Indirect Tax Receipts and the Condition of the Russian Peasantry, 1881–1889," *Slavic Review,* 1984, no. 4, pp. 657–66.

Sanders, Jonathan. "The Union of Unions: Economic, Political, and Human Rights Organizations in the 1905 Russian Revolution." Ph. D. diss., Columbia University, 1985.

Santoni, Wayne D. "P. N. Durnovo as Minister of Internal Affairs in the Witte Cabinet: A Study in Suppression." Ph. D. diss., University of Kansas, 1968.

Schapiro, Leonard. *The Communist Party of the Soviet Union.* London, 1960.

Scharlau, Winfried, and Zbynek A. Zeman. *Freibeuter der Revolution: Parvus-Helphand. Eine politische Biographie.* Cologne, 1964.

Schneiderman, Jeremiah. *Sergei Zubatov and Revolutionary Marxism: The Struggle for the Working Class in Tsarist Russia.* Ithaca, N.Y., 1976.

Schorske, Carl E. *German Social Democracy, 1905–1917: The Development of the Great Schism.* Cambridge, Mass., 1955.

Schwarz, Solomon M. *The Russian Revolution of 1905: The Workers' Movement and the Formation of Bolshevism and Menshevism.* Tr. Gertrude Vakar. Chicago, 1967.

Sef, S. E. *Burzhuaziia v 1905 godu, po neizdannym arkhivnym materialam.* Moscow and Leningrad, 1926.

Seton-Watson, Hugh. *The Decline of Imperial Russia, 1855–1914.* London, 1952.

———. *The Russian Empire, 1801–1917.* Oxford, 1967.

Shatsillo, K. F. "Iz istorii osvoboditelnogo dvizheniia v Rossii v nachale XX veka. (O konferentsii liberalnykh i revoliutsionnykh partii v Parizhe v sentiabre-oktiabre 1904 goda)," *Istoriia SSSR,* 1982, no. 4, pp. 51–70.

———. "Nachalo pervoi russkoi revoliutsii," *Voprosy istorii,* 1975, no. 1, pp. 105–15, no. 2, pp. 109–20.

———. "O sostave russkogo liberalizma nakanune revoliutsii 1905–1907 godov," *Istoriia SSSR,* 1980, no. 1, pp. 62–74.

Shuster, U. A. *Peterburgskie rabochie v 1905–1907 gg.* Leningrad, 1976.

"Sibirskaia ekspeditsiia barona Mellera-Zakomelskogo," *Byloe,* 1917, no. 3, pp. 134–53.

Simms, James Y., Jr. "On Missing the Point: A Rejoinder," *Slavic Review,* 1978, no. 3, pp. 487–90.

———. "Reply," *Slavic Review,* 1984, no. 4, pp. 667–71.

———. "The Crisis in Russian Agriculture at the End of the Nineteenth Century: A Different View," *Slavic Review,* 1977, no. 3, pp. 377–98.

Slusser, Robert M. "The Moscow Soviet of Workers' Deputies of 1905: Origin, Structure, and Policies." Ph. D. diss., Columbia University, 1963.

Smith, Nathan. "The Constitutional-Democratic Movement in Russia, 1902–1906." Ph. D. diss., University of Illinois, 1958.

Snow, George E. "The Kokovtsov Commission: An Abortive Attempt at Labor Reform in Russia in 1905," *Slavic Review*, 1972, no. 4, pp. 780–96.

———. "The Peterhof Conference of 1905 and the Creation of the Bulygin Duma," *Russian History*, 1975, no. 2, pp. 149–62.

Sokolskii, V. D. "Novorossiiskii sovet rabochikh deputatov v 1905 godu," *Voprosy istorii*, 1955, no. 12, pp. 76–86.

Spector, Ivar. *The First Russian Revolution: Its Impact on Asia.* Englewood Cliffs, N.J., 1962.

Startsev, V. I. *Russkaia burzhuaziia i samoderzhavie v 1905–1917 gg.* Leningrad, 1977.

Stites, Richard. *The Women's Liberation Movement in Russia: Feminism, Nihilism, and Bolshevism, 1860–1930.* Princeton, N.J., 1978.

[Struve]. "Iz ruk tsaria—iz ruk Mikado i Anglii," *Osvobozhdenie*, no. 76 (Sept. 2, 1905), pp. 442–44. The article bears the initials "P. S."

———. "Nezhnaia uvertiura k groznomu konfliktu," *Osvobozhdenie*, no. 73 (July 19, 1905).

Surh, Gerald D. "Petersburg's First Mass Labor Organization: The Assembly of Russian Workers and Father Gapon," *Russian Review*, 1981, no. 3, pp. 241–62, and no. 4, pp. 412–41.

———. "Petersburg Workers in 1905: Strikes, Workplace Democracy, and the Revolution." Ph. D. diss., University of California, Berkeley, 1979.

Thaden, Edward C., ed. *Russification in the Baltic Provinces and Finland, 1855–1914.* Princeton, N.J., 1981.

Timberlake, Charles E., ed. *Essays on Russian Liberalism.* Columbia, Missouri, 1972.

Tiutiukin, S. V., et al. *Pervaia rossiiskaia. Spravochnik o revoliutsii 1905–1907 gg.* Moscow, 1985.

Tobias, Henry J. *The Jewish Bund in Russia from Its Origins to 1905.* Stanford, Calif., 1972.

Treadgold, Donald W. *Lenin and His Rivals: The Struggle for Russia's Future, 1898–1906.* New York, 1955.

Trotsky, Leon. *1905.* Tr. Anya Bostok. New York, 1971.

——— [N. Trotskii]. "Sotsialdemokratiia i revoliutsiia," *Nachalo*, 1905, no. 10, p. 1.

———. "Stachka v oktiabre," *Nachalo*, no. 2 (Nov. 15, 1905), p. 5.

Tucker, Robert C., ed. *The Lenin Anthology.* New York, 1975.

Tugan-Baranovskii, M. I. *Russkaia fabrika v proshlom i nastoiashchem.* 7th ed. Moscow, 1938.

Ugarov, I. F. "Bolsheviki vo glave vseobshchei politicheskoi stachki rabochikh Moskvy v oktiabre 1905 goda," *Voprosy istorii*, 1955, no. 10, pp. 3–17.

———, and N. N. Iakovlev. "Pervaia russkaia revoliutsiia 1905–1907 gg. v sovetskoi istoriografii," in M. V. Nechkina et al., eds., *Ocherki istorii istoricheskoi nauki v SSSR*, IV (Moscow, 1966), pp. 411–27.

Valk, S. N., et al., eds. *1905 god v Peterburge.* 2 vols. Leningrad and Moscow, 1925.

Varzar, V. E. *Statistika stachek rabochikh na fabrikakh i zavodakh za 1905 god.* St. Petersburg, 1908.

Vasilev-Iuzhin, M. I. "Iz vospominanii o moskovskom vosstanii 1905 g.," *Proletarskaia revoliutsiia*, 1922, no. 5, pp. 184–93.
———. *V ogne pervoi revoliutsii*. Moscow, 1931.
Verner, Andrew M. "Nicholas II and the Role of the Autocrat During the First Russian Revolution, 1904–1907." Ph. D. diss., Columbia University, 1986.
Veselovskii, B. B., et al. *Agrarnoe dvizhenie v Rossii v 1905–1906 gg.: obzory po raionam*. 2 vols. St. Petersburg, 1908.
Vladimirov, V. *Karatelnaia ekspeditsiia otriada leibgvardiia Semenovskogo polka v dekabrskie dni na Moskovsko-Kazanskoi zheleznoi doroge*. Moscow, 1906.
Volin, M. S., et al. "O gegemonii proletariata v pervoi russkoi revoliutsii," *Istoriia SSSR*, 1973, no. 4, pp. 46–67.
Volobuev, O. V. "Sovremennaia istoriografiia revoliutsii 1905–1907 godov," in *Revoliutsiia 1905–1907 godov v Rossii i ee vsemirno-istoricheskoe znachenie* (Moscow, 1976), pp. 82–96.
Von Laue, Theodore H. "Count Witte and the 1905 Revolution," *American Slavic and East European Review*, 1958, no. 1, pp. 25–46.
———. "Factory Inspection Under the 'Witte System,' 1892–1903," *American Slavic and East European Review*, 1960, no. 3, pp. 347–62.
———. "Russian Labor Between Field and Factory, 1892–1903," *California Slavic Studies*, 1964, pp. 33–65.
———. "Russian Peasants in the Factory," *Journal of Economic History*, 1961, no. 1, pp. 61–81.
———. *Sergei Witte and the Industrialization of Russia*. New York, 1963.
———. "Tsarist Labor Policy, 1895–1903," *Journal of Modern History*, 1962, no. 2, pp. 135–45.
Vucinich, Wayne S., ed. *The Peasant in Nineteenth-Century Russia*. Stanford, Calif., 1968.
Walkin, Jacob. "The Attitude of the Tsarist Government Toward the Labor Problem," *American Slavic and East European Review*, 1954, no. 2, pp. 163–84.
———. *The Rise of Democracy in Pre-Revolutionary Russia: Political and Social Institutions Under the Last Czars*. London, 1963.
Weber, Max. "Russlands Übergang zum Scheinkonstitutionalismus," *Archiv für Sozialwissenschaft und Sozialpolitik*, 23 (1906), pp. 165–401.
———. "Zur Lage der bürgerlichen Demokratie in Russland," *Archiv für Sozialwissenschaft und Sozialpolitik*, 22 (1906), pp. 234–353.
Weinberg, Robert E. "Worker Organizations and Politics in the Revolution of 1905 in Odessa." Ph. D. diss., University of California, Berkeley, 1985.
Weissman, Neil B. *Reform in Tsarist Russia: The State Bureaucracy and Local Government, 1900–1914*. New Brunswick, N.J., 1981.
White, John A. *The Diplomacy of the Russo-Japanese War*. Princeton, N.J., 1964.
Wildman, Allan K. *The End of the Russian Imperial Army: The Old Army and the Soldiers' Revolt (March–April 1917)*. Princeton, N.J., 1980.
Wolfe, Bertram D. "Gapon and Zubatov," *Russian Review*, 1948, no. 2, pp. 53–61.
———. *Three Who Made a Revolution: A Biographical History*. New York, 1948.
"Za glubokoe izuchenie istorii pervoi russkoi revoliutsii," *Voprosy istorii*, 1955, no. 1, pp. 3–10.

Zelikson-Bobrovskaia, Ts., ed. *Pervaia russkaia revoliutsiia v Peterburge 1905 g.* 2 vols. Leningrad and Moscow, 1925.

Zelnik, Reginald E. *Labor and Society in Tsarist Russia: The Factory Workers of St. Petersburg, 1855–70.* Stanford, Calif., 1971.

Zilliacus, Konni. *The Russian Revolutionary Movement.* New York, 1905.

Zimmerman, Judith E. "Between Revolution and Reaction: The Russian Constitutional-Democratic Party, October 1905 to June 1907." Ph. D. diss., Columbia University, 1967.

Index

In this index an "f" after a number indicates a separate reference on the next page, and an "ff" indicates separate references on the next two pages. A continuous discussion over two or more pages is indicated by a span of page numbers, e.g., "pp. 57–58." *Passim* is used for a cluster of references in close but not consecutive sequence.

Manifesto on, 230–31; fear of pogroms in, 255f; compared to Moscow, 304–5, 308f; crackdown in December 1905, 328–29

St. Petersburg Academy, 206

St. Petersburg City Council, 93, 222, 230, 266, 277

St. Petersburg Conservatory of Music, 94–95

St. Petersburg Mining Institute, 200

St. Petersburg Naval School, 270

St. Petersburg Soviet of Workers' Deputies, 217, 232, 306, 309; formation and activities of, 219–21, 277–83; disbanded by government, 298–300

St. Petersburg Theological Seminary, 78

St. Petersburg Union of Janitors, 291

St. Petersburg University, 35, 47, 198–204, 214, 216

Sakhalin Island, 183

Sakharov, Moscow police officer, 318–19

Sakharov, V. V., General-Adjutant, 268

Samara, 32n, 138

San-Galli factory (St. Petersburg), 133

Saratov or Saratov province; unrest in, 108–10, 130, 138, 164, 260, 268; Russian Union of Landowners in, 166; trade unions in, 277

Saratov City Council, 114, 131

Sazonov, I. N., 147n

Schmidt, N. P., 321

Schmidt, P. P., 270–72

Schmidt furniture factory (Moscow), 321

Schwanebach, P. Kh., 178

SDs, *see* Social Democracy

Seasonal workers, 22, 351

Secondary schools, 95, 194–96

Security police, *see* Okhrana

Sedoi, Z. Ia. (Litvin), 318–19

Self-defense groups, 130, 266

Semenovskii Regiment, 320

Semevskii, V. I., 85

Sennitskii, V. V., 334

Serfdom, 18, 27f

Sergei Aleksandrovich, Grand Duke, 25, 112, 157, 227–28, 313f

Sevastopol, 170, 173, 230, 270f

Shantser, V. L. (Marat), 308, 314

Shchepkin, N. N., 66, 177

Shelgunov, N. V., 270

Shidlovsky, N. V., 98, 119–21

Shidlovsky Commission, 119–21, 141

Shipov, D. N., 17, 58, 61, 63–64, 115–16, 235, 248f, 251, 339

Shmakov, A. S., 230

Shtiglits factory (St. Petersburg), 83

Siberia, 27, 49, 272, 291, 323, 330ff, 333

Simbirskii, N., worker-activist, 75

Simferopol (Tauride province), 257

Sipiagin, D. S., 16, 24

Skopin (Riazan province), 195

Slavophilism, 63

Slovo, 128

Smirnov, S. I., 82

Social Democracy, Russian, or RSDWP or Social Democrats (SDs), 6, 34, 60, 121, 170f, 194, 225, 262; formation of, 30; doctrines of, 30–31, 36–38; split within, 38–39; Second Congress (1903) of, 38, 187, 263, 285; compared to SRs, 40; and banquet campaign, 67, 68–69; and Gapon, 80, 84–85, 91, 98; and labor unrest, 137, 150–51; strength of, 184–89, 277; Third Congress (1905) of, 189; and soviets, 220–21; and October general strike, 232–33; activities of in Siberia, 272, 291; and Financial Manifesto, 299. *See also* Bolshevism *and* Menshevism

Social Democratic Party of the Kingdom of Poland and Lithuania (SDKPiL), 156, 185

Social monarchy, 24

Socialist Revolutionary Party or SRs, 5f, 34, 194, 262, 276, 279, 299, 339; formation and doctrines of, 39–40, 191–92, 290–91; and Gapon, 98ff; and labor unrest, 165; strength of, 190–91; and student movement, 198; and St. Petersburg Soviet, 219–20; and Moscow uprising, 307, 313, 316

Society for Promoting Literacy, 326

Sollogub, V. U., General, 328, 333

Solskii, D. M., Count, 179, 223–24, 246

Soslovie (Estate), 117, 117n

Soul tax, 28

Soviet, 3, 280, 306, 309; origins of, 144–50; and October general strike, 217, 219–22, 232; role of during Days of Liberty, 277–83, 291–92, 298–300;

Library of Congress Cataloging-in-Publication Data

Ascher, Abraham, 1928-
  The Revolution of 1905.
    p.   cm.
  Bibliography: p.
  Includes index.
  Contents [1] Russia in disarray. [2] Authority restored.
  1. Soviet Union—History—Revolution of 1905.   I. Title.
DK263.A9   1988   87-26657
947.08'3 —dc19   CIP
ISBN 0-8047-1436-3 (v. 1: cl.)
ISBN 0-8047-1972-1 (v. 2: cl.)
ISBN 0-8047-2327-3 (v. 1: pb.)
ISBN 0-8047-2328-1 (v. 2: pb.)